Child
Welfare
Services

child
welfare
SECOND EDITION # services

ALFRED KADUSHIN, Ph.D.

Professor, School of Social Work
University of Wisconsin, Madison

Macmillan Publishing Co., Inc.
NEW YORK

Collier Macmillan Publishers
LONDON

Macmillan Publishing Co., Inc.
866 Third Avenue, New York, New York 10022

Collier-Macmillan Canada, Ltd.

Library of Congress Cataloging in Publication Data
Kadushin, Alfred.

   Child welfare services.
   Includes bibliographies.
   1. Child welfare—United States. I. Title.
HV741.K26 1974   362.7'0973   73-2760
ISBN 0-02-361800-0

Printing: 6 7 8   Year: 7 8 9

To Sylvia;
to Goldie;
to Raphael
—with love.

Preface

This book is a comprehensive study of the principal child welfare services. It begins by defining child welfare, placing it as a field of practice within social work, and presents a scheme for the categorization of child welfare problems in terms of role theory. It goes on to provide a historical perspective on how and why child welfare services developed and to describe the current socioeconomic context in which they operate. Separate chapters are devoted to each of the principal supportive, supplementary, and substitutive child welfare services: family service and child guidance clinics, the social insurance, aid to families of dependent children, protective services, day care, homemaker service, foster care, adoption, institutional child care. Each chapter includes material on the historical development of the service, the situations for which the service is appropriate, scope of the service, process in offering the service, evaluation of the service, problems encountered by the service, and trends in offering the service.

A chapter on child welfare services in other countries provides an international perspective on the practice of child welfare in the United States. The final chapter is concerned with the sociology of the child welfare worker—characteristics, career routes, occupational problems, and satisfactions.

A special effort has been made to include as much of the relevant research as possible and to supplement material from casework with material available from other practice methods.

The book is directed to the student of social work both at the undergraduate level and at the graduate level. Undergraduate students—whether they plan to work in a social agency after graduation or to go on to a graduate school of social work—will find the material in the text useful preparation. Graduate students enrolled in child welfare seminars or taking courses that are concerned, in part, with child welfare problems will find this a useful, systematic, and detailed review of child welfare services.

The text, then, can appropriately be used at both the undergraduate and the graduate levels. The first edition has been widely used for courses at both levels.

The book is also directed to the child welfare worker currently employed in social agencies. The volume is designed to offer both fully trained professional workers and those with limited professional training a systematic review of the substantive knowledge available concerning child welfare services and to provide a synthesis of widely scattered material for the busy practitioner.

Finally, the book is designed to give the reader a broad knowledge of child welfare services rather than to develop skills for working directly with people who present child welfare problems. The primary purpose of the text is to teach about child welfare—the *what* and the *why*—rather than to teach the *how* of doing child welfare work. It is directed toward developing a knowledge about, concern for, and understanding of child welfare services rather than oriented toward developing technical, professional skills required in treating clients. It is important to note that knowing about a field of social work practice is a necessary prerequisite for effective "doing" and "treating." Charlotte Towle aptly notes:

> Students must have knowledge with which to think. Feeling as a
> professional person must come to feel is developed through, and
> in response to, knowledge. Understanding comes about through
> knowledge that has been integrated through emotional acceptance,
> which permits the faculties of knowing and thinking to function
> in the doing. The nature of doing will, therefore, reflect integration
> or lack of integration of knowledge.*

The presentation is primarily descriptive and expository, concerned with explicating current child welfare practices—how child welfare services actually operate rather than how they should operate. Admittedly, what *is* is a far cry from what *should be*. The detailed material on each of the particular services presented in the text makes it clear that Ameri-

---

* Charlotte Towle, *The Learner in Education for the Professions* (Chicago: University of Chicago Press, 1954), p. 358.

can society has failed large numbers of its children and that child welfare services have relatively low priority in the allocation of national resources. Ours has not been and is not likely to be a filiocentric society. Although the needs and rights of children are a matter of great concern within the individual family unit, this concern has not been reflected in public policy.

The Congressionally appointed Joint Commission on Mental Health of Children, making its report to the nation in 1970 after three years of study, categorically states that "this nation, the richest of all world powers, has no unified national commitment to its children and youth. The claim that we are a child-centered society . . . is a myth. Our words are made meaningless by our actions. . . ." *

Through the detailed exposition on services, this book also makes it clear that in many significant respects the field of child welfare social work has failed large numbers of America's children. In general the field is oriented toward crisis, rescue, and remedy rather than toward prevention and planning. It is reactive rather than proactive, responding primarily in an *ad hoc* manner to emergency situations rather than planning long-term policies. It serves only a limited percentage of America's children and is concerned with life at the margins of society rather than at the center. Services are offered to the few who have limited problems and considerable strengths rather than to the many who have multiple problems and few resources.

The tendency is for "different agencies to respond disconnectedly to a series of discrete crises," so that service to any one family is poorly coordinated. Much of the basic policy in child welfare is founded on intuition and tradition rather than on empirical research and precise information. There is little follow-up and disciplined evaluation of results.

The Child Welfare League of America summarized the situation in 1971: "child welfare services are inadequate, fragmented, poorly financed, and in many communities nonexistent." †

But the text also attempts to make clear the factors that help to explain, although they do not excuse, the failures of society and of the agencies, and to point out the very real achievements of child welfare social work. As a consequence of the efforts of the individual child welfare worker and the agencies under whose auspices he practices, we have rescued for life a sizable number of children. We have found families, protection, care, and physical and emotional support for children

---

* *Crisis in Mental Health: Challenge for the 1970's*, Report of the Joint Commission on the Mental Health of Children (New York: Harper and Row, Publishers, 1970), p. 2.

† *A National Program for Comprehensive Child Welfare Service* (New York: Child Welfare League of America, 1972), p. 4.

who would otherwise have endured greater suffering and pain—if they had lived at all. This is the measure of the victory we have achieved, and it is a record of which we can justifiably be proud.

The need for a revised edition was prompted by the following considerations. Child welfare services are rapidly changing. Some problems and procedures that were current and typical when the first edition of the book was published have been replaced by others. The income maintenance program, discussed in the chapter beginning on page 154, has been the subject of searching inquiry and concern. Social services have been separated from income maintenance administration, and a variety of proposals for fundamental welfare program reform have been widely debated. Substitute care has changed in emphasis, with contractual long-term foster care and subsidized adoptions winning widespread acceptance. There is also greater acceptance of behavioral modification techniques in casework and a greater emphasis on advocacy and brokerage approaches in helping the client as well as on community approaches to child welfare problems. Client rights organizations (in foster care and adoptions, as well as in income maintenance programs) are now part of the reality of child welfare services. Concern with and changes in the service delivery systems are reflected in the development of neighborhood service centers and parent-child centers, and in the employment of paraprofessionals from the local community. There is growing stress on the needs of, and service to, minority-group children. The laws against child abuse, the first of which were adopted shortly before the book was published, have had considerable impact on protective services, and a great deal of new material has become available as a consequence of mandatory reporting under these laws. Head Start and the Federal government Work Incentive program have materially affected day-care practice.

The context in which social welfare and social work programs operate has changed radically. The Federal government is reducing its mandate both for funding and standard setting of such programs and is giving each state a greater measure of responsibility for program support and implementation. In contrast to the national social policy orientation of the period between 1935 and 1970, characterized by an expansion of programs for the deprived, the disadvantaged, the impoverished, and the handicapped, the 1970's is witnessing the elimination of some programs and a considerable reduction in the support of many others.

There is much greater concern with "production" of results, "cost-benefit analysis," and the "biggest bang for the buck." Systems analysis specialists and management consultants are displacing professional social workers as key decision-makers in some program operations. There is a greater, and perhaps desirable, tendency to be critical about the objectives of social programs and what they can accomplish and are accomplishing.

All statistics in the book have been updated. Students and teachers who used the first edition of the book indicated the need for greater selectivity in citing statistics and research results. The problem of selectivity becomes more difficult because there has been a rapid acceleration of research relevant to child welfare services during the past five years, much of which should be called to the reader's attention.

Feedback from students and teachers also made it clear that the chapter on adoption needed a companion chapter on the unmarried mother and the out-of-wedlock child. Such a chapter has been included in this second edition.

A word of explanation needs to be offered for what is excluded from the book. Services to the delinquent child and to the physically handicapped and mentally retarded child have not been discussed. The material on these services has been considered in more specialized texts and is so vast that even a condensed review would have made this book immoderately long and prohibitively expensive. Also, these services have a frame of reference different from that of the services discussed. As Jenkins pointed out:

> Services to the delinquent child must involve detailed consideration of the "legal structure and court apparatus." Services to the physically handicapped and mentally retarded have traditionally been of primary concern to the health and education professions respectively. The traditional child welfare agencies operate in these areas only tangentially. *

The book does not pretend to cover systematically the material on the development, the psychology, or the emotional needs of children: many available texts present this material, from various points of view, in great detail. But it does discuss some of the special problems of child development particularly pertinent to child welfare services: that is, the fatherless child in Aid to Families of Dependent Children, the child of the working mother and day care, the abused and/or neglected child and protective services.

Decisions about what to include and what to omit were difficult to make. Dramatic case history material vitiates somewhat the scholarly posture of the text. Yet, as a practicing social worker and social work educator, the author has great respect for the affective components

---

* Shirley Jenkins, *Priorities in Social Services: A Guide for Philanthropic Funding. Vol. 1: Child Welfare in New York City* (New York: Praeger Publishers, Inc., 1971), p. 25.

of teaching-learning that are communicated through case histories, and so these have been included when appropriate.

The list of people to whom I am indebted is extremely long. It includes teachers and supervisors, students and clients, friends and adversaries, co-workers and colleagues in the United States, the Netherlands, and Israel. It includes the many teachers and students who, having used the first edition of the text, gave me their very constructive suggestions for revision. And it includes the National Institute for Mental Health, the Children's Bureau, and the Silberman Fund, from whom I have received research grants to support the studies that have increased my understanding of child welfare. To name one is to slight another, yet two must be named: Dr. Abraham Lurie, Director of Social Services, Hillside Hospital, New York, a friend of many years with whom I have often discussed social work problems to my invariable enlightenment, and my wife, Sylvia, who has helped me, beyond calculable measure, by being who and what she is.

A. K.

Contents

1

Child Welfare:
Orientation and Scope

Introduction

The term *child welfare* in a general sense has very broad connotations. If we include under the term every activity that either directly or indirectly promotes the welfare of children, we would end by including most of the significant activities engaged in by society.

The sanitary engineer working toward the organization of a physically healthier environment for children, the traffic engineer working toward the reduction of automobile accidents, the research scientist studying congenital anomalies, and the military specialist guarding the country from attack—all promote the welfare of children, and thus these activities may be subsumed under a general definition of *child welfare*. Carstens notes that "child welfare has in the course of time acquired a significance that is so broad and vague that it has come to be applied to almost every effort in social and community work that is likely to benefit children." [10, p. 64] *

Social Work

A more specific and more meaningful definition of child welfare is based on the fact that society has granted to the profession of social work responsibility for helping to resolve many of the problem situations

* References are to be found at the end of each chapter.

encountered by children. In its narrower sense, *child welfare* is regarded as a field of social work practice. Because it is of the genus social work, it shares the characteristics of the genus. To clarify the nature of child welfare, therefore, we must attempt to delineate the normative characteristics of social work. The following illustration may be of help.

Nine years ago Mrs. F., then unmarried, gave birth to a boy, and placed him in the home of a childless married couple whom she knew well. She then left town. Her friends raised the boy as their own, although they never legally adopted him. When Mrs. F. married, she told her husband of her illegitimate child, and he agreed to accept the boy into the family. Mrs. F. visited her friends to tell them of her marriage and of her husband's decision to have the child live with them. Her friends, who had become very much attached to the boy, were reluctant to give him up.

Mrs. F. consulted a lawyer, who agreed to help her establish her legal rights and privileges. However, he felt that aspects of the problem other than the legality of Mrs. F.'s claim to the boy needed to be considered. How would it affect him to be removed from the home in which he was loved and accepted and to be placed in another which was strange and unfamiliar? How would her own marriage be affected? And how would her friends feel when they were suddenly deprived of a child that they had for a long time regarded as their own? These were not questions with which the lawyer was, by training, competent to deal. These were questions involving social relationships, marital relationships, parent-child relationships, and the social institution of marriage and the family. To help Mrs. F. clarify, for herself, the possible social effects of a decision based on her legal rights alone, the lawyer referred her to a social worker.

The inclusion of the word *social* in the title of the profession reflects the social worker's primary concern with the relation of the individual, the group, or the community to the social environment. Early in the profession's history, Mary Richmond defined social work as "those processes which develop personality through adjustments consciously effected individual by individual between man and his social environment." [28, pp. 98–99] More recently, the United Nations Secretariat defined social work as "an activity designed to help towards a better mutual adjustment of the individual and his social environment." [12, p. 5] The Woman's Bureau of the U.S. Department of Health, Education, and Welfare notes that "social work is uniquely concerned with the individual in relation to outer social realities in which he is involved and the satisfactions he gets from them." [39] The Army defines casework as "that process which deals directly and differentially with persons who have problems related primarily to their social situation, and which endeavors, individual by individual, to understand what help is needed and to assist the individual to find and utilize help indicated."

[38, p. 1] Witmer and Kotinsky note that "the profession that takes as its particular task the job of helping individuals, one by one, or in groups, to deal with difficulties they encounter in operating in accordance with the requirements of a social institution is social work. . . ." [42, p. 359] Perlman similarly states that "the person in interaction with some problematic aspect of his social reality is the focus of the social caseworker's concern." [25, p. 130]

The Model Statute Social Workers' License Act defines social work as the professional activity of helping individuals, groups, or communities enhance or restore their capacity for social functioning and for creating societal conditions favorable to this goal (*National Association of Social Workers' News*, May 1970, p. 7).

Because social behavior is carried out primarily in the performance of social roles, there have been attempts to define social work in terms of social role performance. Thus Boehm defines social work as the profession which

> seeks to enhance the social functioning of individuals singly and in groups by activities focused upon their social relationships which constitute the interaction between man and his environment. The focus of activities is the professional intervention in that aspect of man's functioning only which lies in the realms of social relationships or of social role performance. [6, p. 54]

In another article, Boehm notes that

> social work is concerned with enhancing of social functioning of those activities considered essential for the performance of the several social roles which each individual, by virtue of his membership in social groups, is called upon to carry out. . . . Social work intervenes as the interaction (between the individual and the social structure) manifests itself in problematic social relationships. [7]

Physical disease results in the need for the application of specific remedial measures designed to alleviate or cure the disease. Similarly, disabilities in the enactment of social roles require the application of specific remedial measures designed to help people to enact social roles in a more effective manner. Such treatment is made available through the profession of social work.

Other professional groups, notably sociologists, are also interested in the phenomenon of social functioning. However, social work is distinguished from sociology because it is a technology. As a technology, social work is concerned with, and responsible for, helping to "achieve controlled changes in natural relationships via relatively standardized procedures which are scientifically based." [14, p. 24] Sociology has no such responsibility. Sociology is to social work as biology is to medicine: one is the basic science, the other is the technology which applies the findings of the basic science. However, the guidance counselor, the marriage counselor, the clinical psychologist, the psychiatrist are also technologists seeking to effect change in problematic situations similar to those which are the concern of the social worker.

Every situation which social workers, counselors, psychologists, and psychiatrists encounter is a psychosocial situation—the results of man's interaction with his social environment. However, the principal concerns of social work have been, and are, the social antecedents, concomitants, and consequences of the problem situation. The principal concerns of the counselor, the psychologist, the psychiatrist have been the psychological aspects. The social worker is primarily concerned with the psychoSOCIAL situation; the counselor, psychologist, and psychiatrist are traditionally more concerned with the PSYCHOsocial situation.

Admittedly the analysis is not so neat and valid for the social worker offering "psychotherapy" in, let us say, a child guidance clinic. The activity of such a social worker is not clearly distinguishable from that of a clinical psychologist or psychiatrist. Here we have the beginnings of another profession which unites the "psychotherapists," however diverse their formal professional affiliation. [19; 16] Furthermore, in seeking to help clients with seemingly similar psychosocial problems, these different professional groups give different emphases to the variety of therapeutic possibilities available.

Since every difficulty is psychosocial, help can be directed either toward the person or toward the social situation. Thus one can make an effort to help the person cope with the situation or work to change the situation so that it is easier to cope with; one can help to make the person more capable or the situation more "copeable."

All those interventions which focus on the client's adjustive and adaptive capacity and seek to effect changes in the client's functioning through the psychic interaction between client and professional are known as *psychotherapies*. All those interventions which focus on the social situation, the social context of the psychosocial problem, and seek to modify, ameliorate, or change the social situation in favor of the client or to remove the client from a stressful social environment are known as *sociotherapies*. In some measure, all approaches are based on some combination of psychotherapy and sociotherapy. However, social workers have greater access to, and more frequently employ, sociotherapeutic resources. This is particularly true in child welfare services, for the child client has few personal resources which might be exploited for change and his almost total dependency on his environment makes sociotherapeutic resources—homemakers, day care, foster homes, adoptive homes, institutions, and so on—the therapeutic resource of choice.

When a particular kind of social problem, or a difficulty in social role performance, is sufficiently recurrent and widespread, a social agency is organized to help people who encounter this particular problem, and a specialized field of social work is thus institutionalized. For instance, physical illness requiring hospitalization is a recurrent problem that has more than physical consequences: it disrupts family relationships, requiring the reallocation of social roles and the introduction of social role substitutes within the family. If a mother is hospitalized, someone else must perform her activities in the home. In the hospital, the mother assumes temporarily a new social role—that of a patient. If she is to make optimum use of hospital facilities, she has to relate effectively to the hospital, which is a medical institution with a social structure. Medical social workers have the responsibility of helping people to deal with the social concomitants of illness.

Similarly, psychiatric social workers have the responsibility of helping people adjust to the social antecedents, concomitants, and consequences of the recurrent problem of mental illness. School social workers help children who have difficulty in enacting the social role of pupil or in relating to a social institution—the school system. The social worker in corrections has the responsibility of helping the individual with the problems that arise from contact with the legal institutions of society. The social worker in public assistance has the responsibility of helping the client in his role as a wage-earner and with the social antecedents, concomitants, and consequences of the family's relationship to the economic institutions of our society.

Child Welfare as a Field of Social Work Practice

Child welfare is a specialized field of social work concerned with social role enactment. The recurrent problems with which child welfare is concerned are related to the specific relationships between parents and children. According to the Child Welfare League of America, child welfare involves providing social services to children and young people whose parents are unable to fulfill their child-rearing responsibilities, or whose communities fail to provide the resources and protection that children and families require. Child welfare services are designed to reinforce, supplement, or substitute the functions that parents have difficulty in performing, and to improve conditions for children and their families by modifying existing social institutions or organizng new ones. A child welfare service, like any social service, is an "organized formalized way of dealing with a social problem" [35, p. 248], the social problem in this instance arising from difficulty in the parent-child relationship.

Social welfare services are required when a social system such as the family fails to perform the essential functions which society norma-tively ascribes to it. An alternative social system (child welfare ser-vices) then assumes some of the functions ordinarily performed by the well-organized, well-integrated, well-functioning family.

Zitha Turitz, of the Child Welfare League of America, in discussing the distinctive aspects of child welfare, notes that

> any degree of impairment of the parents' ability to provide the care which children need and are expected to receive from their parents results in a major and specific type of social problem for the child. Child welfare services are those provisions which society has made, because of a special concern for children, to deal with this problem in a variety of ways. The purpose of providing child welfare services, and the role of the child welfare worker, becomes that of assuring parental care. . . . [34, p. 1]

A special field of practice arises from the need for specialized knowledge and specialized methods of intervention to deal with clusters of related problems. In order to provide efficient and effective service, agencies and their staffs focus on special problem areas, and thus come to constitute a specialized field of practice. The fact that there is so much to know about child welfare that a textbook of this size with so many references can be compiled bolsters the argument for specialization. Working with a group of clients who share similar characteristics and problems permits the development of expertise and the accumulation of knowledge that assure more effective service. The term *child welfare* as used here applies, then, to a particular set of social problems which become the responsibility of a group of professionals, the child welfare social workers, who attempt to help in the prevention, amelioration, or improvement of such problematic social situations through the develop-ment and provision of particular child welfare services. Our contention is that child welfare services are concerned with a particular set of problems—problems in the social functioning of the parent-child net-work.

The ensuing discussion excludes school social work, for the social problems which concern the school social worker arise from the child's relationship to a particular social institution—the school. The point of entree, the ticket for admission for the services of the school social worker, is some problem in adjustment between the child and the school system, not, as would be the case if a child welfare social worker were being called for, some problem in the parent-child network.

The emphasis on problematic situations is in line with what has been termed the "residual" conception of social welfare, which sees social services as appropriate when normal institutional arrangements for meeting crucial social needs break down. The "institutional" conception of social welfare posits a different point of view: it suggests that, in a complex modern society, social services are appropriately organized and offered to supplement the normal institutional arrangements of society even when these are operating satisfactorily. [17, p. 3; 41, p. 138]

Actually, it is hoped that people will turn to social work agencies, and to child welfare agencies in particular, to enhance social functioning. Just as the World Health Organization has defined *health* as the "state of complete physical, mental, and social well-being, not merely the absence of disease or infirmity" [36, p. 6], adequate social functioning might be defined as the state of optimum satisfaction in social relationships, rather than merely the absence of problems in social functioning.

The fact, however, is that most individuals come to social agencies only when social functioning is problematic. Hence, realistically, we are justified in focusing on problems in social role implementation and performance; we are justified in focusing on the unmet or inadequately met needs of children.

There is considerable justification for the argument that such a view of child welfare does violence to the reality of the child's living situation. Our attention, it is argued, should not be focused narrowly on the parent-child relationship but, rather, on the total family configuration. One might do better to be concerned with family welfare, of which child welfare is a specialized aspect. [18; 29; 31]

The social system of the family might be seen as consisting of three principal interrelated subsystems—the marital-pair system, the parent-child system, and the system of sibling relationships. [27, p. 322] Difficulty in any one of the three subsystems is very likely to produce problems in the related subsystems. But if a conflict between husband and wife is not reflected to any significant degree in the parent-child subsystem, then marital counseling might be more helpful than child welfare services. And one might further argue that, although children live within the family, they have special needs, and that the child welfare specialists have developed a particular understanding of, and experience with, these needs and with the services required to meet them.

Social Roles

Since child welfare services focus on malfunctions in role enactment within the parent-child relationship, it might be helpful at this point to discuss the concept of social role and to clarify the specific role responsibilities inherent in the parent-child role network. A role is the prescribed behavior and attitudes that a person occupying a particular status is expected to assume. As Sarbin says, "A role is a pattern of attitudes and actions which a person takes in a social situation. . . ." [30, p. 224]   Linton states it somewhat more technically:

> The term *role* is used to designate the sum total of the culture patterns associated with a particular status. It thus includes the attitudes, values, and behavior ascribed by society to any and all persons occupying the status. . . . Insofar as it represents overt behavior, a role is the dynamic aspect of status, what the individual has to do in order to validate his occupation of the status. [21, p. 77]

Similarly, Kluckhohn notes:

> The set of behaviors which ego is expected to perform by virtue of his position as father, mother, or child is called a social role. A man in his role as father is expected to behave in certain ways; a woman in her role as mother in certain other ways; and each child according to age, sex, and birth order in still other ways. A role is thus a series of appropriate and expected ways of behaving relative to certain objects by virtue of a given individual's status in a given social structure or institution. [24, p. 350]

As Bernard puts it, "A role, figuratively speaking, is a job description." [5, p. 43]   It is a job description to be followed by the person performing the "job" of parent or child, and includes not only the statement of the expected behavior, but also the statement of the expected accompanying emotion. It prescribes that the parent not only feed the child, but also love him; it prescribes that the child not only obey the parent, but also respect him. Nevertheless, society sanctions a variety of patterns of behavior as well as different levels of adequacy in role performance. [13]

> An important feature of a large proportion of social roles is that the actions which make them up are not minutely prescribed and that a certain range of variability is regarded as legitimate. Sanctions are not invoked against deviants within certain limits. [24, p. 24]

Sanctioned alternatives, however, fall within prescribed limits. Generally, alternative modes of behavior will be sanctioned as long as the responsibility of the role is successfully discharged. For example, spanking and withdrawal of love are both acceptable modes of disciplining a child, but physical brutality is not acceptable because it conflicts with one of the principal purposes of the role of parenthood—care and protection of the child. As Brim says, "role prescriptions include the behavior believed in the society to be the instrumental means to the achievement of some desired result." [8, p. 346]

The role prescription, therefore, will change with changes in society's conception of the purpose of the role. A society that asks parents to prepare the child to live obediently under an authoritarian regime will require forms of behavior in discharging the responsibilities of parenthood different from those required by a society that asks parents to prepare the child to live as a participating member of a democracy. [43] Different subcultural groups in a given society may have differing conceptions of parenthood, so that the role prescription of the white middle-class parent may be different from that to which a lower-class black parent might feel impelled to adhere. [9]

Unlike some other social roles, such as church member, for instance, the parental role, around which a good deal of one's life is organized, demands a high level of involvement and commitment. It can be given up only at considerable emotional, social, and legal cost. On the other hand, it is enacted under conditions of limited visibility. How the parent cares for the child, disciplines the child, or interacts with the child is not generally visible to the community.

Role enactment requires interaction with others; it involves a set of complementary expectations concerning the individual's own actions and those of others with whom he interacts—his counterparts. For the parent, the nature of his counterpart, the child, is always changing, so that the parental role prescription needs constantly to be revised. The parent of the young child is required to meet the child's dependency needs, but the same parent must change his behavior to meet the child's growing need for independence in adolescence. Recognizing that the role prescriptions for parent and child vary with time and with subcultural groups, and that each role description carries with it acceptable alternatives, let us attempt to delineate the normative aspects of role behavior for parent and child in our society.

The Parental Role

The acceptable behavior associated with the performance of a given role includes rights (the behavior expected by us from our reciprocals— the husband from the wife, the child from the parent) as well as obligations (the behavior that others expect us to perform toward them—the husband to the wife, the parents to the child). One person's rights in the role set are the other person's obligations.

What is the parent expected to do and feel in relation to his child in acceptably discharging his parental role?

1. He is expected to provide an income that will permit him to meet the needs of the child for food, clothing, shelter, education, health care, and social and recreational activities.

2. He is expected to provide for the emotional needs of the child—to provide love, security, affection, and the emotional support necessary for the healthy emotional development of the child.
3. He is expected to provide the necessary stimulation for normal intellectual, social, and spiritual development if the family believes this to be important. The parent should see that a school is available and that the child goes to school, that a peer group is available and that the child is encouraged to play, that a church is available and that the child is encouraged to attend services.
4. He must help to socialize the child. Socialization is the process of inducting "new recruits" into the social group, and teaching them the behavior that is customary and acceptable to the group. The parent, in other words, has the responsibility of "transforming a biological organism into a human being."
5. He must discipline the child and keep him from developing patterns of behavior and attitudes disapproved of by the society.
6. He must protect the child from physical, emotional, or social harm.
7. He must present a model for identification of sex-linked behavior.
8. He must help to maintain family interaction on a stable, satisfying basis so that an effort is made to meet the significant needs of all the members of the family. The parent must help to resolve discomforts, frictions, and dissatisfactions, and meet emotional needs by accepting, affectionate responses.
9. He must provide a fixed place of abode for the child and provide a clearly defined "place" for him in the community. Thus the child comes to know who he is and to whom he belongs, and ultimately comes to achieve a stable self-identification.
10. The parent stands as an intermediary between the child and the outer world, defending the child's rights in the community and protecting the child from unjust demands by the community. Since the parental responsibility for socialization of the child is now shared with many community agencies, parents now find that their role requires making "decisions concerning which agencies should do the job for them and which ones should be allowed to exercise influence. Parents are necessarily culture brokers for their children before the age of consent; they encourage and facilitate access to some parts of culture, censor others and unconsciously or ambivalently screen out still others in response to their own preferences and sensibilities." [4, p. 53]

These role functions are applicable to the parental pair, although efforts have been made elsewhere to differentiate the distinctive role responsibilities of father and mother. [11; 32; 44]

The Child's Role

The child's role is inevitably somewhat more limited. As Sarbin notes, "assignment of tasks imposed by a particular role must be appropriate to the physical and intellectual capacity of the role participants." Totally or partially dependent, the child is limited in physical and mental capacity, and possesses a limited repertoire of skills. Nevertheless the status of child carries with it a set of obligations, and these are reciprocal to the parental roles.

1. If the parental role requires that the parent teach the child the appropriate attitudes and values of the society, the role of the child demands that he learn these attitudes and values, that he act in accordance with them and in accordance with the prescription for his age and sex.
2. If the parent's role is to discipline the child when he engages in inappropriate behavior, the child's role is to accept such discipline, to obey the parent, and to make the necessary changes in his behavior. The child is required to display the behavior that is acceptable to the family, to the peer group, and to the community.
3. The child is expected to meet some of the emotional needs of his parents by responding affectionately to them, confiding in them, and respecting them. The child is expected to act in a manner that will reflect credit on his parents and elicit praise for them in the community.
4. The child must cooperate with the parent in protecting himself from danger and harm, and in meeting his physical, emotional, and educational needs. The child is required to eat the food offered, to go to the school provided, and to refrain from activity likely to be physically, socially, or emotionally damaging.
5. The child has some responsibility for maintaining family unity and reducing family tensions by cooperating and sharing with other members of the family, and by showing loyalty to members of the family group.
6. The child is required to perform whatever appropriate chores are asked of him, and to care for whatever clothes, toys, and furniture the parents have provided.

The Community's Role

Although less visible and apparent than either the parent or the child, the community is an authentic component of the parent-child network. The community, represented by the state, is a parent, beyond the biological parent, to all children. This is the meaning of the concept of *parens patriae*. As such the community has some rights and obligations in implementing its role in the parent-child network. When the community fails to implement its role effectively, we have another group of situations requiring the intervention of child welfare services.

The community fulfills its "parental" obligations by exercising its regulatory and legislative powers in protecting children and providing the resources they need for proper biological and psychosocial development. The community protects children by licensing day-care centers, and providing legal sanctions against child labor, neglect and abuse of children, truancy, and the sale of alcohol, tobacco, and pornography to minors. Through legislation establishing adequate programs for social insurance, income maintenance, and health care, public welfare agencies, schools, and recreational facilities, the community provides resources that enable the child to meet his needs. A community which fails to function adequately in behalf of its children becomes a legitimate focus of child welfare services social action.

Problems of Role Functioning: Parent-Child Network

Most children live in a reasonably well-established family group, in which both parents and children are effectively discharging their respective role requirements.

As Le Masters notes, "in a well-organized family, the major roles have been identified, assigned, and are performed with some degree of competence," having been understood and accepted. [20, p. 50] However, the community must still provide school facilities, health facilities, clean water, a decent sewerage system, adequate police protection, and so on. These services, required by normal children in normal families, are not child welfare services as we have defined them here.

Child welfare services are those services required when parents or children are either incapable or unwilling (or both) of implementing their respective role requirements, or when a serious discrepancy arises between the role expectation of the community and the individual's performance. We can now categorize recurrent problems of role implementation and fulfillment that might, and do, require the intervention of child welfare social work services (alternative categorizations are available in social work literature [1; 2; 22; 26]).

1. Parental role unoccupied.
2. Parental incapacity.
3. Parental role rejection.
4. Intra-role conflict.
5. Inter-role conflict.

6. Child incapacity and/or handicap.
7. Deficiency of community resources.

Parental Role Unoccupied

The most obvious difficulty results when the position of parent is unoccupied. The role may never have been occupied, as is true of the paternal role in the truncated family system of the unmarried mother and illegitimate child; death, separation, or divorce may leave the role of the father or the mother—or sometimes both—permanently unfilled; long hospitalizations, military service, or imprisonment may leave the role of the parent temporarily vacant. In all these cases, some essential requirements for the normal operation of the parent-child system remain unmet. As long as the role is unfilled, the child is not incorporated in an adequately functioning family and is likely to be deprived. This, then, is an area of concern for child welfare services.*

Role Unfilled—Death of Mother

Gregory C., thirty-seven, a factory clerk, is devoted to his motherless children—Pete, twelve; Violet, ten; Rose, nine; and Billy, seven—and is determined to keep them together.

Eight months ago Mr. C.'s wife died of cancer. He tried to carry on alone, asking a neighbor to care for the children after school until he returned from work. But the double burden of running the home and providing for his family became overwhelming. Relatives suggested that he divide the children among them, but the children, terrified, begged their father not to send them away.

Upset and confused as to how to proceed in caring for his children, Mr. C. came to an agency.

Role Unfilled—Death of Father

Mrs. Lillian C., thirty-seven, came to the agency for help with her two boys—Ben, sixteen, and Tommy, eleven. While their mother went to work, both boys were playing truant regularly from school. Tommy would idle about the house, awaiting her return. Ben loitered on street corners with a gang of boys and was becoming unmanageable.

During the past five years, Mrs. C. has had little time for the children. When her husband died ten years ago, she managed on their small savings supplemented by financial help from her brother.

* Most of the brief illustrations which follow originally appeared in *The New York Times'* Annual Listing of 100 Neediest Cases, submitted by New York social work agencies. © 1964 by The New York Times Company. Reprinted by permission. Additions have been made from later years and other sources.

But this help stopped when her brother suffered business reverses, and Mrs. C. had to take a job as cashier to make ends meet. Constantly fatigued by the need to be both mother and father to her children, she became hopeless and bitter. She often told her sons that they were being "cheated by life."

Role Unfilled—Physical Illness

Ordinarily, Jack R., ten, and his brothers—William, seven, and Saul, five—are punctual pupils, neatly though poorly dressed, and attentive in class. But recently they began to be tardy and were frequently absent. Jack fell behind in his work; the younger boys were unruly; all three looked unkempt.

When teachers finally enlisted the agency s aid, the social worker found that the boy's mother, Mrs. Janet R., twenty-nine, had been hospitalized for several weeks with asthma, and the boys and their father, Henry R., thirty, were trying to carry on alone. Mr. R., who works long hours as a store clerk, spent nights and weekends doing heavy chores while Jack handled the light tasks and supervised his brothers. But the lunches Jack prepared were skimpy; he couldn't keep up with the dish-washing and the baths and the marketing.

The doctors say it may be several months before Mrs. R. can return home. Mr. R. and the boys would make any sacrifice to remain together, but they cannot manage alone any longer.

Role Unfilled—Imprisonment

Larry V. is ten and normally active and boisterous. He looks like his father. His mother's great fear is that he will follow in his father's footsteps. Mr. V. recently was sentenced to a prison term for purse-snatching. Mrs. Dorothy V., thirty-five, is so ashamed of her husband's criminal record that she has cut herself off from friends and neighbors. She has also become unduly strict with Larry, disciplining him severely and setting inflexible rules about homework and bedtime. The result is that he has grown increasingly rebellious, which has been very upsetting to Mrs. V. The family has been receiving public assistance.

Role Unfilled—Mental Illness

Mrs. Sylvia P., thirty, was lost when she came to the agency several months ago. Last winter her husband Milton, thirty-three, a salesman, suddenly became quarrelsome and erratic. He was dismissed from his job, and soon after was committed to a mental institution.

To support her children—George, nine, and Sue, five—Mrs. P. went to work as a file clerk. But she had to move into an over-crowded apartment with her sister and her ailing mother, both of whom complained endlessly about the children's noise. George became restless and disobedient. Both he and Sue were disturbed by their father's absence, and Mrs. P., ashamed, answered their questions evasively. The children became such a problem that Mrs. P. asked the agency for help.

Role Unfilled—Illegitimacy

A year ago, Betty N., twenty-four, was happy and secure. Now she faces the problem of caring for an illegitimate child.

Betty's fiancé, Stephen S., twenty-five, entered medical school two years ago. A year later, Betty was graduated from college and began to teach, saving for their wedding day. Last summer she became pregnant. Stephen offered financial help for an abortion, but he refused to marry her, saying it would hurt his career. Betty broke off with him.

Betty's parents have agreed to pay for her confinement but they have refused to provide for the baby and have urged her to give it up for adoption. Torn by indecision, Betty came to the agency.

Role Unfilled—Migration

Paul's father, after a long period of unemployment, recently decided to try his luck elsewhere. Because he was uncertain about the job possibilities in Chicago, he decided to go without the family. He left Appalachia six months ago, and is still looking for steady work. Paul, ten, misses his father, with whom he used to hunt and fish frequently. He is becoming depressed and his school work suffers as a result.

Parental Incapacity

Inadequate role implementation sometimes results from incapacity. The role incumbent may be physically present and desirous of fulfilling his role requirements but may be incapacitated by physical, mental, or emotional inadequacy, or lack of preparation, training, or knowledge. A physically handicapped mother may find it difficult to meet the demands of an active, healthy youngster. A mentally deficient mother may be incapable of learning the essential routines of child care. A mother who is herself emotionally immature cannot meet the dependent needs of her infant child. Some parents, deprived in their own childhoods, may have come to parenthood without adequate education or marketable job skills, and without having learned essential child-care skills from *their* parents. Sometimes addiction to drugs or alcohol may render a parent incapable of providing adequate physical and emotional care for his children. In all of these cases, because the role of the parent is inadequately implemented and the child suffers, child welfare services are an appropriate remedial resource.

Role Incapacity—Illness

When Mrs. Rosalie M. came to the agency, she was so depressed by her many family problems that she felt she could not go on. Her husband Morris, forty-one, always was sickly, but up to six months ago he managed to support his family by working as a printing salesman. Then he became so crippled by arthritis that he lost his job. The family has been living on his unemployment insurance, but it will soon expire.

Mrs. M.'s constant worry about finances and Mr. M.'s ill-health have affected the children, who can no longer secure their parents' interest. Daniel, eight, has become listless; and Beatrice, ten, is so nervous that she runs home from school to see if her family is still there. Recently, when the children began failing in school, authorities referred Mrs. M. to the agency.

Role Incapacity—Illness

Frank F. and his wife Rose, both thirty-six, have been married for fifteen years. They have lived from crisis to crisis, but now it has become too much for them. Mr. F. is a laborer; his earnings have never adequately covered the family's needs. Mrs. F. is diabetic; the care of three children leaves her suffering chronic fatigue. She upbraids her husband for being a bad provider. He lashes out at her for being a poor manager. They quarrel bitterly and endlessly.

The continual tension is reflected in the children: Mark, fourteen, refuses to play with other children; Frances, eleven, often cannot eat; Therese, eight months old, cries constantly. Their pastor suggested that they seek the help of a social agency.

Role Incapacity—Physical Handicap

Mrs. Belle H., thirty-two, is crippled in body but not in spirit. A year ago Mrs. H. was stricken with polio and had to be hospitalized. Her husband Victor, thirty-four, sent ten-year-old Shirley to live with relatives. Sylvia, four, was placed in a foster home.

Two months ago Mrs. H. was brought home in a wheelchair, with both legs useless and one arm partially paralyzed. Believing it would aid her rehabilitation, her doctors advised that the family be reunited, and the children are now home again.

Mrs. H. goes to a clinic for therapy several times a week, and eventually will recover partial use of her limbs. Presently, however, her handicap prevents Mrs. H. from adequately caring for her children.

Role Incapacity—Ignorance

Peter's mother was making a small but constant error, out of ignorance, that had serious effects on his health. It was noticed at the well-baby clinic that he was not gaining any weight and that his color was poor. When, at the request of the authorities, the situation was investigated, it was found that Peter's mother had been using teaspoonfuls instead of tablespoonfuls in making up his formula.

Role Incapacity—Emotional Immaturity

Kathy is only eleven, but she bears a burden far beyond her years. Her mother, Mrs. Maureen L., forty, is an alcoholic. Her father, George, forty-one, works nights in a factory and takes little interest in his family, which includes, besides Kathy, George Jr., eight; Louis, seven, and Peter, six. For the past two years Kathy more and more has had to do the housework and care for the children. When her mother disappears, as often happens, Kathy does the marketing and cooking. When her mother has fits of weeping, Kathy anxiously tries to "mother" her, too.

Recently Kathy began to show signs of the strain she is under. She daydreamed in school. She lied to her teacher. She took money from her mother's purse to spend on classmates. Mr. L., alarmed, came to the agency.

Role Incapacity—Mental Retardation

Tommy is four, a bright, sturdy, normal little boy with a quick smile. But he needs help, because his parents are mentally retarded.

Tommy's parents grew up in institutions; there they received enough training to be self-sufficient. His father, who is twenty-eight, works as a dishwasher, and is able to support his family adequately. But his unpredictable attitudes confuse Tommy. When Tommy misbehaves, sometimes his father scolds him, sometimes he laughs at him. Tommy's mother is bewildered by her lively son and is unable to understand or anticipate his actions. He refuses to mind her and lacks the most rudimentary training. It was on the advice of a clinic nurse that she sought the agency's help.

Role Incapacity—Drug Addiction

Ruth, eight, and Jimmy, six, frequently have had to beg food from the neighbors. Their parents are drug addicts, and the children are frequently neglected for long periods of time, when the parents are on drugs. The apartment is barren of furniture, and the children poorly clothed, since all of the limited family income goes to support the habit. Mr. C. finds it difficult to hold a steady, adequately paying job. Neglect and deprivation are beginning to affect adversely the health of the children.

Role Rejection

Inadequate role implementation sometimes results from role rejection. For many people parenthood is a voluntarily assumed role; for others, however, parenthood is an involuntary burden resulting from a biological accident. There is, on the part of these parents, a conscious or unconscious rejection of the parental role, which results in varying degrees of failure in role performance. These parents are apt to be indifferent, neglectful, or abusive. Some totally abandon the role of parents by deserting their families. The child suffers, or is apt to suffer, as a result of rejection of the parental role, and child welfare services are consequently required to protect the child.

Role Rejection—Neglect and Abandonment

Nancy is almost five. She is headstrong and defiant; she tears her dolls apart and bites other children when she quarrels with them. Her sleep is disturbed by nightmares during which she cries out for her "Mummy."

Nancy's parents, an unstable couple in their twenties, were never happy in their marriage. They quarreled constantly, and frequently separated for long periods. Four months ago they left Nancy with a friend, saying they expected to be out late that night. But next day the friend received a letter saying they were leaving town and could no longer provide for Nancy. They asked that she be taken to the agency.

Role Rejection—Abandonment

Freddy is a brown-haired, chubby little boy almost three years old. At times he is sweet and affectionate; at others, for no apparent reason, he throws himself on the floor of his boarding home kicking and pounding. Often he wakes in the night screaming.

Shortly after Freddy was born, his mother asked the Welfare Department to place him for adoption. She said that he was illegitimate and that his father had deserted her. Before her story could be checked, she disappeared. Recently a court determination of abandonment was made, and the Welfare Department turned Freddy over to the agency for adoption.

Role Rejection—Neglect

Mrs. Yvonne E., thirty-one, was sentenced to sixty days in the county jail Wednesday on charges of neglect of children.

The E. case came to the attention of the Police Department's Crime Prevention Bureau July 22, after a neighbor summoned police. An investigation at about 4 A.M. showed that Mrs. E.'s four children were alone in the apartment. The floors were strewed with decayed food and mildewed clothing; windows were broken and insects infested the bedding; food in the refrigerator was covered with insects, and the children were attempting to fry a spoiled, uncleaned fish. Toilet facilities in the apartment were plugged.

Role Rejection—Physical Abuse

A little girl with both eyes swollen nearly shut heard a judge describe her mother as "a savage," as he sentenced the mother to one year in the House of Correction.

Mrs. Barbara F., twenty-one, admitted pummeling the child, Darlene, three, with her fists and striking her time after time with her shoes and belt. Asked whether she loved the child, Mrs. F., a waitress, replied, "I didn't think much of her from the day she was born." Police were called Tuesday after a babysitter, Mrs. Minnie J., noticed that the child's face, legs, back, and stomach were severely bruised.

Role Rejection—Desertion

Steve is only nine. Last year he was an A pupil. This year he has tried so hard to look after his mother and his baby sister Anne, two, that he is failing.

Steve's father, Mr. Malcolm P., thirty-three, a bookkeeper, and Steve's mother, Mrs. Lois P., quarreled incessantly because Mr. P. squandered his money on gambling. Sometimes he would stay away from home for days at a time; six months ago he deserted his wife and children, though continuing to send money for their support.

Mrs. P. grew so ill and despondent that she neglected her home and children. Steve stayed up nights to do the housework and took on much of Anne's care. When Mr. P. delayed sending money for their support, Steve searched in vain for a parttime job as errand boy. But at school he could not concentrate. His teacher, learning of the home situation, advised Mrs. P. to consult the agency.

Intra-role Conflict

Inadequate role implementation sometimes results from problems of conflict in role definition or intra-role conflict. The mother and father may disagree strongly as to who is supposed to do what for and with the child. The mother may expect the father to help her care for the child; the father may define his role more narrowly as primarily that of a provider.

Intra-role conflict may result from the seemingly incongruent demands imposed by the parental role, which requires that one love the child yet discipline him, indulge him yet deprive him, free him yet restrict him. Or conflict may result from differing interpretations of role behavior by the various reference groups with which the person is affiliated; the parents may expect one kind of behavior from their adolescent child while his peer group may define expected behavior in quite another, and conflicting, way. Some parents and children may define their reciprocal roles differently. The frequently cited generation gap refers, in essence, to problems of intra-role definition.

Some parents fail to perceive clearly the requirements of the role, or society may have failed to define the role clearly. In periods when the role of parent is changing, it is not clear how the parent should behave or what is expected of him. Furthermore, even though parental roles generally might be clearly defined, specific aspects of the role might be ambiguous. For instance, the division of parental energy and time between the child's needs and the parent's own needs may be a matter over which society itself is undecided. The problems deriving from these conflicts impede effective implementation of parental role, and the child therefore suffers.

Intra-role Conflict—Definition of Role

Mr. and Mrs. F. were advised by an elementary school teacher to apply for help at a child guidance clinic. Paul, their eight-year-old son, was doing poorly in his studies and frequently displayed disruptive behavior in the classroom. He shouted, fought with other children, and was difficult to discipline.

In talking with the caseworker, Mr. and Mrs. F. revealed that the problem of disciplining Paul was a matter of considerable friction between them. Mr. F. had grown up in a home that emphasized strict obedience, respect for elders, and prompt physical punishment for lapses in behavior. He believed that parents should order and children should obey. Mrs. F. felt uncomfortable with this approach. Her tendency was to be more permissive, to allow more latitude, and to permit the children to "express themselves rather than be squelched." As a consequence of this difference, neither parent took responsibility for disciplining Paul. Each would make an attempt at it when emergencies arose, but neither one felt that he had full right to try his own approach because the marital partner so strongly disagreed with it.

Intra-role Conflict—Definition of Role Behavior

Mrs. R. and her husband might have been able to work out their conflict, but Mr. R.'s mother kept picking at him and urging him to object to Mrs. R.'s approach to child care. Mrs. R. felt that she was still young, that she had a right to go out frequently as long as she had a babysitter to care for the twins, Jerry and Joe, three and one-half. Her mother-in-law, coming from a small Italian village, believed very strongly that Mrs. R. should stay at home all the time and care for the children. All the going out, she felt, was really neglect of the children. Mr. R. was caught between his wife and his mother, but tended to side with the latter in all the arguments. The fights were getting more and more bitter and more and more prolonged, and the twins were beginning to react to them. Joe, who had been toilet-trained by two and one-half years, was beginning to wet the bed; Jerry, who had begun to be weaned, was showing a greater attachment to the bottle.

Inter-role Conflict

Inadequate role implementation may result when the parental role conflicts with another social role. According to Werble,

When the expectation between the vital social roles occupied by a single actor are inconsistent, contradictory, or mutually exclusive so that compliance with one set of role expectations necessarily entails noncompliance with another set of role expectations, we have the problem of role conflict. [40, p. 30]

The occupational role often conflicts with the duties and obligations of the parental role. The father, who is away from the home a great deal because of the demands of his job, faces such a conflict, just as the working mother faces a conflict between her role as a mother and her role as an employee. Also, the demands on a man in his role as son to his own parents may conflict with the demands made on him as a father to his children. The conflicting demands made by different role requirements stemming from the variety of positions people occupy simultaneously in a complex society may result in the inadequate implementation of the parental role. In such situations, the child is deprived, and the intervention of child welfare services is appropriate.

Role Conflict—Working Mother

Mrs. W. needed to work and enjoyed her job. Her husband's income as a postal clerk could not meet the needs of a growing family of six children—five girls and a boy. Mrs. W. decided to go to work when it seemed clear that the family was becoming more and more heavily indebted. But two of the children—Mike, two and one-half, and Ruth, three and one-half—were still at home and needed her, and even the school-age children seemed to react negatively to her absence from home. Mrs. W. wasn't sure that being a salesclerk, when she should be a mother, was the best choice to make. Besides, a good deal of her energy was being absorbed in making arrangements with all sorts of people to care for the preschool children during the time she was at work. Concerned about the situation, Mrs. W. came to the agency to discuss her conflicts.

Role Conflict—Mother-Daughter

During the last four months Mrs. R. had been more of a stranger than a mother to her three children—Nancy, five; Joan, seven; and William, eleven. Mrs. R.'s father, seventy-six, suffered a heart attack about six months ago. A widower, he was living alone in a six-room house that the family had owned for the last thirty years. He refused to go to an institution and Mrs. R., an only child, was very worried that he might overextend himself and suffer another sudden heart attack. As a result, she made an effort to visit him daily and care for him. She left in the morning and did not come home until the children were asleep. Mr. R. had been trying to care for the family in his wife's daily absence. Although she recognized that her children were suffering as a result of the family's disorganization occasioned by the care of her father, she felt great guilt if she neglected her duties as a daughter.

Child Incapacity and/or Handicap

Inadequate role implementation also results from excessive demands on the role incumbents. The physically handicapped or emotionally disturbed child is incapable of performing the role required normally of the child. Such a child imposes on its parents a burden of care, of specialized knowledge, of patience and control beyond that which any society can normally expect of them, and the possibility of adequately meeting the needs of such a child is reduced. The child's failure to meet the expectations of the parents robs them of the emotional satisfactions that are the rewards of fulfilling their many parental obligations and duties, and makes it even more difficult for them to perform adequately the parental role. In such cases, the provision of child welfare services is appropriate.

Excessive Demand—Epilepsy

Anne is only six, but she knows that she is different, that her parents quarrel constantly over her, and that her older brother and sister are ashamed of her. Anne is an epileptic.

Anne's father, Jacob L., thirty-eight, a municipal clerk, has never accepted his daughter. He reminds his wife Lillian, thirty-five, that he never wanted a third child. He complains that Anne takes too much of Mrs. L.'s time. Mrs. L., in turn, accuses him of making Anne's condition worse by his refusal to share the parental burden. The L.'s sense of shame has affected the other children: Joseph, thirteen, shies away from the outside world; Dana, ten, is a behavior problem at school.

Excessive Demand—Mental Deficiency

For years Samuel and Martha W. couldn't understand why their youngest child, Ethel, five, was so different from her four brothers and sisters, ranging in age from seven to fourteen. She could not talk or respond to speech; she had no control over her body functions; yet she was strong and active and kept hurting herself. Ethel is a severely retarded child.

The care of Ethel, on top of the problem of caring for her four children on the meager income of Mr. W., forty-eight, a peddler, became too much for Mrs. W., forty-three. A social worker, disturbed by signs of neglect the other children showed at a free summer camp, visited the home and persuaded Mrs. W. to take Ethel to the agency.

Excessive Demand—Emotional Disturbance

During the past two years, Billy, seven, has been unable to sleep more than four or five hours a night. He would wake up during the night screaming and covering his eyes as though he saw something which frightened him. He would strike and bite his brothers and sisters, and was destructive of neighbors' property. Billy tended to play by himself, carrying on an intelligible conversation with his toys. He had temper tantrums that would last for hours. His behavior was disrupting the entire family and the neighbors were beginning to complain.

Despite their best efforts, Mr. and Mrs. S. seemed incapable of dealing with their son's behavior. They were exhausted by their attempts to help him and frustrated and upset because they did not know what to do next. They felt their failure all the more keenly since they had proved themselves to be reasonably adequate parents in dealing with their other children—Kathy, nine; Frank, fourteen; and Sylvia, three. Billy, however, was too much for them to contend with.

Excessive Demand—Deformity

Mrs. Bertha V., thirty-seven, prided herself on being a good wife to her husband, Louis, forty, a laundry worker, and a devoted mother to her children—Henry, twelve; William, ten; and Bonnie, four.

Four months ago Mrs. V.'s fourth child, Gloria, was born— hopelessly deformed and retarded. Mrs. V. refused to put her in an institution. She became so wrapped up in Gloria's care that she neglected the family. Two months ago, after locking herself in a bedroom with the child every day for a week, Mrs. V. took an overdose of sleeping pills. A neighbor got Mrs. V. to the hospital in time to save her life.

Psychiatric examination revealed that Mrs. V. is near a complete mental breakdown as a result of attempting to care for a child whose needs would tax the capacity of any parent.

Excessive Demand—Brain Injury

Mrs. Janice C., twenty-seven, and her husband Michael, thirty-one, a machinist, face a sorrowful decision. Doctors say their youngest child, three-year-old Susan, must be put in an institution, but they cannot bear to part with her.

Susan is a victim of a progressive brain disease that is expected to take her life within a few years. Mrs. C. is expecting another child, and she finds Susan's care increasingly heavy. Susan cannot sit up by herself or control her movements. She hits her head repeatedly on her crib and high chair, which are carefully padded, and needs constant watching. Moreover, the other two C. children— Lorraine, seven, and Alice, six—resenting the attention given their handicapped sister, are becoming defiant and unruly.

Deficiency of Community Resources

Inadequate role implementation sometimes results from deficiencies in community resources. For instance, a father will find it difficult to implement the income maintenance aspects of the parental role if there are no jobs available. As Spiegel points out, "Insofar as role activities require technical instruments, equipment, furniture, props, customs, climate and other appropriate physical facilities (including money), a lack or insufficiency of these instrumental prerequisites interferes with role transactions." [33, p. 369]   When adequate employment opportunities, schools, recreational facilities, health services are lacking, or when social and racial discrimination, overcrowding, and social disorganization are characteristic of the community, parents may find it difficult to implement their roles. The atmosphere of the community needs to be free of the stigma of racial and class discrimination if the parents are to be expected to raise their child with a sense of dignity and self-acceptance. The problems may result not only from the lack of available resources, but also from the lack of access to them by particular groups. If discrimination operates to keep some kinds of jobs closed to non-whites, women, former offenders, former mental patients, or those who have been mentally ill, the problem is, for these groups, a deficiency in environmental resources available, which adversely affects family role enactment. Efforts to change community conditions which adversely affect social functioning are part of the responsibility of child welfare services.

Community Deficiency—Inadequate Housing

Mr. and Mrs. R. are very much concerned about the threat to their children's healthy development presented by the neighborhood in which they live. Mr. R. has worked steadily for the past fifteen years as an elevator operator in a large office building. They have been living in the same apartment house for the past twenty years. So far they have been able to rear their children—George, sixteen; Alice, twelve; and Susan, seven—without any serious problems. However, the neighborhood in which they live has been rapidly deteriorating. Several women in the apartment house are openly engaged in prostitution. The neighborhood barber shop and candy store are the hangouts for dope-pushers, numbers-runners, and pornography salesmen. They would like to move out of the neighborhood, but cannot find any apartment as large as the one they presently occupy at a rental they can afford. Despite their best efforts at being adequate parents, they feel that the counter-influence of some of the neighborhood elements may negatively affect the behavior of their oldest boy, George, in particular.

Community Deficiency—Unemployment

The men stand around idly on Main Street. There is nothing else to do. Three months ago the local mine, in which most of them have worked for the better part of their employable lives, closed down. The vein was giving out and it was no longer profitable for the mine company to continue operations. Three hundred men were suddenly thrown out of work, and the town industries and services were able to absorb only a small fraction of this large body of unemployed men. For the rest there remained limited savings, unemployment insurance for a limited period, and then, no one knew exactly what. As miners, as wage-earners, these men had been able to support their families. Now there were no jobs available, and they worried about how they might continue to care for their children.

The variety of problems in role enactment, detailed above, is neatly summarized by Bartlett when she says that

the condition with which child welfare services are primarily concerned is the deficiency in these provisions resulting from (1) incapacity of parents, (2) extraordinary needs of certain children, and (3) limitations of opportunities and resources. [3, p. 43]

Two recent studies confirm the contention that the social problems outlined above are, in fact, the primary concerns of child welfare agencies. [15, 23] Both studies attempted a nationwide "census" of the circumstances which resulted in applications for service from child welfare agencies. In both studies, problems in parental role coverage resulting from death, divorce, separation, desertion, imprisonment, illegitimacy; inadequate parental role performance owing to physical and/or mental illness; parental role rejection manifested in neglect and/or abuse of child; and inadequate enactment of the child's role owing to emotional or physical disability accounted, in aggregate, for most of the reasons someone, either the family or the community, had called for the help of a child welfare social worker.

The problems encountered by child welfare agencies change with changes in the society. Earlier in the century, many of the problems which came to the child welfare agencies reflected intergenerational and intercultural conflict. The parents, often recent immigrants speaking no English, brought to the parent-child relationship a definition of the parental role which had been shaped in the context of the "Old World," while the children defined their expectations in terms of the American experience. Currently, however, child welfare agencies encounter problems of intergenerational conflict resulting from different definitions of parent-child roles caused by a fast-changing culture. The over-thirty parent reflects attitudes and convictions very different from those of his child, and the conflict is expressed in bitter battles about hair length, marijuana, sexual relationship, work habits, and so on. A decade ago, parental incapacity arising from alcoholic addiction was a problem frequently encountered by child welfare agencies; today, parental incapacity is often caused by drug addiction.

While 50 years ago child welfare agencies were frequently concerned with children of recently arrived immigrant parents facing difficulties of adjustment to a new and strange world, 50 years from now child welfare agencies may be concerned with families in which the parental role of father is unfilled because he is away on an interplanetary trip that is scheduled to take three to five years to complete.

Problems of role enactment may be the result of social pressures or psychological pressures, or both. In some instances, the most significant component in the problem is a personal pathology; in others, it is the pathology of society. A black man with limited education has difficulty in obtaining and holding an adequate job. Living on a limited income, in crowded substandard housing, the pressure of the social situation may lead him to desert his family. A middle-class engineer living on a decent regular income in a comfortable suburb may also desert his family because he feels tied down, hemmed in, anxious, and depressed. In both instances, the role of parent has been abandoned, although for very different reasons. As far as the child is concerned, the etiology of the problem matters little. What does matter is that something must be done to fulfill the obligations of the rejected position. Each situation may present a unique combination of psychological and social factors resulting in a particular kind of problem.

Some problems are more susceptible to solution through community organization. Others are more susceptible to solution through involvement of the client in group activity. Still others are more susceptible to solution through work with the individual client. It might sometimes be helpful to use a combination of approaches.

For instance, the working mother of a preschool child must arrange for child care while she is on the job. If the community lacks day-care services, and the problem is of concern to a sufficiently large number of women in the community, social workers would then employ the method of community organization in an effort to establish a day-care center.

Sometimes, however, even if a day-care facility is already available in the community, a mother may be anxious about the effects of temporary role substitution on her relationship with her child. The caseworker might discuss with the mother her feelings about relinquishing her maternal role for some part of each day and her anxieties regarding the child's reaction to day care, and help her make a reasoned decision with which she will be comfortable.

Child welfare social work is not synonymous with case work although this is, admittedly, the method of helping most frequently employed. Any and all methods—casework, group work, community organization, social action—are employed, alone and in combination, which can appropriately be applied in effecting some positive change in, and for, the client or client group. Social system change, social reform, is as much a responsibility of child welfare social work as is client symptom change; prevention is as appropriate as rescue-therapy-rehabilitation. These diverse approaches are complementary in this as well as in other fields of social work.

Further, the formulation does not suggest that any one method has to have been defined in a particular way. Casework in child welfare can be defined as a method which includes brokerage and advocacy activity in the client's behalf, and its psychotherapeutic endeavors might as legitimately employ a behavioral modification as a psychoanalytic or a Rogerian nondirective approach.

Categories of Child Welfare Services

Child welfare services, whether designed to help on the level of community action, group involvement, or individual contact, can be categorized as supportive, supplemental, or substitutive. These categories are not mutually exclusive, and they sometimes tend to overlap.

Supportive services include the services of child guidance clinics, the family service agency programs, and the work of child protective agencies. Supportive services are the first line of defense in dealing with actual or incipient problems of child welfare, when the family and parent-child relationship system is structurally intact but subject to stress. If the stress is permitted to continue, it might result in a structural break—divorce, separation, desertion, and so on. Supportive services are designed to use the family's own strength to work toward a reduction of strain in the parent-child relationship system.

The child who is disobedient, rebellious, and incorrigible may be beyond the normal parent's capacity to socialize. In such a case, the child guidance clinic may effectuate sufficient change in the relationship between parent and child so that the child becomes more responsive to the parent's teachings.

Casework services offered by family service agencies on behalf of the child support, reinforce, and strengthen the parents' efforts to discharge adequately their parental responsibilities. And, in dealing with marital friction that would ultimately have deleterious effects on the child, the family agency is offering another supportive service.

Protective services, offered by child welfare agencies for children who have been grossly neglected or abused, are primarily supportive services designed to develop and strengthen any and all factors in the situation that would enable the parents to enact their roles in a more socially acceptable manner.

Supplementary services are the second line of defense, called upon when a parent-child relationship is seriously impaired because a significant aspect of the parental role is inadequately covered but the family configuration is of such a nature that, with supplementation, the child can continue to live at home without harm. Financial maintenance programs of all kinds—assistance as well as insurance—are, in effect, supplementary services. Financial maintenance programs act *in loco parentis* as far as the income-producing responsibilities of the parents are concerned. Homemaker programs and day-care programs are also supplementary, for both are designed to supplement the mother's enactment of child-care functions.

Substitute services are the third line of defense, and are used when the situation is so damaging as to require either a temporary or a permanent dissolution of the parent-child relationship system. A substitute family is offered the child in a foster home, an adoptive home, or an institution. The substitute family may be similar in structure to the normal family, as in the case of the foster family or the adoptive home, or it may be different, as in the case of the institution—the orphan asylum, the residential treatment home, the training school for delinquents, the institution for the physically, emotionally, or mentally handicapped, and so on. The substitution may be temporary (as in the case of a foster home) or permanent (as in the case of an adoptive home). The institution may be employed both as a temporary or as a permanent family substitute. In all substitute family care arrangements, the natural parent of the child yields almost total responsibility to somebody else for the performance of the parental role in relation to the child.

Plan of Book

The plan of the book is to present a detailed review of each of these broad categories of supportive, supplementary, and substitute services, and to examine the specific programs that fall into one or another of these categories: child guidance, family service, protective service, income maintenance programs, day-care service, homemaker service, foster care, adoptions, institutional care.

In the case of each of the services we shall present material regarding the following content areas:

1. General historical background.
2. Situations for which service is appropriate.
3. Scope of service.

4. Process in offering the service.
5. Evaluation.
6. Problems regarding service.
7. Trends in offering service.

Before presenting a discussion of each of the specific child welfare services, we have included a chapter on the historical and current context of child welfare. This material is designed to provide a frame of reference for the discussion that follows. Following the chapters on each of the services there is a chapter on child welfare practices in other countries. This provides an international perspective on our problems and the way we meet them.

Because readers of the book are likely to be interested in child welfare as a career and because the professional subculture of the child welfare social worker affects the services offered, the final chapter is a discussion of the sociology of the child welfare worker—demography, recruitment, career line, value orientations, occupational problems, and so on.

Summary

Child welfare is defined as a special field within the profession of social work. Social work is concerned with man in relation to his social situation. As a technology, it is responsible for effecting change in some problematic aspect of the client's enactment or implementation of his social roles. It may effect such change by preventing the likelihood of impairment of social role enactment, by enhancing social role performance, or by helping to restore the capacity to implement social roles effectively.

As a specialized field within social work, child welfare is concerned with the antecedents, concomitants, and consequences of a particular kind of social problem—the parent-child relationship network, and the enactment and implementation of parental roles and child roles.

The recurrent problems for which child welfare has been given some responsibility include those deriving from roles left vacant because of death, hospitalization, illegitimacy, imprisonment, and so on; roles inadequately implemented because of illness, handicap, ignorance, and so on; role rejection, as in cases of abandonment, abuse, and neglect; intra-role conflict; inter-role conflict; problems resulting from the child's inability to implement his role; and problems resulting from deficiencies in community resources.

In meeting such problems, child welfare has developed a number of services. These may be grouped as supportive services (family service, child guidance clinics, protective services), supplementary services (insurance and assistance income maintenance programs, homemaker programs, day-care programs), and substitutive services (foster family care, adoptions, institutional child care).

Bibliography

1. ATHERTON, CHARLES R., *et al.* "Locating Points for Intervention." *Social Casework,* **52** (March 1971), 131–41.
2. ———— *et al.* "Using Points for Intervention." *Social Casework,* **52** (April 1971), 223–33.
3. BARTLETT, HARRIETT. *Analyzing Social Work Practice by Fields.* New York: National Association of Social Workers, 1961.
4. BENSON, LEONARD. *Fatherhood: A Sociological Perspective.* New York: Random House, Inc., 1968.
5. BERNARD, JESSIE. *Social Problems at Midcentury.* New York: Holt, Rinehart & Winston, Inc., 1957.
6. BOEHM, WERNER. *Objectives of the Social Work Curriculum of the Future.* New York: Council on Social Work Education, 1959.
7. ————. *The Training of Psychotherapists.* Ed. by Nicholas Dellis and Herbert Stone. Baton Rouge: Louisiana State University Press, 1960.
8. BRIM, ORVILLE. "The Parent-Child Relation as a Social System's Parent and Child Roles." *Child Development,* **28** (September 1957).
9. BRONFENBRENNER, URIE. "Socialization and Social Class Through Time and Space," in *Readings in Social Psychology.* Ed. by E. E. Maccoby *et al.* New York: Holt, Rinehart &Winston, Inc., 1958.
10. CARSTENS, C. C. "Child Welfare Services," in *Social Work Yearbook.* New York: Russell Sage Foundation, 1937.
11. DUVALL, EVELYN M. "Conception of Parenthood." *American Journal of Sociology,* **52** (1946).
12. FRIEDLANDER, WALTER. *Introduction to Social Welfare,* 2nd ed. Englewood Cliffs, N.J.: Prentice-Hall, Inc., 1961.
13. GEISMER, L. L., and BEVERLY AYERS. *Patterns of Change in Problem Families.* St. Paul, Minn.: Family-Centered Project, Greater St. Paul Community Chest and Councils, Inc., 1959. Appendix A.
14. GREENWOOD, ERNEST. "Social Work and Social Science—A Theory of Their Relationship." *Social Service Review,* **29** (March 1955).
15. GROW, LUCILLE J., and AMY W. SHYNE. *Requests for Child Welfare Services—A Five Day Census.* New York: Child Welfare League of America, December 1969.
16. HENRY, WILLIAM E., *et al. The Fifth Profession; Becoming a Psychotherapist.* San Francisco: Jossey-Bass, Inc., 1971.
17. KAHN, ALFRED. "The Social Scene and Planning of Services for Children." *Social Work,* **7** (July 1962).
18. ————. "Child Welfare: Trends and Direction." *Child Welfare,* **41** (December 1962).

19. KRAFT, IVOR. *Toward a New Conception of Social Work in American Society.* Cleveland: School of Applied Social Services, Case Western Reserve University, January 1968. Mimeo.

20. LE MASTERS, ERSEL E. *Parents in Modern America.* Homewood, Ill.: The Dorsey Press, 1970.

21. LINTON, RALPH. *The Cultural Background of Personality.* New York: Appleton-Century-Crofts, 1945.

22. MAAS, HENRY. "Behavioral Science Basis for Professional Education: The Unifying Conceptual Tool of Cultural Role," in *Proceedings of the Interdisciplinary Conference.* Washington, D.C.: Howard University, School of Social Work, May 1, 1957.

23. PACKMAN, JEAN. *Child Care: Needs and Numbers.* London: George Allen & Unwin, Ltd., 1968.

24. PARSONS, TALCOTT, and EDWARD SHILS (eds.). *Toward a General Theory of Action.* Cambridge, Mass.: Harvard University Press, 1954.

25. PERLMAN, HELEN HARRIS. "Social Components of Casework Practice." *Social Welfare Forum.* New York: Columbia University Press, 1953.

26. ————. "The Role Concept and Social Casework: Some Explorations. II: What Is Social Diagnosis?" *Social Service Review,* **36** (March 1962).

27. POLLAK, OTTO, and DONALD BRIELAND. "The Midwest Seminar on Family Diagnosis and Treatment." *Social Casework,* **42** (July 1961).

28. RICHMOND, MARY. *What Is Social Casework?* New York: Russell Sage Foundation, 1922.

29. SAMPSON, JEROME. "Is Child Welfare a Specialty?" and the discussion by Zitha Turitz that follows. *Child Welfare,* **41** (November 1962).

30. SARBIN, THEODORE. "Role Theory," in *Handbook of Social Psychology.* Ed. by Gardner Lindzey. Cambridge, Mass.: Addison-Wesley Publishing Co., Inc., 1954.

31. SHULZE, SUSANNE, *et al.* "Symposium: Developing Generic and Specific Knowledge Through the Study of Children Services." *Child Welfare* (April–May 1955).

32. SLATER, PHILIP. "Parental Role Differentiation." *American Journal of Sociology,* **47** (November 1961).

33. SPEIGEL, JOHN. "The Resolution of Role Conflict Within the Family," in *A Modern Introduction to the Family.* Ed. by Norman Bell and Ezra Vogel. New York: The Free Press, 1960.

34. TURITZ, ZITHA. Quoted in Helen Hazen, "Distinctive Aspects of Child Welfare." *Child Welfare* (July 1957).

35. ————. "Development and Use of National Standards for Child Welfare Services." *Child Welfare,* **46** (May 1967), 245–53.

36. UNITED NATIONS, DEPARTMENT OF ECONOMICS AND SOCIAL AFFAIRS. *Training for Social Work—An International Survey.* New York, 1950.

37. ————. *Parental Rights and Duties Including Guardianship.* New York, 1968.

38. U.S. DEPARTMENT OF THE ARMY, HEADQUARTERS. *Army Psychiatric Social Work.* Washington, D.C., Government Printing Office, March 1950.

39. U.S. DEPARTMENT OF LABOR, WOMEN'S BUREAU. *The Outlook for Women in Social Work—General Summary.* Social Work Series Bulletin, No. 235–8. Washington, D.C.: Government Printing Office, 1952.

40. WERBLE, BEATRICE. "The Implications of Role Theory for Casework Research," in *Social Science Theory and Social Work Research.* Ed. by Leonard Kogan. New York: National Association of Social Workers, 1960.
41. WILENSKY, HAROLD, and CHARLES LEBEAUX. *Industrial Society and Social Welfare.* New York: Russell Sage Foundation, 1958.
42. WITMER, HELEN L., and RUTH KOTINSKY (eds.). *Personality in the Making.* New York: Harper and Row, Publishers, 1952.
43. WOLFENSTEIN, M. "Trends in Infant Care." *American Journal of Orthopsychiatry,* **23** (1953).
44. ZELDITCH, MORRIS. "Role Differentiation in the Nuclear Family," in *Family: Socialization and Interaction Process.* Ed. by Talcott Parsons and Robert Bales. New York: The Free Press, 1955.

2

Perspectives on
Child Welfare Services

Factors in the Development
of Child Welfare Services

The social problems that are the proper concern of child welfare are as old as mankind. The orphaned, the illegitimate, the abandoned, and the handicapped child have always been with us. In the first section of the first book of the Bible, Genesis, we encounter a problem of sibling rivalry in the conflict between Cain and Abel and concern on the part of the parents, Adam and Eve, about the trouble in their family. Yet professional social work is less than a century old. The question arises, then: How were the problems of child welfare handled before this network of services was developed? Several significant factors helped to explain the emergence of the field of child welfare social work:

1. The development of a humanitarian ideology and the growing rejection of previously acceptable solutions.
2. Economic and political changes that reinforced and supported changes in ideology.
3. The increased specialization of social institutions.
4. The increase in scientific knowledge.
5. The "discovery" of childhood.
6. The rise in status of the family and the child.
7. Changes in the "arithmetic of child production."

Ideology and Alternative Solutions

Child welfare services are one part of the total social system. It is to be expected, then, that such services reflect the nature of the economy, the family organization, and the position of the child in the particular society. Each society deals differently with the problems of children and families.

One general solution to the problems of child welfare is to eliminate them at their source. Dead children present only a very limited problem —that of disposal. And children who are never conceived do not present even this small problem. So the first line of defense against the development of problems in child welfare is contraception. The solution is an ancient one, but one that has always aroused controversy. Judiciously applied, it prevents the problem presented by unwanted children. Indiscriminately applied, however, it threatens the continued existence of the group.

Himes summarized his detailed historical study of contraception by noting that

> contraception, as only one form of population control, is a social practice of much greater historical antiquity, greater cultural and geographical universality, than commonly supposed, even by medical and social historians. Contraception has existed in some form throughout the entire range of social evolution—that is, for at least several thousand years. The desire for, as distinct from the achievement of, reliable contraception has been characteristic of many societies widely removed in time and space. [30, p. xii]

Egyptian papyri, dating from 1850 B.C., that give contraceptive prescriptions and instructions are part of the elaborate documentary evidence in support of the thesis. [30, p. 61] Primitive contraceptive measures were mechanical in nature. Often, however, they took the form of strong social sanctions regarding the spacing of children. Thus, parents were forbidden to have intercourse during the time that the child was being nursed—which might extend over a two- or three-year period.

> In Fiji the male is actually banished to a hut to live a life of celibacy for the duration of the suckling period of the child—varying from 12 to 36 months. . . . In New Guinea if a second child is born before the first can walk, the parents are ridiculed by the rest of the village. [47, p. 42]

If contraception failed, as it often did, there were socially sanctioned resorts to abortion or infanticide. Thus, in a study of some 350 societies,

Devereaux found abortion practiced in almost all. In some forty of these societies, the practice was approved wholly or conditionally, or was regarded with neutral tolerance. [17, pp. 361–71]   Lecky notes, with reference to abortion, that "no law in Greece or in the Roman Republic or during the greater part of the Empire condemned it." [39, p. 22]

If abortion failed or if it was not applied in time, infanticide, particularly in selective instances, was then resorted to in dealing with child welfare problems at their source.

Lecky also points out that "infanticide was almost universally admitted among the Greeks, being sanctioned and in some cases enjoined upon what we should now call the 'greater happiness principle,' by the ideal legislations of Plato and Aristotle and by the actual legislations of Lycurgus and Solon." [39, p. 27]   Reviewing the relevant, and sometimes contradictory, source material, Hands concludes that "there can be little doubt that the Hellenistic age, with its high incidence of poverty, witnessed infant exposure on a large scale." [27, p. 69]   In the Roman Empire, Lecky notes, "Pagan and Christian authorities were united in speaking of infanticide as a crying vice of the Empire and Tertullian observed that no laws were more easily, or more constantly evaded, than those which condemned it." [39, p. 29]   And Sumner indicates that "For the masses, until the late days of the Empire, infanticide was at most a venial crime." [68, p. 319]

Infanticide often took the form of abandonment. The parents who were unable to care for their child left him to be found and accepted by others who could. If the child was not found or if no one accepted him, nature took its course and neither the family nor the society was further concerned with the child. Parents unable to care for a child, but still concerned over his fate, might choose to abandon him in a well-frequented spot to assure his being found. Thus, in Rome, children were brought to a "column near the Vilabrium, and these taken by speculators who educated them as slaves or very frequently as prostitutes." [39, p. 30]

The abandonment of infants was resorted to for a long time throughout Europe. Caulfield, analyzing the situation in eighteenth-century England, contends that "dropping [abandoning] of infants was an extremely frequent occurrence during this period and was accepted by all classes without comment." [11, p. 31]   McCloy, in a detailed study of social welfare problems in eighteenth-century France, notes that "one of the saddest features of eighteenth-century French history was the wholesale abandonment of infants by their parents." [43, p. 238]   The frequently told tale of Hansel and Gretel is, in effect, a story of attempted abandonment; the motivation of the stepmother may be primarily psychological (the rejection of the children of the former wife), but the father accedes to her plan to "lose" them because there is not enough food for both parents and children.

Although abandonment is a private solution which may leave the community with the problem of providing for the unwanted child, it proved to be a public solution as well. The mortality rates for abandoned children were much higher than the already high rates for non-abandoned children. In Elizabethan England many parents were

> too poor to support their children at all and parish records contain numerous entries concerning the desertion of unwanted children who were found dead on the roads from exposure and starvation— a practice which continued among the poorer classes up to the nineteenth century. [58, p. 22]

As late as 1873 the "medical register of New York reported 122 infants found dead in streets, alleys, rivers and elsewhere." [60, p. 10]

Abandoned children placed in foundling hospitals died at such a rate that, although it is likely that the existence of such facilities decreased the number of infanticides, it "may be questioned whether they diminished the number of deaths." [39, p. 37]   The abandoned children dying in the various hospitals in France, notes McCloy, "probably varied at the frightful rate of 50 to 80 percent, by cities." [43, p. 248]   Such resources for abandoned children may be subject to Mead's accusation (in another context) that they were "only a prolonged, ritualized method of disposing of the infant for whom nobody wishes to care." [44]

Jonas Hanway, an eighteenth-century English child welfare researcher of parish workhouses which received young children for institutional care, made efforts to follow up the history of each child placed. He found that in many parishes "the mortality of all children received was 80 to 90 percent or, if you please, upon those received under twelve months old, 99 percent." [11, p. 140]

Among the poor, another solution was the selling of children.

> In the days of the Later Roman Empire, the spectacle of children being sold became a sight so common that various regulatory measures against it were passed. The Justinian Code of 534 contained a provision by which a father whose poverty was extreme was allowed to sell his son or daughter at the moment of birth, and repurchase the child at a later date. [7, p. 493]

The motives for these expedients indicate the relationship between these "preventive solutions" and potential problems in child welfare. Devereaux states, in reviewing the motives for abortion, "Economic factors play a tremendously important role in the motivation for abortion. . . . Anyone familiar with the tremendous economic burden which primitive women carry and with the great poverty of many groups [will understand this]." [17, p. 13]   Miller notes the relationship of abortion and infanticide in primitive societies to available food supply: "The child must enter the world only when his presence will not crowd or necessitate unwanted economy"; thus infanticide and abortion "are means of restoring the equilibrium between human numbers and natural resources." [47, p. 30]   Sumner notes these practices are "primary and violent acts of self-defense by parents against famine, disease, and other calamities of overpopulation which increase with the number which each man and woman has to provide for. . . ." [68, p. 313]   Hobhouse concurs:

> To primitive man having a severe struggle for existence, the advent of a new mouth to feed is often a serious matter. Hence infanticide is not an uncommon practice in the uncivilized world and coincides with genuine and even devoted attachment to the child if once allowed to live. [31, p. 339]

Infanticide and abandonment resulted more frequently from hardness of life than from hardness of heart. "Urgent want and the sterility of the niggardly earth" were the reasons advanced by the people of Radash Island who allowed each woman only three children, requiring her to kill each succeeding child. [55, p. 37]   Bossard notes this same motive for Greek support of infanticide when he repeats the story of the Greek father who, when asked, "Why do you expose your child?," answered, "Because I love the children I have." [7, p. 614]   Hands points out that "after Emperor Constantine and Theodosius had forbidden the practice of infant exposure, it became necessary to admit the parents' right in extreme cases of poverty to sell a new-born child." [27, p. 71]

Poverty of resources is only one of the motives. If caring for the child is likely to be difficult, abortion or infanticide might be employed. If, for instance, the mother dies in childbirth, the child, too, may be killed:

> In Australia the infant is buried alive with its mother or killed and burnt with her corpse. The Semang of the Malay Peninsula wrap mother and child in one shroud, the child being placed on the mother's breast with its face downward. . . . Among the Chiloctin Indians of Canada the death of a mother during delivery leads to burying the child in its cradle with the mother. [47, pp. 39–40]

Devereaux quotes Denig to the effect that "one-eighth of the children are destroyed *in utero* or after birth by the Crow women. The same is often done by the Assinaboin, particularly if the father of the child has abandoned the woman before its birth." [17, p. 185]   Somewhat similarly, the illegitimate child was aborted or killed not only because of the shame attendant upon the birth of a bastard but also because the mother would have found difficulty in caring for and rearing him. [17, pp. 245–89]   A child conceived in an incestuous union was also likely to be aborted because his birth would present a social problem. The 1890 edition of the *Encyclopaedia Britannica* notes that "The modern crime of infanticide shows no symptoms of diminution in the leading nations of Europe. In all of them it is closely connected with illegitimacy in the class of farm and domestic servants." [quoted in 3, p. 42]

By the same token, deformed or defective children are done away with in some societies. This obviates, once again, a problem in child welfare that is likely to result from the failure of a child to perform adequately the social role requirements expected of a child. "Among the Indians on the Amazon River, the child was exposed to a test for a right to survival, as all infants immediately after birth were submerged in a stream, but the deformed child was never pulled out again." [47, p. 48] Sumner quotes Seneca as referring to the "killing of defective children as a wise and unquestioned custom," and Seneca is seconded by Pliny in this. [68, p. 319]   Aristotle, too, thought that defective children should be put to death, and the exposure of sickly children among the Spartans is well known. The Roman Twelve Tables clearly stipulated that deformed children were not to be given care. And Payne, quoting an ethnographic report, notes that, among the Dieyerie of Australia, "all sickly and deformed children are made away with in fear of their becoming a burden to the tribe." [55, p. 38]

Twins present a special problem because such a birth doubles the burden of care and the number of mouths to be fed. Hence, twin births often result in infanticide in some societies. For the same reason, children born while an older child is still very dependent may be killed because the simultaneous burden of child care is too great. Thus, among the Pima,

> . . . if a woman gets pregnant while lactating, she aborts by pressure on the belly. The unborn is sacrificed to the interests of the previous baby "which the mother loved more because she could see it." [17, p. 310]

Plato's idea was that "men over fifty-five and women over forty should not procreate," and if they did, the child should be aborted or killed, because older parents are not likely to live long enough to see their children become independent. The prevention of child-bearing by older parents obviates the problem of dependent orphans.

Variations in the accepted arrangements of the structure of the family, such as concubinage and polygamy, also contribute to the solution of child welfare problems. Where more than one wife is available to the father, more than one "mother" is available to the child if his own mother falls ill or dies. The widespread acceptance of monogamy in the West makes this solution unavailable, although serial polygamy, in the form of remarriage, helps to refill parental roles left vacant by divorce. Changes in the ideology of the community have reduced the availability of other solutions, such as infanticide and abandonment. Furthermore, there has been a slow but perceptible change in the prevailing attitude toward the ill, the deprived, the handicapped, and the dependent members of society. Children, as a dependent group, have shared in the benefits of such ideological change.

Of course, concern for the needs of the less privileged, less capable members of society is not a modern phenomenon: the Code of Hammurabi and the Old Testament provide humanitarian admonitions about caring for people in need. "Greece in the age of Plato provided funds for soldiers' orphans and free medical service for poor children. The famous *pueri alimentarii* in Rome at the period of the Empire was a special semigovernmental service for the charitable maintenance of the children of indigent citizens." [63, p. 375]

Concern for the dependent and the deprived became one of the central values of Christianity. Christianity preached the sanctity of all human life—even that of the fetus in the womb. This meant that both infanticide and abortion were crimes. The child was guaranteed the right to life and the resources to sustain life. Reinforcing and supplementing these theological presuppositions was the humanitarian ideology of the Enlightenment, which provided a secular foundation for the rights of the child.

As a result, some of the previous solutions to child welfare problems —infanticide, for instance—became ideologically inadmissible. But, when society makes such solutions unacceptable, it must provide alternative solutions. At this point, the necessity for child welfare service becomes evident. This relationship is revealed in the history of Western Europe, and is noted by Sumner, who says that as a "corollary of the legislation against infanticide, institutions to care for foundlings came into existence." [68, p. 319]   In fact, Constantine, influenced by Christian teaching, in A.D. 315 promulgated a law

> . . . to turn parents from using a parricidal hand to their new-born children and to dispose their hearts to the best sentiments. . . . If a father brings a child saying he cannot support it, someone should supply him without delay with food and clothing. . . . [55, p. 264]

The Church became the protector of parentless children, accepting those children whose parents could not provide for them. As early as A.D. 325, the Council of Nicaea prescribed that Xenodochia be established in each Christian village—such an institution to have the responsibility of aiding the sick, the poor, and abandoned children. Although it did not sanction abandonment, the Church recognized the stresses and pressures that made it impossible for many parents to care for their children. At the seventh-century Council of Rouen, the priests of each diocese were instructed to inform their congregation that women might leave at the door of the church any children for whom they could not care. Churches provided the *tour*—a basket in which one placed an abandoned infant inside the church.

Gradually more and more institutions, hospitals, and asylums became available in which to house abandoned and neglected children. A variety of alternative measures arose that predate professional social work—resources such as the workhouse for children, "outdoor relief" (relief outside an institution through a cash grant or the like) for parents who were unable to care for their children, and an elaborate system of "binding out" or apprenticeship training entered into while the child was still very young.

The point, however, is that when a society rejects abortion, infanticide, and abandonment as solutions, it must assume the responsibility to care for the child whose life it has saved. This, then, suggests the need for developing the services and resources that constitute the field of child welfare.

Economic and Political Changes

A humanitarian attitude toward the child cannot prevail if the economic situation is unfavorable. Even after the attitude of the Christian church toward children became dominant, instances of child abandonment and child neglect rose during periods of economic distress. Sumner observes that, "in reality nothing put an end to infanticide but the advance in the arts [increased economic power] by virtue of which parents can provide for their children." [68, p. 321]

The Industrial Revolution, by increasing the productive capacity of all adults, made it possible for them to care for a greater number of dependent children. Society could now afford to support and care for physically handicapped children, mentally defective children, and dependent children whose own parents were unable to care for them.

Bossard, in analyzing the relationship of the productivity of adults to the needs of the child population, notes:

> The status of childhood, as reflected in school, work, and child-care standards of all kinds represents in large measure the relative size of the nonproductive and productive groups and the capacities of the latter to serve the former. [7, pp. 590–91]

Political factors also increased the need for some community-supported institution to deal with child welfare problems. Social institutions evolve in order to perform a useful function in society, and to permit society to operate more effectively, and with less conflict. Child welfare services meet the needs of children, but they also reduce the threat of social disequilibrium. Humanitarian and ethical considerations are often secondary to the need to maintain social stability by providing the necessary social arrangements (in this case, the child welfare services) to deal with problems of social dysfunctioning which did affect a significant number of children. [2]   Failure to provide child welfare service entails a possible increase in the number of children who might become delinquent or develop physical and/or mental illness and constitute both a threat to, and a burden on, society.

Finally, the enfranchisement of nonpropertied classes gave political power to a growing number of poor parents who needed the help of the community in implementing their parental role. Ignoring the needs and demands of this growing group of voters would present an internal political threat.

Failure to provide child welfare services poses an external threat which derives from the dependence of modern nation states on a citizen army for national security. In World Wars I and II, very sizable percentages of men in the United States and Britain were found to be physically, mentally, or emotionally unfit for service, partly as a result of childhood deprivation.

Specialization of Social Institutions

Another factor in the development of child welfare services is the increasing specialization of social institutions and the change, or loss, of functions of some institutions. One such institution is the neighborhood.

Over a long period of history, most people lived in small rural groups in which people grew up together, knew one another intimately, and kept contact with neighboring families over a number of generations. The extended family, including collateral relatives as well as nonrelated but familiar members of the community, assumed some responsibility for maintaining children whose parents were unable to fulfill their role obligations. Problems of child welfare were frequently solved through mutual aid. In underdeveloped countries today, where the organization of communal life resembles that of Europe hundreds of years ago, mutual aid from neighbors and kin is still a frequent source of help. In such societies "there are plenty of orphans but no orphanages." A recent report by the United Nations Children's Fund, describing the effects of urbanization in underdeveloped countries, notes that poverty, hunger, and disease are often a traditional part of the child's life in the rural community, "but there, at least, the child has his natural protection and will seldom be abandoned by the community even if his parents die. In the new environment of the urban slums things are quite different." The impersonal relationships of the city replace the personal relationship of the rural community and require the introduction of child welfare organizations. [64, p. 23]

In an urban society, siblings often live at a distance from each other and from their parents and grandparents. Nor is the obligation to mutual support as firmly sanctioned—the obligations to one's nuclear family take clear precedence over those to the extended family.

The early parish group, too, was a closely knit primary group—the unifying factor being the sharing of significant beliefs. The parish "was a mutual aid group, the members of which looked out for each other especially during the era of persecution." [59, p. 276]   The parish group has lost much of this cohesiveness, and, even if it had not, the secularization of modern society would exclude many people from such aid.

The feudal system, with its elaborate structure of rights and obligations, was a more formally contractual kind of mutual aid. As de Schweinitz says:

> . . . under feudalism there could, at least in theory, be no uncared-for distress. The people who today would be in the greatest economic danger were, in the Middle Ages, presumably protected by their masters from the most acute suffering. . . . Insurance against unemployment, sickness, old age was theirs in the protection of their high lords. [62, p. 2]

Mutual aid was also a feature of another kind of primary group—the occupational family—the guild, which operated like an extended family to protect its members from risks to security. When guilds were small and their members knew one another intimately, they felt a responsibility for one another's welfare and made provisions for the care of the widows and children of deceased fellow members. Queen points out that, for guild members,

> there was a close community of interest and a sharing of the daily experiences of life. The guild itself was just a primary group with intimate personal relations. . . . This being the case, it was quite natural that we should find the guilds assumed responsibility for the bereaved widows and orphans of their members, educated the latter, and, if they were girls, provided them with dowries. [59, p. 282]

Ultimately all the institutions that had assumed responsibility for dealing with child welfare problems diminished their involvement in such problems or else found that social change made previous solutions untenable. With the growth of an urbanized population, with the growing mobility of population attendant upon industrialization, the "neighborhood" is less apt to denote a primary group, so that mutual aid through this source becomes less certain. Both the guilds and their modern counterparts—trade unions, professional associations, merchants' and manufacturers' associations—were institutionalized around a primary function other than child welfare. As this primary function—concern with the problems of the occupation—became more complex, the institutions became less concerned with secondary, nonessential functions. The church's religious function took precedence over its eleemosynary concerns, especially after the Reformation, which reduced the resources available to the church generally and, consequently, the resources it could make available for charitable purposes. Steinbicker notes that "poor relief was the first ecclesiastical institution to be secularized after the religious revolt." [67]

These changes meant that a new institution had to be developed to deal with child welfare problems. The diminished interest and capacity of institutions like the neighborhood, the extended family, the guild, and the church in dealing with child welfare problems created a need for child welfare social work which was designed to fill the gap.

The neighborhood, the extended family, the church, and the occupational group still contribute to helping with child welfare problems. Such resources exist side by side with the more formal professional resources and services, and they are frequently explored by the individual before he approaches the professional services. However, only child welfare social work is explicitly concerned with child welfare problems as its primary, specific, institutional responsibility.

At the same time that many social institutions are disencumbering themselves of concern for the child, one institution—the nuclear family—has developed a more specialized concern for the child. As the modern family loses some of its traditional functions—production, protection, recreation, and so on—the problems and satisfactions of child rearing are becoming its principal business. It is a common enterprise, which for many is the principal ingredient of marriage. With such specialization in family function, children become of increasing importance.

The Scientific Revolution

Advances in scientific knowledge have not only increased the productivity of each worker so that fewer productive adults could support a larger number of dependents, but also made possible the development of a science of child welfare. Greater scientific concern with problems of child development, and the results of such studies, have intensified the importance of childhood. Freud was among the first to call attention to the crucial importance of childhood in shaping human destiny, but his work was followed by a host of other studies, examining and clarifying the effects of childhood experiences. The years of childhood began to assume greater importance and significance vis-à-vis other periods of life.

The Freudian emphasis on childhood was supported by other scientific advances—particularly the Darwinian theories on man's origin and evolution. The genetic point of view—which stresses continuity in development, points to the importance of beginnings, and insists that the past is structured in the present—became a solidly accepted concept. Childhood assumed an unprecedented importance.

But such studies, and the growth in knowledge that resulted from such studies, did more than heighten the importance of childhood; they also gave rise to a new profession. Professions develop in response to a human need, but the attempt to meet the need can be professionalized only if there is a scientific body of knowledge available to form the basis for professional action. The studies regarding childhood and children became the basis for such journals as *Child Development, Child Welfare, Courrier, The International Journal of Child Welfare, Children Today*—none of which existed one hundred years ago. Ultimately, this material is codified and organized so that courses are taught, textbooks are written, and educational programs are developed for the training of professionals in specialties concerned with various aspects of childhood. Thus the expansion and elaboration of special knowledge concerned with welfare services for children made possible a professional field of specialization in child welfare.

The Discovery of Childhood

The recognition of childhood as a distinct period in life is so widely accepted that it is difficult to realize that it was not always so. Biological differences, of course, forced a recognition of the child as a being distinct from the adult. But childhood was believed to be a short period "of transition which passed quickly and was just as quickly forgotten." [2] Throughout most of history, life has been exceedingly short for most people and "maturity" had to be reached earlier in life. It might be remembered that Romeo was not yet sixteen, and Juliet not yet fourteen, when their fervent, tragic romance was in flower. When the average life span did not exceed thirty years, childhood could not be prolonged. "Conscious of the brevity of life . . . parents were eager to introduce their sons and daughters into the adult world at the earliest possible moment." [58, p. 198]

The economic position of the family and of society was such that the individual had to become self-supporting as quickly as possible. Children began to earn their living at six or seven years of age. According to a statute enacted in England in 1535, "Children under fourteen years of age, and above five, that live in idleness and be taken begging may be put to service by the government of cities, towns, etc., to husbandry; or other crafts of labor. . . ." [quoted in 8, p. 64]   William Blake, the poet, began working in a silk mill in 1764 when he was seven years old. An advertisement in *The Baltimore-Federal-Gazette* of January 4, 1808, stated, "This [Baltimore Cotton] manufactory will go into operation this month, where a number of boys and girls from eight to twelve years of age are wanted." [quoted in 72, p. 27]

Older people in small English villages recounting their childhood as they lived it in the latter part of the nineteenth century note how early in life childhood ended for them: "The children helped in their own way. We started field work when we were five or six. . . . I was living in Deplen when I first started ploughing. I was fifteen years old and I had been at work for seven years. . . . I lost my father when I was nine so I had to think about work." [6]

The definition of the term *child* has been, and is, quite elastic. Earlier in history, child welfare problems were dealt with by defining the end of childhood as a period of dependency very much earlier than it is defined today. As children very early in life became responsible for self-support," childhood effectively ended at the age of seven or, at the latest, nine." [58, p. 42]

For a long time, there was no distinctive child dress; it was merely adult dress in miniature, so that there was little symbolic demarcation of childhood and children were very early absorbed into the world of adults.

Aries says that

> . . . in medieval society, the idea of childhood did not exist. . . .
> The idea of childhood is not to be confused with affection for
> children: it corresponds to an awareness of the particular nature
> of childhood, that particular nature which distinguishes the child
> from the adult, even the young adult. In medieval society, this
> awareness was lacking. [1, p. 128]

Just as there is a relationship between greater concern for children and the development of a more productive economy, so there is a relation between the development of modern education and the idea of childhood. The view of childhood as an important and significant period evokes a need for a formal, highly developed system of education, which, in turn, reinforces and supports the idea of the distinctiveness of childhood. Age grading becomes part of the way of categorizing people in society.

Changes in family living arrangements and orientation from one which included many relatives in the household and which viewed the extended family as the primary domestic unit, to a greater focus on the nuclear family and to a living arrangement which excluded all except the nuclear family, contributed toward the enhancement of concern for the child. Farber notes, for instance, that in addition to children, households in seventeenth-century Puritan settlements generally contained servants (including laborers and apprentices) and elderly parents or maiden aunts. [20, p. 4] Pinchbeck argues that:

> Just as the institutional development and acceptance of formal education with the consequent isolation of the child from adult society was a prerequisite of the emergence of modern sociological and psychological concepts of childhood, so also the gradual isolation and individualization of the family as a social and psychological entity ultimately contributed to the same end. The ties between parent and child were necessarily strengthened in a family reduced to parents and children. . . . [58, p. 307]

The Status of the Family and the Child

The status of the child is closely related to the status of the family as an institution vis-à-vis other institutions through which people seek the satisfaction of basic needs. The family is, for the child, the only significant social institution to which he is related for the first years of his life.

The family, although always an institution of importance, came to be overshadowed by other institutions to which adults owed allegiance. The church, the state, the peer group, the army, the guild, the occupation—all have frequently taken priority over the family; and men have devoted their primary attention, energy, and concern to these other areas of their lives.

Aries, in talking about the family in the Middle Ages, indicates that it fulfilled a function—it ensured the transmission of life, property, and names—but it did not penetrate very far into human sensibility. [1, p. 411] According to Aries, the medieval family

> . . . existed in silence: it did not awaken feelings strong enough to inspire poet or artist. We must recognize the importance of this silence—not much value was placed on the family. [1, p. 364]

More recently, however, the family has become the significant center of our lives. Religion, occupation, the friendship of peers, the state—all are subservient to the family. We invest more of ourselves in the family than in almost any other social institution. The fact that family—and the nuclear family at that—has assumed such central importance in our lives results in an increase in the importance of the child, who is a member of this, but of no other, significant social institution.

Changes in the Arithmetic of Child Production

Another important factor that affects the status of the child is what Bossard has aptly termed the *arithmetic of production*—the relationship between birth rate and child mortality rates. For a long time in the history of mankind, many children were born and many died. Parents expected that a high percentage of the children they conceived would be with them only a short period of time:

> The general feeling was, and for a long time remained, that one had several children in order to keep just a few. As late as the seventeenth century in "Le Caquet de l'accouchée" we have a neighbor, standing at the bedside of a woman who has just given birth, a mother of five, and calming her fears with these words, "Before they are old enough to bother you you will have lost half of them, or perhaps all of them." . . . People could not become too attached to something that was regarded as a probable loss. This is the reason for certain remarks which shock our present day sensibility, such as Montaigne's observation, "I have lost two or three children in their infancy not without regret but without great sorrow." [1, pp. 38–39]

His vagueness about the number reveals that children, and childhood, were not matters of great importance or significance: "Indifference was a direct and inevitable consequence of the demography of the period." [1, p. 39]

Cotton Mather had fifteen children, only two of whom survived him. Calhoun, in his *Social History of the American Family*, quotes a Plymouth gravestone: "Here lies . . . with twenty small children" [10, p. 89] and notes the not atypical case of another Colonial mother who, having been married nine years, "had one child living and five dead." [10, p. 106]

The mortality rate of English royal children was very high. Five children of Henry III, seven children of Edward I, and four children of Edward III died in infancy. Queen Anne gave birth to five children and buried them all. Since accurate birth records were not kept for commoners and peasants, infant and childhood mortality rates can only be estimated. Caulfield, reviewing the relevant material, notes that in the two decades 1730–1750 in London "75 percent of all children christened were dead before they reached the age of five." [11, p. 7]

To invest emotionally in children was to invite problems, for one was so often doomed to see the child die. If one was to hope to retain psychological stability, he had to maintain an attitude of restrained attachment toward children. Because the child was a transient in the family and because, even if he survived, the period of his childhood was short, anything peculiarly identified with childhood was relegated to secondary importance. The family was adult-centered, adult-directed, and adult-oriented. Mitchell, noting these factors, concludes that

> it is probable that the modern concept of parental love is of comparatively recent origin, and that throughout most of history interest in, and affection for, infants and young children has been at a much more superficial level. . . . If parents were thus unable to develop deep feelings of affection towards their offspring, they would be unlikely to entertain such sentiments toward the children of their neighbors. [48, p. 301]

Hence it was difficult earlier to get public policy support for child welfare services to meet the needs of the children of the community.

With advances in sanitation, in public health, and in medicine and with the greater availability of more effective contraceptive measures, fewer children were conceived, but those that were conceived had better chances of surviving. One could allow himself to develop a deep feeling for the few children he had, with confident hope that such love would not inevitably be followed by sorrow and pain at the child's untimely death. And because children came to be, for many, the results of careful and restricted planning, they were apt to be highly valued when they were born.

Legal Status of the Child

The legal status of the child has changed over a period of time, making explicit and reinforcing the more favorable position of the child in society. At one time, children had the status of chattel: "The child's position in the average family of the masses was for centuries roughly in this order: father, cattle, mother, child." [16, p. 15]   Hunt points out that comparing children to animals was:

> an image that appears throughout seventeenth-century literature on children. In a total sense the small child was an intermediate being, not really an animal (although he might often be compared to one) but on the other hand not really human either. [33, p. 125]

Early European legal systems gave little, if any, recognition to the rights of the child. The amphidroma ceremony in ancient Athens, performed on the fifth day after birth, symbolized the actual social birth of the child. Before then, the child, alive but not actually a member of the community, could be disposed of. The Roman concept of *patria potestas* gave the father almost absolute power over his children. In early Germanic law the child was under the *munt* of the father, which gave the father authoritative control. Neither the Roman nor the Germanic code made explicit the obligations of the father to maintain and protect the child. Parents in pre-Revolutionary France could obtain a *lettre de cachet* permitting imprisonment of a disobedient child, and the Napoleonic Code clearly defined the subordinate position of the child.

With the gradual acceptance of the rights of the child, parental authority has come to be defined "as a series of rights and obligations on the part of both parents which are to be exercised for the good of the child and which are balanced by a sense of correlative rights and obligations on the part of the child." [90, p. 11]   Parental power, previously exercised in domination over the child in the interests of parents, is now more likely to be regarded as a trust to be employed in the best interests of the child.

The very real change in attitude toward the status of children is exemplified by the fact that in November 1954 the United Nations General Assembly unanimously adopted and proclaimed a Declaration of the Rights of the Child, which affirms the rights of the child to have special protection and to enjoy opportunities and facilities that will enable him to develop in a healthy and normal manner; to have a name and a nationality from his birth; to enjoy the benefit of social security, including adequate nutrition, housing, recreation, and medical services; to grow up in an atmosphere of affection and security, and, wherever possible, in the care and under the responsibility of his parents; to receive special treatment, education, and care if he is handicapped; to be among the first to receive protection and relief in times of disaster; to be protected against all forms of neglect, cruelty, and exploitation; and to be protected from practices which may foster any form of discrimination. The 1970 White House Conference on Children affirmed these rights. [89]

Effective implementation of these rights of children requires the development of a network of child welfare services. Of course, some kind of child welfare was practiced long before the profession of social work emerged. Community efforts took the form of the *pueri alimentarii* of ancient Rome, almshouses, and the "outdoor" poor relief granted to indigent people living in their own homes. For instance, outdoor poor relief in the late eighteenth century in New York City was offered in response to recurrent problems of child welfare: "husband in prison" . . . "husband has broke his leg" . . . "a house full of small children" . . . "husband at sea" . . . "husband bad fellow" . . . "sick and distressed" . . . "her husband has abandoned her and she has broke her arm." [quoted in 50, p. 25]   And side by side with these public efforts to relieve distress and want we have always had the private acts of good will, by benevolent individuals and the activities of organized voluntary groups. Thus Hands notes the distribution of corn and oil and cash in ancient Greece and Rome through the auspices of wealthy benefactors [27, Chap. VII], and in early nineteenth-century New York City child welfare problems were ameliorated by such private benevolent groups as the Society for the Relief of Poor Widows with Small Children, the Female Assistance Society, The Orphan Asylum Society, the New York Society for the Prevention of Pauperism, and the Humane Society. (The latter incidentally dealt with a social situation which no longer presents a problem for child welfare—the imprisonment of a father for debt.) [50]

Professional child welfare workers were preceded by such gifted and dedicated "amateurs" as St. Vincent de Paul, who fought during the reign of Louis XIII for the establishment of institutions for abandoned children; Vives, who in 1525 wrote *On the Relief of the Poor*, the first modern textbook on social work in public welfare; Thomas Carom, who in 1739 energized London into building a hospital for foundlings; Lord Ashley, Earl of Shaftesbury, who tirelessly fought for passage of the Factory Acts, limiting the worst abuses of child labor in nineteenth-century England; Florence Kelly, who performed similar yeoman service for American children; Dr. Bernado and Charles Loring Brace, who nightly collected the abandoned, homeless, parentless children off the streets of nineteenth-century London and New York, respectively.

It would be difficult to measure the influence these individuals had on stimulating a sense of greater community responsibility for services for children. But having noted that the profession of social work and the formal organization of a network of child welfare services was preceded by a variety of preprofessional "social work" efforts to deal with child welfare problems, efforts which existed alongside such responses as contraception, abortion, infanticide, abandonment, child labor, and neighborly mutual aid as procedures for dealing with such problems, it might be noted that the reverse situation exists today. Alongside the formal system of professional child welfare services, society currently employs many of the classical solutions in dealing with child welfare problems. A rich network of neighborly, volunteer mutual aid exists side by side with the formal agency resources responding to child welfare problems. When a single car accident in Mt. Kisko, New York, killed two women and critically injured four others, it left twenty young children permanently or temporarily motherless. Neighbors volunteered to help with babysitting and child care and to collect funds for the families. [25] Ethnic- and church-group mutual aid societies continue to act as family surrogates in times of stress or need. The immigrant *landsman-shaft* organizations are examples of these mutual aid approaches. They continue today in attentuated forms, affected adversely by growing assimilation.

Child labor continues to offer a "solution" to child welfare problems. The American Friends Service Committee, in a study conducted in cooperation with the National Committee on Education of Migrant Children, reported in 1971 that many children under twelve were still employed full-time as farm laborers.

Even infanticide exists as a twentieth-century procedure for dealing with child welfare problems at the source. A government policy of euthanasia in Nazi Germany sanctioned the deliberate killing of defective children; "idiot and malformed children" were killed by "doses of morphine, chloride, and luminol" at the children's institutions to which they had been sent. [49, p. 114]   A court trial in 1963 in Liege, Belgium, was concerned with the "mercy killing" of a child born deformed as a result of the mother's having taken Thalidomide (a tranquilizer) during her pregnancy. The family had prevailed upon their doctor to prescribe a lethal dose of a sleeping drug, and the family and the doctor were charged with homicide. During the trial the city of Liege officially sanctioned a referendum of the local population: of those who voted, 16,732 approved the infanticide, while only 938 disapproved. The doctor and the family were acquitted. [24]

In 1971 a widely discussed case involved a mongoloid child born with an intestinal obstruction. The parents, who already had two normal children to care for, refused permission for an operation to correct the intestinal difficulty. The doctors sought a legal opinion and were told that the court would probably uphold the parents' right to refuse to permit surgery. The baby died of starvation in the hospital about two weeks later.

The most important of the classical measures currently applied to potential child welfare problems are contraception and abortion. Contraception has widespread community acceptance, and abortion is legal in some countries, illegal but openly tolerated in others, illegal and not tolerated in still others, but common everywhere.

The American Experience

In view of the crucial factors that determine the status of children and the valuation of the child, American child-centeredness becomes explicable. The American ethos is grounded not only in the Judeo-Christian tradition, but more particularly in the humanist tradition of the Enlightenment. A humanitarian concern for the dependent and the underprivileged is congruent with our tradition. A highly industrialized nation, the United States is in an economic position to implement its philosophical attitude. Our pragmatic, secular orientation has resulted in a widespread acceptance of contraceptive measures and the idea of family planning. This, along with our highly developed medical and public health resources, has resulted in the kind of arithmetic of child production associated with high valuation of the child. Our respect for scientific research has led to acceptance, however ambivalent, of the teachings of child-care experts—all of whom have a vested professional interest in heightening the status of childhood.

Some particular aspects of the American experience further help to explain the great emphasis on the child in America. In a nation of immigrants, the experience of parents—developed in terms of another time and another place—tends to be discounted. Indeed, parents often had to turn to their children for help in learning the language and customs of their adopted country. The teacher-learner relationship between parent and child, reversed, favors the child.

Even with the slowing down of immigration, some of this attitude remains in the tradition and is reinforced by rapid social change, which, in the context of what Kingsley Davis has called the "de-accelerating" rate of socialization, implies that the parent's knowledge and solutions are not always applicable to the problems faced by children. They are solutions made for another time—as though the parent were an immigrant in his own country. Once again the tendency is to derogate the parents somewhat and to increase the valuation of the child. Upward social mobility also has the effect of derogating parental experience in favor of the child's knowledge.

In a tradition-oriented society, the past is revered, and its custodians —parents and grandparents—are respected. In a society oriented toward change the emphasis is on the future, and hopes, ambitions, and attention are lavished on the child as the future toward which we strive. That orientation of the American culture reinforces the importance of children and childhood, and our positive regard for the individual and for individual development makes the child, not the family, the vehicle for fulfilling the future and reaping its rewards.

The democratic tradition, of necessity, is reflected in family organization. It is difficult for the ethos to sanction autocracy within the family. The tendency toward congruence presses the family in the direction of democratization of internal relationships. This suggests, within the limits of practicability and biological competence, a greater voice for children in the family and less domination of children by parents.

The family that has production as one of its key functions can permit only limited democracy. Somebody has to be "boss" of a productive unit to ensure that the necessary work will get done smoothly, efficiently, effectively. When the family becomes primarily a unit of consumption, family organization can support a greater measure of democracy. This is one of the changes that has taken place for most American families within the last fifty years. With such change has come the possibility of a more democratically organized family, and a concomitant enhancement of the status of children.

These are some of the special factors, unique to the American experience, that reinforce the general factors in the growing importance of children and childhood over a period of time. These special considerations give American culture a filiocentric orientation conducive to the development of child welfare services.

The Current Context of Child Welfare Services

Introduction

A historical overview gives us some perspective on the factors that stimulated changes in child welfare resources and services, but it is also helpful to consider the changes currently taking place in American society that may influence the need for child welfare services.

Historical trends are both more revealing and more relevant than annual statistics, which, because they are ephemeral and soon outdated, will be cited only sparingly, and for illustrative purposes. Throughout, *children* refers to individuals eighteen years of age or younger; *nonwhite* includes Indian, Oriental, and Mexican-American (although black children make up about 95 percent of this group). Most of the statistical data, specific details of which the student might wish to check for himself, are derived primarily from recent government publications. [75; 76; 77; 78; 80; 82; 84; 88]   Additional specific references are cited where appropriate.

The Child Population

In 1970 there were some 73,320,000 children in the United States— a third of the total population of 203 million Americans. *The trend is toward a decrease in the proportion of young children to total population.* In 1960 21.7 percent of the population of the country was composed of young children nine years of age or younger. In 1970 this group made up only 18.5 percent of the total population.

These figures reflect *the trend toward lower birth rates during the decade.* This is true for both white and nonwhite women. The birth rate among nonwhite women, however, is still somewhat higher than that among whites. As a consequence, the median age of the nonwhite population is younger than that of the white group. A larger proportion of the total population of nonwhites, therefore, is concentrated in the younger age groups. This means a somewhat disproportionate nonwhite population of risk for child welfare services.

The decline in birth rates during the 1960's (interrupted only by a temporary upturn in 1969–70) grew sharper during the early 1970's. By September 1972 fertility rate dropped to replacement level, 2.1 per woman of child-bearing age, the threshold of zero population growth (*The New York Times*, September 24, 1972). By the end of the year it had dropped even below the replacement level to 2.08 (*The New York Times*, December 5, 1972) and by April 1973 to 2.03 (*The New York Times*, April 4, 1973).

As a consequence of the slowing down in population growth the Census Bureau in December 1972 reduced its projected estimate of the country's population at the end of the century by at least 20 million people (*The New York Times*, December 18, 1972).

The number of children under five decreased from over 20 million in 1960 to about 17 million in 1970—a decline of 15.5 percent. This unprecedented decrease is the more remarkable because it occurred at a time when the number of young adults of child-bearing age had increased sharply. [26]

The high birth rate in the post-World War II decade produced about 5 million more potential mothers in 1970 than there had been in 1960. An "echo baby boom" had been anticipated as a consequence. Instead the beginning of the 1970's was marked by a "baby bust" or a "birth dearth." Hospitals all over the country began to reduce obstetrical services in the early 1970's in response to the falling birth rates.

Of direct significance to the projected need for child welfare services is the fact that during the 1960's, birth rates among low-income and minority-group women (though still higher) fell even more sharply than those among women in general. Consequently, there was a trend toward a reduction in the disproportionate concentration of children in low-income and minority-group populations (*The New York Times*, March 5, 1972).

Although high unemployment rates during the 1970's may have been a temporary factor in the declining birth rates, the greater availability of adequate family-planning technology, coupled with a decrease in number of children desired, may be a permanent feature of our national life.

Recent reports have shown a significant drop in the number of children women desire. In 1965 women expected to have, on the average, three children; in 1972, the expected average had dropped to 2.3. If other factors remain constant, therefore, the demand for child welfare services is likely to decline during the coming decade.

The trend is toward a more favorable child-dependency ratio. The largest proportionate increase in population projected between 1970 and 1980 is in the 20–39 age group, from 26 percent to 31.6 percent of the total population. This is the age population of productive adults who will be working, producing, and paying taxes. At the same time, the proportion of the population which consists of younger, dependent children will be smaller in the immediate future, so that more productive adults will be available to care for a smaller number of dependent children.

The projected increase in the proportion of the population consisting of productive adults coupled with the decrease in the proportion of the population consisting of young children makes for a more favorable child-dependency ratio—proportionately fewer dependent children being cared for by a proportionately larger population of productive adults. When the ratio of dependent children to productive adults is low—when

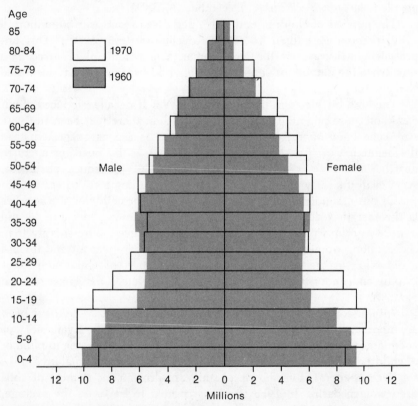

FIGURE 2–1. Changing population pyramid by age and sex. *(Pocket Data Book USA 1971.* U.S. Department of Commerce, Bureau of the Census. Washington, D.C.: Government Printing Office, 1971, Fig. 36, p. 50.)

there is a favorable child-dependency ratio—the community is in a more advantageous economic position to provide adequate services for those children who need them.

Because the child population of the United States is not evenly distributed, child-dependency ratios vary from section to section. For instance, in 1968, there were 59.3 children under eighteen years of age for every one hundred adults under sixty-four years of age in the north-east states; at the same time the ratio in the north central states was 66.6 children per one hundred productive adults.

The child-dependency ratio is only one factor in determining the supply of child welfare services. A second important factor is the attitude of society toward the child. The society itself must decide how its resources are to be allocated. In a gerontocracy, for instance, the needs of older adults might take precedence. But if the children are regarded as having strong claims to available goods and services, they are likely to be favored instead.

The current American attitude stresses the importance of children. Children have high status within the family, and parents devote a considerable amount of their time, energy, and emotional resources keeping children well clothed, well educated, well adjusted, and well amused. Nevertheless, public policy does not always reflect family policy. Dewey's dictum that "what the best and wisest parent wants for his own child, that must the community want for all its children," is frequently violated. Although the society is favorably disposed toward them, children are competing with other age groups in society for available goods and services. The proportion of population sixty-five years of age or older rose from 8.1 percent in 1950 to 10.1 percent in 1970, so that in the future children may have to compete with the aged for adequate services.

The Unwanted Child

We owe the child the right to be conceived and born as a wanted child if we are to reduce the risk for child welfare services. The deliberate decision to conceive implies readiness to have a child and favorable conditions for his reception. An unwanted pregnancy may reflect unfavorable child-care conditions and, hence, increases the probability of need for child welfare services. Family planning involves not only limiting the number of children, but also timing their arrival to coincide with the family's readiness to welcome a new member.

There currently appears to be more effective family planning among all groups in the population, although a higher percentage of unwanted pregnancies occurs among nonwhites and the poor. [9; 91]

The trend is to make family planning programs more widely available so as to increase the likelihood that each child will be born wanted. More widespread dissemination of birth control information and devices may have a significant impact on family planning by the poor and the nonwhite, who currently have proportionately larger families with more limited resources available for self-support. This might reduce the number of children who tax their families' capacity to care for them and who consequently constitute a potential demand for child welfare services.

Genetic counseling, combined with more liberal abortion statutes, may reduce the number of congenitally disabled children, many of whom require child welfare services. Examination of parental chromosomes at some 175 genetic clinics throughout the country can inform parents of their risk in conceiving a child who might inherit some deformity. If such a child is conceived, examination of the cells in the fluid surrounding the fetus can predict the birth of a mongoloid child, a child with sickle cell anemia, cystic fibrosis, and other kinds of congenital deformities. The family may then decide to abort the pregnancy.

The illegitimately conceived child, like the deformed child, runs a high risk of being unwanted and constitutes a higher than normal risk for child welfare services. Making contraceptive information and devices available to the unmarried helps reduce the risk of illegitimate children. And programs of abortion on demand are already beginning to have some impact on the number of illegitimate births.

As a consequence of greater availability of family planning counseling, genetic counseling, and abortions, the *trend is in the direction of a greater number of children being wanted at birth.*

Infant and Child Mortality

Once conceived as a wanted child, we owe the child the right to life. *The trend has been toward a steady decrease in infant and child mortality.* Infant mortality rates have declined steadily from 26 per thousand live births in 1960 to 19.6 in 1970. Nevertheless, our mortality rate was higher than those of thirteen other industrialized countries in 1970. In 1967 President Johnson declared, "Nearly 40,000 babies die each year who would be saved if our infant mortality rate were as low as Sweden's," which had the lowest infant mortality rate in the world at the time. [73] The United States slipped from eighth place in 1955 to fourteenth in 1970 (see Fig. 2–2.) Countries with lower infant mortality rates included the Scandinavian countries, the Netherlands, Japan, the United Kingdom, Australia, France, Canada.

Although the infant mortality rate among nonwhites in the United States is declining, it is still consistently higher than the rate among whites, so that the chances that a black child will die in its first year are some six times higher than those of a white child. In this case, race is a less significant factor than poverty, the lack of adequate prenatal and postnatal medical care available to the poor, and limited access to contraceptive information and devices which would permit more desirable spacing of pregnancies. In fact, the infant mortality rate among poor whites in the United States is still higher than that among equivalent populations in many other countries. If the United States were ranked on the basis of infant mortality rates among whites alone, it would still have a less favorable ranking than ten other countries. [12; 19]

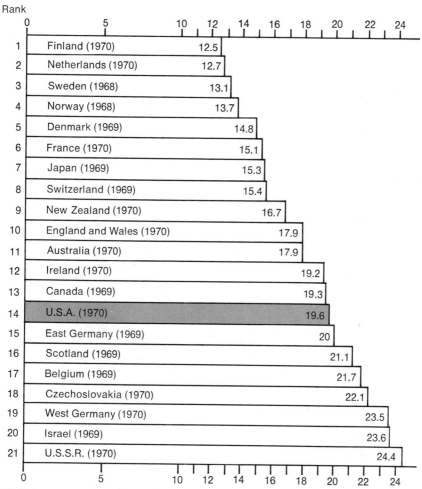

FIGURE 2–2. Infant mortality rates: selected countries in rank order. *(Demographic Yearbook 1970, 22nd issue. Statistical Office, United Nations Department of Economic and Social Affairs. New York: United Nations, 1971, Table 16.)*

Family Disruption: Divorce, Desertion, Illegitimacy

Once guaranteed the right to life, we owe the child the opportunity to grow up in an intact home under the care of both a father and a mother. The loss of either or both parents increases the risk of the need for child welfare service. *The trend of family disruption arising from the death of a parent has been downward.*

Marrying earlier than her counterpart fifty years ago, and bearing fewer children, the modern mother is likely to complete her child-bearing phase earlier in life. This, coupled with an increase in life expectancy for both sexes, means that most parents will live through the full period of dependency of their children. Thus there has been a steady decrease in the absolute and relative numbers of full orphans—from 6.5 million in 1920 (some 16 percent of the child population) to 3.3 million orphans in 1970 (some 4.6 percent of the child population).

Maternal mortality, as one cause of partial orphanhood, has been decreasing, although here, too, our rate is still higher than that of some twelve other countries. While decreasing along with white maternal mortality rates, the rate of maternal mortality among nonwhites was more than three times higher than that among whites at the end of the 1960's. Although life expectancy for both whites and nonwhites has increased, the nonwhite child is more likely than a white to lose a parent as a result of death. By the end of the 1960's, life expectancy was 68.1 years for white males and 75.4 for white females, but only 60.5 years for nonwhite males and 68.9 years for nonwhite females. The difference, however, is narrowing.

While death of parents is less frequently a cause of family disruption, there is an increase in other significant forms of family disruption. *The trend is toward an increase in divorce, in desertions, and in illegitimacy.* All of these trends increase the risk for child welfare services.

In the two decades following the end of World War II, divorce rates stabilized. Since 1965, however, there has been a slow, but steady, rise, from 2.2 per thousand in 1960 to about 3.7 per thousand in 1971. The number of divorce granted increased from 393,000 in 1960 to 768,000 in 1971. Of greater immediate significance for increasing risk for child welfare services is that more and more often children tend to be involved in divorce actions. In 1952 only 46 percent of all divorces involved children, but by 1970, 60 percent of all divorces involved children. Every divorce involving a child precipitates a situation in which child welfare services may be called upon to meet the unfilled paternal roles. Some percentage of these children regain a father on remarriage of the mother, but many continue to grow up in a single-parent home.

Separations and desertions affect almost as many children as divorce, although statistical data on this phenomenon are difficult to compile. Marital disruption is more frequent among urban families, among low-income groups, and among nonwhites. Desertion, traditionally the "poor man's divorce," may run as high as 400,000 to 500,000 each year. [23]

Another factor of significance for child welfare services is *the trend toward a continued gradual increase in both the rate and number of illegitimate births.* The rate is expressed as the number of illegitimate births per thousand unmarried women aged 15–44. In 1968, for instance, 340,000 illegitimate births were reported, as contrasted with some 142,000 in 1950. The rate shows a less spectacular and much more gradual change—from 14 per thousand unmarried women in 1950 to 24 per thousand in 1968. During the 1960's, despite the continued increase in the absolute number of illegitimacies, there was a clearly discernible leveling off of the illegitimacy rate.

There is a significant difference in the incidence of illegitimacy among whites and nonwhites, although the difference is narrowing. In 1950 the rate was nearly twelve times higher among nonwhites than among whites. Since 1960, the rate among whites has increased while that among nonwhites has decreased, so that toward the end of the decade the latter was only eight times higher than the former. (The historical, social, and economic reasons for these differences are discussed in Chap. 10.) Figure 2–3 recapitulates some of the vital statistics.

Rate per 1,000 Population

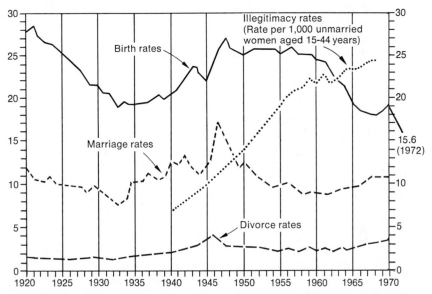

FIGURE 2–3. Vital statistics rates, 1920 to 1972. *(Statistical Abstract of the United States 1972*, 93rd edition. U.S. Department of Commerce, Bureau of the Census. Washington, D.C.: Government Printing Office, 1972.)

The trend is toward an increase in the percentage of children growing up in a broken home. However, the great majority of American children grow up in an intact home under the care of two parents. As a matter of fact, during the past one hundred years, decreases in parental death during childhood dependency have been able to offset the increases in divorce, desertion, and illegitimacy. Consequently, the child today has a better chance of growing up in an unbroken home than a child born in 1870. The short-range trend, however, is toward a slight increase in broken homes.

In 1970 about 83 percent of all children under eighteen were growing up in a home with both parents. This means that about 12 million children were not incorporated in an intact family in 1970. Children growing up outside the care of a two-parent home are most likely to be living with one parent, generally the mother. In 1970 about 9 million children were growing up in a one-parent home. About 3 million children live in institutions, foster homes, with relatives, and so on. [76, Table 159] In this, too, the white child has an advantage: in 1970, about 87 percent of all white children—but only 57 percent of black children—were growing up in a two-parent home. [76, Table 119]   The percentage of white children growing up in an intact home was relatively constant throughout the decade, dropping only slightly, but there was a steady drop in the percentage of nonwhite children growing up in an intact home.

Income is a very significant factor in family disruption, although race plays some part. [4; 15; 21]*   In 1969 for all families with income of less than $3000, 24 percent of black children and 44 percent of white children were living with both parents. For all families with incomes of $15,000 or over, 89 percent of black children and 97 percent of white children were living with both parents.

"The effects of income level . . . [are] about five times as strong as the effects of race. Female-headed families are five times more characteristic of poor families than of black families." [70, p. 153]   Among whites and nonwhites "the percentage of families headed by a woman moves steadily downward as family income rises." [66, p. 5]   But since the percentage of female-headed families is higher among nonwhites at every income level, the factor of race would seem also to be significant. In 1969, at the $2000 income level, 74 percent of all black families, but only 57 percent of all white families, were headed by a woman. For families with income of $10,000 or over, 5 percent of black families, but only 2 percent of white families were headed by a woman.

The evident importance of this material is that a child in a one-parent home, or a child without parents, is a greater than normal risk for child welfare services.

Poverty: A Factor of Risk for Child Welfare Services

Poverty is another factor that increases the potential need for child welfare services. The family living on the edge of poverty faces stresses that increase the probability of failure in parental role performance and the probability of family disruption. We owe the child the right to be wanted, the right to life, and the right to grow up in the loving care of both a father and a mother; we owe him, further, the right to grow up in

---

* See also Robert B. Hill, *The Strengths of Black Families.* New York: Emerson Hall Publishers, 1972.

a family which has sufficient resources to meet his basic needs. *The trend over the past decade has been toward a reduction in the percentage and number of children living in poverty.*

It is difficult to define poverty. There is a controversy over whether poverty can be defined in absolute terms or whether it is a subjective, individual sense of deprivation. Even if one accepts the idea that poverty can be defined in absolute terms, there is still a problem of deciding what standard measures can be applied to calculate the level of income actually needed by a family. [45; 52]   During the 1960's, the Federal government used a poverty index which is widely accepted, and which has been periodically adjusted in response to rises in the cost of living. By 1973 the poverty index for a nonfarm family of four was $4200.

In 1959 it was estimated that some 16 million children—about 25 percent of all American children—were living in poverty. Ten years later, in 1969, some 10.5 million children—about 15 percent of all American children—were living in poverty. While the population of children had increased, the numbers living in poverty had decreased.

It is easier to deal with absolute poverty, however, than with relative deprivation. Although over-all income levels are high and rising, the

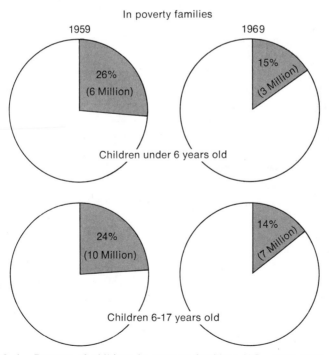

FIGURE 2–4. Percent of children in poverty families: U.S., 1959–1969. (*Profiles of Children.* U.S. White House Conference on Children. Washington, D.C.: Government Printing Office, 1970.)

distribution of income in the United States has remained substantially unchanged in the last twenty years: the lowest 20 percent of households have consistently been receiving about 5 percent of aggregate family income. The gap between the poor and the affluent in America remains almost as wide as ever.

In addition, by the end of the 1960's the advance against poverty was slowing down. Between 1969 and 1970, the country experienced its first reversal in its decade-long war against poverty, as the number of people living in poverty increased by some 5 percent. [74] Furthermore, not all groups shared equally in the benefits from the war against poverty. The principal victories during the 1960's were won for the white family headed by a male. Nonwhite families and families headed by a woman made fewer gains; nonwhite families headed by a woman made fewer still. Finally, although the number of people below the poverty line dropped by almost 40 percent to 24 million from 1959 to 1969, the decline for whites was about 25 percent more rapid than that for nonwhites. Still, the black child had made some progress. In 1959, 65.5 percent of all black children were living in poverty; by 1970, only 40 percent.

Nonwhites made substantial gains in obtaining more desirable jobs during the 1960's. While in 1947 only 3 percent of black families had incomes of $10,000 or more, by 1969, about 24 percent of black families were in this group. Yet nonwhite workers are still heavily overrepresented in low-income groups, and the unemployment rate for blacks was, throughout the decade, nearly double that for whites. Because they hold poorer-paying jobs and are subject to higher rates of unemployment, nonwhite families have lagged substantially behind white families in income. The gap is closing, but very slowly. In 1960, the nonwhite family's median annual income was 55 percent that of the white family —a difference of $2600 a year. By 1969 the nonwhite family's median annual income was 64 percent that of the white family—but the difference was now about $4000.* By the end of the decade, despite twenty years of progress, one of every five black families (but only one of every ten white families) had an income of less than $3000, and black college graduates had lower annual incomes than white high school graduates.

Because there are many more white children in the country than nonwhite, although most nonwhite children are poor, most poor children are white. In terms of the actual numbers of children affected, poverty is a problem for whites, particularly for the white child living in a family headed by a female.

The large family, like the nonwhite family and the family headed by

---

* Since 1969 there has been a reversal of this trend. By the end of 1972 black median income was only 59 percent that of whites (*The New York Times*, July 23, 1973).

a woman, is apt to be poor. Only 8 percent of all three-person families, but 22.8 percent of all families of seven persons or larger, were below the poverty level in March 1971.

There is also a sizable group of American families—"the working poor"—who earn incomes above the official poverty level yet too low to sustain a "modest but comfortable way of life." Although the official poverty level income for a nonfarm family of four was about $4000 in 1970, the U.S. Bureau of Labor estimated that a "modest but adequate" living standard for a family of the same size at this time required about $9500. Many American children live in families whose available income is such that adequately meeting their needs is a constant, enervating struggle.

Poverty is related to some of the other contingencies that tend to increase the likelihood that a family will require child welfare services. Divorce, separation, widowhood (when there are young children in the family), and unmarried motherhood involve not only a problem in family organization resulting from loss of a father figure, but also a great probability of a sharply reduced family income. One of the pockets of poverty in the United States is that of the family headed by a woman.

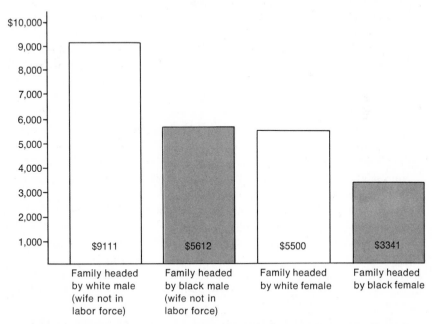

FIGURE 2–5. Median family income by head of family and race, 1969. The richest families are likely to be families headed by a white male; the poorest families are likely to be families headed by a black female. (*Black Americans: A Chartbook.* U.S. Department of Labor, Bureau of Labor Statistics. Washington, D.C.: Government Printing Office, 1971, Table 21, p. 48.)

The highest-income families are those headed by a white male. The next highest is that of the family headed by a nonwhite male. A family headed by a white female has a still lower median income. The family headed by a nonwhite female has the lowest median income.

The consequences for a child of living in poverty are detailed in a recent report by the National Commission on Mental Health after an extensive nationwide study:

> Poverty means that millions of children are at high risk in health and mental health. It means hunger and malnutrition which may cripple intellectual and physical development and undermine a child's belief in his parents and the world in which he lives. It means a crowded, meager home which can offer little to overcome the child's increasingly reduced potentialities. It means life in a neighborhood which probably offers little opportunity for healthy play, privacy, or safety but many opportunities for danger, brutality, and exposure to deviant behavior. It means a stunting of hopes and prospects, a feeling of exclusion and rejection, a sense of rage at injustice, or surrender to defeat. It too often means that the child receives little or no medical and dental services, that he attends schools of inferior quality, that his life prospects are constricted and darkened even before life is barely begun. The wonder is not that so many of the poor continue to have critical mental health and related problems throughout their lives, but that they manage to do as well as they do, and complain so little, especially when they are continuously exposed to the rich and exotic life patterns that are advertised as being "the American way." [36, p. 149]

The connection between poverty and other child welfare problems is indicated by a New Orleans study which showed "that although 26 percent of the female population of reproductive ages were poor, they accounted for 72 percent of the stillbirths, 80 percent of the maternal deaths, and 68 percent of the infant deaths." [86, p. 389]

Malnutrition is one of the serious consequences of poverty and inadequate income. The U.S. Senate Committee on Nutrition and Human Needs reported in August 1969 that "clinically validated malnutrition exists in serious proportions in the United States and is a particularly acute problem among infants, preschool, and schoolchildren from low-income families." [87, p. 5]   The Citizens' Board of Inquiry into Hunger and Malnutrition in the United States reported similar findings in 1968, as did a panel of doctors who undertook a survey under the auspices of the Field Foundation. [13; 32; 37]

Although many mothers work because they want to, most mothers—particularly mothers of preschool-age children—work because they have to. The lower the family income, the more likely it is that the mother will be working. *The trend has been toward an increase in working mothers, particularly mothers of preschool children.*

This poses a problem of inter-role conflict—the role of mother vs. role of employee—and dictates the need for some temporary substitute child-care service for the dependent child. In 1960, 20 percent of mothers with children under six were working; by 1970, 32 percent of such mothers were employed. This meant that over 4 million preschool children shared their mothers with employers. (A more detailed analysis of the working mother is included in Chap. 8.)

The participation of mothers in the labor force has some benefits, however: it increases the income level of many families, thus permitting the families to meet the needs of children more adequately; it also moves the child-dependency ratio in a favorable direction; and it results in an expansion of the work force and an increase in the country's productivity.

Minority-Group Status: A Factor of Risk for Child Welfare Services

Being nonwhite is a major factor increasing the probability that child welfare services may be needed. Every applicable social indicator reveals the relative disadvantage of the nonwhite American. Among nonwhites, infant and maternal mortality rates, illegitimacy rates and family disruption rates, and unemployment rates are higher. The percentage of nonwhites living in poverty is higher than that of whites, as is the percentage of young children whose mothers are working, and the percentage who live in dilapidated, substandard housing. Illiteracy rates are higher among nonwhites, as are high school drop-out rates, crime rates, and rates of victimization from crime. The incidence of disabling illnesses is higher among nonwhites; the percentage of children under seventeen who have never seen a dentist is higher. On the other hand, life expectancy is lower; median income is lower; lifetime earnings are lower; level of education achievement is lower; frequency of accessibility to adequate medical care is lower; accessibility to higher status jobs is lower; home ownership is lower; the percentage of the group covered by any kind of health insurance is lower. [75; 84]

As a consequence of their disadvantaged position, the nonwhite population provides a disproportionately large group of recipients of all of the welfare services and a disproportionately large group at risk for such services.

Table 2–1 recapitulates some of the statistical changes in 1960–70 that are significant for child welfare services. For purposes of comparison, statistics for whites and nonwhites are reported separately.

TABLE 2–1.   Trends Relevant to Child Welfare Services

Relevant Factor	Years	White	Nonwhite
Birth rate (per 1000 population)	1960	22.7	32.1
	1965	18.3	27.6
	1970	15.5	25.2
Infant mortality (per 1000 live births)	1960	22.9	43.2
	1965	21.5	40.3
	1970	17.4	31.4
Maternal mortality (per 100,000 live births)	1960	26	97.9
	1965	21	83.7
	1968	16.6	63.6
Life expectancy at birth	1960	70.6	63.6
	1965	71	64.1
	1968	71.1	63.7
Unemployment rates (annual average)	1960	4.9	10.2
	1965	4.1	8.1
	1970	4.5	8.2
Median annual family income	1960	$ 5,835	$3,233
	1965	$ 7,251	$3,994
	1970	$10,236	$6,541
Percent of population below poverty level	1960	18	56
	1965	13	47
	1970	10	32
Illegitimacy rate (per 1000 unmarried women 15–44 years of age)	1960	9.2	98.3
	1965	11.6	97.6
	1970	13.2	86.6
Percentage of mothers in labor force with children under 6	1966	24	40
	1971	29	47
Own children living with both parents as a percentage of all children in the racial group	1960	92	75
	1965	91	71
	1970	87	57
Divorce (per 1000 total population; not available by race)	1960	2.2	
	1965	2.5	
	1971	3.7	

The figures generally show improvement for both whites and non-whites, but they also reveal the comparatively more favorable situation of the white population.

Urbanization and Services

There is a trend toward urbanization of the nonwhite population and suburbanization of the white population. Between 1960 and 1970 the population of the United States grew 13 percent, but the urban population grew 23 percent. By the year 2000 it is anticipated that 85 percent of our population will be living in metropolitan areas. The past decade has witnessed an increase in percentage of nonwhite living in inner-city areas and an outflow of whites to neighboring suburbs. By 1970 over 73 percent of the total population lived in and around large cities. Three out of every five blacks in the United States lived in the central city of a major metropolitan area, though whites still outnumber blacks in central city areas by four to one.

Since minority groups are likely to incur a disproportionate need for child welfare services, these services, to be accessible, should be located in the inner city. Some services would need to be established in the suburban areas to meet the needs of the groups which had migrated to the outlying districts, but rural areas—having lost some percentage of their population—might require fewer services in the future.

Changing Values

Statistical trends regarding the number of children at risk and trends regarding the social contingencies which directly affect the number of children possibly needing child welfare services are very important factors helping us to understand the context in which such services are offered. Of importance, too, is the nature of ideological changes.

We currently are undergoing a change in attitudes toward parenthood which may affect the context in which child welfare services are offered. The concern with zero population growth and the agitation for changes in the status of women have diminished the prestige formerly accorded the status of parent. Parenthood is no longer unanimously and enthusiastically applauded, and having more than two children may shortly be regarded as socially irresponsible, if not actually illegal.

With fewer children and increased life expectancy, women are currently finding that only a relatively small percentage of their productive years are devoted to the full-time maternal role. The average woman may be a full-time mother for about ten years, and since she is capable of being fully productive for a period of some 30 to 35 years, the woman who has dedicated herself to motherhood finds herself with either a part-time job or no job at all for a good part of her life. This fact supports and reinforces the orientation of women's liberation and population control groups for a de-emphasis on motherhood and a search for alternative life styles for women.

Books such as *The Baby Trap* and *The Case Against Having Children* are receiving attention and comment and suggest a flight from parenthood. [56, 65] A deliberate decision not to bear children has become socially acceptable. In 1972 a national organization of nonparents was formed to agitate for the acceptability of "childfree" marriages—its slogan: "None is fun" (*Time*, July 3, 1972). The teachings of society have hitherto generally reflected and supported the Biblical injunction, "Be fruitful and multiply." Currently the idea of parenthood as an important, significant life goal is open to question and debate, and childless marriages are more acceptable. The greater availability and effectiveness of contraceptive devices help to reinforce these changes in ideology.

The last decade has witnessed a revolution in attitude regarding public support of family planning. Before World War II, some states forbade dissemination of contraceptive information and devices, and there was very strong and effective opposition to the use of public money for support of birth control programs. But by December 1970, Congress authorized the expenditure of $382 million for family planning services and population research over a three-year period. The bill also created an Office of Population Affairs in the U.S. Department of Health, Education, and Welfare. In 1972 Federal appropriations included $90 million for family planning services and $37.7 million for family planning research.

Thus, by the 1970's, public acceptance of birth control was so widespread that public funds were being expended in support of government-sponsored contraceptive programs. Tax dollars were being used to provide contraceptive devices, on request, to public welfare recipients (both married and unmarried). Social workers were generally more involved with offering family planning services than they had been at the beginning of the decade. [40; 42]

An even more revolutionary attitude emerged toward abortion. By 1972 abortion reform acts had been passed by seventeen states and reform legislation had been introduced in many other states. Reform bills liberalized procedures in accordance with the suggestions contained in The American Law Institute Model Penal Code. Legalized abortion was permitted in the case of pregnancy resulting from incest or forceable or statutory rape, or when there was reason to suspect that the fetus might be deformed, or when the mother's physical health might be adversely affected by bearing the child. In four states—Hawaii, Alaska, New York, and Washington—the legislation, in effect, permitted abortion on demand.

Revision of all restrictive state abortion statutes was finally made mandatory by a landmark Supreme Court decision on January 22, 1973, which, in effect, legalized abortion. By a 7–2 decision the Court declared that during the first three months of a pregnancy the decision to abort rests solely with the woman and her physician. During the second trimester the state may not prohibit abortion but may regulate its practice in the interest of protecting the woman's health. Only during the final trimester of pregnancy can the states prohibit abortion. The decision rejected the contention that the fetus is a "person" within constitutional terms and must be protected by the state. While the move-ment to bring state statutes into line with the Supreme Court decision was proceeding slowly, changes were implemented in many states by mid-1973. Extrapolating from previous experience with legalized abor-tion, hospitals were preparing for some 1,600,000 abortions annually (*The New York Times*, January 28, 1973).

The anticipated consequences of this revolutionary decision have direct relevance to projected needs for child welfare services. It will further the likelihood of a decline in the population of children as abor-tion is used as a backstop to contraception; reduce the number of illegitimate births; reduce teenage marriages, frequently contracted in response to premarital pregnancies, and thus the rate of divorce, which is at its highest in this age group; reduce the number of unwanted children and the abuse of such children; lower maternal and infant mortality rates as births to high-risk women—the unmarried, the poor, the very young—decline.

In support of such prognostications it might be noted that within the first two years after the passage of the N.Y. State law, 400,000 abortions were performed in New York City. A disproportionally high percentage of such abortions were requested by the poor and the nonwhite and by single pregnant women. As a consequence, "out-of-wedlock births de-clined for the first time since statistics began to be collected in 1954" in New York City. [18, p. 6]   California reported that about 60 percent of the abortions following liberalization of the statutes in 1967 were per-formed on unmarried women under the age of twenty-five. [53, p. 497] New York showed a decline in maternal and infant mortality rates fol-lowing legalization of abortion (*The New York Times*, January 28, 1973). A rigorously conducted National Fertility Study concluded that some 20 percent of all births between 1960 and 1965 (about 4.7 million children) were unwanted, the largest percentage of such pregnancies occurring among the nonwhite and the poor. [9, p. 1179]

There is currently a greater acceptance of a wider variety of child-rearing contexts and less consensus that the nuclear family is the most desirable. The report of the 1970 decennial conference on children points to the "wide diversity of family forms"—nuclear family, extended family, single-parent family, commune—and supports acceptance of "differential family forms" according to their appropriateness and effectiveness in particular situations. The report noted that "There is a need to make visible the increased variability in family forms and to recognize the right of individuals to live in any family form they feel will increase their options for self-fulfillment." [89, p. 232]

There is a growing acceptance, too, of the idea that the responsibility for rearing a child is shared by the parents and the community. The idea of joint responsibility leads to a greater acceptance of day-care centers and other community-centered arrangements for progressively earlier implementation of the partnership.

There has been an increase in concern in offering service to black families and black children on the part of the child welfare agencies during the past decade, in sharp contrast to the earlier disinterest documented by Billingsley in his historical review of services to black children. [5]   This change resulted partially from the migration of the black population from Southern rural centers to Northern urban centers, where more adequate services are found, and from the relative decrease in demand for services on the part of white families and children. The major cause, however, lies in the ideological shifts which resulted from the Civil Rights movement of the 1960's, which focused attention on the problems of all minority groups. Institutional racism, as manifested in policies of child welfare services, came under critical review and led to recommendations for policy changes.

Summary

The chapter has been concerned with developing an historical perspective on child welfare services and attempting to place child welfare services within the current context of American society. A number of factors were discussed to help explain the fact that, although child welfare problems have been encountered throughout history, only recently has a special institution such as social work child welfare services been organized. Among the factors discussed were the following:

1. The inadmissibility of previous solutions and changes in ideology.
2. The greater productivity of the community in making possible support of a large group of dependents.
3. The increased specialization of social institutions.
4. The "discovery" of childhood.
5. Changes in the arithmetic of production.
6. The increased status of the family and the child.
7. The scientific revolution and the development of a science of child rearing.

The American experience presented some special considerations that heightened the tendency to elevate the status of the child and increase concern for his needs. The immigrant status of most parents and the strong future time orientation in the United States helped to emphasize this filiocentric trend.

Among current trends in American society of relevance to child welfare services, the following aspects were discussed:

1. Recent relative decreases in size of child population.
2. The changes in child-dependency ratios occasioned by the changing demography.
3. Changes in the life cycle of the family and their effect on childhood dependency.
4. Continued decreases in infant, child, and maternal mortality, and increases in life expectancy.
5. The consequences for family disruption rates of the increase in divorce rates, increases in the number of children affected by divorce, increases in illegitimacy rates, and reduction in death rates of the parents. Other factors related to changes in family functioning, such as the increase in number of working mothers, were also discussed.
6. The prevalence of poverty in the United States, particularly among families headed by a woman and nonwhite families.
7. Membership in a minority group as a factor in increasing the risk of need for child welfare services because of higher rates of family disruption (through divorce, separation, death, illegitimacy), lower family income, fewer employment opportunities.
8. Changes in the geographical distribution of the population, such as increases in urbanization and suburbanization.
9. Ideological changes regarding childless marriages, family planning, abortion, and the nature of the family.

Bibliography

1. ARIES, PHILIPPE. *Centuries of Childhood.* New York: Alfred A. Knopf, Inc., 1962.
2. ATHERTON, CHARLES R. "The Social Assignment of Social Work." *Social Service Review,* **43**, 4 (December 1969), 421–29.
3. BAKAN, DAVID. *Slaughter of the Innocents—A Study of the Battered Child Phenomenon.* San Francisco: Jossey-Bass, Inc., 1971.
4. BILLINGSLEY, ANDREW. "Family Functioning in the Low Income Black Community," *Social Casework,* **50**, 10 (December 1969), 563–72.
5. ———, and JEANNE M. GIOVANNONI. *Children of the Storm—Black Children and American Child Welfare.* New York: Harcourt Brace Jovanovich, Inc., 1972.
6. BLYTHE, RONALD. *Akenfield–Portrait of an English Village.* New York: Delta Paperbook, 1969.
7. BOSSARD, JAMES H. S., and ELEANOR S. BOLL. *The Sociology of Childhood,* 4th ed. New York: Harper and Row, Publishers, 1966.
8. BREMNER, ROBERT H. (ed.). *Children and Youth in America—A Documentary History,* Vol. 1, pp. 1600–1865. Cambridge, Mass.: Harvard University Press, 1970.
9. BUMPASS, LARRY, and CHARLES F. WESTOFF. "The 'Perfect Contraceptive' Population," *Science,* **169** (September 18, 1970).

10. CALHOUN, ARTHUR W. *A Social History of the American Family.* Vol. I: *The Colonial Period.* New York: Barnes & Noble, Inc., 1945.
11. CAULFIELD, ERNEST. *The Infant Welfare Movement of the Eighteenth Century.* New York: Paul Hocker, 1931.
12. CHASE, H. C. "Ranking Countries by Infant Mortality Rates." *Public Health Report,* **84**, 1 (1969), 19–27.
13. CITIZENS BOARD OF INQUIRY. *Hunger, U.S.A.* Boston: Beacon Press, 1968.
14. COMMISSION ON POPULATION GROWTH AND THE AMERICAN FUTURE. *Population and the American Future.* New York: New American Library (Signet), 1972.
15. CUTRIGHT, PHILLIP. "Income and Family Events: Marital Stability." *Journal of Marriage and the Family,* **33**, 2 (1971).
16. DESPERT, J. LOUISE. *The Emotionally Disturbed Child—Then and Now.* New York: Robert Brunner, 1965.
17. DEVEREAUX, GEORGE. *A Study of Abortion in Primitive Societies.* New York: Julian Press, Inc., 1955.
18. DUFFY, EDWARD A. *The Effect of Changes in the State Abortion Laws.* Public Health Service Publication 2165. Washington, D.C.: Government Printing Office, February 1971.
19. FALKNER, FRANK. "Infant Mortality—An Urgent National Problem." *Children,* **17**, 3 (May–June 1970), 83–87.
20. FARBER, BERNARD. *Guardians of Virtue—Salem Families in 1800.* New York: Basic Books, Inc., 1972.
21. FARLEY, REYNOLDS, and ALBERT I. HERMALIN. "Family Stability: A Comparison of Trends Between Black and White." *American Sociological Review,* **36**, 1 (February 1971).
22. FELT, JEREMY. *Hostages to Fortune: Child Labor Reform in N.Y. State.* Syracuse, N.Y.: Syracuse University Press, 1965.
23. FREED, DORIS J., and HENRY H. FOSTER. "Divorce American Style." *Annals of the American Academy,* **38**, 3 (May 1969), 71–88.
24. GALLAHUE, JOHN. "Tragedy at Liege." *Look* (March 12, 1963), 72–78.
25. GREHEN, FARRELL. "Mothers, Martyrs of the Speed Age." *Life* (January 18, 1960), 16.
26. GRIER, GEORGE. *The Baby Bust: An Agenda for the 70's Special Report.* Washington, D.C.: The Washington Center for Metropolitan Studies, 1971.
27. HANDS, A. R. *Charities and Social Aid in Greece and Rome.* Ithaca, N.Y.: Cornell University Press, 1968.
28. HARTLEY, SHIRLEY F. "The Decline of Illegitimacy in Japan." *Social Problems,* **19**, 1 (Summer 1970), 78–91.
29. HERZOG, ELIZABETH. "Social Stereotypes and Social Research." *Journal of Social Issues,* **26**, 3 (1970), 109–25.
30. HIMES, NORMAN E. *Medical History of Contraception.* Baltimore: The Williams & Wilkins Co., 1936.
31. HOBHOUSE, L. T. *Morals in Evolution.* London: Chapman & Hall, Ltd., 1951.
32. HOLLINGS, ERNEST. *The Case Against Hunger: A Demand for a National Policy.* New York: Cowles Book Co., 1970.
33. HUNT, DAVID. *Parents and Children in Seventeenth-Century France.* New York: Basic Books, Inc., 1969.

34. HUNT, ELEANOR. "Infant Mortality and Poverty Areas." *Welfare in Review,* 4 (August–September 1967), 1–12.

35. JACOBSON, PAUL. *American Marriage and Divorce.* New York: Holt, Rinehart & Winston, Inc., 1959.

36. JOINT COMMISSION ON MENTAL HEALTH. *Crises in Child Mental Health— Challenge for the 1970's.* New York: Harper and Row, Publishers, 1970.

37. KOTZ, NICK. *Let Them Eat Promises: The Politics of Hunger in America.* Garden City, N.Y.: Doubleday & Company, Inc., 1971.

38. LADAR, LAWRENCE. *Abortion.* Indianapolis: The Bobbs-Merrill Co., Inc., 1966.

39. LECKY, WILLIAM E. *History of European Morals.* Vol. II. New York: Appleton-Century-Crofts, 1869.

40. LIPSCOMB, NELL I. "Casework and Family Planning." *Social Casework,* 50, 4 (April 1969), 204–209.

41. LITWAK, EUGENE. "Occupational Mobility and Extended Family Cohesion." *American Sociological Review,* 25 (February 1960).

42. MAYFIELD, MARY N. "Family Planning in Public Welfare." *Public Welfare,* 28, 2 (April 1970), 161–64.

43. MCCLOY, SHELBY T. *Government Assistance in Eighteenth-Century France.* Durham, N.C.: Duke University Press, 1946.

44. MEAD, MARGARET. "A Cultural Anthropologist's Approach to Maternal Deprivation," in *Deprivation of Maternal Care.* Geneva: World Health Organization, 1962.

45. MERRIAM, IDA C. "Income and Its Measurement," in *Indicators of Social Change.* Ed. by Eleanor B. Sheldon and Wilbert E. Moore. New York: Russell Sage Foundation, 1968.

46. MIDDLETON, NIGEL. *When Family Failed.* London: Victor Golancz, Ltd., 1971.

47. MILLER, NATHAN. *The Child in Primitive Society.* New York: Brentanos, 1928.

48. MITCHELL, R. G. "Children in Society," in *Child Life and Health.* Ed. by Ross S. Mitchell. London: J. & A. Churchill Ltd., 1970.

49. MITSCHERLICH, ALEXANDER. *Doctors of Infamy.* New York: Abelard-Schuman, Ltd., 1949.

50. MOHL, RAYMOND A. *Poverty in New York 1783–1825.* New York: Oxford University Press, Inc., 1971.

51. MORGAN, JOHN, et al. *Income and Welfare in the United States.* New York: McGraw-Hill Book Company, 1962.

52. ORSHANSKY, MOLLIE. "How Poverty Is Measured." *Monthly Labor Review,* 92 (February 1969), 37–41.

53. OVERSTREET, EDMUND W. "Logistic Problems of Legal Abortion." *American Journal of Public Health,* 61, 3 (March 1971), 496–99.

54. PAKTER, JEAN, and FRIEDA NELSON. "Abortion in New York City: The First Nine Months." *Family Planning Perspective,* 3, 3 (July 1971), 5–12.

55. PAYNE, GEORGE H. *The Child in Human Progress.* New York: G. P. Putnam's Sons, 1916.

56. PECK, ELLEN. *The Baby Trap.* New York: Bernard Geis Associates, Inc., 1971.

57. PERLMAN, RICHARD. "Juvenile Delinquency and Some Social and Economic Trends." *Welfare in Review*, 1 (October 1963).
58. PINCHBECK, IVY, and MARGARET HEWITT. *Children in English Society*. Vol. I: *From Tudor Times to the Eighteenth Century*. London: Kegan Paul, Trench, Trubner & Co., 1969.
59. QUEEN, ALFRED S. *Social Work in the Light of History*. Philadelphia: J. B. Lippincott Co., 1922.
60. RADBILL, SAMUEL X. "A History of Child Abuse and Infanticide," in *The Battered Child*. Ed. by Ray E. Helfer and C. Henry Kempe. Chicago: University of Chicago Press, 1968.
61. SCHORR, ALVIN. *Slums and Social Insecurity*. U.S. Dept. of Health, Education, and Welfare, Social Security Administration, Division of Research and Statistics, *Research Report* No. 1. Washington, D.C.: Government Printing Office, 1962.
62. DE SCHWEINITZ, KARL. *England's Road to Social Security*. Philadelphia: University of Pennsylvania Press, 1947.
63. SELIGMAN, EDWIN, R. (ed.). *Encyclopedia of Social Science*. Vol. III. New York: The Macmillan Company, 1930.
64. SICAULT, GEORGES (ed.). *The Needs of Children*. New York: The Free Press, 1963.
65. SILVERMAN, ANNA, and ARNOLD SILVERMAN. *The Case Against Having Children*. New York: David McKay Co., Inc., 1971.
66. STEIN, ROBERT L. "The Economic Status of Families Headed by Women." *Monthly Labor Review*, 93 (December 1970), 3–10.
67. STEINBICKER, CARL R. *Poor Relief in the Sixteenth Century*. Washington, D.C.: Catholic University Press, 1957.
68. SUMNER, WILLIAM G. *Folkways*. New York: Dover Publications, Inc., 1959.
69. SUSSMAN, MARTIN. "The Isolated Nuclear Family: Fact or Fiction?" *Social Problems*, 11 (Spring 1959).
70. TEN HOUTEN, WARREN D. "The Black Family: Myth and Reality." *Psychiatry*, 33, 2 (May 1970), 145–73.
71. THANT, U. *Trends in the Social Situation of Children*. Report on Children of the Secretary General. New York: United Nations Economic and Social Council, January 8, 1970.
72. TRATTNER, WALTER I. *Crusade for the Children*. Chicago: Quadrangle Books, Inc., 1970.
73. U.S. CONGRESS. *Message from the President of the United States: Recommendations for the Welfare of Children*. 90th Congress, 1st Session. Document No. 54.
74. U.S. DEPARTMENT OF COMMERCE. *Current Population Reports: Consumer Income, May 7, 1971*. Washington, D.C.: Government Printing Office, 1971.
75. ———. *The Social and Economic Status of Negroes in the United States, 1970*. Washington, D.C.: Government Printing Office, July 1971.
76. ———. *Census of Population, 1970. General Social and Economic Characteristics—Final Report U.S. Summary*. Washington, D.C.: Government Printing Office, 1972.
77. ———. *Statistical Abstract of the United States, 1972*. 93rd ed. Washington, D.C.: Government Printing Office, 1972.

78. U.S. DEPARTMENT OF HEALTH, EDUCATION, AND WELFARE PUBLIC HEALTH SERVICE. *Facts of Life and Death. Public Health Service Publication* No. 600, Revised 1970. Washington, D.C.: Government Printing Office, 1970.

79.————. *International Comparison of Prenatal and Infant Mortality—The United States and Six West European Countries.* Washington, D.C.: Government Printing Office, 1967.

80. ————. *Trends in Illegitimacy in the United States: 1940–1965.* Washington, D.C.: Government Printing Office, February 1968.

81. ————. *Population and Family Planning—The Transition from Concern to Action.* Report of the President's Committee on Population and Family Planning. Washington, D.C.: Superintendent of Documents, November 1968.

82. ————. *Increases in Divorce in the United States: 1967.* Publication No. 1000, Series 21, No. 2. Washington, D.C.: Government Printing Office, 1970.

83. U.S. DEPARTMENT OF LABOR. *The Negro Family—The Case for National Action* (The Moynihan Report). Washington, D.C.: Government Printing Office, 1965.

84. ————. *Black Americans: A Chartbook.* Washington, D.C.: Government Printing Office, 1971.

85. U.S. SENATE. *The Food Gap: Poverty and Malnutrition in the United States.* Interim Report—Select Committee on Nutrition and Human Needs. Washington, D.C.: Government Printing Office, August 1969.

86. ————, COMMITTEE ON GOVERNMENT OPERATION. *Background Papers Prepared for the 1970–71 White Conference on Children and Growth.* Washington, D.C.: Government Printing Office, 1971.

87. ————, COMMITTEE ON LABOR AND PUBLIC WELFARE. *Hunger and Malnutrition in America—Hearings Before the Subcommittee on Employment, Manpower and Poverty of the Committee on Labor and Public Welfare, July 11–12, 1967.* Washington, D.C.: Government Printing Office, 1967.

88. U.S. WHITE HOUSE CONFERENCE ON CHILDREN. *Profiles of Children.* Washington, D.C.: Government Printing Office, 1970.

89. ————. *Report to the President—1970.* Washington, D.C.: Government Printing Office, 1970.

90. UNITED NATIONS. *Parental Rights and Duties Including Guardianship.* New York: United Nations, 1968.

91. WESTOFF, CHARLES F., and NORMAN B. RYDER. "Recent Trends in Attitudes Toward Fertility Control and the Practice of Contraception in the United States," in *Fertility and Family Planning, a World View.* Ed. by S. J. Behrman *et al.* Ann Arbor: University of Michigan Press, 1969.

3

Supportive Services

Introduction

The first line of defense in dealing with situations requiring child welfare services are those designed to support, reinforce, and strengthen the ability of parents and children to meet effectively the responsibilities of their respective statuses. Supportive services are designed for children living in their own homes. In these instances, both parents are generally present and show some willingness and capacity to enact their roles effectively. However, there may be difficulties in the parent-child relationship as a result of parent-child conflict or as a reflection of marital conflict.

In making use of such services, the family remains structurally intact. The child can remain, and be maintained, in his own home despite some malfunction in the parent-child relationship system. In offering supportive services, the agency does not take over responsibility for discharging any of the role functions of either parent or child. The service always remains external to the family's social structure.

The two principal agencies offering supportive services are the family service agencies and the child guidance clinics. The family service agencies intervene more frequently through service to the parent; the child guidance clinic, through service to the child. Both agencies hope to effect changes that would enable parents and child to live together with greater satisfaction and less friction than was previously experienced. The aim is to lessen the danger of family disruption by improving the social functioning of family members.

Historical Background

The family service agency has its origins in the Charity Organization Societies that were established in the United States during the 1880's. Such societies were organized to coordinate the activities of the many private charities serving the poor. Operating without a full awareness of one another's activities, they often served the same client in a haphazard, contradictory manner.

Until the beginning of the Great Depression in the 1930's, such agencies served primarily an economically deprived clientele and the problems brought to the agency were those that were closely related to economic need. [20]   The service revolved around offering, and helping the client to use, concrete resources, prominent among which were cash relief grants. At the same time, there was emphasis on helping the poor through the personal influence and interest of the social worker—"not alms alone, but alms and a friend" was thought to be the most desirable approach. Such an approach can be viewed as a precursor of the central use of a personal relationship in helping, the principal approach of the family service agency and guidance clinic of today.

When government agencies assumed primary responsibility for relief grants, both the characteristics of clientele and the kinds of primary problems brought to the family service agencies began to change. More and more insistently the agencies defined their function as that of providing help with emotional problems of interpersonal relationships and family adjustment, parent-child problems, and marital problems. By the 1950's this change in emphasis had been successfully interpreted to the community. As a result, the current clientele is more nearly representative of the general composition of the community, since parent-child and marital problems exist at every socioeconomic level. Problems for which the clients currently seek help are now more likely to be those with which child welfare is concerned.

The Family Service Association of America is the national coordinating organization to which almost all of the family service agencies belong. It was established in 1911 as the National Association of Societies for Organizing Charity. In response to changing clientele and ideology, its name was changed in 1930 to the Family Welfare Association of America, and again in 1946 to the Family Service Association of America.

The supportive nature of the family service agency is clearly outlined in the stated aims of the organization. The Family Service Association of America declares that "the central purpose of the family service agency is to contribute to harmonious family interrelationships, to strengthen the positive values in family life, and to promote healthy personality development and satisfactory social functioning of various family members." [28, p. 3]

The second principal child welfare supportive service, the child guidance clinic, has a different history. The forerunner of the modern clinic originated in a concern with the problem of juvenile delinquency. In 1909 Dr. William Healy, working under the aegis of the Juvenile Court of Cook County, Illinois, began a study of juvenile offenders. He attempted to apply some of the newer concepts of psychiatric service derived from Freud's discoveries, and he made explicit efforts to individualize the juvenile offender. In 1917 Dr. Healy's facility, later known as the Institute for Juvenile Research, received state support, and his work was extended to a wider group of emotionally disturbed children, whether delinquent or not. The attempt to individualize each child involved a fourfold approach—"a medical examination to analyze the child's physical assets and abilities, psychological tests to estimate his intellectual capacity, psychiatric interviews to determine his attitudes and the character of his mental life," and a study of the child's developmental history and social situation. [115, p. 47]   Thus Healy's approach considered not only the physical and psychological factors in development, but the social factors as well, and the dynamic interaction between parents and children as causative factors in the child's disturbed behavior. This fourfold approach characterizes the guidance clinic today.

The pioneer work of Healy was widely disseminated as a result of the sponsorship of demonstration clinics by the National Committee for Mental Hygiene in the early 1920's. These clinics, financed by the Commonwealth Fund, were established to demonstrate a method of dealing with juvenile delinquency. Among the objectives that led the Commonwealth Fund to undertake financial support of child guidance clinics were

> to develop the psychiatric study of difficult, predelinquent and delinquent children in the schools and juvenile courts; to develop sound methods of treatment based on such study . . . ; to demonstrate in a number of widely scattered cities the value of such psychiatric study and treatment applied to children of this sort referred from juvenile courts, schools, and other agencies.
> [46, p. 329]

The first demonstration clinic was established in 1922 in St. Louis, with a staff consisting of a psychiatrist, a psychologist, and a social worker. Additional clinics were set up in six cities throughout the country—Norfolk (Virginia), Dallas, Minneapolis, Los Angeles, Cleveland, and Philadelphia. Two traveling clinics were established, operating from three to six months in each city, in an effort to demonstrate the value of such a service and to encourage the community to set up a permanent clinic.

To implement the demonstration, the Fund also set up a program for the training of child guidance workers at the New York School of Social Work. The school established special courses in child guidance and established a psychiatric clinic, The Bureau of Child Guidance, New York City, which was used as a training center for social workers.

Before the demonstration experiment was terminated in 1927, it had established the feasibility and need for such a facility for all children who presented emotional problems. By 1928 a Directory of Psychiatric Clinics for Children in the United States published by the Commonwealth Fund, listed 470 clinics in thirty-one states offering service to 40,000 children during that year. [46, p. 332]

The premise on which the child guidance clinic approach was based was that delinquency was only one manifestation of parent-child difficulties; that emotional disturbances among children, of which delinquency was merely a symptom, resulted from a malfunction in the relationship between parent and child during the early period in the child's development; that the child's behavior was purposive and in response to these developmental difficulties and a reflection of the fundamental problem. If such behavior were to be studied in sufficient detail, with a perceptive knowledge of the critical aspects of child development, one could arrive at an understanding of why the child was behaving in this way. Because the behavioral problem was in response to something that had gone wrong in the relationship between parents and children, one needed to understand, and change, not only the child's behavior but the parents' behavior as well.

And, although the central concern of child guidance clinics was the child, it soon became an axiom of clinic practice that "for every problem child, there is a problem parent." Thus the parent, as well as the child, became an object of concern. The delinquent child shared problems of parent-child relationship with other children, many of whom manifested the results of such disorder in a way that was more disturbing to themselves than to others. There was a movement, then, toward helping all children with problems rather than the delinquent child only. A study of the activities of these clinics indicates that many of the supposedly modern innovations in practice, such as the community mental health orientation, advocacy, and brokerage were integral aspects of their service. [63]

In summary, one might note that the family service agency is a direct descendant of those agencies in the community controlled and administered by social workers. The guidance clinic was fathered by psychiatry and the mental hygiene movement, mothered by the courts and the Commonwealth Fund, and had social work as a godfather.

Situations for Which Supportive Agencies
Are the Appropriate Resource

Any kind of difficulty in the implementation of parent-child roles is an appropriate situation for supportive family service. The parent who has difficulty in disciplining his children, who derives little satisfaction from parenthood, who is concerned about his child's peer group relationships or school performance, a family torn by sibling conflict, an unsatisfactory marital situation to which the children are reacting by disorders in behavior—all supposedly can profit from regular, periodic interviews with a family agency caseworker.

It is difficult to make a clear-cut distinction between the problem that is appropriate for referral to family services and that appropriate for the child guidance clinic. The family service agency is more apt to offer service in those situations in which there are problems of parents to which the child is responding; the child guidance clinic is more apt to offer service in those situations in which there are problems of children to which the parents are responding. The circularity of the problem configuration is evident merely in this statement and the consequent confusion as to where the distinction, if any, lies. Historically, family service has been concerned with the problems of the family, and through this concern became interested in treating the child; and child guidance clinics were concerned with the problems of children, through which they came to be concerned with the problems of parents.

Informational, interpretive material distributed by local family service agencies calls attention to their concern with such problems:

> Who are you? Perhaps you are a mother or a father and concerned about your son because you can't understand or control him . . . or worried and puzzled by your daughter's unhappiness and inability to make friends.

The pamphlet then goes on to indicate that the family service agency helps with these kinds of problems. [33]

Another pamphlet notes that the family service social worker helps with problems such as "a husband [who] feels he can no longer talk to his wife without quarrelling . . . a child [who] becomes unmanageable; a bright teenager [who] starts to play hooky and fails in his studies." [55]

A study of the principal nonsectarian family service agency in New York City—the Community Service Society—shows some of the problems involving children that come to such an agency. As part of the study, the clients' statement of the problem was recorded verbatim. A wife says:

My husband wrote the New York Hospital if they knew of a place where I and my baby could go for a rest. My problem is that I have to live with my mother and twelve other people. It is crowded and we all get nervous. What we need is a place of our own.

A mother says, "I have a boy fourteen who is getting too wild. I can't manage him." A boy of eleven, facing a problem in sibling relationships, says, "I don't want to remain with my brother anymore. I'd rather be sent to a reformatory." A girl says, "I don't get along with my mother. She likes my sister better. I don't feel like one of the family." A father says, "I want to know what's wrong with my son. He's a bright kid yet look at his report card, everything is wrong." [10, pp. 12–13]

Studies of the operations of particular family service agencies substantiate the fact that problems regarding parent and child roles are among those for which clients most frequently seek help. [34, pp. 36–37] Nationwide studies confirm that parent-child difficulties constitute a high proportion of the problems which bring families to a family service agency. In 1970, 42 percent of family agency clients presented a problem of "parent-child" relationship at intake, 26 percent listed a problem of "child rearing or child care," 14 percent were concerned with "personality adjustment of a child under thirteen." Clients presented more than one problem, but the three major areas were personality problems, marital problems, and parent-child problems. [8] Interpersonal adjustment problems are generally given higher priority at intake than situational problems (employment, housing, and the like).

The presenting problem is the "ticket of admission" to an agency. For the child guidance clinics, set up to help the child, the presenting problem is generally formulated in terms of the child's deficiencies in role implementation. A study of over 1600 "presenting complaints" in three guidance clinics in 1966 is shown in Table 3–1.

One can see how much of a strain is imposed on parent-child relationships by the persistence of the types of problems listed in the table. Any child who consistently presents any of these behaviors is not effectively carrying out his role.

Both the child guidance clinic and the family service agency attempt to deal with families in trouble by direct treatment of the child, but the family agency is more likely to try to help the child through help to the parents. Family service agencies, however, do accept responsibility for direct casework with children who have problems and there is no significant difference between the problems coming to the family service agency and those coming to the child guidance clinic. The more severely disturbed children are, however, more likely to be referred to the child guidance clinic if only because of the presence of a psychiatrist-consultant on the clinic team.

TABLE 3–1. Presenting Complaints in Guidance Clinics

General Problem	Specific Presenting Complaint	Number of Children with Specific Complaint	Total
Relations in school or difficulties in learning	Learning problem	370	
	School phobia	36	
	Speech or hearing	30	436
Delinquency or near-delinquency	Aggression, fighting	172	
	Stealing	71	
	Running away or truancy	28	271
Behavior and medical problems	Medical and other	142	
	Behavior problems (nonspecific)	121	
	Obesity	5	268
Neurosis	Night terrors, nervousness	118	
	Enuresis	28	
	Soiling	20	166
Relations with authority	Temper tantrums	58	
	Poor family relations	56	
	Lying	33	
	Obscene language	4	151
Autism	Inhibition or shyness	70	
	Daydreaming	14	84
Relations with peers	Poor peer relations	73	73
Retardation	Retardation	44	44
Depression	Depression	41	41
Sex	Sexual aggressiveness	21	
	Homosexuality	9	
	Masturbation	6	36
Setting fires	Setting fires	25	25
Psychosomatic difficulty	Psychosomatic complaint	23	23
Suicidal threat or attempt	Threatened or attempted suicide	14	14
Separation	Separation problem	8	8
Total			1640

* Number of complaints is larger than the number of cases (1241) because some children had more than one complaint. [106, p. 108]

Scope

By 1970 there were 333 family service agencies employing approximately 3000 professionally trained social workers, serving more than 530,000 families. Based on the approximate average size of a family, it is estimated that some 1.8 million individuals were served during that year, directly or indirectly.

Despite the growth of such agencies, it is estimated that only 63 percent of the population of the United States had such service available and accessible. [31, p. 5]

Thirty percent of all contacts were made by telephone or by letter; 64 percent of the contacts involved in-person interviews with the client. The largest percentage of the in-person contacts with the agency were of short duration—five interviews or less. Only 17 percent of the clients maintained a contact with the agency which exceeded five interviews. [8, p. 19]

Family service at the start of the 1970 decade was essentially an urban service; rural areas remain essentially without the availability of such services. Clients were most frequently referred by friends and relatives, less often through social workers, teachers, or physicians.

Agencies in 1970 were serving a slightly higher proportion of disadvantaged families than they did in 1960. In 1970 some 51 percent of agency client families were of lower or upper-lower socioeconomic status.

Despite the decided effort offered by family service agency to indicate their readiness to serve black families, there was almost no increase in the use of family service by members of the black community between 1960 and 1970. Nevertheless, black clients were served by family agencies in nearly double their proportion to the general population. [8, p. 6]

The children needing help at clinics and family service agencies are difficult to define. The phrase *emotionally disturbed child* is ambiguous, open to a variety of interpretations. Attempts have been made to estimate (either by a comprehensive survey of a particular area or through interviews with teachers) the number of children who might be characterized as emotionally disturbed. As a consequence of such studies the U.S. Public Health Service estimates that 2–3 percent of schoolchildren are in need of psychiatric care and an additional 7 percent in need of some help for emotional problems. [95, p. 50] A more conservative estimate is that some 1.5 million schoolchildren needed psychiatric care in 1966. At that time psychiatric facilities were offering service to some 500,000 children.* By far the largest single group (80 percent of all children served) were being treated at out-patient psychiatric clinics such

---

* By 1971 some 772,000 children under eighteen were being treated through some established mental health facility (*The New York Times*, July 30, 1973).

as child guidance clinics. [95, p. 3]   More disconcerting than the fact that only one third of the children estimated as needing services were actually receiving service is the finding that only a limited number of children seen at the clinics were receiving treatment: two thirds of the 400,000 children seen at clinics were seen for intake, referral, diagnostic evaluation, and testing and had a median number of three interviews. Adolescents (10–14) were the age group most frequently served and twice as many boys as girls received service. The most frequent diagnostic category was "transient situational personality disorder," which reveals little about the actual difficulty which brought the family for service.

The trend has been toward a considerable expansion of facilities, and the number of children receiving care in clinics almost doubled between 1959 and 1970. The development of community mental health centers throughout the country under the Community Mental Health Centers Act of 1963 provided an additional significant resource for both out-patient and in-patient care of children needing psychiatric service. Five hundred such centers were scheduled to be in operation by early 1970, and 2000 more by 1980. Each center is designed to serve a limited population (75,000–200,000) and will be readily accessible to the community it serves. As more community mental health centers are organized, the child guidance clinic may tend to cease to be a discrete entity and become one unit of a comprehensive community mental health program.

Process in Supportive Services

Casework Service Approach

A small percentage of families come to the family agency or clinic after reading or hearing about the work of such agencies through mass communication media—newspapers, radio, television, and so on; these may be regarded as self-referred applicants. More frequently, however, applicants are referred by friends, other social and health agencies, schools, courts, and physicians.

Once the initial contact has been made, the agency and the applicant get acquainted with one another. The agency learns the general nature of the applicant's problems and determines if it is the appropriate agency for helping the applicant. The applicant learns something about how the agency operates and determines if he wants the kind of help the agency has to offer, in the way the agency offers it. If both applicant and agency agree that parents are having a problem with their children and would like to have the help of the agency in dealing with it and the agency feels it can be of help, the applicant becomes a client.

There then follows an effort to get a clearer picture of the problem through a social study. The clinic is more apt than the family agency to offer psychological examinations, as well as an interview between staff psychiatrist and child. In both agencies, however, interviews are held with parents and children, as well as with other members of the community who have some knowledge about the child. The social study covers the developmental history of each of the family members, the developmental history of the family as an entity, and the current relationships and patterns of interaction among family members.

Based on the information developed in the social study, an assessment is made of the nature of the difficulty, and the principal factors in the problem situation. Once again the assessment in the clinic is likely to be more highly formalized than in the family service agency, involving a meeting in which the various professionals who have had contact with parents and child discuss their view of the family. The diagnosis is then used for planning a treatment program. The goals of casework treatment, as described by the Family Service Association of America, are to

1. Support or maintain the client's current strength by helping him mobilize capacity and resources to meet his current life situation.
2. Modify the client's attitudes and patterns of behavior by increasing his understanding of himself, his problems, and his part in creating them.

"The focus of the agency's help is on the specific reality problems that the family is facing and on the ways of reducing pressure and relieving undue hardship. . . . The effect of treatment in both categories is to reduce social and emotional pressures and to increase the client's capacity for satisfactory social functioning." [28, pp. 7–8] Both parent and child, as a result of such treatment, can more effectively implement their respective roles and reduce the possibility of family disruption.

Treatment is based on interviews between parents and caseworker and/or child and caseworker in the family agency. In the clinic, although the parent is most likely to see a caseworker, the child may be seen by either staff caseworker, staff psychologist, or staff psychiatrist. Interviews with the child are supplemented by sessions in which the child communicates his problems, and his reaction to his problem, through the medium of play therapy.

Because it is recognized that the supportive service, the first line of defense in child welfare, is somewhat amorphous, it might be best to amplify this description of process with the following case study.

Mrs. S., a woman with professional background in a field allied to psychology, came to us with her concern about David, age 5.

David was a bed wetter, was refusing to attend kindergarten, and when he did go caused so much trouble by his absolute refusal to conform that his teacher described him as "the worst and most difficult pupil" in a class of 52 children. He could not get along with children of his own age, whom he either attacked or from whom he withdrew. The family consisted of Mr. and Mrs. S., a couple in their early thirties, David, and his younger sister, Rita, age 2.

In the first interview Mrs. S. had no trouble at all in presenting the facts of her situation and her view of the problem in a very poised and intelligent manner. Her interpretation, however, lay very much outside herself. For the first two years of David's life, Mr. S. had been overseas in the armed services. Mrs. S. had moved back to her own parents, who were in good financial circumstances. David had been greatly spoiled by his grandfather and an uncle, Mrs. S.'s married brother, ten years her senior, himself childless and very fond of David, who visited frequently and showered him with expensive gifts. Although soon after Mr. S.'s return to civilian life the S.'s moved into their own apartment, Mr. S.'s relationship to his son was not satisfactory, according to Mrs. S. In a slightly critical and yet triumphant manner, she described how her husband rather awkwardly forced himself on his son and seemed unable to establish a natural relationship with him. The visits and gift-bringing of Mrs. S.'s older brother were still continuing, accompanied by the uncle's rather dramatic show of affection for David, with which Mr. S., an undemonstrative person, felt unable to compete. While his brother-in-law's visits were a continuous source of irritation to Mr. S. and Mrs. S. herself recognized that they were not helpful to the family's attempts to grow into a more cohesive unit, she saw no way of changing this situation since she felt she could not deprive her childless brother of the satisfaction that the relationship to David gave him.

This material came out easily from Mrs. S., who seemed to have it on the tip of her tongue. Only when the counselor asked specifically about her own relationship to David did she begin to talk less fluently and with less poise. While Mrs. S. had made very conscious attempts at giving time and attention to David, which we gathered he was constantly seeking, a note of annoyance crept into her voice as she described his demands, as if she were somewhat resentful of them. When she described playing games with David, a picture of a really competitive situation emerged in which Mrs. S. would get annoyed every time David won, or when he came out ahead of her in solving a puzzle and then tried to help her finish hers. It was hard for the listener to imagine that this was a description of a mother and a child doing things together; it sounded much more like a relationship between contemporaries.

When Mr. S. was seen subsequently, he gave the impression of a man who lived somehow in the shadow of Mrs. S.'s family. Since his return to civilian life he had been working for his father-in-law and his brother-in-law. While he resented his economic dependence on them and their interference with David, he felt quite powerless to bring about any change. He compared his own reticence in showing feeling with the demonstrativeness of his in-laws, and blamed them for standing between him and his son. Like his wife, Mr. S. could not as yet acknowledge his own part in the difficulty, and needed to hold others responsible. Discussion with Mrs. S. during subsequent interviews gradually moved into the area of her relationship to her brother, who, being ten years older, had always made her "feel very inconsequential." She had always felt that he, as the son, had been favored by her mother, and this had left her with a feeling that being a girl did not really amount to much. Fearing a complete loss of love, Mrs. S. could not afford to let herself know her feelings of resentment toward her mother and brother. In her need to keep her feelings hidden, she always met her mother's continuous criticism by trying to please her and conform to her standards.

It now became painfully clear to Mrs. S. how this had affected her relationship to David, whose needs as a child she had not been entirely free to meet. For example, she had begun to toilet train David—one of whose problems was bed-wetting—at an extremely early age, because this was her mother's concept of child rearing and she did not dare oppose it in spite of her professional knowledge that this was harmful to the child. Her inability to assume any control over her brother's relationship to David also began to take on a different meaning for Mrs. S. She realized that her feeling of guilt toward her brother, because of her acknowledged hostility to him, had in a way paralyzed her and driven her to let him have more of David than was his right.

Mrs. S. was now much freer to consider her relationship with her husband. She began to grasp how much she had tried to dominate him since his return from the war. She had encouraged him to move to New York City (his roots and ties were elsewhere), to take a job in her father's business, and to take on her friends, thus leaving very little room for him to find himself again after the war experience. She had not helped him with his need to form a relationship to David, and had really found some satisfaction in the fact that David clung to her and was pushing Mr. S. away. In her relationship to David, too, there had been rivalry, since in Mrs. S.'s concept of the relationship of male and female either the man dominated the woman and made her feel little, or the woman controlled and dominated the man.

For Mr. S. it was very meaningful that from the first moment the counselor, who was a woman, treated him as the man in the family, whose opinion and feelings were very important, and whose active participation in contact was considered essential if David was to be helped. Having felt weak in his silent struggle with his wife, her family, and even his son, Mr. S. immediately gained strength from this attitude on the part of the counselor. The counselor helped Mr. S. to recognize his tendency to withdraw whenever he needed to reveal himself to another person. His reaction was directly linked to his problem with his son, who, he felt, had been taken away from him by his in-laws as a result of their demonstrative ways. Deeply touched by the counselor's recognition of his pain over this, Mr. S. related his pattern of withdrawal to his own background, describing a most ineffectual father and a cold mother who showed her contempt of her husband and of men in general in an unmistakable manner. His wife's domination over him seemed to have brought out the fear that he was destined to suffer his father's fate. He was resentful but unable to express this feeling, since he feared that any show of anger toward his wife might lead her to leave him. He felt he had little to offer her, particularly after his return from the war when he had to make a new beginning.

As a result of sharing his deep sense of inadequacy with the counselor and finding that exposure of these very painful feelings had not crushed him, an emotional change occurred in him which, in his relationship to the agency, found its tangible expression in his decision to take over payment of the fee for the interviews, for which until then his wife had carried responsibility. At home Mr. S. was increasingly able to let his wife know his feelings and thoughts; and Mrs. S., who herself had achieved greater freedom to relate to her husband on a more realistic, mature basis, discovered what an interesting companion Mr. S. really was. In relation to the outside world, the couple felt a unity such as they had never felt before. Suddenly they could quite comfortably handle the question of visits and gift-bringing with Mrs. S.'s brother and experienced much satisfaction in finding that they were able to do this in a natural, matter-of-fact way that was not offensive to the brother and left them without a sense of guilt.

As Mr. and Mrs. S. gained more security in their relationship as husband and wife, they found a way of handling David that gave him the possibility of identification with his father so necessary to a sense of security at his particular age level. As Mrs. S. came to see David as a five-year-old child rather than as another male competitor, she found herself able to meet his demands in a realistic manner. Her attitude became more loving and had in it firmness and consistency, whereas formerly she had swung from one extreme to another in her handling of him. For Mr. S. the realization that he was important to his son and that he as the father had something very special to offer him was possible only because of his increased respect for himself as a man. He was quite startled to find how much the child responded to him when he approached him spontaneously, without his previous fear of being pushed away. David stopped bed-wetting completely and, not needing to cling to his mother any more, was free to form more positive relationships with children of his own age. The school reported tremendous improvement in the child. [pp. 75–79] *

The S. family might have been offered equally effective service at a child guidance clinic. The approach to the family would have been essentially similar except that the guidance clinic record might have included more direct contact and work with the child. The similarity in approach derives from the fact that the family service agency and the child guidance clinics have the same basic set of presuppositions regarding the treatment of parent-child relationship problems.

1. Children have problems because of some serious imbalance in their affectional relationship with parents.
2. Because the problem is the result of faulty interaction between parent and child, it is best not to seek to help either the child or the parent *alone* to change; it is best if both participants in the interactional process are helped to effect some change in the way they relate to each other. Simultaneous treatment of both parents and child is therefore desirable.
3. Behind the parents' own difficulties in acting in an accepting manner toward their children lies some disorder in their relationship with their own parents. Consequently, helping the parents to implement their roles more effectively requires some exploration of their own developmental histories.
4. People can change as they become more aware of the reasons why they behave as they do. One aim of treatment is to help both parents and child to develop more conscious recognition of the purposes their behavior serves. Having become aware of the purposiveness of their behavior, they are in a better position, supposedly, to control and/or change their behavior. It is for this reason that the therapist seeks to establish an atmosphere of psychological safety and acceptance. In response to such conditions, parents and children can risk expressing

* From Elsa Leichter, "Parent-Child Relationship Problems—Participation in Treatment by Both Parents," in Robert Gomberg and Frances Levinson, eds., *Diagnosis and Process in Family Counseling.* New York: Family Service Association of America, 1951. By permission of the publisher.

thoughts and feelings that they may be hiding from themselves, as well as from others. The mother can openly say, for the first time perhaps, that she does often hate her child because it is less dangerous, less likely to lead to rejection, to express this here than elsewhere.

> . . . If a client can be helped to understand why he behaves as he does or to recognize and understand the origin of the neurotic tactics that continually defeat him, he will gradually abandon the inappropriate behavior and substitute therefore more rational tactics in the management of his life. Increased self-understanding is regarded as inherently good and as a means toward the end of good psychological health. [51, p. 741]

5. One might help parents and children to effect changes in behavior by offering the therapist as a pattern for identification and emulation. The therapist stands for, and exemplifies, the "good" parent in his attitudes toward the child and his behavior. The parent in treatment is presented, through the therapist, with an illustration of an emotionally healthier approach toward children. If the relationship between parent and therapist is a positive one, the parent seeks to "imitate" the therapist as a person he admires and respects: ". . . Individuals frequently accept guidance from those they love. They model themselves after them and seek to win their approval." [116, p. 45]

6. For the child, the satisfying, trustful, confident human relationship developed with the therapist is ultimately generalized to other adult figures. Having learned to "trust" himself to risk a loving relationship with one adult without having been hurt and rejected, the child is more likely to risk a similar relationship with his parents. He develops a feeling of security in contact with the people who are emotionally of utmost importance to him—his parents.

   Children who need the help of supportive services often are reacting to negative parental attitudes—rejection, indifference, punitiveness. Consequently they have learned to regard all adults as potentially hurtful. The clinic offers the opportunity for a corrective emotional experience in which the child encounters an adult who explicitly contradicts the anticipated indiscriminating generalization that the child is making from his parents to all adults. Good supportive casework is carefully designed to make it possible for a client to learn to be close to another person without getting hurt. In experiencing this knowledge the child is able to divest the symbol of "adult" of its anxiety-producing potential.

Because they share the same preconceptions, the treatment approaches of the child guidance clinic and the family service agency in dealing with parent-child relationship problems are often indistinguishable. However, there are differences in the way treatment is administered. The family service agency is administered and staffed by social workers, with a psychiatrist frequently acting as part-time consultant. The clinic is more frequently under the directorship of a psychiatrist and includes psychiatrists as active members of the treatment team, in addition to social workers and clinical psychologists. Hence, although at the family service agency, social workers see both parents and children for treatment, in the clinic, the psychiatrist frequently treats the child while the social worker treats the parents. There are a variety of other patterns, however, in the allocation of responsibilities among psychiatrists, psychologists, and social workers in the clinic.

Until fairly recently the approach of the child guidance clinic and the family service agency was based almost exclusively on principles from psychoanalytic psychology. Currently there is more interest in, and utilization of, approaches based on behavioral modification learning theory. Such an approach to children's problems postulates that disturbed or maladaptive behavior is learned behavior. Treatment therefore consists of "unlearning" the maladaptive response. The focus is on the undesirable behavior itself, the "symptom," rather than on resolving any internal condition which is manifested in the symptom. The behaviorist denies that there is any internal conflict sustaining the behavior which might be perceived by others as a symptom.

The difference between the two approaches is a difference in seeing the child's behavior as an expression of underlying conflict or a learned response which must be inhibited or extinguished. There is less concern with "diagnosis" since the "etiology" of the problem is not important. There is more concern with exact definition and delineation of the particular behavior which needs to be changed, and the source and nature of those "reinforcements" which encourage continuation of the undesirable behavior.

Laws of learning can then be applied not only to the elimination of undesirable learned behavior but also to the acquisition of new and desirable patterns of behavior.

The behavior was learned and is sustained by current activities of people in a position to reward and/or punish such behavior, generally the parent. Behavioral modification therapy therefore frequently involves instructing parents so that they support desirable behavior through prompt and appropriate rewards and/or discourage undesirable behavior by nonreinforcement or by appropriate and prompt punishment.

Various techniques have been developed, such as counterconditioning or reciprocal inhibition, operant conditioning, modeling, and aversion therapy, and these have been applied to a wide variety of children's problems—hyperactivity, temper tantrums, phobias and tics, bedwetting, retardation, childhood psychosis, delinquency. [15; 36; 61; 113]

Some of the techniques have been "translated" for social workers, and
their applicability to social work situations has been made explicit.
[54; 107]

The following is an account of the use by social workers of desensitization procedures in treating a school phobia. The child had been
treated at the clinic through use of traditional psychotherapeutic approaches over a period of six months but no improvement had been
noted.

Jimmy, ten, was referred to the child guidance clinic because he was
unable to go to school. A month prior to the referral he had
suffered a bronchial infection, following which the Christmas holiday
season occurred. After that, the youngster refused to return to
school, in spite of efforts by the parents, the teacher, and the
principal. The patient stated that when he thought about going to
school in the morning he became frightened and often vomited.
His previous school attendance record was excellent, as was his
school work performance. Jimmy was described as being high-strung,
sensitive, and preoccupied with high-level performance. As therapy
progressed, secondary problems began to arise, consisting of
avoidance of friends and peers. Apparently, Jimmy could not find
adequate excuses for being out of school, and as his friends
telephoned or visited the home, he became quite anxious and finally
refused any contact with peers at all. The patient indicated that
he did not feel that he could assert himself and that he did not
feel as worthwhile as his brother or sister.

The patient described many arguments at home involving
everyone in the family. He indicated that he would not be overly
concerned if his father moved out of the house, but if his mother
left, it would be quite different. "If she goes, the whole family
would fade away. We would have to go to another home. . . .
If it did happen, it would be horrible. I wouldn't know what would
happen to myself or anyone else. The family would be just all messed
up, and I'd go crazy." This concern about losing his mother
was evidenced at other times; for example, the patient also stated
that if his mother went to the store, he often imagined that she
might get hit by a car. Or even when mother took him to the store
with her, Jimmy would stay in the car and begin to think
that there might be a robbery and that she might get shot. Other
factors that seemed related to his concerns were: (1) Jimmy got lost
as a small child and remembered how terribly frightened he was;
(2) five years previously, when his mother was working, he had
worried a good deal about her; (3) his mother often used the
phrase, "Someday I'll be dead, and you'll wish you had me. You'll

want help, and I won't be there." And, in referring to school, she often said, "One of these days when you get home, I won't be here."

After approximately six months of traditional therapy, shortly before school was to start, the patient indicated that he was nervous about trying to go back to school, but indicated that he felt "bigger" than he had felt six months previously. He also stated that he felt he knew himself better and felt more confident. There appeared to be a good relationship between Jimmy and the therapist. On the day he was to return to school, the patient could not take the step out of the home, and again he panicked.

The desensitization procedure in this case was carried out in the school environment. The school officials were informed of the procedure, and they cooperated fully with the therapist. Jimmy was told that each day the therapist would accompany him to school, and that together they would approach the school gradually. Since it was known that he could tolerate going by the school in a car, the first step consisted of Jimmy and the therapist sitting in the car in front of the school. The other steps were as follows: (2) getting out of the car and approaching the curb; (3) going to the sidewalk; (4) going to the bottom of the steps of the school; (5) going to the top of the steps; (6) going to the door; (7) entering the school; (8) approaching the classroom a certain distance each day down the hall; (9) entering the classroom; (10) being present in the classroom; (11) being present in the classroom with the teacher and one or two classmates; (12) being present in the classroom with a full class. This procedure was carried out over twenty consecutive days, including Saturdays and Sundays. [38, p. 148] *

At the end of the twenty-day period, Jimmy remained in school. A two-year follow-up study has indicated that there have been no subsequent manifestations of the phobia.

The authors of the report, both social workers, explain the success of the program on the basis of reciprocal inhibition. They paired a pleasant stimulus, contact with the workers with whom Jimmy had a good relationship, with an anxiety-provoking stimulus, the school. The pleasure, the presence of the therapist, weakened the anxiety provoked by the school, ultimately resulting in the gradual diminution of such anxiety. Although other, more complex, psychodynamic factors were involved (fear of separation from the mother, hostile wishes that the

* From William P. Garvey and Jack R. Hegrenes, "Desensitization Techniques in the Treatment of a School Phobia," *American Journal of Orthopsychiatry*, 36, 1 (January 1966). Copyright © 1966, the American Orthopsychiatric Association, Inc. Reproduced by permission.

mother be injured, and guilt and anxiety aroused by such wishes), dealing with the behavior, in and of itself, seemed to effect the change
desired by both the family and the child.

Learning theory approaches, it is argued, are particularly efficacious
with children for the following reasons:

1. The world of "significant others" is more restricted in the case of a
   child and hence can be more easily controlled.
2. Those closest to the child in a position of authority, the parents, have
   not only the potential for controlling the child's environment but also
   the desire to do something about changing the child's behavior. Consequently their cooperation in therapy can be enlisted.
3. Maladaptive behaviors for which children are referred often include
   the specific, well-defined behaviors—temper tantrums, bed-wetting,
   phobias—most amenable to behavior therapy approaches.
4. In children, learned patterns of behavior have been recently acquired
   and are not so firmly established as in adults, and behavior more
   recently learned may be more easily unlearned.
5. There is less ethical objection to controlling and "manipulating" the
   child's environment than is true for the more independent adult,
   and there is less objection to establishing behavioral goals for children.

Such an approach might also be more effective for those clients,
generally lower-class, who are uncomfortable with a nondirective relationship centered on "talk" and concern with "self-actualization" and
a search for "meanings." The drop-out rate of such clients might be
reduced by an approach which offers specific directives for action.

Behavioral modification therapists have actively recruited, and
trained, the parents as co-therapists. The parents are trained to respond
to the child's behavior in a manner which is designed to effect changes
in the child's behavior in terms of learning theory. [43; 48; 73; 105; 110;
111; 118]   The following is an account of the way one mother was enlisted as therapist for her child:

> The child in this study was a four-year-old boy, Peter S. He is the
> third of four children in a middle-class family. Peter had been
> brought to a clinic because he was extremely difficult to manage
> and control. His mother stated she was helpless in dealing with his
> frequent tantrums and disobedience. Peter often kicked objects
> or people, removed or tore his clothing, called people rude names,
> annoyed his younger sister, made a variety of threats, hit himself,
> and became very angry at the slightest frustration. He demanded
> attention almost constantly, and seldom cooperated with Mrs. S.
> [48, p. 100]

Clinic personnel observing the mother-child interaction in the home noted the frequency of manifestations of nine specific objectionable behaviors. Included among these were "throwing objects," "biting his shirt or arm," "pushing his sister," "removing or threatening to remove his clothing," and so on.

> The mother was informed of the nine objectionable behaviors which would be treated. She was shown three gestural signals which indicated how she was to behave toward Peter. Signal "A" meant she was to tell Peter to stop whatever objectionable behavior he was emitting. Signal "B" indicated she was immediately to place Peter in his room and lock the door. When signal "C" was presented she was to give him attention, praise, and affectionate physical contact. Thus, every time Peter emitted an objectionable behavior, Mrs. S. received a signal from the clinician instructing her on her response. [48, p. 102]

On the basis of such programmed learning, the mother developed a changed pattern of interaction with Peter, and the mother, as "therapist," applied the behavioral responses designed to effect changes in Peter's behavior. Use of parents as therapists is called *filial therapy.*

Filial therapy is possible because the behavioral modification procedures are specific and action-oriented and can be quickly taught to the parent. The capacity of parents of emotionally disturbed children to "develop behaviors that will contribute to the solution of interpersonal problems that the parents presumably helped create" seems to be demonstrated by empirical evidence. [105, p. 110]

In some instances, nonprofessional community volunteers have been taught behavioral modification procedures which then they used with disturbed children in home and school settings. [10] In response to the considerable interest in behavioral modification procedures employing parents (and teachers) as the primary change agent for disturbed children, the National Institute of Mental Health published, in 1971, an annotated bibliography of articles on this approach. [13]

As a consequence of the influence of behavioral modification approaches on supportive services, there is likely to be, in the future, a greater concern with clearly observable, objectifiable variables for study and change, a greater ability to clearly define the problem that needs to be changed, and a more modest statement of explicit objectives that can be operationally defined, so that outcomes can be measured. Criticism of the behavioral modification approach raises the question about whether or not the mechanical "rat psychology" conception of man's behavior and the "manipulative" nature of the procedure is compatible with the humanistic ideology of social work. [16] The response in the still-continuing debate is the evidence: the parents and children who are living together more satisfactorily as a result of these procedures and the fact that the approach brings to social work a degree of precision and scientific vigor it previously lacked. [17]

Group Service Approach

Both family service agencies and child guidance clinics have adopted a group approach in helping families with parent-child relationship problems. The group may supplement the individual casework service; often, however, this may be the only form of help offered a family. The supportive service agencies have developed two different kinds of programs employing a group approach—family life education programs, and group counseling or group treatment programs. "The proportion of agencies using group treatment has grown rapidly in the last ten years, from 10 percent in 1958 to 62 percent in 1968" and 83 percent reported offering some form of family life education program. [30, p. 13]

Family life education is defined by the FSAA as "a process by which people are helped through group discussion to broaden their understanding of family relationships. . . . The aim of such education is the prevention of unhappy family relationships and the strengthening and enrichment of family life." [32, p. 6] The family life education program of family service agencies is implemented through lectures by agency social workers to community groups, leadership of parent discussion groups, formal institutes on child care and parent-child relationships, participation in radio and television programs on family life education. A few larger family service agencies have staff members who are assigned full-time responsibility for family life education programs. The meetings may be initiated by the agency, but frequently the agency is asked to provide a group leader and a program for groups of parents in various community organizations—PTA groups, women's service groups, and so on.

The group counseling service is frequently difficult to distinguish from the ongoing family life education program. Both kinds of groups consist of limited numbers of parents who come together with some regularity to discuss parent-child relationship problems with the help of a skilled leader provided by the agency. There are some distinguishable differences, however, which have been identified.

The counseling groups are viewed by the agency "as a special controlled environment which offers a corrective emotional experience—a re-education living experience to the client." [22, p. 124] The family life education programs have a more educational, rather than therapeutic, function, so that content and discussion emphasize normal family relationships and rational procedures in dealing with normal problem situations. Group counseling services, unlike parent education services, seek to dissolve pathology in the parent-child relationship.

The group counseling program is likely to include parents who are more disturbed and who face more serious problems. Family life education programs usually involve clients who are educable, who are free to interact with the educational content in a rational manner fully conscious of why they accept or reject the material being discussed. Group counseling programs, on the other hand, usually involve clients who, because of emotional conflicts of some consequence, are not fully conscious of why they react negatively or overenthusiastically to the material being discussed.

Parent life education is based on the assumption that difficulties in parent-child relationships often arise from limited experience and lack of knowledge in the parental role rather than as a result of any personality difficulty. Group counseling programs assume that the parent has some personality difficulty.

The difference in composition of the two kinds of groups also determines differences in the activity of the social worker or discussion leader. In the family life education programs, the leader structures his role, and is perceived, as an educator-expert on parent-child relationships responsible for presenting to the group what research and experience has determined as the best approach in meeting parental problems. In the group counseling sessions, the discussion leader is more apt to be permissive, noncommittal, and neutral.

The family life education program has an orderly progression of meetings, the leader setting out in advance what is, in effect, the syllabus of a course in parent education. The syllabus, however, is kept flexible so as to give group members the opportunity of modifying it to meet their preferences. The content of the group counseling meetings is less structured, being designed primarily in response to the changing emotional needs of the group. The emphasis is on emotional expressiveness and spontaneity, and the leader acts so as to reward such responses rather than more intellectual, more conventional, responses.

Educational group leaders are more apt to be task-oriented—concerned with communicating a body of content. Group counselors are less apt to be concerned with a specific task than with establishing and maintaining an atmosphere conducive to relaxation—full discussion with a minimum of defensiveness. Here the interaction among group members is the primary vehicle for helping parents to effect changes in their relationships with their children.

The group counseling meetings are frequently a later adjunct to casework services being received by the family. In family life education programs, on the other hand, parents who display a need for more intensive, more individualized contact through the group discussions are referred for casework services.

There are significant similarities between the two kinds of groups. Both kinds of groups tend to concern themselves with recurrent situations occasioning difficulties for parents and children—questions about "eating, sleeping, toilet training, the handling of aggression, the question of discipline, how to deal with sibling rivalry, how to handle sex curiosity . . . the child's reactions to disturbing experiences, such as death in the family." [84, p. 200]

Both the family life educator and the group counselor must establish an atmosphere conducive to effective interaction—a warm, psychologically safe, affectively positive atmosphere. In both groups the leader plays the role of stimulating, expediting, and guiding discussion. In both groups the leader must have a permissive, accepting, reassuring manner.

Both kinds of groups tend to draw on the living experiences of the parents with their children and to involve the emotional, as well as intellectual, participation of the group members. Out of a sharing of common experiences and involvement with the content hopefully comes a greater understanding and capacity for parenthood.

The parent education programs sponsored by supportive service agencies have a preventative as well as supportive intent. Brim points out that parents today are less likely to have become socialized to the parental role through traditional channels. [12, pp. 17–18]   Because the grandmother, the experienced parent, does not often live with the new mother, she is not in a position to demonstrate and supervise child-rearing practices. Even if grandmother could do this, the development of scientific knowledge regarding child rearing has supplanted traditional approaches. Science supposedly makes available more desirable ways of rearing children than does tradition. Consequently, parent education programs are designed as formal channels of communication between the expert-scientist and the modern parent. The aim in many of the programs is to help parents "achieve the ability to accept themselves, to discover their own strength, and to develop the ability to find their own answers in handling their children." [12, p. 103]

Both in the individual interviews and in the group meeting it is hoped that the parents will gain increased understanding of children's needs in general and of the needs of their child in particular, some further understanding of the parental role, and increased self-awareness about their reactions to their child and the effects of their behavior on the child. With increased understanding, increased self-awareness, and the support of the caseworker and/or group may come the necessary changes in their relationship with the child that will result in greater satisfaction in the parental role. The aim is to develop greater self-confidence in the parents, to make them feel more at ease and more relaxed in their role as parents. This in itself is believed to create a healthier climate for child development. Parents in the group may identify with a more therapeutic approach to children as exemplified in the attitude of the group leader.

When the group is organized, its purpose is discussed with individuals and with organizations asking for a group leader in behalf of their members. An effort is made to clarify expectations. Individuals may not be admitted to a group if they are so disturbed as to behave in a way that is detrimental to good group functioning. For some parents, however, the group approach is the approach of choice. This is based on some advantageous characteristics of the group approach, such as the following:

1. The group counseling situation may make acceptance of a treatment relationship easier for some clients. The focus of attention is wider in a group, and the relationship with the social worker is not so embarrassingly intense and threatening as it is in a casework situation.
2. In the group, negative feelings toward the worker, the agency, and the child can often be more easily expressed because of the "safety in numbers."
3. The fear of overdependency on the worker, excited in the one-to-one interview relationship, is less intense in the group.
4. Suggestions for changes in child care may be more easily accepted by some parents in the group situation than in individual interviews. Members of the group identify with one another and tend to help each other find solutions to similar problems. Criticism that would not ordinarily be accepted without resentment may often be accepted from a fellow group member.
5. The parent, in exchanging experiences with others facing similar problems, is stimulated to verbalize his often negative feelings about his child with less anxiety, and comes to view his behavior more objectively.
6. The parent's anxiety is reduced as he comes to realize that his child, and his reaction as a parent, is not as atypical, as deviant, as he had supposed. Hearing from other parents that they too have similar difficulties is reassuring.
7. The parent derives value from sharing experiences regarding possible solutions to problem situations. The repertoire of possible solutions available to each group member is increased as those offered by other members are added to those that the group develops in discussing parent-child problems.

Child guidance clinics have developed family life education programs designed to introduce groups of parents to the use of behavioral approaches. [73] Although the success of these programs has been limited, the definite, precise procedures gave the parents a sense of control and relief from feelings of hopelessness about the children's disturbing behavior.

Behavioral modification approaches have also been used to treat children in the context of their peer groups. [93]

Sally was referred to the group because she was shy; that is, she did not play with other children, and, given a choice, she remained with adults. An observer at the first meeting counted fewer than five minutes per hour of playing time with other children. At the second meeting, the therapist smiled and praised Sally whenever she approached other children; when she approached the therapist or the observer, neither responded. At the end of this session she was playing with other children at the rate of twenty-five minutes per hour. At the end of a third session, in which Sally was praised only when playing with other children, she was spending forty minutes per hour with the others; this amount was almost the same as the average for all children in the group. [94, p. 4]

Family Therapy Approach

There has been a strong trend toward the use of family therapy in dealing with parent-child problems. [2; 27; 46; 69; 98]   Family service agencies as well as child guidance clinics have participated in this trend. Both agencies are using joint interview casework sessions in which the married couple meet with the caseworker as well as family interviews (casework sessions which include the couple and one or more other members of the nuclear or extended family).

Family therapy is based on "dynamically oriented interviews with the whole family" viewed as a behavioral and social system. It focuses on the family as an integrative unit, as a special entity greater than the sum of individual family members. The assumption is that the child is what he is because the family is what it is and that if the child is to change, the family must change, too. Since the child does not get "sick" alone, he will not get well alone. Meeting with the family rather than with individual members permits the worker to obtain a more accurate and more relevant diagnostic understanding of the family. Rather than being told about family interaction, she can observe directly the patterns of leadership and control, the allocation of roles, the pattern of intrafamily communication, the nature of conflict, the operation and effectiveness of mutual defenses, the nature of family alliances and rejections, the extent and nature of existing strengths. Intrapersonal problems can be observed as they become visibly manifested in interpersonal encounters.

In family interviewing what one parent conceals the other reveals. What the parents hide together the child blurts out. What one member expresses in a twisted prejudiced way is corrected by another when certain anxiety-filled material is touched on. The family may engage in a silent pact to avoid these areas. But sooner or later such denials are broken through. Family life by its very nature is inimical to the guarding of personal secrets. [1, p. 94]

Through the family interview, "the worker and all participating family members are directly and mutually exposed to each other's impact with the result that the worker is placed in an especially strategic position for intervening directly in the system." [24, p. 280]

1. The worker can stimulate new patterns of interaction, directly encourage expression of feeling, and at the same time provide a safe context for the expression of such feeling and offer protection to the family member against whom negative feelings might be expressed. He can demonstrate, for family observation, consideration and possible emulation different patterns of family interaction and behavior, new ways of relating to each other. In the presence of all, the "worker legitimizes new norms and expands members perceptions of the range of permissible and worthwhile behavior, thus stimulating all (family members) simultaneously to modify basic norms controlling their family interaction." [24, p. 284]
2. Any changes in attitude which take place as a result of individual therapy need ultimately to be translated into actual behavioral changes. Family therapy gives the parent the opportunity of actually experimenting with changed behavior under the direction and guidance of the worker.
3. Any tendency on the part of the worker to overidentify with any one member of the family is open to correction by others in the group.
4. The worker gets immediate feedback of the results of his interventions in the family interaction and can modify his behavior accordingly. The fact that all members of the family participate in the therapeutic encounter enhances and supports everyone's motivation to change.

This is a more difficult situation for the worker, however.

1. Outnumbered, he is exposed to being drawn in and directly involved in the family problems. He needs to be aware of, and to resist, efforts by family members to manipulate him.
2. The worker needs to relate to the action rather than to a recital of action: "The shift is from talking about conflict to direct demonstration and help in dealing with conflict." [24, p. 288]
3. A worker involved in family interviewing needs to relate to different age groups simultaneously, and to sort out and understand the com-

plex communication transmitted by parents and children in one room together for an extended period.
4. There is a problem, too, in deciding limits of communication. To what extent, for instance, should parental concern regarding sexual adjustment and finances be discussed while younger children are present?

Community Organization Approach

In addition to casework and group work, the family service agencies offer a supportive service to parents and children through their community organization activity. These agencies call attention to problems in the community that are likely to have an adverse effect on parent-child relationships, and attempt to mobilize the community to remedy such situations. Child guidance clinics, too, have operated on the community level to develop a more receptive and understanding attitude on the part of community leaders toward parent-child relationship problems and to develop better coordination of services to families presenting such problems.

There has been a very decided shift in the balance between casework and alternative methods in family service agency approaches to problems presented by clients. The emphasis in the illustrative vignettes in this chapter, which present the family agency responding to client problems with a personal counseling approach, may be less typically representative of the work of the family service agency of the future. Not only is there a recent shift in the modality of service, but there is an associated shift in the population to which principal service efforts are to be directed—from middle-class white to lower-class white and nonwhite.

The most notable example of this change in emphasis was the announcement in February 1971 by the Community Service Society of New York that it planned to terminate "123 years of family casework and individual counseling."

The Community Service Society, established in 1848 as the Association for Improving the Conditions of the Poor, is the oldest and largest family service agency in America. It pioneered professional education for social work by establishing a School of Philanthropy in 1898, which became the Columbia University School of Social Work, the first graduate school of social work in the world.

The Society explained the policy change by noting that casework and individual counseling "had proved inadequate for the poor who face overwhelming problems in the slums." The general director of the Society noted that "If the individual is to be helped, someone has to deal with the complex of social ills that bears on the individual, not just the individual himself. Instead of starting out by saying that 'the individual is the client, we're going to say the community is the client' " (*The New*

York Times, January 29, 1971). As an alternative, the Society planned to work directly with existing neighborhood groups to deliver services, to exert pressure on government agencies, and to coordinate existing public and private programs.

Similarly, on January 4, 1972, the National Conference of Catholic Charities, one of the largest of the nationwide denominational agencies, announced that the "organization planned to supplement its traditional social services [which included supportive family services] with a new focus on political activism" (*The New York Times*, January 5, 1972).

The announcement by the Community Service Society of its abandonment of casework as its principal operative approach in helping the client was, however, only a more dramatic and extreme example of a shift previously debated and adopted by the Family Service Association of America. In 1969 the organization adopted a program of family advocacy. This involved helping families

> develop effective strategies to deal with the systems that are failing to meet their needs, secure a fair share of existing resources and services as well as develop new ones. First priority at this time will be given to high risk families suffering most acutely from the impact of racism, dehumanization, poverty, and injustice—
> the Family Service Association of America will begin with an attempt to adapt Family Service to the needs of the poor and non-white communities. [29]

Riley, Assistant General Director of FSAA, defines family advocacy as dealing "with institutional systems rather than with individuals." [89, p. 374] Family service agencies are encouraged by the policy statement to become involved in local social action in behalf of clients—to move from "case to cause." [70]

Advocacy can focus on the needs of one individual or family or on the needs of a group of people faced with similar problems. In either case, the goal is to mobilize resources in the community in the clients' behalf, to remove obstacles to access to the service, to insure the clients' right to service. This may involve seeing that new resources are provided, that regulations and procedures are modified so as to meet client needs.

> The most common targets of family service advocacy are the systems involving education, public welfare, health, housing, and employment. The actions range from seeking changes in operating policies and practices that can be readily achieved at the local level to seeking to influence public attitudes to seeking to change state or federal legislation or administration policy. [89, p. 379]

The efforts of the private agency are supplemented by similar efforts by public agencies. In response to resolutions adopted by the 1970 White House Conference on Children, a Federal Office of Child Advocacy has been established. Currently many states are attempting to develop an organizational structure for programs of child advocacy, coordinating the efforts of private and public agencies and citizens' groups. The child advocate is concerned with the interests and welfare of children, monitoring the local situation to insure that children's rights are secured, and that their needs are met. The activity implies "intervention on behalf of children in relation to those services and those institutions which impinge on their lives." [56, p. 11]   The orientation of advocacy programs suggests a conscious concern with changes in all the institutions, in addition to the family, which may affect a child's life. Such programs are of recent origin and are faced with the problem of differentiating themselves from existing child welfare programs. [56]

At the present writing, while there is considerable pious, rhetorical support for the change in emphasis, and some beginning limited action, most social workers, in most family service agencies, continue day by day to do the work illustrated in this chapter. They are painfully and conscientiously working with conflicted parents and children on an individual family counseling basis to support, strengthen, and reinforce whatever positive aspects there are in the relationship, so that the family can live together with slightly less aggravation, and slightly more satisfaction. This is, after all; an eminently worthy endeavor for which no one needs to apologize.

Given the continuing if not the exclusive need for some kind of casework-individual counseling, the problem then becomes one of increasing the effectiveness of the therapeutic technology of the supportive services caseworker. One way this is being attempted is through the use of radically different approaches to helping, such as behavioral modification as noted above.

Evaluation of Service

Individual Treatment

The extent to which the counseling services help in resolving the problem is not clear. The nationwide study conducted by FSAA suggests that, in many instances, contact is broken before an intensive counseling relationship can be developed. Only 17 percent of all the clients coming to family service agencies continued for more than five interviews. Of significance, however, is the fact that, "on the average, cases focused on children's problems lasted the longest—the family presenting such a problem continuing on an average of 11–12 interviews." [7, p. 21] Altogether, cases centered on children's problems accounted for one third of all of the interviews in the family service agencies. [7, p. 22]

There have been few formal efforts to evaluate the results of casework in family service agencies. One of the more recent studies was conducted with the cooperation of the Youth Consultation Service, a social agency offering service to adolescent girls. [74] Through a review of school records, the researchers identified a group of girls with potential problems. About half of these girls (189) were offered casework and group work services at the agency; the others (192) acted as a matched control group, and were not offered treatment of any kind.

Over the next three and one-half years, about 95 percent of the experimental group received some kind of treatment. The service offered was generally some combination of casework and group counseling, and the median number of such sessions was sixteen. Only forty-seven girls had casework treatment alone and, of these, in only 27 percent of the cases did the worker estimate that the client was "very much or quite a bit" involved in the treatment relationship.

Criteria of outcome included behavioral measures of school performance and out-of-school behavior. These behavioral measures were supplemented by "clinical criteria"—that is, two indirect measures of personality changes, the Junior Personality Quiz and the Make-a-Sentence Test, a projective device. In addition, the researchers used some self-report forms and class sociometrics. The general assumption was that there should be measurable difference in outcome between the group that had received treatment and the group from which treatment had been withheld.

With reference to school behavior (academic performance, awards and service ratings, attendance, truancy, conduct, teacher ratings), the report states:

> We may summarize the findings on all measures that have been grouped together as school-related behavior by noting that none of them supplies conclusive evidence of an effect by the therapeutic program. However, the relatively better showing of experimental cases with respect to truancy suggests that the surveillance that accompanies the rendering of treatment services tends to have some effect and this possibility is by no means a trivial achievement if further research were to show that it does indeed occur. [74, p. 176]

Test data yielded similar results, and the researchers concluded that

> The attitude personality test and sociometric data . . . failed to detect in any important respect an effect of the experimental treatment program. The findings are not entirely negative, since

some of the pattern of responses show slight indications that experimental cases appear somewhat less unfavorable in a number of parallel instances. [74, p. 204]

The general conclusion is that, "with respect to all of the measures we have used to examine the effects of the treatment program, only a minimal effect can be found." [74, p. 204] *

Ripple studied case outcome of 141 clients who received at least five casework interviews at family service agencies in the Midwest. [91] The question asked was: How well off was the client at the closing of the case with respect to the problem which he brought to the agency and with respect to his general adjustment? In the attempt to answer the question, three interrelated criteria were used: "(1) Level of adjustment at case closing, (2) change in level of adjustment from case opening to case closing, and (3) status with respect to the problem at case closing." [91, p. 157]

Two experienced case-record analysts read the case records and made judgments on client adaptation and adjustment, using movement scales developed by the Institute of Welfare Research of the Community Service Society in New York City, one of the largest family service agencies in the country. A separate scale for assessing problem status at closing was developed for this study. A single composite score was computed for each client based on the three criteria of outcome. A favorable outcome composite score was "defined as one in which there was a strongly positive rating on at least one of the criteria and no negative rating." [91, p. 169]

Of the 141 clients in the study group, seventy-five (53 percent) were judged to have "favorable" outcome composite scores; sixty-six (47 percent) were judged to have "unfavorable" scores. [91, p. 169]   Those clients who presented problems involving environmental stress or difficulties of primarily external origin (illness, handicap, unemployment, unmarried parenthood, and so on) had a higher rate of "favorable" outcome (57 percent) than did those clients (49 percent) whose problems were primarily psychological (personality disturbance, maladaptive interpersonal relationships, intrafamilial conflict, and so on). [91, p. 169]

Another detailed study was conducted by the Institute of Welfare Research of the Community Service Society of New York City. Using the movement scale devised by the institute for evaluation, the researchers found sufficient detail in the records to make judgments regarding seventy-eight individuals in thirty-eight families. Of these, some degree of improvement was associated with casework in fifty-nine (76 percent) of those judged. [58, pp. 50–51]   A follow-up interview with these

* See Mary F. Macdonald, "Reunion at Vocational High," *Social Service Review*, **XL** (1966), for a critical evaluation of this research and the researcher's response in the issue following.

families five years after termination of contact with the agency indicated that "a predominant majority of the ex-clients appeared to place a high positive value on the help they had received, the caseworkers who were known to them, and the agency. . . . The gains in general positive movement judged to have occurred during the time casework was offered tended, on the whole, to be sustained subsequent to closing of cases." [58, p. 103]

Geismar studied the effects of intensive casework on a group of thirty multiproblem low-income families with young children. Using the St. Paul Scale of family functioning, which defines the level of family role implementation in nine areas, "three independent judges rated the level of family functioning before the beginning of treatment." [40, p. 320] The source of data on which the ratings were based is not made clear. A control group of fifty-one families from neighborhood AFDC caseloads was selected for study. These families were only loosely matched to the thirty families being offered intensive social work. The control families were interviewed to "establish a quantitative measure of their social functioning" at the start of the experiment, and at two subsequent nine-month intervals. "Data for evaluating change in social functioning of the treatment families was collected [at six-month intervals] by the workers carrying the case—for the control families, the corresponding information was procured by the AFDC worker" serving the family. [40, p. 326]

Evaluations of the family functioning at the end of eighteen months showed that the experimental group had made statistically significantly greater advances than the "comparison" AFDC group. [40, p. 334] The largest gains were made in the area of family health conditions and practices.

More modest gains were made in the area of care and training of children. The researchers conclude that while the tentative nature of the findings "must be stressed in view of the small numbers of families involved, and the problem of matching experimental and control cases," nevertheless the results "affirmed our belief that multiservice intervention could effect measurable changes in social functioning." [40, p. 349]

In another project conducted by Geismar, casework service was offered to a random sample of young urban families with young children. In the Family Life Improvement Program, as it was called, an experimental group of families was matched with a control group of families, and treatment was offered over a four-year period. [41] Once again the St. Paul Scale of Family Functioning was used to obtain a base line of social functioning. In general, treatment families showed improvement in almost all areas, but a comparison of the two groups showed that "differences of a magnitude representing statistical significance were few, suggesting that the Family Life Improvement Program, although affecting many areas, still had a relatively limited impact upon

the over-all functioning of the treatment group families." [39, p. 460]
Treatment families recorded relatively greater favorable changes than
did control families in child care, health practices at home, and household practices.

Geismar concludes that "intervention in instrumental areas of social
functioning improved in some 70 percent of the cases as a result of
effective than service in expressive areas" (parent-child relationship,
marital relationship), because clients "are generally most responsive to
help in areas they can readily perceive and identify." [39, p. 465]

A Child Welfare League study of supportive services offered families
through public and private agencies found clients indicating that family
functioning improved in some 70 percent of the cases as a result of
service, workers noting that case objectives had been achieved, to some
extent, in 75 percent of the cases. [103]   As in the Geismar Study the
greatest positive changes were in the area of specific care of the children
and in the parent-child relationships. The study identified the technique
of support—the expression by the worker of emotional reassurance,
understanding, and encouragement of the client—as the most frequent
and most important worker intervention. Of all the techniques employed
only "support showed a statistically significant relationship to outcome."
[103, p. 127]

A study of brief, planned service evaluated the results of family
agency service. Many of the families included in the study presented
problems of parent-child relationship. Change in family functioning
resulting from the contact was assessed by research interviewers, caseworkers, and clients. About 81 percent of the families presenting parent-
child relationship problems were improved at closing. [86, p. 108]

The Danish Institute of Social Research conducted an experiment in
supportive services, offering family-oriented social work treatment to
seventy families over a two-year period. A corresponding number of
socially similar families acted as a control group. Statistical analysis of
research interviews with experimental and control families before and
after treatment showed "a positive, although modest, net effect with the
supported families as compared to the control group." [60, p. 190]   The
conditions of about 20 percent of the families were somewhat improved
and those of about 8 percent much improved.

A 1970 national census of family service agency clients revealed that
counselors and clients felt that there was improvement in 69 percent of
the cases treated, while in 21 percent there was no change or a change
for the worse. [8]

Levitt has reviewed most of the available research regarding the
results of therapy with children at child guidance clinics. One review,
covering the period 1929–55, analyzed eighteen different relevant research reports; a more recent review covered the 1955–62 period and
included material from twenty-two reports. [65; 66]

The review of more recent studies parallels the details of earlier studies. Improvement is noted for the treated group, but similar levels of improvement are noted for the "defector groups"—that is, children who had appeared at the clinic but who dropped out before being treated. Levitt concludes his second review of the relevant research by stating: "Again, the inescapable conclusion is that available evaluation studies do not furnish a reasonable basis for the hypothesis that psychotherapy facilitates recovery from emotional illness in children." Levitt is careful to point out that this does not mean that psychotherapy is ineffective for children but simply that its effectiveness has not been proven. [66, p. 49]

Of considerable interest, however, is the fact that "improvement rate for therapy is lowest for cases of delinquency and antisocial acting out and highest for identifiable behavioral symptoms like enuresis and school phobia." [66, p. 49]   The question of whether or not such service is measurably effective may not be as appropriate as a question that directs itself to determining those diagnostic categories for which such service is most effective. Doubts have been raised about the adequacy of the studies available to Levitt for such a review, particularly the adequacy of the control group. [49; 52]   The most optimistic conclusion arrived at by Hood-Williams in analyzing Levitt's review is that "as yet there is no satisfactory answer to the question of how effective psychotherapy is with children." [52, p. 87]   Subsequently updating the review of the research on psychotherapy with children in 1972, Levitt comes to similar conclusions. [67]

The majority of available child behavior modification therapy reports are case studies illustrating the success of the procedures employed with individual children or small groups of children. There are few rigorously formulated evaluation studies, and those available tend to support the claims of the behaviorists that they can effect more change in children's behavior more quickly than other approaches, particularly in instances where the nature of the disordered behavior is clearly defined. There is little evidence that the behavioral modification procedures result in substitution of one symptom for another, as those opposed to such procedures charge.

A recent review of the research regarding behavior therapy with children indicates that most of it "did not meet the basic requirements of scientific research. There are serious inadequacies in the areas of observer bias, inadequate follow-up control groups, and insufficient reporting." [82, p. 169]   Another review of behavior therapy with children notes:

> . . . only a small number of studies . . . have attempted to compare behavior therapy with more traditional approaches and the evidence for the superiority of the new technique seems about

equaled by that which shows it to have no advantage. . . . [But] behavior therapy with children, though no panacea, seems likely to bring limited or significant relief at least to certain patients presently unamenable to, or unreachable by, traditional techniques and holds a potentiality for enlarging the theoretical horizons of child psychiatry. [113, p. 370]

Group Treatment

No evaluation studies of any of the family service agency group programs come within respectable range of meeting the requirements of scientific rigor. Some of the reports include, as evaluatory material, statements of reaction to the program by group participants. Such statements, derived from questionnaires generally distributed by the agency at the termination of a series of family life education meetings, reflect some of the values the participants derive from the program:

I usually left the kids for my wife to handle as I thought I didn't have the time. Now I find myself taking more interest in them. I believe these sessions have brought me closer to my children.

I have found that our household runs more smoothly since we have attended these lectures. We give a little more thought to what we are doing with our children.

The topic on discipline brought to my attention my overstressing the nonessential matters with my son. I find I am more patient with him and less apt to blow up. [37, p. 134]

Participation in such groups often is important to parents as a social experience. It affords an opportunity for going out together and meeting other parents of similar age and background, and it mitigates some of the feeling of social isolation. Parents frequently point to this as one of the desirable features of the programs.

The limitations of such self-report procedures as an evaluatory device have frequently been discussed in social science research literature. Brim's review of evaluation studies in the area of parent group counseling programs and parent life education programs concludes by stating that a "brief summary of the nearly two dozen studies leaves little doubt that their results are inconclusive. . . . The issue of how effective is parent education in changing parents or children, therefore, remains unresolved at present." [12, pp. 310, 312] *

* A more recent review of family therapy comes to similar conclusions. See Richard A. Wells, Thomas C. Dilkes, and Nina Trivelli, "The Results of Family Therapy: A Critical Review of the Literature," *Family Process*, **11**, 2 (June 1972), 180–207.

A review of the available experience with low-income groups suggests that they are difficult to organize and very difficult to keep going. Only a very limited number come to the initial meetings and subsequent attendance is limited and sporadic. It is particularly difficult to involve fathers in such programs. The review report notes that the available demonstrations "offer slight or no evidence that the parent education component is effective in altering the attitudes or behavior of low-income families" and that it is an "open question whether parent education can serve as a basic means of combatting the consequences of low-income family life." [59, p. 36]

In 1965 family service agencies in cooperation with the National Urban League and the Child Study Association of America organized the project ENABLE (Education and Neighborhood Action for Better Living Environment). The Office of Economic Opportunity funded these projects through local community programs. The project, although short-lived, was successful in enlisting a group of parents who were more deprived than the usual family service clientele. Although the drop-out rate of both blacks and Mexican-Americans was consistently higher than that for whites, the project revealed that many low-income families could be induced to participate in such groups and that attitudes toward family life would undergo changes as a consequence of such an experience. [96]

Problems

1. Many families who need, and can use, supportive services are reluctant to apply for them. Some of this reluctance arises from lack of knowledge of the availability of the services and may disappear with better dissemination of information. More frequently, however, parents fail to see the agencies as a resource that can help them resolve parent-child difficulties.

2. Another problem is that, having come, many clients drop out before obtaining the full benefit of the contact. A nationwide study of family service clients showed that about 40 percent of all cases were closed because the client was unwilling, or failed, to continue contact. Child guidance clinics face a similar problem: drop-out rates have been estimated at between 35 and 45 percent.

Part of the difficulty is that the parents assume the child will be "straightened out." The suggestion that the parents' behavior is contributing to the child's difficulty and that they must involve themselves in treatment is contrary to their expectations and is viewed as a threat. In place of advice and a prescription, they are invited to engage in a process of self-examination. Their expectation is that the clinic will deal directly and primarily with the child and that the child will be required to change. [68]

This suggests a problem for research in this area—a problem which has been, to some extent, investigated [35; 64; 90]   If we could identify at the beginning contact those kinds of clients who are likely to remain with the agency and to make effective use of the service, we might then be able to deploy our services more effectively, and reduce the expenditure of time and effort expended in working with families who could not, or would not, use the service. Furthermore, the reluctance to contact the supportive service agency and the drop-out rate of those who do come suggests a third problem: the casework-counseling approach of these agencies may not be either appropriate or acceptable to a group of potential clients, and may have to be supplemented by a more active approach in which the client and worker "do" things together, in which direct "advice" on parent-child relationships is prescribed.

A study by Mayer and Timms based on interviews with working-class clients of the Family Welfare Association in London, a British family service agency, suggests some of the reasons for the higher drop-out rate among lower socioeconomic groups. [72]   Although the worker was concerned with determining, and dealing with, the "causes" of the problem, the working-class client was concerned with doing something about the problem directly. Each assumed the other shared his view of what they were doing together. Thus the client soon became puzzled and frustrated by the workers' behavior. The research suggests that the worker would do well to clearly discuss his assumptions and methods.

3. Available research also indicates that it is difficult for people to find their way through the maze of social services or even to obtain the simple facts regarding their availability. Low-income people who might need the services most are often least likely to know about them and least capable of dealing with the red tape surrounding them. In many sections of the country, moreover, no supportive services are available; in others, such services are heavily duplicated. Professionally trained personnel, therefore, may be inefficiently deployed.

4. The problem of "boundaries" also plagues supportive service agencies: Where does the family service agency end and the child guidance clinic begin? The child is part of the family; the disturbed child is still a child and a member of the family. To treat the child apart from the family is as illogical as to treat the family apart from the child. As a result of this ambiguity, some family service agencies and some children's agencies have merged to form family and children's agencies.

5. The results and consequences of supportive programs are still an open question. Such programs face a problem of evaluation that does not bedevil some of the more concrete types of programs (see Chap. 5), where the consequences of service interruption seem self-evident. The

results of present evaluation studies, as we have noted, are certainly not unequivocal in support of the contention that the agencies are successful in effecting change in a statistically significant percentage of the cases treated. Perhaps a philosophical question needs to be raised here: How much difference in how many families is necessary to prove such services worthy of support? In any case, evaluation of results is a problem for supportive service.

Trends

The preceding discussion noted that there is a trend toward more frequent employment of behavioral modification approaches by supportive agencies, a greater emphasis on a family-centered approach and the use of group procedures, and a shift in the balance between casework and community organization approaches to the client's problems.

1. The trend has been toward widening the responsibilities for supportive service to American families. Successive policy changes on the part of the public welfare programs, particularly Aid to Families of Dependent Children, have made the agencies responsible for offering supportive services to low-income families in the community. Comprehensive mental health centers also accept some responsibility for offering supportive services to the family.

A variety of new agencies now include family counseling as part of a complex program of social services. The Neighborhood Service Centers were established in response to the geographical inaccessibility of established agencies, the fragmented nature of their services, and their "formality." The traditional agencies are characterized as "too big, too distant, too self-serving—formal, impersonal, officious"; the neighborhood service center, on the other hand, is seen as "informal, personal, integrated." [77, p. 1]   The centers are located in low-income neighborhoods, often as storefront operations. They are open on weekends, informal in their intake procedures, and staffed in part by local residents.

The recency and rapidity of development of multiservice neighborhood centers can be grasped from the fact that in 1970 there were 2500 such centers, 62 percent of which had been established since 1964. The centers, located in low-income neighborhoods, serve a disproportionately great number of low-income clients. [75]

A supportive function is included among the stated goals of the community service center. Among the objectives of the center is to "maintain and improve parental functioning—to help parents to carry their responsibility for nurturing the health, education, growth and development of their children." [108, p. 14]   The multiservice neighborhood center concept stresses efforts to determine what the "consumer" wants from the agency. The shift in terminology from "client" to "consumer" is in itself a significant exemplification of a change in relationship between agency and those who use the agency service fostered by the multiservice neighborhood center group. There is also a more explicit emphasis on the agency's responsibility for social action, community organization, and advocacy in behalf of neighborhood residents. In a sense, then, the neighborhood center development initiated the orientation recently adopted by the Family Service Association of America and the Community Service Society.

Despite the determined efforts of such agencies to be more responsive to the needs of local residents, preliminary study shows that they face many of the administrative problems which plagued the more traditional agencies. The tendency is to solve these problems by making intake selective and by working toward specialization of service within the agency. [47; 57; 77; 83]   Furthermore, although many multiservice centers were established with the intent of breaking with the casework orientation of traditional agencies serving the family, most centers find that their central activity is counseling—"trying to change the client or at least dealing with his problems"—rather than community action. [76, p. 7]   This is, perhaps, a testimonial to the technological and political difficulties inherent in systems change and a suggestion that, despite social work's best intentions, it may continue to stress individual casework.

Thirty-six parent-child centers established through the Office of Economic Opportunity in 1968 in some thirty states are also competing with the family service agency. Serving low-income families with young children, the parent-child centers include family counseling and family life education as part of their service. [23]   At present, therefore, the family service agency is only one of a series of agencies offering supportive service to the family.

2. There is increasing evidence that brief preplanned service may be as effective as extended service in solving parent-child problems. One careful experiment was conducted with a group of 120 lower-middle-class families seeking family service agency help with marital and parent-child problems who were randomly assigned to short-term or extended traditional service. [86]   Among the cases were the following:

> An eight-year-old boy who is a behavior problem at home and school; mother becomes increasingly frustrated over how to control him; father, a salesman, away a good deal, ineffectual when at home.
>   Chronic marital difficulties brought to a head by a nine-year-old son's disturbed behavior; intense conflicts between them about how the boy should be handled; their request for help

precipitated by their failure to work out a separation; now want to resolve difficulties. [86, p. 47]

The sixty clients in the brief-service group were offered "not more than eight in-person interviews to be conducted within three months after completion of intake"; the sixty clients in the extended-service group were offered up to eighteen months of service.

The results indicated that the first group showed more improvement than the second—84 percent of families receiving short-term service, but only 64 percent of those given extended help were improved at closing. Follow-up studies showed the gains of the two groups to be equally durable. In cases where the problem was one of parent-child relationships, however, the difference in outcome between the two kinds of service was not as great; 84 percent of the first group, and 78 percent of the second, showed amelioration.

In general, then, lower expenditure of casework time and effort yielded better results. Explanations for this unexpected finding relate to the fact that short-term treatment requires the explicit formulation of specific, limited goals which structured the joint activity of worker and client, and that awareness of time limitations might have focused great worker-client effort in problem solving. [87]

Similarly, child guidance clinics have been experimenting with, and evaluating, short-term treatment, with similar positive findings. [4; 5; 97; 102] As L. Parad points out, the largest percentage of clients coming to family service agencies and child guidance clinics has always continued only for a very limited number of interviews. [81] However, a prolonged intensive contact was thought to be most desirable, less "superficial." Currently the change is not as much a change in the percentage of clients coming for a limited number of interviews as it is a change in attitude of professionals toward the desirability and utility of the short contact. There is growing acceptance of the therapeutic value of a limited contact, and more deliberate planning for such contacts by professionals.

3. The trend toward deliberate, consciously planned short contact is supported by a trend toward the more frequent use of "crises intervention" approaches by supportive agencies. [80; 85] "Crises intervention" derives from the concept of psychosocial homeostasis—psychosocial equilibrium. When some stressful situation is encountered by the client—a member of the family falls ill, a man retires, another child is born, a job is lost, and so on—the previously established family equilibrium is disturbed, and if the disturbance is beyond the family's coping capacity, a crisis develops. During the period of crisis "defenses are lowered—motivation is heightened, due to the discomfort of the anxiety created by the disequilibrium. . . . Thus, the individual is usually more amenable to help during crises and a minimum of thera-

peutic effort may have maximal therapeutic effect." [81, p. 139]   If the agency intervenes at the point of crisis to help the family deal with the crisis, the contact is generally of short duration, terminating when some kind of equilibrium is restored.

4. Because some clients are reluctant to make use of the agency, there is a trend toward what is sometimes termed *aggressive* or *assertive* casework. This involves a more active attempt to identify—generally through the help of the schools—those families in the community that are likely to be in trouble. Once the families are identified, the agency takes the initiative in going to them, telling them of the services that are available, and actively attempting to invite their use of the services. [78] The agencies that have adopted such an approach have explored other, less traditional, ways of helping the families deal with parent-child relationship problems. Similarly, group work agencies—settlement houses, community centers, and so on—are reaching out to problem youths in their area who would never go near the agency. "Detached workers" move out of the agency and frequent local candy stores or poolrooms, getting acquainted with the neighborhood gangs and offering their help. [117]

5. Social workers show an increased willingness not only to move out of the agency into the community so as to solicit the interests of families who might profitably use their services, but also to experiment with new approaches. [4; 79; 99]   For the parent who cannot use the kind of supportive services that depend on development of insight, social workers show a readiness to experiment with more directive, more openly educational kinds of procedures. Instead of asking how the client feels and what he wants to do about his situation, the social workers may actively suggest the kind of help their experience has indicated will effect a desirable change and may then help the client to carry through the suggestion. The social worker may go shopping with the mother who finds it difficult to budget adequately for food; he may demonstrate the desirable way of handling an infant.

6. Another trend is the more active solicitation of low-income families in parent education programs, which had been composed, for the most part, of middle-class families. In the attempt to enlist the interest of low-income families, it is felt that "parent educators must go at least 75 percent of the way. Such parents apparently want assurance that they as individuals will be genuinely welcomed into the program; that their everyday clothes are all right; that arrangements will be made for the care of their children." [59, p. 128]   A successful approach has been to tie the parent education group discussions to some practical activity, such as sewing. Yet, despite such efforts, "only a small proportion of mothers in low-income neighborhoods where such parent education programs are offered actually become involved in the programs." [59, p. 131]

7. There has been a trend toward allowing greater choice of agency service through "purchase of care." Public agencies in need of counseling for their clients might arrange to purchase such service from a family service agency or a child guidance clinic. The client might then be permitted to select the agency of his choice; and the public welfare agency, having negotiated a contract with the voluntary agency, would pay for the needed service. [71; 109; 114]

Summary

The first line of defense in meeting child welfare problems is the supportive service. The family service agencies and child guidance clinics are available to support, strengthen, and reinforce the family in dealing with conflicts in the parent-child relationship network. In offering such help, supportive services remain outside the family social system.

Family service agencies have their origin in the charity organizations that sought to make charity more scientific and effective. Child guidance clinics have their origin in the attempts to deal with juvenile delinquency. Family service agencies come to child welfare through treatment of the parent; the child guidance clinics have always been concerned directly with the child.

Both child guidance clinics and family service agencies are unevenly distributed throughout the country and serve a relatively small percentage of the population. It is estimated that all the child guidance clinics and family service agencies in the nation do not serve more than 0.5 million children a year.

Workers in both agencies seek to create a therapeutic relationship with the parent and/or child. The relationship is used as a source of influence, a source of identification, and the basis for a corrective emotional experience.

Evaluation studies tend to suggest that the service is helpful, but available research does not establish this helpfulness at statistically significant levels.

Among the problems faced by supportive agencies are high drop-out rates, resulting in inefficient use of service; reluctance to use the service on the part of many who need it; the inapplicability of a psychotherapeutic approach to the supportive agency client; the limited availability of supportive service; and overlap between the responsibilities of family service agencies and guidance clinics.

Among the trends identified were a greater emphasis on community organization—social action approaches and a decreased emphasis on casework, more frequent use of behavioral modification procedures, increase in diversity of agencies offering supportive services, changes in the service delivery systems, greater acceptability of "aggressive" social work, greater acceptability of family group therapy and brief treatment procedures, and growth of purchase-of-care arrangements.

Bibliography

1. ACKERMAN, NATHAN. *Treating the Troubled Family*. New York: Basic Books, Inc., 1966.
2. ———, et al. *Expanding Theory and Practice in Family Therapy*. New York: Family Service Association of America, 1967.
3. AUERBACH, ALINE B. *Parents Learn Through Discussion: Principles and Practices of Parent Group Education*. New York: John Wiley & Sons, Inc., 1968.
4. AYERS, B., and J. C. LAGEY. *Community Treatment Programs for Multi-Problem Families—A Survey of 260 North American Communities*. Community Chest and Councils of Greater Vancouver Area, December 1962.
5. BARTEN, HARVEY B. *Brief Therapies*. New York: Behavioral Publications, 1971.
6. BEATT, EARL J. "Family Services: Family Service Agencies," in *Encyclopedia of Social Work*, 16th issue. Ed. by Robert Morris. New York: National Association of Social Workers, 1971.
7. BECK, DOROTHY F. *Patterns in Use of Family Agency Service*. New York: Family Service Association of America, 1962.
8. ———, and MARY A. JONES. *Family Agency Clients—Who Are They? What Do They Want? What Do They Get?—The Early Findings of the 1970 Family Service Association of America Census*. New York: Family Service Association of America, 1971.
9. BELL, JOHN E. *Family Group Therapy*. Public Health Monograph 64. Public Health Service, U.S. Department of Health, Education, and Welfare. Washington, D.C.: Government Printing Office, 1961.
10. BLENKER, MARGARET J., et al. *A Study of Intake*. New York: Institute of Welfare Research, Community Service Society, June 1950.
11. BRIAR, SCOTT. "Family Services and Casework," in *Research in the Social Services—A Five Year Review*. Ed. by Henry S. Mans. New York: National Association of Social Workers, 1971.
12. BRIM, ORVILLE, JR. *Education for Child Rearing*. New York: Russell Sage Foundation, 1959.
13. BROWN, DANIEL. *Behavior Modification in Child and School Mental Health—An Annotated Bibliography on Applications with Parents and Teachers*. Rockville, Md.: National Institute of Mental Health, 1971.
14. BROWN, GEORGE E. *The Multiproblem Dilemma*. Metuchen, N.J.: Scarecrow Press, Inc., 1968.
15. BROWNING, ROBERT M., and DONALD O. STOVER. *Behavior Modification in Child Treatment*. Chicago: Aldine Publishing Company, 1971.
16. BRUCK, MAX. "Behavior Modification Theory and Response: A Critical Review." *Social Work*, **13**, 2 (April 1968), 43–55.

17. CARTER, ROBERT D., and RICHARD B. STUART. "Behavior Modification Theory and Practice: A Reply." *Social Work,* **15**, 1 (January 1970).
18. CHILD WELFARE LEAGUE OF AMERICA. *Preliminary Statement on Social Work Service for Children in Their Own Home.* New York: Child Welfare League of America, 1968.
19. CLIFTON, ELEANOR, and FLORENCE HOLLIS. *Child Therapy—A Casework Symposium.* New York: Family Service Association of America, 1943.
20. CLOWARD, RICHARD, and IRWIN EPSTEIN. *Private Social Welfare's Disengagement from the Poor: The Case of Family Adjustment Agencies.* 1964. Mimeo.
21. COLEMAN, JULES, *et al.* "A Comparative Study of a Psychiatric Clinic and a Family Agency." *Social Casework,* **38**, 1 and 2 (January–February 1957).
22. CONRAD, GERTRUDE. "The First Eighteen Months of Group Counseling in a Family Service Agency." *Social Casework,* **40**, 3 (March 1959).
23. COSTELLO, JOAN, and ELEANOR BINSTOCK. *Review and Summary of a National Survey of the Parent-Child Center Program.* Office of Child Development, U.S. Department of Health, Education, and Welfare. Washington, D.C.: Government Printing Office, 1971.
24. COUCH, ELSBETH H. *Joint and Family Interviews in the Treatment of Marital Problems.* New York: Family Service Association of America, 1969.
25. COURSEY, PATRICIA, *et al.* "A Socioeconomic Survey of Family Agency Clients." *Social Casework,* **46**, 6 (June 1965), 331–38.
26. CYRUS, ADA S. "Group Treatment of Ten Disadvantaged Mothers." *Social Casework,* **48**, 2 (February 1967), 80–84.
27. EHRENKRANZ, SHIRLEY. "A Study of Joint Interviewing in the Treatment of Marital Problems." Parts I–II. *Social Casework,* **48**, 8–9 (October–November 1967), 498–501, 570–74.
28. FAMILY SERVICE ASSOCIATION OF AMERICA. *Scope and Methods of the Family Service Agency.* New York: Family Service Association of America, 1953.
29. ——. *Summary of Family Advocacy Program November 26, 1969.* Mimeo. New York: Family Service Association of America, 1969.
30. ——. *Family Service Statistics—Parts II–V: Summary of 1968 Yearly Report Questionnaires.* New York: Family Service Association of America, November 1969.
31. ——. *Facts and Trends on F.S.A.A. Member Agencies 1970.* New York: Family Service Association of America, October 1971.
32. "FAMILY LIFE EDUCATION." *Highlights,* **12** (May 1951).
33. FAMILY SERVICE AGENCY. Pamphlet. Atlanta, Ga., n.d.
34. FANSHEL, DAVID. *An Overview of One Agency's Casework Operation.* Pittsburgh: Family and Children's Service, October 1958.
35. FOWLER, IRVING A. "Family Agency Characteristics and Client Continuance." *Social Casework,* **48**, 5 (May 1967).
36. FRANKS, CYRIL M., and DOROTHY J. SUSSKIND. "Behavior Modification with Children: Rationale and Techniques." *Journal of School Psychology,* **9**, 2 (Winter 1968), 75–88.

37. FUNT, IRENE. "The Application of Casework Principles in Family Life Education." *Social Casework*, **43** (March 1962).

38. GARVEY, WILLIAM P., and JACK R. HEGRENES. "Desensitization Techniques in the Treatment of a School Phobia." *American Journal of Orthopsychiatry*, **36** (January 1966), 147–52.

39. GEISMAR, LUDWIG L. "Implications of a Family Life Improvement Project." *Social Casework*, **52**, 7 (July 1971), 455–65.

40. ———, and JANE KRISBERG. *The Forgotten Neighborhood.* Metuchen, N.J.: Scarecrow Press, 1967.

41. ———, and JANE KRISBERG. "The Family Life Improvement Project," Part I. *Social Casework*, **47**, 9 (November 1966), 563–70. Part II. *Social Casework*, **47**, 10 (December 1966), 663–67.

42. GELFAND, DONNA M., and DONALD F. HARTMAN. "Behavior Therapy with Children—A Review and Evaluation of Research Methodology." *Psychological Bulletin*, **69**, 3 (1968), 204–15.

43. GUERNEY, BERNARD. "Filial Therapy—Description and Rationale." *Psychological Bulletin*, **28**, 4 (1964), 304–10.

44. HALEY, JAY, and LYNN HOFFMAN. *Techniques of Family Therapy.* New York: Basic Books, Inc., 1967.

45. HANE, MARGARIE K. "Shortened Treatment in a Child Guidance Clinic— The Results of 119 Cases." *British Journal of Psychiatry*, **112** (1966) 613–16.

46. HARPER, AMOS, et al. *American Charities and Social Work*, 4th ed. New York: Thomas Y. Crowell Company, 1940.

47. HASENFELD, YEHESKEL. "Organizational Dilemmas in Innovating Social Services: The Case of Community Action Centers." *Journal of Health and Social Behavior*, **12** (September 1971), 208–16.

48. HAWKINS, ROBERT P., et al. "Behavior Therapy in the Home: Amelioration of Problem Parent-Child Relations with the Parent in a Therapeutic Role." *Journal of Experimental Child Psychology*, **4** (1966), 94–107.

49. HEINICKE, C. M., and A. GOLDMAN. "Research on Psychotherapy with Children." *American Journal of Orthopsychiatry*, **30** (1960).

50. HEREFORD, CARL F. *Changing Parental Attitudes Through Group Discussion.* Austin: University of Texas Press, 1963.

51. HOBBS, NICHOLAS. "Sources of Gain in Psychotherapy." *American Psychologist*, **17** (November 1962).

52. HOOD-WILLIAMS, J. "The Results of Psychotherapy with Children—A Re-evaluation." *Journal of Consulting Psychology*, **24** (1960).

53. JANOWICZ, RUTH. "Whom Should the Family Agency Serve?" *Social Casework*, **48**, 2 (February 1967), 85–93.

54. JEHU, DEREK. *Learning Theory and Social Work.* London: Kegan Paul, Trench, Trubner & Co., 1967.

55. JEWISH FAMILY SERVICE AGENCY. Pamphlet. New York, n.d.

56. KAHN, ALFRED, SHEILA KAMERMAN, and BRENDA McGOWAN. *Child Advocacy—Report of a National Baseline Study.* New York: Columbia University School of Social Work, 1972.

57. KIRSCHNER ASSOCIATES. *A Description and Evaluation of Neighborhood Centers—A Report for the Office of Economic Opportunity.* December 1966.

58. KOGAN, LEONARD, et al. *A Follow-up Study of the Results of Social Casework.* New York: Family Service Association of America, 1953.

59. KRAFT, IVOR, and CATHERINE S. CHILMAN. *Helping Low-Income Families Through Parent Education—a Survey of the Research.* Children's Bureau, U.S. Department of Health, Education, and Welfare. Washington, D.C.: Government Printing Office, 1967.

60. KUHL, P. H. *The Family Center Project: Action Research on Socially Deprived Families.* Copenhagen: The Danish Institute of Social Research, Publication 35, 1969.

61. LEFF, ROBERT. "Behavior Modification and the Psychosis of Childhood: A Review." *Psychological Bulletin,* **69,** 6 (June 1968), 396–409.

62. LEVENSTEIN, SIDNEY. *Private Practice in Social Casework.* New York: Columbia University Press, 1964.

63. LEVINE, MURRAY, and ADELINE LEVINE. *A Social History of Helping Services—Clinic, Court, School, and Community.* New York: Appleton-Century-Crofts, 1970.

64. LEVINGER, GEORGE. "Continuance in Casework and Other Helping Relationships: A Review of Current Research." *Social Work,* **5** (July 1960).

65. LEVITT, EUGENE. "The Results of Psychotherapy with Children: An Evaluation." *Journal of Consulting Psychology,* **21** (1957).

66. ———. "Psychotherapy with Children: A Further Evaluation." *Behavioral Research Therapy,* **1** (1963).

67. ———. "Research on Psychotherapy with Children," in *Handbook on Psychotherapy and Behavior Change—An Empirical Analysis.* Ed. by Allen E. Bergin and Sol L. Garfield. New York: John Wiley & Sons, Inc., 1972.

68. MAAS, HENRY, and ALFRED KAHN. "Sociocultural Factors in Psychiatric Clinic Services for Children: A Collaborative Study in the New York and San Francisco Metropolitan Areas." *Smith College Studies in Social Work,* **25** (February 1955).

69. MACGREGOR, ROBERT, et al. *Multiple Impact Therapy with Families.* New York: McGraw-Hill Book Company, 1964.

70. MANSER, ELLEN (ed.). *Family Advocacy—A Manual for Action.* New York: Family Service Association of America, 1973.

71. MANSER, GORDON. "Implications of Purchase of Service for the Voluntary Agencies." *Social Casework,* **53,** 6 (June 1972), 335–41.

72. MAYER, JOHN E., and NOEL TIMMS. *The Client Speaks—Working Class Impressions of Casework.* London: Kegan Paul, Trench, Trubner & Co., 1970.

73. McPHERSON, SANDRA B., and CYRILLE R. SAMUELS. "Teaching Behavioral Methods to Parents." *Social Casework,* **52,** 3 (March 1971), 148–53.

74. MEYER, HENRY S., et al. *Girls at Vocational High.* New York: Russell Sage Foundation, 1965.

75. O'DONNELL, EDWARD L., and OTTO M. REID. "The Multiservice Neighborhood Center—Preliminary Findings from a National Survey." *Welfare in Review,* **9,** 3 (May–June 1971), 1–8.

76. ———, and OTTO M. REID. "The Multiservice Neighborhood Center—Neighborhood Challenge and Center Response." *Welfare in Review,* **10** (1972), 1–7.

77. ———, and MARILYN M. SULLIVAN. "Service Delivery and Social Action Through the Neighborhood Center—A Review of Research." *Welfare in Review*, **7**, 6 (November–December 1969), 11–12.

78. OVERTON, ALICE. "Serving Families Who Don't Want Help." *Social Casework*, **34** (July 1953).

79. ———, and KATHERINE TINKER. *Casework Notebook*, 2nd ed. St. Paul, Minn.: Greater St. Paul Community Chest and Councils, Inc., March 1959.

80. PARAD, HOWARD S., and GERALD KAPLAN. "A Framework for Studying Families in Crises." *Social Work*, **5** (1960).

81. PARAD, LIBBIE. "Short-Term Treatment: An Overview of Historical Trends, Issues and Potentials." *Smith College Studies in Social Work*, **51** (February 1971), 119–46.

82. PAWLICKI, ROBERT. "Behaviour-Therapy Research with Children: A Critical Review." *Canadian Journal of Behavioural Science*, **2**, 3 (1970), 163–73.

83. PERLMAN, ROBERT, and DAVID JONES. *Neighborhood Service Centers*. U.S. Department of Health, Education, and Welfare. Washington, D.C.: Government Printing Office, 1967.

84. POLLAK, G. "Family Life Education, Its Focus and Techniques." *Social Casework*, **34** (May 1953).

85. RAPOPORT, LYDIA. "The State of Crises: Some Theoretical Considerations." *Social Service Review*, **26** (1962).

86. REID, WILLIAM J., and ANN W. SHYNE. *Brief and Extended Casework*. New York: Columbia University Press, 1969.

87. ———, and LAURA EPSTEIN. *Task-Centered Casework*. New York: Columbia University Press, 1972.

88. REYNOLDS, MARY K., and JOSEPH CRYMES. "A Survey of the Use of Family Therapy by Caseworkers." *Social Casework*, **51**, 2 (February 1970), 76–91.

89. RILEY, PATRICK V. "Family Advocacy—Case to Cause and Back to Case." *Child Welfare*, **40**, 7 (July 1971), 374–83.

90. RIPPLE, LILLIAN. "Factors Associated with Continuance in Casework Service." *Social Work*, **2** (January 1957).

91. ———. *Motivation Capacity and Opportunity—Studies in Casework Theory and Practice*. Social Service Monographs, Second Series. Chicago: School of Social Service Administration, University of Chicago, 1964.

92. ROBBINS, LEE N. *Deviant Children Grown Up*. Baltimore: The Williams & Wilkins Co., 1966.

93. ROSE, SHELDON. "A Behavioral Approach to Group Treatment of Parents." *Social Work*, **14**, 3 (July 1969), 21–29.

94. ———. *Treating Children in Groups*. San Francisco: Jossey-Bass, Inc., 1972.

95. ROSEN, BEATRICE, et al. *Utilization of Psychiatric Facilities by Children: Current Status, Trends, Implications*. Public Health Service Publications. Washington, D.C.: Government Printing Office, 1968.

96. ROSENBLATT, AARON, and LEE M. WIGGENS. "Project ENABLE—Characteristics of Parents Service." *Social Casework*, **48**, 10 (December 1967), 639–47.

97. ROSENTHAL, ALAN J., and SAUL V. LEVINE. "Brief Psychotherapy with Children: Process of Therapy." *American Journal of Psychiatry,* **128,** 2 (August 1971), 141–46.

98. SATIR, VIRGINIA. *Conjoint Family Therapy,* rev. ed. Palo Alto: Science and Behavior Books, Inc., 1967.

99. SCHLESINGER, BENJAMIN. *The Multiproblem Family—A Review and Annotated Bibliography.* Toronto: University of Toronto Press, 1963.

100. SCHREIBER, LEONA. "Evaluation of Family Group Treatment in a Family Agency." *Family Process,* **5** (March 1966), 21–29.

101. SCHULMAN, GERDA, and ELSA LEICHTER. "The Prevention of Family Breakup." *Social Casework,* **49,** 3 (March 1968), 143–50.

102. SHAW, ROBERT, et al. "A Short-Term Treatment Program at a Child Guidance Clinic." *Social Work,* **13,** 3 (July 1968), 81–90.

103. SHERMAN, EDMUND A., et al. *Service to Children in Their Own Homes— Its Nature and Outcome.* New York: Child Welfare League of America, 1973.

104. STAMM, ALFRED M. "NASW Membership: Characteristics, Deployment and Salaries." *Personnel Information,* **12,** 3 (May 1969), 1, 34–45.

105. STOVER, LILLIAN, and BERNARD G. GUERNERY. "The Efficacy of Training Procedures for Mothers in Filial Therapy." *Psychotherapy: Theory, Research and Practice,* **4,** 3 (August 1967), 110–15.

106. TECLE, JAMES, and SOL LEVINE. "The Acceptance of Emotionally Disturbed Children by Psychiatric Agencies," in *Controlling Delinquents.* Ed. by Stanton Wheeler. New York: John Wiley & Sons, Inc., 1968.

107. THOMAS, EDWIN J. (ed.). *The Socio-Behavioral Approach and Applications to Social Work.* New York: Council on Social Work Education, 1967.

108. U.S. DEPARTMENT OF HEALTH, EDUCATION, AND WELFARE. *Toward a Comprehensive Service Delivery System Through Building the Community Service Center.* Washington, D.C.: Government Printing Office, 1970.

109. VORWALLER, DARREL J. "The Voluntary Agency as a Vendor of Social Services." *Child Welfare,* **51,** 7 (July 1972), 436–42.

110. WAHLER, R. G., and M. ERICKSON. "Child Behavior Therapy: A Community Program in Appalachia." *Behavior Research and Therapy,* **7** (1969), 71–78.

111. WAHLER, ROBERT. "Mothers as Behavior Therapists for Their Own Children." *Behavior Research and Therapy,* **3** (1965), 113–24.

112. WEISSMAN, HAROLD H. (ed.). *Individual and Group Services in the Mobilization for Youth Experience.* New York: Association Press, 1969.

113. WERRY, J. S., and J. P. WOLLERSHEIM. "Behavior Therapy with Children: A Broad Overview." *American Academy of Child Psychiatry Journal,* **6,** 2 (April 1967), 346–70.

114. WINOGRAND, IRIS R. (ed.). *Purchase of Care and Services in the Health and Welfare Fields.* Proceedings of the First Milwaukee Institute on a Social Welfare Issue of the Day. Milwaukee: University of Wisconsin, 1970.

115. WITMER, HELEN. *Psychiatric Clinics for Children.* London: Commonwealth Fund, 1940.

116. ———. *Psychiatric Interviews with Children.* New York: Commonwealth Fund, 1946.

117. *Working with Teenage Gangs.* New York: Central Harlem Street Clubs Project, 1950.
118. ZEILBERGER, J., *et al.* "A Modification of a Child's Problem Behaviors in the Home with Mother as Therapist." *Journal of Applied Behavior Analysis,* **1** (1968), 47–53.

4

Supplementary Services:
Social Insurance

Introduction

Family service agencies and child guidance clinics, in helping with problems of child welfare, primarily operate to strengthen and reinforce the parents in discharging their parental roles, but they do not in any way attempt to assume the parents' responsibility. The service remains, in effect, outside the family system. Supplementary services, on the other hand, enter into the social system of the family. They are designed to discharge some part, however limited, of the role responsibility of the parent. For the period of time that the supplementary service is offered, the family embodies the biological parent(s) and the supplementary parent in the guise of the agency. Supplementary services include the income maintenance programs, day care, and homemaker service.

There is an overlap between the supplementary services and the supportive services. As one aspect of their role is supplemented, the parents are able to discharge others more competently. Where the parental role is left permanently vacant because of death, illegitimacy, desertion, divorce, or separation, or is temporarily unfilled because of imprisonment, military service, illness, or unemployment, serious dislocation of the parent-child system takes place and necessitates some arrangement for role supplementation.

One of the principal roles of the parent is to provide for the child and insure his healthy development. In our money economy, this means that the family must have a cash income, and the responsibility for implementing the wage-earner role is generally delegated to the father, although the mother may supplement his income. Income maintenance programs are designed to act *in loco parentis*—in place of parents or as supplementary parents—as far as this specific aspect of parental role responsibility is concerned.

Unemployment, disability, or death of the wage-earner may result in the loss of family income. Workman's compensation, unemployment insurance, and the Old Age, Survivors', and Disability Insurance (OASDI) are social insurance programs that provide for income maintenance for the family faced with such situations. Public assistance programs—general assistance and the Aid to Dependent Children program —cover some of the contingencies provided for by the social insurances and for others as well. Thus assistance may be granted to families left fatherless through desertion, separation, divorce, imprisonment, or illegitimacy.

Both the insurance and assistance programs are pertinent to social work because they are concerned with the consequences of failure in adequate implementation of a social role; they are concerned with situations in which the normal institutional arrangements of a family cannot provide the income to meet the needs of the child. Because both kinds of programs are concerned with situations that directly affect children, these programs can be regarded as pertinent to the field of child welfare.

Social Insurance and Public Assistance

The insurance programs and the assistance programs are distinguishable on the basis of the following significant considerations. The insurance programs, unlike the assistance programs, are financed by the employee-beneficiary and the employer or by the employer alone. Thus the OASDI program is financed by contributions from employees matched by contributions from employers. Both workman's compensation and unemployment insurance are financed in most states through a tax on the employer. But these payments made by the employer might be regarded, like wages, as specific conditions of the employment contract, and the insurance benefits might be regarded as deferred wages. Thus, as contributors to the social insurance funds, the employee or employer has a contractual entitlement to these resources—as would be true in any insurance program. Although their right is based on legislation and, unlike insurance, the conditions and nature of the benefits may be changed by legislation, there is acceptance of the insurance idea that the right to benefits derives from participation in the program.

The money spent in meeting the obligations of the public assistance programs, however, comes from general tax revenues, so that all citizens pay to support the program. The right to public assistance is not clearly acknowledged. The claim to benefits is based more on the ethical premise that every citizen in need has a legitimate claim on the group.

There is an essential difference in the basis for eligibility, related to the difference in the sources of funds for the programs. Eligibility for social insurance is based on the existence of a particular contingency— death, unemployment, or accidental injury. The recipient's financial situation is not a question of concern, so that an unemployed millionaire might receive unemployment insurance.

Eligibility for the assistance programs, on the other hand, is based on verification that a particular situation exists and on verification of need. Death of a father covered by OASDI would qualify his family for insurance benefits; but to qualify for assistance benefits, the family would have to prove need as well.

As Burns points out, both programs concern themselves with "need": "But social insurance deals with *presumptive* rather than *demonstrated* need and is a social institution dominated by a concept of *average* rather than *individual* need." [2, p. 36]   Consequently, although the applicant for assistance must demonstrate his need for assistance, the applicant for social insurance benefits does not.

In the case of the insurance programs, statutory provisions clearly delineate the nature of the amount of the benefits, the precise nature of conditions determining eligibility for benefits, and the persons entitled to benefits. The assistance programs can be more highly individualized, so that the amounts granted to each family are determined by a variety of conditions. Insurance payments are determined on the basis of average presumed need but the budget is computed individually for each family receiving assistance. Thus the insurance programs have a greater element of predictability: the potential recipient can predict, in advance, when he will be eligible and exactly how much he will get. The assistance programs, because they are based on need, allow for a much greater play of administrative discretion. The acceptance of the application and the amount granted cannot be as easily predicted.

Because the assistance programs are based on need, the process of determining eligibility must involve detailed study of the intimate family situation. The eligibility study in the insurance program normally concerns itself only with a more objective, factual consideration of the family situation.

In the assistance programs, payment is made in terms of specific budgeted items. Income from the insurance program is entirely discretionary and may be used by the recipient in any way he sees fit.

The major social insurance programs all grow out of job connection. People are covered by the program by virtue of their employment and their benefits are determined, to a considerable extent, by the time on the job and the amount of money earned. But many families face temporary or permanent interruption of income, or inadequacy of income, even though the family head has not been in insured employment. We need, therefore, income maintenance programs that are not job-related. The public assistance programs, unlike the existing social insurance programs, are not related to employment.

Social insurance differs from social assistance, then, in the following ways:

1. It is work-related.
2. There is no means tests.
3. It is contributory.
4. It is compulsory.
5. Benefits are clearly defined in the law.

Basic to the social insurances is the effort to distribute the risks that are an inevitable concomitant of industrialization so that they need not be borne by the worker alone. Unemployment, for instance, most frequently results from causes over which the worker has no control—changing economic conditions, a changing market situation that reduces demands for a particular product, and so on—and it seems right that those suffering from a contingency that arises from the nature of the social situation should be helped by social legislation. Social security is, in effect, "organized social responsibility."

Social insurance programs are operated through public agencies out of concern with the effects on public welfare of recurrent contingencies affecting a sizable percentage of the population. Because the welfare of the public is a basic reason for the existence of the program, it is administered with a sensitive regard for the social effects of the program. This affects the computation of benefits and the determination of premiums and eligibility. The fact that social welfare influences the design and operation of the program distinguishes the social insurances from private insurance, where profit is the key determinant of policy.

Unlike private insurance programs, the social insurances are compulsory, and benefits are not directly related to the extent of contribution, so that those who contribute less may derive proportionately greater benefits than those who contribute more. The benefit formulas are weighted in favor of the lower income wage-earners. Benefits for low-income wage-earners average about three-fifths of wage loss; although the high-income wage-earner gets higher benefits, it is a smaller percentage of former income. Social insurance thus has, as one result, the effect of some redistribution of income in society.

Social insurance and public assistance complement each other. One covers work-related contingencies and benefits only members of the work force, while the other covers contingencies which are not in any way related to work and covers those people who have never been in the labor force. One program is designed to prevent people from slipping into poverty; the other is designed to facilitate the families' exit from poverty. We will consider social insurance in this chapter, public assistance in the next. Each program will be examined in relation to its importance for child welfare.

Social Insurance Programs

Workman's Compensation

Workman's compensation is the oldest form of social insurance in the United States. It provides money benefits and medical care to an injured worker, and cash benefits to the family of workers who are killed. In order to be eligible, the worker must have sustained an injury "arising out of, and in the course of, employment." Thus the program provides some measure of income to the worker—and, through the worker, to his dependents—when injury on the job temporarily or permanently prevents him from fulfilling the role of wage-earner.

The United States lagged far behind European countries in developing a program of workman's compensation. A broad, compulsory program had been enacted in Germany in 1885, and England adopted such a program in 1897, but the first American workman's compensation laws, passed in Maryland in 1902, were declared unconstitutional. The Federal government finally adopted a workman's compensation law in 1908 for a limited number of employees. The first legal state workman's compensation laws were adopted in 1911, when ten states passed such legislation. By 1948, however, workman's compensation laws had been passed in all states.

Prior to the enactment of such legislation, the injured employee had had to sue for redress. Common law held that the employer was not responsible if the employee had, through negligence, contributed to the accident, if the accident was the result of an act on the part of a fellow employee, or if the worker knowingly assumed the risks of dangerous employment. Even if the worker did have a solid case against the employer, he still had to prove his case in court—generally against the more efficient legal talent that the employer could afford to hire.

A review of some six hundred cases of fatal injuries in three states under the old employer's liability law indicated that in "almost one-half of the cases, the amount received did not exceed $500." [9, p. 385] Frequently, in response to the desperate situation in which the families of injured workers found themselves, a collection was taken up—a procedure described as organized begging. The situation is graphically described by Joseph Parkes:

. . . My mind goes . . . back . . . to when I was a little chap
of eleven years of age working in a cotton mill in England. I
remember being in the mill yard, and peering through the window of
the office of the mill. I saw a man sitting on a stool. His hand was
hanging off—there was only a piece of skin holding it in place.
He was receiving no medical attention whatever. I inquired, in my
boyish way, why something was not done for him, and was
informed that a wagon would come for him soon and take him to
the infirmary. I asked why there wasn't some way of helping
him in the mill, and was told the mill did not have anything of a
surgical character. By and by, a wagon came and the man was
bundled off to the hospital. I was informed later that nothing would
be done by the mill in the matter: that there were plenty more to
take the man's place. That made a profound impression on my
mind, one I have never been able to eradicate. [Quoted in 9, p. 426]

As industrial operations became more complex, more highly mecha-
nized, and more rapid, and as they came to involve increasing contact
with injurious physical and chemical processes, the dangers inherent in
the job situation increased. Here were hazards over which the individual
worker could exert only a small measure of control, so that some percentage of accident and injury was inevitable. It was felt that the burden
of such hazards should not, and could not, be borne by the worker
alone: "The framework of modern industrial technology made the common law of negligence an anachronism." [9, p. 390]   The cost of work
injuries became an inevitable part of the expense of production to be
assumed by the community rather than by the injured worker.

The main purpose of workman's compensation laws was to eliminate,
or reduce, the uncertainties of payment of damages for injuries sustained
at work. Under these laws, workers and their dependents are assured
prompt payment for injuries, regardless of fault and with a minimum
of legal technicalities. Benefits are paid when there is an injury that
results in permanent total disability, permanent partial disability, temporary total disability, or temporary partial disability. In each case, the
injury must arise out of, and in the course of, employment.

In most states, there is a seven-day waiting period before the injured
worker is eligible to receive cash benefits. Medical benefits, however,
start immediately. Families profit indirectly from the existence of workman's compensation laws in that such laws act as an incentive to the
employer to institute safety programs and to provide safe working conditions, thus helping to reduce the number of injuries.

The programs are administered by the states and, except for a program for its own workers, the Federal government is not involved.
Consequently, the programs vary from state to state. The programs
provide for the purchase of insurance by the employer to cover worker

claims against the employer for injuries incurred on the job. In all states, only the employer contributes to the program. In some states he is required to carry such insurance; in other states, he is given a choice. The compensation laws are so worded that the employer has "liability without fault" for any injuries sustained by the worker in the course of his employment. But, although the program is predicated on the idea that workmen injured on the job are entitled to compensation, injuries resulting from willful misconduct, gross negligence, or intoxication on the job may not be compensable.

There are special programs of workman's compensation for seamen and railroad workers. Veterans also have a special program of compensation and medical care for disability, primarily service-connected. But not all employed people are covered by some kind of workman's compensation program. The self-employed, domestic workers, farm laborers, and employees of charitable or religious organizations are the largest groups excluded from such protection. Many states have a "size-of-firm" limitation so that firms employing fewer than three to five employees may be excluded from the program. It is estimated that about 84 percent of the workers in this country are covered by workman's compensation laws. [27, p. 6]

The amount and the duration of compensation vary widely from state to state. In twenty-three states, payment is made for the period of disability or for life. In the other states, there may be a maximum placed on the period during which benefits are granted, a limitation on the total amount of benefits, or both.

Variations in benefits as one moves from one jurisdiction to another are graphically delineated by Kossoris:

> A leg is worth 500 weeks in Wisconsin, 300 weeks in Rhode Island—but only 150 weeks in Maine, 160 in South Dakota, and 170 in Vermont. In Oregon, complete loss of hearing is worth 350 weeks; in Arizona, 260; and in Maine, as little as 65. . . . In about two-thirds of the states, a worker's life is worth $10,000 (about 2½ years' earnings) or less. The widow and four children of a worker who earned $75 a week before he was killed will receive $25 a week in Kansas up to a total of $6000. A widow in Indiana, under the same circumstances, would be paid $10,000, but minus the benefits paid before her husband's death. In Ohio, the death benefits would amount to $9000; in Tennessee, $7500; Kentucky, $9500; Virginia, $7500; Vermont, $6500; and in Maine, $6000. But, if the widow remarries, she forfeits all or most of the unpaid benefits. [16, p. 4]

The amounts have changed somewhat since this statement was first published, but the fact of widespread variation has not changed.

Although injuries are covered, occupational diseases arising from employment are not covered to the same extent. Some states do not cover occupational diseases and many states list a restricted number of occupational diseases.

Medical care is furnished, although a third of the programs limit the length of time during which it is furnished, or the total cost, or both.

When injury on the job results in the death of the wage-earner, his widow and children are granted compensation. Here, too, compensation for life, or until the widow remarries or the children reach a specified age, is the exception. Death benefits, in most jurisdictions, are limited to a specific period or until the worker's family has received some maximum amount.

A National Commission on State Workmen's Compensation Laws, appointed by the President in 1970 to study the program, concluded that the protection furnished by the program is, in general, "neither adequate nor equitable" (*The New York Times*, July 31, 1972). The Commission recommended in its report, issued in 1972, that the program be made compulsory rather than elective, that work-related diseases be included for compensation, and that cash benefits should be at least two-thirds of the worker's gross weekly wage.

The importance of the program might be gauged from the fact that, over the last twenty years, the number of disabling work injuries has averaged around 2 million each year. The number of children affected by the programs through injuries sustained by the family wage-earner, therefore, is likely to run even higher. [34]

Because the state programs are so differently organized, over-all statistics on the workman's compensation program are difficult to compile. As a result, it is not possible to state accurately how many children might be affected by the operation of the program. The fact that, in 1971, some $3.5 billion were paid to beneficiaries in cash and medical benefits indicates the importance of the program to the income maintenance of individuals and their families. [31]

Unemployment Insurance

Unemployment represents a greater hazard to family income maintenance than does disability resulting from injury on the job, because more people are affected by unemployment for longer periods of time. Unemployment results in the inability to perform adequately the role of the parent. If the role requires the father to be a wage-earner, the community must provide sufficient opportunities to enact this aspect of the role. If this is not possible, supplementation must be provided. Unemployment insurance is one form of supplementation.

Unemployment insurance is a state-administered program designed to replace part of the income lost by unemployment through the payment to unemployed workers of specific amounts of money for a limited period. [26, p. 81] It is sustained, generally, by employer contributions based on a payroll tax. The Federal government supervises the program through the Bureau of Employment Security of the U.S. Department of Labor.

The United States lagged behind Europe in enacting an unemployment insurance program. France had adopted such a system in 1905; Britain, in 1911; Italy, in 1919; Germany and Denmark, in 1927. In this country, Wisconsin was the first state to pass an unemployment insurance law, in 1932. Three years later, in 1935, the Social Security Act set up a Federal unemployment tax of 3 percent on the first $3000 of each worker's wage, payable by employers having eight or more employees. If, however, the employer was paying a tax to a state employment insurance fund, he could be relieved of paying most of the Federal tax. Consequently, it became highly advantageous for states to organize an unemployment insurance program. Within two years of the passage of the Social Security Act, all states had developed such a program.

Employers who have a good "experience rating," based on stable employment records, may be permitted to reduce the amount of their tax. The Federal program neither requires, nor prohibits, employee contributions but only three states include such contributions today.

The Federal government collects the unemployment insurance funds and pays the total cost of administering the state programs. Through the tax offset provision, the Federal government has some leverage that permits it to set some general standards. For instance, no state can deny unemployment insurance to a worker who refuses to take a job if the position offered is available as a result of a labor dispute, or if wages, hours, and working conditions are substantially less favorable than prevailing standards. Each state has to provide a fair hearing before an impartial tribunal for any claimant who questions the denial of his application. Also, each state must make the necessary reports to the Federal government, and its administrative staff must be appointed in accordance with merit systems regulations. If a state does not conform to such general minimum requirements, its tax offset may be denied.

Within such limitations, each state is free to develop its program in its own way, so that there is considerable diversity among the states in regulations regarding eligibility requirements, the actual amount and duration of benefits, and so on.

ELIGIBILITY

In general, to be eligible for benefits, a worker must indicate that he is available for work—that he is still attached to the labor market—often by registering for work at a public employment office. Some states regard the claimant as complying with the availability for work requirement if he is enrolled in a vocational training or retraining course.

A worker does not qualify for benefits if he voluntarily left his last job without good cause. (A "good cause" is usually one connected with work and work conditions and attributable to the employer. Personal illness frequently falls within the limits of "good cause.") Nor can the worker claim benefits if he was discharged for "willful, deliberate, or gross" misconduct connected with his employment. ("Gross" misconduct includes dishonest or criminal acts.) Unemployment that results from a labor dispute generally makes the worker ineligible for benefits.

If the worker who has qualified for benefits subsequently refuses a suitable job offer, he may be disqualified for benefits. The criteria for determining whether or not a job is "suitable" depends on such considerations as the "degree of risk to claimant's health, safety, and morals; his physical fitness and prior training experience and earnings; the length of his unemployment and his prospects for securing local work in his customary occupation; distance of the available work from his residence." [33]

One can see that many of the eligibility requirements require some interpretation of "eligibility" on the part of the official making the decision, but it should be noted that these factors disqualify the applicant only temporarily. They do not make him ineligible permanently. The length of time and the conditions of requalification vary from state to state.

COVERAGE, DURATION, AND AMOUNT

Not all workers are covered under the program. The Employment Security Amendments of 1970 provided more adequate support for children of the unemployed, and extended protection to those who work in nonprofit organizations, in state hospitals, in institutions of higher education, and in firms employing even only one person. As a result, three-quarters of all employees are now covered under the program.

In addition for the first time since the inception of the program, the wage base, or taxable portion of the employers' payroll, and the gross Federal unemployment insurance tax were raised. This will provide more funds for benefits.

Of greatest importance is the fact that the Amendments provide that, whenever the rate of insured unemployment reaches 4.5 percent for three consecutive months, the worker can receive up to thirteen additional weeks of payments—or thirty-nine weeks in all.

Neither unemployment insurance nor workman's compensation replaces the wage-earner's income at the level each of the programs had hoped to achieve. Workman's compensation seeks to replace two-thirds of the worker's wage loss; unemployment insurance, one-half. In 1970 workman's compensation was replacing, on the average, about 53 percent of the wages lost through accident; unemployment insurance, about 35 percent of the wage loss for a period of about twenty-six weeks.

The situation is improved somewhat for families with children when the program provides for an increase of benefits for dependents. In 1970 such supplementation was provided in seventeen states for families drawing workman's compensation; by eleven states, for families drawing unemployment insurance. Such a provision increases the total level of income available to the family when the father is unemployed or without income because of work-related injury.

The unemployment insurance program, as presently operated in most states, is designed to meet the income maintenance needs of a family only over relatively short periods. It is not designed to cope with income maintenance needs affecting a mass of people over a prolonged period. It has been compared to fire insurance that would provide against holes burnt in the carpet but would not cover the situation if the house burned down. Nor is it designed to cover the situation of loss of income due to illness. To qualify for unemployment insurance, one needs to be ready and able to work.

Consequently, situations such as prolonged unemployment and unemployment due to illness might impose income maintenance difficulties for the family and its children. These difficulties for families became highlighted late in the 1950's when, owing to an economic recession, many workers exhausted their benefits.

The number of beneficiaries of unemployment insurance in 1971, under the state unemployment insurance programs, was 6.5 million. How many of these beneficiaries have children, and how many children are involved, is not known. One might reasonably assume that a considerable number of the claimants are heads of families with dependent children. The amount of benefits paid in 1971 under these state programs was $5 billion, which indicates the extent to which the program contributes to sustaining family life. [31]

Old Age, Survivors', and Disability Insurance

The most important insurance program affecting children is the Old Age, Survivors', and Disability Insurance program. [17]   As originally established in the Social Security Act in 1935, the program was primarily designed to provide old age pensions. A person who had worked for a stated period of time in covered employment could, upon reaching the age of sixty-five, retire and receive a monthly benefit. But if he died before he reached the retirement age, there was no provision for continuing payments to his surviving dependent wife and children.

In 1939 the Act was amended to include provisions for payments to surviving dependents; at this point, the program developed very considerable significance for child welfare. Whereas previously a mother and children faced with the loss of family income as a result of the death of the father had no recourse other than Aid to Dependent Children, such a family was now entitled to benefits under the insurance program. As more and more workers were covered, and as more families became eligible for payments in case of the death of the father, a shift from the assistance to the insurance programs became evident. For instance, whereas death of the father accounted for 37 percent of the cases on Aid to Dependent Children in 1942, in 1960 such a contingency was a factor in only 7.7 percent of the cases.

The 1939 amendments, which changed an old age pension program to an old age pension and survivors' program, still left a sizable group of children unprotected. These were the dependents of the wage-earner who became permanently and totally disabled and whose family was consequently without income. If disability were the result of injury on the job, income maintenance responsibility for the family would, at least for a time, be assumed by workman's compensation. But, as noted, even those workers covered by such compensation had no claim and no security if the injury or disability were sustained away from the job.

In 1956, by the narrowest of margins, Congress amended the program to provide for disability insurance benefits to a disabled worker and his dependents, starting at age fifty. What had started as an Old Age Insurance program (OAI) had, by virtue of the survivors' insurance features, become an Old Age and Survivors' program (OASI), and then had been expanded to an Old Age, Survivors', and Disability program (OASDI).

The Social Security amendments of 1960 further liberalized the disability program by removing the age fifty eligibility requirement, and the 1965 amendments liberalized the disability provisions. Originally the disability had to be "permanent"—one expected to continue for a long and indefinite time or to result in death. As a result of the 1965 amendments, a worker whose disability is expected to last for twelve months, even though he will probably recover and return to work, is eligible to receive benefits during the period of disability.

Determination of disability is made by state agencies, usually the state vocational rehabilitation agency, under agreements between the states and the U.S. Department of Health, Education, and Welfare. Disability is defined by the Social Security Administration as the inability to engage in any substantial gainful activity by reason of any medically determinable physical or mental impairment (including disabling personality disorders and psychoneuroses as well as psychoses) that can be expected to result in death or that has lasted or can be expected to last for a continuous period of not less than twelve months. [32]

Before benefits can actually be drawn, there is a five-month waiting period. During this time an attempt is made to evaluate the response of the disability to appropriate treatment. The disability insurance benefit, plus any workman's compensation to which the worker is entitled, may not exceed more than 80 percent of previous average monthly earnings, and disability payments to the family are discontinued if the parent refuses, without good cause, to accept vocational rehabilitation services.

The question of the existence of a disability is only part of the story. Not only must a disabling condition be present, but this must result in an "inability to engage in any substantial gainful activity." Those handicapped people who can, and do, work are not entitled to benefits. Benefits are continued during a twelve-month trial period if the disabled worker has been rehabilitated to the point at which he can make an effort to return to employment.

Of concern to children is another provision of the disability sections of OASDI: if the dependent child of a worker covered under the program becomes totally disabled prior to his twenty-second birthday, the child can draw monthly benefits indefinitely. In this case, the mother caring for the child can also draw monthly benefits. This is of particular concern to severely retarded children who are likely to remain dependent throughout life. These children can draw benefits indefinitely. The mother of such a child is also eligible for monthly payments for as long as the child is in her care, regardless of her age or her child's age. Thus the parents of the mentally retarded child have some assurance of continued support for the child beyond their death. Benefits for physically or mentally disabled children are not paid until the eligible parent retires, dies, or is himself disabled.

Henry B. is twenty-nine years old and severely mentally retarded. He was alone and helpless after the sudden death of his parents in an automobile accident.

Henry B. was the only handicapped child in a family of six children. He had been mentally retarded since birth and had always been entirely dependent on other people to care for him. At the time his parents died, he was the only child still living with them. One of his sisters wanted to take him into her home, but she and her husband couldn't afford the extra expense involved.

When the Social Security representative got in touch with this daughter about her father's Social Security, he explained that Henry might be eligible for childhood benefits as a survivor of his father. Henry's sister applied on his behalf. He was accepted as eligible for benefits since his disability was incurred long before he reached twenty-two.

With the Social Security benefits, the sister and her husband are able to take care of Henry in their home.

If an insured worker dies, reaches retirement age, or is disabled, his children are entitled to benefits on his Social Security account if they are under eighteen years of age, unmarried, and dependent on the parent.

Children who were living with their grandparents for the year immediately before the grandparent retired, became disabled, or died are entitled to benefits from the grandparents' account. A child who was receiving benefits under his biological parents' account can now continue to receive benefits even after adoption. Furthermore, an adopted child is entitled to benefits on the account of his adopted parents. The illegitimate child is entitled "if the father was supporting the child or had a legal obligation to do so." Benefit payments continue until the age of twenty-two for those children who remain in school as full-time students. [15]   If the child reaches the age of twenty-two in the middle of the semester or quarter, benefits will be continued till the end of the term. However, no benefits are paid the mother of a child if the only child at home is beyond eighteen years of age.

A dependent child not in school ceases to be eligible for benefits when he reaches his eighteenth birthday or when the child, younger than eighteen, marries. A disabled child over twenty-two drawing benefits because of a disability incurred before his twenty-second birthday will face discontinuation of benefits if he refuses, without good cause, to accept vocational rehabilitation services. A child receiving benefits because of the father's disability will have such benefits ended if and when the worker is rehabilitated and returns to work.

The child's monthly benefit rate is one-half his insured parents' primary rate if the parent is receiving retirement age or disability benefits. If the child is drawing benefits as the result of the death of the parent, the benefit rate is three-fourths of the parents' primary insurance amount.

If an insured worker dies, reaches retirement age, or is disabled, his wife is entitled to insurance benefits if she is caring for a child entitled to benefits on his father's Social Security account. The wife's benefits are one-half of her husband's primary insurance amount. The combined benefits of children and mother, in the case of the death of the father, may not exceed a family maximum of $708.

The fact that a child's mother is divorced from the insured worker does not affect the child's right to benefits from the father. If the mother remarries, the child is still entitled to benefits from the first father's account.

The children of a mother who is covered under the program and becomes disabled can draw benefits as a consequence of her disability. If she dies her children can draw survivors' benefits on her record. Benefits to children based on the mother's earning record provide a very important protection for the single-parent family headed by a woman. This additional income is also of considerable importance to the two-parent family if the father must employ someone to help care for dependent children after the mother's disability or death. In December 1971, "460,000—more than one-tenth of all child beneficiaries—were receiving benefits on their mothers' work record. The number of children in this group had increased nearly threefold since 1960, while the total number of children entitled on their fathers' record had doubled." [1, p. 8]

Mr. James Wallingford married Mrs. Judy Anaka in Buffalo, New York, in November 1967. Mr. Wallingford, an accountant, had lost his wife Carole in January 1967 after a lengthy illness. He had three boys—James, 11; Michael, 10; and Bruce, 6. Mrs. Anaka was the widow of an Air Force pilot who was killed in July 1965. She had four children—Karen, 10; Kristen, 8; Kathleen, 6; and Edward Jr., 4. After the wedding, Mrs. Anaka—now Mrs. Wallingford—continued to get $347 in Social Security checks for her four children, and Mr. Wallingford got $122 for his three boys on the work record of their mother. Together, the Wallingford family got a total of $469 each month—covering every one of their children except Kathryn Ann Wallingford, born in August 1968.

Such continued support benefits for children increase the probability of remarriage and make it easier. The child's benefits, in over 90 percent of the cases, are paid to the mother, who is given the responsibility of managing the child's benefits in his behalf. If the mother is not available or is unfit to manage the funds responsibly, or if the child is not living with his mother, designating a responsible representative payee may become a problem. A special unit, the Welfare Branch of the Division of Claims Policy, Bureau of Retirement and Survivors' Insurance, has been organized to help deal with such problems. Its local offices may work with local child welfare agencies in evaluating the acceptability of representative payees. If the child is institutionalized, the institution may be designated as the payee. Some institutions apply the benefits toward the cost of child care but, as the child grows older, may designate some part of the benefits as savings for the child. For a child in foster care, the agency or the foster parents may be the payee, depending on the agency's recommendations.

The tremendous implications of the OASDI program for children are made clear in the following updated and abridged version of an article by economist Sylvia Porter:

Social Security Is Amazing Aid to Young Widow
A young father of three infants was killed in a freak accident in our community the other day, leaving not only a heartbroken widow but also an empty bank account. While we were discussing

with the neighbors how to ease at least her financial tragedy, I volunteered, "One 'good' angle is the fortune she'll get from Social Security from now on. It'll run into tens of thousands of dollars in cash."

The cash stake of this young widow and her infants, as I figured it out with the local office of the Social Security Administration, comes to about $220,000. What's more, this inheritance is free of income and sales taxes.

Her husband would have had to accumulate a nestegg of more than $200,000 and would have had to invest it at 4 percent tax-free to duplicate in part what she is now going to get.

. . . In our neighbor's case the father had been fully insured at the top Social Security salary level of $12,600 a year. His infants are one, two, and three years old. Now:

On application, his widow will get a lump-sum death payment. This amounts to $255 (and is generally regarded as a burial expense payment).

His infants and their mother will get a pension of $708 a month until the oldest child is eighteen. Assuming that she does not remarry during the fifteen-year period, this adds up to $127,440.

For twelve months, his widow and her two children, still under eighteen, will get a monthly pension of $708. This amounts to $8496 over the year.

For twelve months, she and her one child still under eighteen will get a monthly pension of $606.80. This amounts to $7281 over the year. Total benefits would be $143,217.60 over a seventeen-year period if the children don't go to school.

If the children continued school (all three) until age twenty-two the payments would be as follows:

Lump Sum	$ 255.00
(17 years) widow and three children (family maximum)	$144,432.00
(2 years) three students (family maximum)	$ 16,992.00
(1 year) two students (no family maximum)	$ 7,281.60
(1 year) one student (no family maximum)	$ 3,640.80
Total amount to be paid in monthly benefits including the lump-sum burial expense	$172,601.40

This would be a total amount paid until the youngest child no longer qualifies as student (at age twenty-two). Then if the widow did not remarry and started to collect unreduced benefits (82.9

percent at age sixty-two projected to age seventy-four) she would collect $335.40 per month or $4024.80 per year. If she collected for twelve years this would mean another additional $48,297.60, which added to $172,601.40 totals $220,899.00.*

This is the benefit situation for such a family in 1975. The case described is a demonstration of the current program at its very best. The payments made in such cases depend on the length of time in insured employment and the salary received, up to a maximum of $12,600 a year. If the worker was covered for less than ten years, or forty quarters of employment, or if his maximum earnings were less than $12,600 a year, benefits would be reduced proportionately.

In 1971 the average monthly payment made to a widowed mother with three or more dependent children was $315.60. [31]

The lump-sum death benefit payment, designed to meet burial expences, was the maximum amount payable. It may be less in other cases, for the death benefit payment is equal to three times the primary insurance amount, but in no case does it exceed $255.

The level of OASDI benefits has been increased periodically. The formula for computing benefits has been revised periodically, and minimum levels of benefits and maximum allowable benefits have been raised. The average monthly benefit for a child was $12.22 in 1940; this had increased to about $90.95 in 1971. The average mother's monthly benefit was $19.61 in 1940; this had increased to about $95.60 in 1971. [31]

The tax rate advanced to 5.85 percent each for both employee and employer in 1973 and is scheduled to rise to 7.3 percent in the year 2011. The taxable base, the maximum amount of earnings against which the tax rate is applied, was increased to $10,800 in 1973 and $12,600 in 1974. It will be subsequently raised as the cost of living increases. This change in base, plus an increase in the contribution rate schedule, meant an increase in benefits. The maximum benefits that could be paid to a widow and dependent children, therefore, increased. Previously the maximum benefits payable to the widow and children of a deceased worker were $280. The changes provided for an increase in the maximum available to a widow and two or more dependent children to $708. Here, once again, it must be noted that the maximum is available only to the family of the worker if the father had been earning at least $12,600 a year for some time. Because most of the workers in the United States earned less than this in 1974, many of their widows and children will not be entitled to maximum benefits.

Benefits are reduced if the insured worker works after retirement and earns more than $2400 a year; at age seventy-two or older this does

---

* Our thanks to the Madison, Wisconsin, office of the Social Security Administration for providing the updated figures.

not apply. If an auxiliary or survivor works—a wife, a widow, or a child —and earns more than $2400 a year, the benefits of the particular person working are reduced accordingly. Income from annuities, trust funds, stocks and bonds, and rentals from real estate are not regarded as earnings, so that such income does not affect benefits. For earnings in excess of $2400, benefits are reduced by one-half of the excess. If a widowed mother earns $2500, then one-half of the earnings in excess of $2400, or $50, is withheld from benefits.

The amount that one might earn before benefits begin to be reduced is such that it may not affect the right of part-time teenage workers. Mothers' earnings may, however, cut into their benefits.

To recapitulate, OASDI affects children by providing the possibility of continued income in certain situations. These are listed in order of the number of children affected. The number of children listed as receiving benefits as a result of each contingency is, in round figures, for December 1972. [31]

1. Children receiving benefits because their fathers have died: 2.85 million.
2. Children receiving benefits because their fathers were disabled: 1.08 million.
3. Children receiving benefits because their fathers reached retirement age: 585,000.
4. Children over eighteen receiving benefits because their fathers are dead, disabled, or retired and they themselves incurred a disability before their eighteenth birthday: 305,000. (In the greatest majority of instances such persons were mentally deficient or suffering from cerebral palsy, epilepsy, or schizophrenic disorders.)

In 1972 the amount of money granted for the support of children who benefited from the program was about $4.5 billion. As of December 1972 there were 5 million children receiving benefits under the OASDI program. Some 541,000 widowed mothers were receiving benefits as a result of the fact that they were caring for dependent children of OASDI beneficiaries. More than 550,000 youngsters between the ages of eighteen and twenty-two were attending school full time and continuing to draw benefits. The amount of such "stipend" support for this group amounted to $500 million. The average payment of about $90 a month enabled these young people to remain in school. The total yearly amount which such beneficiaries draw as full-time students is greater than all of the scholarship money made available through all of the colleges and universities in the United States.

Nonwhite children are disproportionately represented in the population of beneficiaries. Some part of this is due to the fact that nonwhites die at an earlier age than whites, and nonwhite families are somewhat larger. The average benefits to nonwhite children are about 70 percent of those to whites because nonwhite workers earn lower average wages. [19]

OASDI is of particular value to young families which have not yet had the opportunity of building up reserves and where the father has not as yet attained his full wage-earning potential. [13]

An interview study with a large group of widows with children drawing Social Security survivors' benefits found that

> . . . widowed families with Social Security benefits occupy an intermediate position between other fatherless families and husband-wife families. Their income is much higher than that of the first group but considerably lower than that of the second. The Social Security survivor benefits deserve the main credit for raising the income of widowed families above that of other fatherless families. Without the benefits their income would probably be about the same [as other fatherless families]. [21, p. 63]

The report indicates the successful achievement of one of the principal objectives of the program, to "help moderate the decline in living standards when the earnings of the family head cease because of retirement, disability, or death." [21, p. 55] This is the wage-loss-replacement objective.

The same study demonstrates that level of income replacement is inadequate, that many of the widows had to work to supplement benefits that did not adequately meet family needs, and that the husbands' death created severe economic problems for the families. Once the father is gone, despite OASDI, these families had "little prospect of maintaining the financial position attained by the family prior to the fathers' death and even less of improving it." [21, p. 47] A detailed study of the economic situation of the surviving families of auto-production workers, for example, indicated that "a substantial number of survivors are failing to meet what has been defined as a modest, but adequate standard of living." [11, p. 9] The City Workers' Standard Budget was used to assess the adequacy of survivors' benefits against the sum required to maintain a family "at a level of adequate living according to prevailing standards of what is needed for health, efficiency, the nurturance of children and for participation in social and community activities." [11, p. 18]

There have been substantial recent increases in benefit levels on four different occasions between 1968 and 1972—a 13 percent increase in February 1968, 15 percent in January 1970, 10 percent in January 1971, 20 percent in July 1972. Although benefit levels have kept up with rises in the cost of living, they have not increased as much as wages during a similar period. Provision has now been made for automatic adjustments in Social Security benefits every time an increase of 3 percent or more is recorded in the Consumer Price Index.*

Since the inception of the program, more and more children have been affected, not only because of the fundamental changes in the nature of the program itself, but also because more groups of fathers have been included in the program. By 1973, over nine out of every ten workers and their dependents were covered by OASDI. Some of the excluded groups—such as Federal employees, policemen and firemen in many states, and railroad workers—are covered by special retirement systems.

The OASDI program is the only Social Security program operated directly by the Federal government. The Bureau of Old Age and Survivors' Insurance, Social Security Administration, Department of Health, Education, and Welfare, administers the program through some 600 local district offices in the principal cities and towns in the United States. Application for benefits is made by the claimant at these district offices.

The program is financed by matched contributions from both employer and employee. The money collected is placed in the Old Age and Survivors' Insurance Trust Fund, which is managed by a board of trustees consisting of the Secretary of Labor, the Secretary of Health, Education, and Welfare, and the Secretary of the Treasury. The contributions from employers and employees include a 0.5 percent tax specially assigned to finance the disability provisions of the program; these funds are kept separate. The Old Age and Survivors' Insurance Trust Fund is invested in interest-bearing, guaranteed U.S. government obligations or securities, and this income is added to the fund.

Veterans' Administration Program

For the sake of comprehensiveness, we should note that the Veterans' Administration Program of benefits to veterans and their dependents also affects a sizable number of children, although nowhere near the numbers of children affected by the programs already discussed. Disabled veterans are entitled to compensation, if the disability is service-connected, and some children of deceased veterans are entitled to a pension. [20]

Trends and Problems

The trend in the insurance programs is toward liberalization, which takes the form of increasing coverage of previously excluded groups.

---

* An additional 5.4 percent increase was legislated in July 1973 to take effect in June 1974.

The trend is more pronounced in the OASDI program than in the workman's compensation program or the unemployment insurance program. However, all programs exclude some employed workers, so that some dependent children still lack the assurance of continued income if the parent dies, is injured at work, or loses his job. Currently, some part-time workers and some self-employed groups are not covered by OASDI.

Coverage is also extended by liberalizing definitions of eligibility for benefits. Thus, until 1965 an illegitimate child was eligible for OASDI benefits only if the state in which he resided recognized his rights to inheritance. As a result, some illegitimate children in some states were ineligible. The 1965 amendments established a nationwide definition of eligibility: an illegitimate child is eligible "if the father was supporting the child or had obligation to do so."

Liberalization also takes the form of including contingencies not previously covered by the program. Thus Old Age and Survivors' Insurance was extended to permit payment of benefits for disability, and workman's compensation was broadened to make specific provisions for the coverage of occupational diseases.

Despite this extension, there are specific recurrent contingencies, affecting large groups in the population, which are not provided for by any program. Illness, for example, not only results in the loss of a wage, but also imposes a burden on an already depleted family income; yet we have no national program of health insurance. The loss of family resources that results from illness can be gauged by the fact that "private wage and salary workers in 1964 had a potential income loss of about $8 billion because of nonoccupational short-term sickness and injury (including the first six months of long-term disabilities). Less than one-fourth of this amount was replaced through benefits paid under private and public cash sickness plans, including sick leave." [8, p. 13]

It might be appropriate here to note that liberalization of the social insurance programs is only partly a response to the need for a program of income replacement for all wage-earners and their dependents. It also reflects the recognition that all income maintenance programs are devices required by a highly industrialized economy to maintain economic stability and full employment. Maintenance of a healthy level of economic growth would be more difficult if the large amounts of support poured into the economy through the insurance and assistance programs were withdrawn. Thus the great loss of income cited as a result of illness affects the economy adversely.

Liberalization of the insurance programs also takes the form of increased benefits over longer periods of time. The OASDI program has gone further toward increasing the beneficiaries' real income than either the workman's compensation or unemployment insurance programs. But, despite such liberalization, the adequacy of current levels of payment is open to question. Although the principal purpose of all the social insurance programs is to provide public assurance of a minimum level of income maintenance when the principal wage-earner is removed from the labor market as a result of specific contingencies, the level at which the family is to be maintained is a matter of controversy. At present, average benefits run higher than public assistance payments for comparable situations, but lower than the amounts required to meet the needs of a modest but adequate city worker's family budget as computed by the U.S. Department of Labor.

We noted that the average OASDI benefits for a widow and three dependent children was $315.60 in 1972. The reader might want to decide for himself whether this is sufficient to maintain a family of three at a modest but adequate level of living.

All the insurance programs tend to reflect the concept of "less eligibility," the idea that benefit levels should be lower than the lowest salary levels in the community. This policy is based on the fear that more adequate benefit levels would tempt people to try to live off the program rather than work, although there is little empirical evidence to substantiate the suspicion.

This results in a continuing problem for the insurance programs. Despite efforts to maintain benefit levels by increasing the amount of payments, the cost of living and earning levels are rising more rapidly. The average retired worker's monthly benefit represented a smaller percentage of his average monthly earnings in 1970 than it did in 1940, so a widow and two children in 1970, despite the absolute increase benefits, would have had to do with a relatively smaller amount. Also, those families that most need Social Security are apt to be least adequately protected. There is an "inverse relationship between income and the incidence of the economic and social risks associated with modern industrial life, with the result that those most likely to incur these risks can least afford to protect themselves through private saving and private insurance." [12, p. 31] And since social insurance programs relate benefits to earnings, they are apt to be of less help to those children whose fathers' earnings were inadequate throughout his working life. The inequity is mitigated somewhat by a "floor of protection" that guarantees a minimum benefit to the family of even the lowest eligible wage-earner.

Also, social insurance is supplemented in many instances by employee group life insurance and collective bargaining agreements which provide paid sick leave and pension plans. But in these cases, too, the families with the lowest earnings are least likely to be protected by the more adequate programs. Furthermore, more low-income families are likely to be ineligible for social insurance or union protection because of the intermittent or casual nature of some low-income jobs. Cohen notes that "only 84 percent of poor families were covered by Social Security or other government pensions in 1959 as contrasted with 93 percent of all families." [7, p. xiii]   Another inequity is created by the payroll taxes paid by the worker to finance his Social Security: the low-income worker tends to contribute a larger proportion of his wages than the higher paid worker does.

There is a trend toward making social insurance more family-oriented. The revision of the Old Age Insurance program so that it becomes an Old Age and Survivors' Insurance program reflects this increased concern with the family rather than with the wage-earner alone, as does the modification of the unemployment insurance program (by some twelve states) so as to provide additional payments if an unemployed worker has dependents. There is a trend toward broadening the social insurances programs so that they may become more than mere income maintenance services. Thus the workman's compensation program in some states includes provisions for rehabilitation services for the injured workers, and the unemployment insurance program offers job counseling and help in job placement.

Yet there is much that is of concern to children to which the programs are still indifferent. For example, the noneconomic consequences the child suffers from the injury, death, disability, or unemployment of the father are not regarded as the concern of the social insurance programs, nor are the programs intended to meet this gap. Thus mothers and children are left to struggle with a variety of social problems without assistance. A detailed study of blue-collar families following the death of the father indicated the emotional disruption to which the surviving children were subject.

"The study findings indicate the need for improved and expanded nonfinancial counseling resources to aid the families and particularly the children of recently deceased workers." [11, p. 10]   Casework rehabilitation services (see Chap. 5) have been associated with assistance programs but not with insurance programs, and as a result, Kahn notes a difference in the image of the families who are the clients of these two different programs. [14]   The family receiving insurance is regarded as a "normal" family capable of meeting all its problems except that of income maintenance; the assistance family is regarded as a less capable family requiring casework services as well as income.

The distinction becomes less and less tenable, if it ever was valid, as an increasingly larger proportion of the population comes under insurance coverage. Certainly it is reasonable to suppose that all families with dependent children, eligible for benefits because of injury, disability, or death of the father, are likely to face some serious social problems that derive from the need to reallocate social responsibilities within the family systems.

The growing dissatisfaction with income maintenance programs and the widespread discussion of radical reform of such programs (discussed in greater detail in Chap. 5) have resulted in serious consideration of major changes in the Social Security program. A national health insurance program is currently being discussed, and the possibility of a children's allowance program has been proposed. [2; 10; 24; 25; 35]

Summary

Income maintenance programs are among the supplementary child welfare services. Such programs stand in place of the parents, supplementing a principal component of the parental role: provision of a cash income for the maintenance of the family. Social insurance and social assistance programs are the two principal income maintenance programs. They differ from each other in the following ways:

1. Insurance benefits come out of a special fund to which the beneficiary has contributed directly or indirectly, whereas assistance benefits come out of public revenues.
2. Need is presumptive in establishing eligibility for insurance, but must be established in the case of the assistance programs.
3. The amounts of benefits are individually determined and budgeted for specific items in the case of assistance programs, but are determined by statute in the case of the insurance programs and are entirely discretionary.
4. The insurance programs are connected with employment, so that coverage is job-connected, whereas the assistance programs are not job-related.

The principal insurance programs are workman's compensation, unemployment insurance, and Old Age, Survivors', and Disability Insurance.

More than 90 percent of all families with children are covered by OASDI; more than 80 percent of all families with children are covered by workman's compensation and a smaller percentage by unemployment insurance. In each instance, the program is of considerable importance to children because it provides the incomes that have been interrupted through injury, unemployment, disability or death of the wage-earner, generally the father.

The number of children maintained by the OASDI program alone in 1972 was about 5 million. More children are maintained by the other insurance programs; many millions are benefited by workman's compensation and unemployment insurance.

The trend is toward liberalization of the insurance programs through increased benefits, extended coverage, and broader definitions of eligibility. The insurance programs are becoming more family-centered and more concerned with family problems other than income maintenance. The programs face the problems of erosion of replacement income, the uneven coverage so that those who need it most are least adequately covered, and some ambiguity as to aims of the programs.

The United States does not provide, as do most of the Western European nations, for a system of national health insurance or for a system of children's allowances—a kind of insurance that helps to equalize the burden of family care of dependent children. None of these countries, however, including the United States, has a fatherless-child insurance program, which would provide for the child when a father has deserted, separated from, or divorced the mother, and when payments from the father for support of the child are not forthcoming or inadequate. Divorce, desertion, illegitimacy, and so on are not yet considered insurable risks.

Bibliography

1. Bixby, Lenore E. "Women and Social Security in the United States." *Social Security Bulletin,* **35,** 9 (September 1972), 3–11.
2. Burns, Eveline M. *The American Social Security System.* Boston: Houghton Mifflin Company, 1949.
3. ————. "Children's Allowances and the Economic Welfare of Children—The Report of a Conference." New York: Citizens' Committee for Children of New York, Inc., 1968.
4. Cohen, Wilbur J., and Robert M. Ball. "Social Security Amendments of 1965: Summary and Legislature History." *Social Security Bulletin,* **28** (September 1965).
5. ————, and William Haber. *Readings in Social Security.* Englewood Cliffs, N.J.: Prentice-Hall, Inc., 1948.
6. ————, and William Haber. *Social Security Programs, Problems, and Policies: Selected Readings.* Homewood, Ill.: Richard D. Irwin, Inc., 1960.
7. ————, and Eugenia Sullivan. "Poverty in the United States." U.S. Department of Health, Education, and Welfare Indicators. Washington, D.C.: Government Printing Office, February 1964.
8. Epstein, Lenore A., and Alfred M. Skolnik. "Social Security Protection After Thirty Years." *Social Security Bulletin,* **28** (August 1965).
9. Gagliardo, Dominico. *American Social Insurance.* New York: Harper and Row, Publishers, 1949.
10. Garfinkle, Irwin. "Negative Income Tax and Children's Allowance Programs: A Comparison." *Social Work,* **13,** 4 (October 4, 1968), 33–39.
11. Glasser, Melvin, et al. *Survivors' Benefits and Blue Collar Workers.* Lexington, Mass.: D. C. Heath & Company, 1970.
12. Gordon, Margaret. *Economics of Welfare Policies.* New York: Columbia University Press, 1963.

13. GUILLOT, ELLEN E. "Congress and the Family: Reflection of Social Processes and Values in Benefits in OASDI." *Social Service Review*, **45**, 2 (June 1971), 173–82.
14. KAHN, ALFRED. "Social Services in Relation to Income Security." *Social Service Review*, **39** (December 1965).
15. KIRSCH, BARBARA. "School Attendance Patterns of Student Beneficiaries." *Social Security Bulletin*, **34**, 10 (October 1971), 22–24.
16. KOSSORIS, MAX D. "An Appraisal," in *Workman's Compensation in the United States*. U.S. Bureau of Labor Statistics Bulletin 1149 (1954).
17. LARSON, NOETA. "Children Receiving OASI Benefits." *Children* (September–October 1958).
18. LUBOVE, ROY. *The Struggle for Social Security, 1900–1935*. Cambridge, Mass.: Harvard University Press, 1968.
19. MURRAY, JANET H. "Old Age, Survivors', Disability, and Health Insurance Changes in the Beneficiary Population." *Social Security Bulletin*, **32**, 4 (April 1969), 21–28.
20. NATIONAL ASSOCIATION OF SOCIAL WORKERS. "Veterans' Benefits and Service." *Social Work Yearbook, 1960*. New York: National Association of Social Workers, 1961.
21. PALMORE, ERDMAN, et al. *Widows with Children Under Social Security*. U.S. Department of Health, Education, and Welfare, Office of Security and Statistics Research Report No. 16. Washington, D.C.: Government Printing Office, 1966.
22. PECHMAN, JOSEPH A., et al. *Social Security Perspectives for Reform*. Washington, D.C.: The Brookings Institution, 1968.
23. ROHRLICH, GEORGE F. "The Place of Social Insurance in the Program of the General Welfare." *The Journal of Risk and Insurance*, **36** (September 1969), 333–54.
24. SCHORR, ALVIN L. *Poor Kids*. New York: Basic Books, Inc., 1966.
25. ———. "Alternatives in Income Maintenance." *Social Work*, **11**, 3 (July 1966), 22–29.
26. SCHOTTLAND, CHARLES I. *The Social Security Program in the U.S.*, 2nd ed. New York: Appleton-Century-Crofts, 1970.
27. SKOLNIK, ALFRED M., and DANIEL N. PRICE. "Another Look at Workman's Compensation." *Social Security Bulletin*, **33**, 10 (October 1970), 3–25.
28. TURNBULL, JOHN G., et al. *Economics and Social Security*, 3rd ed. New York: The Ronald Press Company, 1968.
29. U.S. DEPARTMENT OF COMMERCE. *Statistical Abstracts of the United States, 1971*. Washington, D.C.: Government Printing Office, 1971.
30. U.S. DEPARTMENT OF HEALTH, EDUCATION, AND WELFARE. *Social Security Programs in the United States*. Washington, D.C.: Government Printing Office, April 1971.
31. ———. *Social Security Bulletin, Annual Statistical Supplement, 1971*. Washington, D.C.: Government Printing Office, 1973.
32. ———. *Social Security Handbook on Old Age, Survivors', and Disability Insurance*, 3rd ed. Washington, D.C.: Government Printing Office, 1966.
33. U.S. DEPARTMENT OF LABOR. *Comparison of State Unemployment Insurance Laws*. Washington, D.C.: Government Printing Office, 1970.

34. ———. *State Workman's Compensation Laws*, revised 1969. Washington, D.C.: Government Printing Office, 1969.
35. VADAKIN, JAMES C. *Children, Poverty and Family Allowances*. New York: Basic Books, Inc., 1968.

5

Income Maintenance:
Aid to Families
of Dependent Children

Introduction

Social insurance programs provide coverage for only a limited number of situations that are likely to result in a problem of income maintenance. They do not provide protection for the following:

1. A child whose father is ill and partially disabled.
2. A child whose father is unemployed for a long period of time and is not eligible for unemployment insurance or has exhausted his benefits.
3. A child whose father has deserted, or is divorced or separated from, his wife.
4. A child whose father is imprisoned.
5. A child who is illegitimate.
6. A child whose father is dead but was not, while alive, covered by OASDI.
7. A child whose father is dead, retired, or permanently disabled but whose OASDI benefits are below subsistence level for the family.

A supplementary program is needed to provide for these families. The principal program available in filling this gap is the Aid to Families of Dependent Children—the AFDC program (previously known as the Aid to Dependent Children program—ADC).

In discussing the differences between assistance and insurance programs, we noted that the assistance programs attempt to individualize the needs of the client. In doing this, the agency becomes aware of, and takes responsibility for, helping with other social problems that the family faces because the social roles of father and husband are vacant or inadequately implemented.

Historical Background

The precursor of the ADC program in this country was the mothers' pension program, which was a public assistance rather than a true pension program. Earlier in our history, the problem that most frequently resulted in unfilled paternal roles was the death of the wage-earner. The mothers to be assisted were generally widows. The solution, it was felt, lay not with public aid to the family but with reallocation of roles within the family. Children moved up early in life to assume the income maintenance responsibility of the father. The solution was tied to the public acceptance of child labor, defended by Mr. Sherard of the Southern Textile Association before a U.S. House of Representatives committee investigating the question of child labor in 1916:

> Take for instance a widow woman who has two children, we will say under 14 years of age, but of legal age, as we now employ them between 12 and 14. These children can easily make $1 a day. There are $2 a day for the subsistence of that family. If they are deprived of their work, what are they going to do? [1, Vol. I, p. 480]

The adoption of more rigorous legislation against child labor by the states in the early years of the twentieth century, and by the Federal government in 1917, made such a "solution" more difficult and intensified the need for alternatives, such as a mothers' pension program.

Even during the period when it was acceptable for children to work, some widows or deserted mothers had children who were too young to work. In such instances, public outdoor relief and private charity were so inadequate that the children were frequently removed to an institution or foster home. One of the earliest mothers' pension laws, that of Illinois, passed in 1911, "was proposed by Judge Merritt W. Pinkney, of the Cook County Juvenile Court, because he found himself continually asked to take children from poor, but competent, mothers and commit them to institutions." [1, Vol. II, p. 230]

The trend toward such pensions was further influenced by the growing acceptance of the idea of adequate schooling for all children. The relationship between compulsory school laws and mothers' aid is indicated by the fact that as a state raised the age for compulsory school attendance, the age limits of eligible children in the mothers' aid programs were raised accordingly. As a matter of fact, Oklahoma contests

Illinois' claim of passage of the first statewide mothers' pension program, for in 1908 Oklahoma passed a "School Scholarship Law," providing payment to a widowed mother so as to enable her to keep her children in school.

The movement for aid to dependent children received great impetus from the first resolution adopted by the First White House Conference on Children in 1909:

Children should not be deprived of home life except for urgent and compelling reasons. Children of parents of worthy character, suffering from temporary misfortune, and children of reasonably efficient and deserving mothers, who are without the support of the normal breadwinner, should, as a rule, be kept with their parents, such aid being given as may be necessary to maintain suitable homes for the rearing of children. Except in unusual circumstances, the home should not be broken up for reasons of poverty but only for considerations of inefficiency or immorality. [114, p. 32]

The relationship between the income maintenance problem faced by widows and separation of their children from the home was clearly established by a Massachusetts study that showed "that insufficient income of the mother and [the] mother's absence from the home at work were the two largest causes of separation of children from widowed mothers" and "that three-fifths of the children could have been maintained at home if finances for that purpose had been available." [79, p. 127]   According to a similar study undertaken in New York State,

It is a mockery upon the wealth and intelligence of the great Commonwealth of New York that there are at present in institutions at public expense over 2726 fatherless children committed for destitution only and 933 others committed for the illness of the widowed mother—which research proves, is [as] often the result, as the cause, of destitution. [79, pp. 128–29]

Another significant impetus came from the "child-saving" movement of the late nineteenth and twentieth centuries. [53; 105]   The movement focused on social control and the prevention of delinquency, but also stressed the relationship between family life and delinquency and encouraged the preservation of the family. Assistance to "fit and proper parents" in maintaining the home for the child was therefore encouraged as a delinquency prevention procedure.

As a result of the widespread concern with such situations, ten years after the adoption of the first mothers' pension law in 1911, forty states had such legislation. By the time of the Great Depression, Alabama,

Georgia, and South Carolina were the only states that did not have a mothers' aid pension program.

It is interesting that most social workers fought its development. They felt that relief programs under such sponsorship were bound to be inadequate and inefficient. The private voluntary agencies, which spoke for the profession at this time, maintained that a public program of assistance would help "pauperize" the poor by encouraging and perpetuating dependency. "Poverty" was a blameless misfortune experienced by the "deserving" poor; the pauper was a social deviant who had no statutory right to assistance. They therefore opposed "outdoor relief" —public grants to people in their own homes—even before it was proposed in the form of mothers' aid. [25, pp. 55–62]   They preferred that assistance be provided under the auspices of voluntary agencies which could impose "scientific" eligibility standards and follow-up controls to assure that the recipient would use the assistance "wisely" and be helped to become self-supporting. Available studies made clear, however, that the private agencies, even with support of public funds, could not adequately meet the needs of large numbers of economically deprived children [25, pp. 77–78]

In the programs instituted before the Great Depression, few states extended coverage to children of unmarried, divorced, or deserted mothers. Most restricted coverage to the children of widows or of incapacitated fathers. The laws were frequently administered by the courts, chiefly the juvenile courts; the age limit of the children to be assisted, and the amount of aid, varied from state to state. The laws were permissive, so that many counties authorized to grant such aid did not actually do so. This was particularly true in the states that did not share expenses of the program with local communities. In some states (Arkansas, Mississippi, and New Mexico), although legislation had been passed, the programs were largely inoperative. "Not only was coverage sporadic but in the prosperous 1920's maximum grants were at subsistence or less than subsistence levels." [25]   In 1926 mothers' aid maximum grants ranged from a low of $348 a year in such states as New Jersey, Texas, and Rhode Island to a high of $840 a year in such states as California, Michigan, and Connecticut. In 1931 only about 90,000 families were receiving aid under the mothers' pension law, states like Maryland and Virginia having fewer than 200 families on aid. Over 95 percent of the assisted mothers were white and about 85 percent were widows. [132, pp. 395–96]

Conceptions of the program also varied. In some states, the program was designed to compensate children for the loss of a father; in others, it was designed to compensate the mother for the care of the child as her right for service rendered to the community.

The Great Depression imposed a growing burden on the programs, which eventually resulted in the virtual collapse of many. Thus a report on the status of the mothers' pension program in Michigan in 1936 notes:

> The limited resources of some counties, combined with the financial pressure of the last five years, made it impossible for many counties to maintain adequate standards and in certain areas led to the discontinuance of all payments. This collapse of provision for mothers' aid came at a time when the need was greater than ever before, since many mothers who might have remained independent in normal times, had suffered through loss of investments and savings and the absence of normal work opportunities . . . as early as November 1933, 34 counties which had formerly granted pensions had discontinued all grants. [1, Vol. II, p. 273]

Federal participation in these programs was initiated in 1933, with the institution of Work Relief and Home Relief programs administered by the states but financed through the Federal Emergency Relief Administration. These were, however, temporary measures. A more formalized long-range program was necessary, and growing demand for Federal participation in the mothers' pension program culminated with the passage of the Social Security Act in 1935. This included provisions for the formal establishment of Federal grants to the states for Aid to Dependent Children as one of three categories of public assistance established in Title IV of the Act.

Administration

At the Federal level, the Assistance Payments Administration (a branch of the Social and Rehabilitation Service of the Department of Health, Education, and Welfare) administers the program and develops policy for AFDC. Through regional offices throughout the United States it provides general administrative direction and coordination of the program:

1. It assures that Federal grants are disbursed, and used, in compliance with Federal legislation.
2. It assists states in applying Federal requirements to their programs.
3. It works with states to improve the AFDC program.
4. It collects data on the program's operations and on problems related to the program.
5. It improves public understanding of the program and coordinates the activities of the program with related programs.

The agency also offers consultation to the states, reviews and evaluates state programs, and develops program policies and standards to ensure efficient operation of the program.

The Social Security Act provides for Federal participation through Federal grants-in-aid to the states. If the state offers financial assistance to families of dependent children, the Federal government must partially reimburse the states. However, for the states to be eligible for such reimbursement, their assistance programs must meet Federal requirements:

1. All persons should have the right to apply for assistance, and aid should be made available with reasonable promptness if the applicant is eligible.
2. Applicants found ineligible for assistance must be given an opportunity for appeal through a fair hearing.
3. Uniform standards regarding methods of determining need and amount of assistance must be established throughout the state. The program must be available to applicants in every part of the state. This protects against discrimination and assures that applicants in similar circumstances will be accorded similar treatment.
4. Most information which the applicant shares with the agency must be kept confidential.
5. Assistance should be in the form of money payments and the person has the right to determine how best to use the income. This permits the recipient to manage his own affairs and enables him to shop without being differentiated from other members of the community (as would be the case with a voucher grant).

To ensure efficient administration of the program,

1. A single state agency must be set up to administer the program.
2. Personnel standards for employees of the program must be based on the civil service merit system.
3. Records must be maintained and periodic reports made.

Such requirements are designed to protect the public and emphasize accountability for proper operation. An additional requirement, in an amendment to the Social Security Act adopted in 1950, was designed to protect the public from abuse of the program. Known as the NOLEO (Notice to Law Enforcement Officers) amendment, it stipulates that state payments to children who have been deserted or abandoned by their fathers will not be reimbursed by the Federal government unless state public assistance agencies have reported the missing fathers to appropriate law enforcement officers.

A state organizes a plan for administration of its assistance program and submits it for approval to the Federal government. If the plan is approved, the state is authorized to receive Federal reimbursement. The relative distribution of cost of the program varies from year to year, but generally the Federal government contributes about 57 percent of the total cost; the states, 33 percent; and local governments, counties, and cities, about 10 percent. Federal reimbursement covers a percentage of the direct assistance payments and medical expenses, and state expenditure for administration of the program (which includes cost of social service).

The grants-in-aid formula has been modified several times since the passage of the Social Security Act. Generally, the changes have served to increase Federal financial participation in the program.

The Federal share ranges from 50 percent in states with high per capita income to about 65 percent in states with low per capita income. This difference in the extent to which the Federal government will assist the state in meeting the AFDC budget is known as the *variable-grant provision*. The variable-grant provision was adopted to meet the problem resulting from the fact that AFDC payments tend to be lowest in states with below-average per capita income and that such states tend to have a higher proportion of needy children. Thus the need for assistance is greatest in those states least able to pay the cost of it. The variable-grant formula provides for a larger share of Federal participation in those states faced with this problem.

There have also been changes in Federal reimbursement to the states for the cost of administration of the program. This has resulted from an explicit attempt to reorient the program from an income maintenance program, to an income maintenance and social service program, and currently to an income maintenance and employment training and placement program.

In 1962 the focus of the AFDC program was revised to emphasize social services as a significant component of the program along with income maintenance. In signing the legislation which implemented this shift in focus President Kennedy said:

> This measure embodies a new approach—stressing services in addition to support, rehabilitation instead of relief, and training for useful work instead of prolonged dependency. This important legislation will assist our state and local public welfare agencies to redirect the incentives and services they offer to needy families and children and to aged disabled people. Our objective is to prevent or reduce dependency and to encourage self-care and self-support; to maintain family life where it is adequate and to restore it where it is deficient. . . . Public welfare, in short, must be more than a salvage operation picking up the debris of human life. [136, p. 1]

Before the 1962 amendments, the Federal government paid half of the total amounts spent by the state for administration of services. The 1962 amendments increased Federal financial participation to 75 percent of the cost of providing those self-care and self-support services which the Secretary of the Department of Health, Education, and Welfare prescribes, and other services specified as likely to prevent or reduce dependency, and 75 percent of the costs of training staff to administer public assistance programs.

To be eligible for such increased reimbursements, the state must provide for each child whatever services are needed in view of his home conditions and other problems or circumstances. AFDC services must be coordinated with public child welfare services so that all possible and appropriate help reaches each dependent child. Caseloads must be cut to permit workers to offer more effective services.

By 1967 rehabilitation through casework was replaced by rehabilitation through work training and job placement. The 1967 Amendments to the Social Security Act called for a Work Incentive Program (WIN) which provided for training and job placement of AFDC recipients.

By 1971–72 many states perceived the social service provision as a source of extra welfare funds from the Federal government. With the Federal government contributing $75 for every $25 the states spent, social services were cynically defined "as anything you can get 75 percent for" and almost every client-oriented worker activity was listed as a social service. By August 1972 it was estimated that grants to states for social service for fiscal year 1972 would run to $4.8 billion (*The New York Times*, August 9, 1972). As a consequence Congress in October 1972 shifted from unlimited Federal matching of state expenditures to a limit of $2.5 billion of Federal aid.

Although the Federal government offers consultation, guidance, stimulation, and money, administration of the program is a state responsibility. The state's decision to operate an AFDC program with Federal participation is a voluntary one. The state continues to administer the program, determines whether or not local governments will share in the financing, and determines the level of assistance payments and the scope and coverage of the program. Thus the program remains consonant with the particular state's capacities and objectives.

All this makes for wide variations throughout the country, particularly in eligibility standards and the amount of assistance. The Federal government makes no attempt to assure that children in different states will be treated equally, nor that the grants will be large enough to provide the minimum necessities of life.

The AFDC program, according to the Social Security Act, is set up to aid "needy" children under eighteen years of age who have been "deprived of parental support or care by reasons of the death, continued absence from the home, or physical or mental incapacity of the parents." In 1961 Congress added another condition for eligibility: dependency due to the unemployment of the father (AFDC-U).

States may choose to provide coverage for only some of these contingencies. For example, by the end of 1972, only twenty-six states had extended coverage to dependent children because of the father's unemployment. Opposition to the measure has stemmed from the fact that, although the Federal government is ready to participate, some part of the expense of the program will have to be borne by the states. In some states it was felt that the problem of the unemployed father was not sufficiently severe to warrant inclusion of another category in the AFDC program.

The states can also restrict eligibility in any category. For instance, the definition of *unemployment* varies from state to state. In those states that have passed implementing legislation for AFDC-U, some exclude seasonal workers, the self-employed, and so on. [135]   The definition of *physical or mental incapacity of the parent* can vary so as to exclude, in some states, parents who might be eligible in another state. Some states set no residence requirements; others require a year's residence before an applicant is eligible. Some states have a waiting period of three months in cases of desertion before the family is eligible, to eliminate cases where the father deserts but returns home within a relatively short period of time. States may set the age of the child who is eligible for help so that one state gives aid to needy children under twenty-one, whereas another state might offer aid only to needy children under eighteen.

Whatever the problem—death, desertion, separation, divorce, incapacity, unemployment—and however it is defined, the child and the family are not eligible unless they are "needy." However, the determination of "need" is left to the state. *Need* is defined as the gap between the total cost of living essentials set by the state and the family's income from all sources.

To identify the gap, a budget is computed that includes essentials of living—food, rent, a clothing allowance, and fuel. If the income of the family, from all and any sources, is equal to, or greater than, the budget computed, the family is deemed not to be in need. If the family's income is less than the computed budget, the family is eligible for assistance, and the amount of the grant is equal to the difference between the income and the computed budget. In addition to providing for the budgeted items, the agency pays the medical and pharmaceutical expenses for members of the family. (These are paid directly to the doctor and the pharmacist.)

Items included in the budget, and the level of liberality with which budgets are computed, vary from state to state. For instance, in December 1972 the average monthly payment to an AFDC recipient was $14.41 in Mississippi and $81.24 in Wisconsin.

In summary, then, AFDC is an assistance program financed by Federal, state, and local governments. Federal requirements, enforced through the sanction of grants-in-aid, have resulted in some basic uniformity in the program throughout the United States, but because the program is administered by the states, there is still considerable variation from state to state.

Situations for Which AFDC Is an Appropriate Resource

The situations for which AFDC is an appropriate resource are limited by the eligibility requirements of the program. Table 5–1 indicates the major crisis situations that have led to the application for AFDC and the percentage of families that have applied because of the particular contingency. The data are for the month of January 1971.

TABLE 5–1.   Families Receiving AFDC (1971)

Status of Father	Percentage of Families Receiving AFDC
Dead	4.3
Incapacitated	9.8
Unemployed	6.1
Other status	3.4
Alive but absent from home	76.2
Not married to mother	27.7
Separated	15.8
Deserted	15.2
Divorced	14.2
Imprisoned	2.1
Absent for other reasons	1.2

If the three categories that reflect family disruption—desertion, separation, and divorce—are combined, they account for about 45 percent of all of the cases. Because "need" is also a requirement, it is not surprising that in most of the cases the families had been living at a marginal economic level for a long time and that many parents had come from homes in which income was marginal. There was thus little opportunity to build economic reserves against crises precipitated by death, desertion, incapacity, and so on.

Scope

In December 1972 there were a total of about 11 million persons receiving assistance under the AFDC program. This includes about 8 million children plus their "caretakers"—generally their mothers. The program is, therefore, by far the largest single public welfare program in the United States affecting children. It is, perhaps, the only public welfare program affecting children that is available in every county of the United States. It is estimated that, since its inception, the program has helped over 100 million children to remain and grow up in their own home. At any given time, about 10 percent of all of the children in the United States are receiving AFDC, and about one out of every five children has received financial assistance and services under the AFDC program at some time or another during his life. This means that about 20 percent of all the children in the United States have been helped by AFDC at one time or another.

Between 1965 and 1972, the numbers of children receiving all, or part, of their maintenance from AFDC rose sharply and dramatically. In December 1965, some 4.4 million children and their mothers were receiving aid under the program; by December 1972, this had increased to 8 million children and 3 million parents, mostly mothers. The rate per thousand children under eighteen assisted rose from forty-five in 1965 to ninety in 1972. In the single month July–August 1970, AFDC recipients increased by 214,000—the largest monthly increase in the history of the program (see Fig. 5–1). Expenditures for such assistance rose from $1.7 billion in 1965 to $7 billion in 1972. Some of the increase is due of course to higher prices, but more than half of the increase was the result of expanded assistance caseloads, and somewhat more adequate assistance payments.

There was increasing public puzzlement over the continued, very sharp rise in the numbers and rate of AFDC recipients. The 1960's were a period of continuing high rate of prosperity and employment. Social Security was extended to cover more people and pay more benefits. The percentage of people living in poverty was slowly but consistently reduced. What factors then accounted for the rapid rise in the number of AFDC recipients? The following reasons have been advanced to explain the rapid expansion in the program in the late 1960's.

Eligibility for aid was broadened by changes in policy. AFDC-U, adopted as an emergency measure in 1961 to meet the consequences of rising unemployment, became a permanent part of the program.

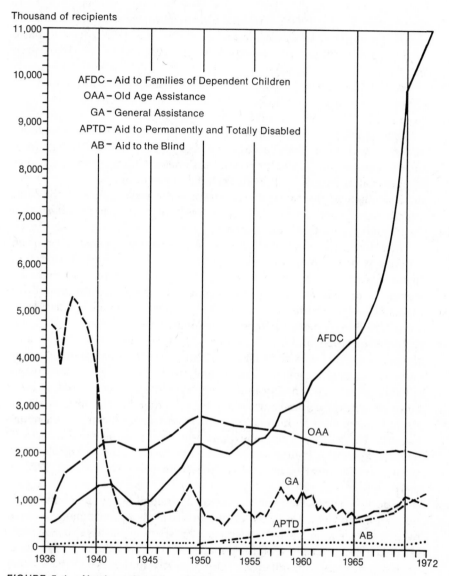

Thousand of recipients

FIGURE 5–1. Number of public assistance recipients of money payments by program: June and December of each year, 1936 to 1970, and through September 1972. (National Center for Social Statistics, Social and Rehabilitation Service, U.S. Department of Health, Education, and Welfare.)

Families with children whose father was in the home, but unemployed, could now be eligible for AFDC assistance. By the end of the decade, some twenty-six states had added AFDC-U, and assistance to unemployed parents accounted for 5 percent of the total caseload.

Similarly, AFDC-FC, assistance to children in foster care, was initiated early in the 1960's. A child placed in foster care for whom the AFDC program was responsible and who received AFDC prior to placement could continue to be supported by the program after placement.

As a consequence, some states transferred large numbers of foster children from programs financed with other funds to AFDC, and again the number of recipients increased.

Liberalization of the program by Congressional action in the 1960's also extended other kinds of coverage. Congress increased the age range of children eligible for Federal reimbursement. Children up to 21 years of age, if attending school, were declared eligible. In 1962 a change was made to include the father in the grant if he were living in the home and if family dependency was the result of the father's physical or mental incapacity or unemployment.

Increases in benefit levels further acted to include in the programs families which had previously been ineligible. The 1967 amendments to the Social Security Act required that all states reappraise their cost standards to reflect changes in prices and to make appropriate adjustments in their definition of *need* by July 1969. As a result, benefit levels were raised, and more families were covered by the program.

Between 1963 and 1971 average AFDC payments increased more rapidly than the increase in wages. [77, p. 14]   In some states the total value of all possible benefits came close to the earnings of low-income wage-earners. "The measurable value of belonging to the public assistance system for a family of four with no other income in Chicago (in 1971) was equal to an income received from full-time work at an hourly wage of $2.30. . . . The same female-headed four-person family with no earnings could receive in cash payments, food stamps, or surplus commodity and medical benefits about $4938 in New York City." [77, pp. 3–4]

Court decisions have made previously ineligible groups eligible. The U.S. Supreme Court declared unconstitutional two provisions which had been widely employed by the states to restrict eligibility: the one-year residence requirement and the "man-in-home" regulation. The denial of assistance (in some nineteen states) to any family which had a man living in the house or visiting the mother regularly was based on the assumption that such an able-bodied male was a "father substitute" who could be expected to support the children. The Court decided that for purposes of AFDC eligibility only those men who had a legal obligation to support the children—that is, their real fathers or their mother's husband—could be treated as "parents." Thousands of families, by virtue of this ruling, became eligible for assistance.

The Supreme Court rulings reflected the development during the 1960's of a new specialization in law which concerned itself with laws and administrative procedures affecting the poor. [39; 50; 116]   The result of these activities was to increase the flow of eligible applicants for AFDC.

These efforts were supplemented by the organized activities of the welfare recipients themselves. The Welfare Rights Organization, established in 1967, distributed information to families technically eligible for assistance, but who had not applied, informing them of their rights to assistance and actively helping them to make application. Representatives of the Welfare Rights Organization stationed themselves near or in public welfare offices to advise applicants about procedure and rights. Their efforts were reinforced by the greater tendency on the part of the casework staff to accept applications. Studies in eleven major cities revealed that "the extent of utilization of AFDC by the city's poor population was associated positively with the rate of caseworker turnover, the relative youth of caseworkers, and the caseworkers' recipient orientation and inversely with caseworkers 'professionalism.' The evidence is persuasive that caseworkers can ration welfare" on the basis of their attitudes toward the applicants. [77, p. 13]

Between 1960 and 1970 the proportion of applicants accepted for aid by caseworkers rose sharply. [77, p. 12]

The widespread discussion of poverty and welfare policy during the 1960's made more people aware of such programs. The "discovery" of poverty, the establishment of the Office of Economic Opportunity, and the development of community action councils in low-income neighborhoods called attention to the assistance program and increased the readiness and willingness to apply on the part of those eligible.

Medicaid, and the realization that paid medical care was available to AFDC recipients, prompted additional numbers of people to apply.

The war against poverty reduced the number of white two-working-parents families below the poverty level, but had less effect on nonwhite families and very little effect on female-headed families. Hence, whatever positive changes were taking place in the poverty picture, they had little impact on the group of families that formed the pool of AFDC applicants. The sharp increase in the cost of living in the 1960's meant that such families fell further and further behind. The fact is that only a limited number of poor families apply for and receive public assistance; most of the families struggle to maintain themselves even on marginal and subsistence incomes without aid. [95, pp. 216–17] But this also means that there are many families who can, by a slight change of circumstances, be precipitated from precarious independence to a need for assistance.

Even if the percentage of those receiving assistance remained the same throughout the 1960's, the very increase in population would have produced an increase in the number of people receiving assistance. During the 1960's the young adult population most likely to need AFDC increased more rapidly than any other age group.

Also, increases in the rates of divorce and illegitimacy meant an increase in the number of family disruptions, and a consequent increase in the number of families eligible for assistance. Furthermore, work incentive amendments permitted disregard of some percentage of earned income in order that some families might continue to receive aid who would otherwise have been ineligible for continued support. They, therefore, remained on the rolls, increasing the number of recipients.

In attempting to assess the relative importance of these factors Gordon examined the welfare situation in New York City. Analyzing income distribution in the city, changes in welfare policy, and changes in grant levels in particular, he concludes that:

> the largest source of increase in welfare stemmed from the increase
> in real grant levels (which increased the number of people eligible
> for aid), that changes in the income distribution accounted for a
> smaller share, and that those eligible for welfare showed no greater
> propensity to join the rolls. . . . The cause of the welfare "crisis"
> is simply the widespread poverty in the city—not chiseling or
> welfare rights organizations or liberal administrative policy. [42,
> pp. 83, 87]

Process in the AFDC Program

Intake and Eligibility

In 1971 the statistically typical AFDC Jones family consisted of a mother, thirty-one, and three children, one under six, one between six and thirteen, and one between thirteen and eighteen years of age. The father is absent from the home rather than ill or dead. The family lives in an urban area and, since 51 per cent of all recipients were nonwhite, there is a slightly better than even chance that the Jones family is nonwhite. The mother has had ten years of education, but did not complete high school (only 19 percent of AFDC recipients are high school graduates). She is probably not employed (only 14 percent of the AFDC mothers are employed full- or part-time, and only 7 percent are enrolled in the Work Incentive program).

Mrs. Jones did not apply for assistance immediately after trouble struck, but made an effort to remain independent by utilizing the family's limited personal and financial resources. [14; 44] In a little more than five months, Mrs. Jones exhausted those resources and applied to the Department of Public Welfare in the county where she resides. The first interview focused on her "presumptive" eligibility and reviewed the general factors in her situation that determined her eligibility. Having been deserted or divorced or separated, and having three children under the age of eighteen, all attending school, Mrs. Jones was presumed eligible for assistance under the program. However, every state has a number of other eligibility requirements that must be satisfied. Because this is an assistance program, Mrs. Jones had to prove that the family was in need—that its income, from whatever source, was less than the standard budget computed by the state. If there was some income (let us say that Mrs. Jones was receiving some support from her divorced husband), but the amount was $20 a month less than the computed budget, she would be eligible for the difference and would receive a total AFDC grant of $20. If Mrs. Jones had an insurance policy of sizable cash surrender value, it would have to be converted, as would any valuable real property. This would apply, however, to few applicants. A study in California showed that only 4.4 percent of AFDC families has as much as $300 in personal property (automobiles, life insurance policies, and cash or readily convertible securities). Only 2.1 percent of the cases had real property that might have been used to decrease their public assistance need. [24, p. 44].   Generally, an applicant is permitted to keep a car or a phone only if it is necessary for transportation or health.

If it is established that Mrs. Jones' income, from all sources, is short of the basic budget, there are still additional considerations before the family's eligibility is acknowledged. If Mrs. Jones is applying because her husband deserted her, she is required to charge him with abandonment so that legal efforts can be made to obtain support. And if Mrs. Jones is in a position to take a job without injuring her health or neglecting her home or children, the agency may require her to find work as a condition of offering assistance. If Mrs. Jones has relatives who are legally responsible for, and capable of, supporting her, she may be denied assistance.

After the first office interview, a visit to the home would generally be made. Mrs. Jones would be required to produce documentary proof of eligibility—birth certificates proving the children's ages and establishing the fact that she is indeed their mother, her marriage certificate, proof of residence, canceled bank books, insurance policies, rent receipts, utility bills, and information regarding income from any sources. Mrs. Jones is encouraged to take the initiative in providing the documentation necessary to support the application but if, for any reason, she has difficulty in obtaining any of the documents, the caseworker stands ready to help her.

Eligibility, once established, must be periodically reaffirmed. Any change in the client's situation—if the husband returns, if the mother remarries, if the absent father starts making payments, if money is

earned by Mrs. Jones or any of the children—must be reported immediately to the agency so that the budget may be revised accordingly.
Eligibility is, therefore, a continuing concern of the program administrators.

These initial interviews also deal with other important matters. An
attempt is made to help Mrs. Jones resolve any conflicts she may have
regarding her application for assistance. An assessment is made, with
client participation, of alternatives either considered by the client or
suggested by the worker. As a result, resources for support occasionally
come to light about which the client has not been aware. Any problems
faced by the family, in addition to that of income maintenance, are clarified. The AFDC program and agency policy are interpreted, as clearly as
possible, in terms of their applicability to the situation faced by Mrs.
Jones.

If Mrs. Jones can satisfy all of the conditions of eligibility, her children are less than eighteen years of age (or less than twenty-one years
of age if attending school), her husband is absent from the home, the
family is in need as defined by the state, she has charged her husband
with abandonment, and she is ready to accept suitable employment. How
much assistance can she hope to receive if she is receiving no income
from any source?

Each agency has a budget sheet based on data supplied by home
economists. A food budget is computed for each child and for Mrs.
Jones. The food budget varies with the age of the child, so that that of a
fifteen-year-old boy is greater than that of a five-year-old boy. Rent is
included on an as-paid basis, although some of the states set a limit on
how much they will allow. Clothing allowances are included although
these, too, vary with age. Fuel and electricity are also included, as well
as some basic household items, which vary from state to state.

The average national monthly financial payment per AFDC family
in December 1972 was $191.17 per month. Mrs. Jones, head of the
average AFDC family, would receive for herself and her three children
a total monetary grant of about $191.17 a month or about $2300 a year.
The "poverty index," established by the Federal government, described
a city family consisting of mother and three dependent children as "in
poverty" if their income in 1972 was less than about $4200 per year
(or about $350 per month). The Jones family, living on their average
AFDC income, would then be far below the poverty level. Some of the
gap is reduced by medical assistance and food stamps, which are in
addition to the monthly grant.

Although the amount computed for the assistance budget is very
modest, in many states the family will not receive even that amount.
Some states have set a maximum on the amount of money they will
grant a family, regardless of need, so that not all AFDC families are
granted the amount required to meet the budget as computed by the

agency. The average amount of recognized unmet need for AFDC families in January 1971 was $29.72 per month.

Some extent of the level of deprivation experienced by children in AFDC families is suggested by the responses to a nationwide questionnaire sent to such families: 30 percent of the mothers replied there were not enough beds for everyone in the family; 25 percent of the families lack enough furniture for everyone to sit down together for a meal; in 17 percent of the families children had stayed home from school at one time or another because they did not have shoes or clothes. [41] More detailed studies of the living situation of particular AFDC families emphasize the same depressing, spirit-corroding living situation— crowded, dilapidated housing and barely adequate meals. [3; 11; 29; 74]

Thus, having overcome the barrier of eligibility, the Jones family has to contend with an even more formidable hurdle: the continuing problem of survival on the grant allotted. Mrs. Jones may improve her position by working part-time. Allowance is made for lunches, equipment, clothing needed for work, transportation, and child care, so the sum covering these expenses is not deducted from her grant. But because these are additional expenditures that result from Mrs. Jones' having accepted employment, there is no net gain in family income. The first thirty dollars of her earnings and one-third of the remainder are excluded from the computation of her budget. Such a change in procedure, adopted in 1967, is designed as a work incentive.

Mrs. Jones receives some additional kinds of support under the program. All recipients are eligible for either food stamps or free food. A dollar's worth of food stamps can be exchanged for more than a dollar's worth of food so the stamps stretch family income, and limited varieties of foodstuffs are available free under the commodity distribution program. In addition, Mrs. Jones and her children are provided free medical care, direct payment being made to doctors and pharmacists by the local Department of Public Welfare.

Problems Requiring Services

In addition to money, medical or remedial care, food or food stamps, a fourth kind of assistance comes in the form of social services. Every study points to the fact that the AFDC families have multiple problems —child-care problems, personal and family problems, health problems, economic problems, home management problems, housing problems, and so on. [14; 44; 46; 69; 71; 76; 103; 120]

Financial need itself has several consequences. The family with limited income has fewer real choices in planning life in the present and in the future; its range of social and recreational activities is limited. Members of such families feel less adequate, more vulnerable, more submissive than others; they lose their sense of self-esteem and self-respect.

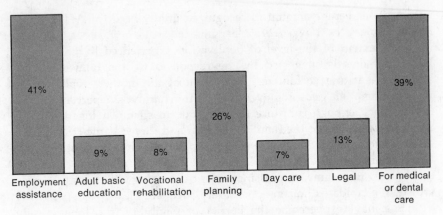

FIGURE 5–2. AFDC families receive a wide variety of services (for 1970). (U.S. Department of Health, Education, and Welfare.)

Some feel a sense of isolation from others, a fear of rejection as "free loaders," "welfare chiselers." Many such families live on the fringes of society, reflecting society's contempt for, and rejection of, them.

There are some problems that the AFDC family shares with many families on all income levels—problems of emotional disturbances in children and marital maladjustment; some it shares with other low-income family groups—problems of housing, medical care, money management. Some, however, are more or less peculiarly typical of the AFDC family and therefore may require the special understanding and the special help of the social worker.

One of the principal social problems faced by the AFDC family is the fact that it is generally a fatherless family. The primary effect of fatherlessness and husbandlessness on the family group is, of course, the necessity of adjusting to living on a reduced income (see Chap. 2). It is the loss of income that causes the family to apply for AFDC. But the absence of father-husband has more far-reaching consequences than the loss of income. Other aspects of his paternal role are uncovered, or inadequately covered, and the children suffer as a result. Some of the effects on the children are indirect: they are consequences of the effects of husband deprivation on the mother. In the one-parent family headed by a woman, some of the mother's most basic needs are denied. [68; 85; 153]

1. *Emotional support.* The mother is denied a socially sanctioned source of affection. Even though the marital relationship may have had conflicts, there were times when the wife-mother could turn to the husband-father and receive some support.
2. *Socially sanctioned sexual satisfaction.* Despite conflicts, the presence

of the husband-father in the home permitted occasional release from sexual tension—a satisfaction now denied the mother except through guilt-producing illicit channels.

3. *A companion for leisure-time activities.* Social life, beyond adolescence, is organized by couples. The single woman is difficult to fit in; she feels odd, is regarded as a "fifth wheel," and is not readily invited. The social role of the husbandless mother, of the divorcée, is an ambiguous one. In some respects the single-mother status is a minority-group status with some of the difficulties this implies socially. One of the recurrent complaints expressed by the husbandless mother is that of loneliness and social isolation.

4. *Help in caring for the home.* The mother is denied help in performing household chores and repairs normally delegated to the father. The mother now has to assume the burden of fixing, repairing, keeping accounts, paying the bills, lifting and hauling, and so on. The sheer mechanics of keeping a family and living quarters in operating condition becomes greatly complicated in the absence of a father-husband.

5. *Help in the routine care of the children.* Most husbands share some of the responsibility for child care, shopping, and covering for the mother when she is ill or indisposed. Now the total unrelieved burden of a twenty-four-hour day, seven-day week care of the children falls on the mother. She is the sole caretaker, the sole disciplinarian, the sole provider of affection, in health and in illness.

6. *Help in sharing the burden of responsibility for making significant decisions regarding the children and the home.* As one husbandless mother said: "Twenty-four hours a day, I have to decide what to do, what not to do, what's right for us, what's wrong for us, without help of anyone. I am just one person but I have to work and worry for two." [31, p. 19]

The deprivations suffered and the additional burdens imposed on the husbandless mother often result in a kind of chronic physical and emotional fatigue. Anxious and heavily burdened, the mother has less time, less physical and emotional energy to make available to the children. Thus, some of the impact on the children of the father-husband's absence is the indirect consequence of the impact of such absence on the mother. The children are required to carry some part of the mother's burden of unhappiness.

It is also felt by the children in the mother's changed emotional relationship to them. The single mother is apt to feel guilty toward the children because they are deprived of a father; hence, she tends to become overprotective, overanxious, more permissive, in an attempt to "make it up" to them. "The trouble with single parents," one child said, "is that they are afraid to say 'no.' They feel guilty, the kid knows it, and he can sometimes persuade a parent to let him do almost anything he wants to." [31, p. 151]

Meeting the child's needs means putting aside one's own needs, but doing this means further self-deprivation. If the mother does accept the frustration of her own needs, she develops a feeling of hostility toward the child, which leads to guilt and further discomfort.

Deprived of affection, the mother may exploit the children's emotional resources. The children, in such instances, have to "make it up" to the mother for the deprivation she suffers. In the father-husband's absence, a mother may turn more often to the children, especially the male child, for expressions of love and affectional response normally received from the father. Conversely, the mother may identify the child, particularly the boy, with the absent parent and some of the hostility toward the father-husband, an unavailable target, may be expressed directly against the child. She may demand a reallocation of roles and ask him to accept the burden of discharging some of the responsibilities left uncovered by the father's absence. This might result in denying the boy some of his childhood and imposing on him a kind of pseudo-maturity. [81, p. 258]

Or, the mother may have many conflicting feelings about her relationship with the absent father. This depends to some extent on the reason for his absence. If he is dead, and the relationship was a good one, there is a feeling of grief and mourning which must be lived through. There is, however illogical, a feeling of resentment at being deserted. If the father is absent because of divorce, separation, or actual desertion, the mother might feel some guilt about her possible contribution to the marital failure. There is the constant hope and anxiety that the father might return. Death is final; divorce, separation, and desertion always leave the possibility of reconciliation. Hostility and bitterness toward the absent parent may be communicated to the children and generalized—"men are no good," "don't trust men," and so on. There is a sense of personal failure, a suspicion of personal inadequacy at the inability to succeed in the most personal of all relationships—marriage. [36, p. 47] In divorce, separation, desertion, or imprisonment, the mother is also faced with the problem of explaining the father's absence to the children in a manner that has fewest negative psychological consequences.

The children themselves also face some direct consequences of their father's absence. For one thing, they are denied a source of male sex role identification. The father serves as a model to the boy; he provides some opportunity for the girl to sharpen her own sex role identification by practicing reciprocal role behavior with a member of the opposite sex. Identification involves more than exposure to examples of male behavior; it involves an emotional commitment to the "teacher" and an emotional disposition to emulate him.

The fatherless child also loses a source of discipline and socialization. The father is generally the firmer disciplinarian and representative of the world outside the home. He tends to bring into the socialization process the tenets of the wider community, of the world of work.

The fatherless child also loses the emotional support of another parent. The child who depends on one parent for satisfaction of emotional needs is in a precarious position. It is imperative that he maintain a good relationship with the sole source of supply. Having two parents makes the child feel more secure and less anxious of pleasing either parent. Having temporarily angered one parent, he can turn to the other parent for emotional support. The resources at the child's disposition are less meager and the threat of failure to obtain needed emotional support is not so great. The hostility and aggression that every child occasionally feels toward the parent are likely to be inhibited, and ultimately repressed, where there is dependence on one parent for affectional needs; expressing such hostility poses too much of a threat to the child.

The fatherless child also loses the companionship of a father. Going places, doing things, talking and joking with a father are a source of considerable satisfaction for the child, part of the joy of living. Having two parents permits variety in companionship and activities. It permits more diversification and more complexity in adult-child relationships. This is denied the fatherless child.

Lack of a father makes it impossible for the child to engage in some of the symbolic rituals in which his peers enthusiastically participate— Father's Day, proud recital of their father's occupational activities, and so on. It intensifies the sense of difference between the child and his peers.

Children feel deserted and abandoned at the death of a father. They might feel rejection and some sense of guilt at having contributed to the parent's leaving in cases of divorce, separation, or desertion. They might feel that if they had been "better" children, perhaps the father would have remained. The child is faced with a conflict of loyalties between the mother and the absent father and confusion as to how he should feel toward the father. The father's absence permits an unrealistic idealization of him, an image uncorrupted by exposure to the unpleasant realities of day-to-day living.

The nature of the problem posed for the children by the father's absence depends, of course, on the age of the child. Loss of the father when the male child is between three and six is, supposedly, anxiety-provoking because it fulfills the child's Oedipal wish to get rid of the father so that he might possess the mother. Loss of the father during early adolescence, when the child is faced with the problem of consolidating and integrating a stable sexual identification, intensifies problems for the child.

All this tells us something about what the family loses when it loses a father-husband. As Hill says,

> [The father is] . . . manifestly much more than a meal ticket. He is a source of companionship, is confidant and friend to the mother and children. He provides security against crises, supplies intimate masculine response to all members, and is particularly necessary to keep the mother normal and happy. [56]

And it tells us about the kinds of interpersonal problems with which many of the one-parent, fatherless, AFDC families may need help.

Although it might be suggested that there are, for many children, father-substitutes available in the extended family and in the community, an interview study with AFDC mothers in Chicago indicated that "70 percent of the mothers said that no man did things with, or for, their children that were usually done by a father." [103, p. 83] Another study of a sample of 515 families with 1280 children in Maine found that in only "about a third of the homes some male is participating in caring for the children and in recreational activities with them." [120, p. 12]

It is clear, then, that the AFDC family presents some characteristic social problems affecting children and deriving from the unusual social organization of the family which leaves a key social role uncovered. It is for help with such problems that social service is offered to the AFDC family.

Of course, not all AFDC families need, or want, social services. Some can, and do, manage without such help, so an adequate monthly check is all they need from the agency. Fatherlessness is not necessarily productive of pathology, and studies on the functioning of the single-parent family, summarized by Herzog and Sudia [55] and Kadushin [63], indicate that in many instances the family adequately copes with the problem of fatherlessness, so that the children grow up to become adequately functioning adults. There are other families, however, that do need, and can use, social services.

An analogous statement might be made regarding the needs of adults in AFDC families. There was a gradual shift in social work orientation during the 1960 decade, so that greater emphasis is currently placed on the contribution of pathology in the social system to the situation of the AFDC family. This was, in general, a desirable corrective to a previously unwarranted overemphasis on the pathology of the recipient families as the sole or principal factor in accounting for their difficulties. Like many corrections, however, it generates its own errors.

While *many* AFDC families find themselves on welfare because of failings and imperfections in the social system—discrimination, structural unemployment, unjust distribution of income and resources—*some* recipients are on welfare partly because of the personal, physical, and/or psychological difficulties they bring to their situation. A study in California carefully compared 600 welfare families with a group of 600 nonwelfare families matched for income, ethnic origins, and family composition.

> [The families on welfare] showed the highest percentage of ill health and lack of skill as barriers to work. . . . They were high on psychological dependency and high in anomie. . . . The data from the attitude tests suggest that personality factors and present conditions of life probably interact in producing the long-term aid case. His outlook is characterized by a strong inner feeling of dependency and a high degree of hopelessness and alienation. [128, pp. 198–99]

The researchers conclude:

> The provision of increased employment opportunities for the very low-status worker is a necessary but not sufficient condition to alter the feedback cycle which is the true cause of welfare dependency. Social, psychological, and health factors that narrow the worker's flexibility of response and lower her capacity to deal with crises also need to be altered if any large-scale reduction in welfare dependency is to be expected. [128, p. 247]

While this does not, obviously, argue against the need for changes in the social system, it calls attention to the need for concomitant efforts to help individuals to change so that they can more adequately take advantage of changes in the social system. One can, then, repeat in an altered context what was noted above—that while many AFDC families might be able to manage with a monthly check, the provision of employment training and job placement, and so on, some AFDC families might need, and want, a more personalized social service.

Social Service in the AFDC Program

Service, in AFDC, has been defined as purposeful help provided to individuals and families with financial and social difficulties to find, and effectively use, resources in themselves and in the community. It is an attempt to motivate the client to do something constructive about his situation, to help him decide what he wants to do, to assist him in doing it, and to support and encourage him while he is engaged in making such changes. In the context of child welfare social work, it means maintaining and strengthening the ability of the parents to implement their role responsibilities in the physical, social, and emotional care, protection, and support of their children.

The worker may attempt to help mother and children with any of the consequences of fatherlessness. He may attempt to help with maintaining ties with the absent father, with effecting a reconciliation between the parents, or with getting the absent parent to agree to some support payments. The worker may help with these or with any other problems the family might face. A report of a project established to give service to AFDC families by trained caseworkers, working with a limited caseload, summarizes the help offered:

> Primarily what the workers did in their contacts was to provide a learning experience in which people were helped to deal more effectively with practical aspects of daily living. Although most of the families presented serious and complicated problems, the worker helped family members concentrate their sometimes limited capacities on solving one small and tangible problem at a time— one which had possibility of successful solution.
>
> Examples are help in consolidating debts and budgeting income, in getting children to school on time, in securing more adequate housing, in planning regular meals, in preparing for employment, and especially in getting medical care when needed. The latter was something most clients could see as of practical and immediate advantage to themselves. Moreover, adequate medical care helped restore physical energy badly needed to deal successfully with other problems.
>
> Besides its practical benefits, this kind of help in coping with everyday problems gave people experience in how it felt to be successful, and in how to use orderly methods of going about something in at least one specific area in their lives. Since "nothing succeeds like success," such experience, with the continuing help of the worker over a period of time, proved a considerable incentive for people to come to grips successively with other unsatisfactory aspects of their lives. [124, pp. 36–37]

As Meier says, "the best way to help a person *feel* more adequate is to help him *be* more adequate." [87, p. 20]

The worker helps by consistently demonstrating interest and concern in the client's problems. The assumption is that the client will respond to the interest and concern of the worker, that the interest and concern reflects the worker's evaluation of the client as a person of worth and importance, that this interest and concern can be best expressed—at least initially—by meeting the critical needs of the client. The worker is in a position to do this because there is a broad area of discretion in the administration of the grant which is limited only by the worker's willingness to extend himself on the client's behalf.

The following are some illustrations of such an approach from public welfare units offering casework services to AFDC families.

Mrs. S., divorced from her husband, with three small children, was suddenly cast in a situation she had not anticipated. As the sole parent in the family, she now was to be homemaker, supervising adult, and manager of the family affairs. The job was too much for her and the stresses of the job showed their mark through her poor management of the money made available to her through AFDC.

In other areas of adult functioning, she performed in an adequate manner. Upon exploration we found Mrs. S. a somewhat immature person who had previously depended heavily upon her husband. We faced with her realistically the fact that now it was necessary for her to learn how to manage on her own. We viewed her current situation as an opportunity for learning and provided the atmosphere and support through our supportive services and practical homemaking services through the agency homemaker. We allowed her to move at her own rate and develop her own potentials as she saw them.

We noted that, in the past, workers had attempted to convince her that with her family situation she could make arrangements for the care of her children and find employment in order to be independent of us. We also noted she had consistently resisted these efforts. She had real fears about leaving the home and going to work. She had never worked previously. She was married early in life and, as mentioned above, developed a strong dependency upon her husband. Rather than try to convince her of the capabilities for employment, we recognized and accepted with her the validity of her feelings and allowed her to feel completely comfortable in her dependency upon us. As she responded to our acceptance of her dependency and the services provided to strengthen her functioning, she demonstrated less fear of doing more for herself.

Eventually she was able to try employment through the County Works Project department. This was looked upon with her as a "sheltered workshop environment" whereby she could practice leaving the home and working. The experiences through this sheltered workshop situation gave her a feeling of confidence; and in fact, her fears dissipated quickly, for in a matter of months she was able to locate employment in a local industry. Her earnings were sufficient to cover her needs.

Although through this employment there was one less family

receiving financial assistance, the more important achievement
was that now we have a more self-confident person who is capable
of providing a more adequate adult figure to the three dependent
children in this home. [90, p. 11]

Mrs. J. applied for aid when her husband left home during an
acute alcoholic episode. She was too distressed to plan for her
future, but felt reconciliation would not work because of her
husband's long history of alcoholism. She expressed interest in
providing a better life for herself and her children. When Mr. J.
returned to the home they decided on separation, and he was
committed to a state hospital for treatment as an alcoholic. Frequent
interviews were arranged to support Mrs. J. through the crisis
and to help her consider her future. At first she alternated between
being demanding and in tears, but with the help of the worker she
was able to turn her attention to securing much needed medical
and dental care for the children. Later, she was able to think
through her feelings toward her husband and to view his condition
in a more objective manner. She began to plan toward his release
from the hospital and return home.

When Mr. J. was released, the agency provided new glasses
which relieved his persistent headaches. He joined Alcoholics
Anonymous. The agency referred him to California State
Employment Service, through which he found a job. Mrs. J.
supplemented his earnings through part-time evening work in a
restaurant (her working earlier had not been encouraged because she
was not then considered ready for it). Mrs. J. felt that with her
increased understanding of her husband's condition, with her
ability to accept more responsibility in the home, with the treatment
he had received in the hospital and the support of the AA, the
family would probably get along. After receiving services for three
months, this family was reunited and self-supporting. [124, p. 32]

These case reports reveal the personalized counseling aspects of
social services. Yet they also indicate that in helping the family it is
necessary that personalized counseling be supplemented by the employment of what has been termed *hard services*—helping the family by
providing "social utilities" such as homemaker service, day care, sheltered workshop experience, job placement. Personalized counseling is
further supplemented by helping the client with access to necessary
medical and dental care.

They are not typical, however, of casework contact with clients of
public welfare agencies. An interview study with some 800 AFDC clients
in six Wisconsin counties indicated that even when a family was a

"defined service case" workers rarely visited more than once every three months and visits were generally brief.

> [The evidence] strongly indicates a very low level of social services activity. . . . For the vast majority of AFDC families social service means a caseworker's visit a little more than once every three months, for a little less than forty minutes per visit with an occasional client's call to her caseworker. . . . The main social service activity is little more than a relatively infrequent, pleasant chat. It is somewhat supportive, it is rarely threatening, but also not too meaningful in the sense of either helping poor people get the things they need or changing the course of their lives. [52, pp. 126–27]

Studies also indicate that what the client more frequently wants from the social worker is not personalized counseling but more tangible kinds of help, such as income supplements, housing, health care, and jobs.

A 1967 nationwide mail questionnaire study of some 3000 AFDC recipients asked, "Besides giving you money, has welfare helped you in any other ways? In what other ways has welfare helped you?" [141] The noncash help most frequently cited by clients was tangible service—medical care (45 percent), clothing and household effects (22 percent), and surplus food (20 percent). Social and emotional support (cited by 14 percent of the clients) was defined as "welfare workers listening to, understanding advice about, and helping to solve problems; feeling of security, peace of mind, and moral support." A contact between worker and client once every two or three months was regarded as "often enough" by most clients—hardly enough for intensive casework; a third of the respondents, however, suggested more frequent contact.

The limited available data suggest that the service most AFDC clients want and see themselves as needing is, in effect, an extension, in kind, of income maintenance—medical care, food, clothing. Counseling services dealing with personal and family problems are important only to a small number of clients and an acceptable, but not very meaningful, adjunctive service to many of the clients. [12; 52; 106; 108; 109; 141; 154] A 1966 interview study with 1800 AFDC mothers in New York City showed that clients knew little of available social services other than income maintenance and medical care. [109] When particular topics and problem areas were discussed with the caseworker, the exchange seems to have been diffuse in nature. There was little hostility toward the system and the caseworkers, but also little confidence "in the capability of the system and its representatives to effect service and [in] the relevance of service to the client." [108, p. 72] While income maintenance, income supplements, and medical care had high priority, discussion of child behavior, child care, and the children's adjustment was a frequently offered service. [154, p. 53]

Workers are generally liked, respected, and trusted, and most clients feel that they can discuss their problems with their workers. Clients agree that workers try to help and, for the most part, really care about the welfare of their clients. When the family had contact with one worker over an extended period of time rather than a succession of different workers, and when interviews took place in the home, the worker-client relationship was regarded by the client as more satisfactory. Such clients were more likely to have discussed the children's adjustment with the worker. A single long home visit was regarded as more satisfactory than a series of short ones. [106; 108; 109]

Perhaps the lack of sharp need for counseling derives from the fact that many recipients are imbedded in a network of significant social relationships. When 1200 AFDC mothers were asked in a survey if there was "any one person you go to with your troubles and problems?" over half answered "yes" and the person was usually a friend or relative. Many of the mothers had relatives in the same city or the same neighborhood, and about 90 percent had a "best friend." There was a good deal of mutual aid in child care. [107, pp. 149–50] Primary group support is also clearly noted in an intensive study of the lives of AFDC recipients by a social worker who moved into a housing project to do a participant-observation study. [61]

For many of the AFDC mothers their neighborhood constitutes a social system through which they give and receive help of various kinds and through which they exchange information or misinformation about the vital social and economic processes of their daily lives. Neighbors helped each other in times of illness and in times of "troubles," caring for each other's children and lending and borrowing scarce resources; they shared information regarding child rearing, welfare, marketing, and homemaking, and they enjoyed recreational activities together—watching television, playing cards, shopping. This does not deny that some percentage of the families (approximately 30 percent) were poorly integrated into the neighborhood and were socially isolated.

The objectives of AFDC social services are stated in general terms—to "strengthen family life and enhance family stability, so that children may have a home life conducive to healthful physical and emotional growth and development; to maximize the level of personal and social functioning; to help the recipients realize their full capacity for self-support and independent living." The justification for providing service has been more frequently stated, and more receptively presented, in terms of helping the recipient become self-supporting than in terms of any intrinsic value to the family. While services may help improve the quality of life of the family on welfare, the primary intent of legislative support for these social services is to reduce the number of families on welfare. Consequently, the services emphasized by Congress are related to employment and dependency reduction—job training, job placement, day care, and family planning.

Termination of Assistance

The average family received assistance for about twenty months in 1971. AFDC is, then, for most families a temporary expedient rather than a way of life. However, in 1971 about 17.7 percent of AFDC families had been receiving assistance for five or more years. [145; 149] Families requiring assistance because of desertion, divorce, or illegitimacy received assistance for longer periods of time than was true for families needing assistance because of incapacity of the father. [14]

Most cases were closed because the families' economic circumstances improved. However, many cases are closed because the family is no longer eligible for assistance, though still in need. The youngest child, for instance, may have reached eighteen years of age, or the father may no longer be technically incapacitated.

Although there is great concern about intergenerational dependency, one study revealed that only about 15 percent of the mothers on AFDC had parents who had ever received public assistance. [107]   Another study by Greenleigh Associates showed that only 11.1 percent of public assistance recipients had received aid as children (*The New York Times,* August 10, 1969). Most of the families on AFDC (65.8 percent) in 1971 have not previously applied for or received aid. [145]

In summary then, our typical client, Mrs. Jones, a thirty-one-year-old mother with three children in need because the husband was out of the home, would have struggled along for about five months before applying for assistance. Having applied and been found eligible, she would have received a financial grant of about $191 per month plus medical assistance and social service help. She would have received assistance for a period of about 20 months, and then would have gone off the program because, through some change in her situation, she was no longer in need.

Group Approaches in the AFDC Program

The group approach has been used to supplement casework activities with AFDC clients. [4; 19; 22; 29; 34; 57; 62; 65; 67; 88; 94; 115; 122; 130; 155]. "Group services are defined as those social services of staff directed towards helping clients cope better with problems through a group experience." [94, p. 5]

Much of the time-consuming repetitive information that needs to be presented to the client at the point of application might be advantageously presented to a group of prospective AFDC clients. This has been attempted in California, with good results. [19]

More frequently, group meetings have been organized for clients already receiving aid. Prospective members for such groups are selected by the caseworkers and an invitation is issued to them to join. It is made clear that participation is voluntary and in no way affects eligibility for assistance. Average attendance at such groups has been small (four to eight mothers). The meetings revolve around problems of mutual interest—rearing children in a fatherless family, public attitudes toward AFDC recipients, the group members' own feelings about receiving assistance, social activities for single women, relationships with absent fathers and husbands, money management on the AFDC budget. Transportation expenses to the meeting are furnished and child-care arrangements are made by the agency to permit the mothers to participate. [57; 92] Knowlton points to the fact "that the two greatest problems in starting a group of AFDC recipients center around planning and financing baby-sitting and transportation." [67, p. 212]

The following is an excerpt from one of the group meetings on a problem of recurrent concern to the AFDC mother—the problem of their relationship with men:

> GINNIE: I would like a good, pat answer to give a man when they come up with this bit about "You need sex in order to be a complete person." That people who are not having sex are balling up inside. I've been told this I don't know how many times and I'm sure there's a good answer that will stop them in their tracks right now, but I can't find it.
>
> DEBBY: All I can think of to say is, "I don't need a man," and this sounds so silly, because you know you're telling a lie right there.
>
> CHARLOTTE: If it were just a matter of satisfying a physical need, like drinking water or eating breakfast, it would be different. But it's so wrapped up in morals and things. We're all conditioned the way our parents conditioned us. We'd be injuring ourselves emotionally, often, much more than the physical injury we may do ourselves by abstaining.
>
> GINNIE: That's right. This would be fine for the minute, but I have to get up in the morning and look at myself in the mirror and I'm not going to be so happy with myself if I'm going to fool around like this.
>
> DEBBY: I've got to the point now where everybody thinks I'm stuck-up because I feel this way. Just to go out and date a guy and have him expect you to pay for the date, I don't believe in that. When you're single and a virgin, you can always fall back on "I'm waiting for marriage," but when you've been married and have children, you can't say that.

CHARLOTTE: And you can't say you're not frustrated, either!
(Laughter from the group.)
DEBBY: Well, I want some security, a home, a companion, someone I can respect. But I find, to a lot of men, love means nothing but a mattress and two sheets.
GINNY: They're trying to prove to themselves that they are a man and that they're capable of subduing all these women. [57, pp. 203–204] *

The following is an excerpt from another group discussion by AFDC mothers about another recurrent problem—explaining the father's absence to the children:

Mrs. Pierce said sometimes you had to think about yourself and find out what you thought about different kinds of things. She said it was after the third group meeting, when we had been talking about what you tell your children about their father, and she didn't agree with everything that was said at that meeting. She said that she knew it was right to tell the children or anybody else the truth, but she didn't see any reason to make the children feel badly by telling them that their father and she didn't live together any more. She said as she thought about herself and why she felt this way, she began to wonder if it wasn't because it would be harder on her than it was on her children. She had decided that you don't take the easy way out for you, but tell your children the truth when they ask and let it go at that. Miss Watson said, "But nobody ever gave me an answer to my question, since my children's father and I weren't married!" Mrs. Pierce expressed agreement and said that was true, and Miss Elliott nodded and they all looked at me.

I said perhaps there wasn't a specific answer to Miss Watson's and Miss Elliott's problem, but is the truth any different for one than for the other? Can we make a mistake right by denying it? All nodded in agreement and we talked about the fact that one cannot make a wrong right, but we can move on from that mistake and be different, if we recognize and face the mistake.

Mrs. Thompson said, "You know what? I've told my kids that their father and I have had a disagreement and that is why we aren't living together." She explained that the children seemed to understand and accept this, and laughingly told the story of her little boy who asked her later, "When are you two going to get over your disagreement?" [155, p. 29]

* From Norman Fenton and Kermit T. Wiltse, eds., *Group Methods in the Public Welfare Program.* © Copyright 1963 by the Institute for the Study of Crime and Delinquency. Used by permission of Pacific Books, Publishers, Palo Alto, California.

Another group shows the mothers helping one another express some of their resentment at carrying the total burden of child care:

> MARY: (*Interrupting.*) But when you sit at home all by yourself—
> HELEN: (*Interrupting.*) But you can't! That's just it! You can't stay home all the time. You love your children, you do your duty by them, but then the time comes when you need a little outing . . . something to look forward to . . . other people's outlook on life. I don't know, it just, well, gives you a lift, and when you go home and go to get dinner, you feel a little bit freer.
> JANE: Sometimes you feel like screaming at the children. You know, you're hot and tired and confused and . . . and you go to the refrigerator, and you don't know what you're there for—
> ALICE: (*Interrupting.*) But if you could just have a breath of fresh air, like if you didn't get out for a few minutes, you'd feel, oh, all stuffed up. And then you turn on the gas to cook and you *really* feel hot.
> JANE: (*Dryly.*) Cooked! Cooked! [57, p. 199] *

Sometimes groups have been formed around specific problem situations. In one instance a group of mothers interested in making application for employment was organized. The group role played employment interviews and discussed civil service testing and child care for the working mother. [22] In another instance, the group grew out of the problems a number of different mothers were encountering with their teenage daughters. [62] In another instance, group meetings were held for mothers who had a delinquent child in a training school; the meetings were oriented around helping the mothers understand the child and helping them prepare for his return home. [155] Group educational meetings have been held with AFDC mothers to help them with purchasing and preparing food, budgeting, and homemaking. [29] Group programs of parent education have been sponsored jointly by the Department of Public Welfare and the local Family Service Agency for AFDC clients. [4]

During such group meetings of these various kinds, clients have shared information that they had not previously disclosed to their caseworker, and agency staff members have been given an opportunity of gaining additional understanding of their clients.

One worker with an AFDC caseload had been concerned that so few of the mothers arranged for their school-age children to buy school lunches at the special reduced rate for recipient families. Their reasons were vague and unrealistic. Some time later, when

---

* *Ibid.*

the same worker was serving as a group leader with some of the same mothers, the subject was introduced by a client new to the agency. The reaction of the other mothers was immediate and volatile. The children who bought the reduced tickets were publicly identified as "welfare" and were given a different colored ticket; they were made to stack dishes and clean the tables; they felt themselves discriminated against in other ways. Even though it meant financial hardship, no mother in the group was using the "special" school lunch program.

When the worker asked why none of them had mentioned this to him before in the office interview, several reasons were given. They hadn't known him so well, he wouldn't have understood, they didn't want to cause any trouble, it wasn't important enough, etc. [94, pp. 9–10]

Through observing the clients in group relationships, the agency has been able to get feedback information on their feelings toward the agency and on their lack of knowledge, or misunderstanding, of agency regulations. Wiltse suggests that group meetings are a device "for learning more about the culture of the public assistance clients, their value systems and family pattern." Because clients "outnumber the workers at group meetings, they feel more comfortable about expressing their true feelings regarding the agency." [152] Such groups provide the client with the opportunity to share with the agency some of his negative feelings about the agency and agency workers. This permitted them to accept, through interpretation by the leader, a better understanding of agency policy and procedures. They were able then to accept greater responsibility for their share in the process—for instance, providing the necessary information to maintain eligibility.

The group meetings of AFDC mothers have also provided an opportunity for improving the public image of the program. One group invited a reporter to attend a meeting so he could get a better idea of the problems faced by its members. An understanding article in the local press on the program resulted from this contact. [57]

The literature detailing the activities of such groups rarely includes material on the formal evaluation of the results. The reports occasionally include details of self-evaluation by members of the group. The reports include instances of clients who obtained employment and clients who remarried, partly as a result of the increased self-confidence and improved relationships with people that derived from the group meetings. It is also noted that the groups provide a social and recreational benefit for many of the mothers who are socially isolated. It permits others to get a sense that they are, and can be, doing something about their problems.

Few evaluation studies in social casework have attempted a comparison of outcome between an experimental and control group. There are fewer such studies in social group work. Navare and Glasser completed such a study with AFDC mothers. [100]   Group work services were offered to 89 AFDC families whose children had school-related problems. The group sessions were designed to help the mothers develop skills in problem solving, and to apply these skills in dealing with parent-child interaction concerning school problems. The control group consisted of 73 AFDC mothers with similar problems who attended none, or only one, of the group meetings. Outcomes were measured by a test of changes in generalized anxiety level, the Parent Attitude Research Instrument (the PARI), A Day at Home Test, which solicits reports from the mother of specific family behaviors during the course of the day, and a Pupil Behavior Inventory completed by the teacher. A comparison of the outcome measures of the experimental group of mothers (most of whom had attended six group meetings) and the control group showed that mothers offered group treatment had significantly improved attitudes of responsibility toward their children's adjustment in school, task performance, and decision making in the home, and lower generalized anxiety levels. The children of the mothers in the experimental group showed significant improvement in classroom conduct, but there was no difference for such factors as academic motivation, grades, or school attendance.

Lawrence reports a study of the use of group techniques to improve nutritional and marketing practices among AFDC mothers. [73]   A client-directed approach characterized by group control, group determination of content, and expression of feelings was contrasted with a worker-directed approach characterized by focus on task rather than feelings. The worker-directed group improved marketing practices more than the client-directed group, but there was no difference in nutritional practices. The researcher notes that it might be desirable to consider a worker-directed, advice-oriented approach in attempting to change specific behaviors.

Evaluation

Evaluation of Aims Achieved

The principal stated aims of the program are to provide the child with the following:

1. The economic support and services he needs for health and development.

2. The opportunity to grow up in a setting of his own family relationships.
3. A share in the life of the neighborhood and the community.
4. An education that will help him to realize his capacities.

In a great measure, many of these aims have been achieved by the program. However inadequate the grants, the program has provided a basic income for children who might otherwise have had none, and has made it possible for children to live in their own homes under the care of their own mothers, instead of being divided among relatives, left without supervision, or sent to foster homes. In the thirty-five years since the inception of the program, the program has been the means of keeping together the families of some 100 million children. "Without this assistance, it is certain that many of these families would have dissolved completely and the children would possibly have suffered permanent emotional and even physical damage." [10, p. xxii]

Maintained at home in their own families, these children have also been afforded the opportunity to share in the life of the neighborhood and the community. A sizable percentage of the children have participated in community youth organizations and activities. [14]

The educational goal has been achieved: "The evidence clearly demonstrates that, as a group, these children have already gone much further than their parents." [97, p. 11]   However, it appears that the educational achievement of AFDC children, as a group, is lower than that of their peers.

Studies of AFDC families show that "there appears to be very little basis for viewing the AFDC family as disorganized or severely deviant— the families as a whole present a profile of functioning that is quite stable." [8]   Relatively few AFDC families have been charged with child neglect or abuse, and the level of delinquency of AFDC children is similar to that of their peers. [14; 44]

The fact is that since its establishment in 1925 the AFDC program has distributed billions of dollars to families caring for millions of children who would otherwise have been seriously deprived. In one study which asked mothers who had left the welfare program what they thought it had done for them, over half said "it provided basic economic security; it prevented the family from breaking up." [52, p. 188]

Intensive Service

Another important aspect of evaluation is the data on the effects of intensive service offered AFDC clients. During the past decade, various intensive casework demonstration projects have involved permitting highly trained and experienced caseworkers to work with a limited caseload of some forty to sixty-five families. In each case, the information regarding the family was carefully reviewed, an explicit diagnosis made, and a treatment plan formulated. Consistent contact was attempted with the family to implement the treatment plan and available community resources were enlisted in the client's behalf.

In summarizing ten such studies that illustrated the "practical value of social work services" (not all of them concerned with the AFDC program), Bell notes that the "ten projects reviewed returned a significant number of families to self-support and decreased both the duration of grants and the incidence of applications." [6, p. 2]   The studies cited suggest that much in the way of rehabilitation can be achieved with concerted effort on the part of trained, adequately supervised personnel with reduced caseloads. But too few of the projects had been set up with sufficiently rigorous procedures and controls to enable us to say with any confidence that specific results are consistently attributable to the intensive service offered.

A more carefully controlled experiment was attempted in Chemung County in New York State. [13; 147]   From a pool of AFDC clients, two groups, consisting of fifty families each, were chosen. One group received intensive casework services by trained workers over a period of three years; the other group received only the usual service.

Because the project ran over a three-year period, there were difficulties occasioned by turnover in personnel, changes in policy of the agency, and so on. However, most clients in the demonstration group received about two years of casework service from one or another trained caseworker, and the experimental group had more than twice as many contacts with the worker as the control group had.

The principal criterion for determining the results of the experiment was on an eight- to twelve-page description of family functioning in terms of explicit dimensions developed by Geismer. [37]   There were two summaries for each case: one prepared at the opening of the project; the other, at closing. The research summaries were given to independent teams of trained judges, who rated each dimension of family functioning. The difference between the scores at opening and those at closing was used as a measure of "movement." As an additional evaluation procedure, the same material was given to a second set of judges trained in the use of the Community Service Society Movement Scale. [60]

The evaluation procedures established that the demonstration and control groups "started at comparable levels of family functioning at the opening of the project," but that the demonstration group, as a whole, "made a modest relative gain over the control group," although the difference in scores between the two groups at closing was not statistically significant. Essentially the same results were obtained by the judges using the Geismer Scale as by those using the Community Service Society Movement Scale.

The researchers concluded that, "after two years of service to multi-problem families . . . by trained caseworkers operating with reduced caseload, and greater than usual cooperation of the community's resources, the demonstration group showed a small, but statistically non-significant margin of superiority over the control group who received only routine service from the regular public assistance workers." [13, p. 151]

After the report was written and circulated, a persistent question was raised: How "good" was the casework that had been offered the client? The demonstration project assumed that "good" casework was whatever a trained caseworker did. At the conclusion of the experiment, however, the researchers asked two leading caseworkers to make an independent evaluation of the level of casework performance of the project workers, based on a review of the case records. When the level of rated performance was checked against movement in individual cases made by families in the experimental group who had received treatment, it was noted that the workers who had a higher performance rating were able to achieve a greater amount of movement in the cases for which they had responsibility. This would suggest that achievement of results is possible if the level of casework performance is sufficiently high.

The Chemung County study results are supported by a study of public welfare families in Puerto Rico. [83]

A third study involved a cooperative effort between a public welfare agency and the New York City Community Service Society, an agency which offers a highly professionalized casework service. [98; 99] Seventy-five families receiving public assistance and who were seen for five or more in-person interviews with Community Service Society caseworkers were compared with a control group of sixty-eight families who received public assistance but who had no contact with Community Service Society. Based on a comprehensive research interview the functioning of the two groups of families was assessed approximately fourteen months after the beginning of casework contact on the part of experimental group of families. Contrary to expectations, the families in the experimental group who had received the casework help did not, for the most part, "appear to be functioning differently at the conclusion of the project than those in the control group." [98, p. 194]   A section concerned with assessing behavioral changes in the children in the two groups of families concludes that "there is no indication on the basis of the items examined that the collaborative service has a significant measurable effect on the psychosocial functioning of the children." [98, p. 151]   It might be noted, however, that whatever slight differences were detected invariably were in favor of the experimental group which had received the casework treatment.

A study designed to assess the effectiveness of social services in the AFDC program was commissioned by the California State Assembly.

[18]   One hundred fifty-eight matched pairs of California AFDC social workers and their clients were interviewed in 1968. Workers and clients were asked identical questions so that the research yielded two versions —that of the worker and the client—of the same set of events. The criterion was a subjective one—the extent to which the recipients themselves "believed they had been helped by the social services offered." One-third of the recipients stated that the social worker had "helped" with a problem. Most frequently these were concrete problems such as illness, rent and housing, job training and employment, and problems with children. In contrast to the clients, the workers felt they had been helpful in somewhat more than half of the cases. There was little consensus, however, about the helpfulness of the contact—often when the client thought she had been helped the worker did not agree and when the worker thought she had been helpful the client did not agree. In only 15 percent of the cases did both the worker and the client agree that the client had been helped by the social service intervention. Neither length of contact nor the worker's level of training seemed related to outcome.

Rudoff and Piliavin conducted a study evaluating the effects of reduced loads and intensive casework service in the Aid to Needy Children Program—The California AFDC Program. [121]   Clients were randomly assigned either to the special unit offering intensive service to a reduced load of clients or to the regular service units. One hundred twenty-two clients in the special experimental unit were matched with a similar number of clients in the regular service unit. Both groups were given the California Psychological Inventory at the beginning of the experiment and then once again some twelve months later. Before and after changes in the California Psychological Inventory responses were used as the criteria for change in intrapersonal functioning. Changes in social functioning were assessed on the basis of employment rates and discontinuance from assistance. In general, the researcher concluded that intensive service unit workers "were apparently unable to achieve clearly better results than workers carrying normal agency caseload." [121, p. 25]   However, within the larger group of clients in the experiment a smaller subgroup of thirty highly employable clients in the intensive service unit were matched with a group of thirty highly employable clients in the regular service unit. "The assessment of the effect of the Special Services on employable Aid to Needy Children mothers revealed that significantly more mothers receiving intensive service were able to find employment." [121, p. 27]   It is suggested that intensive service, to be effective, needs to be employed selectively: with some groups of clients it may make a significant difference.

A study reported by Wilson of an intensive casework experiment with AFDC families in Delaware tends to support this conclusion. [151] In this experiment an intensive service unit was also established and the workers were given a limited caseload. After a two-year demonstration period, the experimental group was compared with a matched group of clients who had received standard service. The comparison was made on the basis of follow-up interviews with clients and content analysis of the case records. A significantly higher proportion of the families in the demonstration group had become independent of public assistance. [151, p. 303] The most notable difference was found among those families with "high rehabilitation potential." The researchers conclude that "intensive casework cannot remake the basic family structure of a large segment of our society—that counseling and guidance alone cannot effectively solve the AFDC mother's predicament," but that it is effective when it is "directed deliberately and systematically toward its most vulnerable target—the family with a profile of high rehabilitation potential." [151, p. 304] *

Problems

1. One of the problems faced by the AFDC program is that it is badly in need of reform, but efforts to change the program have not yet been successful. The Ninety-Second Congress ended in 1972 without approving legislative proposals for AFDC reform which had been introduced in 1969, studied and debated over a three-year period, and passed twice by the House of Representatives.

During the last half of the 1960's criticism of the AFDC program came from taxpayers, recipients, social workers, citizens' groups, and government officials at every level. [17; 38; 43; 91; 104; 126]

As average AFDC benefits rose, those on relief in some high-grant states were receiving almost as much as poor full-time working families. [49] As Lampman notes, "such an inequity is an affront to the value of work and tends to drive a wedge of bitterness between the low-income worker and the welfare poor." [70, p. 8]

The working poor regarded the program as discriminatory because it excluded them from assistance. The program thus provided an incentive to family disruption since a father earning low, intermittent wages could insure a steady, improved income for his family by deserting, making his family eligible for AFDC.

Clients and social workers, on the other hand, felt that the amount of aid was too low—in most states, well below the official poverty level. Clients regarded the eligibility test as demeaning and social workers complained that it robbed them of the time to offer service to the client.

---

* See also a more recent recapitulation of studies concerned with casework effectiveness: Joel Fisher, "Is Casework Effective? A Review." *Social Work*, **18**, 1 (January 1973), 5–20.

Each one of a series of government commissions and task forces appointed to study the program—The Advisory Council on Public Welfare (1966), The Advisory Commission on Rural Poverty (1967), the Kerner Commission on Civil Disorders (1968), and the President's Commission on Income Maintenance Programs (1969)—called for fundamental changes in the nature of the program and a uniform national standard of assistance implemented by Federal grants based on one eligibility requirement—need.

In addition to the proposals to revise and amend the welfare system, serious consideration was given to abolishing the current programs and substituting a guaranteed annual income, a negative income tax, or a children's allowance scheme.

The debate was temporarily ended by President Nixon's proposal that AFDC be replaced with an entirely new structure: the Family Assistance Program.

In presenting the case for such a change to the public in 1969 President Nixon said,

> Whether measured by the anguish of the poor or by the drastically mounting burden on the taxpayer, the present welfare system has to be judged a colossal failure. . . . The tragedy is not only that it is bringing states and cities to the brink of financial disaster, but it is also failing to meet the elementary human, social, and financial needs of the poor. . . . It breaks up homes. It often penalizes work. It robs recipients of dignity. And it grows. . . . If the present trends continue another 4 million will have joined the welfare rolls by 1975. The financial cost will be crushing; the human cost will be suffocating. [101]

The proposal was introduced by the President in a message to Congress in August 1969. The rhetoric was conservative, the policy implications were radical. Emphasis was placed on the preservation of the work ethic, on job training of welfare recipients, on a requirement that application for assistance be accompanied by registration for training or work. "Workfare" as a substitute for "welfare" was the keynote of the message. The proposal made need the basic eligibility requirement, so that, for the first time, the working poor family, with the father in the house and employed, would be eligible for assistance. A uniform nationwide basic income floor was established and guaranteed by Federal responsibility for payment up to this basic minimum level. Emphasis was to be placed on requiring training and work placement by eligible recipients, and a graduated scale of payments was introduced to maintain a work incentive. The emphasis on employment was to be implemented by support for an expanded program of day care, job training, and job placement. [53]

The President's bill was amended and passed by the House of Representatives as the Family Assistance Act of 1970, but it failed to get Senate approval. The bill was reintroduced and passed by the House in June 1971. The Senate passed another version of the bill in October 1972. The Conference Committee appointed by the two houses of Congress to settle the differences between the two bills ended in failure. Congress did, however, radically revise the adult assistance categories—aid to the blind, aid to the permanently and totally disabled, and old age assistance—by making these Federal programs and guaranteeing to all recipients a Federal standard of assistance higher than grant levels under the AFDC program. This action prompted *The New York Times* to question editorially whether we were, indeed, a child-centered society.

> No legislative body could be more compassionate than the Senate when dealing with the financial needs of the 3.2 million aged, blind, and permanently disabled people on the nation's welfare rolls. . . . But that same solicitude makes doubly shocking the very different, or more accurately, indifferent attitude most senators appear to take to the 11 million needy mothers and children who make up the biggest and most deprived element in the tragedy of welfare (*The New York Times*, October 3, 1972).

The Family Assistance Plan passed by the House in 1971 guaranteed an income of $2400 to every family of four in the United States, to be provided by the Federal government, and available solely on the basis of need. However, since AFDC grants for a family of four were higher than $2400 in 1971 in most states, the bill provided that states would be urged to continue to supplement the minimum $2400 standard for families eligible for AFDC. As an incentive to work, families could continue to draw the full $2400 if they earned $720; beyond this first $720 "income disregard" Federal benefits would be reduced $2 for each $3 earned. Table 5–2 summarizes this aspect of the plan.

With its emphasis on work incentives, the bill required that every

TABLE 5–2.

Earnings	Benefit for a Family of Four	Total Income
$ 0	$2400	$2400
720	2400	3120
2000	1547	3547
3000	800	3800
4000	213	4213
4320	0	4320

employable applicant register with the Department of Labor for work or work training. A mother caring for children over three years of age was designated as employable. If she refused to register for work, the grant to the family would be reduced by $800. Applicants would be required to accept "suitable" employment, defined as any job that paid at least 75 percent of the Federal minimum wage—in 1971, this amounted to $1.20 an hour. Funds were authorized to increase the number of training opportunities, public service jobs, and day-care facilities.

For families with employable applicants, the program would be administered by an Opportunities for Family Program established in the Department of Labor; all other families would be enrolled in the Family Assistance Plan administered by the Department of Health, Education, and Welfare.

The bill gave little emphasis to the social services aspects of the program and further reduced any encouragement to the states to establish and support such services.

The bill, if passed, would have increased the total number of people receiving assistance in 1973 to an estimated 25 million and would have increased the total public assistance bill by some $4 billion.

The debate over the Family Assistance Plan bill raised little question about whether or not the mother's place was in the home with her children or in the work force. In 1967, with inauguration of the Work Incentive program requiring AFDC applicants to work, this question had been settled. The answer was further confirmed by Congressional approval of the Talmadge bill in 1971, which strengthened and tightened the Work Incentive program. The welfare reform debate in the 1972 Congress was primarily over how extensive and coercive the work test should be.

There seemed to be general agreement about the need for a federally guaranteed income and the necessity of including the working poor in the program. The controversy was over the level of income and the level of tax on earned income so as to insure a work incentive. The Welfare Rights Organization asked for a $6500 guaranteed income and minimums of $2600 and $3000 were introduced by some Congressmen to replace the $2400 minimum finally included in the bill.

With the failure in passage of the proposal, these questions still remain matters of debate and discussion. We have reviewed the proposals in some detail because the material is of historical interest, because it indicates the direction of planning for change in the AFDC program, and because these proposals are likely to be the starting point of recommendations for changes that probably will be considered in the near future.

2. A continuing problem for the AFDC program is likely to relate to unrealistic public expectations of major reductions in the number of families receiving assistance. Our experience with the Work Incentive program since 1967 and the results of studies of the background of

AFDC recipients should reduce these expectations. [2; 15; 20; 27; 40; 48; 54; 59; 75; 96; 97 102; 110; 118; 148]

Available data indicate that the AFDC recipient's potential for self-support is such that only a very modest percentage will be able to move off the program. The studies show that there are real and significant barriers to the employability of the 3 million adults on the AFDC program who care for 8 million children. Employment potential is associated with such factors as parental educational level, previous job experience, employment skills, physical and mental health status, some general competence in handling personal affairs, and conditions in the local labor market. The dilemma is that those who score high on all of these factors do not need much help and effectively use whatever service they do need. Those who score low need a great deal of help but cannot make effective use of the services available.

In reality, if the recipient's situation and capacity had permitted independence he would not be on assistance, unless one assumes that the typical recipient does not want to work. Yet every study that tests this assumption concludes that there is little difference between the welfare population and the rest of the community regarding readiness and willingness to work. [41]

The Work Incentive program, as amended by the Talmadge bill, requires a careful review of the AFDC caseload in a search for all employables, followed up by work training and job placement, with day care provided for the young children of employable mothers. As of 1972 the program had had very limited success. *The New York Times* reported, for example, that the program in New York State "has been found to have minimal effectiveness in reducing welfare rolls and in putting clients to work according to reports made in May (1971) and September 1972. . . . Three evaluations of the California WIN Program, all released in early 1972, found that the program had failed to provide meaningful training or permanent jobs" (*The New York Times*, October 9, 1972).

A recent detailed study of employment programs for AFDC recipients in Michigan concludes that "full-time employment is not a feasible alternative to welfare for most recipients." [59, p. 1]

As a matter of fact, a coercive work program which fails to fulfill its promises may decrease the incentive to work on the part of AFDC mothers. Reid and Smith, studying AFDC mothers' experience in the Work Incentive program in Chicago, Detroit, and Cleveland, found that the majority accepted the program and were anxious to obtain work. However, "almost two years later very few had obtained jobs through the program. . . ." [118, p. 359]

The researchers note:

The low job-placement rate for WIN recipients had already been well established in national and local WIN statistics. This study adds nothing new in that respect. What it does add is evidence that the inability of the program to deliver jobs may also mean frustration of the AFDC mothers' own aspirations. Even though they may have realized some sense of accomplishment and tangible benefits from their participation in educational and vocational programs, most of the mothers left WIN with their original goals unrealized. In that respect another disappointment or another failure to achieve has been added to their lives. [118, p. 359]

The problem appears to be the lack of enough steady jobs at the level of skill which the AFDC recipient can offer, paying a wage adequate enough to cover the basic living needs of the family. Nevertheless the studies do show that if we cannot justifiably expect to reduce sharply the number of AFDC recipients, a concentrated effort at training and placement can lead to a modest increase in the job possibilities available to some.

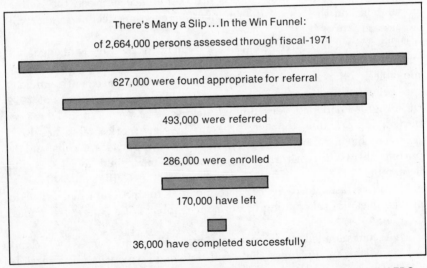

FIGURE 5–3. With special help and special effort a limited number of AFDC parents find employment. (U.S. Department of Health, Education, and Welfare and U.S. Department of Labor.)

The magnitude of the problem is indicated by the material made available in 1972 from employment surveys conducted by the U.S. Census Bureau covering fifty-one urban areas populated by 13 million people. It was found that large numbers of people who work for a living do not earn a living wage. For instance, 60 percent of the manufacturing jobs in New York City in 1970 paid less than was required to sustain a decent minimum standard of living as determined by the U.S. Bureau of Labor Statistics. [123, p. 43]   The AFDC mother, in trying to achieve independence, will be competing with many workers who earn, and live, at a near-welfare level. The failure, ultimately, lies in the job market and the limited possibility that the economy will provide full employment at a living wage.

Despite attempts to maintain work incentive by permitting recipients to keep some percentage of earnings, current public assistance regulations impose a very heavy "tax" on employed recipients. For instance, a New Jersey mother of three receiving benefits from AFDC, Medicaid, food stamps, and public housing would gain only about 20 percent of the total income derived from a full-time job paying as much as $700 per month: a $4.00 an hour job is worth only 80¢ an hour in increased family benefits to such a mother. [133]

The community may face a further disappointment when it becomes clear that, ultimately, many of the efforts designed to help the recipients achieve independence will require the expenditure of more public funds than would be needed if the family were maintained on the AFDC program. It was estimated that in 1970 reasonably decent day care cost about $1600 a year per child; at the same time the average yearly AFDC grant per child was only about $600. It is clear that offering day care as a procedure for helping AFDC mothers train for and obtain employment does entail considerable additional financial expense.

3. One of the most difficult problems faced by the AFDC program is its negative public image and, as a consequence, the public's ambivalent attitude toward it. The amount of support allotted the program, as contrasted with that given other assistance programs, tends to substantiate the hypothesis of a negative attitude toward AFDC and confirms the fact that this attitude is a problem for the program. Levels of aid per recipient in the adult assistance categories—old age assistance, aid to the blind, aid to the totally and permanently disabled—have always been higher than aid to children in the AFDC program. The complete federalization of the adult assistance categories in 1972 and the failure by Congress to federalize the AFDC program confirms the differences in the level of public acceptance of these different programs.

A nationwide sampling of public opinion in 1969 revealed that a sizable percentage of the population felt that responsibility for poverty was largely located "in the character of the poor persons themselves" rather than in social and economic factors, and that a clear majority felt that there are too many people receiving welfare who can and should be working. [33]   The 1969 survey indicated a widespread negative view of welfare recipients.

First, the public finds it difficult to understand why, in a period of prolonged, continuing prosperity, the program continues to grow. The fact is that AFDC is the most expensive of the assistance programs, for, although the individual grants are smaller than those in other assistance programs, the number of recipients is very much larger. This cost engenders a negative attitude toward the program.

Furthermore, the nature of the problems that bring people to the program aggravates the negative public attitude toward the program. There has been a shift in the social composition of the recipient group served by the program. The mothers' aid program, which was the precursor of the AFDC program, was formulated to meet the problem of widowhood. The development and success of the OASDI program, the widespread development of insurance programs as a fringe benefit, the changing longevity statistics which make less probable the death of the younger husband-father—all tend to make death a less frequent contingency requiring application for AFDC. But as dependency arising from the death of the father has declined, the relative importance of dependency arising from his absence from the home as a result of illegitimacy, desertion, divorce, separation, and imprisonment has increased.

Death and disability are "respectable" reasons for dependency. While the "line between personal inadequacy and victimization by circumstances is not an easy one to draw" [150, p. 25], the widow is clearly a victim of circumstances. But the public can more easily view illegitimacy, divorce, and desertion as examples of personal inadequacy. Thus the public tends to view AFDC recipients as a socially undesirable group. It seems to many that the program rewards nonperformance of parental duties and that the program thus poses a threat to the solidarity of all families.

The attitude toward the program is also influenced by the strong feelings generated by racial conflict. Mr. Mitchell, City Manager of Newburgh, New York, who achieved national prominence in 1960–61 when he developed and attempted to enforce the Newburgh Code of Restrictive Regulations regarding relief recipients, felt that "a shiftless, unskilled, and immoral influx from the South was crowding the public assistance rolls." For those unfamiliar with the delicate euphemisms he employed, Mitchell would amicably spell out their significance. "Negroes —that's what the influx is," he said. [30, p. 96]

It is true that blacks form a disproportionately large percentage of AFDC recipients. Although they constitute approximately 11 percent of the population, they make up 43.3 percent of all families receiving AFDC in 1971. [149] *

* Although blacks currently form a considerable proportion of AFDC families, this upholds a generalization that has been true throughout our history. The immigrant minority group that is striving for full membership in American society has always constituted a larger percentage of those obtaining public welfare. At one time this was true of the Irish immigrant group, of the Italian immigrant group, and so on. The Know-Nothing movement, which had as one of its cardinal tenets restrictive immigration, pointed to indigency of immigrants as an argument in favor of such a proposal.

Kallen interviewed at length 300 white and 300 black women living in Baltimore about attitudes toward welfare, race, and so on. The research notes that there was a high relationship among whites between antiblack and antiwelfare attitudes. "It would appear to be a reflection of the general attitude among whites that it is the blacks who are the prime recipients of welfare. In fact, it seems fair to say that many of the objections expressed by whites to current welfare programs were in effect antiblack biases not always so thinly disguised." [64, p. 89]

The public image of the program also tends to be shaped by the recurrent widely publicized "exposures" of "abuses" of the program. Articles in popular national magazines point to "countless examples of indolence and sloth," showing "how the taxpayer supports men and women who not only don't work but who are breeding a society of illegitimates besides." [93, p. 32]   The articles publicize the atypical cases— "one family with twenty-three children—fifteen of them illegitimate— drawing $969 a month in welfare aid. Another woman with fourteen illegitimate children had received $61,525 during her eighteen years on the Newark relief roles." [66, p. 31]   As a consequence there is a persistent and pervasive conviction that the AFDC rolls are filled with "chiselers" and "freeloaders."

Periodic determined efforts have been made to review the eligibility of AFDC recipients to ascertain the truth of such accusations. Studies in Cook County, Illinois [45], in California [125], in Washington [46], and studies by the field staff of the U.S. Department of Health, Education, and Welfare [146] show that fewer than 5 percent of the recipients are ineligible for assistance. A 1970 nationwide review found that the number of cases identified by state public assistance agencies as involving a question of fraud represented 1.4 percent of the AFDC caseload. In more than half these cases, "sufficient facts to support a question of fraud were not available." [143]   Such a level of ineligibility is clearly within acceptable administrative limits in any complex large-scale program, and within the tolerance level of 4 percent ineligibility set by the Federal government.

Critics of the program discount the findings, pointing out that the nationwide U.S. Department of Health, Education, and Welfare study was a case of an agency investigating itself.

New York City's experience during 1970–72, when it was treated to a "press release" war regarding "ineligibles," is typical. Mr. Sugarman, Director of the Human Resources Administration, responsible for the AFDC program in New York City, issued a series of carefully developed reports indicating that only 2–5 percent of recipients were ineligible. The New York State Welfare Inspector General, Mr. Berlinger, on the basis of his staff's investigation, issued a series of equally carefully prepared reports indicating 15–20 percent recipient ineligibility. The New York Controller, Mr. Levitt, on the basis of his staff's review of the situation, estimated 7–10 percent ineligibility. The New York State Social Services

Commissioner, Mr. Lavine, making his own study, concluded that 7.5 percent of recipients were ineligible.

The problem seems to result from the fact that the studies involve highly complex judgments regarding eligibility decisions made by workers at some time in the past, such decisions having been made in terms of eligibility criteria open to differing interpretations. Consequently, the same case might be regarded as eligible if a liberal, applicant-oriented interpretation of policy is applied or ineligible if a strict, highly restrictive interpretation of policy is employed. Furthermore, there can be sharp differences in opinion about the extensiveness and detail of documentation which the client needs to provide to "prove" eligibility.

There is much less fraud than is suggested by many critics of the program but somewhat more fraud than social workers would like to believe is true. But as one welfare director said, "You don't stop a good program because one in a hundred recipients is bad any more than you abandon checking accounts because some people forge checks." [47, p. 69]   To this general conclusion one would need to add, in all justice, the note of comparison advanced for consideration by the Welfare Rights Organization. They point to the far larger percentage of "chiseling" on tax returns by various groups in society. [149, p. 10] The WRO also lists the many groups in America who do get assistance from the community without incurring public disapproval. [91, pp. 140–46]   It has been suggested that the oil depletion allowance should be entitled the Oil Producers' Public Assistance Program, airline subsidies should be called Aid to Dependent Airlines, and the $1200–$1500 it costs the community to educate a college student for a year in state-supported universities should be termed Aid to Needy Students.

Another approach to demonstrating eligibility is through studying the consequences of a denial of aid. When aid is denied through the AFDC program, applicants—because they are still in need—seek, and receive, assistance through other sources. For instance, a study by Lewis in Connecticut establishes that as categorical aids, such as AFDC, become more restrictive in their eligibility requirements, general assistance costs are increased. [78]

An Ohio study shows that when a county discontinued general assistance in 1961 after voters rejected a local tax levy for welfare, responsibility for maintenance of the family was shifted to other programs. The report states that, "in some form, the community has paid, and is still paying, maintenance costs for most of these families since the needs of the families and the children have continued." [138, p. 17]   There was a 54 percent increase in money owed landlords, grocers, doctors, and so on, during the fifteen-month period after curtailment of aid, and the medical needs of dependent children suffered. Of 250 children affected, only eighteen were reported to have received immunization against smallpox, diphtheria, and tetanus; only fifteen had received polio inoculations. The report concludes that the community "has been irreparably damaging its children during the vital growing years, thereby perpetuating, rather than alleviating, problems confronting the community" (*The New York Times*, November 10, 1963).

The problem of the unmarried mother and the illegitimate child contributes to the negative public image of AFDC. Many contend that AFDC "rewards" and encourages illegitimacy by reducing the deterrents to unmarried motherhood. In response, public welfare officials point out that unmarried mothers are only one part of the AFDC caseload, and that only a small percentage of illegitimate children in the United States are supported on the AFDC program. An extra illegitimate child involves a monthly increase in income that varies from state to state, but averages, nationwide, less than $45 a month. A dollar or a dollar and a half a day hardly compensates for the additional expense in caring for an extra child, aside from the physical and emotional burden of care imposed on the mother. Henry McCarthy, former Commissioner of the New York City Department of Public Welfare, said that "if this contention were true, it would be the first time in history that a statute fathered a child." Unmarried mothers on AFDC, aware of these facts, are generally unhappy about their out-of-wedlock pregnancy. [45, p. 19]

Denial of AFDC to the unmarried mother does not solve the problem of illegitimacy. Bell, citing a relevant study, notes:

> In a randomly selected sample of 323 families who had been denied ADC between June 1954 and June 1956, the incidence of illegitimacy soared after the families were rejected by the program. . . . When ADC was discontinued, . . . 45 percent of the children were illegitimate; when the families were interviewed in 1957, 91.4 percent of the children born in the intervening period were illegitimate. . . . It seems to be true that depriving families of public aid only increases their vulnerability to out-of-wedlock pregnancies. [5, pp. 70, 183]

Chilton, studying the effects of another such punitive state program, concludes that "it did not noticeably reduce the number of out-of-wedlock children nor did it discourage illicit sexual relations. . . . The practical effect of the law was to remove from the AFDC rolls, for different lengths of time, a large number of children who were otherwise eligible," to the possible detriment of the children's development. [23, p. 22]

Restrictive measures are proposed in the belief that illegitimacy increases as aid is made available for the support of mother and child. One would expect, then, that there would be a relationship between increases in illegitimacy and AFDC recipient rates and certainly a relationship between the level of aid in a state and the number of out-of-wedlock families on AFDC. A careful examination of these considerations shows that such a relationship does not, in fact, exist. [28] Illegitimacy in states with very low AFDC benefit levels increased at the same rate as it did in states with very high benefit levels. However, this does not seem to offset the criticism that derives from the fact that, over the years, a growing percentage of children on AFDC are born out of wedlock and that the burden of caring for out-of-wedlock children on AFDC has been growing steadily.

Of even greater concern, in terms of public reaction to the program, is the AFDC mother who gives birth to an out-of-wedlock child during the time that she is receiving assistance. Punitive proposals have been made—compulsory sterilization of unmarried mothers receiving aid, imprisonment of the unmarried mothers, denial of aid on the birth of the second illegitimate child. Public welfare officials point out that some of these proposals would be harmful to the children and costly to the community. To punish the mother by taking the child from her deprives the child of care by a generally adequate mother. Few of the unmarried mothers caring for the children with the help of AFDC have been found to be neglectful.

The importance of the program to the future of the illegitimate child and the fact that AFDC does permit the child to grow up in a favorable setting were confirmed in an interview study of thirty mothers who had been receiving AFDC for more than two years, each of whom had two or more illegitimate children. These mothers gave their children very good care, had a deep feeling of responsibility toward the children, and were ambitious for them. They definitely did not see public assistance as a desirable "way of life" for the child, although they themselves had no alternative. [7]

Denial of AFDC to the unwed mother and the illegitimate child is an expensive policy in terms of the emotional cost to the children and the financial cost to the community. A former Commissioner of the City of New York Department of Public Welfare notes:

> A program of institutionalization of the illegitimate children receiving AFDC would cost the City for the 55,000 out-of-wedlock children now [1959] on AFDC about $110 million more annually than it is now spending. This does not include a capital outlay of about $1 billion for institutional facilities. The abandonment of the AFDC program for out-of-wedlock children would bankrupt the city.

The numbers and cost are higher today, and the point made is therefore even more valid. However, the problem still remains: How does one provide for the illegitimate child without *seemingly* subsidizing unmarried motherhood?

4. A problem results from the fact that the program is in conflict with itself regarding its relationship to the father-husband. Supposedly, the agency is responsible for helping the father as well as the mother and the children, helping to reduce tension between the father and the rest of the family, and implementing, if possible, an eventual reconciliation. At the same time, the program stands as an adversary to the father, which makes achievement of the stated aims difficult.

The NOLEO Amendment made it mandatory for the deserted mother, in applying for aid, to be willing to take legal action against her husband if she wanted to qualify for assistance.* Responsibility for following through was placed on the Department of Welfare. "In this way the Public Welfare Agency, in addition to being the instrument of providing financial assistance and services for rehabilitation, becomes a vehicle of social compulsion." [86, p. 5]

A mother may hesitate to initiate action to compel support from the absent father because she may see such action as reducing the chance for reconciliation. "She may be concerned about the effect of such action upon the attitude of the children toward herself or toward their father." [86, p. 65] Yet, unless she agrees to the action, neither she nor her children are eligible for assistance.

The entire question of support payments to the family from divorced, deserted, or putative fathers is a problem for the program. Congress has repeatedly attempted to legislate procedures which might effectively increase the amount of such support payments. Over time the amount of such payments recovered barely exceeds the administrative expense involved in enforcing the regulations. However, the cost-benefit aspects are less important than communication of community support of the concept that the divorced, deserted, or putative father is responsible for the support of his children. This principle is difficult to implement because such fathers are hard to locate; once located, they are often unable to make support payments for their children.

There is a conflict between the general aims of the program, the nature of program administration, and the level of assistance grants. The question has been raised as to whether the program, which offers assistance at a level that barely meets minimum need, is not self-defeating. As Burns says, niggardly assistance levels "are not calculated to enhance self-respect, normal participation in community life, or a

---

*The procedure, in effect, demands of the applicant what is not demanded of deserted mothers in the community who are not applicants for assistance. This, it is pointed out, is in conflict with the principle that acceptance of assistance "should not result in the recipient's acquiring a different status from others in the community." The same might be said about suitable home provisions. The AFDC client may have to be more rigorous than others in complying with the verbalized mores of the community.

spirit of enterprise among the young," nor are they likely to help the children to "feel that they are part of, and owe loyalty to, the aims and traditions of their society." [17]

The executive director of the Child Welfare League of America, in discussing this problem, says:

> It is folly—if not hypocrisy—to plan for and talk about providing casework services and educational resources for people who are miserably housed and hungry. It is equally unrealistic to think that parents who are deprived of basic physical needs, and who are given even these by a resentful society, will be able to meet the needs of their children. [117, p. 12]

The negative relationship between assistance levels and rehabilitation efforts is noted in the report on the work of a special intensive casework unit with AFDC families in Cleveland, Ohio. During the time that the project was in operation, grant budgets were cut. The report notes:

> It is necessary to face the question whether any program of service and rehabilitation can succeed when clients must live on such inadequate allowances. In the meeting of the project staff held at the time the 30 percent cut in grants was announced some of the workers questioned whether it was worthwhile for the project to continue under these conditions. They recognized that many AFDC mothers are almost completely preoccupied with the struggle to meet the family's basic needs and have no heart for planning for the future. When assistance is inadequate, the underlying suspicion and distrust of many clients, growing out of earlier life experiences, is accentuated. Their hostility is likely to be projected upon the case worker, who is already uncomfortable about the limited help she can give. While adequate assistance grants do not automatically insure rehabilitation of clients, inadequate assistance definitely makes rehabilitation more difficult. [131, p. 70]

No amount of social service can substitute for inadequate assistance. Under such conditions it is difficult to implement the rehabilitative aims of the program. The question, of course, remains whether or not social services have an effective technology available which will implement the rehabilitative objectives of the program even if adequate assistance is given.

Trends

We have noted above some of the trends in the AFDC program during the past decade: (1) the sharp increase in the number of recipients; (2) the increase in cost; (3) the change in the nature of the problems which bring people to apply for aid; (4) the liberalization of eligibility requirements by Congress and through U.S. Supreme Court decision; (5) the shift in orientation of the program from income maintenance to rehabilitation through social services to vocational training and job placement; (6) the development of a new legal specialization concerned with due process for assistance recipients; and (7) the development of an organization of welfare recipients to educate recipients and agitate for their rights.

In some instances what were formerly trends during the 1960's have become established parts of the program. There is little question now about family planning as an AFDC service and little question about providing contraceptive devices to clients, married or single. In New York State the program will pay the medical costs of an abortion if the procedure is desired by a recipient.

Most agencies have moved toward a consolidation of the previously independent child welfare services and AFDC social services, which are now generally administered through a single organizational structure.

1. There is a trend toward a program of socialized medicine for a very sizable proportion of the child population through the public assistance program. The 1965 Social Security amendments, in addition to authorizing a program of Medicare for the aged, authorized a program of public medical care for all "medically needy children" in Title 19 of the Act. The need for such a measure became clearly evident in the findings of the Head Start program. Physical examinations given routinely to children from low-income families enrolling in Head Start programs across the country revealed serious medical problems in a large proportion of the children. In Boston, one-third of the children were found to have serious illnesses or defects; in Chicago, 5000 of 13,000 children from low-income families needed medical attention.

Implementation of this provision requires action on the part of the individual states, but if a state chooses to come under the program any medically needy child or youth under twenty-one can receive, at public expense, whatever medical or health care he needs. Before the 1965 amendments, children in families receiving assistance were granted medical care on a vendor payment basis. This group of children will continue to receive such help—although the amendments call for upgrading this health program as well. The significant change made by the amendment is the inclusion, in the program of publicly supported health service, of children in those families who are not receiving assistance but whose income is too low to allow for medical expenses. If a state chooses to set up a program to include this group of children in addition to those already receiving medical service because they are AFDC clients, Federal reimbursement will cover some percentage of the expense involved.

Originally the Federal government did not set any limits on its reimbursement to the state, permitting the states to determine the levels which defined *medically needy*—families whose income is too high for public assistance programs but not high enough to cover medical care. Currently, however, the Federal government will not reimburse the state for medical assistance to families whose income is more than 133 percent of the state AFDC payment level. Although states had faced penalties for failure to establish a medical program, these penalties have been rescinded. Because Federal pressure to develop programs of medical assistance for the "medically needy" poor and near poor has been reduced, it was estimated that, in 1970, two out of three children in such families were not included in any medical assistance program. [139, p. 104]

2. There is a trend toward separation of income and services in the AFDC program. The separation of social services from the determination of eligibility for assistance and the administration of financial maintenance is now the accepted policy of the Social Rehabilitation Services of the U.S. Department of Health, Education, and Welfare. [140]

For years social workers have complained that the red tape involved in determining eligibility and administering financial assistance has robbed them of the time to "do service." Separation reflects the recognition that "social services" and "income maintenance" are two discrete functions which are more effectively performed by different staff units possessing different qualifications. Income maintenance might be standardized and computerized so that it could be administered by a nonprofessional staff; "social services" could then be offered by a professionally trained staff. Specialization of function would make the social services staff and their function clearly identifiable.

A family may receive assistance without "risking" services, and another family may seek services even though they are not eligible for, or do not want, assistance. Separation is based on an assumption, yet to be tested, that the "services" can be clearly defined and that the need for, and discussion of, service-related problems can be divorced from income maintenance problems. Early experience with separation suggests that this is very difficult to achieve (*The New York Times*, December 27, 1970). [58; 111; 127]   A positive relationship with AFDC clients, currently based on demonstrated capacity to help through provision of financial assistance, may be more difficult to develop where such help no longer comes from the worker. Furthermore, separation involves a risk as well as an opportunity for social workers. Separation permits an examination of the effectiveness of service uncontaminated by its relationship to income maintenance and it permits a count of the number of clients who will choose service in its own right. Divorced from maintenance, and operating on its own, "social services" may be vulnerable to reductions in governmental support.

3. There has been a trend toward the use of simplified methods for determining eligibility of applicants. In November 1968 the Social and Rehabilitation Service of the Department of Health, Education, and Welfare required that states develop and test a plan for the use of declaration forms—simple objective forms to be filled out by the applicant and carrying, when legally signed, the force of an affidavit.

A simple application form requires less time and effort and is less demeaning to the client. Those states which have experimented with a declaration form note that the amount of fraud was minimal. These conclusions were based on a detailed follow-up investigation of the eligibility of a random sampling of cases previously accepted for assistance on the basis of the declaration form alone. [112, pp. 6–9]

The new, simplified procedure, however, poses a problem for individualized social work services. The "declaration form" elicits only limited, factual data that reveal little about the family's possible need for services. Because the form might be completed and sent in without personal contact with the caseworker, a family may have no opportunity to be informed about services which they might be interested in using. To meet this problem, some of the declaration forms have provided the client with an opportunity to request service. One form includes the following section:

Other Family Needs

I want to talk with a caseworker about our needs and problems. Briefly, these are ⎯⎯⎯⎯⎯⎯⎯⎯⎯⎯⎯⎯⎯⎯⎯⎯⎯⎯⎯⎯

The trend toward the substitution of a simple declaration form was slowing down by 1972. By that time, the Federal government was no longer exerting influence in encouraging such a change, and some jurisdictions, notably New York City, which had briefly moved to using such a system, returned to the more detailed eligibility tests.

4. Public dismay over the increase in the number of welfare recipients became increasingly evident in the early 1970's. In many cities efforts were made to actively deter people from applying and to interpret eligibility requirements more strictly. Some nineteen state legislatures voted welfare cuts in the early 1970's. The trend at that time seemed to suggest a turn in the direction of greater political conservatism and a movement away from programs of social reform.

5. There is also trend toward computerization of the AFDC program and increasing emphasis on the use of budget management procedures to provide more precise accountability for funds expended and to evaluate the social and economic returns achieved by the AFDC program. Social workers in administrative positions are being replaced by professional systems engineers with management training. Independently operated management consulting firms are more frequently being employed by welfare agencies to study their operation and make suggestions for change.

6. There is a trend toward purchase of service by the AFDC program. Instead of providing the services the client may need, the welfare agency contracts for the purchase of such services from another agency or private organization. Day-care services, homemaker services, and family-planning services are often contracted and purchased on this basis. [134] The trend has been toward developing greater specificity in purchase-of-care procedures and tightening controls to insure that the public welfare agency is actually getting what it contracted to purchase.

Summary

Because the social insurance programs cover only a limited number of the contingencies that result in income loss for the family, further income maintenance programs in the form of public assistance are necessary.

The assistance program directly affecting children is Aid to Families of Dependent Children. A precursor of the program, developed by the individual states earlier in the twentieth century, was known as the mothers' aid or mothers' pension program. Development of such a program was encouraged by passage of legislation prohibiting child labor and by legislation making school attendance compulsory. During the Great Depression, the bankruptcy of state programs resulted in the acceptance by the Federal government of responsibility for support, and the Social Security Act in 1935 provided for grants to the state for a program of assistance to dependent children.

Currently, the AFDC is a program in which service is offered directly to the recipient by the county, supervised by the states, and supported by local, state, and Federal funds. The Federal government, in administering its grants-in-aid reimbursement, makes certain minimum requirements with which the states, requesting reimbursement, must comply. Such requirements protect the recipient and establish some broad uniform standards. However, essential details of the program are left to the discretion of the individual states, and there is considerable variation in the program from state to state.

The program is designed to provide an income for children who are "needy" because their fathers are absent from the home, disabled, or unemployed. "Need" is determined by the state and is defined as the difference between an assistance budget for the family computed by the local agency and family income from all sources.

In December 1972, the program, available in every county in the United States, offered assistance to 8 million children and some 3 million parents. The typical AFDC family consisted of a mother and three children, and required assistance because of family disruption (divorce, desertion, separation). It had attempted to maintain itself without recourse to assistance for a period of some five months, and will be on assistance for a little over two years. It will, during the time it is on assistance, attempt to live on a budget that is only a little larger than one-half the amount determined as the "poverty index" level for a family of four.

In addition to the problem of living on a limited income, most AFDC families have additional problems of health, housing, and child care. The largest percentage of the children face the problem of living in a family without a father.

The program has succeeded in its major aim of maintaining dependent children in their own homes under the care of their mothers. It is less successful in keeping the children in school through high school graduation. Although AFDC children were ahead of their parents, educationally, they were behind their non-AFDC peers.

A review of the research regarding a special intensive casework approach to helping AFDC families suggests that such a program appears to be helpful, although clear attribution of results to intensive efforts is somewhat hazardous. Widespread efforts have been made to supplement casework by a group approach to AFDC families. The following problems are identified as a matter of concern to the program:

1. There is a need for general reform of the program to provide an adequate minimum income to all families in need. Recent legislative attempts toward such change were reviewed.
2. The general public may have unrealistic expectations concerning a sharp drop in the number of welfare recipients as a consequence of training and employment programs.
3. The negative public image of the program has reduced public willingness to provide the program with the resources it needs.
4. There are conflicts within the program concerning its attitude toward the father out of the home.
5. There is a disparity between the aims of the program and the levels of assistance it provides.

The following trends were discussed:

1. Changes are taking place in the nature of the problem situations that prompt families to apply for AFDC.
2. There is a trend away from concern with income maintenance toward a greater concern with casework services and vocational training and employment.
3. There is a continued increase in the number of recipients and in the cost of the program.
4. There is a greater concern for the legal and civil rights of recipients and the development of recipients' organizations.
5. There is a movement toward broader medical care coverage for children.
6. There is a trend toward the separation of income maintenance and social services.
7. Simpler eligibility procedures, based on client declaration forms, are being developed.
8. Agencies are contracting for the purchase of services to meet client needs.

Bibliography

1. ABBOTT, GRACE. *The Child and the State.* Chicago: University of Chicago Press, 1949, 2 vols.
2. ARNER, FREDERICK B. *The Work Incentive (WIN) Program: Establishment and Early Implementation.* Legislative Reference Service, Library of Congress, Washington, D.C., June 5, 1969.
3. ATHERTON, C. R. "Growing Up Obscene: The By-Product of Life on AFDC." *Public Welfare,* 27, 4 (April 1969), 371–75.
4. BARNWELL, JOHN. "The Mother's Club as a Setting for Group Counseling," in *Group Methods in the Public Welfare Programs.* Ed. by Norman Fenton and Kermit Wiltse. Palo Alto, Calif.: Pacific Books, Publishers, 1963.
5. BELL, WINIFRED. *Aid to Dependent Children.* New York: Columbia University Press, 1965.
6. ————. *The Practical Value of Social Work Services.* Bureau of Public Assistance, U.S. Department of Health, Education, and Welfare. Washington, D.C.: Government Printing Office, April 1961.
7. BERG, RENEE. "Utilizing the Strengths of Unwed Mothers in One AFDC Program." *Social Work,* 9 (July 1964).
8. BERKOW, RUTH, et al. *A Study of Patterns of Social Functioning of Families in the ADC Program in Essex and Somerset Counties, N.J.* An unpublished M.S. thesis. School of Social Work, Rutgers University, New Brunswick, N.J., June 1962.
9. BERNARD, SYDNEY E. "Innovation in Public Assistance: The Case of Eligi-

bility Declaration." *Social Work Practice*. New York: Columbia University Press, 1968.

10. BLACKWELL, GORDON, and RAYMOND GOULD. *Future Citizens All*. Chicago: American Public Welfare Association, 1952.

11. BONEN, GIL, and PHILIP RENO. "By Bread Alone and Little Bread: Life on AFDC." *Social Work*, **13**, 2 (April 1968), 5–11.

12. BRIAR, SCOTT. "Welfare from Below: Recipients' Views of the Public Welfare System." *California Law Review*, **54**, 2 (May 1966), 370–85.

13. BROWN, GEORGE E. *The Multiproblem Dilemma—A Social Research Demonstration with Multiproblem Families*. Metuchen, N.J.: Scarecrow Press, 1968.

14. BURGESS, M. ELAINE, and DANIEL O. PRICE. *An American Dependency Challenge*. Chicago: American Public Welfare Association, 1963.

15. BURNSIDE, BETTY. "The Employment Potential of AFDC Mothers in Six States." *Welfare in Review*, **9**, 4 (July–August 1971), 16–19.

16. ———. "Changes in AFDC 1969–1971." *Welfare in Review*, **10**, 2 (April 1972), 28–32.

17. BURNS, EVELINE. "What's Wrong with Public Welfare?" *Social Service Review*, **36** (June 1962).

18. CALIFORNIA STATE ASSEMBLY. *California Welfare: A Legislative Program for Reform*. California Legislature, Sacramento, Calif., 1969.

19. CAMERON, F. J. "The Use of Preintake Meetings for Prospective ANC Applicants," in *Group Methods in the Public Welfare Program*. Ed. by Norman Fenton and Kermit Wiltse. Palo Alto, Calif.: Pacific Books, Publishers, 1963.

20. CARTER, GENEVIEVE W. "The Employment Potential of AFDC Mothers: Some Questions and Some Answers." *Welfare in Review*, **6**, 3 (July–August 1968), 1–11.

21. ———. "Research in Public Welfare," in *Research in the Social Services—A Five-Year Review*. Ed. by Henry S. Maas. New York: National Association of Social Workers, 1971.

22. CHAMPION, BERNICE, and ARNOLD GEIN. "Group Meetings for Mothers on ANC as Preparation for Employment," in *Group Methods in the Public Welfare Program*. Ed. by Norman Fenton and Kermit Wiltse. Palo Alto, Calif.: Pacific Books, Publishers, 1963.

23. CHILTON, ROLAND. "The Consequences of Florida's Suitable Home Law—A Case of Ineffective Intervention." *Welfare in Review*, **7**, 5 (September–October 1969), 17–22.

24. CLAYTON, NORMAN. *Status of the Aid to Needy Children Program, Part I*. Department of Social Welfare, State of California, July 1960.

25. COLL, BLANCHE D. *Perspectives in Public Welfare—A History*. Social and Rehabilitation Service, U.S. Department of Health, Education, and Welfare. Washington, D.C.: Government Printing Office, 1969.

26. COSTABILE, JANE. *The AFDC Client in Small Group Settings*. Ann Arbor, Mich.: University of Michigan School of Social Work. April 1966. Mimeo.

27. COX, IRENE. "The Employment of Mothers as a Means of Family Support." *Welfare in Review*, **8**, 6 (November–December 1970).

28. CUTRIGHT, PHILLIPS. "AFDC, Family Allowance and Illegitimacy." *Family Planning Perspectives*, **2**, 4 (October 1970), 4–9.

29. DE MELTO, JUNE. "The Crises of the Tenth of the Month." *Public Welfare*, **21** (October 1963).

30. ECHMAN, FERN M. "Crusade Against the Poor." *Redbook* (February 1963).

31. EGLESON, JIM, and JANET EGLESON. *Parents Without Partners*. New York: Ace Books, Inc., 1961.

32. EPPLEY, DAVID B. "The AFDC Family in the 1960's." *Welfare in Review*, **8**, 5 (September–October 1970).

33. FEAGIN, JOE R. "We Still Believe That God Helps Those Who Help Themselves." *Psychology Today*, **6**, 6 (November 1972), 101–10.

34. FEIN, ARNOLD, and MARION SAMSON. "Group Meetings for Mothers on ANC as Preparation for Employment," in *Group Methods in the Public Welfare Program*. Ed. by Norman Fenton and Kermit Wiltse. Palo Alto, Calif.: Pacific Books, Publishers, 1963.

35. FENECHIL, OTTO. *Psychoanalytic Theory of Neuroses*. New York: W. W. Norton & Company, Inc., 1945.

36. FREUDANTHAL, KURT. "Problems of the One-Parent Family." *Social Work*, **4** (January 1959).

37. GEISMER, LUDWIG, and BEVERLY AYERS. *Measuring Family's Functioning*. St. Paul, Minn.: Family-Centered Project, Greater St. Paul Community Chest and Councils, Inc., 1960.

38. GELL, FRANK. *The Black Badge—Confessions of a Caseworker*. New York: Harper and Row, Publishers, 1969.

39. GELLHORN, WALTER. "Poverty and Legality: The Law's Slow Awakening." *William and Mary Law Review*, **9** (Winter 1967), 285–301.

40. GOLDSTEIN, JON H. *The Effectiveness of Manpower Training Programs: A Review of Research on the Impact of the Poor*. Studies in Public Welfare Paper No. 3. Joint Economic Committee, Congress of the U.S. Washington, D.C.: Government Printing Office, 1972.

41. GOODWIN, LEONARD. *Do the Poor Want to Work?* Washington, D.C.: The Brookings Institution, 1972.

42. GORDON, DAVID M. "Income and Welfare in New York City." *The Public Interest*, No. 16 (Summer 1969), 64–88.

43. GRANN, RICHARD P., *et al.* "How Well Does the System Work? Welfare Clients Speak Out." *Public Welfare*, **30**, 3 (Summer 1972), 34–38.

44. GREENLEIGH, ARTHUR. *Addenda to Facts, Fallacies, and Future: A Study of the Aid to Dependent Children Program of Cook County, Illinois*. New York: Greenleigh Associates, Inc., 1960.

45. ———. *Facts, Fallacies, and Future: A Study of the Aid to Dependent Children Program of Cook County, Illinois*. New York: Greenleigh Associates, Inc., 1960.

46. GREENLEIGH ASSOCIATES, INC. *Public Welfare: Poverty, Prevention, or Perpetuation*. New York: Greenleigh Associates, Inc., 1964.

47. GROSS, LEONARD. "Are We Paying an Illegitimacy Bonus?" *Saturday Evening Post* (January 30, 1960).

48. GRUSON, KERRY. "Welfare Women and Work Registration." *Human Needs*, **1**, 2 (August 1972), 17–18.

49. HAMILTON, JOHN. "Why It May Not Pay to Work." *New York Times Magazine* (Sunday, December 21, 1969).

50. HANDLER, JOEL, and MARGARET K. ROSENHEIM. "Privacy in Welfare: Public Assistance and Juvenile Justice." *Law and Contemporary Problems* (Spring 1966), 378–412.

51. ———, and ELLEN JANE HOLLINGSWORTH. "The Administration of Social Services and the Structure of Dependency: The Views of AFDC Recipients." *Social Service Review,* **43,** 4 (December 1969), 406–20.

52. ———, and ELLEN JANE HOLLINGSWORTH. *The "Deserving Poor"—A Study of Welfare Administration.* Chicago: Markham Publishing Co., 1971.

53. ———. *Reforming the Poor—Welfare Policy, Federalism and Morality.* New York: Basic Books, Inc., 1972.

54. HAUSEMAN, LEONARD. *The Potential for Work Among Welfare Parents.* U.S. Department of Labor. Manpower Research Monograph No. 12. Washington, D.C.: Government Printing Office, 1969.

55. HERZOG, ELIZABETH, and CECELIA SUDIA. "Fatherless Homes—A Review of the Research." *Children,* **15,** 5 (September–October 1968), 179–81.

56. HILL, REUBEN. *Families Under Stress.* New York: Harper and Row, Publishers, 1949.

57. HOFFMAN, JEAN. "Group Counseling with ANC Mothers," in *Group Methods in the Public Welfare Program.* Ed. by Norman Fenton and Kermit Wiltse. Palo Alto, Calif.: Pacific Books, Publishers, 1963.

58. HOSHINO, GEORGE. "Separating Maintenance from Social Services." *Public Welfare,* **30,** 2 (Spring 1972), 54–61.

59. HOUSTON, R. BERNARD, *et al. The Employment of AFDC Recipients in Michigan.* State of Michigan, Department of Social Services, June 1972.

60. HUNT, McVEIGH J., and LEONARD S. KOGAN. *Measuring Results in Social Casework: A Manual in Judging Movement,* rev. ed. New York: Family Service Association of America, 1952.

61. JEFFERS, CAMILLE. *Living Poor.* Ann Arbor, Mich.: Ann Arbor Publishers, 1967.

62. JOHNSON, LEONORA B. "A Child Welfare Worker Uses the Group Method with ADC Families." *Child Welfare,* **42** (January 1963).

63. KADUSHIN, ALFRED. "Single-Parent Adoptions: An Overview of Some Relevant Research." *Social Service Review,* **44,** 3 (September 1970), 263–74.

64. KALLEN, DAVID J., and DOROTHY MILLER. "Public Attitudes Toward Welfare." *Social Work,* **16,** 4 (July 1971), 83–90.

65. KEVIN, DAVID. "Group Counseling of Mothers in an AFDC Program." *Children,* **14,** 2 (March–April 1967), 69–74.

66. KNEBEL, FLETCHER. "Welfare: Has It Become a Scandal?" *Look,* **25** (November 7, 1961).

67. KNOWLTON, DEREK, and DOROTHY KEELING. "The Use of Group Counseling with Mothers in One-Parent Families in ANC Program," in *Group Methods in the Public Welfare Program.* Ed. by Norman Fenton and Kermit Wiltse. Palo Alto, Calif.: Pacific Books, Publishers, 1963.

68. KRIESBERG, LOUIS. *Mothers in Poverty—A Study of Fatherless Families.* Chicago: Aldine Publishing Company, 1970.

69. Kronick, Jane, et al. "The Legitimacy Status of Children Receiving AFDC." Child Welfare, 42 (July 1963).

70. Lampman, Robert. Nixon's Choices on Work for the Poor. Madison, Wis.: Institute for Research on Poverty, University of Wisconsin, May 1969.

71. Langer, Thomas, et al. "Psychiatric Impairment in Welfare and Non-welfare Children." Welfare in Review, 7, 3 (March–April 1969), 10–21.

72. Lansdale, Robert T. The Florida Suitable Home Law. Tallahassee, Fla.: School of Social Welfare, Florida State University, August 1962.

73. Lawrence, Harry. "Comparative Group Leadership Styles with Welfare Mothers." Public Welfare, 30, 3 (Summer 1972), 39–47.

74. LeBeaux, Charles. "Life on ADC: Budgets of Despair." New University Thought, 3 (Winter 1963).

75. Levinson, Perry. "How Employable Are AFDC Women?" Welfare in Review, 8, 4 (July–August 1970), 12–16.

76. ———. "The Next Generation—A Study of Children in AFDC Families." Welfare in Review, 7, 3 (March–April 1969), 1–9.

77. Levitan, Sar, et al. Work and Welfare Go Together. Baltimore: Johns Hopkins University Press, 1972.

78. Lewis, Verl S. "Local General Assistance Costs and Restrictive Categorical Aid Policies." Social Work, 6 (October 1961).

79. Lundberg, Emma O. Unto the Least of These . . . Social Services for Children. New York: Appleton-Century-Crofts, 1947.

80. Lynch, John M. "Case Turnover in AFDC." Welfare in Review, 2 (July 1964).

81. Lynn, David, and William Sawry. "The Effects of Father-Absence on Norwegian Boys and Girls." Journal of Abnormal and Social Psychology, 59 (September 1959).

82. MacLatchie, Elizabeth. Simplifying Application and Investigation Processes. Chicago: American Public Welfare Association, September 1968.

83. Marin, R. C. A Comprehensive Program for Multiproblem Families—Report on a Four-Year Controlled Experiment. Puerto Rico: Institute of Caribbean Studies, University of Puerto Rico, 1969.

84. Marks, Leah. Your Right to Welfare—A Statement of the Facts About Public Assistance in New York City. New York: Citizens' Committee for Children and Youth, Inc., and Columbia University Center on Social Welfare Policy and Law, July 1968.

85. Marsden, Dennis. Mothers Alone—Poverty and the Fatherless Family. Baltimore: Penguin Press, 1969.

86. McKeany, Maurine. The Absent Father and Public Policy in the Program of Aid to Dependent Children. University of California Publications in Social Welfare, I. Berkeley and Los Angeles: University of California Press, 1960.

87. Meier, Elizabeth. "Casework Services to ADC Families." Public Welfare, 19 (1961).

88. Miller, Florine. "Pioneering Group Counseling with A.N.C. Mothers," in Group Methods in the Public Welfare Program. Ed. by Norman Fenton and Kermit Wiltse. Palo Alto, Calif.: Pacific Books, Publishers, 1963.

89. MILLER, WALTER. "Implications of Lower-Class Culture for Social Work." *Social Service Review*, **33** (September 1959).
90. MILWAUKEE COUNTY DEPARTMENT OF PUBLIC WELFARE. *1960 Annual Report.* Intensive Case Unit, Department of Public Welfare. Milwaukee County Department of Public Welfare, Milwaukee, Wis., 1960. Mimeo.
91. MILWAUKEE COUNTY WELFARE RIGHTS ORGANIZATION. *Welfare Mothers Speak Out—We Ain't Gonna Shuffle Anymore.* New York: W. W. Norton & Company, Inc., 1972.
92. MINYARD, OLIVE, and DENZIL JOHNSTON. "The Use of Group Counseling with Mothers in an A.N.C. Program," in *Group Methods in the Public Welfare Program.* Ed. by Norman Fenton and Kermit Wiltse. Palo Alto, Calif.: Pacific Books, Publishers, 1963.
93. MOLLOY, PAUL. "The Relief Chiselers Are Stealing Us Blind." *Saturday Evening Post* (September 8, 1951).
94. MONTELIUS, MARJORIE. *Working with Groups—A Guide for Administration of Group Services in Public Welfare.* Washington, D.C.: Government Printing Office, 1967.
95. MORGAN, JAMES N., et al. *Income and Welfare: The U.S.* New York: McGraw-Hill Book Company, 1962.
96. MORSE, HAROLD. "Measuring the Potential of AFDC Families for Economic Independence." *Welfare in Review*, **6**, 6 (November–December 1968), 13–18.
97. MUGGE, ROBERT. "Education and AFDC." *Welfare in Review*, **2** (January 1964).
98. MULLEN, EDWARD S., et al. *Preventing Chronic Dependency—An Evaluation of Public–Private Collaborative Intervention with First-Time Public Assistance Families.* New York: Institute for Welfare Research, Community Service Society, December 1970.
99. ———, et al. "Services for the Newly Dependent: An Assessment." *Social Service Review*, **46**, 3 (September 1972), 309–22.
100. NAVARRE, ELIZABETH, and PAUL GLASSER. *Group Work Practice with AFDC Mothers—An Evaluation Study.* Ann Arbor, Mich.: School of Social Work, University of Michigan, April 1969. Mimeo.
101. NIXON, RICHARD. "Message to Congress." *Welfare in Review*, **7**, 5 (September–October 1969).
102. OBERHEU, HOWARD. "AFDC Mothers—Employed and Not Employed." *Welfare in Review*, **10**, 3 (May–June 1972), 58–61.
103. O'REILLY, CHARLES T., and MARGARET M. PEMBROKE. *Chicago's ADC Families—Their Characteristics and Problems.* Chicago: Loyola University School of Social Work, 1960.
104. PIVEN, FRANCES F., and RICHARD A. CLAWARD. *Regulating the Poor—The Functions of Public Welfare.* New York: Pantheon Books, Inc., 1971.
105. PLATT, ANTHONY. *The Child Savers—The Invention of Delinquency.* Chicago: University of Chicago Press, 1969.
106. PODELL, LAWRENCE. *The Attitudes Toward Social Services of Mothers on Welfare.* New York: Human Resources Administration, Department of Social Services, n.d.
107. ———. *Families on Welfare in New York City.* New York: Center for Study of Urban Problems, City University of New York, 1968.

108. POMEROY, RICHARD. *Studies in Public Welfare—Reactions of Welfare Clients to Caseworker Contact.* New York: Center for the Study of Urban Problems, City University of New York, n.d.

109. ———, et al. *Studies in Public Welfare: Reaction of Welfare Clients to Social Service.* New York: Center for the Study of Urban Problems, City University of New York, n.d.

110. PRESCOTT, EDWARD, et al. "Training and Employability." *Welfare in Review,* **9**, 1 (January–February 1971), 1–6.

111. PUBLIC WELFARE REPORTING CENTER. *Social Services in Public Welfare.* New York: Public Welfare Reporting, National Study Service, Inc., August 1969.

112. ———. *Facts About Welfare—Declarations or a Simplified Method of Eligibility Determination in the Administration of Public Assistance.* New York: National Study Service, Inc., May 1969.

113. ———. *Are People Treated Equitably in Our Public Welfare Program?* New York: National Study Service, Inc., March 1969.

114. PUMPHREY, RALPH E., and MURIEL M. PUMPHREY. *The Heritage of American Social Work.* New York: Columbia University Press, 1961.

115. PURDY, DELOREZ. "A New Approach Toward Helping Public Assistance Families," in *Group Methods in the Public Welfare Program.* Ed. by Norman Fenton and Kermit Wiltse. Palo Alto, Calif.: Pacific Books, Publishers, 1963.

116. REICH, CHARLES. "Individual Rights and Social Welfare: The Emerging Legal Issues." *Yale Law Journal,* **74**, 7 (July 1965), 1245–57.

117. REID, JOSEPH, and ELIZABETH GLOVER. "Unmet and Future Need. Programs and Problems in Child Welfare." *Annals of American Academy of Political and Social Science,* **355** (September 1964).

118. REID, WILLIAM J., and Audrey D. SMITH. "AFDC Mothers View the Work Incentive Program." *Social Service Review,* **46**, 3 (September 1972), 347–61.

119. REIN, MILDRED, and BARBARA WISHNOV. "Patterns of Work and Welfare in AFDC." *Welfare in Review,* **9**, 6 (November–December 1971), 7–12.

120. ROMANYSHYN, JOHN. *Aid to Dependent Children in Maine—A Study of Family Management.* State of Maine Department of Health and Welfare, June 1960.

121. RUDOFF, ALVIN, and IRVING PILIAVIN. "An Aid to Needy Children Program: A Study of Types and Responses to Casework Services." *Community Mental Health Journal,* **5**, 1 (1969), 20–28.

122. SHOEMAKER, LOUISE P. "Social Groupwork in the ADC Program." *Social Work,* **8** (January 1963).

123. SPRING, WILLIAM, et al. "In Much of the Inner City 60 per cent Don't Earn Enough for a Decent Standard of Living." *The New York Times Magazine* (November 5, 1972), 42–60.

124. STATE OF CALIFORNIA DEPARTMENT OF SOCIAL WELFARE. *A Study of Marin County, California.* Sacramento, Calif.: State of California Department of Social Welfare, n.d.

125. ———. *Fraud—The Aid to Needy Children Program.* Sacramento, Calif.: State of California Department of Public Welfare, July 1960.

126. STEINER, GILBERT. *The State of Welfare.* Washington, D.C.: The Brookings Institution, 1971.
127. STERN, SOL. *The Screws Are On the Welfare System—Down and Out in New York. The New York Times Magazine* (Sunday, October 22, 1972), 46–65.
128. STONE, ROBERT C., and FREDERIC T. SCHLAMP. *Welfare and Working Fathers—Low-Income Life Styles.* Lexington, Mass.: D. C. Heath & Company, Inc., 1971.
129. TRECKER, HARLEIGH. *Group Service in Public Welfare.* Bureau of Family Services. U.S. Department of Health, Education, and Welfare. Washington, D.C.: Government Printing Office, 1964.
130. TURMAN, GEORGE. "A Chronological Report on the Use of Group Counseling with ANC Recipients," in *Group Methods in the Public Welfare Program.* Ed. by Norman Fenton and Kermit Wiltse. Palo Alto, Calif.: Pacific Books, Publishers, 1963.
131. TUTTLE, ELIZABETH. *Narrative Report of the Special ADC Project.* Cuyahoga County Welfare Department, Cleveland, Ohio, January 1963.
132. U.S. CHILDREN'S BUREAU. "Mothers' Aid 1931." Reprinted in *Children and Youth—A Documentary History.* Ed. by Robert H. Bremner. Cambridge, Mass.: Harvard University Press, 1971.
133. U.S. CONGRESS. *Income Transfer Programs: How They Tax the Poor.* Subcommittee on Fiscal Policy, Joint Economic Committee. Washington, D.C.: Government Printing Office, 1972.
134. U.S. DEPARTMENT OF COMMERCE, NATIONAL TECHNICAL INFORMATION SERVICE. *Purchase of Social Services—A Study of the Experience of Those States in the Purchase of Service by Contract Under the Provisions of the 1967 Amendments to the Social Security Act.* Washington, D.C.: Government Printing Office, January 1971.
135. U.S. DEPARTMENT OF HEALTH, EDUCATION, AND WELFARE. "Aid to Dependent Children of Unemployed Parents: The First Seven Months of Operation." *Social Security Bulletin,* 25 (August 1962).
136. ———. *Serving People in Need—Public Assistance Under the Social Security Act.* Washington, D.C.: Government Printing Office, 1964.
137. ———. *Social Development, Key to the Great Society.* Washington, D.C.: Government Printing Office, 1966.
138. ———. "Study of Effect of Relief Curtailment in an Ohio County." *Social Security Bulletin,* 27 (February 1964).
139. ———. *Report of the Task Force on Medicaid and Related Programs.* Washington, D.C.: Government Printing Office, 1970.
140. ———. *The Separation of Services from the Determination of Eligibility for Assistance Payments—A Guide for State Agencies. A Draft.* Washington, D.C.: Government Printing Office, 1970.
141. ———, National Center for Social Statistics. Social and Rehabilitation Service, *1967 AFDC Study—Preliminary Report of Findings from Mail Questionnaire.* January 1969. Mimeo.
142. ———. *Graphic Presentation of Public Assistance and Related Data 1970.* Report 1f-4(70). Washington, D.C.: National Center for Social Statistics, August 1971.

143. ———, Social Rehabilitation Service. *Report on the Disposition of Public Assistance Cases Involving Questions of Fraud, Fiscal Year 1970.* Washington, D.C.: National Center for Social Statistics, 1971.

144. ———, Social Rehabilitation Service. *Public Assistance Statistics.* Washington, D.C.: National Center for Social Statistics.

145. ———, Social Rehabilitation Service. *Findings of the 1971 AFDC Study, December 22, 1971.* Washington, D.C.: Government Printing Office, 1972.

146. Vernier, Paul, and Robert H. Mugge. "Findings of the AFDC Eligibility Review." *Welfare in Review,* 1 (October 1963).

147. Wallace, David, and Jessie Smith. *The Chemung County Research Demonstration with Dependent Multi-Problem Families.* New York: State Charities Aid Association, 1965.

148. Warren, Martin, and Sheldon Berkowitz. "A Pilot Project Assesses the Employability of AFDC Mothers and Fathers." *Welfare in Review,* 7, 4 (July–August 1969), 1–7.

149. Welfare Rights Organization. *Six Myths About Welfare.* Washington, D.C.: Welfare Rights Organization, February 1971.

150. Wickenden, Elizabeth, and Winifred Bell. *Public Welfare—Time for a Change.* New York: Columbia University School of Social Work, 1961.

151. Wilson, Robert C. "An Evaluation of Intensive Casework Impact." *Public Welfare,* 25, 4 (October 1967).

152. Wiltse, Kermit. "New Approaches to Administration of ADC Programs." *Casework Papers* (1959).

153. Wynn, Margaret. *Fatherless Families.* London: Michael Joseph Ltd., 1964.

154. Yahr, Harold, et al. *Studies in Public Welfare: Effect of Eligibility Investigation on Welfare Clients.* New York: Center for the Study of Urban Problems, City University of New York, 1967.

155. Youngman, Louise. "Social Groupwork in the AFDC Program." *Public Welfare,* 23 (January 1965).

# Protective Services

Introduction

It is difficult to neatly classify protective services as either supportive, supplementary, or substitutive. Protective services are called upon in a variety of situations, characterized by a similar factor: neglect, abuse, or exploitation of a child. The protective service agency is organized around the nature of the problem, and uses a wide variety of services—supportive, supplementary, and substitutive—in trying to help the family deal with it. The agency may seek to protect the child by strengthening the home (*supportive*), by supplementing the parent's own efforts to care for the child (*supplementary*), or by removing the child from the home and placing him in another home (*substitutive*).

Definition

The Child Welfare League of America defines *child protective service* as "a specialized child welfare service which carries a delegated responsibility to offer help in behalf of any child considered, or found to be, neglected. . . . Its distinctive aspects are related to the social problem of child neglect." [34, pp. 1–2] *Neglect* is broadly defined to encompass both passive neglect and active abuse or exploitation, and covers the social, emotional, educational, and physical needs of the child.

Protective service is "based on law and is supported by community standards. Its purpose is protection of children through strengthening the home or, failing that, making plans for their care and custody through the courts. . . . [It is] a service on behalf of children undertaken by an agency upon receipt of information which indicates that parental responsibility toward those children is not being effectively met." [32, p. 8]

The Children's Division of the American Humane Society, the national body coordinating the work of protective agencies, defines *protective service* as "a specialized casework service to neglected, abused, exploited, or rejected children. The focus of the service is preventive and nonpunitive and is geared toward rehabilitation through identification and treatment of the motivating factors which underlie" the problem. [39, p. 2]

The problems with which the protective agencies are concerned arise from gross parental inadequacy in role performance and from active role rejection. The parent may be present, but incapable of caring for the child, or unwilling to do so. Under the concept of *parens patriae*, the state has an obligation, as a "parent" to all children, to defend the rights of the child. The problem, however, is to avoid "infringing on the rights of the general parent population while simultaneously insuring the rights of a specific child." [23, p. 8]   One might, however, say that parental rights derive from parental obligations. When these obligations and responsibilities are unfulfilled, the corresponding rights may be abrogated. Currently, the right of the parent to the control of his child is regarded as an inherent natural right subject to the protection of due process. The natural right is not regarded as absolute; it is in the nature of a trust.

Judicial power of the community to intervene in behalf of the child against the parent "has rarely been challenged; only its *extent* has been questioned." [137, p. 353]   The justification for community intervention is based on the need for community self-preservation. The continuity of the group rests with children. Any danger to the life of the child threatens such continuity. Thus, intervention in cases of neglect and abuse is merely an extension of the community's need to intervene against infanticide. More immediately, however, the community's justification for intervention lies in the fact that neglect or abuse of the child is likely to result in an expense to the community: the child may need care or medical attention at community expense; the neglected child is less apt to grow up to be a self-sustaining adult.

The humanitarian justification goes beyond these considerations: a child should not be abused or neglected; he has a right to expect protection and care.

It is often suggested that urban living makes imperative a more formal, legalized expression of such concern.

In stable, closely knit communities, informal supports and restraints contributing to the protection of children were exercised by public opinion and by concerned relatives, friends, and neighbors, who were aware of problems within the family group. The absence of these supports and restraints, related to the anonymity made possible in mobile, urban, populations, has created a vacuum. The community can no longer rely completely upon public opinion, relatives, friends and neighbors, to provide protection to the child whose health and life are in danger. [23, p. 8]

Jules Henry, an anthropologist, notes:

There is minimal social regulation of parent-child relations in our culture; this is, above all, what makes lethal child-care practices possible. In a primitive culture, where many relatives are around to take an active interest in one's baby, where life is open, or in large households, where many people can see what a mother is doing and where deviations from traditional practice quickly offend the eye and loosen critical, interested tongues, it is impossible for a parent to do as he or she pleases with his child. In a literal sense, a baby is often not even one's own in such societies, but belongs to a lineage, clan, or household—a community—having a real investment in the baby. It is not private enterprise. The almost total absence of the social regulation of parent-child relations in our private-enterprise culture is a pivotal environmental factor making it necessary to institutionalize community concern in an agency offering protective service. [68, p. 332]

All agencies concerned with child welfare may be said to be protective agencies. In the more specialized use of the term, the protective agency is an agency that is given special responsibility in cases of child abuse, exploitation, and neglect. Such agencies are often delegated, usually by charter, some specific authority to act for the community in its collective expression of concern for children.

Others have questioned the distinctiveness and uniqueness of the protective service agencies. It is pointed out that all agencies have a responsibility to intervene when a child is abused or neglected, that authority is inherent in all social work, and that the protective agency, in petitioning for court action, has no greater mandate than any other agency. [127] Nevertheless, the fact is that other agencies in the community tend to attribute to the protective service agency greater responsibility for problems of abuse and neglect.

Kahn aptly notes that "the protective responsibility is lodged in the whole community" and it is the total configuration of all the agencies serving children which are, in aggregate, capable of "protecting" children so as to insure all their rights. However, the protective service agency does have a special function: "The protective service moves into action only when socially defined minimums are not met or where children are in clear and present danger." [75, p. 325] And Boehm indicates that the protective service agency itself "appears to accept the role of 'agency of last resort.' " [25, p. 46]

This may in fact be desirable, because it permits a clear delineation of function, giving one agency responsibility for court action, freeing the "family agency to continue to concentrate on those families who are motivated to seek service and to refer others elsewhere. . . . The family agency can continue to be perceived as a source of help, not a source of threat." [124, p. 66]

Historical Background

In earlier periods of history, the child was regarded as a chattel of his parents. In its most unrestricted expression, this gave the parents the right to kill the child at birth, to sell him, to exploit his labor, or to offer him as a sacrifice to a deity. Although almost every community restricted and regulated such rights to some extent, until recently parental power over the child was subject to relatively few limitations. Blake's poem "The Chimney Sweeper," written in 1788, illustrates the extent of parental control:

> When my mother died I was very young,
> And my father sold me, while yet my tongue
> Could scarcely cry weep, weep, weep,
> So your chimneys I sweep and in soot I sleep.

Acceptable, sanctioned procedures for disciplining the child differ with the culture and the times. The Biblical injunction in Proverbs 23:13–14 might be regarded as sanctioning what might today be termed child abuse, "Withhold not correction from the child for if thou beatest him with the rod he shall not die; thou shalt beat him with the rod and shalt deliver his soul from Hell."

In one of the earliest (English) handbooks on the upbringing of the young, parents were advised:

> If thy children rebel and will not bow them low
> If any of them misdo, neither curse nor blow
> But take a smart rod and beat them in a row
> Till they cry mercy and their guilt well know. [119, p. 157]

Henry IV of France, whom "contemporaries regarded as an especially easygoing father" [72, p. 138], writes to those caring for his young son:

> I have a complaint to make: you do not send word that you have whipped my son. I wish and command you to whip him every time that he is obstinate or misbehaves, knowing well for myself that there is nothing in the world which will be better for him than that. I know it from experience, having myself profited, for when I was his age I was often whipped. That is why I want you to whip him and to make him understand why. [72, p. 135]

Until the early part of the twentieth century, parents were allowed to exploit the labor of their children:

> In the silk mills children were generally taken about seven, but some as early as six, principally, it was said, to oblige their parents. . . . "If there was a restriction as to the work of children under ten years of age," said William Sedgwick, a cotton spinner of Skipton, "I think the parents would be injured thereby because many children under ten aid the sustaining of their family by their wages." [71, p. 81]

A Manchester merchant, testifying in the nineteenth century at a hearing regarding child labor, noted that if a proposed bill safeguarding the health of children in factories were passed, "parents would conceive it a loss of the British birthright, that of control of a parent over his child." [71, p. 47] In 1880, Lord Shaftsbury, when his attention was called to the manifestations of child abuse and exploitation, said:

> The evils you state are enormous and indisputable, but they are of so private, internal, and domestic a character as to be beyond the reach of legislation and the subject would not, I think, be entertained in either House of Parliament. [1, p. 16]

In a general way, the neglected child has always been an object of concern in America. [52, pp. 167–69] But the agencies concerned with child protection trace their origin to the dramatic case of Mary Ellen in 1875. The child was cruelly beaten and neglected by a couple with whom she had lived since infancy. There seemed no appropriate legal measure available to protect her. Community leaders, concerned with the situation, appealed to the Society for the Prevention of Cruelty to Animals. This organization brought Mary Ellen to the attention of the court as an "animal" who was being mistreated. Because the law did protect animals from abuse, the complaint was accepted, protection was granted Mary Ellen, and her guardians were sent to prison. As a result of this case, a Society for the Prevention of Cruelty to Children was organized.

The organization of the New York County Society for the Prevention of Cruelty to Children in 1875 was a signal for the development of similar societies elsewhere: San Francisco, Boston, Rochester, Baltimore, Buffalo, and Philadelphia. Many of the Societies for Prevention of Cruelty to Children were originally organized as separate voluntary agencies; others were organized as subdivisions of the existing agencies concerned with the protection of animals, because "there was acquiescence in the view of the fundamental similarity of protective work for children and of animals." [90, p. 138]   Over the course of time, some of these agencies have merged with social agencies concerned with child welfare, while others have maintained their separate identity. The American Humane Society, originally organized for the protection of animals, established a Children's Division in 1887 to coordinate the activities of the various voluntary protective service associations that were developing throughout the country. By 1900, 161 such societies had been established throughout the United States. [52, p. 173]

The work of these agencies centered around "child rescue." The agency "uncovered" the cases of children who were neglected, abused, or exploited, and worked to remove the children from their homes. The emphasis was on legal action and the agency agitated for, and supported, efforts to enact legislation for the protection of children and to enforce these laws. Thus, as Sandusky notes, "such agencies performed a law enforcement function primarily rather than a social service function." [127, p. 579]

One of the earliest of these societies, the Massachusetts Society for the Prevention of Cruelty to Children, was established in 1878 for the purpose, as stated in its charter, "of awakening interest in the abuse to which children are exposed by the intemperance, cruelty, or cupidity of parents and guardians and to help in the enforcement of existing laws under the subject, procure needed legislation, and for kindred work." [124, p. 1]

Almost from the start, however, another orientation, less legalistic and more social, was evident. It suggested that the primary rationale of protective services was to help the parents, not to punish them, to keep the family together, rather than to disrupt it. It is a difference between seeing the protective service agency as a law enforcement agency and seeing it as a social agency. This orientation was given considerable emphasis by the First White House Conference on Children, in its declaration that the child should not be removed from the home for reason of poverty alone. It was given further impetus by the growing recognition, based on the developing science of child psychology, of the importance of the home to the child.

However, despite the fact that the current definitions of protective services express a social work rather than a legal emphasis ("protection of child through strengthening of the home"; "preventive, nonpunitive service geared toward rehabilitation"), the two points of view are inherent in the operations of all agencies. What has been achieved is the greater stress on one, not the elimination of either.

The rapid development of protective agencies in the late nineteenth and early twentieth centuries was followed by a period of very limited growth. In fact, even today many areas of the country do not have such agencies. Impetus to the formation of such agencies was supplied by Title V, Part 3, of the Social Security Act, which granted Federal funds to states for the care of "children who are dependent, neglected, or in danger of becoming delinquent." Further impetus was given by the 1960 Golden Anniversary White House Conference on Children and Youth, which recommended that states enact legislation authorizing communities to charge a specific social agency with responsibility for receiving complaints regarding child neglect and to provide services to the children and parents involved. Further development of protective services resulted from the 1962 amendments to the Social Security Act, which required each state to develop a plan to extend child welfare services—protective services among them—to every political subdivision of the state.

Distinctive Aspects

The state is, ultimately, a parent to all children. When the natural parents neglect, abuse, or exploit the child, the state has the legal right and responsibility to intervene to protect him. The state delegates this authority to the protective service agency, so that, in effect, the agency operates as an arm of the state and operates with legal sanctions. In such situations not only does the protective service agency have the right to intervene, they have the duty to intervene. All social agencies have an obligation to concern themselves with any situation of danger or potential danger to children, but the protective service agency has an explicitly delegated responsibility to intervene in such situations.

It follows, therefore, that protective services may be initiated on the basis of a request by someone other than a member of the family. In the case of services discussed earlier, client participation was voluntary; in the case of protective services, client involvement may be involuntary. Protective services deal with those instances of failure in parental role performance in which the parent is unaware of the need for service, or is unwilling and/or unable to avail himself of the services the community has provided.

Once involved, the agency cannot withdraw until the child is clearly no longer in danger. Just as the family is not permitted to decide whether or not they want the agency's help, the community does not permit the agency to decide whether or not it should offer the service. "The agency cannot leave a client free to accept or reject its services; nor can it withdraw only because the parent has refused or is unable to take help." [32, p. 8]

The agency's responsibility of staying with the situation as long as danger to the child exists is illustrated in the following case:

Neighbors complained that a young mother was seriously neglecting her four-month-old daughter, the first and only child. When the child welfare worker visited the home, she found the baby looking very pale and listless and apparently not in good physical condition. She persuaded the mother to take the baby to a clinic, where the child was found to be seriously malnourished and to have a severe diaper rash. On her next visit to the home, the worker found that the mother had apparently done nothing to carry out the doctor's instructions. As the worker talked to the mother about her lack of care and the seriousness of the baby's condition, the mother ordered her out of the house. The worker agreed to go, but explained that she would have to continue her responsibility for seeing that the baby had more adequate care even to the point of filing petition at court, if necessary. The worker called in a public health nurse, who helped the mother follow the doctor's instructions. The mother told the nurse how sorry she was about the way she had treated the child welfare worker and asked the nurse to tell her to return. The worker went back promptly and from then on was able to help the young mother and her husband grow in their ability to care for their child. [128, p. 24] *

Because the agency operates on the basis of delegated authority, it may invoke legal sanction, if necessary, to protect the child and his rights. Although all agencies have the right to petition the court for protection of the children with whom they are concerned, the protective agencies are viewed by themselves, by other agencies, and by the client group as the agency having special responsibility for invoking such sanctions.

---

* From Annie L. Sandusky, "Services to Neglected Children," *Children* (January–February 1960). By permission of the author and *Children*, U.S. Department of Health, Education, and Welfare, Social Security Administration, Children's Bureau.

Situations for Which Protective Services Are Appropriate

The situations in which protective agencies intervene are those in which the parent is unable and/or unwilling to enact the parental role effectively, and his failure constitutes an actual danger to the normal physical, emotional, and social development of the child. The statutory definition of *neglect* suggests the different kinds of situations. Although they differ from state to state, these definitions generally include the following:

1. Physical abuse.
2. Malnourishment; poor clothing; lack of proper shelter, sleeping arrangements, attendance, or supervision.
3. Denial of essential medical care.
4. Failure to attend school regularly.
5. Exploitation, overwork.
6. Exposure to unwholesome or demoralizing circumstances.

Social workers and mental hygienists are concerned about still another kind of neglect rarely mentioned in the statutes: emotional neglect, a denial of normal experiences that permit a child to feel loved, wanted, secure, and worthy.

Physical Abuse

Physical abuse refers to those situations involving a child who is beaten to the point where he sustains physical damage. The line between physical abuse and harsh parental discipline is difficult to define. As Arnold says, "forms of punishment considered proper, and even wholesome, in Elizabethan or Victorian days would be considered as abuse today." [6, p. 3] Silver raises the question of limits:

For example, if a parent punishes a child with a belt, is it after the fourth slash with the belt that parental rights end and child abuse begins; is it after the belt raises a welt over two millimeters that it becomes abuse versus parental rights? [125, p. 804]

Yet there would be little doubt that the following examples, reported by local newspapers, would be generally considered physical abuse.

A five-year-old girl wandered innocently onto a porch after being instructed not to do so. She was kicked back into the house, thrown across the room and hit on the head and face with a skillet.
    The father of a nine-month-old boy blackened his son's eyes,

burned his face, hands, and neck, and fractured his skull. [31, p. 126]

A national newspaper survey of published reports of physical abuse conducted by the Children's Division of the American Humane Society revealed that in 1962 children were beaten

. . . with various kinds of implements and instruments. The hairbrush was a common implement used to beat children. However, the same purpose was accomplished with deadlier impact by the use of bare fists, straps, electric cords, T.V. aerials, ropes, rubber hose, fan belts, sticks, wooden spoons, pool cues, bottles, broom handles, baseball bats, chair legs, and, in one case, a sculling oar. Less imaginative, but equally effective, was plain kicking with street shoes or with work shoes.

Children had their extremities—hands, arms, and feet—burned in open flames as from gas burners or cigarette lighters. Others bore burn wounds inflicted on their bodies with lighted cigarettes, electric irons, or hot pokers. Still others were scalded by hot liquids thrown over them or from being dipped into containers of hot liquids. . . .

What kinds of injuries were inflicted on them?

The majority had various shapes, sizes, and forms of bruises and contusions. There was a collection of welts, swollen limbs, split lips, black eyes, and lost teeth. One child lost an eye.

Broken bones were common. Some were simple fractures; others, compound. There were many broken arms, broken legs, and fractured ribs. Many children had more than one fracture. One five-month-old child was found to have thirty broken bones in his little body. [37, p. 6]

In some instances cruelty is episodic and nonrecurrent. Frequently, however, an abused child has suffered abuse before.

In the late 1960's, in response to the growing concern with the "battered-child syndrome," all states adopted child abuse reporting laws. As Paulsen notes, "Few legislative proposals in the history of the United States have been so widely adopted in so little time." [116]

The laws generally require that professionals in contact with a possibly abused child report the incident to some agency. Social workers and doctors are the professionals most frequently identified as being required to make such a report. The agencies to which reports are to be made are generally the public welfare agency or the legal agencies of the community. The laws grant civil and criminal immunity to the professionals required to make such reports, provide penalties for failure to report, and sometimes provide for follow-up. The abuse-reporting laws are essentially a case-finding device that helps the community to identify the abusive family and the abused child. [147]

A recent nationwide study of child abuse reports found that slightly more than half the abused children were boys, 46 percent were over six years of age, and a disproportionate percentage were nonwhite. [58] Abuse occurred in the child's home, most frequently shortly before and after dinner. Most often the children suffered "bruises, welts" or "abrasions, contusions, lacerations," as a result of "beating with hands" or "beating with instruments."

The abuser was most frequently the child's own mother, partly because a very high percentage of abusive families were headed by a woman, partly because the mother is in more constant contact with the child. While some college graduates and professional workers were reported among the abusers, the largest percentage of the reported group had low educational attainment and occupational status. Family income was low and expenses were high since almost half the families had four or more children. Only about 11 percent of the abusive parents had themselves experienced abuse as children.

About half the children and at least 60 percent of the parents involved had showed noticeable deviations in social, behavioral, physical, or intellectual functioning in the year before the abusive incident.

In most cases, the victim's own family sought help—their first choice, medical services; second, the police; and third, some social agency. Social agencies carried the major responsibility for helping the family and the children after the incident became known, eventually becoming involved in service to 90 percent of the families. About a third of the children were placed away from home by agencies after the abuse.

Neglect

Child neglect may be regarded as another kind of problem. The parent who abuses or cruelly mistreats the child is guilty of a crime of commission; neglect is more frequently a problem of omission. The ultimate in neglect, of course, is child abandonment. The abandoned child is, by virtue of his abandonment, a client of the protective service agency. [63] In less egregious instances, the child is found to be living in filth, malnourished, without proper clothing, unattended, and unsupervised.

The neglectful parent may be rejecting his parental role; more frequently, however, he is merely inadequate in performing it—and he is suffering along with the child.

A woman charged with child neglect described her third-floor cold-water flat to the judge at the hearing:

It is an awful place to live. The wallpaper is in strips, the floor board is cracked. The baby is always getting splinters in his hands. The bathroom is on the floor above and two other families use it. The kitchen is on the first floor. I share it with another woman. I have no place to keep food. We buy for one meal at a time. [63, p. 5]

The following instances detail the social worker's description of situations encountered in investigating complaints of neglect:

The family of ten is living in two rooms. The plaster is falling down; window panes were out; the plumbing leaked. The wind howled through cracks and it was bitterly cold. Two young children with frostbitten hands and feet were removed from this home to a hospital. [63, p. 10]

What I saw as I entered the room was utter, stark, disorganization. The room was a combined kitchen-dining room. At the other end of the room two scrawny, owl-eyed frightened children—a girl of about four and a boy of three—stared silently at me. Except for thin cotton undershirts, they were stark naked. They had sore crusts on their legs and arms. They were indescribably dirty, hair matted, body and hands stained and covered with spilled food particles. Sitting on a urine-soaked and soiled mattress in a baby carriage behind them was a younger child—a boy about two.

The floor was ankle deep in torn newspapers. There were feces in about a half-dozen spots on the floor and the air was fetid and saturated with urine odor.

There were flies everywhere. What seemed like giant roaches were crawling over the paper-strewn floor. The kitchen sink and gas stove were piled high with greasy and unwashed dishes, pots, and pans. [41, p. 11]

Another report reads:

The eight children are cold and hungry. There is no heat in the home and the children have been observed begging for food in the vicinity of a diner. [124, p. 42]

The police are frequently the first to be involved, and police patrol-car reports often detail cases of neglect:

Responded to a complaint concerning three children, ages two to six, left alone in a parked car for several hours. Observation indicated that the children were dirty and unkempt, cold and hungry, poorly clothed, and in need of medical care.

Responded to a domestic disturbance where drinking parents had been fighting, children were frightened and appeared to be abused by parents. The home was in disorder.

Responded to a complaint about several children ages three to seven, left alone in a small apartment for several hours. [143, p. 44]

These dramatic accounts might be balanced by a more "typical" illustration of neglect.

The father, an unskilled laborer, had only seasonal jobs which paid poorly. Public funds supplemented their meager income. The mother handled the budget poorly and frequently did not pay rent or gas and electric bills so that the family was periodically threatened by eviction from their poor slum dwelling or the cutting off of utilities. A [social] worker, who could see her only briefly once a month at the time of the arrival of the check, simply went over the budget. The mother would agree to carry out the budget but the next month it would be the same story.

Meantime the children were out of school frequently with respiratory illnesses. Sometimes they just truanted. When they truanted, they stayed out of sight of the mother and the house. Miraculously, they got into no more difficulties than a few minor thefts. When the attendance officer visited the home, the mother said in despair that she could do nothing with the children. At other times it was noted that she made all kinds of excuses to protect the children, and even hid them when she spotted the attendance officer or the social worker coming.

The mother told of the woeful life she had had since she was ten after her mother died. She had been very dependent on her own mother. She had stopped school in a few years, having reached only the sixth or seventh grade. Her father became demoralized after his wife's death; she went out to work and married very early.

She married an older man whose work potential was low, so she still had not found the dependency and security she sought as an extension of her own dependent and deprived childhood. But she told with pride about how she had helped her husband through a long and serious illness early in their marriage, and how her children had been sickly but she nursed them.

The mother was not strong. She never got out of the home although her husband did have a glass of beer with some of his friends occasionally. She "borrowed" money from the rent or the gas and electricity to let the kids go to a movie every week or two. When they were out of the house, it gave her rest, too, and she knew where they were if they were in the movies and that they were warm.

It was an extremely poor and bare small apartment they lived in. Discouraged about their drab living quarters, she also, with some guilt, had "borrowed" money from another part of the tight budget to buy some brightly colored oil cloth for the dining table and to edge some shelves.

The mother told of making over an old calico housedress of hers, in hopes of enticing her ten-year-old daughter back to school with a "new" dress. The mother showed a genuine but not too effective effort at maintaining some kind of home. The mother functioned like a retarded person although we did not know how much of the retardation was due to limited endowment and how much was due to years of living under depressing life conditions. It was probably some of both. [151, pp. 5–6] *

Neglect also refers to consistently inadequate supervision or control of the child. Such complaints might read "A ten-year-old girl smokes and goes with her mother to bars"; "seven- and eight-year-old boys are encouraged to drink and smoke and walk around the house undressed"; "children are wild and undisciplined, parents seem unable, or unwilling, to control them and they run around the neighborhood like little savages, destroying property and terrorizing the smaller kids." [124, p. 41]

In this general category, one might also include educational neglect and medical neglect. In such cases, the parents make no effort to see that the child attends school or to provide the medical care he needs. "One child was covered with sores but not brought to the doctor. In another case, a mother refused the medical advice for follow-up care after a serious illness." [124, p. 44]

Medical neglect is illustrated in the following instance (Sally, the child in this instance, was a two-and-one-half-year-old English girl):

Someone noticed that her eye was closed and badly swollen and when nothing seemed to be done about it, he rang up the police, who told the protective agency. When the worker called on her, Sally's mother told him she thought the little girl had run into the end of her brother's toy pistol when they were playing in the garden. She added that she had been bathing the eye to see that it would be all right. The worker asked permission to call a doctor who took one look at Sally and said, "Hospital." There they decided that an immediate operation was necessary. Her father gave his consent and they removed Sally's eye to find that the trouble had not been caused by her running into anything but by an air-gun dart which had entered her eye and had lain there for twenty

* From Exie Welch, "Sustaining the Child in His Impaired Home," *Child Welfare*, 33 (July 1953). By permission of the Child Welfare League of America, Inc.

days. If the operation had been delayed, the hospital believed that the infection would have spread to her other eye and then probably she would have been blind for life. [1, p. 48]

Exposure to Unwholesome or Demoralizing Conditions

Children living with parents who engage in prolonged, severe alcoholism, prostitution, criminal activity, and drug addition are also considered to be in danger. Such behavior on the part of the adult, which is "morally injurious to the child," is illustrated in the following reports:

Mother had intercourse with several men in the same room in which the three young children slept.
Mother and father were found in a drunken stupor when [the social] worker arrived and neighbors reported that parents frequently engaged in prolonged drinking bouts.

The child may be living in an illegal environment, such as a house of prostitution or a gambling establishment, or the child may be living in an environment that is likely to contribute to his "moral degradation and/or delinquency." An example is that of a "mother and teenage girl living above a bar where the only entrance to the apartment is between a bar and a pool hall." [154, p. 5]

Emotional Neglect

A parent may provide adequate physical care for the child and yet manifest his rejection by starving or abusing the child emotionally. Deprivation of affectional support can be as harmful as denial of physical needs. [55; 102; 103; 150] But only rarely do legal statutes explicitly recognize emotional neglect. In 1970 Minnesota and Idaho were the only states that had such legislation. The fact that the social definition of neglect is broader than the legal definition is sometimes attributed to the fact that most of the laws concerned with defining neglect were written when perception of, and concern with, emotional neglect were less sharp. Of greater significance is the fact that emotional neglect is difficult to define in the precise terms required by law, and its consequences are equally difficult to establish conclusively. Whatever the reasons, emotional neglect is a psychosocial concept, which yet has only limited legal support.

Because emotional neglect is generally accompanied by physical neglect, the procedure is generally to make a case on the basis of physical symptoms, although the emotional damage may be the more significant injury sustained by the child.

The following examples of emotional neglect suggest the validity of the agencies' concern:

Eleanor, ten years old, was referred to the Massachusetts Society for the Prevention of Cruelty to Children as an emotionally deprived child, completely rejected and suffering from malnutrition, although the parents were able and willing to provide adequate food, clothing, and shelter. There was no evidence of physical neglect, but Eleanor would not eat and was gradually losing weight to the point where the psychiatric clinic, to which the protective agency referred her, felt that placement was necessary. Both the clinic and the protective agency tried to help the parents accept placement, but without success. The mother, who was completely rejecting, was an unhappy, unstable person not amenable to treatment. The father, who had some warmth for the child, was not strong enough to assert himself and meet Eleanor's emotional needs. There was little evidence on a physical level for court action. Conferences with lawyers and even with the juvenile court judge resulted in the decision that successful court action could not be sustained to remove the child. [102, p. 6]

Judy's misery was exacerbated by the fact that she was the only child in her family to be treated badly, her two- and four-year-old brothers having a good family life with all the normal treats, outings, and sweets. But not only did she have none of these things, but when her father came home from work she had to leave the room instantly and play either in the kitchen or upstairs in her unheated bedroom. She was never allowed in the same room as her father, even if this meant her being sent to bed as early as five o'clock and never allowed to watch television or sit down to a meal with the rest of the family.

At the age of seven, the inspector found her a "curious mixture of aggressiveness and being on the defensive, looking as though she expected a blow although no evidence of physical violence has come to light, underweight and pale compared with her two sturdy little brothers."

The mother's attitude was negative and she seemed anxious only to placate her husband and have a good home for herself and the two younger children. The father made no pretense about his hatred and repudiation of the child, although he admitted that he had no reason to suspect that she wasn't his own. This case came to light because a teacher realized that the child was becoming rude and was bullying the other children to an exceptional degree. [1, p. 113]

Exploitation

The child may be forced to work at unreasonable tasks for unreasonably long hours. Often this is in contravention of child labor laws; sometimes, although technically legal, the workload suggests neglectful exploitation. In either instance, the child is denied opportunity for normal recreational activities and other opportunities for social and intellectual development. Exploitation also involves encouraging the child to beg, to steal, or to engage in prostitution for the benefit of the parents.

Although not spelled out in the statutes, another kind of neglect affecting the child should be explicitly noted: *community neglect*, which might be defined as a persistent failure on the part of the community to take action to provide adequate child-care resources despite the clearly established deprivation suffered by a significant group of children in the community. The community is guilty of neglect when it fails to provide adequate housing, adequate levels of public assistance, adequate schooling, adequate health services, or adequate recreational services, or when it allows job discrimination or makes no effort to control an open display of vice, narcotic traffic, and other illegal activity. Malnutrition in children which results from inadequate welfare grants can be regarded as an example of community neglect. The protective service agencies have as great a responsibility to protect the child from community neglect as they have to protect him from parental neglect.

Scope

Scope of Services

Because neglect, abuse, and exploitation are legal problems as well as social problems, all states recognize the need to do something about such situations. The laws vary from state to state: some define these situations very clearly; others define them broadly or leave definition "to administrative discretion." [86, p. 34]   However, although all jurisdictions have laws against neglect, abuse, and exploitation, not all have social agencies with clearly recognized responsibility to act in such situations.

By 1966 a nationwide survey indicated that protective services under public welfare auspices were reported to exist in forty-seven states. However, it was noted "that much of what was reported as child protective services was in reality nonspecific child welfare services or nonspecific family services in the context of a financial assistance setting."

[38, p. vii]   The survey showed a long-term decline of such services under voluntary agency auspices. The public agency, particularly the local department of public welfare, was more and more frequently given the responsibility for offering such services. However, there is no clearly identifiable specially designated protective services unit in many of the public welfare agencies. The scope of service is such that one agency or another in the community is available to intervene in problems of serious neglect, abuse, and exploitation. The limited number of private agencies suggests, however, that only rarely is there available a highly professionalized service to deal with the problems involved on a long-term basis.

Scope of Problem

Protective service agencies deal with a problem of very sizable proportions. A 1961 nationwide study of children receiving child welfare services from public as well as voluntary agencies indicated that "the most important single problem presented by the 377,000 children served by public agencies was neglect, abuse, or exploitation by parents or others responsible for the child's care." [73, p. 2]   Neglect, abuse, and exploitation ranked third among the problems faced by the 49,000 children receiving service from the voluntary agencies.

Lewis, reviewing a number of unpublished studies done at the University of Pennsylvania School of Social Work, concludes:

There is more parental neglect than is detected—much more than is reported and a great deal more than becomes known to the protective agencies and the courts—less than half the cases of neglect identified by persons professionally involved in serving the families of [low-income] neighborhoods get reported to the protective service agency. [88]

The most frequently encountered kind of situation is that of a child who, although not abused, is receiving substandard care. Neglect of one kind or another accounts for the preponderant number of situations in which the protective service agencies must intervene. [124, pp. 35–37; 25, p. 460]   Both Boehm and Rein noted that the situations referred to protective service agencies contained a sizable percentage that might be defined as emotional neglect. [124, p. 46; 25, p. 460]

The nationwide passage of abuse-reporting laws has made possible the gathering of statistics regarding abuse. It should be noted that there is some gap between incidence and reporting; more children are actually abused than are reported as abused. However, the nationwide reporting statistics reviewed by Gil show child abuse to be less of a problem than had been anticipated. [58]   In 1967 some 6000 cases of abuse were reported; in 1968 6600 cases were reported. In 53 percent of the cases, the injuries were considered to be "not serious"; in 37 percent, they were rated as "serious, no permanent damage expected"; in 5 percent, they were "serious with permanent damage"; and in 3 percent, they were fatal.

Gil concludes:

> Physical abuse of children does not seem to be a "major killer and maimer" of children as it was claimed to be in sensational publicity in the mass media of communication. Such exaggerated claims reflect an emotional response to this destructive phenomenon which, understandably, touches sensitive spots with nearly every adult, since many adults may themselves, at times, be subject to aggressive impulses toward children in their care. In spite of its strong emotional impact, and the tragic aspects of every single incident, the phenomenon of child abuse needs to be put into a more balanced perspective. [18, p. 137]

Process in Protective Services

Intake

In the case of protective services, contact is generally initiated not by the client but by neighbors, relatives, school authorities, a visiting nurse, or another social agency. Case finding is, therefore, primarily through a complaint referral. A complaint is, in effect, a report of a condition of neglect or abuse which needs exploration.

The most frequent sources of referral are other community agencies —schools, public welfare departments, hospitals, family service agencies, police, the courts, and so on. Members of the child's family are likely to be the second most important source of referral (usually a complaint is made by one parent against the other), and members of the community are the third main source of referral. [25, p. 461; 124, pp. 12–18] Agencies also feel obligated to accept anonymous complaints, but they do so with some reservations.

Not all complaints are given extended active service by the protective service agency. Continued service is reserved to those situations that represent a clear hazard to the well-being of the child. Where the situation relates more directly to a threat to the community rather than the child, or where violation of community mores are involved, continued service is less likely. Continued service is more likely if referral has been made by a community agency rather than by a private individual. Because agencies are not likely to make a referral unless there is some substance to the complaint, they are more likely than individuals to make an appropriate referral. [25]

Some complaints are unfounded, falling into the categories of "summer neglect," "spite neglect," and "crisis neglect." Cases of "summer neglect" refer to the increase in complaints during summer when, with windows open, people can hear what goes on next door; those of "spite neglect" refer to complaints made by relatives, spouses, or neighbors who call the agency as a way of seeking revenge on the parent; and those of "crisis neglect" refer to the sudden increase of calls to the agency when the newspapers report a case of a serious injury or death of a child because of mistreatment. [124, p. 73]

When a complaint is initiated by an individual in the community, the agency accepts the responsibility not only for investigating the situation, but also for helping the person who makes the complaint. Some people may feel guilty at having made the report or about "interfering" in the affairs of another family; consequently, they need reassurance that their communication is held in confidence.

The first contact by the agency is generally made with the person, or agency, who has initiated the complaint. If the situation seems to warrant further exploration, contact is initiated with the family against which the complaint has been made. Many agencies suggest that the initial contact with the family should be by letter. [30, p. 14]   The letter, it is argued, identifies the agency, gives a general explanation of the service and the community's concern, suggests that help is needed, and gives the parent a chance to react in privacy and consider what to do. Other agencies prefer to make an unannounced visit. Henry's study of the effects of such a procedure demonstrates that this approach does not necessarily have the negative consequences usually anticipated by social workers. [67]

Whether the contact is initiated by letter or by an unannounced visit, the approach is direct and frank. It involves a clear statement by the agency that it has learned that a situation of potential danger to the child exists and, representing the community, it would like to enlist the aid of the parents in determining what is happening. The focus of the inquiry is not on the investigation of the truth or falsity of the allegation, which would put the parents on the defensive. The focus is on what should be done—by agency and parents together—for the optimum benefit of the child. Protective service agencies prefer to "evaluate" rather than "investigate"—and this is an important attitudinal difference: an investigation may be conducted without involving the client; an evaluation implies a joint process, with the parents' active participation.

The parents are not given the right to refuse an exploration. "We accept the parent's right to make his own decision, but we question the wisdom of having him base it solely on his impulse to resist help and not include his wish to help his child." [85]   The agency does not regard its approach as an intrusion but, rather, as a demonstration of concern and an active implementation of its desire to be helpful to both parents and children. As one client noted, "what they do here is protect parents from being cruel to their children." [20, p. 83]

The caseworker tries to get an accurate and objective picture of the situation. He is concerned with specifics: "the dates and times when the children have been left alone unattended for hours at a time; when they have been absent from school without sufficient reason; when the parents have been intoxicated and unable to function adequately as parents." [67, p. 5] Such details will be required as evidence if and when a petition is made to the court, but even more important, it can be used as a basis for discussing with the parents why the community, as represented by the agency, is concerned about the situation and why the parents themselves should be concerned. Getting evidence of neglect and/or abuse and establishing a relationship with the client are not antithetical procedures. Obtaining such information is, in effect, part of the social study step in the casework process—a prerequisite for diagnosis and treatment—that is helpful in establishing a relationship. Almost always an effort is made to see the child in behalf of whom the complaint was initiated.

The agency does not disclose to the client the identity of the complainant, because they do not feel it is helpful. However, Varon suggests that this compounds one of the psychological problems faced by the client: feeling impotent and helpless in the face of social forces that "victimize" him and over which he has no control, he is made to feel more vulnerable and more impotent by an "anonymous" complaint against which he cannot contend. [149] The worker must be aware that the initial contact is apt to arouse the hostility, the guilt, and the defensiveness of parents, for their adequacy as parents is being called into question, their authority over their children is in danger, and the autonomy of the family is being threatened. The parents must be given an opportunity to ventilate their hostility.

Benjamin has aptly described the prescribed effective professional approach in protective service situations:

Protective service should reach out to the negligent parents with
feeling for them as troubled people, with discernment that life
may not have given them sufficient opportunities to develop their
capacities for parenthood, and with sympathetic understanding for
their inability to cope with their problems alone. Kindness
and acceptance should form the basis for every helping relationship.
However, understanding is not enough for helping negligent
parents. Since they are often disorganized, at times confused or
belligerent and destructive in their attitudes, it takes firmness to
stop them. . . . Expectations clearly and strongly stated in specific

terms give direction to the unorganized client, lift him out of confusion, and help him partialize problems that might otherwise be overwhelming. . . . Implied in the concept of expectation is a concern for the other person and respect for his potential ability to accept his responsibility. [14, pp. 12–17]

The approach is based on a number of assumptions:

1. The parents are not deliberately or perversely willful in their behavior; neglect, abuse, and exploitation are not the result of happenstance but are responses to the difficulties, social and/or personal, which the parents face. The behavior toward the child is symptomatic of some serious difficulty in the parents' and/or the family's situation.
2. There is, consequently, a cause for such deviant behavior which, if understood, might be subject to change; people can, and do, change with the help of the agency.
3. The parents themselves are unhappy about the situation. However resistant and defensive they may be to the community's intervention in the family's life, they welcome, in some measure, the opportunity to see if they can be helped to effect changes.
4. For the good of the child, the family, and the community, the first efforts should be directed at helping the parents make the necessary changes which would permit the child to remain in his own home without danger.

It may, however, be difficult to communicate these assumptions successfully to the client group. Varon, in interviews with thirteen former clients of a protective service agency and fifty of their nonclient neighbors, discovered that the agency was generally perceived as investigatory and punitive: "Only a fraction of the former clients interviewed appeared able to conceptualize something as complex as authority that is simultaneously coercive and benevolent." [149, p. 57]

The basic approach—one that combines acceptance and firmness, an attempt to understand rather than to judge, and respect for the parents as people while in no way condoning their behavior—is illustrated in the following case:

> The C. family was referred to the child welfare agency by a hospital which treated the six-year-old boy, Wade, for a broken arm suffered in a beating by his mother. Mr. C. began the first interview with the [social] worker by saying, "I want to say directly at the beginning that I approve of all my wife has done." He said the neighbors were prying into his business and they were "neurotic about the whole affair." Mrs. C. agreed with him.
>
> Mr. C. then tried to deflect the conversation from the beating of

the child by talking about the neighbor's interference in the past. The worker listened attentively but brought the subject back to the beating by saying that he could see they had had some trouble with their neighbors but the report of serious abuse of the children was the main concern now. Both parents said they whipped the children because they believed in firm discipline and they challenged the worker's right to question this. Mr. C. again attempted to avoid the subject of Wade's beating by describing at length how strict his parents had been with him. Mrs. C. said the children had "evil in them" which had to be controlled.

The worker said he could understand how Mr. and Mrs. C. felt about his being there. He granted that the parents had the right to discipline their children, but pointed out that when a child is injured "the community wants to find out what the problems are and try to help the family. That's why I am here."

Mr. C. maintained that there was not any problem. He began talking about one of the other children's difficulties in school, and with Mrs. C. went into a long tirade about "young teachers" not being firm enough with youngsters.

Again the worker brought the conversation back to the C.'s own disciplinary practices by saying that children had to be dealt with firmly, but the injury of a child was a serious matter. He added, "I can understand that one may be so upset he has trouble controlling himself." Mrs. C. hesitatingly said, "I was so upset and too angry," and broke into tears. The worker replied that, if together they could try to understand why Mrs. C. gets so upset, perhaps the behavior would not continue. Mr. C., who had been silent for a while, said he realized it was serious and that he did not approve of Mrs. C. beating the children but did not know what to do. He had told her that this was bad for the youngsters, but she continued. Mrs. C. remarked that looking back on Wade's beating was a terrible experience. She did not realize she had injured him until his arm became swollen. She supposed it was her anger and her temper that did it. She would like to talk to someone and she does need help. [128, p. 24] *

The decision to provide continuing service is based on such factors as repetitiveness of the parents harmful behavior, the degree of guilt expressed, the acceptance of "blame," and the nature of the situation which triggered the incident. The following incidents indicate the differential response to these factors.

* From Anna Mae Sandusky, "Services to Neglected Children," *Children* (January–February 1960). By permission of the author and *Children*, U.S. Department of Health, Education, and Welfare, Social Security Administration, Children's Bureau.

A hospital reported that a nine-year-old had been brought to
the Emergency Room for treatment of a fractured wrist. The mother
admitted that the father had caused the injury. The child was
treated on an out-patient basis.

An appointment letter was sent to the parents, and both came
to the office. Both parents readily admitted what happened. The
mother was working, the father was resting after coming home from
work. A policeman came to the door with the boy, explaining
that he had just caught him on the railroad tracks. The father
became upset for various reasons: the shame of having a policeman
bring his boy home, knowledge that his son had disobeyed home
rules and the law, and anxiety for the injuries that could have
occured if a train had come. The father had a finger missing which
made him even more sensitive to the loss of a limb. The father
grabbed the boy to discipline him with a belt, they struggled, and
somehow in the process the wrist was broken.

The father expressed appropriate guilt for hurting the boy, as
he certainly had no intention of breaking his wrist. It was clear
that he rarely used a belt, and both parents felt they had pretty
good children. There was no expression of any family problems. In
this situation, there was no need to protect the child, and the
parents were not asking for help with any other problems. Therefore
there was no role for continued social work intervention. A letter
was sent to the reporting hospital explaining the disposition, with
a copy to the parents.

A hospital reported the admission of a twenty-month-old boy
with multiple old fractures, numerous scars, head wound, and a
hematoma on the back. The mother said he fell down the stairs,
and that he was an "evil" child. She entered a hospital the following
day to deliver her third child.

A visit was made to the mother in the hospital. She denied
any trauma, and gave no recognition to the seriousness of his injuries.
She was told that the matter would be presented to the Court
before the child's discharge. She did not object, but did verbalize
that she didn't want the child removed from her.

In subsequent visits it was determined that the newborn and
older child received adequate care and were not abused. The mother
was unable to talk about the abused child, and often sat silently
with tears rolling down her face.

A trial was held in Family Court, where medical testimony was
presented. The mother offered no objections, although she continued
to deny the abuse.

The child was placed in a foster care home as soon as he

was ready for discharge and continued service was provided to the mother by the social worker in that department. [145, pp. 42–44] *

Diagnosis

Some tentative efforts have been made to identify the distinctive attributes of the parents who neglect or abuse their children. One of the principal conclusions reached by Young, in her study of the records of 180 families referred for neglect or abuse, is that the two groups of parents may have little in common. [158, p. 135] It has been suggested that a common causative factor is the "emotional immaturity" of the parents. The term generally includes lack of impulse control, an inability to love or to feel genuine concern about the needs of others, an inability to learn from previous experience, and an inability to make or implement long-range plans. The difficulty supposedly results from a lack of stable love relationships in the parent's own childhood, and inadequate gratification of early emotional needs. Furthermore, it is believed, many such parents have been denied the opportunity to identify with adequate parental figures and, consequently, lack an effective pattern for their own parental behavior. On the contrary, they have supposedly identified with the aggressive, neglectful parents and in enacting the parental role themselves are, in fact, compulsively repeating what they themselves experienced. According to the Child Welfare League of America, "parental neglect is usually a symptom of severe personality disturbances." [34, p. 6]

This suggests that neglectful and/or abusive parents are acting in response to the deprivation they themselves experienced in childhood. They themselves are still children—in their narcissism, their selfishness, their dependency, and their impulsiveness. Young notes that a very large percentage of her sample of abusive and neglectful parents "came from homes where they were physically neglected or abused. . . . The vignettes of their past, their own spontaneous comments about it, picture parents who themselves never had a childhood." [158, p. 75] But Meier, in a follow-up interview study of sixty-one adults who had been under foster care for long periods in their childhood, noted that, although these parents had themselves been neglected, the quality of care of 149 children born to these adults was questionable in only two cases. In this study, the experience of neglect did not result in a repetition of this pattern in adulthood. [96]

Boehm suggests another view regarding the significant factors making for parental neglect:

* From Ellen Thompson and Norman Paget, *Child Abuse: A Community Challenge.* Buffalo, N.Y.: Henry Stewart Publishing Co., 1971. By permission of the publisher.

Because of the strong psychodynamic orientation of social work, attention has been focused largely on the personality disturbance of parents as a major causal factor in neglect. Thus, the focus would make it logical to assume that such disturbance would occur among families regardless of social class or other demographic characteristics. . . . Analysis of the characteristics of families involved in neglect complaints, however, shows that assumption of random distribution does not hold up and that the educated, economically independent family is the rare exception among neglect referrals. The preponderance of the families referred for neglect comes from the lower socioeconomic strata of the community and differs markedly from the general population in education, income, neighborhood, race, and family structure. . . . [25, p. 459]

Of Boehm's sample of 183 neglectful families in the Twin Cities, 60 percent consisted of broken, one-parent families, as against 7 percent of broken families in the general population of the Twin Cities; 42 percent of the neglectful families were receiving public assistance, as against 3 percent of such families in the total population. [25, p. 459]

Similarly, a study of cases referred to the Massachusetts Society for the Prevention of Cruelty to Children in 1960 indicates that 60 percent of the families were one-parent families. In comparison, in 1960 only 13 percent of all families in the country were one-parent families, emphasizing the extent to which neglectful families are atypical in this crucial respect. [124, p. 49]   Sixty-three percent of the families in the Massachusetts study had sought financial assistance from community agencies at one time or another. [124, p. 128]   Most of these clients came from the lowest socioeconomic ranks in the community, and people from this level are the most likely to become the chronic neglect cases. [124, p. 55]

Boehm's summarizing comments are applicable to the population of both studies cited:

Two major aspects of stress are immediately apparent: the stress of financial deprivation and the stress of living in a one-parent family. . . . When the stress of financial need is combined with the psychological stress inevitable in the one-parent family in which the single parent, usually the mother, carries the total responsibility for management, guidance, and physical care, the resultant stress is often overwhelming. [25, p. 464]

An intensive study of forty-three families who received protective services in Denver supports these findings: in only 26 percent of the cases were both parents in the home. [130, p. 115]

Further stress is imposed by the unusually large size of neglectful families. Rein noted that 42 percent of the families referred to the Massachusetts Protective Agency in 1960 had four or more children. [124, p. 48]   And an intensive study of neglectful families noted that 27 percent of the families had between seven and thirteen children. In this study also, the extent of family disruption was much higher than in the general population and "a large number of the families were living on substandard incomes." [27, pp. 30–31]

Hancock, studying 112 mothers imprisoned in New Jersey for child neglect, notes that the "two social problems that stood out significantly" for this group were the problems of destitution and "grossly inadequate housing." "Many of these families were without sufficient funds for basic maintenance. Out of the total group, only a slim 7 percent had earned income sufficient to meet reasonable family budgets." [64, p. 12] Here, as in the previous studies cited, one of the outstanding characteristics of the neglectful parents was the atypically large number of children for whom they had responsibility. Nearly half of the families involved included five or more children. [64, p. 14]   The significance of the heavy burden of care imposed by the number of children in the neglected family may be appreciated when it is remembered that only 10.5 percent of all families in the United States in 1962 had four or more children in the family. [146, p. 42]

Studies in England of the neglectful family tend to substantiate the association among neglect, income, and family size. According to Wilson, reporting on a detailed study of fifty-two such families,

The size of the families is over three times the national average and the income per head much below the average. Indeed, it has been shown that in the majority of cases where there are more than five children the income is below subsistence level. . . .

There are certain patterns of adverse economic conditions in all of the families which are at least partly responsible for the existence of physical neglect of the children. Tables correlating fathers' work and health records with mothers' health records and the sizes of the families have shown that the struggle to bring up very large families on low incomes is a test that would break all but the most resourceful and capable personalities.

. . . It is unfortunate that, in the literature dealing with families who are suspected of child neglect, these extreme stress situations are rarely discussed. An emphasis is put instead on the parents' inability to make a success of their lives. This inability is frequently interpreted as an immaturity of personality. This character traces back to a childhood of much insecurity which can only be dealt with by some sort of relationship therapy. While this diagnosis may be a correct one in many cases, it is obvious that it does not give a complete explanation. The conditions described above are bound to produce a considerable amount of anxiety and strain and as the economic problems presented to these families appear to be insoluble, they generate continuous frustration. [152, p. 62]

Other studies have pointed to the physical and mental limitations of neglectful parents and the possible relationship between such factors and neglectful behavior. Sheridan, in a study of one hundred mothers charged with neglect, notes: "It is clear that this series of mothers shows a formidably large number of mentally subnormal women (27 percent classified as imbeciles or feeble minded, an additional 43 percent classified as dull or backward on a Terman-Merrill test scale)." [132, p. 91] In another study of one hundred mothers charged with neglect, one of the characteristic features noted was physical impairment. They are described as "undersized, with pale expressionless faces, dragging feet, drooping posture," and seemingly physically and emotionally exhausted. [133, p. 722]

Kahn summarizes a study made by the Women's Group on Public Welfare in England:

. . . [It] showed the neglectful mothers to be in poor health and without anybody who would help care for their children or relieve them, even briefly. The families were often broken, subject to extreme poverty, residing in poor housing, and suffering from mental defect or illness. Analysis suggested, in fact, that misfortune, rather than neglect, was a more appropriate designation for 50 percent of 234 cases studied intensively. [75, p. 322]

Young also reports very considerable social deprivation, poor health, and mental retardation among her population of 180 neglectful, abusive parents. Over half of them had serious health problems and 58 of 110 parents who had received psychological exams were found to be mentally retarded. [158, pp. 69–71]

Some studies indicate that, although there is great social stress, the parent is less able to cope with such stress because of personality disturbances. Thus, a Canadian study of 147 neglectful parents indicates that emotional immaturity of the parent was noted in 70 percent of the cases analyzed intensively, but inadequate income and the absence of one parent were also associated with child neglect. [32, p. 12]

Polansky and his co-workers identified clusters of behavior typical of some neglectful mothers. [120; 122] One group of neglectful mothers manifesting an "apathy-futility syndrome" was "socially withdrawn, physically slow, or immobilized, generally ineffectual." Another group was "childishly impulsive," dependent on others for guidance and approval, unable to control tension or excitement.

Another report summarized twenty cases of gross neglect that came to the attention of a medical social worker assigned to a pedriatics ward:

> In the twenty case studies, at least five common factors can be isolated: a long history, in one or both parents, of family and social breakdown in their own childhood and youth; repeated illegitimacy; severe neurotic or character disorders; grossly inadequate housing; striking poverty based on lack of employment, underemployment, or insufficient financial assistance. [104, p. 35]

A question arises: Is poverty the cause or the result of basic psychosocial pathology that makes the parents unable to cope with their environment? Whether poverty is the primary cause or is secondary to some "immaturity," there seems less question about the fact that, to cope adequately with the conditions under which most of these families are forced to live, a level of maturity is required that few of the families possess—if indeed any level of maturity could make it possible to cope with such conditions.

Because income maintenance programs, available throughout the country, supposedly provide for the subsistence needs of the child, neglect is assumed to be the result of factors more complex than poverty alone. Nevertheless, assistance levels are such that the real deprivation —exhaustion, frustration, failure of hope, apathetic indifference, despair —that comes from living day after day on the edge of poverty, amidst squalor, plays a part in the parents' inability to mobilize themselves to care for the child. Having studied 180 families referred to agencies for neglect or abuse, Young recapitulates by noting that, "If the behavior of neglecting parents toward their children could be summed up in one word, that word would be *indifference*." [158, p. 31]   One learns to ignore that about which he can do little.

Such a situation is fertile soil for neglect. As Meier says, "The grinding harassments of constantly doing without the things that are needed, and the small daily discouragements and disappointments that poverty-stricken parents suffer, deplete the energies of parents and render them less able to meet the social and emotional needs of their children." [95, p. 172]   Environmental stress may be a significant, necessary condition for neglect, although the sufficient conditions include the factor of personal pathology. The statistics show that neglect is related primarily to great social stress associated with factors of "inadequacy" or "immaturity." The available statistics indicate that the protective service agent's client is usually a woman struggling alone to raise a family of larger than average size on a poverty-level income in a slum area. The neglectful mother is frequently physically exhausted, mentally impoverished, emotionally deprived, and socially isolated.

According to Chesser:

> . . . Though they are dealt with under the same heading, there is a
> radical difference in character between cases of neglect and cases
> of cruelty to children. . . . Positive cruelty . . . is less often
> related to those conditions which cause or encourage neglect; it is,
> in its nature, more likely than neglect to arise from deep-seated
> deficiencies in character. . . . Neglect, which is far more common
> than cruelty, is mainly caused through the reaction upon reasonably
> normal parents of intolerable conditions. [33, p. 133]

Abuse may, on occasion, result from a distorted definition of parental
role behavior. More frequently, however, it is symptomatic of role rejection—the parent rejects parenthood and, in his frustration, practices a
form of limited infanticide. There is a deliberateness in the behavior of
abusive parents that is not as frequently found in neglect cases. There is
also more personality pathology associated with abuse than with neglect.

Two lines of evidence suggest that abusive parents are somewhat
different from neglectful parents. First, although abuse, like neglect, is
more heavily concentrated among lower socioeconomic classes, it is more
randomly distributed throughout the population. Such a finding is congruent with an explanation of abusive behavior based on personality
factors.

Second, there seems to be considerable distortion of reality in the
abusive parents' perception of their child. As one study of 115 abusive
families concluded, "The behavior of these children seldom provoked or
warranted the abuse they received; instead, they seemed like innocent
victims of something far more complicated than their own behavior."
[31, p. 129]

Frequently, one child becomes the target for abuse, as though he
represented, symbolically, some conflict for the parent. Nurse noted that
"The victims were set apart from other children in their families by the
parents, who regarded them as mentally slow or potential delinquents,
without clear-cut evidence." [108 p. 204] This suggests that "parental
abuse expresses [the] overdetermined needs of the parent rather than a
reality-based reaction to a provocative child." [108, p. 25] Boardman,
studying hospitalized abused children, indicates that "because in almost
all cases only one child is the victim, hospital members believe that the
child has become a symbol of some kind to the adult." [22, p. 45] The
child who is abused may, therefore, be a victim required for the maintenance of the psychic stability of the family. Removal of the child, without any modification of the family's emotional configuration, may result
in the substitution of another victim.

Other frequently encountered characteristics of abusive parents further suggest the dominance of psychological factors over social factors

in the explanatory configuration. [141; 160]   There often is an absence of guilt [93; 100; 158] and a tendency toward social isolation. [50; 70; 99; 100; 129; 158]   There is little concern with what "others" think, for there is little contact with others.

There is little valid evidence to support the theory that abusive parents were themselves abused as children. However, abusive parents seem generally to have been deprived of a positive relationship with parental figures which might have served as a constructive model of good parental behavior. [58; 93; 135; 158]   Other studies show a high level of general aggressiveness and deviant behavior among abusive parents. [46; 65; 97; 105; 126; 138; 141]

Abuse, like suicide, may be a cry for help. "Parents who neglect and batter their children are actually speaking their parental incapacities in action language and are asking to be stopped in behaving the way they do." [100, p. 56]   As Kaufman notes, such parents, being unconsciously afraid of their own aggression, may feel some security in finding someone who wants to stop this destructive force. [78; 79]

Billingsley's research offers perhaps the best methodological attempt to sort out the characteristics which distinguish the neglectful parent and the abusive parent from the adequate parent and to further distinguish the neglectful parent from the abusive parent. [18]   Billingsley selected parents who had been identified by protective services agencies as abusive or neglectful, and matched them with parents who had been identified by visiting nurses or AFDC caseworkers as adequate. Intensive interviews with the mothers were conducted by second-year students of a graduate school of social work, who were not told to which group the mothers belonged. Information was elicited concerning the mothers' social and family background, their current social situation and social functioning, and their child-rearing practices. Interviews were supplemented, in some instances, by psychological tests such as the Minnesota Multiphasic Inventory, Barron Ego-Strength Scale, California Psychological Inventory, and IQ tests.

While such factors as "family structure, family stability, and patterns of parental role dominance" did not tend to be associated with different levels of maternal adequacy, the mothers who do not mistreat generally reported a "more emotionally satisfying relationship with their parents and were more likely to have had continuous experiences with at least one individual who provided an adequate model for the kind of identity formation which would foster superego development." [18, p. 149]

Comparisons of the three groups of families in terms of alcoholism, mental disorder, and sexual promiscuity of the mother revealed that

Whatever the disorder, it was least often observed in adequate families, next often in neglectful families, and most often in abusive families—thus the impression that abusive parents demonstrate a higher incidence of intrapsychic and behavior disorders is supported by this data. . . . Neglectful families are not without observable intrapsychic distress, but less often exhibit such disorder than do abusive families. . . . Further, families who mistreat their children in general are more apt to exhibit such disorder than those who do not. [18, p. 142]

"However, it is clear that the personalities of the neglectful women and the abusive women have different underlying mechanisms." The women who abuse their children are seriously disturbed individuals, "suspicious, withdrawn, socially alienated, prone to impulsivity and the projection of blame, generally presenting more psychotic tendencies." [18, p. 150] The picture of the neglectful mother is more diffuse, showing poor socialization and general neurotic tendencies which are in part a reaction to external stresses.

Comparisons of neglectful and adequate mothers from the same low-income population revealed that the neglectful families faced considerably more stress. "The neglectful mothers were much more likely to have more children, to be without a husband, to have experienced recent marital disruption, to be poorer, to be without necessary material resources for caring for their children." [18, p. 203] They were more likely to be estranged from their extended family, and so deprived of its physical and emotional supports. "The low-income neglectful parent is under greater environmental and situational stress, and has fewer resources and supports in coping with these stresses than does the adequate mother who is her low-income neighbor." [18, p. 203]

Clinical contact by psychiatrists, psychiatric social workers, and clinical psychologists with a group of sixty parents who came to a hospital for treatment of their abused children tends to confirm the results of Billingsley's research.

With few exceptions our patients had emotional problems of sufficient severity to be accepted for treatment had they presented themselves at a clinic or psychiatrist's office. . . . From direct observation of parents with children and the descriptions given by them of how they deal with their offspring, it is obvious that they expect and demand a great deal from their infants and children. Not only is the demand for performance great, but it is premature, clearly beyond the ability of the infant to comprehend what is wanted and to respond appropriately. Parents deal with the child as if he were much older than he really is. Observation of this interaction leads to a clear impression that the parent feels insecure and unsure of being loved, and looks to the child as a source of reassurance, comfort, and loving response. It is hardly an exaggeration to say that parent acts like a frightened, unloved child, looking to his own child as if he were an adult capable of providing comfort and love. [83, p. 109]

These parents tend to regard the behavior of even small children as willful, deliberate disobedience. Strict discipline is then perceived as justified since the child is consciously disobeying the parent.

Kempe and Helfer, the research psychiatrists associated with this study, feel that the act of abuse requires a parent who has the potential for abuse, a child who may be somewhat different and/or difficult and who fails to respond in a manner expected by his parents, and a crisis situation, which triggers the abusive act. The probability of abuse is increased in a context of social isolation, which reduces the ready availability of help and support from other people.

The following case illustrates the complexity of contributing factors:

Larry, age twenty-seven, is a quiet, shy, unassuming little man who works as a welder's assistant. Since childhood, he has been plagued by a deep sense of inferiority, unworthiness, and unsureness of himself in his work and in all human relations. There is also a deep resentment, usually very restrained, against a world which he feels is unfair. . . . Larry does not recall either mother or father spanking, as a routine, but there were constant verbal attacks and criticism. He felt that neither of his parents, particularly his mother, really listened to him or understood his unhappiness and his need for comfort and consideration.

While he was in the army, Larry and Becky planned to marry. She was to come to where he was stationed, and they were to be married at Christmas time. He waited all day at the bus station, but she never appeared. Sad and hopeless, he got drunk. Months later, a buddy told him she had married somebody else the first of January. He saw her again a year later when home on leave. She had been divorced; so they made up and got married. She had a child, Jimmy, by her first marriage. . . . They have had three more children of their own. Mary, age four, is liked very much by both parents. . . . David, age two-and-a-half . . . is "a very fine, active, alert, well-mannered little boy." He is quite responsive and both parents like him and are good with him. Maggie, four-and-a-half-months old, was thought by both parents to be "a bit different" from birth. She seemed to look bluer and cried less strongly than their other babies and was also rather fussy. . . . Maggie was admitted to the hospital with symptoms and signs of bilateral subdural hematoma. She had been alone with her father when he noticed a sudden limpness, unconsciousness, and lack of breathing. He gave mouth-to-mouth respiration, and she

was brought to hospital by ambulance. There was a history of a
similar episode a month before when Maggie was three-and-a-half-
months old; when alone with her father she had become limp,
followed by vomiting. . . . The circumstances of the attack were
as follows: Larry's boss told him that his job was over. The
construction contract had been suddenly cancelled and there was
no more work. Feeling discouraged, hopeless, and ignored, Larry
went home, shamefacedly told Becky he had lost his job, and
asked her if she wanted to go with the children to her family.
Saying nothing, Becky walked out of the house, leaving Larry alone
with Maggie. The baby began to cry. Larry tried to comfort her,
but she kept on crying so he looked for her bottle. He could not
find the bottle anywhere; the persistent crying and his feelings
of frustration, helplessness, and ineffectuality became overwhelming.
In a semiconfused "blurry" state he shook Maggie severely and
then hit her on the head. Suddenly aware of what he had done,
he started mouth-to-mouth resuscitation; then Becky came home
and Maggie was brought to the hospital. [83, pp. 133–34] *

In this case, Larry, whose history predisposed him to feelings of
insecurity and rejection, enters into a marriage in which his position is
uncertain, finds himself the father of a child who is difficult to care for
and makes heavy demands on parental patience. These factors provide
the potential for abuse, which is then precipitated by a crisis situation
during which the child acts in a way to increase the already considerable
momentary stress, becoming the immediate target for all past and
present frustrations.

The child himself often makes some "contribution," by imposing
a greater than normal burden on parental patience. Johnson, in a detailed
study of 101 abused children, found that most of the children "were hard
to care for." Some were subject to severe temper tantrums; some had
feeding, toilet-training, or speech problems; some were mentally retarded. About 70 percent of the group showed "physical or developmental deviation before the injury was reported." The younger children
in the group were described by the child welfare workers as "whiny,
fussy, listless, chronically crying, restless, negativistic, unresponsive";
the older children as gloomy, impertinent, and sullen. [74, pp. 149–50]
Gil notes that 24.5 percent of the child abuse cases registered in the
national study checked as a factor the "persistent behavioral atypicality
of the child; e.g., hyperactivity, high annoyance potential." [58, p. 127]

Protective service cases present a problem for data assessment or
diagnosis in that there are no "typical" neglectful or abusive parents.

* From Henry C. Kempe and Ray E. Helfer, The Battered Child. Chicago: University of Chicago Press, 1968. By permission of The University of Chicago Press.

In developing a typology of child abuse, Gil notes that causation is multidimensional and includes such factors as the prevailing cultural ideas about the limits of permissible parental discipline, the child-rearing practices of different class groups, environmental stress factors, the level of biopsychosocial functioning of the child's caretakers, and situational factors. [58]

The diversity may reflect further the fact that all parents are potential child abusers. All children impose heavy physical, emotional, social, and economic burdens on the parents. Along with parental love, there is resentment. Bakan [7] points out the persistent hostile themes in the nursery songs sung by generations of parents, as illustrated by the following, which suggests child abuse:

> Hush-a-by baby on the tree top,
> When the wind blows, the cradle will rock,
> When the bough breaks, the cradle will fall,
> And down will come baby, cradle, and all.

Both *neglect* and *abuse* are terms used to describe a wide variety of behaviors that have in common only certain affects on the child. No single cause can explain such behavior. However, abuse may be more often a response to psychological stress, whereas neglect may be more often a response to social stress.

Evaluation

Diagnosis is followed by an effort to evaluate the parents' capacity to change—to determine the degree of modifiability of the child's environment. If it is clear that change will be minimal, one has to assess the relative dangers, to the child, of remaining in the home as compared with those involved in separation and placement in substitute care.

The agency must also consider the importance of siblings to the child. One survey of 147 families noted that positive relationships in the sibling-sibling subsystem frequently existed side by side with the overwhelmingly negative relationships in the parent-child subsystem. [32, p. 13] Thus the sibling relationship, as a possible source of strength and support to the child, is an important factor in any decision regarding the child.

One must recognize, too, that no home is wholly bad. His parents are the only ones the child has known and, despite neglect and abuse, he has developed some ties to them. Protective agencies have often found— to their surprise and, perhaps, chagrin—that they were attempting to "rescue children who did not want to be rescued." Young, however, found that some children in her sample of abusive and neglectful families were ready and willing to be removed from their homes. [158, p. 99]

There is potential for change in the fact that the parents themselves are unhappy and ambivalent about their situation. The degree of ambivalence present in these situations, which the agency can use in helping the parents, is indicated by the fact that one or another of the parents is, on occasion, the source of complaint to the agency. In fact, Kaufman cites an instance of a mother calling an agency to report herself as a parent maltreating a child. [78]   On the other hand, these are difficult clients to work with generally—not hard to reach but rather hard to change. Frequently others have tried before the client was referred to the protective service agency. Thus "60 percent of the cases which eventually come to the Massachusetts Society for the Prevention of Cruelty to Children had been in contact with a casework or guidance agency at some time or other before the protective service contact." [124, p. 133]

The lack of leverage for therapeutic action which characterizes contact with such families is substantiated by Young:

> Neglectful and abusive families show a conspicuous absence of any feelings of guilt about their behavior toward their children; . . . they rarely saw any association between their behavior toward the child and the undesirable behavior in the child, and they showed little awareness of the unacceptability of their behavior until the community intervened. [158, pp. 175–76]

One of the difficulties in working with such families is that they are not responsive to the informal network of social control, which often acts as an ally to the worker in motivating for change:

> A conspicuous distinction with these families is their seeming indifference to social control. The social pressures which in other groups compel at least minimum outward conformity have little effect upon the families in this study except as they are officially and specifically implemented. . . . Most of the families in this study had little to lose—social status, economic security, community respect, the good opinion of other people were all lacking and, for most of them, always had been. They may have wished they had some or all of these advantages, but if so, their wishing was a wistful longing for the moon, not a force compelling them to effort. They had no incentive to change their behavior or to limit it—they feared no loss and expected no rewards. Social control had lost its major weapons and relinquished its place to official and legal controls. [158, p. 84]

Treatment Aims and Approach

The core of the agency's work is with the parents, the objective being to prevent further neglect and/or abuse of the child and to alleviate or correct those problems that have led to the situation. The ultimate aim is to preserve the home so that the child can have his needs adequately met within his own natural family.

In visits to the home, it may be desirable to focus on the needs of the parents, because meeting the parents' needs results in the parents' greater capacity to meet the child's needs. Also, any attention paid to the child during a visit may alienate the parent, who may feel that his deficiencies in child care are being emphasized by the worker's satisfactory interaction with the child. Furthermore, as a part child himself, the parent's sense of rivalry with his own child for the worker's attention may further excite his animosity toward the child.

Parental behavior concerns the protective service agency only in its effects on the child. The parent is not necessarily asked to change himself; it is the situation detrimental to the child that must be changed. As Kahn says, the obstacles to thoroughgoing change are so great "that more modest attainments are more common—sustaining the child in his own home without damage, correcting specific defects in parental care, correcting and alleviating the effects on the child of prior parental mishandling." [75, p. 335]   The very presence of the agency may tend to activate latent factors so as to make for a positive change:

> The K. family, consisting of Mr. and Mrs. K. and five children ranging in age from eleven years to a few months, were referred to the child welfare agency because of gross neglect of their children. Living conditions were deplorable. The children were usually dirty and unkempt, and school attendance was poor. Work with the parents revealed marital difficulty to be one of the major problems underlying the neglect. Mr. K. was about to leave Mrs. K. for another woman.
>
> While Mr. and Mrs. K. were discussing their marital difficulties with the [social] worker at their home, eight-year-old Jean came into the room quietly crying. When the worker asked what was troubling her, Jean came to the worker, put her head on her shoulder, and sobbed. She finally said, "I want to live with Grandma." The worker asked Jean if she was worried about things at home and the child replied that she was. When asked where she would rather live, Jean said, "With Mommy and Daddy, but they don't seem to want me." The worker said a problem like that must be very hard for a little girl to think about. Jean tearfully and vigorously nodded. The worker then asked if Jean was afraid she had come to take her away. Again the child nodded, sobbing uncontrollably.

The worker assured Jean that she was there to help Mommy and
Daddy make things better for her and not to take her away.

Mr. and Mrs. K. sat silently watching. The worker turned to
them and asked whether the incident had meant anything to them.
Mr. K. replied, "It meant a lot. We have been so concerned with
our own affairs we haven't thought what this was doing to the
children."

Concern for the children was, in this case, latent and submerged
under the parents' exclusive concern with the marital problem.
In this case "improvement" in the care of the children came slowly,
with some reversal to former habits of uncleanliness and careless-
ness. But they did stay together and family relationships did
improve. [128, p. 23] *

The very demonstration of community power and concern, expressed
in the act of intervention, may induce change. The parent, impressed by
the community's power as represented by the agency, may become less
abusive, less neglectful. This change in behavior, "of which the obvious
cause is caution lest legal action be taken, is often discounted as an
unimportant indication of a client's likelihood of changing his behavior
. . . but it *is* constructive behavior though it is reactive to authority.
If no more, it shows that the parent recognizes another standard." [12,
p. 87]

What has been achieved is compliance. [81] The client has accepted the social worker's efforts because of his concern over the possible
social consequences of his behavior and his desire to avoid certain specific punishments. The new behavior is not adopted because the client
believes it to be good or desirable; the new standards remain external;
he has learned to do or say what is necessary but there is no inner conviction in the values followed. Continued supervision is necessary
because the client has to be kept constantly aware of the possibility of
negative consequences for failure to provide adequate care.†

The more desirable goal is to change behavior through the inter-
nalization of new standards of child care. To support such a change in
values and beliefs, the agency must be certain that the living situation—
housing, income, and so on—provides a realistic possibility for the
mother to act in accordance with a changed attitude toward child care.

* Sandusky, *op. cit.*

† We have not included a discussion of authority and its use in casework. For
a discussion of such factors, see Sidney Moss, "Authority—An Enabling Factor in
Casework with Neglectful Parents," *Child Welfare*, 42 (October 1963), 385–91; Elliot
Studt, "An Outline for Study of Social Authority Factors in Casework," *Social Case-
work* (June 1954); Robert Foren and Royston Bailey, *Authority in Social Casework*.
New York: Pergamon Press, Inc., 1968; Shan Kar A. Yelaja, *Authority and Social
Work: Concept and Use.* Toronto: University of Toronto Press, 1971.

Agency intervention imposes a penalty—the loss of privacy. The agency claims the right to know what is going on. Out of a sense of shame and discomfort at exposure, the client may be prompted to change in order to get the agency out of his life.

Despite the claim that intensive work is done with such families, the one study that provides such information indicates that the worker has, on the average, 7.3 contacts with each family between opening and closing of a case—hardly enough for any possibility of personality reorganization. [124, p. 57]

Of course, families charged with neglect are apt to be multiproblem families facing severe social and physical deprivation and, because of limited education, are less likely to make effective use of a psychotherapeutic approach to problem situations. The agencies usually have to prove their value to the client by taking concrete steps to alleviate some of the burdens faced by the family. The agency may have to take the initiative in doing for the clients some of the things they are incapable of doing for themselves—even such simple things as completing an application form for new housing or a new job.

The most successful approach seems to be one that directs itself to situational changes rather than psychological changes. Neglectful parents appear to be childlike in their dependency, their disorganization, their impulsiveness, their inability to plan, their lack of judgment regarding the damaging consequences of foolish decisions. They are helped by a casework approach designed to encourage the development of some kind of routine around which they can organize their lives. Like children, they simultaneously welcome and resent being told, in clear, unequivocal terms, what to do. As Young says, such parents "want borrowed strength, not freedom of choice—a freedom they lacked the strength to use. The authority of the protective caseworker not only protects the children from parents, it protects the parents from themselves." [158, pp. 125–26] The caseworker acts as a good parent—direct, frank, firm, but nonpunitive. According to Kaufman, "The worker assumes the role of autonomous ego for these parents. He adopts a kindly but firm supportive parental role." [79, p. 196]

A study by Kelly of the factors associated with improvement in clients notes that "the problems with which protective service was most often successful were those where what was not being done for the children and what needed to be done for them was made clear and readily understandable to the parent." [80, p. 25]

Such clients, in short, require a highly structured definition of unambiguous expectations. In reciprocation, the worker has to show the client that he is ready and willing and able to help to effect some improvement, however slight, in the client's living situation. He has to prove, as Overton says, his "utility value to the client." [109, p. 50]

The change effected needs to be direct, immediate, observable, and in line with what the client considers desirable.

A relationship of trust in the worker is hard to establish and, initially, the client may be a passive recipient of service rather than an active participant in his own treatment. The social worker has to be frank in exercising the authority of his agency affiliation and the authority of his position. Young suggests that abusive parents respond primarily to authority used without hesitancy or apology, but at the same time without punitiveness:

> The caseworker who faces abusing parents cannot be afraid of them. They exploit fear and they deride weakness. Neither can the caseworker afford any illusions about them; with intelligence they can be very convincing and remarkably adept at saying what the caseworker wants to hear. . . . Primarily they respect power, and there is substantial indication that they evaluate any caseworker, or anyone else for that matter, in terms of how much power over them that person has. . . .
>
> By and large, abusing parents were respectful to those they feared, manipulative with those they could use, and indifferent to everyone else. . . .
>
> The greatest asset a caseworker can have in dealing with these families is a deep conviction that no one has the right to abuse the helpless. It is out of such conviction, not anger at the parents, that help is best offered. [158, pp. 95, 127]

Furthermore, the structure of contact must be informal, more often in the home rather than in the office. One intensive-casework demonstration project with neglectful parents indicated that it is helpful to plan interviews for the same hour of the same day each week to "establish a pattern that our clients could remember and rely on." The procedure also was designed to help the client develop a greater sense of planning in their lives. [21, p. 15]

The worker needs to accept the expectation of small gains, limited goals, as well as the initial dependency of the client. Expectations set should be realistic; they should be set with some appreciation of class and ethnic differences in the approach toward child care and should, in no instance, be different from those expected from most parents in the community. Drawing on his experience in helping neglectful mothers in Appalachia, Polansky notes that forming a relationship with such mothers

> . . . depends on a worker who has strong convictions about the needs of children and no great need to be popular with every one she meets. . . . The worker can be pretty sure that the mother

will be more afraid of him than he is of her. . . . It does not hurt to let the mother save face by expressing her resentment. It is not so necessary to answer an attack as to hear it out. The aim is not to win an argument with her about whether she has a right to be angry, but to win a relationship for the sake of the children. Strength and calmness in the face of attack, even if directed at the worker, usually has a settling effect, and increases her respect for one. If one asks how these characteristics are acquired, we can only reply, "The more you do it, the easier it becomes." For after a time, an experienced child welfare worker handles anger like an electrician deals with current. We respect its force and potential for danger, but we are not all that frightened when we believe we know what we are doing. [122, pp. 56–57]

Bandler aptly summarizes some of the problems in working with such families and the workers' response to these difficulties:

The nature of the families' processes of communication is extremely complicated and requires special attention in achieving involvement. Language is not a familiar vehicle for communication of feelings, or for identifying and categorizing, or conveying information. These families are action-oriented, concrete in their thinking, and not used to introspection or abstract thinking. They have little or no psychological insight into themselves or their behavior and little or no perception of conflict areas or psychological problems. Their solutions of economic, social, and psychological problems are impulsive and for immediate gain. The future is not taken into account. Consequently planning does not enter into their solutions. Problems in communication are compounded by their failure to trust anyone or any institution. Traditional casework methods, which are based on the assumption of trust and which are developed through ordinary avenues of communication, are not adequate. Consequently certain adaptations of casework concepts and techniques were necessary to achieve the initial goal or involvement. Our families had not initiated help or even recognized that they needed it, so the classic setting of the agency was not possible. The primary setting of the home, and the worker's participation in the family-life activities as a primary figure—virtually a member of the family—were central to any real involvement [p. 260]

Mutual involvement and the gradual establishment of trust in the worker are achieved through the worker's gratification of dependency needs, which need not lead to insatiable demands. During the period of testing the social worker gradually emerges as a constant object and a figure who establishes some order, and a priority of problems, in their chaotic lives. Through such a relationship there appears to develop some enhancement of self-esteem and some improvement in the management of household and children. [8, p. 291]

The worker has to be ready to perform a wide variety of roles with these families—advisor, teacher, enabler, intervener, coordinator of treatment, expediter, supporter, and confidant. There must be constant effort to identify concrete needs and provide concrete services. Professionals who have worked with such parents have remarked on their emotional inaccessibility, the persistence which one has to display in going out to them physically and emotionally, and the difficulty in liking them while aware of what they did to a child. [36]

Another difficulty encountered by many workers dealing with neglect and child abuse is the acceptance of the "banality of evil." The expectation is that the parent who abuses or neglects his child would look and act markedly different from the general run of parents. Instead, such parents are, for the most part, relatively indistinguishable from anyone else.

Workers must also be ready to work with related professional groups —the doctors treating the abused child, the lawyers representing the agency or the parents, and the courts.

The worker has to consider also the treatment needs of the children. Because the child's parents are not providing a good parental model, the worker must present himself to the child as an example of how good parents should act. If the child feels hostile to his parents he may react with guilt to this feeling of hostility, however justified. He may be anxious about what is going to happen and fearful that the family may break up. He may have been forced to assume responsibility for himself and for younger siblings because of parental default, and may resent the fact that he is being denied a true childhood. These are some of the problems with which the caseworker can help the child.

It might be obvious, but the protective service worker should be aware of the need to turn off the lights and lock the door of any home which is entered in order to remove a child who has been temporarily abandoned; and in transporting a child to make certain, lest she herself be accused of neglect, to put seat belts on the child and use the safety latch on the car door.

A protective agency, if it is to do its work effectively, needs a wide variety of resources. The agency may make regular payments to emergency foster families who stand ready to accept any child on short notice. The agency also needs babysitters or homemakers who are able to go into homes and care for children temporarily abandoned. It needs access to foster homes in which children might be placed for longer periods of time. The protective service agency may itself provide a variety of services—day care, counseling, vocational guidance—or may purchase such services from another agency. The following example of the use of day care involves a father who was abusing his four preschool children:

> He explained that he worked at night and tried to sleep and keep his children during the day while his wife worked. He and his wife were having serious marital problems which frequently erupted in verbal and physical attacks upon each other and the children. The father explained that he realized he had whipped the children too hard, but that the problems presented by the conflict between him and his wife, and his inability to get his sleep and watch the children were just too much for his nerves. When the children failed to obey him, he lost his temper and whipped them too hard. Obviously, day care alone is not the answer to this problem but it was one way of reducing the demands made by the children upon their father and of meeting their need for supervision. [94, p. 9]

Termination

The agency should plan with the family a target date for termination. The normal family is not one without problems, but one that copes with its problems without the support of a social agency. But because the agency is responsible for seeing that the child is safe, it—rather than the family—has the obligation to make the decision regarding termination. When the parents demonstrate that they can function so that the child is no longer in significant danger, it is time for the agency to consider termination. Termination should involve a recapitulation of the changes that have taken place, an explicit expression of commendation and support for the changes made, and a review of some of the difficulties that the parents will inevitably face.

Court Action in Protective Services

The process of assuring more adequate care for the child may involve changes in the child's own home or, if this is impossible, a substitute home. If the parents are unwilling or unable to plan the necessary changes, or if the situation involves so clear and present a danger to the child that he can be protected only by being removed from the home, the agency may have to obtain court action. In taking such action, the principle followed is that "use of the court should be constructive—as a resource, not as a last resort." The court process needs to be seen as "a means of protecting the child rather than prosecuting the parents." [145, p. 44]   The caseworker attempts to exercise his authority in a positive, supportive manner. In every instance, the rights of the parents to the child must be safeguarded, and the abrogation of such rights— however brief—can be sanctioned only by the court.

If the caseworker feels that the children must be removed from the home, he first seeks the parents' voluntary consent. If they refuse, the agency has no alternative but to begin court action. Actually, however, according to the limited statistics available, recourse to legal action is atypical and most protective service cases are closed without it. Robert Mulford, general secretary of the Massachusetts Society for the Prevention of Cruelty to Children, states that his agency finds it "necessary to take only a small percentage of their cases to court, actually less than 10 percent. . . ." [103, p. 3]   Also, Vincent DeFrancis, Director of the Children's Division of the American Humane Society, notes that "the experience of the better protective agencies shows that fewer than 10 percent of the cases coming to their attention require the exercise of the court's authority." [40, p. 11]

Of the 1350 cases accepted for service by the Children's Aid and Society for the Prevention of Cruelty to Children of Buffalo, New York, only 10 percent faced court action initiated by the agency. [111]   An analysis of child abuse cases in New York City showed that "only 10 percent were referred to the Family Court for action and of this comparatively small hard-core group, the court removed the children in approximately one-quarter of the cases. Such removal thus constituted only 2.5 percent of the reported child abuse cases." [123, p. 216]

A study of 250 cases of confirmed abuse attempted to assess the factors which distinguished those cases in which the protective agency sought court action. There was a greater likelihood that court action would be taken in the case of the younger child who sustained serious or multiple injuries, and who lived with a single parent who tended to deny having abused the child. [145, pp. 125–34]

In those limited number of instances in which court action appears necessary, the agency files a "formal application to invoke the judicial authority of the court." This is different from a complaint that "reports a condition of neglect which needs exploration." [3, p. 19]   In many jurisdictions, children who are in imminent danger may be removed from the home by an officer (employees of protective service agency may be invested with this authority) or through an application to the family court for an immediate hearing on the case.

Invoking legal sanction changes the worker, however temporarily, from helper to adversary. The worker should attempt to help the family understand that the use of legal sanction is an effort to motivate the family to mobilize whatever strengths it has in dealing positively with the problem. Many families may find that this sounds much like the "this hurts me more than it hurts you" gambit, and they find it difficult not to see the worker as pitted against them. However, parental hostility supposedly can be mitigated if the worker explains clearly the action he proposes to take and the reasons for it, and presents the material in court in such a way as to emphasize the helpfulness of the action to the family. [101, p. 387]   The petition should be presented not as a procedure directed against the parents but as a procedure in behalf of the child. [101, p. 387]

The petition, which is a statement to the court of the fact that the child needs protection, should include "evidence concerning the social and family background, specific conditions and frequency of occurrence of neglect as seen by the worker, parents' attitudes toward the children, whether the family used agency help, and, if so, how they used it." [101, pp. 385–86]   The material in the petition should be supported by data from schools, medical facilities, other social agencies, law enforcement agencies, and so on.

The very fact that a legal procedure has been initiated may help the parents to mobilize themselves to make the necessary changes. As Hancock says, "The agency's authority to insist on more responsible care often induces parents to examine their own situation. . . . While they may protest vigorously, they are actually relieved to find strength in an outside factor that requires something of them." [64, p. 8]   The seriousness of the situation exemplified by the agency's recourse to the court may support and reinforce the positive components of a parent's ambivalence—that part of him that wants to do right by the child.

The petition that initiates the court process is followed by a preliminary hearing within two or three weeks. At the preliminary hearing, the parents indicate whether or not they will consent to or contest the petition. The hearing also is designed to determine whether the allegations of the petition are true, and whether the established facts constitute neglect. The parents are free to hire a lawyer and, in many jurisdictions, to ask for a jury trial. However, a survey conducted in 1966 by the *Columbia Journal of Law and Social Problems* in New York City found that while parents are told of their rights to counsel in neglect cases, little is done to implement those rights. As a consequence "76 percent of all respondents in neglect cases in the Kings County Family Court" were not represented by an attorney at any hearing. [35, p. 230]

Because the judge is concerned with protecting the rights of the parents as well as those of the children and the community, the material presented by the caseworker in support of the petition should follow the rules of evidence generally deemed admissible by courts of law. The material presented must be relevant, based on actual knowledge rather than hearsay, and supported by sufficient facts. A worker's certainty that he "feels" a child is neglected or abused finds little sympathetic response in a court of law; the burden of proof rests with the social worker. [134]   "Social workers have a habit of using such words as *seem, appear,* and *wonder* as if they were not sure of what they are saying. . . . The court respects the confidence of a worker who *is* rather than *appears*, who *says* rather than *implies*, and who *tells* rather than *shares*." [130, p. 119]   In filing a petition, the social worker accepts a responsibility—to the court, the community, the child, and the parents—to prepare the material in a manner that will withstand challenge.

Criminal prosecution in cases of child abuse is difficult and often ineffective. The child is frequently too young to testify; the parents cannot be made to testify against themselves; the incident has generally taken place without eyewitnesses. Consequently proof "beyond reasonable doubt" is difficult to obtain.

> P. was an Air Force technical sergeant on foreign duty. His wife, twenty-three, and their daughter, two, continued to live in a trailer at their last Stateside duty station. Mrs. P.'s own family lived in another part of the country, and she had few friends or confidants where she lived.
>
> A complaint of child abuse, made by neighbors, resulted in investigation and a criminal prosecution. Mrs. P. was represented by court-appointed counsel. At the trial, when the State concluded its evidence, the case was dismissed for lack of proof "beyond reasonable doubt." Because of this outcome, the civil abuse case was also dismissed and Mrs. P.'s child was then returned to her, with no follow-up surveillance or service. Within three months she had killed the child.
>
> On a prosecution for homicide, Mrs. P. was convicted of manslaughter, and was given a short prison term. [84, p. 192]

In some states the law accepts "preponderance of evidence" rather than evidence "beyond reasonable doubt," and assumes that any serious and unexplained injury to the child in the home results from neglect or abuse by the parent. Since the U.S. Supreme Court decision in Gault (1967) required a stricter adherence to due process in matters concerning juveniles, however, there has been a growing reluctance on the part of family and juvenile courts to accept "preponderance of evidence" as a basis for action. [12]   In the future, such courts are more likely to require proof "beyond reasonable doubt."

In making a disposition of the case the judge may decide that there is not sufficient evidence to warrant any action by the court. If, however, he decides that there is sufficient evidence, the judge may make one of several decisions. He can permit the child to remain in his own home but place the family under the supervision of the court. Responsibility for supervision may be delegated to the probation department of the court or to a public or private social agency. The agency has a continuing responsibility to report to the court regarding the conditions under which the child is living. The parents' refusal to make necessary changes can be brought to the immediate attention of the court. As Beck says, the value of protective supervision is that "the agency's legal responsibility to the court, in reference to the family, is brought into focus and made specific for all concerned." [11, Part II, p. 17]

The judge can also place the child under protective legal custody. The child may be permitted to remain in his own home but under the legal custody of a social agency. This is a step beyond protective supervision because the agency given protective legal custody has the "right to care, custody, and control of the child." The agency may remove the child to another home if the parents refuse to make the changes necessary to mitigate the dangers the child faces.

He can also terminate parental rights and order the child removed from the home and placed under the guardianship of the agency.

All these procedures are designed to prevent hasty or arbitrary action and to make certain that any action taken is in accordance with due process. The court's decision also gives legal sanction to a desirable casework plan and reinforces the authority of the worker or the agency. Legal sanctions can do little to help a child other than reduce the probability of his being injured. The law can dissolve a child's family relationship; it cannot preserve or rebuild it. This is the responsibility and the capability of the social services.

Use of Group Approach

Contacts with individual families may be supplemented by group meetings of parents to discuss child-rearing problems and marital difficulties that affect their handling of children. McFerran [13; 91; 92] stresses that such meetings have to consider not only lack of motivation but financial problems, which may "make it impossible for prospective participants to hire babysitters and pay for transportation" so that they can attend meetings. [91, p. 31] The agency, therefore, may have to pay for both sitters and transportation.

Parents' attendance at group meetings is interpreted as a demonstration of cooperation with the agency. The agency, however, must be prepared to "require" attendance. Although the size of the group is limited, many of the members benefit from the knowledge they acquire and are stimulated "to examine their methods of handling their children and to look at themselves critically." The meetings have, in addition, a "social value for many of the members, especially for some husbands and wives who rarely, if ever, had shared an activity of mutual interest." [91, p. 33]

The response to some of the activities scheduled for such meetings is illustrated in the following.

The Andrews family was referred to us on complaint of abuse of a sixteen-month-old child. Mrs. Andrews was harassed by the care of six children. Over a period of time, we found no recurrence of the abuse, but did spend much time trying to motivate the parents to seek necessary medical attention for the family. Mrs. Andrews would appear to accept the worker, and would make plans for obtaining medical care, but later she would change the plans or put them off. At first she was quite defensive about the abuse charges and tried to convince the caseworker that everything was all right. Both parents were finally induced to attend the parents' meetings.

Immediately after the first meeting, Mrs. Andrews kept her first appointment at the agency's office. During that interview she broke down, saying, "That movie at the meeting was intended for Ira and me." The group leader had shown a film concerned with marital difficulties; it depicted a husband going out and getting drunk because of pressures at home. Mrs. Andrews then brought up her concern about her marital problems and her husband's drinking. Up to this point she had defensively denied any marital or drinking problems. Participation in the meeting had helped her bring out and discuss her need for help. [92, p. 227]

Group programs have been developed through the cooperative efforts of the courts, social agencies, and educational institutions. In one instance, the court ordered parents adjudged to be neglectful to attend group sessions devoted to family life education. Failure to attend was regarded as contempt of court. Some of the group meetings were devoted to a didactic presentation of material about children's needs and child development, family finances and budgeting, and health care of children. Other meetings were structured to permit a general nondirective discussion among the parents of problems they were having in rearing their children. According to a newspaper account of such a group experience,

Mostly the leaders listen quietly, ask an occasional question to clarify a viewpoint or throw an idea into focus. They may encourage a timid member to tell his opinions or steer a wandering conversation back on the track, but they do not forcefully direct the discussion and they do not tell people what to do.

The parents tell each other that—and one value of the discussion group is that they'll listen to each other. Members of a group understand each other's problems pretty realistically; they have the same problems. And their advice is apt to be blunt.

When a mother casually mentioned dividing a bottle of beer with her fourteen-year-old, she was plainly taken aback to learn that other parents in her group were appalled. "If I only want half the bottle, why shouldn't she finish the rest if she wants to—right in her own home?" the mother demanded. "What's next for her—whiskey at fourteen?" a father inquired sourly. [156, Secs. 1–2]

Evaluation

There are no well-designed evaluation studies to establish the exact degree of success achieved by protective services. There are studies, however, that give some indication. For example, a 1960 study of help offered 115 families who had abused their children indicated that 66 percent of the families had remained "structurally intact," 16 percent had accepted voluntary placement of the children, and in only 8 percent of the cases had court action been necessary to remove the children from their homes. [98, p. 7]   A study of improvement in client problems encountered in the caseload of one public protective service agency indicated some improvement in 128 out of a total of 246 problem situations listed. [80, p. 23]   Another study of 5095 neglected children given service by the Child Welfare Division of the Missouri Department of Public Welfare in 1958–59 showed that, "in approximately 66 percent of the situations, the children remained in their own homes and benefited from the service to parents." [129, pp. 67–68]

A follow-up study of a group of families in Denver indicated that children in three out of four families were better off after they had received protective services. [131, p. 43]   And Varon, conducting follow-up interviews with thirteen former clients of a highly professionalized protective service agency in Boston, found that "five have been helped by the agency, three had been unaffected by it, and five were still disturbed at the time of the study." (Criteria for categorization are not given.) Those who were helped were those least identified with the working-class community in which they lived, and "they were mostly strong individuals who could assume a position of leadership." [149, pp. 55–56]

Young's detailed study of the records of 180 families, however, although not focused on evaluation of services, suggests that the protective agencies were not particularly successful in effecting change in client behavior:

Even when outside intervention occurred, sometimes including temporary removal of the children, there was no visible change in parental behavior. This was true for 95.4 percent of the "severe abuse" group, for 78 percent of the "moderate abuse" group, for 82.5 percent of the "severe neglect" type, and for 69.7 percent

of the "moderate neglect" group. . . . Of all the groups, the
"moderate neglect" group showed the greatest tendency toward
change of parental behavior, although even here the proportion
was not great. [158, p. 175]

More recently, however, Young described an experimental program
with a group of 125 families referred for child neglect. Living in chronic
poverty, family members were apathetic and impulsive and family life
was disorganized: there was little family cohesion, and much friction
and frustration. The experimental approach involved the agency's active
attempt—through casework, group work, and coordination of community services—to help the family achieve some order in their lives.
By the end of the first year, deterioration had been checked in 90 percent
of the families; during the second year an estimated 55–60 percent of
the families showed progress in at least one area of family functioning—generally income management and household practices. [157,
p. 379]

An intensive-casework protective service project involving one hundred families used a judgment scale completed by the workers at the
beginning of contact and at termination. The judgment scale, an adaptation of a casework movement scale, was developed by the Community
Service Society in New York to permit the caseworker to evaluate the
client's level of functioning in significant areas. At initial contact, 74
percent of the families were described as functioning at a "poor" level;
the other 26 percent ranked as "fair"; none of the families ranked as
"adequate" or "better than adequate."

At the end of intensive service, 32 percent of the families were
judged "poor" in terms of their over-all level of functioning; 42
percent were ranked as "fair" and 25 percent were reported as
"adequate" or "above adequate" in functioning . . . thus, 25
percent raised their over-all level of functioning from either a "poor"
or "fair" rating to an "adequate" or "above adequate" level. . . .
[27, p. 33]

It might be noted that families for the project were selected from the
agency's total caseload, and that the workers on the project were
assigned to a limited number of cases (fifteen) and held weekly interviews with parents.

Rein notes that "situation improved is officially the reason for closing
in well over half of the 2367 cases closed by the Massachusetts Society
for the Prevention of Cruelty to Children in 1960." However, he points
out, "this optimistic appraisal must be weighed against the fact that
close to half of the requests for service involve cases which have been
known to the Society before." [124, p. 29]

Basing his conclusion on a number of unpublished research projects and theses, a social work researcher states:

Such studies are consistent in reporting that current [protective] services achieve only partial success with many families and little or no success with problem-ridden families—those families known to many community agencies over long periods of time. Rather the studies show that families once provided protective service often come to [the] attention [of the agency] again with recurring evidence of neglect. In many communities existing organizational patterns and the programs they offer do not achieve a high level of success in helping neglecting parents and their child; they are even less successful in preventing neglect. Of all cases previously served [by the principal protective service agency in one large urban community], close to 60 percent returned again for service within five years after the termination of the agency's service and many returned three, four, or even more time. [88, pp. 115–16]

Johnson and Morse, evaluating the effects of service to about one hundred abusive families, note that "though significant improvement in ability to function and ability to care for children occurred in many families, most were still at a low level of adequacy at the time the service was discontinued or at the end of the study." [74, p. 151] Child care had improved in thirty-three families and the workers felt that about 80 percent of the children were no longer in danger of subsequent injury. Including a sizable number of children who were removed from the abusive home and placed in substitute care, about 67 percent of the children were receiving adequate care at the end of the study. Thus, while the service may have changed the pattern of behavior in only a limited number of parents, for most of the children the intervention of the agency led to improved living situations.

The agencies have apparently achieved some modest measure of success. The amount of change one might expect the agencies to effect must be assessed against the great social and personal deprivation characteristic of the families who are the clients of such agencies. Even the modest success achieved may have been more than could have been initially expected.

Problems

1. The problem of establishing explicit standards in determining neglect has not yet been solved by protective agencies. Acceptable minimum levels of parental adequacy vary from community to community and

among different groups within the same community. For the agency this means that "since criteria for evaluation of family adequacy have not yet been clearly defined, it is extremely difficult to formulate standards of minimum levels of adequacy in child care below which no child shall be allowed to continue." [24, p. 12] Actually, such standards tend to become established empirically in legal norms as the courts are forced to make definite decisions in particular situations.

State statutes, of course, include a legal definition of neglect, but this merely sets broad limits within which each community may define the specifics of neglect. As Meier notes, "The paradox of neglect laws is that they teem with adjectives and adverbs—*properly, improper, necessary, unfit, insufficient, inadequate*—thus requiring a judgment to be made by the court in each specific instance of alleged neglect to determine whether the child is indeed neglected." [95, p. 158] Downs quotes a legal decision which points to this dilemma:

> There is such a diversity of religious and social opinion, social standing, intellectual development and moral responsibility in society at large that courts must exercise great charity and forbearance for the opinions, methods, and practices of all different classes of society; a case should be made out which is sufficiently extravagant and singular and wrong to meet the condemnation of all decent law-abiding people, without regard to religious belief or social standing, before a parent should be deprived of the comfort or custody of a child. [45, p. 134]

The problem of ambiguous definition is frequently expressed as a conflict between the social worker and the community. Not atypical is the case of what appears to be physical neglect ("children are dirty, clothes all torn and ragged; they never have a bath") in a home in which the parent-child relationship is emotionally and socially wholesome; or the case of a loving mother who is somewhat casual in her sexual relations. Although the community may press for action in such cases, the social worker may believe that the situation does not require intervention.

The problem may be expressed as a conflict between the court and the social worker. Situations that appear to the social worker to be clear-cut cases of emotional neglect may be rejected by the court because no evidence of physical damage is available.

The problem of defining minimally acceptable standards of care is related to the problem of defining the respective rights of parents and children. The balance between the two differs from community to community, as Maas found, in a study of child care in nine different communities throughout the country. [89] Earlier in the nation's history, the law jealously guarded the rights of parents while according little attention to the rights of children. This attitude is still a strong influence in our current approach to the problems of abuse, neglect, and exploitation. The protective service agency has to move with considerable circumspection, and with clear evidence of harmful conduct, lest it be accused of unwarranted meddling. "The rights of parents are protected by tradition and precedent" [45, p. 133]—a tradition and precedent older and more firmly established than any tradition or precedent in favor of the child.

If it is difficult to establish a basis for justified intervention in cases of physical neglect and abuse, it is even more difficult in cases of emotional neglect and abuse. A broken arm is a broken arm, but a damaged psyche is more difficult to establish unequivocally. This elusiveness of definition is a problem for the protective service agency because it is not always clear how much, or in what situations, intervention will be supported by the community.

Boehm asked 1400 respondents to indicate whether or not they thought it desirable for the community to intervene in a series of typical neglect situations. "Three general types of situations were chosen and the questionnaire comprised six vignettes." One type involved abuse such as "Jane, eight, stole some small articles from the school. Her mother beat her and burned her fingers as punishment." A second type involved hazards to healthy emotional development and socialization of the child. Mother takes good care of her only child, a girl of eight, "but is extremely worried that the child will contract a disease. She keeps her home after school and on weekends to protect her from germs." The third type of situation was one in which parental behavior was "contrary to community norms and values, but no immediate threat to the child's welfare was apparent." A divorcée with three children is fond of them and gives them good physical care. "She is sexually promiscuous, however, and has often had men staying overnight in her apartment." [25]

Community leaders felt that protective intervention was necessary and justifiable in the first case, which involved physical danger to the child; they were divided with regard to the need for protective action in the third case, which involved a difference between the values of the family and those of the community. In the second case, however, which involved emotional neglect or danger, they were opposed to protective action. Boehm summarizes by pointing out that "strong support for protective action exists in the community only when the situation presents a gross physical hazard to the child and that little or no weight is attached to behavior that suggests a mental health hazard to the child." [25, p. 456] Interestingly enough, the attitude of social workers in the sample was congruent with the general community opinion in their unwillingness to opt for protective service intervention in the emotional hazard situations.

Nettler used another approach but obtained somewhat similar results. [106]   As part of a larger study on community leadership opinion regarding child welfare, 939 community leaders in Texas were given a list of thirteen situational statements. These were graded from situations involving obvious physical danger to the child ("About two to three times a week a father whips child black and blue"; "Parents lack money with which to feed the child adequately") through more ambiguous situations ("Mother 'parties' and does not feed children regularly although food is available"; "Parents fight frequently and curse and strike each other") to situations involving potential psychic danger ("One parent is emotionally disturbed in a household that can provide adequate material support"). Respondents were asked to check those situations in which they felt the community must intervene. The only situations for which more than 60 percent of the respondents supported intervention were those involving physical danger to the child. Potentially emotionally damaging situations received little support for intervention. [106, p. 94]

To some extent, the reluctance to interfere with parental rights leads to reluctance to report instances of neglect or abuse. Consequently, such cases come to the attention of the protective service agency only when the neglect and abuse has become extreme. The reluctance may ultimately have tragic consequences.

In 1953, a boy of thirteen was referred to a children's court because of chronic truancy. A psychiatric examination established the fact that the boy was "drawn to violence" and represented "a serious danger to himself and to others." Psychiatric treatment was recommended by the psychiatrist and social workers concerned with the boy's situation. The mother refused to accept the recommendation and refused to bring the boy back for treatment. Should the mother have been forced to accept treatment for the boy? This is the question of limits of protective intervention. Nothing was done. Ten years later the boy, Lee Harvey Oswald, assassinated President Kennedy.

The clearly deleterious effect on the child of the parents' behavior rather than the parents' behavior itself should be the basis for a neglect action. If the parents' circumspect promiscuity or discreet alcoholism has no damaging effects on the child, the state should not intervene. More frequently, parental "fitness," rather than demonstrated danger to the child, seems the criterion for intervention. Katz points to a double standard here—the parental fitness of the poor is examined, while the parental fitness of the wealthy parent is assumed. [76; 77]

That considerations other than the physical and mental health of the child can intrude in determining state intervention was illustrated by one of the most publicized cases of the 1960 decade. Harold Painter's wife and daughter died in an automobile accident in 1962. Mr. Painter, unable to care for his son Mark, four, sent the boy to live temporarily with his maternal grandparents. When he remarried two years later, he requested return of his son. The Iowa Supreme Court agreed that the boy should remain with his grandparents, in order to avoid the trauma that might be precipitated by separation from a home to which he was well adjusted. But the court also based its decision on the fact that Mr. Painter, an artist, was either "an agnostic or an atheist, and has no concern for religious training," and that life with such a father "would be unstable, unconventional, arty, bohemian." [113]

Another example which might be cited is the case of the Mineola, Long Island, parents of a thirteen-year-old boy, who were charged with neglect when their son was absent from school one semester while participating in anti-Vietnam War demonstrations (*The New York Times,* January 4, 1970).

As concepts of children's needs and the context for child rearing change, the protective service agency may be faced with some difficult questions. Is a parent who fails to provide psychiatric treatment for an emotionally disturbed child guilty of neglect? Is provision of orthodontia or plastic surgery required of the parent when the child's emotional and social adjustment may be materially improved as a consequence? Is a child cared for in a hippie commune where marijuana may be frequently used or a child living with a lesbian "couple" in need of protective service intervention?

Neglect statutes presuppose that we know the nature of the favorable child-rearing context. But given the wider variety of ways children are being cared for currently, on what basis does the agency decide which ways are deleterious for the child? How far may the state intrude into what is an essentially private relationship between parents and child? However benevolent the intention, such intrusion, unless clearly limited, may pose a danger to freedom.

The liberalization of abortion and birth control laws is based on the premise that these decisions are private family matters which should be free from community control. The development of a more active role for protective services is a move toward the broadening of community responsibility for intervention in private matters.

2. The implementation of child abuse reporting legislation represents a problem for the protective service field. Frequently, despite the law, professionals are reluctant to fill out the forms and are discouraged further by a lack of faith that anything constructive will result from reporting. But beyond this, there is criticism of such laws as being discriminatory.

Dembitz, a New York State Family Court judge experienced in child abuse litigation regards child abuse reporting laws as class legislation. She notes that the middle-class parent is rarely charged with abuse:

> Doubt that a middle-class parent is a child-abuser; reluctance to attempt to establish child abuse as against the sophisticated defenses and expert witnesses the middle-class parent can muster; and the genuine belief that he has the resources to deal with parent-child

problems without public intervention account for the infinitesimal number of middle-class parents in court on charges that their children's injuries are due to their abuse, as compared to the number of lower-class parents who are so charged. [43, p. 623]

Reports on child abuse currently are most frequently made by hospital personnel located in larger urban area hospitals serving minority families in deprived areas. Very rarely are such reports made by private physicians. [84, pp. 218–19] Although abuse is found in all socio-economic groups, it is most frequently reported among the poor. This may be an artifact of reporting; it may be a function of the heavier emphasis on physical discipline among lower-class groups, or it may be a consequence of the fewer opportunities for temporary "escape" from children—through babysitters, an evening out, a vacation weekend— among the poor. [19]

3. Protective service agencies face a problem in differentiating their area of activity from that of agencies providing general services to children in their own home. Children who require protective services generally come from families with a great variety of problems. All social services to families with children at home are designed to prevent neglect and protect the child from harm. The dilemma within the profession has been manifested in the tendency for agencies established to offer protective service to merge with the child welfare agencies offering a general service.

4. There is a problem of overlapping concern in situations calling for protective service not only within the family of social work agencies but also between social work and other professional groups. Law enforcement agencies—the police, the courts—also are involved in protective service situations. Neglect, abuse, and exploitation are not only social problems, they are also legal problems. Many communities have not yet clearly outlined the respective areas of responsibility of the police and social agencies in protective cases or defined the procedure for effective coordination of the activities of these different agencies in such cases.

The police are also involved in receiving and investigating complaints of neglect, and in verifying and evaluating complaints. In some communities the police become involved in neglect situations because no protective service social agency is available, or none is available around the clock, as are the police.

Attempts have been made for explicit cooperation between police and existing protective social agencies. These involve a definition of the respective appropriate roles and administrative liaison; referral procedures are spelled out; a police officer may be assigned to a social agency; or police and social worker may jointly investigate a complaint. But because of the lack of clear-cut assignment of responsibility in many communities, there are no "clearly defined channels of communication that enable responsible citizens to know how and where to take action" if they become aware of a situation requiring action. [158, p. 137]

5. Although all child welfare agencies face the problem of personnel shortage and high turnover rates, the protective service agencies face particular problems in recruiting staff, especially professionally trained social workers. The problem results partly from the nature of the clientele served and the problem situations for which protective service agencies have responsibility. Because the clients do not initiate the request for service themselves, the social workers may, and do, encounter a great measure of critical hostility and resistance. This requires of the worker a great deal of patience, strength, and persistence.

Also, many of the clients have been referred to the protective service agency before. For example, a study of neglect cases in the area of Manchester, England, indicated that, of 118 families surveyed, sixty-one had received service from one to three agencies, thirty-one from four to six agencies, fifteen from seven to nine agencies. [44, p. 23] And over 85 percent of the families referred to the Massachusetts Society for the Prevention of Cruelty to Children in 1960 had some contact with a social agency prior to their referral—45 percent had been known to between two and four agencies, 36 percent had been known to five or more social agencies: "45 percent had been referred to the agency for the neglect of their children on at least one previous occasion. Nearly 25 percent had been referred three or more times." [124, p. 49] As one protective service worker notes:

> Most cases which eventually land with the protective agency have been "around the horn" of community services. They display amazing consistency in their "inability to use help" but the protective agency must do something with them! Thus it finds itself with a large and concentrated load of seriously pathological case situations. [118, p. 7]

Given the same expenditure of effort, the worker is more likely to be rewarded by gratifying client change in contact with the more voluntary client of the family service agency or child guidance clinic. Young, noting the great turnover of workers who were assigned to neglectful families, reports that "a good number of the workers said that the apparent futility of their efforts was one of the chief causes of change for them." [158, p. 114]

In addition to the emotional discomfort involved in working with resistant, seemingly unappreciative clients, there is the physical discomfort and occasional revulsion experienced by the worker in his encounter with the stink and dirt and disorder characteristic of many neglect cases.

Another aspect of the problem lies in the fact that the social workers in a protective service agency face a conflict between their professional image and the demands of the job. In a study of 110 social workers, Billingsley concluded that this discrepancy between the realities of practice and the preferences of workers "is significantly more prevalent among social workers in a child protective agency than among their counterparts in the family counseling agency." [15, p. 477]   The worker's professional orientation emphasizes voluntarism and self-determination, but the job frequently requires him to seek legal sanctions and other action that is in opposition to the parents' wishes.

> Thus, with a given client, the social worker in a child protective agency is required to be a kindly, understanding, nonjudgmental, and accepting therapist; and, at the same time, a firm, resolute, and determined representative of the formal authority of community norms. [16, pp. 17–18]

There is a further conflict between the social worker's image of what he *should* be doing and what he *can* do, given the nature of the client group. "Warranted" intervention implies severity, but increased severity and treatability are often inversely related. "In the voluntary casework agencies and the mental health clinics, the choice of priority has traditionally been focused upon the most treatable cases, so that the protective agency departs markedly from the usual orientation in casework services." [25, p. 462]

As Billingsley notes, the type of client served by the protective service agency "does suggest that a greater degree of flexibility, creativity, perseverance, and deviation from the professional casework model is required to work with these clients." [16, p. 19]

These, then, are some of the factors that affect recruitment and turnover in protective service agencies.

Trends

1. The most significant, long-term trend in protective services has been the move from a punitive approach to a cooperative one. At one time, the tendency was to remove the child from the home; now much more emphasis is being placed on constructive efforts to rehabilitate the family. The neglectful parent is now less frequently viewed as a willful criminal who should be punished and from whom the child needs to be rescued; he is seen as a troubled person needing help. The trend is to view neglect as a defect, not a vice. The focus of protective service is not protection of the child from the parent but protection of the child from neglect. As Moss notes, "children are best protected by adequately functioning parents." [101, p. 386] Thus the approach now involves identifying and treating the factors that underlie parental neglect as against a previous focus on investigation, adjudication, and punishment.

2. There is also a trend toward greater public agency involvement in protective services. At one time, most protective service agencies were voluntary. During the past decade, however, the most substantial growth in services has occurred in the public welfare agencies.

3. In line with the growth of greater explicit responsibility of public agencies for protective services, there has been an introduction in some states of public round-the-clock social work services. Illinois has initiated such a system of statewide emergency service, which can be reached by calling a well-publicized telephone number. [29]

4. Another trend is that toward a broader definition of *neglect* so as to include emotional neglect. The focus has been, and to a considerable extent still is, on physical neglect and abuse, but the protective service agencies have recognized that emotional neglect and abuse can result in great damage to the child, and there is a greater tendency to perceive emotional neglect as warranting community action.

5. There is also a trend toward more active case finding. Recent large-scale demonstration projects illustrated by such efforts as the New York City Youth Board's Program of Reaching-the-Unreached and the Twin-Cities Project suggest the new trend in what has been termed *aggressive* or *assertive* casework. [107; 109] Here the agencies feel an obligation to seek out those families involved in a situation potentially harmful to children, rather than waiting for the client to come for service or for someone else to initiate a complaint.

6. Another change has been the growing emphasis on helping the client through direct practical measures rather than seeking to effect change in the the client's emotional functioning. This new approach involves a more active, more directive attitude—taking people to clinics and employment agencies, showing the mother how to shop and cook, giving direct advice where warranted.

The change in approach is empirically based—some things seem to work. Behind it, however, is the assumption that a therapeutic approach based on a meaningful relationship and dependent for its success on highly developed communication skills between a worker and client who share some understanding about psychological causation of problems has not proven to be an effective approach for the kinds of families who make up a considerable segment of the protective service agency caseload.

7. Imaginative new resources are being introduced. In one California county, a network of "Good Neighbor Homes" was established, licensed foster homes which agreed to accept children, at any hour on any day, who needed shelter care. The homes were selected so as to be in the neighborhood of children likely to need such care so that they could be

continued in familiar surroundings and in the same school while in short-term substitute care. [117; 140]

A protective service agency in Buffalo, New York, developed a list of "emergency parents" who were available at all times to go into a home and stay with a child who had been left unsupervised and unprotected. [112]   Each "emergency parent" agrees (for a small fee) to be available for one night of each week. Each is provided with a kit which includes "blankets, food, cooking equipment, rechargeable flashlight, first-aid kit, light bulbs, disposable diapers, insect spray, and an aluminum folding cot." [112, p. 128]   The work of the emergency parent is described in the following:

> The police called the agency saying that they had heard from a neighbor that four children were in a home alone, the oldest nine years of age. A caseworker had to enter the home by a window. He found that an unvented gas stove was filling the home with fumes. All children were asleep, one youngster at the very top of the stairs. There was no doubt that a tragedy had been averted. An emergency parent was placed in the home and the sleeping children were guarded from possible accidents. The emergency parent remained all night and part of the morning, when the single parent returned. [112, p. 130]

> On a Sunday afternoon a neighbor complained that eight children, aged twelve to one and one-half, were left alone. The father had deserted some months previous and the mother had "just walked off." The caseworker visited the home, and tried to locate the parent without success. The oldest child had set out to find relatives ten miles away. A husband-wife team of emergency parents was called into the home to look after the children. The children were fed from supplies in the emergency kit since there was no food in the house. The husband and wife stayed on during the night and were relieved by another emergency parent in the morning. On Monday, the caseworker learned that the mother had voluntarily admitted herself into a psychiatric ward. [136, p. 130]

Some attempts have been made to provide a comprehensive, readily available, coordinated range of services to neglectful families. [117] The Protective Services Center, established in Chicago by the Juvenile Protective Association, offers under one roof and under its own administrative control the following services: casework, group work, a day-care center for preschool children, homemaker service, an emergency shelter, temporary foster care, tutoring for children with learning problems, pediatric care, financial aid for special rehabilitative needs, an after-school day-care program, transportation for children to and from the center. One goal was to help the families establish some predictable routine in their lives. The agency not only had to take children to school, but also had to have staff members participate in awakening the children, dressing them, and getting them ready to go. Because of the heavy demands made by the families, only a very limited group could be served by this elaborate program—twenty-six families with a total of 104 children.

Since crisis triggers the abusive act, the availability of some "escape," some support at the time of crisis, might prevent it. If some person could be called at any time to provide a warm, interested, reassuring response, the crisis might be weathered without abuse. It has been proposed that a corps of parent aids be organized as part of a protective services team to act as "good-mothers" and to be available to potentially abusive parents in moments of crisis. [69]   Such a program has been successfully developed at the Pediatric Service at Colorado General Hospital. [84, pp. 42–43]   It has also been suggested that drop-in crisis nurseries be provided where a child can be placed for a few hours "without much explanation or preparation—in moments of great stress—for no other reason than that the mother wants relief." [84, p. 48]

Parent-child center programs have been established to deal specifically with the problems of child abuse. [54]   The mothers meet in a parents' group under the leadership of a social worker; the children are cared for separately. Thus the parents gain some relief from child care while the child enjoys some therapeutic and protective separation from the parent.

A social worker in California helped organize "Mothers Anonymous," a group of abusive mothers (*The New York Times*, November 5, 1971). Membership requires that the mother make an open admission of child abuse and express a desire to change. In addition to group therapy, members of the organization come to each other's assistance at moments of crisis. "When a mother feels she is at a breaking point, she can call for help to another Mothers Anonymous member with whom she has swapped telephone numbers."

The founder of Mothers Anonymous (currently being changed to Parents Anonymous, since fathers are also child abusers) describes the approach by saying:

What we have here is not a confrontation group, not sensitivity training, not Freudian analysis. I guess you might call it layman's reality therapy. We just don't let people moan about how they were beaten when they were three; we say, "You're thirty-three now. The problem is to stop doing what you're doing to your children." [84]

The organization's bulletins indicate that meetings are designed to help members share their feelings about incidents of child abuse, and to express their fears of parenthood or their inability to handle the parental role in a constructive and healthy way. As a result of sharing their feelings and attitudes, members begin to understand themselves better and can start suggesting alternatives and answers to themselves and others. The groups developed through such meetings act as "surrogate families."

The organization requires that every member "admit that our children are defenseless and that the problem is within us as parents." As a consequence of membership in Mothers Anonymous, one mother can now "tell her son to go take his bath, whereas she used to scream, 'Get your bath, you bastard, before I drive your ass right up the wall!'" [84, p. 51]

8. There is increasing recognition that child neglect and abuse, despite its legal aspects, is a problem for social work. Legal sanctions can do little beyond restraining the parents from inflicting harm and damage on the child, while the major problem involves providing for the child's adequate continuing care and custody. For this reason, the best protection for a child is an adequately functioning family in which parental roles are effectively implemented. Thus this is a problem for child welfare agencies, not for the police and the courts.

Summary

Protective services are organized in response to the community's responsibility to protect the child from neglect, abuse, exploitation, and the dangers of living in a morally hazardous environment. Protective services have some distinctive attributes.

1. The client is generally involuntary; agency action is initiated by a person other than the client, or by a community agency.
2. The agency is obligated to offer the service to protect the child, and to remain in the situation until satisfied that the child is no longer in danger.
3. The agency operates with legal sanction delegated by the community, and can invoke legal sanctions to protect the child.

Neglect is the most common kind of complaint requiring protective service. This may manifest itself as neglect of the child's needs for adequate food, shelter, clothing, medical care, or education. Less frequently is neglect of the child's emotional needs a cause of a complaint. Abuse, although dramatic in nature and serious in consequences, accounts for less than 10 percent of the protective service cases.

Neglect appears to be a response to social stress. More often than not, the neglectful mother has no husband, is living on a marginal income and in substandard housing, and is responsible for the care of an atypically large family of children.

Abuse appears to be a response to psychological stress. The parent is reacting to internal conflicts, selects one child in the family as a victim and responds to his misbehavior in a disproportionate manner. Families referred for protective service are generally socially isolated families.

Many areas in the country have no agency with explicitly delegated protective service responsibilities. More recently, county welfare agencies have been accepting responsibility for the service as part of their general services to children.

Although the child is the client, the parent is the focus of service. The general social work orientation that views the client, despite his defects, as someone who should be approached with an attitude of understanding and acceptance is applicable, with modifications, in protective service cases. Here, however, the worker needs to be free to exercise authority in order to protect the child and needs to make unambiguously explicit to the family the nature of agency expectations regarding more adequate care of the child.

The few studies available on the evaluation of protective services suggest that the program is effective in ensuring more adequate care for children in danger. Among the problems noted were the following:

1. The lack of norms regarding standards of adequate parental care that would permit identification of those situations warranting community intervention.
2. The lack of consensus regarding the respective rights of parents and children so that it is clear when the child's rights are being violated.
3. The difficulty in clearly differentiating protective services from general child welfare services to children in their own homes.
4. The difficulties in recruiting protective service workers because of the resistant, multiproblem clientele served and the conflict, for the worker, between professional ideology and the requirements of the service.

Among the new trends noted were the following:

1. The move from a punitive, law enforcement orientation to an approach centered on working cooperatively with the family to effect change.
2. The diminishing extent of voluntary agency responsibility for protec-

tive services, and the increasing public agency responsibility for the service.
3. The development of more active case-finding procedures, as exemplified by the "aggressive" or "assertive" social work approach to multiproblem families.
4. The modification of the traditional psychotherapeutic approach to the client to include a greater emphasis on sociotherapy and a more directive approach.
5. The concern with child abuse and the widespread adoption of legislation to permit identification of, and action with, abusive parents.
6. The growing acceptance of protective services as primarily a social work function and the development of new resources and innovations such as Good Neighbor Homes and Emergency Parents and client organizations such as Parents Anonymous.

Bibliography

1. ALLEN, ANNE, and ARTHUR MORTON. This Is Your Child. London: Kegan Paul, Trench, Trubner & Co., 1961.
2. AMERICAN HUMANE SOCIETY. Protecting the Battered Child. Denver: American Humane Association, 1963.
3. ———. Report of National Agencies Workshop on Child Protective Services, Part I. Denver: American Humane Association, 1957.
4. AMERICAN MEDICAL ASSOCIATION. "The Battered Child Syndrome—Editorial." Journal of the American Medical Association, 181 (1962).
5. AMERICAN PUBLIC Welfare ASSOCIATION. Preventive and Protective Services to Children: A Responsibility of the Public Welfare Agency. Chicago: American Public Welfare Association, 1958.
6. ARNOLD, MILDRED. Termination of Parental Rights. Denver: American Humane Association, 1962.
7. BAKAN, DAVID. Slaughter of the Innocents. San Francisco: Jossey-Bass, Inc., 1971.
8. BANDLER, LOUISE S. "Casework, a Process of Socialization: Gains, Limitations, and Conclusions," in The Drifters, Children of Disorganized Lower-Class Families. Ed. by Eleanor Pavenstedt. Boston: Little, Brown and Company, 1967.
10. BARTA, RUDOLPA, and NATHAN SMITH. "Willful Trauma to Young Children." Clinical Pediatrics, 21 (October 1963).
11. BECK, BERTRAM. "Protective Services Revitalized." Child Welfare, 34 (November–December 1955).
12. BECKER, THOMAS T. Due Process and Child Protective Proceedings—State Intervention in Family Relations on Behalf of Neglected Children. Denver: American Humane Society, 1972.
13. BELLUCCI, MATILDA T. "Group Treatment of Mothers in Child Protection Cases." Child Welfare, 41, 2 (February 1972), 110–16.

14. BENJAMIN, LISELOTTE. *Protective Services: A Guide to Its Concepts and Principles.* Pennsylvania Department of Welfare, Bureau of Children's Services, May 1958. Mimeo.

15. BILLINGSLEY, ANDREW. "The Role of the Social Worker in a Child Protective Agency." *Child Welfare*, **43** (November 1964).

16. ———. *The Role of the Social Worker in a Child Protective Agency: A Comparative Analysis.* Boston: Massachusetts Society for the Prevention of Cruelty to Children, January 1964.

17. ———. "Agency Structure and Commitment to Service." *Public Welfare*, **24**, 3 (1966), 246–51.

18. ———, et al. *Studies in Child Protective Service: Final Report to the Children's Bureau*, September 1969. Mimeo.

19. ———, and JEANNE M. GIOVANNONI. "Child Neglect Among the Poor: A Study of Parental Adequacy in Families of Three Ethnic Groups." *Child Welfare*, **49**, 4 (April 1970), 196–203.

20. BISHOP, JULIA ANN. "Helping Neglectful Parents." *Programs and Problems in Child Welfare. Annals of the American Academy of Political and Social Science*, **355** (September 1964).

21. ———. *An Intensive Casework Project in Child Protective Services.* Denver: American Humane Association, 1963.

22. BOARDMAN, HELEN E. "A Project to Rescue Children from Inflicted Injuries." *Social Work*, **7** (January 1962).

23. ———. "Who Insures the Child's Right to Health?" in *The Neglected and Battered Child Syndrome.* New York: Child Welfare League of America, July 1963.

24. BOEHM, BERNICE. "An Assessment of Family Adequacy in Protective Cases." *Child Welfare*, **41** (January 1962).

25. ———. "The Community and the Social Agency Define Neglect." *Child Welfare*, **43** (November 1964).

26. ———. "Protective Services for Neglected Children." *Social Work Practice.* New York: Columbia University Press, 1968.

27. BOURKE, WILLIAM. "The Overview Study—Purpose, Method, and Basic Findings," in *An Intensive Casework Project in Child Protective Services.* Denver: American Humane Association, 1963.

28. BREMNER, ROBERT H. *Children in South America: A Documentary History*, Vol. 1: *1600–1865.* Cambridge, Mass.: Harvard University Press, 1970.

29. BRIELAND, DONALD. "Protective Services and Child Abuse: Implication for Public Child Welfare." *Social Service Review*, **40**, 4 (December 1966), 369–77.

30. BROMBAUGH, OLIVE. "Discussion." *Child Welfare*, **36** (February 1957).

31. BRYANT, HAROLD D., et al. "Physical Abuse of Children: An Agency Study." *Child Welfare*, **42** (March 1963).

32. CANADIAN WELFARE COUNCIL. *Child Protection in Canada.* Ottawa: Canadian Welfare Council, 1954.

33. CHESSER, EUSTACE. *Cruelty to Children.* New York: The Philosophical Library, Inc., 1952.

34. CHILD WELFARE LEAGUE OF AMERICA. *Standards for Child Protective Service.* New York, 1960.

35. Columbia Journal of Law and Social Problems. "Representation in Child Neglect Cases: Are Parents Neglected?" *Columbia Journal of Law and Social Problems*, 4, 2 (July 1968), 230–54.

36. Davoren, Elizabeth. "The Role of the Social Worker," in *The Battered Child*. Ed. by Ray E. Helfer and C. Henry Kempe. Chicago: University of Chicago Press, 1968.

37. DeFrancis, Vincent. *Child Abuse: Preview of a Nationwide Survey*. Denver: American Humane Association, 1963.

38. ———. *Child Protective Services in the United States: A Nationwide Survey*. Denver: American Humane Association, 1967.

39. ———. *The Fundamentals of Child Protection*. Denver: American Humane Association, 1955.

40. ———. *Interpreting Child Protective Services to Your Community*. Denver: American Humane Association, 1957.

41. ———. *Special Skills in Child Protective Services*. Denver: American Humane Association, 1958.

42. Delsordo, James. "Protective Casework for Abused Children." *Children*, 10 (November–December 1963).

43. Dembitz, Nanette. "Child Abuse and the Law—Fact and Fiction." *The Record*, 24 (December 1969), 623–27.

44. Dennison, David V. *The Neglected Child and the Social Services*. Manchester: Manchester University Press, 1954.

45. Downs, William T. "The Meaning and Handling of Child Neglect: A Legal View." *Child Welfare*, 42 (March 1963).

46. Ebbin, Allan J., et al. "Battered Child Syndrome at the Los Angeles County General Hospital." *American Journal of Diseases of the Child*, 118 (October 1969), 660–67.

47. Elmer, Elizabeth. "Abused Young Children Seen in Hospitals." *Social Work*, 5 (1960).

48. ———. "Identification of Abused Children." *Children*, 10 (September–October 1963).

49. ———. *Progress Report—Fifty Families Study*. Pittsburgh: Children's Hospital, January 20, 1964. Mimeo.

50. ———. *Children in Jeopardy—A Study of Abused Minors and Their Families*. Pittsburgh: University of Pittsburgh Press, 1967.

51. Flato, Charles. "Parents Who Beat Children." *Saturday Evening Post* (October 6, 1962).

52. Folks, Homer. *The Care of Destitute, Neglected, and Delinquent Children*. New York: The Macmillan Company, 1902.

53. Fontana, Vincent S. *The Maltreated Child*, 2nd ed. Springfield, Ill.: Charles C Thomas, Publishers, 1971.

54. Gladston, Richard. "Violence Begins at Home: The Parents' Center for the Study and Prevention of Child Abuse." *Journal of the American Academy of Child Psychiatry*, 10, 2 (April 1971), 336–50.

55. Gibbens, T. E. N., and A. Walker. "Violent Cruelty to Children." *British Journal of Delinquency*, 6 (April 1956).

56. Gil, David G. "Incidence of Child Abuse and Demographic Characteristics of Persons Involved," in *The Battered Child*. Ed. by Ray E. Helfer and C. Henry Kempe. Chicago: University of Chicago Press, 1968.

57. ———, and JOHN H. NOBLE. "Public Knowledge Attitudes and Opinions About Physical Child Abuse—The United States." *Child Welfare*, **48**, 7 (July 1969), 395–401.

58. ———. *Violence Against Children: Physical Child Abuse in the United States.* Cambridge, Mass.: Harvard University Press, 1970.

59. ———. "A Sociocultural Perspective on Physical Child Abuse." *Child Welfare*, **40**, 7 (July 1971), 389–95.

60. GORDON, HENRIETTA. "Protective Services for Children." *Child Welfare*, **25** (May 1946).

61. ———. "Emotional Neglect." *Child Welfare*, **38** (February 1959).

62. GWINN, JOHN, et al. "Roentgenographic Manifestations of Unsuspected Trauma in Infancy." *Journal of the American Medical Association*, **176** (June 1961).

63. HANCOCK, CLAIR. *Children and Neglect—Hazardous Home Conditions.* Washington, D.C.: Government Printing Office, 1963.

64. ———. *Digest of a Study of Protective Services and the Problem of Neglect of Children in New Jersey.* Trenton, N.J.: State Board of Child Welfare, 1958.

65. HARDER, THOGER. "The Psychopathology of Infanticide." *Acta Psychiatrica Scandinavica*, **43**, 2 (1967), 197–245.

66. HENLEY, ARTHUR. "The Abandoned Child." *McCall's* (May 1964).

67. HENRY, CHARLOTTE. *Hard-to-Reach Clients.* Cleveland, Ohio, May 1958. Mimeo.

68. HENRY, JULES. *Culture Against Man.* New York: Random House, Inc., 1963.

69. HOLLIDAY, KATE. "Dial-a-Family." *This Week* (August 4, 1968).

70. HOLTER, JOAN C., and STANFORD B. FRIEDMAN. "Principles of Management in Child Abuse Cases." *American Journal of Orthopsychiatry*, **38**, 1 (January 1968), 127–35.

71. HOUSDEN, L. G. *The Prevention of Cruelty to Children.* London: Jonathan Cape, Ltd., 1955.

72. HUNT, DAVID. *Parents and Children in History.* New York: Basic Books, Inc., 1970.

73. JETER, HELEN. *Children, Problems, and Services in Child Welfare Programs.* Washington, D.C.: Government Printing Office, 1963.

74. JOHNSON, BETTY, and HAROLD MORSE. "Injured Children and Their Parents." *Children*, **15**, 4 (July–August 1968), 147–52.

75. KAHN, ALFRED. *Planning Community Services for Children in Trouble.* New York: Columbia University Press, 1963.

76. KATZ, SANFORD. "The Legal Basis for Child Protection," in *Proceedings of Institutes on Protective and Related Community Services.* Richmond, Va.: Richmond School of Social Work, 1968.

77. ———. *When Parents Fail—The Law's Response to Family Breakdown.* Boston: The Beacon Press, Inc., 1971.

78. KAUFMAN, IRVING. "The Contribution of Protective Services." *Child Welfare*, **36** (February 1957).

79. ———. "Psychodynamics of Protective Casework," in *Ego-Oriented Casework.* Ed. by Howard Varad and Roger Muller. New York: Family Service Association of American, 1963.

80. KELLY, JOSEPH B. "What Protective Services Can Do." *Child Welfare*, **38** (April 1959).
81. KELMAN, HERBERT E. "Processes of Opinion Change." *Public Opinion Quarterly* (Spring 1961).
82. KEMPE, C. HENRY, *et al.* "The Battered Child Syndrome." *Journal of the American Medical Association*, **181** (1962).
83. ———, and RAY E. HELFER (eds.). *The Battered Child*. Chicago: University of Chicago Press, 1968.
84. ———, and RAY E. HELFER (eds.). *Helping the Battered Child and His Family*. Philadelphia: J. B. Lippincott Co., 1972.
85. LANE, LIONEL. "Aggressive Approach in Preventive Work with Children's Problems." *Social Casework*, **33** (February 1952).
86. LAURIN HYDE ASSOCIATES. *Protective Service for the Children of New York City: A Plan of Action*. New York: New York City Department of Welfare, May 1962.
87. LEVY, DAVID M. *Maternal Overprotection*. New York: Columbia University Press, 1943.
88. LEWIS, HAROLD. "Parental and Community Neglect—Twin Responsibilities of Protective Services." *Children*, **16**, 3 (May–June 1969), 114–18.
89. MAAS, HENRY, and RICHARD ENGLER. *Children in Need of Parents*. New York: Columbia University Press, 1959.
90. McCREA, ROSWELL. *The Humane Movement*. New York: Columbia University Press, 1910.
91. McFERRAN, JANE. "Parents' Discussion Meetings: A Protective Service Agency's Experience." *Child Welfare*, **36**, 7 (July 1957), 31–33.
92. ———. "Parents' Groups in Protective Services." *Children*, 5 (November–December 1958).
93. McHENRY, THOMAS, *et al.* "Unsuspected Trauma with Multiple Skeletal Injuries During Infancy and Childhood." *Pediatrics*, **31** (June 1963).
94. MEDLEY, H. EARL. *A New Approach in Public Welfare in Serving Families with Abused or Neglected Children*. Nashville, Tenn.: Department of Public Welfare, May 25, 1967.
95. MEIER, ELIZABETH G. "Child Neglect," in *Social Work and Social Problems*. Ed. by Nathan Cohen. New York: National Association of Social Workers, 1964.
96. ———. *Former Foster Children as Adult Citizens*. Unpublished Ph.D. Thesis. Columbia University, New York, April 1962.
97. MELNICK, BARRY, and JOHN R. HURLEY. "Distinctive Personality Attributes of Child-Abusing Mothers." *Journal of Consulting and Clinical Psychology*, **33**, 3 (March 1969), 746–49.
98. MERRILL, EDGAR J., *et al. Protecting the Battered Child*. Denver: American Humane Association, 1962.
99. MOORE, CAROL W., *et al.* "A Three-Year Follow-Up Study of Abused and Neglected Children." *American Journal of Diseases of Children*, **120**, 5 (November 1970), 439–46.
100. MORRIS, MARIAN, and ROBERT GOULD. "Role Reversal: A Concept in Dealing with the Neglected-Battered Child Syndrome," in *The Neglected-Battered Child Syndrome*. New York: Child Welfare League of America, July 1963.

101. Moss, SIDNEY. "Authority—An Enabling Factor in Casework with Neglectful Parents." *Child Welfare,* **42** (October 1963), 385–91.
102. MULFORD, ROBERT. *Emotional Neglect of Children.* Denver: American Humane Association, 1959.
103. ———, et al. *Caseworker and Judge in Neglect Cases.* New York: Child Welfare League of America, 1956.
104. MUSSING, ROSE. "Neglected Children: A Challenge to the Community." *Social Work,* **3** (April 1958).
105. MYERS, STEVEN A. "The Child-Slayer: A Twenty-five-year Survey of Homicides Involving Preadolescent Victims." *Archives of General Psychiatry,* **17**, 2 (1967), 211–13.
106. NETTLER, GWYNNE. *A Study of Opinions on Child Welfare in Harris County.* Houston, Tex.: Community Council of Houston and Harris County, October 1958.
107. NEW YORK CITY YOUTH BOARD. *Reaching the Unreached.* New York: New York City Youth Board, 1952.
108. NURSE, SHIRLEY M. "Familial Patterns of Parents Who Abuse Their Children." *Smith College Studies in Social Work,* **35** (October 1964).
109. OVERTON, ALICE, and KATHERINE TINKER. *Casework Notebook,* 2nd ed. St. Paul, Minn.: Family-Centered Project, Greater St. Paul Community Chests and Councils, Inc., March 1959.
110. PAGET, NORMAN K. *Protective Service, A Case Illustrating Casework with Parents.* New York: Child Welfare League of America, 1947.
111. PAGET, NORMAN. "Child Protective Services—History, Theory and Practice," in *Proceedings of Institutes on Protective and Related Comunity Services.* Richmond, Va.: Richmond School of Social Work, 1968.
112. ———. "Emergency Parents—A Protective Service to Children in Crises." *Child Welfare,* **46**, 7 (July 1967).
113. PAINTER, HAL. *Mark, I Love You.* New York: Simon & Schuster, Inc., 1967.
114. PAULSON, MORRIS, and PHILLIP BLAKE. "The Physically Abused Child: A Focus on Prevention." *Child Welfare,* **48**, 2 (February 1969), 86–95.
115. PAULSON, MONRAD. "The Law and Abused Children," in *The Battered Child.* Ed. by Ray Helfer and C. Henry Kempe. Chicago: University of Chicago Press, 1968.
116. ———. "Legal Protection Against Child Abuse." *Children,* **13** (1966), 42–48.
117. PENNER, LEWIS G. *The Protective Services Center—An Integrated Program to Protect Children.* Denver: American Humane Association, 1968.
118. PHILBRICK, ELIZABETH. *Treating Parental Pathology—Through Child Protective Services.* Denver: American Humane Association, 1960.
119. PINCHBECK, IVY, and MARGARET HEWITT. *Children in English Society. Vol. I: From Tudor Times to the Enlightenment Century.* London: Kegan Paul, Trench, Trubner & Co., 1969.
120. POLANSKY, NORMAN, et al. "Two Modes of Maternal Immaturity and Their Consequences." *Child Welfare,* **49**, 6 (June 1970), 312–23.
121. ———, et al. "Verbal Accessibility in the Treatment of Child Neglect." *Child Welfare,* **50**, 6 (June 1971), 349–56.

122. ———, et al. *Child Neglect: Understanding and Reaching the Parent.* New York: Child Welfare League of America, 1972.

123. POLIER, JUSTINE W., and KAY McDONALD. "The Family Court in an Urban Setting," in *Helping the Battered Child and His Family.* Ed. by C. Henry Kempe and Ray E. Helfer. Philadelphia: J. B. Lippincott Co., 1972.

124. REIN, MARTIN. *Child Protective Services in Massachusetts.* Papers in Social Welfare, No. 6. Waltham, Mass.: Florence Heller Graduate School for Advanced Studies in Social Welfare, November 1963.

125. REINHART, JOHN B., and ELIZABETH ELMER. "The Abused Child." *Journal of the American Medical Association,* **188** (April 1964).

126. RESNICK, PHILLIP. "Child Murder by Parents." *American Journal of Psychiatry,* **126,** 3 (September 1969), 325–34.

127. SANDUSKY, ANNIE L. "Protective Services," in *Encyclopedia of Social Work.* New York: National Association of Social Workers, 1964.

128. ———. "Services to Neglected Children." *Children,* **7** (January–February 1960).

129. SCHERER, LORENA. "Facilities and Services for Neglected Children in Missouri." *Crime and Delinquency,* **6** (January 1960).

130. SCHMIDT, DOLORES M. "The Protective Service Caseworker: How Does He Survive Job Pressures?" *Child Welfare,* **42** (March 1963).

131. ———, and BETTY JOHNSON. "Facilities and Services for Neglected Children." *Crime and Delinquency,* **6** (January 1960).

132. SHERIDAN, MARY. "The Intelligence of 100 Neglectful Mothers." *British Medical Journal,* **1** (January 7, 1956).

133. ———. "Neglectful Mothers." *Lancet,* No. 1 (April 5, 1959).

134. SHERIDAN, WILLIAM, and PAT MANCINI. *A Social Worker Takes a Case into Court.* Washington, D.C.: Government Printing Office, 1962.

135. SILVER, LARRY, et al. "Does Violence Breed Violence? Contribution from a Study of the Child-Abuse Syndrome." *American Journal of Psychiatry,* **126,** 3 (September 1969), 404–407.

136. SIMMON, HAROLD E. *Protective Services for Children—A Public Social Welfare Responsibility.* Sacramento: General Welfare Publications, 1968.

137. SIMPSON, HELEN. "The Unfit Parent." *University of Detroit Law Review,* **39** (February 1962).

138. SKINNER, ANGELA, and RAYMOND CASTLE. *Seventy-eight Battered Children: A Retrospective Study.* London: National Society for the Prevention of Cruelty to Children, September 1969.

139. SMITH, DAVID H., and JAMES STERNFIELD. "The Hippie Communal Movement: Effects of Childbirth and Development." *American Journal of Orthopsychiatry,* **40,** 3 (April 1970), 527–30.

140. SOMAN, SHIRLEY C. "Emergency Parents." *Parade* (January 29, 1967).

141. SPINETTA, JOHN J., and DAVID RIGLER. "The Child Abusing Parent—A Psychological Review." *Psychological Bulletin,* **77,** 4 (1972), 296–304.

142. STEELE, BRANDT F., and CARL B. POLLOCK. "A Psychiatric Study of Parents Who Abuse Infants and Small Children," in *The Battered Child.* Ed. by Ray E. Helfer and C. Henry Kempe. Chicago: University of Chicago Press, 1968.

143. SWANSON, LYNN D. "Role of the Police in the Protection of Children from Neglect and Abuse." *Federal Probation,* **25** (March 1961).

144. TERR, LENORE, and ANDREW WATSON. "The Battered Child Rebrutalized—Ten Cases of Medical–Legal Confusion." *American Journal of Psychiatry*, **124**, 10 (April 1968), 1432–39.

145. THOMSON, ELLEN M., *Child Abuse—A Community Challenge*. Buffalo, N.Y.: Henry Stewart, 1971.

146. U.S. DEPARTMENT OF COMMERCE. *Statistical Abstract of the United States —1963*. Washington, D.C.: Government Printing Office, 1963.

147. U.S. DEPARTMENT OF HEALTH, EDUCATION, AND WELFARE. *The Child Abuse Reporting Laws—A Tabular View*. Washington, D.C.: Government Printing Office, 1966.

148. ———. *Bibliography on the Battered Child*, July 1969, revised. Washington, D.C.: Government Printing Office, 1969.

149. VARON, EDITH. Communication: Client, Community and Agency." *Social Work*, **9** (April 1964).

150. WALD, MAX. *Protective Services and Emotional Neglect*. Denver: American Humane Association, 1961.

151. WELCH, EXIE. "Sustaining the Child in His Impaired Home." *Child Welfare*, **33** (July 1953).

152. WILSON, HARRIETT. *Delinquency and Child Neglect*. London: George Allen & Unwin, Ltd., 1962.

153. ———. "Problem Families and the Concept of Immaturity." *Case Conference*, **6** (October 1959).

154. WILSON, THELMA GARRETT. *Ventura Ventures into Child Protective Service*. Denver: American Humane Association, 1960.

155. WINKING, CYRIL H. "Coping with Child Abuse—One State's Experience." *Public Welfare*, **26** (July 1968), 189–92.

156. *Wisconsin State Journal*, Madison, Wis. (May 24, 1964), Sec. 6.

157. YOUNG, LEON R. "An Interim Report on an Experimental Program of Protective Service." *Child Welfare*, **45**, 7 (July 1966), 373–81.

158. YOUNG, LEONTINE. *Wednesday's Child*. New York: McGraw-Hill Book Company, 1964.

159. ———. "The Preventive Nature of Protective Services," in *Proceedings of Institute on Protective and Related Community Services*. Richmond, Va.: Richmond School of Social Work, 1968.

160. ZALBA, SERAPIO R. "The Abused Child—A Survey of the Problem." *Social Work*, **11**, 4 (October 1966).

7

Homemaker Services

Introduction

The social insurance and social assistance programs are designed primarily to meet the needs presented by the fatherless family. Homemakers service is designed primarily to meet the needs of the motherless family, to provide for those crucial aspects of the mother's role—child care and maintenance of the home—when the mother cannot perform these functions adequately.

Historical Background

These services, under another name, were being offered as early as 1903, when the Family Service Bureau of the Association for the Improvement of the Conditions of the Poor in New York City employed a number of visiting cleaners who supplemented nursing services by "lifting temporarily the simple everyday domestic burdens from sick mothers." These women were later given the title *visiting housewives*. The Association's Annual Report mentioned their functions: helping in the renovation and restoration of homes; washing, cleaning, and sometimes preparing meals when the condition of the mother prevented her doing so, and demonstrating the art of good housekeeping. After 1918, care of the children, which was to be the principal reason for such services during many years of homemaker development, begins to be stated in these reports as the purpose of assignments. Although this was always a small service—no more than four visiting housekeepers were employed at any one time from 1903 to 1924—it had much in common with present-day homemaker service. [86, p. 1]

Although Breckinridge and Abbott, in a 1912 study of the delinquent child, list "visiting housekeepers" as a service provided to families whose children were in danger of becoming delinquent [7, p. 173], the first organized homemaker program in the country is generally considered to be that established by the Jewish Family Welfare Society of Philadelphia in 1923. The purpose of the program was to provide housekeeper services to families during the temporary absence of the mother. The Jewish Home-Finding Society of Chicago inaugurated its housekeeper service in November 1924. This agency, on the basis of a standing arrangement with family welfare agencies and other welfare organizations of the community, had assumed responsibility for the care of children during the mother's absence from home. Prior to the introduction of housekeeping services, all such children had been placed with foster families. Because many of these children required only temporary care during the hospitalization of the mother for observation, surgery, or childbirth, approximately 40 percent of the total volume of the work of the agency consisted of short-term foster placements. [49] This proved to be an unsatisfactory method of meeting the situation, because of the continual need to find foster homes and the emotional harm the children suffered by removal from their homes. Homemaker services seemed to be a logical alternative.

Goodwin describes some of the experiences that prompted the Associated Charities of Cincinnati to institute a visiting housekeeping service in 1933:

> As family caseworkers, we had witnessed the turmoil in homes that had to be temporarily broken up because of the mother's illness, and had sensed the anxiety which so frequently resulted from this step for both children and husband. Caseworkers had seen, too, a great many of our mothers postpone much-needed operations or periods of complete rest away from home because they could not face the threat of a broken home. Our experience in attempting to meet these situations on an individual basis, through a neighbor's help, or through employment of another client, had not been satisfactory because we felt that in these situations they had undertaken too great a responsibility without sufficient system of supervision and follow-up. [38, p. 281]

The Housekeeping Aid Program, as it was then called, received considerable impetus during the Great Depression under the auspices of the Works Progress Administration (WPA). Women in need of financial assistance were assigned to families in which the mother's illness or temporary absence required supplementation of the maternal role. Although fewer than a dozen family agencies were sponsoring any form of housekeeper services in 1937, almost 500 projects were operating under the WPA at that time. [38, p. 279]

Kepecs notes [49, p. 267] that in Chicago alone in 1938 about 150 motherless families were kept together through housekeepers furnished by WPA. The final report on the WPA notes that housekeeping aide projects

> . . . furnished assistance in housekeeping, care of children, and elementary care of the sick in the homes of needy families in times of illness or other emergency. . . . The services of the housekeeping aides not only provided assistance in emergency situations, but also helped to establish the social principle that services can be extended to needy people in their homes in a more satisfactory and economical manner than through institutional care. . . . Through June 30, 1943, women employed on housekeeping aide projects had made more than 32 million visits into homes where the homemaker was ill or where some other emergency existed. [93, p. 69]

As a result of the developing interest in this service, the Children's Bureau sponsored a conference on housekeeper services in Washington, D.C., in November 1937. The conference had the stated purpose of "thinking through the possibilities for the future development of housekeeper services in terms of the fundamental principles of organization and satisfactory standards of services and . . . consider[ing] the various means by which the development of such services might be guided along sound lines." Participating in the conference were representatives of public and private agencies in the field of social work, public health nursing, home economics, vocational training, and the employment of women workers.

In 1939 a national committee was organized to promote homemaker services. By 1971 this had developed into an independent national organization, the National Council for Homemaker-Home Health Aide Services. It promotes the cause of homemaker service by sponsoring national meetings; developing, collecting, and exchanging information regarding homemaker services; establishing standards and accrediting agencies; publishing a newsletter as well as books and pamphlets; and providing consultation to communities interested in developing homemaker services.

Partly as a result of the stimulation provided by such organizations, homemaker services have developed very rapidly since World War II. In 1954, the Children's Bureau published a directory of homemaker service agencies in the United States. [83]   At that time, they listed ninety-seven agencies located in twenty-nine states, the District of Columbia, and Puerto Rico. In 1972, it was estimated, there were some 3000 homemaker-home health aide services programs offered in the United States. Different reasons have been advanced for the rapid growth of homemaker services in the United States. Among these one might cite the following:

1. The continuing trend toward a nuclear family system, which arises from the continuing mobility of our population. As a result, fewer members of the extended family are readily available to substitute for the mother when she is incapacitated or absent.
2. The reduced availability of foster homes, which requires that other resources be developed to meet children's needs when the mother is not available.
3. The cost of placement for large sibling groups, even if foster homes were available.
4. The growth of hospital insurance programs, which results in increased use of hospital resources—by mothers, among others.
5. Improved techniques for treatment of illness, which permit early return of the mother from the hospital and her rehabilitation at home. Once the mother might have been discharged only when she was ready to resume her functions in the family; now she is encouraged to convalesce at home.
6. The increasingly large proportion of children in our total population, which increases the population of risk of need for homemaker services.
7. The lessened availability in American society of women who are willing to accept jobs that involve living in with families and caring for children.
8. The increasing tendency for men to be employed at a distance from their homes, which decreases the possibility of their taking over their wives' responsibilities in times of illness.
9. The growing appreciation of the value to a child of his own home, even one with some limitations, and of the emotional consequences that accompany his separation from his family and his placement in a foster home.

Definition

The National Council for Homemaker-Home Health Aide Services defines homemaker service as follows:

Homemaker-Home Health Aide Service is an organized community program provided through a public or voluntary nonprofit agency. Qualified persons—homemaker-home health aides—are employed, trained, and assigned by this agency to help maintain, strengthen, and safeguard the care of children and the functioning of dependent, physically or emotionally ill or handicapped children and adults in their own homes where no responsible person is available for this purpose. The appropriate professional staff of the agency establishes with applicants their need for the service, develops a suitable plan to meet it, assigns and supervises the homemaker-home health aides and continually evaluates whether the help given meets the diagnosed need of its recipients. [56, p. 5]

Beatt emphasizes the fact that homemaker service is essentially a casework service:

Homemaker service, as a social service to children, is offered by an agency to give casework help and provide the necessary direct care of children through a supervised homemaker. It makes it possible for parents to keep children in their own homes. It is offered where parents, whose ability to provide home care and guidance has been impaired by some crisis, will with this help be able to function effectively and the children will be assured a proper home. Its goal is to strengthen, support, supplement, and/or restore parental capacity to care for children and to prevent the unnecessary and/or precipitous removal of children from their own homes. As in any other tangible social service, casework helps the family and children to use the homemaker's direct care constructively, and to deal better with the problem that has necessitated the service. [3]

As the definitions indicate, homemaking service differs from maid service or housekeeping service in at least two important respects:

1. The homemaker goes beyond merely doing the housework and feeding the family. She accepts some responsibility for meeting the emotional needs of the children, minimizing their anxiety and maximizing their feeling of security.
2. The homemaker is, in effect, a member of a team charged with the responsibility of implementing a casework plan "to help restore and strengthen parental functioning or otherwise assure that the child has the care he needs." As a member of the team, the homemaker is supervised by the social agency.

Homemaker service is based on the premise that the best place for the care of the child is in his own home, that this is the most favorable environment for the development of a healthy personality. Tied to this premise is the conviction that society has the responsibility of assisting the parents to fulfill their role to the best of their ability; that services should be provided by society which would enable the parents, with the assistance of such service, to care for their children in their own home.

Administration of Homemaker Service

Recruitment

Many types of methods have been emphasized in recruiting homemakers. The public welfare agencies do most of their recruiting through the merit system. Homemaker positions are generally civil service positions, and some kind of examination is given for interested applicants.

All the mass communication media are employed to acquaint possible recruits with the positions available, and appeals are made to groups in close contact with women who might be interested in such a job. In Fort Wayne, for instance, a homemaker agency contacts local industrial concerns that retire their women employees at fifty-five. Once homemaker service has been established and a homemaker staff has been recruited, the staff and the clients are significant sources of contact with potential recruits. The commercial employment agencies have also been used as a source of recruitment. Although most agencies have no real difficulty in securing well-qualified women for normal full-time service, homemakers with special qualifications—the ability to speak a foreign language, the willingness to work for twenty-four-hour periods or at long distances from home—are somewhat more difficult to find. The 1967 amendments to the Social Security Act, which require the use in welfare programs of subprofessional staff and volunteers, recruited if possible from recipient groups, has given considerable impetus to the development of homemaker service. In almost every state the poor, the near-poor, and the welfare recipients have been recruited to fill the position of homemaker. [69]

A large-scale community action program in New York City employed indigenous homemakers who, because they lived in the neighborhood and were familiar with the language, background, and lifestyle of the families they were serving were able to form quick and firm relationships with the families. [36]   Their intimate knowledge of how to cope with the family's problems was of great value—particularly if the homemaker's role was that of teaching more efficient homemaking and child care on a low-income budget.

One report of the work of a group of indigenous homemakers notes:

. . . [They] were untrained, but they were not unskilled. They had considerable ability to cope with their environment, and therefore much to offer clients who were less resourceful than they. They knew how to live on a low income, how to stretch leftovers, how to use surplus foods (including powdered skim milk and canned meat, which must have the preservative removed before it is edible), where to buy inexpensive material, and how to sew an attractive garment with it, how to recognize a bargain. They knew which detergents would best clean an icebox or a stove and which made sense on a low income. They knew their neighborhood, which stores were good, and where bargains could be found. They also had learned how to deal with the local merchants. They were familiar with the neighborhood clinics, the welfare center, the child health stations, and the schools, and they could show a client how to fend with these institutions—not in the manner of a professional, who relies partly on the agency's power and partly on his polish, but the way a lower-class person does it for himself. Most of them had taken care of a large family and had planned their schedules well enough to have some time for themselves. They were both skilled and experienced in caring for young children. [36, p. 191]

The indigenous homemakers were also of help to the staff in educating them to the realities of slum living, and to the perceptions and viewpoints of low-income families.

Because heavy physical demands are often made on the homemaker, good health—including freedom from contagious diseases and disabling handicaps—is an important qualification. Agencies also prefer somewhat older women, perhaps because such women are easier to recruit and are more likely to have had experience in child care and home maintenance.

Personality attributes are also important. Social agencies stress maturity, emotional stability, and a liking for children, and several detailed statements of the agencies assessment procedures in homemaker selection are available in the homemaker service literature. [8; 32; 34] Educational requirements for homemakers are more flexible: most have a grade-school education. [84, p. 30]

Training and Duties

Once the homemakers have been hired, most agencies make provisions for training them. One of the most elaborate of such programs is conducted by the Visiting Homemaker Association of New Jersey in cooperation with Rutgers University. The University Extension Division offers a course to homemakers consisting of some twenty-two hours of instruction. The faculty consists of social workers, nutritionists, home economists, nurses, occupational therapists, and supervisors of homemaker services. The course includes material on child care and development, child psychology, agency policies and procedures, the responsibilities of the homemaker, people's reaction to illness, the purchase and preparation of food, and home management. [63]   A similar course is offered by the University of Illinois School of Social Work. [88]

The training of homemakers is accepted by most agencies as a continuing responsibility. Before new homemakers join the staff, provisions are generally made for group meetings at which they discuss with agency social work supervisors the problems encountered on the job. Individual supervision by the caseworker is an additional form of training offered to the homemaker.

The homemaker's duties are frequently described as "those of the usual feminine head of the household"—care and supervision of the children, family laundry, planning and preparation of meals, cleaning and maintenance of the house, shopping, and so on. They may also include the care of a sick member of the family when no actual nursing is involved. Many agencies protect the homemaker by limiting the amount of heavy work that might be required of her. [84, p. 25]   An effort has also been made to define the limits of the homemaker's activities as they relate to the nursing of the ill mother at home.

Because homemaker service is offered the family to supplement, rather than substitute for, an inadequately implemented maternal role, the nature of the service varies with the family. In general, the homemaker does not fulfill those duties which the family can perform for itself without undue stress. But, unlike a housekeeper, the homemaker must—if the situation demands it—supplement all components of the parental role: maintenance of the home, socialization of the children, and so on. [18, p. 9]

Organization

Homemaker service units are most frequently organized within the agency's administrative structure. Because homemaker service is closely related to the agency's casework functions, it is generally located in, or coordinated with, the unit of the agency offering such service.

A supervisor of homemaker service is assigned full-time responsibility for the administration of the service, and the person so assigned frequently has the title Supervisor of Homemaker Services, Homemaker Supervisor, or Director of Homemaker Services and is charged with recruiting, training, and supervising the activities of the homemakers. If the number of homemakers is too small to warrant the appointment of a full-time supervisor, responsibility for administration of the program may be delegated to a staff member, in addition to his other duties. And in large organizations with a substantial homemaker service program, the caseworker working with a particular family may supervise the homemaker assigned to the family.

Agencies that have an organized homemaker service program may make such service available to clients of other social agencies, a charge being made to the agency with which the client is associated. Also, homemaker service has, on occasion, been organized as a separate social agency which furnishes homemaker service independently to clients of all of the community social agencies.

Scope

A 1958 nationwide study found that there were 143 agencies employing 1700 homemakers providing homemaker service to about 2200 families during the week the study was conducted. In 1972, a similar study found that there were 3000 agencies employing 30,000 homemakers providing service to an indeterminate number of families during the study week. Impressive as such phenomenal growth is, there is an estimated need for 300,000 homemakers. England, with a population of 50 million, has 70,000 "homehelps," and Sweden, a country of 7.5 million people, had 3300 homemakers in 1961.

Homemakers serve a relatively limited number of children. On any one day in 1967 only about 3700 children were receiving such service and throughout that year a total of about 50,000 children were served. [88] This is less than 1 percent of the children served by public and voluntary child welfare agencies within a year.

An increasing percentage of homemaker service is offered under public agency auspices. By 1972, somewhat more than half of all such services were offered by public agencies, and an increasing percentage by health-oriented agencies.

Situations for Which Homemaker Service Is Appropriate

Unlike foster care or institutionalization, which involve temporary substitution of one set of parents for the biological parents, the situations to which homemaker service is thought to be applicable and appropriate are those that are responsive to some degree of role reallocation within the child's own family. The principal aim in providing such service is to enable the family to remain structurally intact during the period when an essential aspect of the role functions performed by the parental pair is being inadequately implemented.

The role that most frequently needs to be supplemented in homemaker service situations is that of the mother. Homemaker service may be offered when the mother is temporarily absent because of physical or mental illness or convalescence. Generally the father is called upon to cover the role functions of the mother, but sometimes they are allocated to the older child or children. What may also happen is that some less significant, less essential aspect of the mother's role is neglected, while the activities that must be performed if the family is to continue to function successfully are performed with the expenditure of additional energy and time on the part of incumbents of other positions—father, daughter, student. Because their own primary roles make heavy demands on their time and energy, and because they may never have learned the skills required for the effective discharge of the maternal role functions, considerable tension may be generated. The presence of a homemaker permits a continuation of the usual pattern of role functions in the family, and helps to maintain family stability.

> Mr. A.'s wife was commited to a mental hospital and he came to the homemaker agency when he had to cope alone with the problem of caring for his three small children. An elderly relative had tried to take over while he was at work, but the situation became too much for her. Mr. A., a factory worker, could not afford to hire help nor could he bring himself to put the children in foster homes. A homemaker was sent to give day care to the youngsters during the months that Mrs. A. must remain hospitalized. The assignment to the family will continue during Mrs. A.'s subsequent period of adjustment and psychotherapy. [84, p. 43]

Homemaker service may be appropriately offered when the mother is physically present but has lowered capacity to cope with the ordinary demands of her position because of "physical or mental illness, disabilities, convalescence, residuals of illness, [or] complications of pregnancy." [18, p. 5]

> A young mother suffered a postpartum psychosis following delivery of the third child. In this situation, the father was able, by taking his vacation and availing himself of the offers of help made by neighbors, to manage care of the two other children, aged five and two, until his wife was ready for discharge from a psychiatric hospital where she had responded quickly to treatment which relieved the acute phase of her illness. However, the psychiatrist stipulated that she could not assume the responsibility or the pressure of care of her children, and would require further out-patient therapy before she could function adequately as a mother again. Homemaker service made it possible for this mother to return home, where she could oversee her children without assuming full responsibility for their care. [64, p. 31]

A mother of three children, fifteen, thirteen, and eleven, lost
interest in herself, her home, and her children after the death of
her husband. Housekeeping standards became progressively worse.
During the winter months they were without heat, water, and gas,
but this mother somehow never followed through to see about
getting something done. She appeared depressed and withdrawn,
sometimes to the point of seeming out of touch with reality,
and was unable to make any plans concerning her children. The
home was dreary and in semidarkness, as the shades were down and
doors closed. This mother seemed to be living in the past, which
represented happiness to her, and she made no effort to form any
relationships in the present.

With the concerted effort of both homemaker and caseworker,
this mother has "come out of herself" enough at times to work
along with the homemaker in housecleaning, sorting mounds of
trash and unneeded clutter, and on occasion even being able to plan
ahead in discussing needed major repairs, new painting, etc.
[57, p. 60]

The homemaker service may be offered to help the mother develop
more adequate skills in child care and home maintenance. In such cases,
role implementation is inadequate because of lack of preparation, training, or knowledge regarding the requirements of the role. The homemaker service has an educational focus in such cases. The teaching
might be focused on such concerns as household organization, meal planning and preparation, maintenance of clothing, child rearing, health care
and use of health resources, and money management. [61]

In other cases, the problem of inadequate role implementation may
arise from the mother's ambivalence regarding acceptance of her role.
Here the homemaker, in her behavior toward the children, offers herself
as an example of the "good mother," which the client may emulate. The
following illustrates the use of a homemaker in a teaching capacity:

Mrs. Harvey's situation was referred to the agency by the police,
who alleged that she was a neglectful mother and recommended that
her children "be taken away from her and placed in foster homes
at once." The police had been called to her home the previous night,
upon complaint of neighbors that Mrs. Harvey's six children,
ranging in ages from one to six years, were alone in the apartment
and were not being cared for. The landlord claimed that this was
a frequent occurrence. The police described Mrs. Harvey's children
as dirty and unkempt. The two-year-old twins were unclothed
except for undershirts. They had remnants of feces on their bodies,
and were sleeping in a bed with a worn-out dirty mattress. The
baby was nursing a bottle of curdled milk. All of the children

seemed to be underweight and malnourished. Mrs. Harvey was hostile toward her landlord for reporting the situation to the police, whom she felt had made an unfair evaluation of the previous night's incident. She was resigned to the possibility of having her children removed, but defended her care as being the best possible under the circumstances. Given these circumstances, one would reasonably question Mrs. Harvey's capacity to use help. But she said, "Everybody tells me I don't take good care of my children, but nobody shows me how."

Over a period of months a caseworker-homemaker team worked closely with Mrs. Harvey and accomplished the following:

(1) The homemaker, through her close contacts in the home, learned exactly what basic essentials in clothing, bedding, cleaning equipment, and cooking utensils were needed by this family and the caseworker tapped community resources to meet these needs, which required large immediate outlays of money. (2) Mrs. Harvey learned, by the homemaker's example, to give better care to the children, giving attention to their diet, hygiene, rest, and supervised play. The caseworker helped Mrs. Harvey to secure medical care, as needed. Mrs. Harvey also learned to intervene in the children's quarrels calmly, and was able to give up her past screaming, ineffective efforts at discipline. (3) The homemaker helped Mrs. Harvey to learn better to shop and to plan expenditures now that she had a predictable, though still limited, income. They watched the newspapers for bargains, budgeted, and went shopping together. [59, p. 47–48] *

In some instances, the use of the homemaker fulfills all the purposes previously mentioned.

Mrs. M. came to the Family Service Agency to request homemaker service because she was expecting to be hospitalized for surgery in the near future. At the time of Mrs. M.'s application for homemaker service, Mr. M. was working steadily and was earning a good salary. Mrs. M. felt that it would be impossible for her daughter, Marian, age sixteen, and her husband to care for the other six children without help.

Homemaker service was provided to the M.'s because it was felt that Marian could not assume major responsibility for caring for her six younger brothers and sisters, which she would have

* From National Council for Homemaker–Home Health Aide Services, Inc., *A Unit of Learning About Homemaker–Home Health Aid Services—Teachers Source Book.* New York, 1968. By permission.

had to do because of Mr. M.'s long hours of work. Because of the emotional problems which two of the children, Dorothy, ten, and Victoria, nine, were displaying in their behavior, it was also felt that a homemaker would be needed to help give the children—and particularly these two—a feeling of security during the time their mother was away. It was expected that the homemaker's observations of the children would give the worker a better understanding of each child and his needs, and would also give the caseworker a clearer picture of inter- and intra-family relationships.

The homemaker was with this family for thirteen weeks. At first it was difficult for the children to accept a stranger in their home, and they directed much of their hostility because of their mother's absence against the homemaker by not speaking to her. It was not very long, however, before they responded to her warmth and interest. After Mrs. M. returned home, she had to be completely immobilized so that it was still necessary for the homemaker to continue to assume most of the care needed by the children. However, as Mrs. M. gained strength, the homemaker gradually returned this responsibility to her. During Mrs. M.'s hospitalization, the homemaker had been able to feed the family more adequately on less money than the family used to spend. Mrs. M. asked the homemaker to help her with menu planning and shopping lists. By the time the homemaker left, Mrs. M. had learned a great deal in this area. To help keep Mrs. M. occupied during her convalescent period, the homemaker also taught her how to mend and darn. [24, pp. 1, 2, Appendix 3] *

Homemaker service may be offered to supplement the mother's activities when she is so burdened by the demands of a handicapped or sick child, as to neglect the needs of her other children. This is an instance of inadequate role implementation in relation to care of the normal siblings due to the excessive demands of the sick child. "The homemaker can share in the care of the handicapped child or, by assuming some responsibility for the other children and the home, will free the mother so that she can give more time to the handicapped child." [85, p. 4] The homemaker and the caseworker can also help the family develop a more understanding attitude toward the handicapped or ill child.

A middle-aged mother applied [for help] at the suggestion of a friend who knew about homemaker service. The mother said she was physically exhausted and going to pieces from the demands of

* Community Service Society, *Report of the Extended Homemaker Service Project*, prepared by Adelaide Werner. New York: Community Service Society of New York, June 1958. By permission of the publisher.

caring for her three-year-old son. He had been born prematurely and weighed only one and one-half pounds at birth. When he was a year old, it was discovered that he was blind. He has been in and out of hospitals for a respiratory ailment; he whines and wheezes even while he is asleep. Recently there has been a diagnosis of cerebral palsy. Tests show that he is not mentally retarded. He cannot sit up and becomes fretful lying in one position. He shrieks in panic when he cannot hear his mother's voice. The father, an artist, had to travel on his job, but took a job as a laborer to be at home. The father made a device to prop up Eddie, but his balance is poor and he topples over. The mother has to reprop him and reprop him. The mother was told that Eddie would never speak, but she patiently taught him to say a few words. The child has to be taken to the clinic three times a week, and the mother was traveling three hours a day to take him there. The mother was troubled about their neglect of Betty, aged seven. Any occasion in school, Sunday school, or neighborhood from which Betty could get pleasure was denied her because her mother could not leave Eddie. Lately Betty is overeating, stealing money, slashing her dresses, and being openly resentful of her brother. Eddie is on a four-hour sleeping schedule, but the mother tries to protect the father's rest. When pressures get too great for the father, he reacts with acute migraine headaches. The mother said she had closed out Betty and her husband and concentrated her whole life on the handicapped child.

The homemaker in this family is gradually establishing herself with Eddie, who formerly would not let anyone but his mother touch him. The homemaker persuades the mother to rest. The homemaker admires the mother's courage and is helping her to take short cuts in housework so that she can spend more time with Betty.

The mother, who was eager for help, unloosed an avalanche of feeling to the caseworker, saying they lived in a house divided. She and Eddie sleep in one room, her husband and Betty in another. The aim of the homemaker service is to relieve the pressures on both parents and on Betty, to help Eddie be less fearful, and to achieve better balance in their lives. [85, p. 4]

Homemaker service may be offered when the mother role is left permanently vacant. In these instances, the mother has died, deserted, or divorced, and custody of the children has been awarded to the father. The aim in such cases is not to effect a permanent reorganization of the family group with the homemaker as a mother-substitute but, rather, to relieve stress and pressure on the father so as to permit a reasoned discussion of his long-range plans. Stressful situations may precipitate a decision made on the basis of expediency; with the intervention of the homemaker, the stress is mitigated and the situation is stabilized long enough to permit formulation of an acceptable plan.

Such use of homemaker service may also permit more adequate preparation for the placement of children into a more or less permanent substitute family arrangement.

> Mr. L., age thirty-nine, his son, age twelve, and his daughter, age five, lived in an adequately furnished apartment in a public housing project. Mrs. L. had died giving birth to a third child which had also died. This had been a happy, stable, lower-middle-class family until the mother's death. Mr. L. was steadily employed as a semi-skilled worker only a few blocks from his home. Relatives and neighbors had been helping to care for the children since his wife's death, but they could not go on doing so indefinitely. Also, Mr. L. recognized that it was not good for the children to have so many different persons care for them and he was getting so much advice that he was not able to think about what he really should do. He did not want to give up his children, but he did not know how to care for them properly and manage his home. His daughter, who had been happily attending a nursery school before her mother's death, no longer wanted to go to school. He had not been able to tell her that her mother had died. His son missed his mother a great deal and stayed alone in his room much of the time. A social worker in the hospital in which his wife had died had suggested that he apply to Community Service Society, Division of Family Service, for homemaker help. The services of the homemaker were provided to the L. family for twenty-three weeks to stabilize the home situation for Mr. L. and his children while the father and the caseworker considered plans for their future welfare and care. It was also hoped that, during the homemaker's stay with the family, the caseworker would be able to get a better understanding of the children and their reaction to their mother's loss. Such information would contribute greatly in deciding the kind of care that would be best for them. [24, pp. 32, 33] *

All situations are subject to change and what may have been initially a plan to provide help during the temporary absence of the mother becomes, owing to her permanent absence, a plan to relieve stress to permit reasoned planning.

> When Mr. F.'s wife was hospitalized with leukemia, he came to the homemaker agency for help in caring for his four small children.

---

* *Ibid.*

The children's grandmother, who suffered from crippling arthritis, had tried to take over while Mr. F. was at work, but the burden of running the home and caring for the youngsters was too much for her. Mr. F., a laundryman, could not afford to hire help, nor did he want to place the children in foster homes. A homemaker was sent in to give day care to the youngsters during the period of Mrs. F.'s hospitalization and now, after her death, the home-maker will continue to help until Mr. F. can make permanent plans for his family. [66, p. 1467]

Homemaker service may also be offered as a diagnostic aid in determining the best plan for a handicapped child or in evaluating possible neglect in homes where child care is reputed to be marginal, as well as in testing parents' ability to modify homemaking standards and parent-child relationship patterns.

A young mother looked up the name of our agency in the telephone book and came in asking for day care for her eight-year-old boy. The parents had recently been divorced. The mother had just begun a new job and her private arrangements for day care for John had fallen through. She said "other people" told her that John teased younger children and had temper tantrums in school. John was born with a cleft palate which has been repaired and was attending speech classes. During the intake study, he talked with the caseworker in floods of words about noise and killing the people who bothered him and his mother. He said that his father beat his mother and that he would strangle his father. His stories were rambling and filled with fears and fantasies. We placed a home-maker to hold the situation, to observe, and to help clarify the child's needs. The homemaker gave a graphic view of the mother's relationships with John. The mother did not come home on time, left no food, never said goodbye to him when she left, nor greeted him when she returned. When he came close to her, she shoved him away and immediately poured out her own problems to the homemaker. The homemaker described Johnny as overactive, with the personal habits of an infant. When she took him to the park, the friendships he initiated with other children immediately resulted in fights. He cautioned her constantly to give a false address lest his father find them. The caseworker asked the mother if she would be interested in having John go temporarily to our small group residence for children. The mother grasped the suggestion eagerly, said she was at the end of her rope, and began discussing John not in terms of what other people were saying but what she herself knew and felt about him. Caseworker, homemaker, and mother worked together toward getting the care and treatment John needs

in our cottage for emotionally disturbed children. The caseworker
has been seeing the mother regularly to help her with her own
problems, which are broader than her inability to rear her boy.
[85, p. 2]

Less frequently, homemaker service has been offered in the following
circumstances:

1. As an alternative to placement of a child in a detention home or
   shelter while suitable arrangements for care are being explored. [46]
   New York City has been considering "establishment of an auxiliary
   corps of homemakers who will be available to the police when children are deserted by their parents." [86, p. 166]
2. As a supplement to day care, when the employed mother could not
   remain at home to care for a temporarily ill child, or when day care
   for the child of a working mother is inappropriate or unacceptable.
3. To supplement the mother's activities "during the summer months
   for families of migrant farm workers." [83, p. 6]
4. To help adoptive parents make the difficult transition to parenthood.
   This "crisis of parenthood" is a problem of role transition during
   which supplementation in adjusting to the new, unfamiliar role is
   helpful. Similarly, homemaker help is offered to parents after the
   birth of their first child. [9, p. 11]
5. To permit a mother to attend a clinic on a regular basis or to receive
   hospital out-patient treatment.
6. To supplement the mother's unfilled role when she must be absent
   from home because of the illness or death of close relatives, or for
   educational reasons. For instance, in June 1971 about 500 children
   under six whose mothers were enrolled in the AFDC Work Incentive
   Program were cared for by homemakers.

Although homemaker service, if imaginatively exploited, is a valuable
and appropriate resource for a variety of problem situations, statistics
reveal that the service is most frequently used for limited kinds of situations. A detailed study of 1183 cases of families with children indicates
that homemaker service was requested in some 88 percent of these cases
because of the illness of the mother or because of her absence from the
home because of illness. [84, p. 67]   Currently, homemaker service is
most frequently offered to families with young children to cover emergency situations of limited duration in which the mother is incapacitated
or hospitalized.

The Casework Process in Homemaker Service

The most distinctive aspect of homemaker service is that it is generally offered under agency auspices in a casework context, as part of an over-all treatment plan, and that the homemaker is under agency supervision to ensure that her activity will contribute to the fulfillment of the treatment plan. The source of referrals for homemaker service depends on whether the agency is private or public. Seventy-four percent of the referrals to public agencies come from caseworkers and other staff members within the agency; the rest come primarily from doctors and medical institutions, or from other public welfare agencies that lack a homemaker service. By contrast, 86 percent of the referrals to voluntary agencies come from outside the agency, and the largest single referring source consists of family, neighbors, and friends. [84, p. 48]

Intake

Intake in homemaker service has the responsibility for achieving the same general purposes that it has in any agency setting. The worker must help the client articulate the problem with which he needs help, and make clear to the client the kinds of service the agency has available. The worker also tries to make clear the conditions under which the service can be offered—that is, the conditions of client eligibility. He then tries to help the client decide whether or not he wants to use the services available, and explores with him the alternative solutions of his problem. Because agency resources are limited, the worker has to be sure that the client not only wants the service, but can effectively use it.

There might also be discussion of the question of payment for the service. Private agencies require the client to pay something toward the cost of the service, the amount being determined by the client's income and the number of members in the family. At intake the client must show readiness to "share financial information including verification of income and to pay toward the service in accordance with his ability." [17, p. 113]

The family's expectation regarding the homemaker is also discussed, as well as the agency's expectation regarding the adjustments that might be required of the family members in assisting the homemaker to fulfill the functions of the missing mother. The structure of service needs to be agreed upon—who does what, when—and an explicit effort is made to help the client understand the distinction between homemaker service and maid service. Also, because in most cases the need for homemaker service is related to the illness of the mother, an attempt is made to obtain a clear picture of the mother's medical condition and the prognosis, her own and the family's attitude toward the illness, and their adjustment to it.

When a beginning relationship between client and agency has been established, the client is given some conception of the casework process, and the agency worker helps the client to learn to play the rather novel, specific, social role of a client in a social agency. Finally, some specific clear preparation has to be made for transition to the next step in the process—continuing with the agency, referral to a more appropriate resource, and so on.

Not all problem situations which might be helped by homemaker service are regarded as appropriate for homemaker service. Certain additional factors are significant in the agency's decision to offer service.

Because the aim of homemaker service is to preserve the family unit, the worker must determine whether a family worth attempting to save does in fact exist. Although the general assumption is that the child's own family offers the best environment for healthy development, in some instances the family situation is so damaging that a substitute family would offer the child a better chance for growth. As Dornenberg says, "The homemaker cannot create a home—but merely sustain what is there." [82, p. 1]   Thus the worker evaluates the family's emotional, structural, and physical resources. The level of family cohesiveness and stability must be such as to make it likely that it will not fall apart. The service must be given with the expectation that the family will again function normally some time in the future.

An experienced executive director of a homemaker service agency sets the program in realistic perspective:

> Those of us who have worked for some years in homemaker service must sadly admit that it is quite rare that we are asked to come into a family situation in which everything is normal in the relationship, in which the standards of living are somewhat middle-class or approaching middle-class, and in which temporary illness or dislocation threatens an already intact family life which we can protect and preserve with the simple addition of this one very good service. I say we rarely see it, although I admit that it occasionally does happen. [59, p. 74]

She continues by pointing out that it is not always, or even frequently, "a cheerful service in a cheerful situation which makes everybody extremely happy because it is successful." [59, p. 48]

The agency also must be sure that the client clearly understands and accepts the service. Here the term *client* refers not only to the individual formally representing the family but to all members of the family who have significant power in determining family decisions and whose patterns of life will be significantly affected by the service. Homemaker service may fail if the father accepts the service without consulting the mother or older siblings, who may be unprepared for the plan, or actually opposed to it. The worker also needs to assess the client's willingness and capacity to work with the agency. The agency selects the homemaker to be assigned and determines some of the conditions under which she works. Thus, through the homemaker, the agency will be in constant contact with the client. In a study of forty-seven unselected clients who were given homemaker service by well-trained and experienced homemakers, the most important single predictive factor relating to successful use of the service was found to be the applicant's attitude toward the part played by the agency in providing and supervising the homemaker. "In 83 percent of the cases using the service successfully, the family was accepting the agency, whereas 92 percent of the families using the service unsuccessfully were resistive, or indifferent, to the agency." [71, p. 345]

Many agencies, however, specifically point out that the willingness or ability of parents to accept help with personal problems is not necessarily a condition for providing homemaker service for children.

The worker also must determine whether or not the client has explored other possible resources—a nondamaging reallocation of responsibilities among family members, the help of available relatives, and so on. If resources that might be exploited do exist, the caseworker has the responsibility of helping the client to plan their effective use.

Unless a twenty-four-hour, seven-day-a-week service is contemplated, the agency must have some assurance that there will be a responsible person available, generally the father, to take over during the time the homemaker is not on duty. Although most agencies prefer that there be a father available in the home to which homemaker service is being offered, Watkins has shown that homemaker service can be effectively offered to the fatherless AFDC family. [90]

The interview, or series of interviews, may end with an offer of service, or it may end with service being refused. The most important single reason for the decision not to offer service is actually a tribute to casework efforts at intake. For instance, in a 1958 nationwide study, 21 percent of the families not accepted for homemaker service had been helped by the caseworker to use their own resources to move toward a solution of the problem. [84, p. 81]   And in another study of homemaker service in New York City in 1959, the Community Council found that 22 percent of the requests for service were not accepted because the family had been helped by the caseworker to use other resources. [23, p. 11]

The second most frequently cited reason reflects the tragic shortage of services available. In the two studies cited above, 17 percent and 20 percent, respectively, of the requests for service had to be denied because a homemaker was not available.

Despite all the concern in the social work literature with capacity to make profitable use of the service, this does not show up in any of the studies as the reason for denial of service in a sufficiently large number of cases to be claimed as a special category.

If homemaker service is offered, contact between the client and the caseworker is maintained. One important reason is that introduction of the homemaker into the family creates a unique situation. It involves the problem of temporary accession into the family system of an adult person who has no legal ties to the family, and who substitutes only in clearly defined areas for a key member of the family incapable of adequately performing the allocated roles. The homemaker has a clearly delineated, restricted relationship with the total family system, but one which involves intimate contact and a sharing of parental prerogatives.

The caseworker, working with the family and the homemaker, is often helpful in preventing problems that might arise from this situation and minimizing tension in case problems do arise.

The introduction of a stranger into the family's social system poses the problem of her acceptance by family members both as a person in her own right and as a mother-substitute. The homemaker, in turn, faces the problem of accepting the members of the family. An additional problem is posed by the fact that the family may have one idea of the way the assigned role of homemaker is to be enacted while the agency and the homemaker have another. The caseworker operates as a resource person facilitating the process of mutual accommodation and helping both the family and the homemaker to cope with problems in failures in understanding.

Still another problem is the danger of a competitive situation developing between homemaker and mother. "The mother may feel her position in the home challenged by the homemaker." [40, p. 14] Because the homemaker may care for the children and manage the home somewhat more efficiently, the mother might fear "that this may make her husband critical of her management." [50, p. 185] In a study of families receiving extended homemaker service care, it was noticed that

> Initially, many of the mothers, including the more adequate ones, evidenced great anxiety about their own displacement and fearfulness around the homemaker's role and function in the home. . . . In the more disturbed and deteriorated family situations . . . the adequacy of the homemakers seemed to threaten these mothers. Competition with the homemaker was increased by the positive reports they received from thoughtless, or malicious, relatives or from friends who told them how much calmer and better behaved their children were and how much better organized their households were now that the homemaker was in charge. Not infrequently, these mothers attempted to alienate their children from the homemaker. . . . [19, p. 103]

Thus the mother may react to the threat to her position by seeking to frustrate the purpose of the service. The mother may press to "give up the homemaker before her physical condition warrants it" [51, p. 135] or overexert herself by assuming functions beyond her physical capacity even while the homemaker is present.

In some cases, problems arise because homemaker and mother have different conceptions of how the mother's role is to be performed.

The homemaker and Mrs. F. complained of feeling uncomfortable with each other. The homemaker felt that Mrs. F. was a dominating kind of person who had outbursts of anger. The caseworker thought that one of the problems was that, with Mrs. F.'s improvement and the encouragement given her to take over little parts of the household management, the very different orientations toward household management in the homemaker and Mrs. F. came to the fore and caused, or helped support, some tensions between the two. The homemaker tended toward a high degree of organization and efficient economies. Mrs. F.'s tendency in household management was toward haphazard, less organized methods. In respective individual contacts with the homemaker and Mrs. F., these differences in household management were discussed; an attempt was made to remove any emphasis on one way being better than another and to help each of them accept the fact that there were different, equally acceptable ways of managing a household.

The children may find it difficult to accept the homemaker without feeling conflict over their "disloyalty" to their own mother. The situation poses a problem for the children regarding their response to a woman who acts as a mother without at the same time being a mother. The child might feel conflict about accepting discipline from such a person because disciplining is clearly a prerogative generally reserved to the true parent. As Baldwin says, "Children feel suspicion and mistrust of the woman who tries to replace, even in part, the mother." [2, p. 125] In such situations, the caseworker may discuss with the children their anxieties about what is happening to the family, helping them to understand and accept the mother's limited capacity for child care while she is ill.

The situation also poses problems for the father. As Gordon notes, "The father may feel his position as provider of the family threatened because the agency selects the homemaker, pays her—at least in part—and it is to the agency that she is responsible." [40, p. 14] The father may also be threatened by the necessity of taking over some of the mother's functions. Acting as a mother, even in a limited way, may create anxiety for the man who is tenuously holding on to his sense of masculinity, as shown in the following case record:

We discussed, at some length, the duties Mr. F. expected of a homemaker. He was somewhat embarrassed at going over these details such as ironing and so forth. When I mentioned that, as a man, he might be unaccustomed to some of this "business" but that illness in the family often changed people's roles, he was reassured.

The father may also have difficulty in accepting the assumption of certain aspects of the maternal role by the homemaker.

Mr. B. had always depended upon his wife to discipline the children, but he resented the homemaker doing it and he would not do it himself. [48, p. 292]

The inability of the father to work cooperatively and effectively with the homemaker may result from feelings and attitudes toward women and mother surrogates stemming from his own developmental experience.

Mr. Madison, a widower of thirty-five with three children under four years of age, could not get along with homemakers. He was surly, curt, and critical. He was unable to show any appreciation of what was being done for the children. Homemakers tried hard to accept his inability to show any graciousness, but none of them cared to remain long in the home. Gradually, as he and the caseworker discussed the needs in his home and the way he handled these, he was able to talk about some of the experiences that had made him distrustful of women. As he gained some understanding, he found ways to handle more satisfactorily his feelings about women and to find pleasure in friendly, warm relationships with them. [2]

The father and the children may be reluctant to permit any changes in the house, out of "loyalty" to the sick mother. The family may feel its privacy is being violated by the intrusion of the homemaker into the family, and may feel anxious about the possibility that she will disapprove of their ways of rearing the children or managing the home. In the course of one demonstration project, it became clear that some of the more disorganized parents "were fearful that the homemaker would learn too much about some aspect of the family's life that they preferred to keep hidden—such as the whereabouts of the children's father, an illegal source of income, an extramarital affair, or the extent of disturbance in their children." [19, p. 103]

Because the request for homemaker service results from some crisis

in the family's life, the caseworker may be needed to help with the social
and emotional consequences of the crisis situation.

Thus Mr. W., in discussing his wife's hospitalization, expressed
some defensiveness about his inability to visit more often. He
suggested that his guilt about this was further intensified by letters
from his wife's family which questioned whether his wife was
getting the best possible attention at the hospital. He wondered
if he should try to visit even more often, although this would mean
even greater neglect of the children until the homemaker could
be placed. We discussed the care his wife was receiving and his
own opinion was that the hospital was doing all it could, that
additional visits on his part would not make a difference.

Mr. K. called the agency for homemaker help in caring for his
two children, Mary, eleven, and Raymond, eight and one-half. He
was upset about his wife's hospitalization in the middle of the night
because of an acute psychotic break. He was overwhelmed with
guilt about his wife's hospitalization, thinking that he had contributed to it because he had been unable to face the beginning
signs of her disturbance despite his knowledge of a former psychotic
break. [24, pp. 26, 27] *

The father may need help in facing a new, threatening situation occasioned by the change in family structure.

In the E. family, with four children, twenty-four-hour service was
necessitated by the hospitalization of the mother and the long and
irregular working hours of the father. Mr. E. was overwhelmed and
became agitated when the caseworker or the homemaker tried to enlist
his help in planning for the family. He had been overly dependent
on his wife and had never participated in the management of the
household or the children. With encouragement from the homemaker and the caseworker during the two months his wife remained
in the hospital, he gradually assumed a more positive and meaningful
place in his family. [19, p. 103]

The availability of the caseworker is of special importance when the
introduction of the homemaker leads to an intensification of the family's
difficulties.

In working with Mr. S., the caseworker learned that he needed
to feel totally responsible and to be the only giving person in his

* *Ibid.*

family. He had a pathological need to assume both the female and male roles in the family, which made it difficult for him to accept a woman in the home. With his lessened responsibility because of the homemaker's presence, his control weakened so he began drinking, staying out late, and buying for the family in ways which threatened the health and nutrition of the children. The presence of a responsible and efficient woman relieved him of the need to be responsible, while at the same time it threatened his own adequacy. [24, p. 45, Appendix]

The caseworker, aware of the underlying problems that may make the service a pathogenic rather than a therapeutic agent, can work toward effecting a more positive use of the homemaker.

Work with the Homemaker

In response to the conflicting reactions to the presence of the home-maker in the home, the caseworker has regularly scheduled conferences with the homemaker as well as with members of the family. This is a service to the family, although an indirect one, for it enables the home-maker to work more effectively with the family.

The social worker is generally responsible for the supervision of eight to ten homemakers. The caseworker sees that the homemaker is assigned to a family and that the assignment is responsibly covered. She sees that each homemaker has an equitable and diversified caseload, that assignments coincide with the special competencies and interests of the individual homemakers.

The caseworker helps the homemaker move into the family situa-tion as unobtrusively as possible, "to fit into the family as a source of strength with the least possible threat to the status of any member of the family." [87, p. 9] In order to be able to prepare the homemaker for working with the family, the caseworker has to explore the details of family schedule and routine, the pattern of family activities, the special needs and preferences of the various children, and special family problems of which the homemaker might need to be aware. Cook County Department of Public Welfare assigns

> . . . the homemaker prior to the date of expected confinement or hospitalization in order to give the mother and children a better chance to get acquainted with her. . . . This alleviates the fears of the mother as to the care her children will receive during her absence and [helps] the children to adjust to the presence of a stranger. [91, p. 30]

The caseworker also helps the homemaker with her struggle to accept the different ways people may organize their home and their routines; she helps the homemaker accept the difference between these children who "belong" to other parents and her own children.

> Mrs. C., the homemaker placed with a family of four school-age children while the mother was in the hospital, felt puzzled and unsure as to how to handle the problem of discipline. She had, in raising her own children, successfully resorted to reasoning with the child and deprivation of privileges as the means of maintaining discipline. This approach did not seem to work with the R. children. They refused to obey her, saying she was not their mother and no amount of talking to them seemed to be of help. She wondered what to do next and brought this question for discussion to her conference with the caseworker.

Because the homemaker will directly encounter many situations that tend to activate strong emotional reactions—mental illness, a neglectful mother—she needs to have someone with whom she can talk over her feelings. An opportunity for catharsis may allow the homemaker to return to the family ready to work more comfortably in the situation. The caseworker offers this opportunity as well as an emotionally supportive relationship to the homemaker so as to dissipate feelings of discouragement and anxiety regarding her competence. Equally important, the caseworker helps the homemaker to become aware of any "projection of expectations of herself upon the mother or her attitude toward her own husband on the father of the family." [39, p. 368] She also helps her to keep from overidentifying with, or rejecting, any one member of the family. [20, p. 2] She helps the homemaker to counter any tendency to take sides with a child against the parent, or with the family against the agency, to compete with the natural parents for the love and respect of the children, or to compete with the mother for the affection of the father.

The caseworker also helps the homemaker understand and modify some aspect of her behavior which may be having a deleterious effect on family relationships.

> Mrs. Emmons, twenty-eight years old, was hospitalized for a postpartum depression shortly after her second child was born. She left behind a dirty home, a frightened seven-year-old, the three-week-old baby, and a depressed husband. A homemaker about the same age as Mrs. Emmons was placed in the home. This was one of her first assignments and she was eager to make a good impression. She performed many extra chores as well as restoring order, cleanliness, and regularity in the household. Soon glowing reports came to Mrs. Emmons from her husband of the homemaker's skill and many achievements. Mrs. Emmons' depression increased and she showed much apprehension.

Through counseling with her supervisor the homemaker came to understand the effects of her actions on the absent mother. She telephoned Mrs. Emmons at the hospital to ask for advice instead of waiting for Mrs. Emmons to telephone the home. The homemaker sent notes and pictures of the children to the mother. When the mother came home six weeks later, the two women were able to work well together, with homemaker's services gradually diminished to two half-days each week until termination some months later. [59, p. 125]

Finally, the caseworker helps the homemaker to become aware of any behavior on the part of members of the client family that may be symptomatic of emotional stress—withdrawal, enuresis, thumb-sucking, temper tantrums, and so on. Through the homemaker, the caseworker keeps informed of any significant changes in the family situation that might require the help of the caseworker. She helps her to understand and meet the needs of the children.

Although the homemaker and the caseworker ideally cooperatively complement each other, there is potential for friction. The homemaker is concerned with the immediate practical needs of the family; the caseworker is more apt to focus on long-range psychological goals. The homemaker knows the family intimately and has the allegiance of the family, which may cause the caseworker to feel resentment. [15] The caseworker acts as "consultant" rather than a "doer," as an infrequent visitor rather than a temporary "member" of the family. The homemaker may feel she has greater familiarity with the situation and may tend to discount much of the caseworker's advice.

Termination

Eventually, the homemaker and caseworker work together to help the family accept termination of the service, with the homemaker gradually doing less and less for the family while the family does more and more for itself. The caseworker helps the family with problems attendant upon the homemaker's leaving.

Mrs. H., who had trouble with her back so that she could not lift her baby, had been referred for some special orthopedic exercises to strengthen the affected muscles. She resisted working on them and seemed to be slipping into a pattern of letting the homemaker do all the work while she sat by giving orders and criticizing the homemaker.

Mrs. H. had to be helped to consider whether she wanted to get well and to face the fact that the homemaker was placed to afford her the chance to try to recover. [40]

The caseworker helps the homemaker change, as the situation changes, by gradually taking less direct responsibility for the care of the children and the home as the mother is able to assume more of her normal role.

Evaluation

Homemaker service has a number of advantages over alternative plans for dealing with the problems presented by the motherless family. The most important single advantage is that it permits the child to remain at home during the time that the mother is incapable of fully implementing her role. Homemaker service imposes a far smaller burden of adjustment on the child than foster care, for the child adjusts to the homemaker in the comforting familiarity of his own home, his own family, his own neighborhood. The homemaker might be regarded as a "traveling foster mother" who comes to the child.

In a study of the values of long-term homemaker service, one agency noted:

Service to fifty families involving 194 children prevented the placement of children in the majority of situations. In several where placement eventually proved necessary, the homemaker and case-worker's knowledge and evaluation of the children and their problems made possible more adequate preparation and planning. [12, p. 7]

As the New York City Department of Public Welfare notes,

. . . [Since the] inception of the program in 1945, Department of Welfare homemakers have cared for over 30,000 children in their own homes, thus avoiding placement and the consequent breakdown of family life that so often results from the separation of children and parents. [75, p. 1]

In 1967 Homemaker Service of the Children's Aid Society of New York served 138 families enabling "109 children to remain in their own homes during periods when parents were faced with illness or some other crises that would otherwise have propelled the children into placement in foster homes."

More methodologically rigorous studies of family situations which resulted in child placement show that, in the worker's judgment, home-maker service might have prevented placement in some of the cases. [45; 73] The studies, however, point to the need for greater flexibility in work schedules for homemaker service, and for the recruitment of "persons whose own background provides them with a familiarity and an understanding not only of the language, but also of the customs and mores of the families they are called upon to assist." [45, p. 189]

The larger the number of children in the family, the more economical homemaker service is for the community, for "homemaker costs are relatively fixed, regardless of the number of children in the family, while costs for foster care rise in direct proportion to the number of children in the family." [12, p. 18]

The availability of a homemaker on a twenty-four-hour basis materially reduced the number of children who might previously have been taken to children's shelters when parents were suddenly taken ill at night.

Homemaker service also provides greater assurance that the solidarity of the family will be maintained. The children remain at home and the father continues to carry full, direct responsibility for the discharge of his role functions vis-à-vis his children.

Homemaker services also contribute to the efficiency and effectiveness of available medical services. Mothers are more likely to accept the necessity for hospitalization if they have assurances regarding the care of their children. Once hospitalized, they are likely to remain as long as is medically necessary and when they return home they are likely to follow a prescribed medical regimen rather than attempt to take on too much too soon. Furthermore, because homemaker service permits earlier discharge on convalescent care of many hospital patients, it makes possible a more efficient use of available hospital bed space. According to Justiss:

> Homemaker service provides a type of care which the ill mother can accept more readily and thus it permits her to accept hospitalization. Many mothers have told us that they would rather stay in their own home and die rather than see their children "sent away" to some stranger's home. Offering such service in a rural county in Texas "where, because of inadequate diet, lack of medical care, overwork, and poor health standards, incidence of tuberculosis is extremely high" has resulted in amelioration of a previously dangerous practice. It is reported that "there has not been a single instance of a mother returning home from a hospital against medical advice since the homemaker program has become well established." [48, pp. 291, 294]

In the Brown family the father had deserted. The mother kept postponing an urgently needed operation because she dreaded leaving her seven children placed as they had been when she was previously hospitalized. When 24-hour homemaker service was provided, she left calmly for the hospital. All of the children quickly became devoted to the homemaker and mentioned how lonely and nervous they had been when they were separated the year before. [19, pp. 101–102]

A report of the Visiting Home Aid program in Monroe County, New York, indicates that, "when a patient is referred by a hospital, the agency inquires as to what will happen to him if they did not admit him to the Visiting Home Aid Service. If they are told he will have to remain in the hospital, it is considered that his admission to the service releases a hospital bed." This happened ninety-two times in the first twelve-month period of the agency service. And Brodsky notes that "homemaker service might make it possible for a not too severely mentally ill mother to have hospital day-care treatment service." [10, p. 15]

Equally important, homemaker service reduces the danger of damaging effects of role reallocation. Without homemaker service, fathers may miss many days of work in an effort to hold the family together. Even in those instances where the father remains on the job, his enactment of the wage-earner role may be impaired because of anxiety about what is happening at home. Homemaker service permits the father to devote himself to the demands of his job with less anxiety. Furthermore, if older siblings are forced to assume the responsibility for performing the functions previously allocated the mother, their enactment of their own student role is impaired through reduced attendance and inadequate preparation. Thus, homemaker service reduces the tendency for family members to assume a burden of responsibilities that impairs effective enactment of their central roles.

Another advantage of homemaker service lies in the fact that it may make a family more amenable to needed casework help with other problems. As Johnson notes, "giving families a tangible service of immediate practical value often makes them more receptive toward help with less obvious problems." [46] The following case illustrates her point:

The F.'s had originally come to the family service agency to seek help with their marital problem. Income was marginal, and many conflicts arose between Mr. and Mrs. F. around the inadequacy of his earnings and their inability to manage within their income. The children were all being affected by their parents' constant quarreling.

Shortly after they came to the agency for marital counseling, Mrs. F. and one of the children were hit by an automobile. Mrs. F.'s thigh and arm were fractured and she had to wear a heavy cast on her leg. As a consequence she could not care for her family and home. The agency, therefore, provided homemaker service during the period of time that Mrs. F. was recovering from the accident.

The concrete services which the homemaker had provided to the family were a demonstration to it of the agency's wish to be helpful and cut through some of Mr. and Mrs. F.'s distrust of the caseworker. This enabled the parents in marital counseling to discuss much information with the caseworker which they had previously withheld. The observations of the family relationships which were made available through the homemaker had helped the caseworker to grasp the family problems more quickly and to focus more contact with more economy of time. [24, pp. 18, 19, App. 3] *

Some of the values of homemaker service may be illustrated by the problem situations that develop in its absence. A study by the Almeda Council of Social Agencies of how a sample of families managed in the absence of the mother and the lack of available homemaker service indicates the older children were kept out of school to care for younger children; one parent took an unpaid vacation from work; one parent took his younger children to work; children were left with relatives at a distance from home; children were left at home without supervision of any kind. [30]

Any evaluation of homemaker service would be incomplete without some effort to review the client's assessment of the value of the service, but there is only one study available which attempts follow-up interviews with clients. [24] The project was conducted primarily as a demonstration and "not as a scientifically planned and controlled piece of research." The follow-up report notes:

It seems reasonable to conclude that the majority of the thirty-five families who received homemaker service in combination with casework and other services were measurably benefited by the help received. In general, benefits took the form of restoration to former role and/or assumption of more adequate roles by the parents or parent, preservation of the family unit from disintegration, and preservation of the individual and collective strength of family members. [24, pp. 45, 47]

The study cites some of the clients' responses regarding the values of homemaker service:

Their comments indicated that, for their children, it had meant that they could remain in their own home and that they had good

* Ibid.

care from the warm, understanding homemaker instead of being placed. To many of the fathers, it meant that they had discovered that they had strength and resources within themselves to meet a family crisis and that, with the help of the caseworker and homemaker, they could care for their children and assume many new responsibilities. Some of the fathers elaborated on this and brought out how they had learned to know and understand their children better. Some fathers also stated that their anxiety was greatly relieved when the homemaker came to help them care for their children and homes, and this had made it possible for them to talk with their caseworkers about other problems which troubled them. To many of the mothers, it meant peace of mind and more rapid recovery because they knew that their children were being cared for by a responsible, well-trained person. . . .

[In those families where homemakers continued with the family after the mother's return home], mothers commented on the tactful way in which the homemakers had helped them gradually resume their responsibilities as they regained their strength. One mother who had been apprehensive about returning home from a mental hospital said "that the homemaker made me feel at home in my own home." Mothers commented on the things they had learned from the homemaker which they had found helpful and were continuing to put to good use. Some had benefited from watching the way in which the homemaker handled their children, others from the way she organized and carried out household duties. . . .

A handicapped mother who needed help in caring for her infant said that she could not have kept her baby with her without the help of the caseworker and homemaker. If she and her husband had placed the baby, he would have been deprived of care by his parents and they would have been also deprived of the experience of caring for their own child. . . .

A mother who had received homemaker help because "she was too emotionally disturbed to care for her own family at home," in expressing gratitude for the help given to her by the caseworker and homemaker, said, in speaking of the homemaker, "she was a warm person who was not only very good with the children, but very good to me. She respected me and treated me like a human being. The homemaker spent all day long with me. She saw me at my worst but still wanted to stick it out to help me. If she hadn't come, I would have ended in a hospital and my husband would have placed the children." . . .

The father of three children whose wife had died and who had applied [for] and received homemaker service, in evaluating the value to him of the service, said, "I have had a chance to look around and see how other families with only one parent who must work can manage. The most important thing you people have helped me with is that you have given me a chance to see that I do not have to rush into a lousy second marriage like my mother did because she was afraid we would not survive. That is what I feared most." [24, pp. 34, 35, 44] *

Problems

1. A controversy exists as to the most appropriate auspices for home-maker service. Because the need for the service is almost always precipitated by a health problem, there is some argument for tying the service to health, rather than welfare, agencies. In 1972 about 40 percent of all homemaker services agencies were operating under the auspices of health agencies or visiting nurse organizations. The current name of the national organization which has accepted responsibility for advancing the cause of homemaker service—the National Council for Homemaker-Health Aide Services—symbolizes the dual allegiance of the service to both health and welfare. On the other hand, the service is designed to deal not with the health problem but, rather, with the social consequences of illness. It is further argued that tying the service to health agencies might tend to foster a narrow view of the appropriateness of the service and tend to keep it restricted to situations involving illness. If viewed from the point of view of illness, homemaker service becomes focused on the patient; if viewed from the point of view of social dislocation, the service is more frequently directed in terms of the needs of children and it is more legitimately classified as a child welfare service. This ambiguity of emphasis may create a problem during the course of offering the service. When a homemaker enters a family because the mother is ill, "who should be the homemaker's primary concern, the incapacitated adult or the insecure child?"

2. A second controversial question arises: "Is casework an essential part of homemaker service?" If so, it seems logical that homemaker service should be offered primarily, as it is now, by social agencies. Some point out that the selective, appropriate offering of a resource, supported by community funds, requires an intake casework interview; that the effective use of the service requires the kind of coordination and ongoing help provided by the caseworker; that in all instances families needing homemaker services are facing some crisis and the caseworker can be helpful in dealing with its consequences. [2; 8; 9]   Aldrich points to the fact that even the seemingly uncomplicated situations actually require the caseworker's continuing help. [1]   This point receives some empirical

* *Ibid.*

support from one nationwide study, which indicates that "about six out of every seven families served in the study were provided casework services as well as homemaker service." [84, p. 65]

Others, however, suggest that, although casework service is needed to determine if the situation calls for a homemaker as an appropriate resource, "this is quite different from requiring a family to be engaged in a continuing casework relationship. If the public gets the idea that, in order to obtain a homemaker, it is necessary to be involved in a continuing casework relationship, the service either will not be used or will be obtained through auspices other than a social agency." Richman points to the "advisability of accepting families who wish to meet their personal needs through homemaker service but who may not need, or want, help with personal problems." [82]   And, as the report of the 1959 Homemaker's Conference suggests, "In many cases the family's only need is for the help of a homemaker in an emergency. They neither require nor want counseling or casework. To add such families to the load of the caseworker is not only burdensome but unrealistic." [86, p. 21]

3. Another problem derives from the fact that the essential differences between homemaker and housekeeper services are very often blurred in the minds of the laymen and, on occasion, in the minds of professionals. In offering the service, this problem of distinction and definition sometimes arises as the agency strives to keep the service from degenerating into a routine, mechanical housekeeping service. A detailed study of home help services in Great Britain, in which extensive interviews were conducted with homemakers, clients, and the public, made clear that the public and clients had difficulty in perceiving homemaker services as differentiated from maid service. [43]

4. There is also a question as to the proper allocation of the limited homemaker service resources. Many of the agencies offer the service to the aged as well as to families with young children. Which group can legitimately claim priority when the decisions regarding service limitations need to be made?

5. Agencies are "frequently insufficiently flexible" in the number of hours per day and length of time for which homemaker service is offered. [23, p. 5]   Some agencies will not provide service if the homemaker is required for more than eight to ten hours a day; others will refuse service if the homemaker is likely to be required for more than three months. National organizations interested in homemaker service have urged that family need, rather than arbitrary limitations, determine the way the service is offered.

6. Another problem involves lack of public knowledge and acceptance of homemaker service. A study of homemaker service in New York City in 1959 revealed that approximately two-thirds of a group of people identified as needing some kind of a home aide because of illness "had neither contacted an agency nor had been referred to one." [23, p. 5]

An English study of motherless families indicated that relatives and friends were the principal source of help. [35]   The relevant social services, such as homemaker service, was a source of help in only a small percentage of cases, mostly to lower-class families and for a limited period. Many of the fathers indicated they would have preferred homemaker services if these had been more readily available. Accepting the help of friends and relatives incurs an obligation and one may not be able to reciprocate the favor. A Dutch interview study of some sixty families who received homemaker services indicated that they preferred them to the help of relatives and/or friends and neighbors. [62, p. 75]

7. There is the problem of recruitment. The prestige of the homemaker is not high enough to permit easy recruiting of competent personnel, and the limited availability of professionally trained casework supervisors makes difficult the expansion of service to meet the growing demand. Furthermore, the service has limited prestige within the agency. [86, p. 5]   Social workers are oriented to thinking in terms of the better established resources, such as foster care, for dealing with the kinds of problem situations in which a homemaker might be appropriately employed. This tends to the neglect and derogation of homemaker service. [86, p. 6]

8. Funding of homemaker service is an ongoing problem. The service has low visibility and low priority for community support either through community chest funds or tax funds. Although there are some sources of funding available, these are far from adequate. While there is some possibility of Federal reimbursement for the expense of providing homemaker service to families receiving public assistance, the service is not specifically identified in Federal legislation, as an essential mandated service, as are, for instance, foster care, protective services, and family planning.

Trends

1. One trend in homemaker service is toward an expansion of the service, a broader definition of situations in which the service might be used. Families that required extended homemaker service once found it difficult to obtain. As a result of several special projects illustrating the value of extended homemaker service [12; 19; 24] and the growing recognition of the clear need for such service, more agencies may make homemakers available either over a longer period of time, or for more hours each day. It is likely that the present trend toward an expansion of homemaker service will continue. Growing difficulties in finding foster homes, and growing dissatisfaction with the program of foster care, will

continue to provide an impetus to explore alternative means of meeting the needs of the motherless family.

Developments in other social problem areas are likely to reinforce the need for homemaker service. For instance, the trend toward community-centered psychiatric services, which help to keep more and more of the mentally ill in the community, requires—for its success—supplementary services such as homemaker service.

The trend toward growth of homemaker service has received considerable impetus from the trend toward social work services in public assistance programs. Through the Children's Bureau, the Federal government had previously made grants, covering 100 percent of costs, available to local public welfare agencies in order to help establish homemaker services on a demonstration basis, but continuing support for the programs was not provided. The 1962 amendments to the Social Security Act, however, made it possible for the Federal government to provide 75 percent of the costs of homemaker service in the public assistance programs. Such reimbursement is available not only for the families receiving assistance but also for those families which, because of limited income, are potential recipients of public assistance. Use of the service is designed to prevent the family from becoming dependent. The Federal grant also requires that the service be made available as one means of implementing the case plan developed to meet the needs of each child in the family, and that it be closely coordinated with all other services provided for the family. Federal encouragement of such service supports a trend toward an increase of homemaker service under public welfare auspices.

2. The increased availability of public funds is part of a general trend toward a greater variety of sources of support for homemaker service. Because the need for homemakers is so frequently occasioned by illness, some hospital insurance programs that finance posthospital care now pay for homemaker service as well. Medicaid also makes funds available for homemaker service needed because of illness or disability. Blue Cross covers 50 percent of the cost of the service in some areas.

Another source of support is the family receiving the service. Over 50 percent of homemaker agencies charge fees, based on the family's ability to pay. In New Jersey, 85 percent of a very extensive homemaker program costing about $900,000 in 1963 was financed by fees. However, this is atypical, because an earlier nationwide study showed that only 9 percent of program financing came from fees. [84, p. 86]

3. There is also a trend toward a more imaginative use of homemaker service. For instance, California has used funds available through the Children's Bureau Crippled Children's Program to provide homemakers for the mothers of crippled children so as to relieve them for a few hours a day. Homemakers have also been used with families charged with neglect "in homes in which standards of household management was so poor as to seriously jeopardize the health and welfare of children in the family." [72, p. 12]   The homemaker assisted these mothers in the care of their children and instructed them in better methods of child care. The reports of homemakers have also been found to be of great help in determining actual conditions in families suspected of child abuse. [57, p. 59]   And in families with very young retarded children, homemaker service has been used in order to relieve family pressures and tensions. It was hoped that, as a result, "energies might be released to work out not only appropriate planning for the retarded child, but also to examine and work through family problems created or aggravated by a retarded child." [70, p. 10]   Homemakers have also been used effectively with families threatened with eviction from public housing because of poor housekeeping standards, as well as with migrant workers and Indian families on the reservations. [57, pp. 61–62]

4. Homemakers have been taught the essentials of behavior modification approaches and have been given responsibility for observing, recording, and reporting behavior and implementing techniques for changing maladaptive behavior: "In essence the homemaker serves as the agent through whom the behavior change program is implemented." [79, p. 4]

5. There is a growing recognition of the need for homemaker services in segments in the community other than the economically deprived. Because illness strikes all groups, because mothers at any socioeconomic level may become incapacitated, there is growing pressure to make homemaker service available at all levels.

Summary

Homemaker service is a supplementary service that originated in response to the need to assume some aspects of the mother's role for a limited period when she was ill at home or in the hospital. Homemaker service obviates the necessity of placing children in a foster home or institution for short periods, and prevents family disintegration during a crisis.

Homemaker service is appropriately offered when

1. The mother is temporarily hospitalized.
2. The mother is in the home, but ill or convalescing.
3. The mother needs tutorial help in developing homemaker skills.
4. The mother needs assistance in caring for a handicapped child.
5. The mother has died or deserted and the father needs time to make adequate, more permanent plans for the care of the children.

6. The agency needs further information about family functioning to permit an accurate diagnostic assessment of a child's needs.

Despite the diverse situations in which homemaker service may be appropriate, its greatest use involves situations in which the mother is ill.

The distinguishing aspects of homemaker service lie in the fact that the responsibility assumed by the homemaker goes beyond the mechanics of housekeeping to include concern with the social, interpersonal effects of the mother's inability to discharge her role, and that homemaker service is offered as part of a total social work plan for the family.

Homemakers are generally older women of limited education who have raised their own children and whose skills center on home management and child care. In October 1972 there were about 30,000 homemakers employed by 3000 agencies offering service to an indeterminate number of families, some percent of which included children. The number of children affected by the program is very small, then, compared with programs such as OASDI and AFDC.

The caseworker helps prepare the family and the homemaker for each other, and works with the homemaker and the family on any problems that might result from her introduction into the family.

Evaluations of homemaker service indicate that

1. It has been successful in preventing the need for short-term foster care for many children.
2. It has permitted the care of the child in his own home at a more limited expense to the community than would otherwise have been the case if the service were not available.
3. It increases the efficiency and effectiveness of medical service for mothers.

Problems regarding homemaker service include the following:

1. The controversy as to auspices.
2. The necessity for casework as an accompaniment to the service.
3. The confusion between homemaker service and housekeeping service.
4. The limited public knowledge of the program.
5. The low status of the program both in the mind of the public and within the social work profession.

Among the trends identified were the following:

1. A greater flexibility in the use of homemakers for situations requiring twenty-four-hour-a-day coverage and a seven-day week.

2. The continued rapid expansion of the program.
3. The increasing interest of public welfare agencies in homemaker service.
4. A greater diversification of sources of financing for such service.
5. A greater diversification of situations for which homemaker service has been found to be appropriate.

Bibliography

1. ALDRICH, C. KNIGHT. "A Psychiatrist Looks at Homemaker Service." *Child Welfare,* **35** (October 1956).
2. BALDWIN, RUTH M. "Values in Long-Time Homemaker Service." *Social Casework,* **34** (March 1953).
3. BEATT, EARL J. "Community Organization to Meet Homemaker Service Need." *Child Welfare,* **36** (July 1957).
4. BODE, GRETCHEN. "Visiting Housekeeping Service." *The Family,* **19** (April 1938).
5. BOGGS, MARJORIE H. "Homemaker Service Helps a Motherless Family." *The Child,* **14** (May 1950) and **14** (June–July 1950).
6. ———. "Some Treatment Implications in the Use of Homemaker Service." *The Family,* **24** (May 1943).
7. BRECKINRIDGE, SOPHONISBA, and EDITH ABBOTT. *The Delinquent Child and the Home.* New York: Russell Sage Foundation, 1912.
8. BRODSKY, ROSE. *Homemaker Service: Under Whose Auspices and for What Purpose?* Jamaica, N.Y.: Jewish Community Service of Long Island, September 1957.
9. ———. "Philosophy and Practices in Homemaker Service." *Child Welfare,* **37** (July 1958).
10. ———. *Use of Homemaker Service for Families with Psychiatric Disorders of Adults.* Paper presented at Eastern Regional Conference, Child Welfare League of America, New York, April 20, 1961. Mimeo.
11. ———. "Administrative Aspects of Twenty-four-Hour Homemaker Service." *Child Welfare,* **45**, 1 (January 1966), 34–39.
12. BROOKLYN BUREAU OF SOCIAL SERVICE AND CHILDREN'S AID SOCIETY. *Long-Term Homemaker Service—Project Report.* New York, September 1958.
13. BURFORD, ELIZABETH. "A Formalized Homemaker Training Program." *Child Welfare,* **41** (September 1962).
14. BURRS, MARY E., and JULIA A. GOODMAN. "The Teaching Homemaker in a School Project." *Children,* **14**, 5 (September–October 1967), 170–74.
15. CASSERT, HILDA P. "Homemaker Service as a Component of Casework." *Social Casework,* **51**, 9 (November 1970), 533–44.
16. CHAMBERS, KATHERINE N. "First Steps in Homemaker Service: A Study of Applications." *Social Casework,* **35** (March 1954).
17. ———. "The Intake Process in Homemaker Service Cases." *Social Casework,* **36** (May 1955).

18. CHILD WELFARE LEAGUE OF AMERICA. *Standards for Homemaker Service for Children.* New York, 1959.
19. CHILDREN'S AID SOCIETY OF NEW YORK CITY. "Nine- to Twenty-four-Hour Homemaker Service Project." *Child Welfare,* **41** (March 1962) and **41** (April 1962).
20. CLOUGH, TRACY C., and JANET C. WOOD. "Homemaker Service to Children in a Multiple-Function Agency." *Child Welfare,* **37** (December 1958).
21. COMMUNITY CHEST AND COUNCIL OF THE GREATER VANCOUVER AREA. *Homemaker–Housekeeper Services: Technical Committee Report.* Vancouver, February 1962. Mimeo.
22. COMMUNITY COUNCIL OF GREATER NEW YORK. *Homemaker Services Programs in New York City: 1959.* New York, December 1959.
23. ———. *Home Aid Service-Needs of Health Agency Clientele.* New York, June 1961.
24. COMMUNITY SERVICE SOCIETY OF NEW YORK. *Report of the Extended Homemaker Service Project,* prepared by Adelaide Werner. New York, June 1958.
25. COMMUNITY WELFARE COUNCIL, HENNEPIN COUNTY, MINNESOTA. *Homemaker Service in Hennepin County.* Minneapolis, June 1958.
26. COMMUNITY WELFARE COUNCIL OF GREATER SACRAMENTO AREA, INC. *Homemaker Service: A Report and Recommendation of the Need for Homemaker Service in Sacramento.* Sacramento, May 1961. Mimeo.
27. COUNCIL ON SOCIAL WORK EDUCATION, NATIONAL COUNCIL FOR HOMEMAKER SERVICES, INC. *A Unit of Learning about Homemaker–Home Health Aide Services.* New York, 1968.
28. DIEBOLT, MARTHA C., and MANYA A. DAVIS. "So You Want to Start a Homemaker Service?" *Child Welfare,* **48**, 4 (April 1969), 223–29.
29. EINSTEIN, GERTRUDE. "The Homemaker's Role in Prevention and Treatment of Family Breakdown." *Child Welfare,* **39** (May 1960).
30. FEDERATION OF COMMUNITY SERVICE. *Report of the Need for Homemaker Service.* Almeda County, Tex.: Federation of Community Services, January 1959. Mimeo.
31. FENGER, BODIL. "Selection of Homemakers for a Family Agency." *Journal of Social Casework,* **29** (June 1948).
32. FITZSIMMONS, MARGARET. "Homemaker Service as a Method of Serving Children." *National Conference on Social Welfare.* New York: Columbia University Press, 1951.
33. ———. "Homemaker Service: Current Practice and Future Planning." *Social Casework,* **38** (June 1957).
34. GILES, JOHN ROBERT. "Individualized Selection of Homemakers." *Social Casework,* **38** (May 1957).
35. GEORGE, VICTOR, and PAUL WILDING. *Motherless Families.* London: Kegan Paul, Trench, Trubner & Co., 1972.
36. GOLDBERG, GERTRUDE. "Nonprofessional Helpers: The Visiting Homemakers," in *Community Action Against Poverty.* Ed. by George A. Brager and Frances P. Purcell. West Haven, Conn.: New Haven College and University Press, 1967.
37. GOLDFARB, DORA, and PHYLLIS MANKO. "Homemaker Service in a Medical Setting." *Children,* **4** (November–December 1957).

38. GOODWIN, MARION SCHMADEL. "Housekeeper Service in Family Welfare," in *Proceedings of the National Conference of Social Work, 1938.* Chicago: University of Chicago Press, 1939.

39. GORDON, HENRIETTA. *Casework Services for Children—Practices and Principles.* Boston: Houghton Mifflin Company, 1956.

40. ———. "Homemaker Service as a Children's Casework Service." *Child Welfare,* 34 (January 1955).

41. HEALTH AND WELFARE COUNCIL OF THE BALTIMORE AREA, INC. *Study of Homemaker Service Needs in Metropolitan Baltimore.* Baltimore, June 1962. Mimeo.

42. HEALTH AND WELFARE COUNCIL, INC., DELAWARE, MONTGOMERY, AND PHILADELPHIA COUNTIES. *The Need for Homemaker Service in Delaware, Montgomery and Philadelphia Counties.* Philadelphia, April 1959. Mimeo.

43. HUNT, AUDREY. *The Home Help Service in England and Wales.* London: Her Majesty's Stationery Office, 1970.

44. HUNT, ROBERTA. "Homemaker Service," in *Encyclopedia of Social Work,* 16th Issue. Ed. by Robert Morris. New York: National Association of Social Workers, 1971.

45. JENKINS, SHIRLEY, and MIGNON SAUBER. *Paths to Child Placement.* New York: The Community Council of Greater New York, 1966.

46. JOHNSON, NORA PHILLIPS. "Creative Uses of Homemaker Service." *Child Welfare,* 35 (January 1956).

47. ———. "Homemaker Service for Children with Psychiatric Disorders." *Child Welfare,* 40 (November 1961).

48. JUSTISS, HOWARD. "Hidalgo County Homemaker Program." *Public Health Reports,* 75 (April 1960).

49. KEPECS, JACOB. "Housekeeper Service for Motherless Families," in *Proceedings of the National Conference of Social Work, 1938.* Chicago: University of Chicago Press, 1939.

50. LANGER, MARIAN. "A Visiting Homekeeper's Program." *The Family,* 26 (July 1945).

51. LEACH, JEAN M. "Homemaker Service as a Way of Strengthening Families During Illness," in *National Conference on Social Welfare: Casework Papers, 1958.* New York: Family Service Association of America, 1958.

52. LEVINE, SARAH C. "Integrating Homemaker Service with Casework." *Journal of Social Casework,* 28 (May 1947).

53. MARGOLIS, PHILIP M. "Stabilizing the Family Through Homemaker Service." *Social Casework,* 38 (October 1957).

54. MORLOCK, MAUD. "Homemaker Services—Major Defense for Children," *Children,* 4 (May–June 1957).

55. ———. "A New Look at Homemaker Service," *Children,* 6 (May–June 1959).

56. NATIONAL COUNCIL FOR HOMEMAKER–HOME HEALTH AIDE SERVICES, INC. *Standards for Homemaker–Home Health Aide Services.* New York, 1965.

57. ———. *Report of the 1965 National Conference on Homemaker Services.* New York, 1965.

58. ———. *Homemaker–Home Health Aide Services for Families with a Mentally Retarded Member.* New York, 1966.

59. ———. *A Unit of Learning About Homemaker–Home Health Aide Services: Teachers Source Book.* New York, 1968.

60. ———. *Readings in Homemaker Service.* New York, 1969.

61. ———. *Homemaker Service to Strengthen Individual and Family Life—A Focus on the Teaching Role of the Homemaker.* New York, 1970.

62. NETHERLANDS INSTITUTE FOR SOCIAL WELFARE RESEARCH. *Some Selected Studies.* The Hague, June 1972.

63. NEW JERSEY STATE DEPARTMENT OF HEALTH. *Homemaker Service Training Course: A Cooperative Project*, rev. ed. New Brunswick, N.J.: Rutgers, the State University, December 1, 1960.

64. ———. *New Jersey Visiting Homemakers—Proceedings of Homemaker Development Seminar*, Princeton, N.J., April 1961. Supplement to *Public Health News* (July 1961).

65. PARKINS, JUANITA. "Homesaving Through Housekeeping Service." *The Child,* 5 (October 1940).

66. PENNELL, MARYLAND Y., and LUCILLE M. SMITH. "Characteristics of Families Served by Homemakers." *American Journal of Public Health,* 49 (November 1959).

67. PRESTON, FRANCES, and RITA MacLENNAN. "Homemaker Service for Parents and Children," in *Proceedings of the National Council of Social Workers, 1947.* New York: Columbia University Press, 1948.

68. REID, JOSEPH H. "Homemaker Service for Children." *Children,* 5 (November–December 1958).

69. REPORTING CENTER OF NATIONAL STUDY SERVICE. *Training and Use of Subprofessionals and Volunteers. Facts About Welfare No. 7.* New York, July 1970.

70. RETARDED INFANTS' SERVICE, AND ASSOCIATION FOR HOMEMAKER SERVICE. *The Value of Homemaker Service in the Family with the Retarded Child Under Five—Final Report.* New York, November 1965.

71. SANTULLI, MARY. "Criteria for Selection of Families for Housekeeper Service." *Smith College Studies in Social Work,* 15 (1944–45).

72. SHAMES, MIRIAM. "Use of Homemaker Service in Families that Neglect Their Children." *Social Work,* 9 (January 1964).

73. SHYNE, ANN. *The Need for Foster Care.* New York: Child Welfare League of America, 1969.

74. SNYDER, RUTH. "Homemaker Service of the New York City Department of Welfare." *Homemaker Services Bulletin,* 2 (September 1961).

75. ———. *Homemaker Service—A Supportive and Protective Service for Children and Adults.* New York: New York City Department of Welfare, May 1962. Mimeo.

76. SPAULDING, RITA G. "Work with the Father in Homemaker Service." *Social Casework,* 35 (January 1954).

77. STRINGER, ELIZABETH. "Homemaker Service Under Private Auspices." *Child Welfare,* 43, 3 (March 1964), 128–30.

78. STRINGER, E. A. "Homemaker Service to the Single-Parent Family." *Social Casework,* 48, 2 (February 1967), 75–79.

79. TALSMA, EUGENE. "The Homemaker Carries Key Role in Child Behavior Modification." Paper presented at National Council for Homemaker Service, May 1970.

80. TAYLOR, ELEANOR. "Integrating Homemaker Service into Agency Program." *Child Welfare*, **34** (January 1955).
81. U.S. DEPARTMENT OF HEALTH, EDUCATION, AND WELFARE. *Children*. Washington, D.C.: Government Printing Office, March–April 1961.
82. ———. *Homemaker Services: A Preventative to Placement of Children in Foster Care*. Washington, D.C.: Government Printing Office, 1952. Mimeo.
83. ———. *Homemaker Services in the United States: A Directory of Agencies, 1954*. Washington, D.C.: Government Printing Office, 1955.
84. ———. *Homemaker Services: A Nationwide Study*. Washington, D.C.: Government Printing Office, 1958.
85. ———. *Homemaker Services: Twelve Descriptive Statements*. Washington, D.C.: Government Printing Office, 1958.
86. ———. *Homemaker Services in the United States: Report of the 1959 Conference*. Washington, D.C.: Government Printing Office, 1960.
87. ———. *Homemaker Services in Public Welfare: The North Carolina Experience*. Washington, D.C.: Government Printing Office, 1961.
88. UNIVERSITY OF ILLINOIS SCHOOL OF SOCIAL WORK. *Training Course for Homemakers*. Chicago, 1960.
89. WATKINS, ELIZABETH G. "So that Children May Remain in Their Own Homes: Homemaker Service Strengthens Aid to Dependent Children Program." *The Child*, **18** (October 1953).
90. ———, and LAURA TURTT. "Short-Term Homemaker Service." *Child Welfare*, **37** (May 1958).
91. WOLDMAN, ELINORE R. "Care of Children in Their Own Homes Through Supervised Homemaker Service." *The Child*, **5** (September 1940).
92. WOLFF, MYRTLE P. "Surmounting the Hurdles to Homemaker Services." *Children*, **6** (January–February 1959).
93. WORKS PROGRESS ADMINISTRATION. *Final Report on the W.P.A. Program, 1935–43*. Washington, D.C.: Government Printing Office, 1944.

8

Day-Care Service

Introduction

Day care is a supplementary child welfare service employed when family care for the child must be supplemented for some part of the day. The use of such supplementation is designed to permit the child to be maintained in his own home. Although the primary purpose of day care is to supplement parental role enactment, it also operates to strengthen and support positive parental role enactment. Like homemaker service, day care is primarily concerned with helping the temporarily motherless family—motherless because the mother is enacting the role of employee.

Definition: Day Care and Nursery School

According to the Women's Bureau of the U.S. Department of Labor,

A day nursery or day-care center has as its primary function the provision of good group care and supervision of supplemental parental care during the day because their parents are unable to care for them due to employment, sickness, or for some other reason. [80, p. 6]

A United Nations report defines day care as "an organized service for the care of children away from their own homes during some part of the day when circumstances call for normal care in the home to be supplemented." This definition is based on the conception of day care "as a supplement to, but not as a substitute for, parental care." [74, p. 18]

In each case, these definitions are followed by some discussion of the differences between day care (a child welfare service) and nursery school (an educational service). Despite any overlap, the central purposes of these programs are essentially distinguishable.

The emphasis in day-care programs is on the primary provision of care and protection—food, shelter, adult supervision, supplementation of primary parental roles. The day-care facility may, incidentally, educate. In fact, it is desirable that the good day-care facility use its time with the child to further his development, but care and protection are the first responsibilities of day care. By contrast, "the true nursery school, unencumbered as it is by the need to aid the mitigation of the child's deprivation of normal maternal care, can concentrate on its proper role of preschool education." [75, p. 9] As Moustakas says, "Parents usually send children to nursery school because they wish to do so; they often send children to a child care center because they must." [53, p. 154]

Consequently, the clientele of the day-care center is apt to come from lower socioeconomic groups; that of the nursery school, from a college-educated middle-class group. The day-care center schedule is apt to be congruent with a normal working day; the nursery school schedule is apt to be for a more limited period. The nursery school, growing out of the movement for childhood education, is more apt to have trained professional teachers on the staff than is true for the day-care center, which grew out of a child protective orientation.

The distinction is clearly made by the Children's Bureau, which, in a report of a 1962 national survey of licensed day-care facilities, defined them as those which have as their principal purpose the provision of "care and protection for children either during the parents' working day or for part of the day and for reasons not necessarily connected with parental employment. . . . Nursery schools and kindergartens were not to be considered day-care facilities within the meaning of this definition since the chief purpose of these facilities is education." [48, p. 29]

There has been a steady movement, however, toward reducing these distinctions, partly because it is believed that all children, having similar needs, should be provided with similar advantageous developmental experiences during the crucial years of early childhood. Thus the Child Welfare League of America, in its 1969 revisions of standards for day-care service, notes:

Day care as a child welfare service [is] . . . designed to supplement . . . daily care, health supervision, and developmental experience needed for optimum development. Any form of day care should be designed as a developmental service that fosters the child's potentialities for physical, emotional, intellectual, and social development. [12, pp. 9–10]

Similarly, the Day Care and Child Development Council of America defines day care as

a service which provides essential care and protection to children outside their homes for a major part of the day on a regular basis. Good day care assures opportunities for physical, emotional, and intellectual growth to the maximum of the child's capacity through group programs for preschool and school-age children as well as through family day care. [18]

Congregate and Family Day Care

Another desirable aspect of a good program of day care is the availability of the diversified facilities. Day care may be given in a congregate or group setting (a center), or it may be given on an individualized home basis, sometimes called foster day care or family day care.

For some kinds of situations, individual family day care is the more desirable alternative. If, for instance, the child is less than two years old, he has not progressed to the point where he can effectively operate in a group situation. He is less capable of contributing to or profiting from a group experience. In addition, the child is not capable of handling, without assistance, many of the simple routines of self-care— feeding himself, dressing himself, and so on—so that he requires more individual attention than is often available in a group situation. Being more vulnerable, both physically and emotionally, the younger child requires the special attention and "mothering" that can be more adequately provided by individual day care. [25, p. 69]   It is often argued, too, that children two years of age or younger are more likely to encounter increased danger of infection in a congregate setting.

Individual care is also desirable for the older child who is emotionally disturbed. The child may be three or four years of age, but he may still be exhibiting the emotional needs of a child of one or two years of age. He is not, therefore, ready for a group situation and needs the support available through individual family day care.

It is also desirable to keep a group of siblings together. Rather than break up the sibling group and deny them the support of familiar and possibly well-liked faces, the group might better be provided with a foster mother for the day.

In addition, there are some practical, situational considerations that may dictate the desirability of family day care over group day care. A day-care center requires a sizable population of working mothers in a community to make operation feasible. Family day care is a more flexible arrangement; it can be expanded or contracted according to need. It also permits more individualization of arrangements. However flexible a day-care center may be, it must maintain a schedule of one kind or another. In rural areas, or where the mother's working day begins or ends at some unusual time, family day care may offer the necessary flexibility.

As a matter of fact, the origin of family day care lay in its greater potential for meeting the individualized needs of particular situations. "Early in 1927 a survey made by the Philadelphia Association of Day Nurseries had shown that care in a day nursery did not meet the requirements of the mothers due to inflexibility of hours, quarantine problems, and exclusion of children suffering from minor illness." [73, p. 3]   Individual day care was suggested as a solution, and was first used in Philadelphia in late 1927.

Historical Background

It is difficult to know where the first day-care center was established. Jean Frederick Oberlin, a Swiss minister, opened a *garderie,* or day nursery, in 1767 for children whose mothers worked in the fields. Robert Owen is sometimes given credit for an early nursery established in 1816 in response to a recognition of the need for child care and protection resulting from the employment of mothers. [57, p. 11]

The first day-care center in the United States was established in 1854 at the Nursery and Child's Hospital, New York City. Employed mothers who had been patients at the hospital left their children under the care of the nurses when they returned to work. But the first permanent day nursery in the United States was established in 1863, to care "for the children of women needed to manufacture soldiers' clothing and to clean in hospitals." [57, p. 91]   By 1900 it was estimated that some 175 such centers had been organized in cities throughout the United States, many of them under the auspices of neighborhood settlement houses. The service was so well established by this time that a National Federation of Day Nurseries was founded in 1898.

The period of the 1920's was characterized by important changes. The parallel growth of the nursery school movement during this period accentuated the educational needs of the preschool child and resulted in a growing shift in day-care programs from a purely protective emphasis to one that included a concern for education. Furthermore, the increasingly greater acceptance of mental hygiene principles in casework and the professionalization of casework itself resulted in more frequent efforts to include casework services as integral elements in day care.

The Great Depression initially had an adverse effect on the day-care-center movement. Increasing unemployment returned many mothers to full-time homemaker status, and limited funds forced the closing of many centers (in 1934 only some 650 were in operation). Ultimately, however, the Depression, through the Work Projects Administration (WPA), provided a large-scale demonstration of some of the values of day care. Such centers were established by the program throughout the country to provide employment for teachers, nurses, nutritionists, and so on. The service they offered was not designed primarily to meet the child-care needs of the working mother but, rather, to provide a healthier environment for children from low-income families. Only children of parents who could not afford the tuition of privately operated nursery schools were eligible for admission to the WPA centers. As the final report on the WPA program notes:

> Many young children from low-income families were cared for in WPA nursery schools. The children were given a daily health inspection and necessary medical services in addition to well-balanced meals, play, and rest in an environment conducive to normal development. . . . These nursery schools everywhere demonstrated their value as an efficient and beneficial mode of child care. [96, p. 62]

Some idea of the scope of the program established is suggested by the fact that in 1937, 40,000 children were in attendance in the WPA nursery schools during a one-month study period.

This program, established under Federal impetus and support, was continued during World War II. But, with the start of the war and the tremendous increase in the need for manpower, the day-care program became part of a systematic national effort to shift women from homes into factories. More than three million married women entered the labor force between 1940 and 1944, many of them mothers of preschool children. The care of the children of working mothers became a problem of concern to many communities. "Increased juvenile delinquency in some communities and high absenteeism in some war manufacturing plants often were attributed to a lack of adequate child-care services." [80, p. 16]

A national conference convened in July 1941, and this was followed by the formation of statewide child-care committees in many states. In July 1942 a sum of $400,000 was allocated to the U.S. Office of Education and the Children's Bureau; grants were made available to states to help establish programs for extended school service and to public welfare agencies to set up day-care centers and other services for children of working mothers.

In further support of this explicit public policy, $6 million, allocated in July 1942 to the WPA, was designated for use in reorganizing its nursery school program in order to meet the needs of employed mothers. When the WPA was abolished by Presidential order at the end of 1942, this project was maintained with Federal funds made available through the Lanham Act. This Act, concerned primarily with defense housing and public works for defense, was reinterpreted so as to permit the allocation of funds to communities in support of child-care facilities and service. Public programs for day care were supplemented, in some instances, by large industrial firms engaged in war work. The Curtiss-Wright plane factory in Buffalo and the Kaiser shipyards established day-care centers for their employees.

> At its peak, the wartime program of day-care centers for children of working mothers had an enrollment of 129,357 children (July 1944) in 3102 units. By the end of the war, every state, except New Mexico, had submitted request for and received Federal funds under the Lanham act for operation and maintenance of child care programs and some $52 million of Federal funds had been expended for this purpose. . . .
> It has been estimated that between 550,000 and 600,000 children received care, at one time or another, under the auspices established through the help of the Lanham act. This, despite the serious handicaps which the program faced due to lack of suitable physical accommodations in many communities and shortages of adequately trained personnel. [80, pp. 9, 19]

Despite urging, on the part of the Children's Bureau, that local communities establish planning groups to ensure the continuation and development of day-care facilities, despite the fact that mothers using the centers organized to agitate for a long-range program that, unlike the emergency one, which was based on the needs of industry, was planned to meet the needs of children, the end of the war saw a sharp contraction of facilities. The principal factor was the withdrawal of Federal funds through termination of Lanham Act support in February 1946. The shortage of trained personnel, the high costs of operation, and the reduction in the number of working mothers also contributed to this change.

The Federal government, in justifying termination of its support, noted that assistance under the Lanham Act for child care had been based on the recruitment and retention of workers for war production and essential supporting services. The Women's Bureau, in evaluating the experience, stated that the wartime program

> . . . undoubtedly marked a far more general understanding than ever before, both by many cooperating agencies and by the public

in general, of the working mother's problems and the community's responsibilities in assisting with them. Employers also testified that the nurseries had great value in reducing absenteeism and turnover in their plants. Perhaps one of the more lasting effects was that the planning and operation of the program brought educational and welfare authorities to a better understanding of each other's policies and objectives and created a more general public knowledge of the standards recommended by educational and welfare agencies. [80, p. 20]

In recapitulating the history of day care in the United States, it is significant that widespread support of day-care facilities did not result primarily in response to the needs of children, but in response to the needs and demands of adult society—to increase job possibilities during the Great Depression, to increase the availability of womenpower during periods of critical labor shortage such as occurred during war periods.

The Social Context of Day Care: The Working Mother

Because the question of the working mother is so intimately related to the question of the need for, and use of, day-care facilities, it would be helpful to present some of the more important data concerning the working mother. This material is essential to understanding the context of day care in the United States today.

Over the past eighty years we have experienced a trend toward an increase of women in the labor force. In 1890 only 18 percent of all women were in the labor force, and they constituted 17 percent of all workers; in 1971, 42.8 percent of all women over sixteen were in the labor force, and they constituted 37 percent of all workers.

Although the proportion of women workers has increased, it is of greater significance that the number of working mothers with preschool children has increased, too. The numbers change from year to year, but the trend is constant. As Oettinger, former Chief of the Children's Bureau notes, "the hand that rocks the cradle must often also punch the time clock." In March 1971 about 4.3 million working women were mothers of children under six years, and about 2.3 million of such mothers had children under three. One out of every three working mothers had a preschool child at home. The number of working mothers with children under six rose rapidly between 1950 and 1971. In 1971 there were 5.6 million children under six whose mothers were employed (see Fig. 8–1).

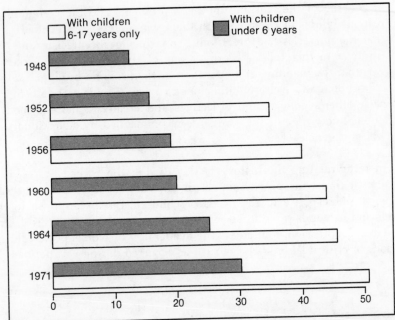

FIGURE 8–1. Percent of mothers with children under eighteen years of age who were in the labor force: United States, 1948–1971. (*Statistical Abstract of the United States 1972*, 93rd ed., Social and Economic Statistics Administration, Bureau of the Census, Washington, D.C.: U.S. Government Printing Office, 1972, Chart 100, Table 92.)

Once the mother contributed to family income by producing goods and performing services in the home. The shift to an industrial economy brought the demand for a cash income, which can be acquired only outside the home in a factory, a store, or an office. As Ogburn and Nimkoff note, "whereas the farmer and his wife jointly produce food and other goods, the trend is for husbands and wives to produce a joint income, although not from a joint enterprise." [58, p. 144]

The changing nature of jobs to be done has increased the likelihood of women working. In 1919, about two-thirds of the labor force was centered in the production industries—agriculture, mining, manufacturing, and construction. In general, such industries offer few employment opportunities for women. Since 1919, however, the sharp increase in the relative number of workers employed in wholesale and retail trades, transportation and communication, government agencies, and service industries has provided a very considerable increase in the employment opportunities for women. The rationalization of industrial production so that each job is broken up into small, manageable components has also helped to increase employment opportunities for women. Also, a greater percentage of women currently have the educational background which would permit them to take advantage of employment opportunities.

Changed child-bearing patterns have also resulted in an increase in the number of women working. In 1890, the last child born was likely to enter school when the mother was about forty years old; in 1973 this was more likely to happen when the mother was about thirty-one. [27] With her children in school the mother is more likely to seek employment. Also, increases in rates of illegitimacy, divorce, family disruptions of all kinds, have resulted in an increase in the number of families headed by a woman. There is considerable pressure for such a woman to find day care for her children and to seek employment for herself.

Two world wars in a period of twenty-five years have also affected the pattern of changing employment of women: on both occasions, women were encouraged to accept paid employment. Although many of the women returned to the home at the termination of the conflict, levels of employment for women continued at higher than prewar levels. The actual experience with women employees changed many fixed ideas about the capacity of women as workers. It also gave many women a more positive acceptance, for themselves, of the role of employee. The civil rights movement has intensified concern with women as a minority group, impelling legislation defending womens' right to employment opportunities. The womens' liberation movement has increased the political power of women and resulted in expanded job opportunities.

The fact that so many goods and services previously produced in the home are now available commercially not only opens employment opportunities for women but also provides the time for such employment. Labor-saving equipment and the lessened burden of housework free women for outside employment. Finally, the ever-rising standard of living exerts pressure for an increase in family income. The more things a family needs or wants to buy, the greater the need for supplementation of the income of the principal wage earner.

But the probability that the mother will be working is related to a number of variables, such as age of the children, family income, and family composition. The younger the child at home, the less likely it is that the mother will be working. Since economic necessity is the major reason women work, labor force participation rates decrease as family income increases. Women with husbands are less likely to work than mothers in fatherless families. Because nonwhite mothers are more likely to be living in low-income families and are more likely to be without husbands, the rate of labor force participation of nonwhite mothers is higher than that of white mothers.

Although the data suggest very clearly that most mothers work because they have to work, it must be remembered that some mothers work primarily because they find a greater sense of self-fulfillment in employment, because they dislike housework and child care, because they have questions about their adequacy as homemakers and mothers, or because they are stimulated by the social contact a job provides.

Because of the steady, sharp increase in working mothers of children under six years of age, increasing numbers of mothers are potentially interested in day care. Industry, which employs the working mother, is also increasingly interested in day care. The considerable interest in day care which developed during the 1960's resulted from a number of other factors as well.

1. Increasing costs of the AFDC program have sparked interest in day care. The effort to reduce welfare rolls by requiring work and training, has, as a corollary, provision of day-care services for the dependent children of the AFDC mother. Thus the 1962 Social Security amendments provided that the Federal government would reimburse 75 percent of the state costs of providing day care for any family currently on AFDC as well as for those families who had been recipients or who were in danger of becoming recipients. The Work Incentive program (WIN) provides special day-care funding to enable AFDC mothers to accept work or training. Agencies are authorized to "purchase" day care for recipient families from any licensed agency that meets Federal government standards. The proposed Family Assistance program provided a special appropriation for day care to implement the requirement that recipients with children accept work or training.

2. Recent research on the educability of young children and pressure from the civil rights movement have generated an interest in day care as a compensatory educational experience. Developmental day care could be provided for children of low-income families whether or not the mothers are working. Here the interest in day care derives from a concern with enriching the supposedly limited educational stimulation available in low-income homes in order to prepare the child for his role as student in the public schools. This is the intent of the Head Start program.

3. Child care provides an excellent opportunity for increasing the number of jobs available to human services paraprofessionals. It is potentially one of the most productive areas for the expansion of the concept of new careers for the poor. The day-care center can utilize the qualifications of many lower-class women who seek employment but whose only marketable skill is experience in caring for children, and many have been recruited as aides of one kind or another. For this reason, among others, expansion of day care is one of the high-priority demands of the Welfare Rights Organization and other groups representing low-skilled nonwhite job-seekers.

4. Advocates of participatory democracy see day care as an excellent vehicle for politicizing local residents. Parents are concerned with, and responsive to, the needs of their children, so day-care centers can often

be organized by action of community volunteers. As a matter of fact, a study of the Head Start program suggests that its effects on parents and community may be as great as the effects on children: a sizable percentage of Head Start programs had increased the involvement of the poor with local institutions, "particularly at decision-making levels and in decision-making capacities." [43, p. 6] Consequently, community action groups of one kind or another have contributed to the growing support for day care.

5. For women's liberation groups, day care is crucial for freeing women from their "primary identification as mothers and from the sole responsibility for child rearing." The community, it is argued, shares with the parents the responsibility for child rearing. Consequently such groups are actively supporting the development of day-care centers available to all mothers, employed or not, on a twenty-four-hour basis.

Caretakers of the Employed Mother's Child

Statistics indicate that many mothers are not available to cover their maternal functions during some part or all of the normal working day. Who cares for the child during this period? Studies of arrangements made for care of the preschool children of working mothers indicate that only 5.6 percent of such children are in day-care centers (see Fig. 8–2). Many children are cared for by relatives, in their own home, or in the home of relatives. Many are cared for by nonrelatives on the basis of private, personal arrangements made by the mother. A very few (0.5 percent) care for themselves. While children over six in school most of the day might be regarded as self-sufficient for a short part of the day, certainly a child of six or younger is clearly dependent. Yet it is estimated that in 1970, 20,000 children under six were left to care for themselves, as were 0.5 million children between six and twelve. One can say with some justification that the adequacy of care for these children is open to question. [49]

Effects on the Child

There is considerable research available regarding the effects of mothers' employment on children. A recent review of the relevant literature summarizes what is known as follows:

On the whole, the studies that have been done make these points: (1) There is no higher rate of delinquency among children of working mothers than among children of nonworking mothers, if quality of child care is taken into account; (2) husbands and children

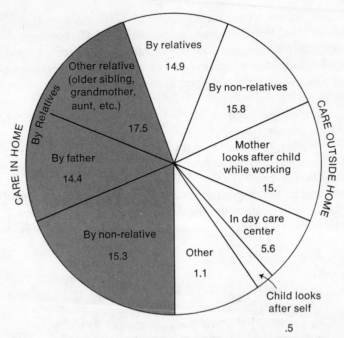

FIGURE 8–2. Child-care arrangements of working mothers with children under six years of age. (*Profiles of Children—1970 White House Conference on Children,* Washington, D.C.: U.S. Government Printing Office, 1970.)

become more involved in housework and other domestic chores when the wife-mother works, but there is no concomitant blurring of basic role distinctions; and (3) the evidence on either impairment or improvement in husband-wife or parent-child relations, or in the social development of the children, when the mother works, is inconclusive. Most studies suggest little or no change; some suggest differential effects depending on the sex of the child. Again, however, most of these studies have been limited in scope and methods, and because of this and their often contradictory findings, it is impossible to draw firm conclusions.

In sum, we can say that neither common observation nor the starts in research have as yet shown anything to support the early prognostications of dire consequences. Perhaps the safest conclusion at this time is that we simply do not know what the long-term effects of maternal employment are for the society as a whole, for child development or family life generally. [64, p. 7]

Similarly, Stolz says, in summarizing an earlier review of research in this area:

. . . . When one concludes a review of this kind, one is impressed with the number of different and opposing findings which research concerning the effects of maternal employment on children has produced. One can say almost anything one desires about the children of employed mothers and support the statement by some research study. [71, p. 25]

Reflecting the lack of clear-cut answers, Oettinger, former Chief of the Children's Bureau, states:

We at the Children's Bureau are often asked these days what are the effects on children of maternal employment? To that question we have a single answer loud and clear: "It depends."

It depends on the kind of mother, the kind of child, the kind of family. It depends, among other things, on why the mother works, how much she works, what she does, what work does to, or for, her, how old her children are, what provisions she makes for them while she works, how they perceive the fact of her working. [56, p. 134]

Although stating a belief in the "absolute indispensability of adequate care and supervision for children where mothers are working," Oettinger notes that, "on the basis of present information, we do not believe that it is necessarily damaging to a child to be separated from his mother during substantial periods during the day if adequate substitute care is provided." It might be noted that the research tends to show some positive consequences of the mother's employment: relief from financial strain, increased sharing of responsibility in family life by father and children, widening of mother's interests, increased independence of children.

Scope

Statistics on the scope of day-care facilities are based on licensing requirements which enable such facilities to be located and counted. The accuracy of these statistics depends, then, on the adequacy of licensing procedures.

In March 1971 a total of 18,435 day-care centers were licensed with an aggregate capacity of 719,232 children. There were 55,366 family-day-care homes licensed with a capacity to serve 192,469 children. Together both kinds of facilities then were capable of providing care for 912,000 children. It was noted above that, in 1971, some 5.6 million children whose mothers worked were under six years of age. Consequently the licensed day-care facilities available were capable of offering care to about 16 percent of the total population of risk. [77, Table 13]

Between 1960 and 1971 there was a very decided increase in reported enrollment capacity of day-care centers and family day-care homes—from less than 200,000 in 1960 to 910,000 in 1971. During the 1960 decade more states and localities adopted licensing procedures and some of the increase merely reflects the inclusion, for counting, of previously existing but unaccounted facilities. It is also true that even if there was a rapid true increase in facilities available, the number of children under six whose mothers were working increased at an even more rapid rate between 1960 and 1971. [86]

In 1970 about half of the day-care centers and about 90 percent of the family-day-care homes were offered under proprietary auspices for profit. Some 35 percent of day-care center facilities were under the auspices of voluntary nonprofit agencies and about 15 percent under public auspices. This distribution has not changed very significantly over the 1960–70 decade.

Despite all the talk about day care as a "social service," then, more than half of all such facilities are operated as a business venture. Many of those operating under voluntary auspices are organized by women's clubs, professional women's groups, patriotic organizations, and church organizations. Only a limited percentage of all licensed facilities under voluntary auspices is administered by what might be regarded as social work agencies, such as settlement houses or community centers and child welfare or family welfare agencies.

Administrative Aspects

Financial Support

Commercial facilities are supported by parents' fees; publicly supported facilities, by public funds; the voluntary agencies, by a combination of Community Chest funds, public funds, and parents' fees. Fees in voluntary agencies are set up in terms of a graduated scale in accordance with income and size of family, and account for 15–30 percent of the total budget. Subsidization of day care by industrial concerns, found during World War II, has all but disappeared. [15]

Except for special emergency periods, such as the period of the Great Depression, and in time of war, the Federal government has not offered support for day-care services. Since 1962, however, acting under Title V of the Social Security Act, the title which gives the Children's Bureau responsibility for establishing, extending, and strengthening public welfare services for the care of dependent and neglected children, the Federal government can make, and has made, grants to states for day care under special circumstances. The 1962 Social Security amendments specifically designated day care as one of the required services to be included in the public child welfare services program in each state.

Under Title IV of the Social Security Act as amended, the Federal government can provide funds for support of day care to families currently receiving AFDC as well as to former and potential applicants and recipients of AFDC. The Federal government guarantees to reimburse the state on the basis of seventy-five cents for every dollar spent on day care. In October 1972 Congress set a limit of $2.5 billion on the extent of Federal government support for designated social services provided by the state in behalf of AFDC recipients. The public welfare agency can provide day-care service or can purchase the service from any other public or voluntary or proprietary day-care center that is licensed and meets certain minimum Federal requirements.

A number of other Federally sponsored or assisted programs are related to day care. The most notable is the Head Start program, which provided *full* day care in 1971 to some 80,000 disadvantaged children age three to five, many of whom had working mothers. The Parent and Child Center is another Federal effort to meet the needs of low-income children. Establishment of Parent and Child Centers resulted from the realization that even Head Start was not early enough, that by three years of age many children had already incurred deficits in development. The Parent and Child Center program was formulated to reach such children prior to Head Start. With the help of funds from the Office of Economic Opportunity, thirty pilot Parent and Child Centers were established throughout the United States in the last half of the 1960's. The centers were established to provide comprehensive services to children three years of age or younger from low-income families.

The 4C program (Community Coordinated Child Care) is another Federal program concerned with day-care needs. Designed to help communities mobilize and coordinate their resources to meet the needs of young children, the program is an outgrowth of the Interagency Federal Panel on Early Childhood established in 1961 to coordinate the activities of the large number of Federal programs concerned with day care.

There is further subsidization of day care through income tax deductions permitted for the expenses of child care associated with employment. The Tax Revenue Act of 1971 allows up to $400 a month deduction for "employment-related expenses" for full-time working families with combined incomes of up to $18,000 a year.

Currently the national organization primarily concerned with promoting and developing day-care programs is the Day Care and Child Development Council of America, formerly the National Committee for Day Care of Children. The Council publishes a monthly newsletter,

Voice for Children. The organization was formed in 1968 to promote good standards of day care, to stimulate the exchange of information, ideas, and experience in the field of day care, and to mobilize support for expansion of day care.

Licensing

"Day care licensing refers to the requirement by law that a license, permit, or certification be secured before a person, agency, or corporation takes on the care of children away from their own home during the day." [87, p. 27]   It may include registration, licensing, and inspection. The licensing procedure rests on a delegation of legislative power to an administrative agency. The required standards for care become in effect "little laws." Licensing insures the maintenance of some minimum standards of day care and reflects the community's concern for the physical and psychosocial safety of its children. [14; 18; 33]   By 1970 almost all states had made licensing of day-care centers mandatory.

Fewer states, however, had made licensing of day-care homes mandatory. [87]   While 90 percent of the day-care centers are licensed, fewer than 2 percent of the family day-care homes are subject to licensing, because most states do not require licensing if such homes offer care to fewer than three children. "Family day-care homes, then, are generally unregulated and unsupervised by any governmental or social agency. Hundreds of thousands of children, including those whose fees are paid by government funds, are cared for in these homes, about which very little is known." [87, p. 89; see also 42]

Licensing regulations are likely to cover such factors as physical facilities, safety standards, health standards, provisions for adequate number and training of personnel, and educational facilities and equipment. They may also indicate the special kinds of provisions to be made for special kinds of children—for instance, a higher ratio of caretakers to children may be required in day-care facilities serving the handicapped. [10; 76]

In the discussion of quality of child care within day care there are repeated references to adult-child ratios. The ratio itself is no certain measure of the level of warmth, maturity, concern, interest, and so on, with which a caretaker may interact with a child. However, while we find it difficult, if not impossible, to measure such qualities with confidence, we can and do measure adult-child ratios. They do, in a rough way, suggest the necessary, if not the sufficient, condition for quality child care. The ratio has become the objective indicator operationally defining the quality of child care.

There are differences, from state to state, with regard to the specificity of the regulations, the nature of the penalties for violations, the kinds of facilities covered, the regularity and frequency of inspection, and the provisions available for consultation and assistance. There have been some efforts to develop national standards in a model licensing code. Currently the Federal government sets guidelines required of a day-care facility if it is to be eligible to receive Federal funds.

The state departments of public welfare are generally given responsibility for implementing licensing legislation; less frequently, such responsibility rests with the state department of health or the state department of education. In any case, the office responsible for licensing may provide supervision and consultation and arrange educational programs, institutes, and workshops to help agencies reach, and maintain, an acceptable level of service.

Social workers who implement the state day-care licensing procedures for the state departments of public welfare thus have two major responsibilities: a supervisory-regulatory function and a consultation function. The supervisory-regulatory function assures the parent and community that conditions at the day-care center are satisfactory. In discharging the consultation responsibility, the social worker helps the day-care center maintain and, if possible, improve conditions for children at the center.

Licenses, once issued, need to be renewed generally every year. Consequently there is provision for periodic re-evaluation of the day-care center. In many localities, however, the licensing staff is too small to do more than keep up with complaints received and have little power to impose adequate penalties for violations. In addition, licensing laws frequently exclude from the licensing requirement sizable groups of centers, such as those run by religious organizations and public school systems.

Licensing procedure involves considerable administrative discretion on the part of the social worker licensing agent. Basic standards for group care of children must be applied sensibly and with some flexibility. The licensing social worker attempts to apply the regulations in a spirit of cooperative mutuality, rather than in a spirit of evaluative assessment. The stance should not be the use of regulations to deny a license, but rather the use of regulations to educate toward the desirability of standards and to motivate their acceptance. Licensing standards should be applied fairly, uniformly, and promptly. A day-care applicant should know what the decision is as soon as possible, and should be clearly informed of the basis of the decision.

Day-care administrators frequently challenge the social worker to justify the standards he is attempting to enforce. They question the validity of required child-care ratios and the validity of credentials demanded for various categories of day-care-center personnel. They are also keenly aware of inequities in licensing resulting from differences in the application of administrative discretion. Objections frequently come from groups of ghetto residents who have organized a day-care center on their own initiative. The director of one such center comments on licensing requirements:

> The center can help to upgrade the community by giving jobs or on-the-job training to persons among the poor who want to work in day care. They could be people who are qualified and talented with children even though they do not necessarily meet the formal licensing requirements. What does a credential or degree tell you about how good a teacher is? [50, p. 72]

Different agencies involved in licensing different aspects of a day-care center may fail to coordinate their activities or may even require contradictory standards. One center was criticized by the fire department because the yard-door latch was too high for the children to reach in case of fire. Another department then criticized the center because the yard-door latch was so low children could open it and run into the street.

Each of the requirements for a license, designed to protect the children, makes establishment of a center more difficult and more expensive. At what point does the need for adequate care and adequate facilities seriously limit the availability of day care? What specific standards, flexibly enforced, are the minimums which are acceptable to the community? This is still a matter for discussion. Licensing regulations which demand too high a standard substitute a problem of low quantity for a problem of low quality.

Cost

Minimum day care, defined as "the level essential to maintaining health and safety of the child, but with relatively little attention to his developmental needs" was estimated to cost $1250 per year per child in 1970. Desirable day care, defined as including "the full range of general and developmental activities suitable to individualized development," was estimated to cost $2370. [87, p. 11] Families debating whether or not it would be economically advisable for the mother with young children to work need to consider the expense of day care, which, in 1971, amounted to $15–$20 a week per child. The community debating provision of day care for children of welfare recipients needs to be aware that such care may actually cost more than paying the current assistance grants, which permit the mother to stay home and care for her child.

Situations for Which Day Care
Is an Appropriate Resource

Day care is most frequently used by the working mother. Day care assumes the role functions relinquished by the mother while she is working. This is a problem of inadequate role implementation that results from inter-role conflict.

> A harassed young mother of twenty-four asked to have her two little boys—Johnnie, aged four, and Jimmie, aged three—enrolled in the nursery so that she might look for a job. She was anxious and pushed by the strain of trying to make ends meet. "We had big doctor bills when Johnnie was born and we have never caught up. How can you have a good family life if you can never pay your bills?" [51, p. 23]

> The S.'s have one child, age three months. Mr. S. is a medical student; Mrs. S. is employed as a secretary. In order for Mr. S. to remain in medical school, mother will continue to work until husband's education is completed. [98, p. 43]

> Mr. G. died of a sudden heart attack. The family had no savings, limited life insurance, and the OASDI payments do not permit Mrs. G. to support her two children—Jane, three, and Bill, four and a half—without supplementation. She is returning to a job she held before marriage as a typist and placing both children in day care.

Psychological desire, preference, and need may be the determinant of the mother's working in some instances. This is true in the case

> . . . of a bright little boy of two whose mother, a compulsive neurotic, found herself unable to adjust to the new duties of a parent. A highly creative, extremely intelligent woman, this young mother was advised to work, thus giving constructive outlet to her compulsive pattern, and to forestall a complete breakdown. Working seemed one way to achieve satisfaction from the drudgeries of home plus the burden of motherhood, yet partially functioning as a mother. In this case, making day care available served to sustain this mother as well as the artistic father, and contributed greatly to the stability of this family. [31, p. 303]

More often, however, children in day-care programs are likely to be members of a family headed by a woman who works because she has to.

Day care may also be provided in situations where the child, because of mental, physical, or emotional handicap, presents an unusually heavy burden. Relief to the overburdened mother during part of the day may be sufficient to obviate the necessity for institutionalizing the child. The need for specialized knowledge in dealing with children who are different may be provided by the day-care facility, staffed by people with specialized education. Daily, time-limited group care also provides an opportunity for normal contact with peers for those children who, because of their handicap, might otherwise tend to be isolated from such normal activities.

The Community Welfare Council of the Greater Sacramento area undertook a survey, in 1960, of parents' attitudes toward the possible use of day care for their retarded children; of 199 questionnaires mailed, sixty-six were returned, forty-seven of which indicated a positive response to the use of day care. The need for day care was felt by the parents for reasons that related to the needs of the family and the needs of the retarded child. [54]

> Most parents feel the need for relief from the demands of constant supervision of their handicapped child in order to meet some of their own personal needs, provide more adequate attention to other children in the family, find employment, and reduce emotional tension within the family.
>
> Parents see the value of day-care services as providing essential social experiences for their children as well as training, therapy, and education that they, as parents, are unable to provide.

The two sets of reasons are related. One parent said, in talking about his retarded daughter:

> The few children in the neighborhood recognize the "difference" and do not want to play with her. The lack of companionship and play affects her to such an extent that she is becoming extremely irritable. This, with the hyperactive personality, is such a burden on my nervous system that I, in turn, cannot always be as objective as I know I should be. A service such as this would be a great help and aid to parents like us with similar problems. It would afford us the relaxation from these tensions, just as I'm certain it would be beneficial to my little girl.

Another parent said:

> The important thing about the program for my child was the opportunity to play with other retarded children as the neighborhood children ignore him. We have been unable to get a babysitter

because of his retardation, and some feel he is catching—people just refuse. I need some time away from him so that I can get some of my work done.

Some day-care centers have been organized as a special therapeutic facility for emotionally disturbed children. [5; 8; 22; 47; 66]   The Virginia Frank Child Development Center in Chicago, for instance, describes itself as "a specialized therapeutic nursery and kindergarten for children three to five years of age who are showing signs of emotional and behavioral problems." The center supplements individual therapy by making available a therapeutic environment for part of the day. Actually, however, very limited day-care facilities are available to serve the physically, mentally, or emotionally handicapped child.

In some cases, day care may offer temporary relief when the parent-child relationship is disturbed. The mitigation of constant stress permits reorganization of psychic forces so as to allow the possibility for altering the interaction in a more positive direction. Day care supports the parents' ability to care for the child, and reduces tension and conflict, increasing the possibility that the child might be maintained in his own home.

The S. family presented a picture of serious emotional disturbances for which they have sought counseling in a family agency for some time. Both parents, threatened by their own pathological background, were showing unrealistic fears and anxieties over their two-and-a-half-year-old son's "wild" behavior and his refusal to speak. On psychiatric exams, the child was found essentially normal and his behavior not inappropriate to his age. Both parents genuinely rejected any thought of full-time placement but, with help, could accept the partial separation of day placement which would lessen the heavy burden of living with their youngster. [31, p. 301]

The following situation illustrates the complexity of interaction in a difficult situation for which day care can be a helpful resource:

J., five-and-one-half, was referred to the [center] by the Riley Hospital Child Guidance Clinic. She had been blind since birth as the result of oxygen exposure. Although both parents were medical students, the mother was regarded as an emotionally and mentally disturbed person. She resisted enrolling J. in the Nursery and did so only at the insistence of the Clinic. The psychiatrist felt it extremely important for the child to be separated from her mother and to have a normal group experience. She made a fine adjustment in our group and will eventually attend the State Blind School. The mother's attitude also improved. [39, p. 31]

Day care may also be used as an alternative to homemaker service when the mother has died or deserted or when her hospitalization will be prolonged.

> One mother who is suffering from phlebitis is not able to give her active three-year-old son full-time care but, with sufficient rest while he is away from home during the day, she can be relaxed and carry on well for the rest of the time. Her husband brings the child to the center. [98, p. 7]

> L.'s mother was in the hospital for an extended time following delivery of a stillborn child. L.'s father, a Presbyterian minister, arranged for day care for the child in the nursery. Although the mother is now convalescing at home, L. is so happy and contented with the group that the parents plan to permit him to continue. [39, p. 31]

> S. has now been in the center nearly two years. Her maternal grandmother made arrangements for her enrollment as her mother was a mental patient in the psychiatric ward of a local hospital and her father was diagnosed as having multiple sclerosis. S. was quite withdrawn when entering our group, but has made slow but steady progress and now plays well with the other children and participates in our group activities. [39, p. 31]

The day-care staff, like the homemaker who is assigned to a family to help educate the parents to more adequate child-rearing methods, attempts to communicate knowledge about feeding, discipline, child protection, and so on.

> . . . [When the mother] came to observe the children in the day care center, she noted with some relief that Joe was not the only child who threw things. She has seen that there are other children who "can't cut on the line," as she has tried to force Joe to do. Mrs. B. was most interested to learn from the teacher that Joe is too young to be expected to cut "on the line." Since her anxiety over unrealistic expectations for her children has been relieved, the neighbors report that Mrs. B. doesn't spank her children as much as before. [35]

Day-care facilities have also been used as a remedial measure for a seriously deprived home environment. A United Nations report points out that, where "shortage or inadequacy of housing leads to overcrowding and to unhealthy living conditions," where "sufficient play space is not available," where there is "concern about child health and a desire to improve the nutrition of certain categories of children," day-care centers may play a role in child protection, "in combating child morbidity and mortality . . . in improving the conditioning of underweight children." [74, p. 23]   In such situations the day-care service assures the children "better care than they would receive if they remained at home." [35, p. 180]   Here inadequate parental role implementation results from deficiencies in the environment—lack of adequate living space, play space, toys, food, and the like.

As Merriam says, "A mother living on the third floor of an apartment building with a four-year-old child and two younger children may be up against a very real problem of being unable to supervise the older child for any outdoor play while also meeting the demands for the care of the young ones." [51, p. 22]

> The oldest of Mrs. B.'s four children was four when this family came to the attention of the Seven Hills Neighborhood House in Cincinnati. Mrs. B. felt that she was going to have to resort to desperate measures to solve her problems, and she told the agency director that she had decided to place her children in foster care. Beset by an inadequate welfare allotment, substandard housing (four children and herself in two rooms), marital difficulties, and full-time care of the children, Mrs. B. was finding life "too much" for her. The day-care center was suggested as a means of relieving some of her child care burdens so that she could re-establish herself. [35, p. 181]

> . . . The family lived in a flat overrun with roaches. During our first visit we found two of the children in cribs and two in playpens. Because Mrs. B. was unable to supervise them when they were about on their own, she decided they were safer there, even though she was well aware that it was very wrong to keep toddlers so confined. . . . [35, pp. 181–82]

> Mary, aged three and one-half, was taken to the pediatric clinic at the hospital by her grandmother, Mrs. C., because Mary was losing weight (she had lost three pounds in a two-month period), was fretful and not sleeping well at night. The physical findings were negative. The pediatrician recommended a play experience, such as a day-care center could provide, since Mary was the only child in a home of four adults. The family lived on the second floor over an unfriendly landlady who would not even permit Mary to play in a small yard. [70, p. 230]

Some day-care facilities suggest other uses of such resources. Large transatlantic liners provide day-care centers that free the traveling parents of the care of the child during the day. Large department stores and shopping centers provide such resources to permit the parents to shop freely. Similar resources might also be used to permit parents to take part in educational or cultural programs, or to take advantage of regular medical or psychiatric treatment programs on an out-patient basis. In each instance, the day-care facilities might, by permitting the parent a greater measure of freedom, contribute to a reduction of parental resentment and parent-child friction, and enhance the parent-child relationship.

Illustrating the use of day care in more normal situations is the following news report:

> The YMCA of Eastern Union County will start a curb service "Mothers Service" on wheels in Linden next month. The YMCA has acquired a thirty-five-foot mobile housetrailer and converted it into a "Jack and Jill" playmobile. The playmobile will set up shop in three different locations in Linden to give mothers two to three hours relief from their youngsters, aged three to five, and time to do some much-needed shopping or other chores (*New York Sunday News*, November 18, 1962).

Such use of day care suggests its appropriateness for keeping tensions within the family at a manageable level by providing periodic relief from the burdens of child care. Of even greater potential importance is the value of such a service to the single parent, who must be mother, father, nurse, teacher, disciplinarian, provider, and housekeeper without possibility of a break.

Evaluation

The most important value of day care is that, like other supplementary services, it increases the probability that the child may be maintained in his own home. The mother who must work can do so without finding a substitute home for the child; the handicapped child may not have to be institutionalized; the family facing a crisis may find sufficient relief and support in day care so that it can be held together for the child.

Some two million children of working mothers, who might otherwise need public assistance, are supported independently of the assistance program. The mother's salary, either as a sole wage in a female headed family or as a supplementary wage in a family headed by her husband, lifted these families out of poverty.

Recent studies by Shyne [68] and Jenkins [40] indicate that the need for foster care might have been prevented in some instances if adequate day care had been available.

A study of a demonstration project by a private agency of the value of family day care to forty-two families noted:

> . . . in ten instances—before day-care service was requested—application for full-time care placement had appeared imminent. In nine other situations—though difficult to establish with absolute certainty—from the prevailing evidence of uneasy parent-child relationships and fear of overwhelming responsibilities, it would appear that full-time placement might have eventuated.
>
> In fourteen situations an application to public relief was prevented. [23, p. 14]

The value of day care in preventing foster placement is illustrated in the following case:

> Mrs. F., a young divorcée with a child of two, was originally referred . . . by a shelter care agency, where the child had been placed for two months pending admission to a full-care foster home. Realizing that she did not really want complete separation from her child, but rather had been overwhelmed by the failure of her marriage and her personal involvements, Mrs. F. withdrew the child from the shelter home. Subsequently she applied to Family Day Care Service for placement of her child, to enable her to go to work. Our accepting this child for day-care placement gave Mrs. F. an opportunity to begin to consider what she wanted for herself and her child.
>
> Day-care service was arranged for Jerry in a home nearby. He remained there for a period of nine months, after which he was ready for admission to a group care center. [32, p. 20]

In a study in California of the possible value of day care for retarded children, one parent stated:

> I tried six weeks ago to see if we could take my son back home from [an institution for the retarded], but was unable to find a babysitter while I was at work, and if there was such a center I know I could have my son at home as that was one of my biggest problems during the summer months when he was at home. [54]

The director of a day nursery details the cooperative action between her agency and a family service agency in holding a family together:

The mentally ill mother and the four-year-old child were in such a constant state of friction that the father was afraid his wife would do some harm to the child in his absence at work. We were able to arrange for the father to bring the little girl in the morning and call for her on his way home from work in the evening. On week-ends he is able to act as a "buffer" between mother and child. With the continuing work of the Jewish Family Service with the mother, the home has remained together. . . . [28]

Some family problems are related to income deficiency. The mother might provide the necessary increment of income necessary to maintain family stability. Day care, which ensures adequate care of the children, makes this solution one that might be sensibly considered and comfortably accepted. Thus, some families, the exact number being difficult to ascertain, are able to maintain themselves independently of public assistance, because the mother is able to go to work where adequate provision for child care is available.

Testimony regarding California's network of day-care facilities indicated that, if the program had been closed down in 1957, it would have "cost the state $7.75 million in relief. By contrast, advocates quickly pointed out, working parents contributed $28 million in taxes during that year—five times the cost of the entire child care program." [60, p. 80]

Conversely, the lack of day-care services can jeopardize the success of efforts being made to help people currently receiving assistance to achieve independence. The Federal government reported that in June 1971, 4000 AFDC mothers could not be enrolled in the Work Incentive program "for the sole reason that child care was not available." [78]

Day care also is a resource that permits a more natural, more acceptable route to help for families with problems. "Parents who are unlikely to seek professional services on their own initiative often respond to help when it is offered along with day care for their children." [26, p. 416] Some families that might not otherwise have obtained treatment for problems adversely affecting children are, through day care, more accessible to such help.

Children who might not otherwise have a safe, stimulating place available for play are provided such a facility; children who might otherwise be deprived of an experience in group interaction under guided supervision are provided with this kind of enriching experience; and children who might otherwise be left to care for themselves, or left to haphazard, uncertain arrangements for care, are more adequately, more safely cared for as a result of the availability of day-care facilities.

Although the following reported incidents may be atypical, they illustrate the possible dangers to which children might be exposed if the mother has to work and cannot make adequate provisions for child care:

> Concrete examples of the physical danger to which children are exposed when left alone while parents work frequently appear in newspapers or are reported by local social workers. Fire is probably the most frequent disaster. For instance, in a small city in Ohio, an eight-year-old girl was burned to death and her six-year-old brother was severely burned in the roominghouse in which the family lived. Their parents were at work. As a result of the death of a five-year-old girl, burned to death in a Connecticut city while her mother was working, labor leaders made plans for the establishment of additional day nurseries for the care of children of employed mothers.
>
> Too great responsibility is often given to the oldest child in a family. An eight-year-old, left in charge of three younger children until midnight while her mother worked on the swing shift and her father was taking a training course, was unable to give proper aid when one of the younger children was injured.
>
> . . . [In one Iowa] city, when a child was hurt in a playground accident, it was discovered that no member of her family was at home all day. The child, too young for school, was just packed off to the playground with a lunch.
>
> . . . In a large Missouri city, four of the children in a family are in school but the fifth, three years old, wanders around the neighborhood, returning home at mealtime to search the icebox for food. In a city in New York, five small brothers and sisters were locked in an apartment without supervision from 10:00 p.m. until 2:00 a.m. From Michigan comes the report of twenty small children found herded into a chicken-wire inclosure in a house basement while their mothers were [at] work. [24, pp. 165–66]   (See Fig. 8–3.)

Day care as a supplementary service, then, has great preventive value. It acts to prevent breakup of families, separation of children from their parents, increased dependency on public aid, and dangers and hazards to children.

The Social Worker and Day Care

An adequate day-care program requires a team approach, because it involves a partnership of three professions—education, health, and social work. [1; 9]   Some families who seek day-care service know very

FIGURE 8–3. A place to play and a place to stay. Top: amid tenement ruins, New York City (photo by Ken Wittenberg). Bottom: story-telling time at a day-care center, New York City (courtesy of New York City Department of Welfare).

clearly what they want, why they want it, and how to use it. In such instances the social worker's only responsibility is to see that the community makes the necessary services available and that the potential applicant is aware of their existence. For some families, however, the decision to use day care is reached only after many interrelated questions have been resolved. In such instances, casework services can be of help.

It is not always clear to the applicant that the mother's employment is the most desirable—or, in fact, the only—solution to the family's problems. For the widow, the divorced mother, or the unmarried mother, AFDC may not have been seriously considered as an alternative or, having been considered, may have been rejected without a full knowledge of the program. The opportunity to talk it over with a social worker having detailed knowledge of the program may result in a decision to stay at home and apply for such assistance rather than to seek employment.

If it is decided that some alternative plan is more desirable, the caseworker can help the applicant in implementing such alternative plans—in making application for AFDC, for instance, or in dealing with the problem of role reallocation in the family so that the child can be cared for at home, or with budgeting so that the mother may not have to work. The caseworker acts as the link between the day-care applicant and resources in the community.

On occasion when a family has an opportunity to explore the additional expenses involved in employment and to estimate the exact additional net income such employment is likely to yield, they may decide that it isn't worth the trouble. Or, having decided that it is advisable, the discussion has at least prepared them for the reality they encounter.

Even when the mother is convinced that employment is the preferable alternative, she may still be ambivalent and anxious about the step she is about to take. Such a mother welcomes the opportunity, if available, to discuss her doubts and fears with a caseworker. The caseworker helps her to clarify exactly what effects she thinks her employment will have on the children; she shares with the mother the knowledge that research has made available regarding the specific effects of mothers' employment on children in different situations and discusses with her what precautions might be taken to mitigate any negative effects. Frequently mothers are less explicitly aware that employment affects not only the younger preschool children but also the older children in the family. Sibling-sibling relations might also be affected. The caseworker helps the mother to become aware of the changes her working will entail for all her children.

The mother's employment also has effects on the marital pair subsystem. The change from mother-wife to mother-wife-employee necessitates some reallocation of role responsibilities in the family. Both the father and the mother are involved, by the worker, in exploring the changes that might be made in order to accommodate the mother's plans for employment, the degree of acceptance of such changes on the part of both parents, and the possible dangers and advantages of alternative modes of accommodation to the wife's working. In addition, she helps the family to determine whether the mother's employment, with day care, is the most appropriate solution to the problems faced by the family and to explore the availability, feasibility, and acceptability of alternative solutions.

If the mother's employment is the only feasible plan, she may have doubts about her capacity to meet the test of job demands. For women who have been out of the labor market for some time—especially for women who have never been in it—self-doubt about adequacy may act as a block to performance. They may use discussions with the social worker to reassure themselves and to test the demands they may have to face. Such discussions take the form of anticipatory socialization to the new role of employee.

The discussions, which attempt to help the family to clarify the decision regarding day care, indirectly have value for the child. They tend to reduce the rate of turnover and assure the child a continuity of experience; they reduce the difficulties the child may have in moving into the day-care situation, because the child's feelings about the program reflect, in some measure, those of his parents. "It is only as the parent's anxieties are relieved and she is reassured that her plan to work and use day care is in the best interest of herself and child that the mother is able to use day care to the best advantage." [30, p. 58]   The family's feeling of comfort with their decision is an important factor in determining the child's capacity to adjust positively to any kind of care.

The application for day care, as is true for similar services, has generally been prompted by some problem in family living—low income, disruption, illness, death, inadequate housing—and the family may need help in dealing with these problems.

The M.'s, a young couple, applied for day-care placement of their two-and-a-half-year-old son, to leave Mrs. M. free to look for employment and enable her to support the family. Mr. M., a commercial artist unemployed for several months, expressed confidence in finding work in his own line, at the same time holding to his unwillingness to accept a job outside his field. Both parents emphasized that day placement of little Andy would solve their present need, and that relief of their financial stress was the ultimate answer to their problem. Using the placement period, which became a very constructive experience for the youngster, as a dynamic situation for the entire family as well, Mr. and Mrs. M. came to see their actual situation in a different perspective. Soon they could acknowledge a marital problem, which had enmeshed and overwhelmed them for some time [and] to which they had closed their eyes. Both admitted that their conflicts were increased by family interferences. The difficulties emerging pointed up Mrs. M.'s disappointment in her husband as an inadequate provider, in spite of his grandiose ideas about himself, and with his inability to take hold of his family responsibilities.

Mr. M., too, began to display some awareness of doubts over his wife's feelings toward him as indicated by her indifference to his sexual demands. In the ongoing interview processes, he was able to acknowledge some connection between his personality pattern and the deterioration of their marital relationship. Although, in the beginning, he held staunchly to his belief that financial security and the advent of a well-paying job would cure their difficulties, both of the parents began to recognize that their deeper personal problems threatened to break down their marriage, and both willingly agreed to accept counseling help from a family agency. [31, p. 302]

For some mothers, the use of day care and the acceptance of employment may be the first step in establishing independence with the anticipation that this will culminate in divorce. The anxiety and the doubts about day care reflect questions regarding the advisability of breaking up the marriage. The mother may use day-care application to discuss this more significant decision.

Mrs. M. applied for day care for Harry, four years old, after an argument with her husband. She had threatened a divorce and he had taunted her with the statement that she could never support herself. She had been employed as a file clerk before marriage and she wondered if she could find a job now. "Maybe," she said, "if I could really prove to myself that I can get a job, I wouldn't have to take all that stuff from my husband. I would really mean it when I say I am walking out."

The decision to use day-care services results in another series of problems with which the families may need help. The child who is being enrolled begins the first formal prolonged separation from the family. The caseworker helps the mother to prepare the child for the transition by discussing with her how the child might react and how the mother might respond to the child's ambivalence and resistance and by reassuring her of the "normality" of the child's anxiety.

The child faces the problem of multiple adjustments. He is separated from the mother and expected to accept the care of adults who are strangers to him. He is placed in unfamiliar physical surroundings, generally far from his own neighborhood. Frequently the behavior expected of him may be different from, or in conflict with, what has been demanded of him at home. Therefore the mother must be prepared for some regression on the part of the child, who may temporarily display more infantile behavior. The need for such preparation is confirmed by Thenaud, who, in a study of requests for day-care service, noted that the mothers showed general lack of understanding of the possible reaction of the children. [72]

The caseworker tries to help the mother understand that children might feel rejected and not altogether certain that the mother will return. It takes repeated experiences of separation and return for confident assurance to develop that the mother will be back. Time sense is so poorly developed in children that for the mother to say she will be back "in a few hours" may have little meaning for the child. This knowledge supposedly helps the mother to accept, without undue embarrassment, the child's crying when she leaves. It also helps to clarify the day center staff's suggestion that the mother explain repeatedly to the child why she is going, what is going to happen, and that she will be back.

Generally, the family applies for day-care service when the mother and father are ready. The child's readiness for the experience, a most important factor in assuring success of the plan, is often not given explicit consideration. The social worker has to make some evaluation of the child's readiness, based on observation of his behavior and information provided by the family. It is suggested that, if the child has recently undergone some difficult change (the birth of a sibling, a recent operation, a serious illness in the family), entrance into the day-care situation be delayed. This reduces the imposition on the child of too many difficult adjustments at once.

But the decision to enroll the child also produces a variety of conflicts for the mother. She may have questions about the child's negative reaction to her because she is leaving him. She may have questions about her adequacy as a mother for giving up the care of her child, however temporarily, to strangers. She may be concerned about the transfer of the child's affection to the "mothers" in the day-care center. She may have some anxieties about the child's adequacy as a reflection of the family's previous care of the child. This derives from the fact that now, for the first time, the child is performing publicly in a uniform test situation and is being measured by professionals, however informally, vis-à-vis his age mates.

The mother reflects some of the general ambivalence toward day care and needs reassurance that she is not a "bad" mother for leaving the care of her child temporarily to others. She may feel happy at being relieved of some of the burden of child care and feel guilty about her reaction.

Mrs. M., a friendly, intelligent mother, wanted to place Charles, aged five, and Peter, aged two, so that she could go to work. Mr. M. was employed full-time but his earnings were marginal. . . . The arrangements for her job were practically completed when she applied. The carrying out of the total family plan hinged entirely, however, on the admission of the children to the day-care center. Although working meant a great deal to Mrs. M., she expressed many anxieties about leaving her children. She spoke with emotion as she told the worker, "I want to feel sure that the people taking care of my children are responsible. It's been a hard decision to make, even to consider leaving them for two days a week; but five whole days is even more difficult. . . . Maybe in a year's time I'll be able to take them away from you and go back to being a mother again."

Mrs. M.'s concern about leaving the children was real, and yet she was eager to relieve the financial stress. At the end of the first interview, she was not certain that Charles and Peter were to come to the day-care center. Within a few days she talked with the worker again and at this time she said, "I've thought it over. I am giving them up for a while but I am not really losing them." After these interviews, Mrs. M. actually followed through her decision by taking the children for vaccinations, toxoid injections, and other health measures required. [88, p. 101]

Especially for the mother of the very young child, there should be some preparation for the fact that she will be missing much of the gratification of experiencing the development of the child. One working mother whose friend looked after her eighteen-month-old child said, "After a couple of months I find that my friend can understand what my baby is saying; I cannot. He learns new things from her and I feel I am beginning not to know him." [99, p. 131]

Even if day care is desirable, there must be some discussion of the optimum choice of day care for the particular child. Is group day care the best alternative, or may individual family day care be better?

The social worker attempts to obtain a comprehensive picture, from the parents, of the child's level of functioning—his likes and dislikes, his physical status, his aptitudes and limitations, his habitual modes of reacting to stress, the most effective ways of motivating the child and of disciplining him, his reaction to adults outside the family, and his reaction to care by them. All this helps the staff to work with the child in a way that is best for the child and for the peer group into which he will be moving. It helps the staff to estimate the difficulty that the child will have in accepting this initial separation.

Some time at intake is devoted to discussing the structure of service and the questions the mother may have about this—fees, family responsibility for bringing and picking up the child on time, care of the child if he becomes ill, health examinations, the schedule of periodic conferences with various members of the staff, the nature of day-care routines, the things the child should bring and those he should not bring.

Arrangements are made for preadmission visits to the center and for preliminary acquaintanceships with the people on the staff who will be working with the child. The contacts between the family and the caseworker, the family and the teacher, help to identify day care with the family in the mind of the child and help him to see this as an extension of the home situation. For some children, arrangements need to be made for gradual desensitization to, and acceptance of, separation from the mother. The child may be made to come only for a few hours initially, and gradually the length of his stay is increased. It may help to have the mother remain with the child for progressively shorter periods of time after his enrollment in the program.

The visit to the center permits the parent to see for herself what is done there for children and tends to eliminate any fears or illusions she may have regarding operation of the center. The visit to the center also has diagnostic value for the staff.

> The way the child leaves the mother and takes to the teacher and to the [day care] environment, and the mother's reaction to this, begins to indicate to the worker what value the child has to the mother, the kind of relationship there is between them, and how ready she is to turn him over to another person . . . to use the . . . [day care] for his benefit. Sometimes, if her tie to him is weak, just seeing that he takes to the [day care] . . . and can bear separation from her will make her decide that she is in danger of losing him and that she must not let him go. In a surer relationship, however, this experience may be the very thing to settle her doubts about how he will take day care and separation and reassure her that it is all right to go ahead. [63, p. 20]

Later, the caseworker can be helpful to the family in working with any situations which adversely affect the child's adjustment to the center. Paradoxically, even the child's positive adjustment to day care may create a problem for the mother.

> Bobby got along unusually well for a child of his age in making the adjustment to the changed surroundings. Mrs. R. was seeing the caseworker at regular intervals and gradually she told us that Bobby liked the nursery so well that he was making a nuisance of himself week-ends because he was constantly asking if this was the day to go to the nursery. She could not understand this attitude on the part of any child. With much concern she said, "It makes me feel that maybe my home is not as good as it should be. Otherwise Bobby would not seem to prefer the nursery." [88, p. 100]

The necessity of carrying multiple burdensome roles—wife, mother, and employee—may produce cumulative stress which the mother may wish to discuss. The difficulties of doing justice to all of her responsibilities without feeling guilty and/or inadequate may require the opportunity for periodic discussions with a sympathetic, understanding person.

Problems may arise because of differences between the expectations of the parents and the day-care personnel in regard to the child's behavior. If the child has learned to dress himself at the center, to feed himself more adequately, the parents should be encouraged to expect the same independent behavior at home. This may create a problem for the mother who finds satisfaction in the child's dependency and feels threatened by a child's developing independence. Sometimes the family sets no limitations on the child's behavior and the day-care center institutes some controls.

Social workers in day care need to be aware of some of the general disadvantages of congregate day care for children. The fact that a sizable number of children need to be dealt with requires some regulation of behavior. Some kinds of behavior are encouraged by day-care personnel if they are to retain control and their sanity, and other kinds of behavior discouraged. Studies by Prescott and Jones indicate that "programs in day-care centers are marked by an absence of strong feelings and of activities that might evoke them. Many staff members appear to be afraid that open expression of strong desires in the form of anger, dependency, or abandoned exuberance would lead to behavioral contagion and chaos." [61, p. 55] There is less access to adults, less opportunity to meet highly individual needs in privacy away from the group, less possibility of contact with a wider range of age mates, more scheduling, and more control than is experienced in the home.

Throughout the contact with the family, the caseworker tries to help the parents with problems in child rearing which, in time, would be likely to affect the child's adjustment in day care.

A young father was turning away from his four-year-old son because he was becoming such a "brat" since the birth of his baby sister. The caseworker was able to add to the father's understanding of the emotional strain the coming of a new baby put upon the older child. He was then able to turn positively to the child again and to give him needed support and affection during a difficult time. [51, p. 25]

A mother of a three-year-old had been finding his thumbsucking a problem. She first taped the child's thumb to the rest of his hand and, when that failed, applied a bitter chemical which had been recommended by the drugstore. When she learned more about the meaning of thumb-sucking to the child, she was able to deal with it with less rigidity, and could feel less guilty and tense about the behavior, which she had thought was an indication of her failure as a mother. [51, p. 25]

Changes in the home situation may be reflected in changes in the child's behavior in day care. Discussing such changes with the parents helps them in understanding how changes in the home are affecting the child.

Bobbie, aged five, was extremely demanding of his teacher, using various methods to keep her attention on him and away from other children. His mother had given little indication of such behavior at home in [the] application interview and the need for a picture of the home environment did not seem important. When seen by the caseworker, a more detailed picture of the home situation was obtained. This was an only child of middle-aged parents. They lived in a three-room apartment due to [a] housing shortage. Bobbie shared a small room with his parents. Frequently the father worked late at night so that Bobbie was alone with his mother, who centered attention on him. Such information would have been helpful in understanding the child in his environment. After discussion with the mother, a plan was worked out to change the household arrangement to permit Bobbie to sleep in a room by himself, gradually helping him to feel that this was not a punitive move but a step toward his own independence. His behavior in the nursery school showed distinct changes and helped him to a more satisfying experience. [36]

Here, as is true for other child welfare services, casework acts to help the client learn what is expected behavior in a new and unfamiliar social role—for the mother and father, the role of partial parent; for the child, the role of member of a day-care group. Once having accepted the designated role, the parents and the child are helped to enact it effectively.

Part of the caseworker's responsibility lies in service to the staff in contact with the child, as well as to the family. [19]

Melvin, four years old, became extremely upset each day at the beginning of nursery school, usually at the point of separating from his family. The mother, a schoolteacher, was unable to remain in school with him during this period. The grandmother, who usually took responsibility for his care, expressed resentment at the need to stay with him and constantly threatened to leave him. The teacher became quite hostile to this mother; blamed her for Melvin's extreme behavior, and felt extremely frustrated in her ability to handle the child.

In interviews with the caseworker, the mother expressed negative feelings for the child and said, "My children in school need me too." She described a history of forced separations in an earlier nursery school experience and also in hospitalization for a tonsillectomy.

In staff meetings, the caseworker, in discussing the information obtained in her interviews with the mother, was able to help the teachers see this mother (and others too) as an individual with many personality problems, and that these disturbances were reflected in the child but that the nursery school could offer Melvin a positive experience through his acceptance by the teacher. [36]

Casework also can contribute to successful termination of service. Termination may result from situational factors such as the family's moving, the mother's remarriage, or the mother's return to the home as a full-time mother. It may come as a result of the child's growing beyond the age when family day care or congregation day care is appropriate. It may come because it seems clear that either the child or the family is not able to use the service effectively.

Withdrawal from the service may frequently give rise to no undue difficulty. This is more likely to be true if the child is leaving, along with other children in his group, at the end of a semester. On occasion, however, the reorganization in the life of the child and the family occasioned by termination of service may require some preparation and discussion. If the contact has been satisfactory, the child is likely to have developed relationships of some intensity with the teacher, the family day-care mother, and the peer group of which he has been a part. It is not easy to give this up without some sense of loss.

Much of what has been said relates both to group day care and to family day care. There are some special features of social work in family day care that must be recognized, however.

Family day care shares many similarities with foster care, generally. It involves, as does foster care, a process of recruitment, evaluation, and selection of day-care parents. The sources of recruitment and the process of selection is similar. This is confirmed by the fact that some agencies find that, with few exceptions, their "foster family home and family day-care home are really interchangeable." [39, p. 4]

There are some special aspects of family day care, however, that derive from the important fact that the child returns to his own home every night. This implies that contact between the day-care parent and the child's own parent is frequent and regular, so that although the day-care mother is less deeply involved with the child than is the foster mother, she has a tendency to be more deeply involved with the child's mother. And because the child experiences separation every day and lives, in effect, in two homes, he might need help in integrating the two major experiences in his life.

Casework with child and mother is similar to group day care in individualized day-care service in that the family is helped to resolve problems that might reduce satisfactory use of the resource.

> Johnny, aged twenty-two months, was a relatively easy child to get along with after his mother left him in the day-care home. He ate and slept well and played contentedly with the toys. As soon as his mother appeared on the scene, however, he ran rampant—jumping on furniture, touching things on tables which had been prohibited, and so on. So serious was his behavior when the mother brought and called for him that the day-care mother didn't feel she could continue to care for him unless the mother began taking some responsibility for disciplining him. It was her impression that the mother never said "no" to him, and never corrected him. There was no question but what Johnny was making life difficult for her but she did nothing about it.
>
> Contact with the mother revealed that because she felt so guilty about leaving Johnny (her relatives all disapproved of her plan to work even though father was in service), she tried to make it up to him by keeping the time they were together free of restrictions and discipline. She wanted it to be a happy, carefree period. Of course it was not. Not only was Johnny's behavior at home upsetting, but he was sleeping poorly and was chronically constipated. It had not occurred to the mother that her indulgence was confusing the child.
>
> With the help of the caseworker, she was able to see how important it was that what was expected of the child in each of his two homes be as consistent as possible. She was helped to see, too, for the first time, perhaps, that parenthood carries with it the responsibility for setting the "do's" and "don't's" which are the basis of habit and character formation in children. [30, p. 58]

Turnover in family day care is high and, as studies show, the child faces the risks of frequent discontinuity in care and adjustment to a new family-day-care mother. [16]

An Explanation

A major controversy revolves about the question of whether day care is a social utility (like public schools and parks) which every family might need and use at some time or whether the need and use of day care implies that this is a "problem" family. Ruderman's survey of day care in the United States leads her to conclude that

. . . great numbers of normal, middle class, intact, responsible families with working mothers need day-care services and even greater numbers of such families want it. In fact, as we get away from the problem situations cited in welfare documents [it becomes clear that] day care is primarily a child care program on all levels of society for normal children and normal families. [64, p. 341]

It is becoming more widely accepted that day care is a "normal" arrangement required by "normal" families. Why then the illustrative material which emphasizes "problem" situations? This follows from the fact that our primary focus in this chapter is really *not* with day care as a recently developed social utility to meet the needs of the contemporary family. The primary focus *is* on the special functions of the child welfare social worker in day care and the kinds of help he can offer to those limited number of families who may have problems in effectively utilizing a social utility available to all. One may accept an "institutional" orientation toward day care as such, and at the same time hold a "residual" orientation toward the particular functions of the child welfare social worker in day care.

Consequently, our concern in this chapter is not with the greatest majority of families who might perhaps effectively utilize day care without, at any point, requiring the intervention of the social worker. Our concern is with those limited number of families who come to day care as a result of some problematic social situation, and with those parents and children whose use of day care produces, or exacerbates, social problems.

The fact that specialized social work functions are an important component of day care for the *limited* number of families who *might* need it is recognized in the Federal Interagency Day Care Requirements, which state that in order to be eligible for support, a day-care center must provide "social services which are under the supervision of a staff member trained or experienced in the field." [76]   The social service functions to be performed for those families who need and want such service are spelled out in the document and in another Federal guide, *Specifications for Positions in Day-Care Centers*. These include "counseling and guidance to the family to help determine the appropriateness of day care," as well as "continuing assessment with the parents of the child's adjustment in the day-care program and of the family situation," and "liaison activity which helps make available to, and coordinates for, the family, any additional community resources which the family might need." [79]

Similarly, Head Start guidelines require that every Head Start program must have a social service program to link the center with the family and the related community services and resources. The social worker in Head Start is charged with the responsibility of being a "strong advocate in obtaining services from local agencies and in referring families to them." Where needed services do not exist he should "work to develop more effective social services."

The social worker in the day-care center thus acts as liaison between the center and the family, the center and the community, and the family and the community. He helps inform the families about relevant community programs and refers them to services they may need, as well as counseling parents on family planning, nutrition, health care, and family budgeting, and providing them with information about food stamp programs, Medicaid, employment, housing, and public assistance. [3]

In a follow-up study of forty-two families involved in a demonstration project in family day care, twenty-nine clients indicated that they were helped by the caseworker in "understanding the child's behavior . . . relieving strain . . . adjusting to [the client's] new life . . . [and] getting . . . [the] child established in nursery school." [23, p. 11]   A detailed study of the need for casework services in a California day-care center indicated that of the 197 families using the center, about seventy families acknowledged concern over some family problem, though only twenty-three families actually asked for help. The parents who sought help were concerned about "children's aggressiveness, hyperactivity, temper, excessive demands, [and] attention-getting behavior." [62]

The social work component in day care, as described in *Standards for Day Care Service*, published by the Child Welfare League of America, and as reviewed in this chapter, exists in only a limited percentage of day-care centers. There is a wide gap between the literature and the actuality. Prescott, who did an intensive study of day-care centers in California, notes that the "social work component as described in the Child Welfare League of America Standards for Day Care is virtually nonexistent. . . . The literature on day care has been concerned primarily with day care as it ought to be or as it has been assumed to exist." [61]

Only a limited number of social workers are employed in day care. Ruderman notes in her study that "only 7 percent of the day-care centers have the regular services of a social worker." [64, p. 102]   If Ruderman's estimate were applied to the 167,000 licensed day-care centers throughout the country in 1970, one might estimate about 1200 full-time social workers employed by day-care centers. Ruderman's findings are confirmed by a study of 98 hospitals operating child care facilities for use of their personnel. "Only 7 percent indicated they provided any type of social service for the family." [64, p. 13]

On the other hand, a national survey of some 300 day-care facilities by the National Council of Jewish Women found that 68 percent of nonprofit centers and 21 percent of the proprietary centers surveyed claimed that they employed a social worker. [42, Table 26, p. 112]   It appears that while social workers can make a specific contribution to more effective use of day-care services, they are currently found in only a limited percentage of day-care facilities.

Problems

1. Although the percentage of working mothers with young children will continue to increase, there is limited, though growing, public support for the development of day-care resources. An intensive study by the Child Welfare League of America of leaders in selected communities throughout the United States shows that "most respondents assigned day care moderate rather than high—or low—priority." [11, p. 33]

2. In part, the priority accorded day care is a reflection of the general lack of knowledge about day-care needs and facilities and the low visibility such problems have, in contrast to the dramatic impact of juvenile delinquency and the problems of emotionally disturbed children.

Day care is primarily a preventive program; the children served do not yet have any problems that are disturbing to the parents or the community, though these may develop later as a result of inadequate child-care facilities available to the family while the mother is working.

The Child Welfare League Study suggests that the reluctance to support day-care services is also related to a negative view of the working mother—a view which sees her as working because she chooses to do so and/or because she is not primarily concerned with, or interested in, the care of her children. One respondent said, "Nothing should be done to encourage any further tendency for mothers to find excuses for avoiding the responsibilities of caring for their children." Another said, "I am strongly opposed to any measure aimed at making private or government agencies devices to have mothers unload their responsibility for their children so they can work." [11, p. 83]

3. The Child Welfare League also found that most respondents preferred some form of in-home individual care by a relative:

> Child care has always been a family responsibility and if the child's own mother is unable to care for him the traditional solution has always been an approximation of maternal care . . . in the child's own home, involving other members of the family. This is customary and seems natural. Other arrangements, perhaps, especially organized ones, have been less common and therefore may seem strange or unnatural. [11, p. 49]

This attitude is reflected in a recent British study of working mothers, few of whom made use of available day-care facilities. A "shocked denial" was noted when the question of use of day-care facilities was raised. "This hinted that in Bermondsey [the locale of the study] the use of an institution, however admirable, was a reflection on the home, whereas to have the child minded by a known individual was not." Child care by relatives gave the "parents fewer misgivings. Relations' ways were 'like my mum's' and even the toddler . . . would sense the family ties." [41, pp. 144–45]

The monetization of child care makes people uneasy since it contradicts the usual family arrangement of child care out of concern and love. The private family-day-care arrangement which the mother organizes for herself with some neighboring person, while it has contractual and financial elements, resembles the mutual aid system of an extended family. Hence it is ideologically a more acceptable arrangement to many mothers.

Thus, although statistics and studies show a large and increasing number of children who might need day care, there are persistent reports that many centers are not utilized to capacity. Ruderman found that "unmet need and at the same time underuse of existing resources is a striking characteristic of the day-care situation today." [64, p. 94] Some explanation for this lies in some of the negative attitudes toward the use of the service by working mothers. Ruderman found that 53 percent of working mothers who were asked said they would be reluctant to use a day-care center if it were available. Among the reasons for opposition were the lack of personal attention they anticipated for their children, the fact that it is likely to be excessively structured and too much like a school, the danger to a child's health of congregate care, and the fact that their child was likely to be in contact with children from "less adequate families." [64, pp. 315–17]

4. There is a problem in deciding the desirable balance of investment and effort in day-care center and the informal, but much more extensive system of the individually operated family-day-care. Agencies and professionals in the field favor an expansion of day-care centers because they control these facilities and they can there implement a program for which their training has prepared them. Family day care is controlled by amateurs and eludes supervision and regulation, but it is and will continue to be used by many families.

Emlen, closely studying family day care over a number of years, found that mothers prefer child care "within three blocks of home," "within five minutes of home," "within easy walking distance of home," "in the immediate neighborhood," "near enough so that my older children can join the little ones after school." He reports that many of the mothers also prefer family day care not only because it was "physically convenient, flexibly accommodating, socially approachable, and consumer controllable, but also because it is perceived, and correctly so, as a comfortable and familiar setting in which the working mother finds a responsible, nurturant caregiver who is capable of providing love and comfort as well as new social learning. . . ." [21, pp. 178–79] Still, many of the mothers would have preferred congregate day care, if it had been available, because of its greater continuity and its provision of better learning opportunities. [42; 64; 94]

Family day care is frequently brought to the family's attention through a newspaper advertisement or a notice tacked up on the local supermarket bulletin board. Although professionals may tend to deplore such informal arrangements, Emlen found that the majority "are not so bad as people suppose, and the sample reported in this study reveals an environment for children the potentialities of which are favorable enough to justify an organized effort to strengthen this type of care as a major resource for day care." [21, p. 3; see also 94; 95] The researchers note "that it is fallacious to assume that family day care is inevitably poor if it is not supervised by a social agency." [16, p. 528] Despite some clearly hazardous examples, many of the family-day-care mothers are personally adequate and capable of meeting the needs of children.

Since informal family day care will continue to be used by working mothers, professionals concerned with child care are making efforts to help improve it. The Neighborhood Day Care Exchange Project in Portland, Oregon, locates women interested in providing day care in their homes, offers them training and consultation in child care, and puts them in touch with mothers needing day care for their children. [16]

Recent efforts also include special publications and newsletters developed by state departments of public welfare for distribution to day-care mothers, special training programs developed by community colleges in cooperation with public welfare agencies, and the development of day-care homes as satellites of day-care centers, with training of the day-care mothers by the day-care center.

5. Following from the view that the family should provide individual care for the child in his own home, day care is often perceived as an exceptional procedure. One might point once again to the results of the Child Welfare League study of community attitudes toward day care, which suggests that respondents generally saw the service as needed by those families who were "different"—the low-income family and the "broken family headed by the mother." [11, p. 93]

This image of the day-care center is reinforced by the fact that because public day-care resources are in short supply, they are currently reserved (through eligibility requirements) for low-income families, single-parent families, and families on public assistance. Socioeconomic segregation often means racial segregation as well. Thus public day-care programs tend to serve children of low-income, nonwhite families, while proprietary day-care centers, supported by fees from parents, tend to serve middle-class white families. While middle-income families are "defined" out of publicly supported facilities, low-income families are "priced" out of proprietary facilities. Minority-group children and children of single-parent households are, in fact, heavily overrepresented in nonproprietary day-care centers.

The association between day care and welfare led to a reluctance on the part of some families, noted during World War II, to apply for day care if this had to be done through a social agency. [34; 35] It has been suggested that information about, and application for, day care should be handled by some agency with more neutral connotations for the public, an agency which is more directly related to the situation that usually prompts the needs for day care, such as the employment services.

6. Another problem is posed by the question of responsibility for day care. Day care meets the definition of a child welfare service. It is an institution organized in response to a social problem, and the social role changes in relation to it. Yet the profession of social work is not certain that it has responsibility for day care. As Host says, "Too often the recent social work graduate has expressed surprise when day care is described as a child welfare service." [37, p. 3] And Kuhlmann notes, "Day care has not yet arrived at the place in the child welfare field where it is viewed as an essential social work program." [44, p. 23] Although this was written in 1955, it appears to be essentially true today.

Some argue that responsibility for day care should be delegated to the educational institutions rather than to the social service organizations. They note that the school is accepted in all communities as a center for child care; that the school district has an established administrative organization, and housing and playground space for such centers; that it has available personnel who can assist in the organization, supervision, and training of staff; that, in effect, the day-care center merely extends the educational system downward (to include a younger group) and outward (to lengthen the school day of older children).

The problem of responsibility for day care is compounded by other considerations. Although day care meets the criteria for inclusion in any listing of child welfare service, it requires the joint cooperative activity of three professions—health, education, and social work—for effective implementation. Each of these, consequently, has vested interest in the service. As it stands, however, day care currently belongs more to the commercial-proprietary group than it does to any of the professions. This raises a problem of social policy.

It is argued that the care and the concomitant education of children (because all care involves some education, however informal) should be matters of public concern and support; that permitting day care to develop largely in the hands of proprietary-commercial interests is irresponsible, and that child-care centers ought to represent a community investment in its families rather than a business venture.

The fact that day care has a variety of different possible goals presents a problem of identification. Industry sees day care as desirable in providing a larger and more dependable female labor force; government officials see day care as helpful in moving people off welfare and into employment; educators see day care as early compensatory education which will more adequately prepare disadvantaged children for school; health officials see day care as a case-finding procedure which will bring to light health deficiencies in young children; women's liberation groups see day care as providing women more alternative options in life styles; social workers see day care as insuring adequate care and protection for the child of the working mother. The working mother sees child care as a dependable, stable source of care for her child, giving him the opportunity of playing with his age mates under the supervision of people who are competent to offer some education and training as well. This has resulted in attempts by the different professions involved to incorporate it within their own particular spheres of influence. As a supplementary parental care facility it has a social work goal; as a supplementary or compensatory educational program it belongs to education; as a facility for the physically or mentally handicapped it can be viewed as a public health resource. Consequently, not only are there differences in orientation among health workers, educators, and social workers as to what is important in day care, but there is competitive disagreement concerning who should control the day-care "turf."

7. A problem that has been generally slighted is the need for supervision and care of the school-age child of the working mother. Studies show that the mother often has to leave for work before the child has breakfasted and is ready for school, and is not available to the child during lunch or between the time school lets out and the end of the work day. School holidays and vacations are a problem, for they do not always coincide with work holidays and vacations. When the child is ill and out of school, most mothers absent themselves from work—at an anxiety-provoking loss of pay for the mother who is head of a family.

This raises the question of public policy with reference to an extended school day. Such measures have been advocated in some communities where there is considerable concern about "latch-key" children—school-age children who wear a latch-key on a cord, which symbolizes their responsibility for self while their mothers are employed.

8. Ideally day care should be available to any mother who needs to work, wants to work, or merely wants to share the care of her child. The facility should be of high quality, conveniently located, and low in cost. Personnel should be professionally trained and sufficiently numerous to permit individualization of the child. But the actual situation is far different.

A 1971 national study conducted by the Westinghouse Learning Corporation for the Office of Economic Opportunity concludes:

Day care for young children in the United States today is an
institution lagging far behind the social change that has brought
about the need for it. It is an unorganized, largely unregulated and
unlicensed service provided in ways that range from excellent
to shockingly poor and yet it is indispensable to a growing number
of people in present-day America: the force of working women of
child-bearing age. [91, p. 95]

The family which has the greatest difficulty is the one whose income
is just high enough to render it ineligible for publicly supported day
care but too low to permit proprietary day care. For this family, the
working poor, the mother's employment is often a clear economic necessity.

Shortage of trained staff is endemic. Low salaries make difficult the
recruitment of adequate numbers of adequately trained people.

Frequently care is not available when the mother needs it. Many
women—hospital nurses, waitresses, hotel maids, telephone operators,
saleswomen—work weekends or evenings. Yet very few centers are
open seven days a week, twenty-four hours a day.

To meet the needs for personnel anticipated by increases in day care
in the near future, the Federal Office of Child Development is actively
sponsoring the development of a new profession, the Child Development Associate, who, after a two-year program in a junior or senior
college and a fieldwork internship, will act to assist day-care-center
teachers.

9. There is a bewildering array of sources of government support for
day care. Manpower development and training legislation makes funds
available to increase the supply of personnel; educational legislation
makes funds available to provide compensatory education; social security legislation provides funds to reduce dependence on welfare; housing
and urban development legislation and model cities legislation make
funds available to achieve the purpose of urban change. Community
groups seeking sources of support need considerable expertise in merely
knowing where and how to apply for funds. The multiplicity of sources
of funding and aims creates a problem for the day-care services.

There is a problem regarding who should be eligible to apply for
Federal funds in support of day care. Community-action groups argue
that they should be eligible to initiate application for such funds. Direct
access by each community-based group is opposed by others since they
regard such a procedure as administratively difficult and inefficient. It
could mean that the Federal government would have to deal with thousands of different community groups to which it might grant funds
directly. Consequently, it is argued that only state or city governments
should be permitted to act as "prime sponsors" in application for, and
distribution of, such funds. Community-action groups argue in rebuttal

that such a procedure may be administratively more efficient but it also permits tighter control of funds so that the more militant social action groups can be "frozen out."

Trends

1. The change in women's employment situation has been revolutionary, but cultural attitudes are changing more slowly. However, there is a growing acceptance of the fact that mother's employment is "normal," that in most cases it is necessary, that it does not reflect child neglect, and that it is not necessarily harmful to the child. All this suggests a trend toward greater concern with the need for day care and a greater acceptance of day care. The 1970 White House Conference on Children recommended that "a diverse national network of comprehensive developmental child care services be established to accommodate approximately 5.6 million children by 1980 through consolidated Federal efforts via legislation and funding as well as through coordinated planning and operation involving state, local, and private efforts. . . . The ultimate goal is to make high-quality care available to all families who seek it and all children who need it." [93, p. 283]

There is growing recognition that failure to build an adequate number of day centers does not result in a reduction of the number of mothers working, but merely leads to less adequate arrangements for the care of children. The change of public attitude is documented by the results of a 1969 nationwide public opinion poll, in which 64 percent of respondents favored expenditure of Federal funds for the establishment of community day-care centers (*The New York Times*, July 12, 1969).

Further exemplifying the change in national attitude was the approval by Congress in late 1971 of a bill which included provisions for extensive public support for day care for a large segment of American families. For low-income families day care would have been provided without cost; a sliding-scale fee would have provided day care to middle-income families at a very low cost. The bill was vetoed by President Nixon, despite widespread support, on the grounds that it was too costly, administratively unwieldy, and "would commit the vast moral authority of the National Government to the side of communal approaches to child rearing over against the family centered approach" (*The New York Times*, December 10, 1971).

As against this feeling that day care might undermine the American family, there is growing acceptance of the idea that day care might, in fact, help to strengthen the family by facilitating mothers' employment, by intervening to prevent development of problems in parent-child relationships, and by providing the possibility of maintaining children in the community who might otherwise have to be institutionalized.

It is easy, however, to exaggerate the depth of this trend. Public funding of day care for all families who want and can use it would signal a major shift in the relative distribution of responsibility between parents and community for care and socialization of America's children. Traditionally, and currently, the principal responsibility for the care and socialization of the preschool child has rested with the family. Even for the older child, communal responsibility has been narrowly defined as being concerned with his education during a limited segment of the twenty-four-hour day. As a consequence of an extensive public day-care program, the community will begin to share with the parent earlier and more extensive responsibility for the child.

The cost of such a commitment has been conservatively estimated at \$5 billion a year with expectations that this "could easily" mount to between \$12 billion and \$15 billion by 1977. [65, p. 252]   Yet only an estimated \$1 billion of Federal money was made available for day care and preschool educational programs in fiscal 1973. It is for these ideological and financial reasons that the controversy over day care in the 1970's as a social policy innovation is comparable in its intensity to the controversy over Medicare in the 1960's.

2. There is among professionals a growing acceptance of congregate day care for very young children. This trend is stimulated and supported by special projects which have yielded reassuring results. Because care outside the home involves special hazards for the young child, many of the licensing regulations have forbidden group care for children younger than two. Preliminary reports indicate that the needs of infants can be adequately met through group-care arrangements if these entail sensible precautions and a high caretaker-child ratio.

In reviewing her own as well as other similar programs, Caldwell notes that the intellectual or cognitive development of very young children is not harmed by "experiences in a day-care environment at a very early age . . ." and, in fact, many young children benefit significantly from such an exposure. Furthermore, "the children who had been enrolled in day care and had been exposed to several adults daily since before their first birthday were just as attached to their own mothers as were the children who had remained at home during this period." [6, p. 8]   As a consequence of these studies, Caldwell states that "the implicit equation of day care with institutionalization should be put to rest." [7, p. 411]   It should be noted, however, that the demonstration projects which contributed to the research findings were high-quality, stable day-care arrangements.

A recent analysis of relevant international research literature concludes:

All in all, the investigations suggest that sufficient high-quality day nurseries can assure completely normal development for the child's health, motor activity, and intellectual and social abilities. Moreover, for children from poor home milieus, the day nursery can insure development better than they would otherwise have had. The question of the child's emotional development remains unanswered. On this question, the most hotly debated aspect of day nurseries research has not yet given definitive results. [69, p. 23]

In response to the greater interest in day care for very young children, the Committee on the Infant and Preschool Child of the American Academy of Pediatrics recently formulated standards for day-care centers for infants and children under three years of age. Twenty-seven states were licensing infant day-care centers in 1971. However, in some states the licensing standards explicitly forbid congregate care for the very young child. Nevertheless, in exemplification of this growing change in professional orientation, there are now a sizable number of congregate day-care-center facilities which accept young infants for care. [38]

3. There is a trend toward a diversification of auspices under which day care is offered. Employers have indicated a growing interest in offering day care for the children of their employees because such a service might increase recruitment of female workers, reduce absenteeism and job turnover, and improve labor relations. For the employee it means being closer to the child during the day, reduces her anxiety and problems about finding day care, and provides continuity of care for the child. Children will have contact with the world of work, the opportunity of seeing their parents in the work role, and a greater likelihood of contacts with males.

Despite the advantages, a 1970 study revealed that only about a dozen companies, with predominantly a female work force, operated day-care centers for their employees' children. Frequently hospitals operate such facilities for use of their personnel. The U.S. Departments of Labor, of Agriculture, and of Health, Education, and Welfare have provided similar facilities. The Amalgamated Clothing Workers' Union is building, and will operate, a network of day-care centers for its members. [82; 83]

There is a trend toward making day care a franchise operation. For instance, E. C. K. Chivers and Associates, which handles the franchise for such national operations as Black Angus Steak House and Lums, also handles the franchise of what it is hoped will become a national network of Kindercare day-care centers. Similarly, franchises are available nationwide for Mary Moppet day-care schools. The national organization provides a two-week training period, helps locate a site, provides standard architectural plans, makes available promotional and advertising campaign material, and provides consultation on selection and purchasing of building and playground equipment. After the establishment of the center, the national organization provides monthly menus and a newsletter concerned with current advances in day care. In response to the trend, the Child Welfare League of America has published a statement of advice and warning to interested investors. [13]

The need for day-care centers and the need to increase self-employment opportunities in the ghettos might be complementary. Subsidies might be made available to qualified people in the ghettos to establish proprietary neighborhood day-care centers. Low-income families needing assistance in purchasing day care might be given vouchers and left free to choose the day-care center—which might then be the proprietary center owned by a neighbor.

4. There is a trend toward a greater explicit diversification of day-care facilities. Previously the literature made distinctions primarily between a day-care center (a congregate-care resource) and family day care (a more individualized care of a child in a home) and between nursery care with a primarily educational purpose and day care oriented more toward care and protection. Currently the literature identifies a "child-development center," a "play-group facility," a "preschool-child-care center," a "school-age-child-care center," a "family-day-care home," a "group-day-care home," a "family school-age-day-care home," and a "group school-age-day-care home." Distinctions revolve around the age and size of the group offered service, and the primary orientation of the facility.

Diversification involves not only different kinds of day-care facilities available providing care for groups of different ages and sizes, but also timing. Since many women work at night, day-care centers in large cities have developed night-care centers and family night-care homes.

5. There is a trend toward the employment of welfare recipients as family-day-care mothers. The New York City Department of Social Services established the Family Day Care-Career Program. The program provides, for the children of welfare mothers interested in a job or job training (called *career mothers*), care in the home of other welfare recipients (called *day-care mothers*). The exchange frees the career mother to obtain, or prepare for, employment while providing extra income for the day-care mothers. The homes are selected and approved by the Department of Social Services and the money earned is not regarded in computing welfare benefits. A training program and follow-up consultation provided child development education for the day-care mothers. Milwaukee [89] and Baltimore [20] report similar programs.

6. The Head Start program confirmed and intensified the trend toward parental involvement in day-care-center activity. It also tended to

enlarge the focus of such involvement. Head Start guidelines require the employment of parents as paraprofessionals and aides in the program whenever possible, and require parent participation in day-care decision making and administration. Similarly Federal Interagency Day Care Guidelines require that "whenever an agency provides day care for forty or more children there must be a policy advisory committee or its equivalent at that administrative level where most decisions are made. The committee membership should include not less than 50 percent parents or parent representatives, selected by the parents in a democratic fashion." [76, p. 14]

7. There is a growing interest in developing day care for special groups—emotionally disturbed children, mentally handicapped children, and children of migrant workers. The care of such children requires special equipment, and personnel with special training who are willing to devote extra time and energy to children. Such day-care centers also make an explicit effort to involve the parents so that the training and/or therapy achieved in the center is sustained and supported by parents in the home. The National Association for Retarded Children has been very active and successful in extending day-care services to such children.

Summary

Day care is a supplementary service designed to provide care for the child during the part of the day when the mother is unavailable. Day care, concerned first with care and protection of the child, is distinguished from nursery school, which has a more explicit educational focus.

There are two principal kinds of day care—congregate day care and day care offered in the family day-care home. Family day care is the more appropriate resource for the child younger than two years of age.

Day care is an appropriate resource for the child whose mother is working, for the handicapped child who does not need institutionalization, for the child living in a deprived environment, and in cases of parent-child conflict when the parent can respond to some relief in care of the child.

In reality, day care is used most frequently to care for the child of the working mother. The problem of day care is thus closely related to the problem of the working mother. The trend is toward an increase in labor force participation on the part of mothers. This trend is related to (1) a change in the family from producer to consumer unit, (2) the family need for a cash income, (3) changes in the nature of the jobs available, (4) changes in the life cycle of the family.

In 1971 there were about 4.3 million working mothers with children under six years of age. The probability that a woman will work is related to the age of her children, the presence of a husband in the home, the level of the husband's earnings.

But, despite the sharp increase in the number of working mothers, only a limited number of day-care places are available—about 910,000 in 1971. Most often children of working mothers were cared for in their own home by the father or by older siblings. Thus, only 6 percent of the children six years of age or under of working mothers were cared for in formal day-care arrangements. Some 20,000 children under six had no regular provision made for their care while their mothers worked.

Social workers form part of the day-care-center team, which includes teachers and health personnel as well. Social workers help to prepare the child and the family for the movement into day care, help them with the social and emotional consequences of the use of day care, and act as the liaison between the family and the child in the center.

Problems related to day care include:

1. The low priority given to day care as compared with other child welfare services.
2. Negative attitudes toward the working mother and toward day care as a supplementary care arrangement.
3. Family day care versus the day-care center as the arrangement of priority.
4. Association of day care with public welfare.
5. The confusion over the professional identity of day care.
6. The problem of neglected age groups.
7. The inadequacy of current resources.
8. Multiple funding sources.

Among the trends identified were the following:

1. A growing acceptance of day care.
2. Increased public support of day care, available to all families.
3. A growing acceptance of day care for infants.
4. A diversification of kinds of day-care arrangements and their auspices.
5. The employment of welfare mothers as caretakers.
6. An increase in parental involvement.
7. An increase in day care for children with special needs.

Bibliography

1. ALLEN, WINIFRED, and DORIS CAMPBELL. *The Creative Nursery Center: A Unified Service for Children and Parents.* New York: Family Service Association of America, 1948.
2. AMERICAN ACADEMY OF PEDIATRICS. *Standards for Day Care Centers for Infants and Children Under Three Years of Age.* Evanston, Ill.: American Academy of Pediatrics, 1971.
3. ARCHINARD, ENOLIA, et al. "Social Work and Supplementary Services," in *Day Care: Resources for Decisions.* Ed. by Edith H. Grotberg. Washington, D.C.: Day Care and Child Development Council of America, 1971.
4. BEER, ETHEL. *Working Mothers and the Day Nursery.* New York: Whiteside, Inc., 1957.
5. BLOCH, JUDITH. "A Preschool Workshop for Emotionally Disturbed Children." *Children,* **17**, 1 (January–February 1970), 10–14.
6. CALDWELL, BETTYE M. "What Does Research Teach Us About Day Care for Children Under Three?" *Children Today,* **1**, 1 (January–February 1972), 6–11.
7. ———, et al. "Infant Care and Attachment." *American Journal of Orthopsychiatry,* **40**, 3 (April 1970), 397–412.
8. CHAZIN, ROBERT M. "Day Treatment of Emotionally Disturbed Children." *Child Welfare,* **48**, 4 (April 1969), 212–18.
9. CHILD WELFARE LEAGUE OF AMERICA. *Tri-Profession Conference on Day Care—Daytime Care: A Partnership of Three Professions.* New York, 1946.
10. ———. *Standards for Day Care Service.* New York, 1960.
11. ———. *Day Care Project Report.* New York, September 1962.
12. ———. *Standards for Day-Care Services: Revised 1969.* New York, 1969.
13. ———. *Small Children as a Small Business—A Primer for Potential Investors in Day Care Centers.* New York, 1971.
14. CLASS, NORRIS E. "Licensing of Child Care Facilities by State Welfare Departments." *Children's Bureau Publication, No. 462.* Washington, D.C.: Government Printing Office, 1968.
15. CLOSE, KATHRYN. "Day Care Up to Now." *Survey Mid-Monthly,* **79** (July 1943).
16. COLLINS, ALICE, and EUNICE L. WATSON. "Exploring the Neighborhood Family Day-Care System." *Social Casework,* **50**, 9 (November 1969), 527–33.
17. COOPER, SOPHIA. "Labor Force Projections to 1975." *Monthly Labor Review* (December 1957).
18. DAY CARE AND CHILD DEVELOPMENT COUNCIL OF AMERICA. *Basic Facts About Licensing of Day Care.* Washington, D.C., October 1970.
19. ECKSTEIN, ESTHER. "The Function of the Caseworkers in Day Care Centers." *Child Welfare,* **41**, 1 (January 1962).
20. EDWARDS, ELVA. "Family Day Care in a Community Action Program." *Children,* **15**, 2 (March–April 1968), 55–58.
21. EMLEN, ARTHUR C., et al. *Child Care by Kith: A Study of the Family Day Care Relationships of Working Mothers and Neighborhood Caregivers.* Portland, Ore.: DCE Books, 1971.

22. FADDIS, GABRIELLLE. "Interaction Between a Nursery School for Disturbed Children and a Nursery School for Normal Children in a Child Guidance Clinic Setting." *National Association of Nursery Centers Bulletin* (Spring 1956).
23. FOSTER FAMILY DAY CARE SERVICE. *Follow-up Study of Foster Family Day Care*. New York, November 1962. Mimeo.
24. FREDRICKSON, H. "The Problem of Taking Care of Children of Employed Mothers." *Social Service Review*, 17 (1943).
25. FREUD, ANNA. "Nursery School Education—Its Uses and Dangers." *Child Study*, 26 (Spring 1949).
26. GILFILLAN, VIOLA. "Day Care as a Therapeutic Service to Preschool Children and Its Potential as a Preventive Service." *Child Welfare*, 41, 9 (November 1962).
27. GLICK, PAUL. "The Life Cycle of the Family." *Marriage and Family Living* (February 1955).
28. GODDARD, GLADYS. "Potentialities of Day Care." *Child Welfare*, 36, 10 (December 1957).
29. GOLDEN ANNIVERSARY WHITE HOUSE CONFERENCE ON CHILDREN AND YOUTH. *Focus on Children and Youth*. Washington, D.C.: Government Printing Office, 1960.
30. GOLTEN, MARGARET. "Family Day Care: What It Means for the Parent." *The Family*, 26, 4 (April 1945).
31. GORDON, BERTEL. "Criteria for Determining Type of Placement." *Journal of Jewish Communal Service* (Spring 1957).
32. ———. "Foster Family Day Care Service." *Child Welfare*, 38, 6 (June 1959).
33. GRANATO, SAM J., and E. DOLLIE LYNCH. "Day-Care Licensing." *Children Today* (January–February 1972), 23–24.
34. GUYLER, CATHRYN. "Social Responsibility for the Development of Day Care," in *Proceedings of the National Conference of Social Welfare*. New York: Columbia University Press, 1942.
35. HANSAN, J., and K. PEMBERTON. "Day-Care Services for Families with Mothers Working at Home." *Child Welfare*, 42 (April 1963).
36. HARPER, MIRIAM C., and CECILE SCHWARTZMAN. "Casework Counseling Service in a Nursery School." *Child Welfare*, 32 (May 1953).
37. HOST, MALCOLM, and PATRICIA HASSETT. "Day-Care Services and the Social Work Profession." *Social Work Education*, 11 (April 1963).
38. HOWARD, MARION. *Group Infant Care Programs—A Survey*. Washington, D.C.: Cyesis Program Consortium, February 1971.
39. JACKSON, THERESA. *Day-Care Services as Administered Under Various Auspices*. New York: Child Welfare League of America, n.d.
40. JENKINS, SHIRLEY, and MIGNON SAUBER. *Paths to Child Placement*. New York: Community Council of Greater New York, 1966.
41. JEPHCOTT, PEARL. *Married Women Working*. London: George Allen & Unwin, Ltd., 1962.
42. KEYSERLING, MARY D. *Windows on Day Care*. New York: National Council of Jewish Women, 1972.
43. KIRSHNER ASSOCIATES, INC. *A National Survey of the Impacts of Head Start*

Centers on Community Institutions, Summary Report. Washington, D.C.: U.S. Department of Health, Education, and Welfare, May 1970.

44. KUHLMANN, FRIEDA M. "Casework Supervision in the Day Nursery." *Child Welfare,* **34** (March 1955).

45. LANSBURGH, THERESE W. "Child Welfare—Day Care of Children," in *Encyclopedia of Social Work,* 16th Issue. Ed. by Robert Morris. New York: National Association of Social Workers, 1971.

46. LEWIS, LUCILE. "Strengths in Day-Care Licensing." *Child Welfare,* **38,** 6 (June 1959).

47. LOVATT, MARGARET. "Autistic Children in a Day Nursery." *Children,* **9** (May–June 1962).

48. LOW, SETH. *Licensed Day-Care Facilities for Children: A Report of a National Survey of Departments of State Governments Responsible for Licensing Day Care Facilities.* Washington, D.C.: Government Printing Office, 1962.

49. ———, and PEARL G. SPINDLER. *Child Care Arrangements of Working Mothers in the U.S. Children's Bureau, Publication 461–1968.* Washington, D.C.: Government Printing Office, 1968.

50. LYNDEN, PATRICIA. "What Does Day Care Mean to the Children, the Parents, the Teachers, the Community, the President?" *The New York Times Magazine* (February 15, 1970).

51. MERRIAM, ALICE H. "Day Care of the Young Child: A Community Challenge." *Child Welfare,* **38** (October 1959).

52. MOORE, WINIFRED A. "What Makes a Good Day-Care Licensing Law." *Child Welfare,* **37** (April 1958).

53. MOUSTAKAS, CLARK E., and MINNIE P. BENSON. *The Nursery School and Child-Care Center.* New York: William Morrow & Co., Inc., 1955.

54. NATIONAL ASSOCIATION FOR RETARDED CHILDREN. Leaflet DR741. New York, n.d.

55. NATIONAL MANPOWER COUNCIL. *Women Power.* New York: Columbia University Press, 1958.

56. ———. *Work in the Lives of Married Women.* New York: Columbia University Press, 1958.

57. NATIONAL SOCIETY FOR THE STUDY OF EDUCATION. *Preschool and Parental Education, 28th Yearbook.* Bloomington, Ind.: Public School Publishing Co., 1929.

58. OGBURN, WILLIAM, and MEYER NIMKOFF. *Technology and the Changing Family.* Boston: Houghton Mifflin Company, 1955.

59. PARKER, RONALD, and JANE KNITZER. "Background Paper on Day Care and Preschool Agencies: Trends in the 1960's and Issues for the 1970's." Background paper prepared for the 1970–71 White House Conference on Children and Youth Committee on Government Operations, U.S. Senate. Washington, D.C.: Government Printing Office, 1971.

60. POLLOCK, S. H. "Schools that Save Families—California Meets Need for Day Care of Children." *Nation's Business,* **4** (September 1952).

61. PRESCOTT, ELIZABETH, and ELIZABETH JONES. "Day Care for Children— Assets and Liabilities." *Children,* **18,** 2 (March–April 1971), 54–58.

62. RAPOPORT, LYDIA, and DONNA M. CORNSWEET. "Preventive Intervention

Potentials in Public Child Care Centers." *Child Welfare*, **48**, 1 (January 1969), 6–13.

63. RAWLEY, CALLMAN. "Casework and Day Care—Beginnings of a Municipal Program." *The Family*, **24** (March 1943).

64. RUDERMAN, FLORENCE A. *Child Care and the Working Mother: A Study of Arrangements Made for Daytime Care of Children*. New York: Child Welfare League of America, 1968.

65. SCHULTZE, CHARLES L., et al. *Setting National Priorities–The 1973 Budget*. Washington, D.C.: The Brookings Institution, 1972.

66. SELLIGMAN, AUGUSTA. "A Day Residential Program for the Disturbed Pre-School Child." *Child Welfare*, **37** (July 1958).

67. SHERIDAN, MARION L. "Family Day Care—For Children of Migrant Farm Workers." *Children*, **14**, 1 (January–February 1967), 13–18.

68. SHYNE, ANN W. *The Need for Foster Care*. New York: Child Welfare League of America, 1969.

69. SJOLUND, ARNE. *The Effect of Day Care Institutions on Children's Development—An Analysis of International Research*. Copenhagen: The Danish National Institute of Social Research, February 1971.

70. STARK, MARY. "Casework Service at Intake in a Day Nursery." *Journal of Social Casework*, **29**, 6 (June 1948).

71. STOLZ, LOIS M. "Effects of Maternal Employment on Children: Evidence from the Research." *Child Development*, **31** (1960).

72. THENAUD, AGNES. "Survey of Requests for Day Nursery Care with Reference to Post-war Planning." *Smith College Studies in Social Work*, **15** (1945).

73. TROUT, BESSIE, and DOROTHY E. BRADBURY. *Mothers for a Day. The Care of Children in Families Other Than Their Own*. Washington, D.C.: Government Printing Office, 1946.

74. UNITED NATIONS. "Day Care Services for Children." *International Social Service Review*, **1** (January 1956).

75. ———. *Mental Hygiene in the Nursery School*. New York: UNESCO, 1953.

76. U.S. DEPARTMENT OF HEALTH, EDUCATION, AND WELFARE. *Federal Interagency Day Care Requirements*. Washington, D.C.: Government Printing Office, September 1968.

77. ———, Social and Rehabilitation Service. *Children Served by Public Welfare Agencies and Voluntary Child Welfare Agencies and Institutions— March 1971*. Washington, D.C.: National Center for Social Statistics, March 1973.

78. ———. *Child Care Arrangements of AFDC Recipients Under the Work Incentive Program—Quarter Ended June 30, 1971*. Washington, D.C.: National Center for Social Statistics, February 1972.

79. ———. *Guide Specifications for Positions in Day Care Centers*. Washington, D.C.: Social and Rehabilitation Services, 1967.

80. U.S. DEPARTMENT OF LABOR. *Employed Mothers and Child Care*. Washington, D.C.: Government Printing Office, 1953.

81. ———. *Facts About Children—Working Mothers and Day Care Services in the United States, 1962*. Washington, D.C.: Government Printing Office, 1962.

82. ———. *Day-Care Services: Industries Involvement.* Bulletin 296–1971. Washington, D.C.: Government Printing Office, 1971.
83. ———. *Child Care Services Provided by Hospitals.* Bulletin 295. Washington, D.C.: Government Printing Office, 1970.
84. ———. *Day Care Facts.* Washington, D.C.: Government Printing Office.
85. ———. *Working Mothers and the Need for Child Care Services.* Washington, D.C.: Government Printing Office.
86. U.S. SENATE, COMMITTEE OF FINANCE. *Who Are the Working Mothers?* Washington, D.C.: Government Printing Office, 1972.
87. ———. *Child Care Data and Materials, June 16, 1971.* Washington, D.C.: Government Printing Office, 1971.
88. VOILAND, ALICE P. "Casework in a Day Nursery." *The Family,* **23** (May 1942).
89. WADE, CAMILLE. "The Family Day-Care Program in Milwaukee." *Child Welfare,* **49**, 6 (June 1970), 336–41.
90. WALDMAN, E., and K. R. GOVER. "Children of Women in the Labor Force." *Monthly Labor Review,* **94**, 7 (1971).
91. WESTINGHOUSE LEARNING CORPORATION AND WESTAT RESEARCH. *Day Care Survey 1970: Summary Report and Analysis.* Washington, D.C.: Evaluation Division, Office of Economic Opportunity, 1971.
92. WHITE, BENJAMIN, and ELLA BEATTIE. "Day Care for the Mentally Retarded as Part of Local Health Services in Maryland." *American Journal of Public Health,* **56**, 11 (November 1966).
93. WHITE HOUSE CONFERENCE ON CHILDREN. *Report to the President.* Washington, D.C.: Government Printing Office, 1971.
94. WILLNER, MILTON, "Unsupervised Family Day Care in New York City." *Child Welfare,* **43**, 6 (June 1969), 342–47.
95. ———. "Family Day Care: An Escape from Poverty." *Social Work,* **52**, 4 (April 1971), 30–35.
96. WORKS PROGRESS ADMINISTRATION. *Final Report on the WPA, 1935–43.* Washington, D.C.: Government Printing Office, 1944.
97. YEOMANS, ALFREDA. "The Role of the Caseworker." *Inside the Day Care Center.* New York: Child Welfare League of America, 1951.
98. ———. "Day Care—An Alternative to Placement Away from Home." *Child Welfare,* **32** (October 1953).
99. YUDKIN, SIMON, and ALTHEA HOLME. *Working Mothers and Their Children.* London: Michael Joseph Ltd., 1963.

9

Substitute Care:
Foster Family Care

Introduction

Foster family care, institutional care, and adoption involve substituting another family for the child's own family, so that someone else takes over all aspects of the parental role.

Such a drastic change is necessary when the child's own home presents deficiencies so serious that it cannot provide the child with minimally adequate social, emotional, and physical care. It involves, for the child, not only temporary total separation (except for visits) from his own family and adjustment to a new family, but also a change of location, a change of school, and a change of peer and sibling group.

Because of the pervasiveness of the change in the child's life, substitute care is regarded as the third line of defense in caring for the child. The stipulation that follows from the need to avoid such drastic social surgery is that every effort be made to keep the home intact for the child and to keep the child in the home.

Substitute care in foster family homes or institutions involves a change in legal custody of the child. Adoption involves going beyond a change in legal custody to a change in legal guardianship. Legal custody is concerned with the rights and duties of the person (usually the parent) having custody to provide for the child's daily needs—to feed him, clothe him, provide shelter, put him to bed, send him to school, see that he washes his face and brushes his teeth. It permits the person, or agency, having custody to determine where, and with whom, the child shall live. Consequently, the agency having legal custody of the child can move him from one foster home to another. But although the agency usually obtains legal custody in foster family care, the child still legally "belongs" to the parent and the parent retains guardianship. This means that, for some crucial aspects of the .child's life, the agency has no authority to act. Only the parent can consent to surgery for the child, or consent to his marriage, or permit his enlistment in the armed forces, or represent him at law. Only with a change of guardianship is the natural parents' tie to the child completely severed.

Actually, many long-term foster family placements become *de facto* adoptions. But the fact that legal guardianship of the child—actual legal ownership of the child—has not been transferred from the natural parents to the foster parents has very considerable implications for the nature of the relationship established between foster child and foster family, and it does permit the return of the child to his natural home at any time.

Definition

The term *foster care* is often applied to any type of substitute care facility—boarding home, adoptive home, or institution. However, the Child Welfare League of America's definition is: "A child welfare service which provides substitute family care for a planned period for a child when his own family cannot care for him for a temporary or extended period and when adoption is neither desirable nor possible." [22, p. 5]

Note that according to CWLA it is care in a *family*, it is noninstitutional substitute care, and it is for a *planned* period—either temporary or extended. This is unlike adoptive placement, which implies a *permanent* substitution of one home for another, one family for another. To distinguish this use of the term *foster care* from other kinds of foster care arrangements, we will refer to it in this chapter as *foster family care*.

Historical Background

Foster family care was probably practiced on a limited basis in antiquity. "Under ancient Jewish laws and customs, children lacking parental care became members of the household of other relatives, if such there were, who reared them for adult life." [162, p. 27]   The early Church boarded destitute children with "worthy widows."

Indenture was an early form of foster family care that was extensively employed. The Elizabethan Poor Laws provided for the apprenticing of dependent children until their twenty-first year. The master accepted the dependent child into his home, provided him with food, clothing, and the necessities of life, and accepted the responsibility for teaching him a craft or trade. In addition, provision was usually made for some extra payment in the form of clothes and/or money at the termination of the indenture. In return, the child was to work for the master around the house and in the craft or trade as an "employee." Indenture was recognized as a "business deal from which the person accepting a poor child on indenture was expected to receive from the child, a full equivalent in work for the expenses of his support, care and teaching." [171, p. 10]

This is set forth clearly in the following indenture contract:

By the Massachusetts indenture the selectmen of the township of Leicester bind Moses Love, a poor child two years and eight months old, to Matthew Scott until the boy shall become twenty-one years old, and dwell with as an apprentice during the term of eighteen years and four months (*viz.*) until he shall arrive to the age of twenty-one years—he being a poor child and his parents not being well able to support it. Dureing all which the sd apprentice his sd Master his heirs Execvtors & Adminrs shall faithfully serve at such Lawfull imployment & Labovr as he shall from time to time Dureing sd term be Capable of doing and performing & not absent himself from his or their service without Leave & In all things behave himself as a good & faithfull apprentice ought to do and the sd Matthew Scott for himself his heirs Execvtors & Adminrs do Couenant promise . . . that he the sd Matthew Scott his heirs Execvtors & Adminiss shall & will Dureing the term aforsd find and provide for the sd apprentice sufficient Cloathing meet drink Warshing and Lodging both in Sickness & in health & that he will teach him or cavse him to be tavght to read & write & siffer fiting his degree if he be Capable of Learning and at the Expiration of the term to Dismiss him with two suits of apparril one to be fitt for Lords day. [171, pp. 15–16]

The preamble of an eighteenth-century Maryland statute on indenture illustrates the relationship between indenture and the problem of child care.

Whereas, it has been found by experience that poor children, orphans, and illegitimate, for want of some efficient system have been left destitute of support and have become useless or depraved members of society; and, Whereas it would greatly conduce to the good of the public in general and of such children in particular that necessary instruction in trades and useful arts should be afforded them, therefore, the justices of the orphans' courts were authorized to bind out orphans, and such children as are suffering through the extreme indigence or poverty of their parents, also the children of beggars, and also illegitimate children, and the children of persons out of this state where a sufficient sustenance is not afforded. [15, p. 266]

Despite the fact that the indenture permitted all sorts of abuses and exploitation, that "it is morally certain that the experiences of indentured children varied all the way from that of being virtual slaves to that of being real foster sons or daughters," [171, p. 17], and that there was little guarantee of protection for the child other than public indignation or the foster parents' desire to keep the good opinion of their neighbors, indenture persisted in the United States until the first decade of the twentieth century. It did provide for many children a family life and at least the minimum of regular care.

A number of factors accounted for the gradual decline of the indenture as a means of foster family care. It was not always profitable for the foster family because children, if taken young, had to be supported for a period of time before they could make a return on their investment. With growing industrialization and the movement of crafts and trades out of the home, the idea of an apprenticeship located in the family became less feasible. But perhaps of greater importance was the impact on indenture of the abolition of slavery, after which it was hard to justify an indenture that required the apprehension and return to the master of a runaway apprentice and that had some of the characteristics of bondage arrangements. In fact, Folks notes: "It has been seriously suggested that, with the adoption of the Constitutional Amendment in 1865, forbidding 'involuntary servitude,' the indenture system became unconstitutional." [52, p. 42]

The real origin of modern foster family care lies with Charles Loring Brace and The Placing Out System of the New York Children's Aid Society. In the middle of the nineteenth century, New York City faced a problem of dealing with a large number of vagrant children who existed with minimal adult care, protection, and support. In 1849, the New York City Chief of Police called attention to the fact that

. . . there was a constantly increasing number of vagrant, idle, and vicious children of both sexes who infest our public thoroughfares, hotels, docks, etc., children who are growing up in ignorance and profligacy, only destined to a life of misery, shame, and crime and ultimately to a felon's doom. . . . Their number[s] are almost incredible and to those whose business and habits do not permit them a searching scrutiny, the degrading and disgusting practices of these almost infants in the school of vice, prostitution, and rowdyism, would certainly be beyond belief. [Quoted in 94, pp. 1–2]

At about this time the Chief of Police reported 10,000 vagrant children in New York City. [171, p. 97]

Brace, a young minister who became the first secretary of the New York Children's Aid Society upon its organization in 1853, developed a new and distinctive method of dealing with the problem presented by these children. The Society would "drain the city of these children by communicating with farmers, manufacturers, or families in the country who may have need of such for employment." The appeal was to Christian charity and to the need for labor on the farms. It involved relocating children from the pernicious influences of urban areas, where there was little for them to do, to rural areas, where there was much for them to do and where the environment was regarded as morally sounder. There evolved a particular program of group emigration and placement technique that resulted in finding foster family care in free foster family homes for about 100,000 children between 1854 and 1929. [94, p. 27]

The procedure was first to collect a group of children in New York City. Many of the children were known to be orphans; some had been abandoned so that the status of their parents was unknown. But many of the children were half-orphans or children with both parents living. In the latter cases, an attempt was made to obtain parental consent to the child's relocation. The largest numbers were provided by institutions in the city, but the Society's agents also had responsibility for locating vagrant, uncared-for children. As Folks says, "The children were received from the newsboys' lodging houses, from orphan and infant asylums, and directly from the parents." [52, p. 67]

In forming the group, some effort was made to eliminate the physically ill, the mentally handicapped, and the incorrigible. After a group was formed, the children set out for the West or South in the company of one of the Society's workers. The community to which the children were to be sent was encouraged by the Society to set up a committee of prominent citizens. The committee had the responsibility of arranging temporary care for the children upon their arrival. Of greater importance was the committee's responsibility to publicize the coming of the children, to encourage families to take them in, and to evaluate the suitability of those who indicated interest. Upon the arrival in town of the group of children, arrangements were made for their distribution to homes in accordance with the preliminary work done by the local committee.

A report by a pioneer child welfare worker, Dr. Hastings Hart, to the National Conference of Charities and Corrections in 1884 describes the "placement" procedure:

I was a witness of the distribution of forty children in————County, Minnesota. . . . The children arrived at about half-past three P.M.

and were taken directly from the train to the Court House, where a large crowd was gathered. Mr. Matthews set the children, one by one, before the company, and in his stentorian voice gave a brief account of each. Applicants for children were then admitted in order behind the railing and rapidly made their selection. Then, if the child gave assent, the bargain was concluded on the spot. It was a pathetic sight, not soon to be forgotten, to see those children, tired young people, weary, travel-strained, confused by the excitement and the unwonted surroundings, peering into those strange faces, and trying to choose wisely for themselves. And it was surprising how many happy selections were made under such circumstances. In a little more than three hours nearly all those forty children were disposed of. Some who had not previously applied selected children. There was little time for consultation, and refusal would be embarrassing; and I know that the Committee consented to some assignments against their better judgment.

The Committee usually consists of a minister, an editor, and a doctor, lawyer, or a businessman. The merchant dislikes to offend a customer, or the doctor a patient, and the minister fears to have it thought that his refusal is because the applicant does not belong to his church. Thus unsuitable applications sometimes succeed. Committee men and officers of the Society complain of this difficulty. The evil is proved by the fact that, while the younger children are taken from motives of benevolence and are uniformly well treated, the older ones are, in the majority of cases, taken from motives of profit, and are expected to earn their way from the start. [70]

Although it did not involve a formal contractual arrangement, and the Society retained control of the child's custody and could remove the child if it was felt that he was being unfairly treated, the free foster family arrangement was still based on the exchange of child labor for child care. As Thurston says in summarizing the program, "It is the wolf of the old indenture philosophy of child labor in the sheepskin disguise of a so-called good or Christian home." [171, p. 136]

Factors contributing to the decline of this procedure were the opposition of Western states to the "extraditing" and "dumping" of dependent children in their area, the opposition of the Catholic Church to what was regarded as an attempt by a Protestant organization to wean children from their Catholic heritage by their placement in non-Catholic homes, the decline in the number of orphans, and the closing of the frontier which reduced the need for such labor as the "emigrant" children could profitably provide. Of considerable influence in effecting a decline in the program was the increasing criticism by the growing number of child welfare professionals. The proceedings of the Annual National

Conference of Charities and Corrections frequently included attacks on the dangers involved in the method of selecting free foster homes for children and the looseness and infrequency of supervision following placement. Although Brace sought to meet these attacks by reports of "research" by agency workers indicating that only a limited number of children were maltreated or turned out poorly, the criticism was never adequately met. The data of much of Brace's research leave much to be desired in terms of their objectivity, the nature of sampling methods employed, and the somewhat haphazard way in which they were obtained. The distances over which the Society operated, and the limited number of workers employed, precluded any careful selection or supervision of homes.

The first annual report of the Massachusetts State Board of Charities states the core of the problem succinctly.

> As a general rule, the persons who now take children into their
> families from the State institutions do so primarily for their
> own advantage, and only secondarily, if at all, for the good of
> the child; but it frequently happens that the child who was taken
> as a servant secures a place in the affections of the family taking
> him, and so the connection ceases to be a mercenary one. These cases,
> however, do not form the rule, it is to be feared.

The system exacted a price from natural parents as well. "Placing out" at a distance meant a kind of pseudoadoption, and the intent actually was to prevent the return of the child to his own home—this, despite the fact that a considerable number of such children did have two living parents. As Thurston notes, "It does not seem fair to the relatives that they be compelled to surrender a child permanently in order to get whatever care he may need temporarily." [171, p. 135]

Before a change took place, however, the program stimulated the development of similar programs of foster family placement in free homes by organizations established to do this within particular states. Such State Children's Home Societies, as they were called, originated with the work of Martin Van Buren Van Arsdale in 1883 in Indiana and Illinois. (Van Arsdale, like Brace, was a minister.) The purpose of the State Children's Home Societies was

> . . . to seek the homeless, neglected, and destitute children and to
> become their friend and protector, to find homes for them in
> well-to-do families and to place them wisely; to look occasionally
> with discretion into the homes, and thus prevent abuse and
> neglect, and to replace children, when necessary; to make it possible
> for persons (without children of their own) to adopt a child; to
> minister, in comforting assurance to parents in fear of leaving their

children penniless and homeless; to protect society by guaranteeing proper home training and education to the unfortunate little ones against its greatest enemies, ignorance and vice; to extend our organization into sister states. [Quoted in 171, p. 156]

By 1923 there were thirty-four states in which such State Children's Home Societies had been established. The activities of these agencies were, and continue to be, supplemented by sectarian agencies in larger cities, such as the Jewish Child Care Association in New York City and nonsectarian agencies such as the Boston Children's Aid Society.

At the same time the public agencies were pioneering other alternatives. The Michigan State Public School (in reality an orphanage) opened in 1874; it was created to be a temporary home for all destitute children who had become public charges, until the children could be placed in foster family homes. Some nineteen other states soon adopted the same plan.

In the late 1860's, Massachusetts pioneered in paying board money to foster families for the maintenance of children who might otherwise have been placed in institutions and who were too young to be profitably indentured. This state also pioneered in more careful supervision of those children who had been indentured by the state.

The Boston Children's Aid Society, under the leadership of Charles Birtwell between 1886 and 1911, carried foster family care a step further. For each child, Birtwell asked, "What does the child really need?" rather than "Where shall we put the child?" The aim, Birtwell said, "will be in each instance to suit the action to the real need, heeding the teachings of experience, still to study the conditions with a freedom from assumptions and a directness and freshness of view as complete as though the case in hand stood absolutely alone." [171, p. 200] This required individual study of the child and a variety of different kinds of substitute care—an individualization of need and diversification of services. Such a procedure, when followed, might mean that no substitute service would, indeed, be offered. The study might show that, with some help, the child could be maintained in his own home. Birtwell showed an appreciation of the potentialities of the preventative placement aspects of supportive and supplementary services. Until such an approach gained acceptance, as it did following its affirmation by the First White House Conference on Children in 1909, foster family care was offered to "rescue" the child from his family.

For Brace, the long-time placement suggested that the foster parent was, in fact, replacing the natural parent in a pseudoadoptive situation. Given Birtwell's approach, the foster parent-foster child relationship becomes something distinctively different—a means through which the child is ultimately restored to his parents.

Birtwell developed a systematic plan for studying foster home applicant families and a systematic plan of supervision once the child was placed. An effort was made to keep detailed records and to develop principles of action. He was, in effect, attempting to build a science of foster family care and to professionalize practice.

These ideas resulted in a changed emphasis in foster family care. Brace and Van Arsdale depended primarily on free foster homes, which meant that the agency did not pay any of the cost of boarding the child; the expense was assumed by the foster home. The gradual acceptance of boarding foster family care, in which the agency pays for the support of the child, gave the agency greater freedom in selection and less discomfort in closer supervision of the home. A greater acceptance of the need to individualize the child led to a diversification of foster care facilities and less exclusive reliance on the free foster family home. Furthermore, the growing recognition of foster family care as a temporary substitute care facility, an interim provision while the child's own home was being reorganized to reaccept him, meant that the agency worked to keep intact the relationship between the child and the natural parents.

The history of substitute care in institutions and that of substitute care in foster family homes are interrelated. The mixed almshouses (see Chapter 11) were at one time a frequently employed resource for the institutional care of children. When, toward the end of the nineteenth century, one state after another began to pass laws prohibiting the use of mixed almshouses for children, they recommended that such children be placed in foster homes instead. Thus the closing of mixed almshouses for children increased the tendency to resort to foster family care. [52, pp. 74–80]

Orphanages frequently used foster family care as a supplementary resource both in the early years of the life of the child, and then again as the child moved toward greater independence. In taking responsibility for infants, before the advent of pasteurized milk and formula feeding, the institution had to provide nursing care. Consequently, orphanages would often place the infant in a foster family for wet-nursing.

When the child reached early adolescence, the institutions, in preparing the child for independence, once again placed the children in foster family homes. As Slingerland says, "All child-caring institutions must at some age dismiss their wards and the usual method when that age arrives is to obtain a place for a child in a private home as an accepted inmate or paid worker before withdrawing institutional care and support." [162, p. 39]

Throughout the nineteenth century and the early part of the twentieth century controversy raged between the advocates of institutional care and the supporters of foster family care over which was the more desirable method. Foster family care was given official sanction in 1899 by the National Conference of Correction and Charities. At that meeting, a report was presented by J. M. Mulrey in behalf of a special committee of prominent child welfare workers appointed to study the problems of the dependent child and to make recommendations. The report adopted by the Conference stated that, when a child needed substitute care, consideration should first be given to a foster family arrangement. [118, p. 167] The First White House Conference on Children in 1909 stated that "the carefully selected foster home is, for the normal child, the best substitute for the natural home." Thus foster family care was given a clear preference.

It might be noted that the history of foster care echoes with the cry that has accompanied many child welfare innovations. The contention was that providing adequate substitute care for the child would encourage parents to desert or neglect their children since they need not feel guilty that their dereliction would deprive the child of care. As a matter of fact it was argued that some poor parents would feel it their duty to desert the child in order that he might be given more adequate care in a foster family home. [54, p. 10]

Scope

In March 1971 some 266,000 children were in foster families or foster family group homes under the auspices of public and voluntary agencies. [178, Table 8] Relatively few (6000 children, 2.3 percent) were in group homes; most were in foster family homes under state or local public welfare agency auspices. Voluntary agencies were responsible for only (15 percent) of the placements. [178] The rate of children in substitute care of all kinds had declined sharply after the passage of the Social Security Act in 1935, a confirmation of the potency of the social insurance and public assistance programs in maintaining children in their own homes. There has been a recent increase as a result of increases in family disruption from all causes. (see Table 9–1).

TABLE 9–1. Children in Foster Family Care and in Child Welfare Institutions for the Neglected, Dependent, and Emotionally Disturbed

Year	Children in Substitute Care (rate per 1000 children)	Children in Foster Family Care (rate per 1000 children)	Children in Institutions (rate per 1000 children)
1933	5.9	2.5	3.4
1960	3.7	2.4	1.3
1965	4.0	2.9	1.1
1969	4.5		
1975 (projected)	4.7	3.9	0.8

Along with changing trends of the rate of children in substitute care, there has been an accompanying long-term trend in differential use of foster family care and the child-care institution for those children needing substitute care.

Table 9–1 notes both the changing rate of children in substitute care and the changing proportionate use of foster family care and child-care institutions. It is estimated that if current gradually increasing levels of need for substitute care are sustained and if the current relative distribution of children between institution and foster family care continues, by 1975 some 300,000 children will be living in foster family care, the rate being 3.9 per 1000 children.

Situations for Which Foster Family Care Is an Appropriate Resource

Foster family care is appropriate when the child's own parents are unable and/or unwilling to care for the child at home, even when supplementary services—income maintenance, day care, and homemaker service—are made available.

Several recent studies have attempted to determine the reasons which prompt the need for foster family care. [65; 144; 160] In one study, interviews were held with the families of all the children who had come into foster family care during a four-month period in 1963. [144] In another, all requests for foster care received over a three-month period by all the child-care agencies in seven selected cities in 1966 were reviewed in detail. [160] The "principal reasons" for the request for placement fell into two major groups: (1) child-related difficulties ("child's physical handicap," "child's mental retardation," "child's socially deviant behavior," "child's emotional disturbance"); (2) parent-related difficulties ("death or desertion," "divorce of parents," "physical and/or mental illness of parent," "neglect," "abuse," "inadequate financial resources").

The largest percentage of children required foster care because of parent-related difficulties, and physical or mental illness of the mother was the most frequently cited reason. The precipitating situation, such as the mother's illness, obtained its potency for requiring placement of the child because, in most instances, the underlying family situation was highly problematic. Family disruption, marginal economic circumstances, and poor health consistently emerge as factors associated with the need for foster family placement. "Although it is usually a specific crisis that brings children into social agency foster care, during the year prior to placement these families, by and large, were functioning marginally and had experienced difficulties so severe that it might have been anticipated that further stress could not be tolerated." [144, p. 111] "The over-all picture of the retrospective year prior to placement shows marginal families without sufficient resources to sustain themselves in the community when additional pressures or problems are added to their pre-existing burdens." [144, p. 61].

A disproportionate number of families were one-parent families, nonwhite, and on public assistance. [144, pp. 12, 14; 160, pp. 29, 41; see also 140, pp. 18–19] The most vulnerable group, then, is likely to be composed of black children living "with mother only" on a poverty-level income.

The precipitating problem in the context of a deprived structural and economic family situation could not be solved by mobilization of any resources available to the family: neither friends nor relatives were available who were willing and able to care for the children.

Some typical statements of parent-related placement situations follow:

I felt very tired and sick, and I went to a hospital in my neighborhood where they told me I need to be hospitalized immediately since I had hepatitis. I told them I had no one to take care of my children and the doctor took me to Social Service, and the children were placed. I have no friends here in New York, and the only one to take care of my children was my mother-in-law and she was in Puerto Rico. [144, p. 82]

I had a nervous breakdown and I knew I was not myself. I asked my neighbors to call the police because I was so nervous and confused. My vision was blurred. I could not touch anything that was not colored blue. I was not paying attention to the baby. I would feel sad for long periods of time. My sister committed suicide four years ago, so when I began not to feel myself I got help. The police came for the baby. [144, p. 104]

My wife became mentally ill after the baby was born in March, and went into [a city hospital] for two weeks, and then into [a state hospital]. Relatives cared for the children for a while, but I had trouble with them because they didn't take good care of the children. I had to do it myself, and I cared for them one and one-half months, but I couldn't continue so I went to the police, who sent me to the Welfare Department. They put the children in homes. My wife came out of the hospital two weeks ago and she's going to a clinic. The children will come home as soon as the clinic says she is well enough to take care of them. [144, p. 119]

The mother was going out a lot to beer gardens, leaving the children alone most of the time, neglecting them. She would stay

out all night. The Court investigated the house; they found the
place filthy and just terrible and then decided it wasn't livable
for the children. The mother didn't care for them. All the kids ate
was canned food, crackers, pretzels and stuff like that. They didn't
eat good food. They were left alone and not given affection. [144,
p. 156]

There was lots of fighting between the parents. The father beat
the children in the head. He fought with the mother because
she would not clean the house, fix food for the children, or generally
care for them. She was always out in the streets. [144, p. 143]

The families requiring foster family care because of child-related
problems came from a wider range of socioeconomic backgrounds, were
more apt to be intact, and were more apt to be white. Requests for placement because of child-related reasons constituted a smaller percentage of
requests (15–20 percent) and were more likely to result in an offer of
institutional care rather than in an offer of foster family care. The child's
behavior had exhausted the emotional resources of the family; other
relatives were unwilling to undertake the burden of care of such a child;
and the cost of private treatment was beyond the family's capacity.

Referrals come from a variety of sources and are related to the nature
of the difficulty. The most frequent initiators of foster care are the
parents themselves and/or close relatives in instances of parents'
physical or mental illness or inability to care for the child because of
social stress, and when the child's behavior makes it difficult for him to
live at home. The police and the courts initiate placement in cases of
neglect and/or abuse.

The nature of foster family care suggests that it is a feasible resource
for the child who has the capacity to participate in, and contribute to,
normal family living. Such care would be inappropriate in the following
cases:

1. When a child presents problems of behavior that would not be
   tolerated in the community, or when he presents problems of behavior that militate against his living in a family group.
2. In the case of a child whose handicap requires some special care
   and/or training beyond that which can be offered by the family or
   the community.
3. When the natural parents are persistent in their objections to the
   child's care in a foster family. The objection may be based on the
   threat of another family succeeding where they have failed; the insti-
   tion is sufficiently different from the normal family setup so as to pose
   less of a threat to such parents.
4. Similarly, when a child is very much threatened by the divided loyalty

to parental figures that is engendered in his placement in another family.

5. When it is desirable to keep a large group of siblings together, and finding a foster family willing to take such a group is unlikely, or when substitute care is necessary for a very limited emergency period.

The present feeling is that all children under six requiring substitute care should be offered foster family care. The need for continuous close mothering supposedly dictates this. On the other hand, foster family care is less desirable for the adolescent. Here the demands made by such care for integration into a foster family conflict with one of the significant developmental tasks of adolescence—achieving independence from the family group. Placement of children of this age in a more impersonal setting might be advisable.

Available studies reveal that some placements might have been averted if appropriate kinds of supportive and supplementary services had been available. For instance, one study noted that 53 percent of the placements were unavoidable but that, in the judgment of the caseworker, 17 percent might have been avoided if more adequate homemaker service or day care or income supplementation had been available. [144, p. 185; see also 160, p. 48] However, there is a residual group who would still need placement if even the best and most adequate of such services were available. The following situations illustrate the need to go beyond supportive and supplementary services to the use of substitute care services:

A mother and father were referred by a family service agency for the placement of their ten-year-old son. They had been pressed into requesting help at the family service agency by the school because of the child's chronic school problems, which dated back to kindergarten. He was withdrawn, could not be motivated to learn, was unable to concentrate, and had poor relationships with teachers, who found him unresponsive to any approach. His other problems included unrealistic fears, hoarding, nightmares, wandering away from home, stealing, inability to make friends, thumb-sucking—all of which dated back to preschool years. The parents, in treatment at the family agency for a year, had made no progress. [92, p. 175]

The need for protective care of four children was reported by a visiting nurse. The children were ill, undernourished, and dirty; they foraged for food in the neighborhood, and they were not sent to school. The mother appeared to be mentally ill, sitting and staring into space as these conditions surrounded her. The father, employed as a garbage collector, was away during the day.

His own mental and emotional condition was such that he did not perceive that there was anything seriously wrong in his home. The extent of his disturbance precluded the use of homemaker service. [92, p. 169]

A divorced mother applied to an agency for placement of two preschool children. Although she worked as a secretary and was able to manage her job successfully, she felt overwhelmed and incapable of caring for the children. The five-year-old boy had developed problems of extreme self-destructiveness, emotional isolation, and nightmares. The day-care center refused to continue his care. The three-year-old boy reacted to the day-care arrangement with increasing anxiety and resistance to habit training for bowel and bladder control. The mother had secured personal psycho-therapy in a clinic, but her problems were found to be too pervasive and deeply entrenched in her character for modification on a short-term basis. [92, p. 174]

The standards set by The Child Welfare League of America indicate that foster care is not appropriate when it is used only because supportive and/or supplemental resources are not available. [22]

Recruitment, Assessment, and Selection of Foster Family Homes

The essential resource of the program is, of course, the foster home. Such homes have to be recruited, assessed, and ultimately selected for a particular child. A great deal of agency work is devoted to each of these steps in the process.

Recruitment

Recruitment involves a program of interpretation to the public of the need for foster homes for children and the satisfactions to be derived from fostering a child. All mass communication media have been used by agencies in recruitment efforts—newspaper ads, radio, television, billboards, placards in buses and subway trains. On occasion, such advertisements have been supplemented by making speakers available to church groups, PTA groups, women's clubs, and so on. Experienced foster parents are asked to participate in campaigns and are asked to speak to local groups. They are effective recruiters, and they are apt to convey a realistic conception of foster care.

Such activity is reinforced by visible enhancement of the symbol of the foster parent. The mayor proclaims a Foster Parent Week, and an award is given to a couple selected as the Foster Parents of the Year. All of this develops a "climate of awareness" of the need for foster parents in the community.

The literature on foster family recruitment suggests, however, that continuous rather than sporadic, intense recruitment drives yield the best results. Some larger child welfare agencies have their own central home-finding department with special workers assigned to this task. In other agencies all workers take responsibility for finding and evaluating foster homes. And usually, for greater effectiveness, several agencies in a community conduct their recruitment efforts jointly. In fact, some communities have developed a central home-finding service under the aegis of the community welfare council. [132]

The following is the text of a typical pamphlet distributed through the community by the central home-finding service of one community:

Home and family, warmth, and the joy of sharing . . . things that are commonplace to most of us are rare in the experience of these children. These things that provide the foundation for future good citizenship have been denied them, and instead they have come to know rejection and misunderstanding, loneliness, and insecurity. . . . The love and care they find in a foster home can help set their lives right and start them toward healthy, productive adulthood.

What Are the Children Like?

The children are of all ages, from infants to teenagers up to eighteen years. Some are quiet, some talkative, some shy, others are mischievous or a bit rebellious. They are of many nationality backgrounds, races, and religious faiths. Some have special needs because of emotional problems or physical disabilities. Otherwise, they are like any other group of average children, with this one exception: they have no home. In facing the many problems of growing up, they are without the love and guidance and example usually provided by parents in a normal home.

What Does It Take to Be a Good Foster Parent?

You need not be wealthy or own your own home. You should have a steady income. You and your family should be in good health and able to provide normal family and community life. But there's more than providing good food, physical care and wholesome surroundings. While the foster parents provide something which the natural parents cannot, the foster child will not be their child. The agency, the courts, and the natural parents retain certain rights. Giving and receiving love, no relationship will ever draw more heavily on your capacity for kindness, patience, flexibility, and sense of humor. Nor will any relationship provide richer rewards.

Will I Get Any Help?

Of course. Throughout the time when the child is in your home, you will be in partnership with the agency. All costs of board, clothing, medical and dental care, and any special aids or services will be paid for by the agency. A trained social worker who is acquainted with the child, his background and needs, will work with you, answering questions and meeting problems as they may arise. The worker's goal, like yours, will be to help the child over the rough spots in his disrupted young world.

What Do I Do Next?

The need for foster homes is urgent and immediate. If you would like to explore further the possibility of becoming a foster parent, please contact the Central Homefinding Service. There is no obligation, and your phone call or letter will mean only that you have questions which have not been answered. May we hear from you soon? (Central Homefinding Service, Madison, Wis.)

Studies of the outcome of foster care recruitment show a great attrition rate among the families that express initial interest. The largest percentage of those who inquire about foster care withdraw voluntarily; a smaller percentage are rejected often for very clear and unambiguous reasons such as overage or poor health. Often less than 10 percent of the original group are licensed, and very rarely more than 20 percent. [27; 29; 34; 56; 125; 180]

In one instance a special television program on foster care in Chicago, "The Children Are Waiting," provided viewers with a battery of fifty phones manned by volunteers ready to accept inquiries following the telecast. Some 5850 people called in response to the program to inquire about foster care, but fewer than 500 families were recruited.

Agency refusal is, in most instances, not the main factor in attrition. Why do so few apply, and why do so many withdraw their applications? Interviews with a randomly selected sample of one hundred people in St. Louis regarding their attitude toward foster care indicated that many people did not "perceive" the agency's publicized need for foster families. There was little prior interest in fostering, so the publicity was largely ignored. Outside employment competes with foster care as a possible satisfying activity for women with limited or no child-care responsibilities, for in 40 percent of the families interviewed the woman was employed outside the home. Also, many of the respondents just did not want to offer a home to a foster child—and not entirely because of selfishness. The researcher, Dick, says:

> Perhaps the equilibrium of these people's lives, the solidarity of the family and the satisfactions achieved in it, outweigh the factors that might lead them to want to board a child. Herein may lie the dilemma of the agencies. The people with the best potential for foster parenthood are the hardest to motivate. [36, p. 50]

Wakeford's study of foster parents in England suggests that motivation is related to class differences regarding the role of mother. [181] Interviews with sixty-six foster parents and a group of 148 controls selected at random from among nonfostering married couples showed that foster families had significantly fewer children of their own and were more likely to be headed by unskilled or semiskilled laborers. Even when class level is held constant, the foster mother "spends less time shopping, less in social organizations, and given an extra free hour each day would be more likely to spend it in the home." [181, p. 340]   There was a clear-cut preference, on the part of foster mothers, for more children. Wakeford concludes that the relationship between socioeconomic class and foster parenthood is not related to income, but to the higher value and prestige accorded the maternal role in working-class families. The foster mother accepts fostering "as an alternative to maximizing income" by working outside the home. "She is more family-oriented than average. She values the home; there she finds most of her satisfactions and employs most of her skills. There she is in her element." This preference is reinforced by the working-class setting, which offers the mother fewer alternative sources of prestige than are available to her middle-class sister. The working-class mother needs children to give significance to the one role that is given prestige according to working-class standards. If she has fewer than an average number of children, and foster mothers had smaller families than average, she can add to their number by fostering. Foster parenthood thus primarily fills a sociopsychological need rather than an economic one.

Both Fanshel and Babcock found, in their detailed studies, that many of the foster mothers came from families with many children, had highly developed homemaking skills, and were positively oriented toward child care and home-centered activities. [6; 42]   Babcock notes that foster mothers "regarded the role of mothering as a main task in life, a task they expect to enjoy." [6, p. 373]   They had little interest in a paid job outside the home, and, in general, tended to disapprove of women working.

Clinical case histories suggested a variety of psychological motives for foster parenthood:

1. It is an alternative to adoption for people who may want the experience of raising a child but cannot adopt one.
2. It provides a "replacement" for a child who has died.
3. It furnishes a companion for their child, when they cannot have, or do not want, additional children of their own.
4. It manifests compassion for children in need.
5. It is attempted compensation for a denied or unsatisfactory relationship. Thus one foster father said that "he thought he was acting out the role of a father that he himself had missed," and another woman was interested in taking a foster child so as to develop the mother-daughter relationship she herself had missed. [60, p. 215]
6. It fulfills the desire to repeat the happy relationship they had with their own (now grown) children.
7. It fulfills a masochistic need to make restitution for having given their own parents "a difficult time."
8. It fulfills a need to seek a second, and perhaps more successful, parental experience after having failed, in some way, in rearing their own children.
9. It results from a frank desire to augment family income, when the wife is reluctant to work outside the home, or has no readily employable skills, or feels that the satisfactions of child care are greater than any possible satisfactions she might derive from any other job.

The idea for foster family care generally originates with the foster mother and is generally engaged in to satisfy her needs. For the foster fathers, "pleasing their wives rather than satisfying pressing internal needs was an important element in the decision of these men to become foster parents." [42, p. 156]   Satisfaction for the father in providing a masculine model for the foster child is also a prominent theme. [33]

The question of motivation becomes even more complex when we recognize that children of different ages may appeal to different patterns of motivation. This is confirmed by Fanshel's study, based on interviews with 101 foster couples, data derived from the Parent Attitude Research Instrument (PARI), and ratings by social workers. [40]   "A rather basic dichotomy appeared in the study between those foster parents who cared primarily for infants and those who cared for older children": those who cared for infants were more oriented to private gratifications ("enjoying the presence of a cuddly baby in our home"; "I like the affection I get from children"); those who took older children were oriented toward social gratifications ("knowing I am doing something useful for the community"; "I like helping the unfortunate, downtrodden people"). [41, p. 18]

The readiness to accept a child for foster family care is likely to stem from multiple reasons. Furthermore, a motive that is inappropriate in one family may, expressed somewhat differently, have positive implications in another. Josselyn points this out very clearly in a cogent analysis of the implications of motives for foster family care. [85] Even the desire to find a "replacement" or companion for one's own child does not necessarily imply failure. A study by Jenkins of ninety-seven foster homes showed that parents expressing these motives were frequently successful. [78, p. 212] "It is unrealistic to expect to find many foster homes free from neurotic motivations and needs since the seeking of a child is usually to some degree the family's way of solving a conscious or unconscious problem." [107, p. 14] You will recall that Dick, in his study of attitudes toward fostering, concluded that people whose needs were generally fulfilled are not likely to be interested in becoming foster parents. [36]

This suggests that applicants respond to the agencies' appeal out of some need of their own. "In the wish to serve there is the need to serve." This in no way implies a derogation of foster parents' readiness to accept a child or their capacity to do a good job. If their needs are complementary to those of the child, they can be, in fact, the best kind of foster parents. It does indicate, as is true for all behavior, that only those people who anticipate some compensation—emotional, social, or economic—will be prompted to apply for foster parenthood.

Requirements for foster parents may legitimately differ from those for adoptive parents. There need be less concern with the age and income of foster parents than is true for adoptive parents. Foster parents are generally recruited from upper-lower- or lower-middle-class groups, are frequently blue-collar workers, and are generally older than the child's biological parents. Foster parents may be capable of accepting and loving only children of a particular age. (This would pose a problem for adoptive care where the need to love the child through all stages of development is necessary.) Foster parents must be able to use an ongoing relationship with the agency. (The adoptive parent-agency relationship is terminal.) Foster parents must be able to accept the child into the family and to adjust to the loss of the child when he leaves.

Assessment

The agency has the grave responsibility of finding the best possible substitute home for the child needing care. A detailed study of all applicants is necessary not only because the agency feels an ethical and professional responsibility to children and their natural parents, but also because it has a legal responsibility to the community. Foster homes are licensed in most states and the agency must certify that the home meets the license requirements.

Some preliminary screening and selection usually proceeds on the basis of objective criteria outlined in state licensing standards. The state normally requires that there be both a father and a mother in the home, that they be young enough and healthy enough to provide adequate care, and that they have an income adequate to meet their needs. It also stipulates that the home must provide adequate space for the child, that it must meet adequate sanitary and safety standards, and that it must be located in a community that offers adequate school, health, church, and recreational facilities. Preliminary investigation indicates whether or not the family can meet these basic requirements.

The more difficult aspects of assessment involve the socioemotional factors that are thought to be desirable in a foster home. These are assessed on the basis of a series of interviews with the prospective foster parents, conducted both in the office and in the home. If there are children in the home, some effort is made to obtain their reaction to the parents' plan to accept foster children. An effort is also made to determine the origin of the applicants' interest in foster care, their expectations concerning foster care, and their experience as parents or (if childless) with children generally. Also of interest are the satisfactions and problems they experienced in rearing their own children and the ways in which the introduction of a foster child might require modification in their child-rearing practices, the developmental history of both husband and wife, the history of their marriage and current marital interaction, the changes they anticipate in the organization of the home and in the interpersonal relationships of family members as a result of the introduction of another child, and their preferences in foster children.

The social worker also explores with the applicants their attitudes regarding visits by the child's natural parents, their attitude toward parents who place their children in substitute care, their probable reaction to the child's eventual departure. And, because the agency has a continuing responsibility for the child, some attempt is made to assess the applicant's willingness to work cooperatively with the agency.

The assessment is designed to inform the applicant about the agency, as well as to inform the agency about the applicant. The applicant is given the opportunity of assessing foster care so that he may decide whether or not he wants it. After learning what is involved in becoming a foster parent, some applicants voluntarily withdraw.

Foster family care poses a paradox for the applicant. The foster family must want a child very much in order to be motivated to engage in foster family care, yet they must feel comfortable in giving up the child placed with them. Not only does the foster parent have to accept the possibility of removal of the child, but he is asked by the agency to participate in a plan that would ensure the probability of the child's removal. One applicant who failed to follow through said, "I saw those lovely babies and when she [the agency worker] told us they did not have a home my heart sort of went out but I am afraid I would get so attached and then they would be moved out to another place again." [34, p. 46]

In addition to the interviews and home visits, agencies ask for and contact references provided by the applicant in aiding the worker to make a decision. The agency's image of the "good" foster parent, used as a generalized standard against which the qualifications of applicants are assessed, has been explicated by Wolins. [187]   A form was devised that included such statements about family functioning as the following: "Children should be allowed to disagree with their parents"; "You have to punish a child to teach him things"; "If you can help it, it's better to have few, if any, strangers come into the house." These forms were given to 343 workers in the county welfare department of three states. The workers were asked to fill out the forms as they imagined the "best" foster couple and then again as the "poorest" foster couple might. Although the results do not indicate what the foster parents are actually like (as has been pointed out in a critical analysis of the research [106]), it does reveal the attitudes the worker associates with the desirable foster parent.

> The workers' projection revealed their image of the good foster family to be a product of the Protestant ethic, substantially modified by Freudian psychology and nineteenth-century humanism. Rationalism and planfulness are important in this family; so are fatherly bossiness and some motherly possessiveness. The mother appears as something of a martyr for her children. Both parents consider it reasonable to proceed in accordance with planned objectives that are not very different from the aspirations of their neighbors. These are reflected in substantial occupational and educational achievement, in the possession of "two or three" children, and in relatively low residential mobility. Along with these nineteenth-century, middle-class virtues, which in themselves seem rather cold and harsh, a good lacing of friendliness appears in the image. It rejects authoritarianism in child rearing and the family is seen as open to strangers and visitors. In family relationships, especially those pertaining to child rearing, the psychologies of interpersonal adjustment have had their impact. Individualization of the child and moderate (and feasible) parental ambitions for him are their primary legacy. . . .
>
> The family we have been describing very much resembles the current general image of an average American middle-class family. Perhaps the workers' good foster family is a somewhat better adjusted family; it is a less conforming family than usual, but all in all it is a planful family with achievement expectations for children, a family in which there is a balance between respect for discipline and appreciation of flexibility and individuality. [187, pp. 97–99]

Wolins took the research one step further by testing the extent to which the image actually influenced decisions about applicants. He tested the image against a group of 1649 foster parents already in the program and a group of 907 prospective foster parents whose applications were pending. The principal finding was that, although the image was clear and consistent, it was not being applied. The foster parents selected did not necessarily conform to the image, and the discrepancy seemed to be widest in those counties where demand for foster homes was greatest. In other words, the balance of supply and demand tends to modify application of the "image."

Another factor seemed to be operating: the worker tended to select applicants who were similar to himself. This tendency, which in the Wolins study is dubiously supported by the data, receives some confirmation in a study done by Dingman, which indicates that foster families rated as "good" by the social workers were those whose attitudes were similar to the attitudes held by the social workers. [37]

In empirically studying assessment of foster parents in England, George found considerable disparity between the theory and practice. Despite the great concern with personality factors as criteria, "there was nothing in the [agency] reports to justify the conclusion that the applicant's character structure was investigated, objectively assessed, and its relationship to the proposed foster child examined." [54, p. 115] Reports by trained as well as untrained workers were highly impressionistic, but without any specific evidence offered in substantiation of the impressions.

Another approach to developing valid criteria for assessment lies in attempting to study the factors that distinguish the "successful" foster parent from the less successful one, or that distinguish the accepted applicant from the rejected applicant.

Etni asked workers in a large New York City agency to designate the "best" and the "worst" foster parents in their caseloads. [26, p. 47] The findings suggested that the better foster parents were younger, and more flexible in their statements of the children they were willing to accept for foster care. When the responses to the question on the application form, "What are your reasons for wanting to take foster children?" were analyzed, it was found that the most adequate foster parents tended to respond in child-centered terms, whereas the least adequate foster parents tended to respond in self-centered terms. Word choices used in the responses were "strikingly different," most adequate parents using the words *love* and *give* more frequently than least adequate parents, who showed a tendency to use the word *take*.

Kinter and Otto compared a group of twenty-four accepted foster parents with a group of fifteen rejected applicants. The result showed that the accepted group saw such factors as "love" and "understanding" as an attribute characterizing their family more frequently than did the rejected group. The findings also seem to suggest the ability to communicate between husband and wife is a distinguishing characteristic of accepted foster parents. Statistical material on levels of significance is not given. [90, p. 364]

Although Etni found younger foster parents more successful, Trasler found that success was associated with foster parents over forty. [175, p. 219] The child's tendency to feel disloyal to his own mother is reduced as he develops an affectional relationship with the older foster parent. Also, older foster parents are more likely to have had experience in rearing a family. Consequently, while such parents may have a need for satisfaction in contact with children, such needs, having been met in their own life experience, are not likely to be so imperious and urgent as to make for heavy demands on the foster child. Age may also be related to less of a need to establish a permanent relationship to the child. Weinstein noted that younger foster mothers tended to "structure the placement situation in terms of adoption rather than boarding care." [183, p. 53] This may create demands on the child that are incompatible with his view of the situation and may make it difficult for the foster parent to share the child with either the agency or the natural parents.

Cautley attempted to analyze the level of correlation between foster home factors and foster home "success." "Success" was defined as the extent to which the goals of the placement were being met as judged by the caseworker assigned to the family. [20] Few of the foster parents' developmental history factors correlated with "success" except religious orientation of the foster mother's parents which was negatively associated with success. Information provided by the foster father that his parents were "affectionate" toward him correlates positively with success. Parents with more children of their own and hence more experience in child rearing were more successful, as were families where foster parents "received encouragement from each other." Although the socioeconomic range was narrow, "success" was positively related to "general economic level of the family."

Fanshel supports the contention that the "good" foster parent is difficult to identify as a separate identifiable entity.

In the research reported here and in other studies of parent behavior, it has become clear that parenthood cannot be studied in isolation from childhood. . . . Many of the foster parents in this study showed a fairly broad range of behavior with the foster children placed with them. One kind of child could evoke a positive, nurturing kind of response; a child with different characteristics could bring forth almost rejecting behavior from the same foster parent. Although one would expect foster parents who reveal strong ego structures and sound superego values to do uniformly with most children placed with them, their parental capacity must nonetheless be seen as a variable phenomenon. The aim of high-level child welfare practice should be to maximize the parental potential of foster parents through the placement of children who can evoke a positive response in them and the provision of professional casework support to foster parents in order to help them withstand the negative and often seemingly unchangeable behavior of upset foster children. [42, p. 162; see also 93; 122; 126]

Accepted applicants are generally required to take a medical examination to establish that they are physically capable of caring for a child and have no infectious diseases. Then a license is issued which certifies that this home is authorized to accept children for foster care. The license, in many states, indicates the specific number of children that the home may accept at any one time. Generally, not more than four older children are allowed at one time and not more than two children under two years of age. A license is usually issued for a one-year period, at the end of which the agency must review the situation and relicense the home.

Selection

Placement of a child involves the selection of a particular home for a particular child. "The focus has shifted from choosing the 'best adjusted parents' to selecting foster parents whose needs meet the needs of the child to be placed." [90, p. 361] Selection, then, is on the basis of complementarity of needs.

This is not entirely a new idea. In 1867 the Massachusetts Board of State Charities recommended "that a child of passionate temper should not be placed in a family where the master or mistress is of a similar disposition. When such instances do occur there is apt to be trouble pretty soon." Placements of children evacuated from London during the war indicated that "nervous children were best placed in quiet, conventional types of home while the active, aggressive children were best in free and easy homes with companions." [13, p. 127]

Colvin reports on an investigation of the extent to which the foster parent-foster child relationship was "growth-producing and mutually satisfying":

With regard to the success of the mothers with children of different temperaments, our findings indicated that mothers showing a high need for play did best with children of low impulse control. Similarly, mothers with a high need for order did best with children showing high withdrawal, whereas mothers with a high need for play and nurturance did best with children showing a low degree of withdrawal. [26]

In general, both for mothers and fathers the study indicated that "parents with specific needs do relatively well or poorly with children showing specific personality characteristics." [26, pp. 45–46]

The home that might be good for a child early in life might become unsuitable later. Jenkins, in the course of studying ninety-seven foster homes, noted that in one group of five homes the mothers took young children for short periods of time and were uniformly successful with them. If the children stayed to the point where they were growing in independence, these mothers found that they were developing difficulties in relation to the child. [78, p. 217]

The age and sex of the foster parents' own children are also significant. Several studies [13, p. 129; 175, p. 223] have shown that failures in foster placement, which results in the child's removal from the home, are associated with the fact that the foster parents had a child of the same sex and age as the foster child. The explanation is that such a situation sets up an undesirable competition.

Foster family care of an emotionally disturbed child may require greater impersonality, less involvement—a relationship that approximates, in some essential ways, the professional relationship. Thus the foster parent who can maintain more emotional reserve may be selected for such a child.

It must be noted that selection of a home is not always a conscious, deliberate process. It is often a "search, seek, find" operation of expediency rather than an exercise of professional judgment.

Types of Foster Care

The process of selection requires a decision on the part of the agency as to the kind of foster family care it should offer the child. The agency may choose from among the following kinds of noninstitutional, twenty-four-hour-a-day arrangements:

1. *Receiving homes*—specialized boarding homes designed to care for children on short notice for limited periods of time. This service is offered primarily to babies and younger children for whom an institutional arrangement is felt to be undesirable even for a short period of time [107] and in situations requiring emergency removal of a child from a home.
2. *Free, work, or wage homes.* The child is placed in a free home, in which the agency pays no board rates, when it is anticipated that the child will be adopted by the family. Work or wage homes may be

appropriate for the older child who can make a contribution in recompense for care.

3. *Boarding homes*, in which the agency and/or natural parents pay the foster parents a board rate. This is, by far, the most common type of foster family care arrangement. According to the Jeter study, about 95 percent of all children in foster family care were in family boarding homes in 1961—only some 4 percent were in free foster family homes and 1 percent in work or wage homes. [83, p. 77]

4. *Group homes*, which may be viewed as a large foster family unit or a small institution. It is a living facility within the normal community simulating a family for a small group of unrelated children. The group home requires more extended discussion, not because it offers service currently to any significant number of the children in foster family care but because it is likely to be an increasingly significant facility in the foster care field. In 1971 there were about 800 agency-operated group homes caring for about 2.3 percent of the children in foster care. [178]

The group home may be that of a private family whose members have been recruited because of their understanding of, and willingness to work with, a large group of children. More frequently it is a single home or apartment owned or rented by the agency and staffed by "foster parents" who are employed by the agency. [64; 115] It is established in a residential community and is indistinguishable from neighboring units. A married couple is employed on a free-rent-and-board basis, plus board rate for each child, or on the basis of a straight monthly salary. The "foster parents" work around the clock, much as they would if these were their own children. From four to twelve children, all of the same sex, are generally accommodated in such a home.

Children selected for group homes must be able to work with the group, and not endanger themselves and others. The children need to be well enough to attend school regularly—as many of them do. An attempt is made to preserve some balance in the group, so that some aggressive youngsters are tempered by some quieter ones, and some relatively normal adolescents. Gula estimates that group homes, "accepting referrals from a wide range of referral agencies, admit less than half." [68, p. 13]

The group home, whether owned and operated by an agency or by a private family licensed to accommodate a large group of children, is an intermediary facility. It offers some of the personalization of family living typical of family care, yet permits some of the distance from adults possible in an institution. It provides the normal community environment found in the foster family home, yet, like the institution, it offers the "opportunity to form peer relationships which are not as threatening as sibling relationships or as different as relationships between foster children and the natural children of the foster parents." [68, p. 28]

This permits the child to feel less threatened and less guilty about establishing a competitive relationship with his foster parents and reduces the threat to biological parents that is posed by another set of "parents" who may succeed where they failed. Consequently, the group home is selected for "emotionally detached youngsters who are either too fearful to risk exposure of their feelings in close relationships or simply do not know how to find their way in close relationships" but who can operate without difficulty in the normal community. [147, p. 10] It is also selected for adolescents because their principal developmental tasks revolve around establishing independence from parents and parental surrogates and it is desirable to offer the kind of diluted, attentuated parental relationships characteristic of the family group home.

The group home has greater therapeutic potential than the family foster home, particularly for the adolescent. Therapeutic changes in the child's behavior in the foster family home depend on what the foster parents can make available, in terms of relationships with the child and models of acceptable behavior. The group home makes these available, but it also provides a peer group, interaction with which helps to control and modify undesirable behavior.

The group home owned and staffed by the agency has additional advantages for emotionally disturbed children. The pay may be high enough to permit the employment of foster parents with some professional training; the fact that it is operated by the agency may allow heavier demands on the "foster parent" staff in meeting the special needs of emotionally disturbed children and in providing the scheduling necessary for special classes, appointments with psychotherapists, and so on. The group home owned and operated by the agency has the additional advantage of permitting the foster parents to be somewhat more relaxed, tolerant, and accepting of the inevitable minor destructiveness of emotionally disturbed children.

The group home may be selected for some emotionally disturbed children for whom the agency does not want to risk the possibility of removal and replacement. Such children are frequently difficult for the normal foster family to keep. In the usual foster home, the foster parents share in the decision whether or not the child stays. In the agency-owned home, the agency alone makes this decision. Thus the group home provides the feeling of permanence and continuity for the child who needs this security.

The group home may also serve as a "halfway house" for children who are ready to be discharged from an institution but who are not yet ready to return to their own families. It permits the orderly, progressive reintroduction of the child back into the community. And it has been used as a service following treatment of emotionally disturbed children in residential care. [123]

Some of the thinking involved in making a decision regarding the selection of the appropriate kind of care is illustrated in the following case:

The conflict between Sarah W., age eleven and one-half, and her mother had become too difficult for Mrs. W. to stand. The father had deserted them several years prior to the present request. Sarah felt that both she and her mother had been abused and rejected by the father.

Sarah responded with extreme rage to her mother, who subtly provoked these outbursts. But she got along well at school with her teachers and classmates and was able to establish a good relationship with the girls and the leader in her Girl Scout troop, even though she was not able to reach out to and initiate a personal friendship with children individually. Sarah was, indeed, a very lonely child and had no intimate friends.

The mother became ill from cancer, and a homemaker was placed in the home. Sarah got along well with the homemaker although whenever she tried to approach her in a motherly way, Sarah would remark irritably, "Now don't start mothering me!"

The child welfare worker concluded that a foster home did not seem wise for Sarah at this time. To be placed in a family would be too threatening for Sarah since she was clinging so tenaciously to her mother now that separation was pending. Sarah could respond positively to adults only when the relationship was not too intense or personal and spread over many children, as with her teachers and the scout leader. . . .

A group home would offer Sarah the advantages of group living and the support of a group. All of the girls in the home would have been placed there for many of the same reasons as Sarah and some, if not all, would have difficulties in the parent-child relationship. She would have a relationship with a house mother, yet this would not be highly personal. She would have the advantage of living in the community and continuing to meet the demands of community life. At the same time, because of the smallness of the group, she would have an opportunity to develop personal relationships with individual girls—and the intimate climate of the group home would help Sarah come to grips with the basic problem affecting her relationship with her mother. [176, pp. 52–53]

In summary, then, foster parents need to be recruited, assessed, and then selected. A constant recruitment effort is necessary to provide the field with the number of families it needs. Foster care appeals to only a limited group of families—generally to families in the upper-lower and lower-middle socioeconomic level who feel some social or emotional imbalance. The worker, in assessing the family, uses as a guide the licensing regulations, which require certain minimum levels of physical adequacy of the home and neighboring community. In addition, workers have a clear image of the "good" parent, which generally follows the middle-class mental health image. However, workers do not always apply the image in assessing foster parents because of the pressure for homes. Selection is in terms of complementary needs of children and foster parents, and the placement has to be individualized so that a good "fit" is obtained.

Process

Intake

Children come into foster care through two principal routes:

1. Parents may make application to the agency for such service.
2. The child may be committed to the agency for foster care after having been adjudged neglected, dependent, or delinquent.

Neglect is a frequently encountered contingency, so many children come into care via this second route (see Chap. 6). In such cases, there is no application for service; the decision concerning the children is some-times made over the parents' opposition or with their passive acquiescence. But for parents who come to the agency of their own volition, there is more of a possibility for casework help in coming to a decision. The very availability of supplementary and supportive services intensifies the problem of decision by increasing the range of choices. Of course, the parents may not be aware of the services—or, being aware, may have some objection to using them. If so, the social worker informs them of the availability of such services and helps them to resolve some of their negative feelings about the services:

> Mrs. M., a mother of two preschool children, has recently been deserted by her husband after years of marital conflict. The family had only limited savings since Mr. M. was a semiskilled punch press operator who had earned little more than a marginal income. Mrs. M. had some experience as a beautician before she was married six years ago. She wanted to place the children, go back to school, upgrade her skills, and then have the children come live with her. She had heard about AFDC but was reluctant to consider it. The worker helped her to feel somewhat more accepting about being "on welfare" particularly because a plan was

worked out for part-time day care for the children while Mrs. M. enrolled in a beautician course. As a result, she withdrew her request for placement.

If there are some strengths in the client or the client's situation that might permit the child to remain at home, the worker explores them with the client. However, if it is clear that the child's own home is "predominantly injurious to the child" and that the family situation is "unmodifiable," or if the parents insist that the child be placed, the agency works with the parents toward the placement of the child. A parent may express a desire for placement but not necessarily accept it. Successful placement needs the continuing active participation of the natural parent and his conviction that this decision is the correct one.

Bowlby, quoting a study done at the Maryland Children's Aid Society in 1942, notes that where both the child and the natural parent accepted placement, the chances of success for the foster placement were very great. In few cases was the child able to show an accepting attitude toward placement if his parents did not themselves hold and sanction such an attitude. [13, p. 119]

The decision to support the parent's desire for placement, or to press for placement despite the parent's opposition, is very difficult for the social worker. [113] In many instances, the decision is made for him—by the situation (as when there is no one available to care for the child at home and substitute care is the only feasible alternative), by the limitations of placement resources, or by parental rights and strongly expressed parental preferences.

Studies of the factors which determine the social workers' decisions conclude that the "drastic step of separating a child from his family is likely to be taken only if there is evidence of considerable deviance or pathology in the child, his parents, or his living conditions." [127, p. 87] Inability to provide adequate care and the mother's pathology were the most frequently cited factors determining placement decisions. [150, p. 222] There were also likely to be fewer interpersonal resources such as relatives, friends, or neighbors to whom the families could turn for help. Placement was less likely when the mother was concerned about the child and motivated to attempt to change. Placement was more likely when the child was receiving "grossly inadequate care in the area of feeding, supervision and guidance, warmth and affection, protection from abuse, and concern regarding schooling." [127, p. 44] Mothers whose children were placed were much more likely to be overwhelmed by responsibility for the family, to show emotional disturbance and low impulse control, and to lack motivation or desire for keeping the family together. [150, p. 119] In two-parent families, the father's functioning took clear precedence over the mother's functioning in determining the placement decision. [127, p. 87] The Child Welfare League of America has, in response to such findings, developed and tested a model for such decisions. [128]

There is considerable variation in the placement decision-making process. In one study workers given the same cases to review "agreed among themselves on slightly less than half of the decisions." [127, p. 88] In a second study there was some 71 percent agreement. [150, p. 243] The latter level of agreement is significantly better than chance, and is typical of the level of disagreement among experts in any complex situation—in the reading of X-rays, in the admission of college students, in decisions concerning the necessity for surgery, and so on.

A nationwide study indicated that the decision to use or reject foster family care is also influenced by community attitudes, community resources, and the orientation of the community legal system. [104] Thus the percentage of children in foster family care varies widely in different communities, although the need may not. [160, p. 58]

If the social worker, in collaboration with the parents, has decided that placement is indeed the best and most feasible choice, he must then make clear to the parents that foster care does not relieve them of the burden of parenthood indefinitely, and that such care is, ideally, temporary. Foster family placement is, in effect, a sociotherapeutic resource permitting a temporary reduction in whatever stress is imposed on the parent by his need to care for the child. Like any treatment resource, it is best used either as a means of effecting change, or as increasing the possibility of effecting change, following a clear diagnostic evaluation of the total situation. Responsible placement requires that the parents be helped to plan the necessary changes that will ultimately permit the child to return. Ideally, planning for the child's return begins at the same time as does planning for the child's placement.

Although it may be clear to both parents that placement is designed to allow them to work toward achieving the changes that will permit the child to return home, placement of a child relieves the crisis; there may consequently be less motivation to do anything about anything, particularly if doing something involves some effort on the part of the parents to effect changes in themselves. To keep participation and motivation high, and to maintain parent-child ties, the agency involves the natural parents in what has been called the *structure of service*.

However limited their contribution may be, the agency seeks to have the natural parents pay for some of the board rate of the child. Even a limited amount symbolizes the parents' responsibility for the child. Actually, however, relatively few parents actually pay any part of the cost of such care: payment comes primarily from county or state funds, in the case of public agencies, and agency funds, in the case of the voluntary agency. The agency encourages parental visits to the child in the foster family home, and all forms of communication for continuing contact. One agency's insistence on these obligations ultimately helped to permit some children to return to their own homes—children toward whom the parents had been largely indifferent until the agency began to require board payments. [17]

The agency encourages the parents to share as much information as possible about the child so that the agency will be able to select the optimum foster family. The agency also involves the parents in preparing the child for placement, helping them to deal with the child's reaction to placement. The act of separation itself is used to maintain the parents' sense of responsibility to the child. The agency helps the parent to feel that, in helping the child to make a comfortable adjustment to separation, he is fulfilling his obligation to the child and demonstrating his concern for the child. It may even ask them to visit the prospective foster home so that they will be assured of the adequacy of care the child will receive. All of this serves to keep parental participation and responsibility at a high level.

Thus far, we have discussed two different ways in which the agency seeks to help the child through casework with the parent:

1. It helps the parent come to the decision that placement will be of greatest benefit to the child.
2. It helps the parent to maintain intact his responsibility to the child and his contact with the child, and it plans with the parent from the start for the child's return.

The agency also seeks to help the parent directly by helping him to deal with some of the disturbing feelings that may result from the necessity to place the child. Although all parents fail at one time or another, the failure is usually limited and private—a family affair. Here, however, the extent of failure is almost total and knowledge of it has to be shared with the agency and, ultimately, with the foster parents. This involves a loss of self-esteem, an anticipation of rejection and censure, an intensification of feelings of inadequacy and shame. This feeling is apt to be intensified with placement and with the pressure to recognize the fact that the foster parents are daily demonstrating more adequacy in the care of the child than the natural parents can themselves show.

For some parents, the placement of the child is an enactment of their desire to get rid of him. The parents feel great anxiety and guilt as a consequence of those desires and as a result of the sense of relief and release they feel in having someone else accept the burden of responsibility for the care of the child. For other parents, placement might be a gratifying way of punishing the child and, once again, this gratification might engender guilt. Relieving guilt while keeping the sense of responsibility high seems like a delicate task for the worker—and it is.

Acceptance of foster family care by the natural parents involves acceptance of an anomalous position. They retain the status of parents, but they no longer practice directly the daily responsibilities of the role. They have to relinquish some of the prerogatives of parenthood to another set of parents. They may fear that, in doing so, they might lose the child's affection and respect to the foster parents. The agency has to help the parents in their struggle with these fears.

Finally, although placement relieves the parent of the burden of care for the child and the loss of some prerogatives regarding his control, it also involves the loss of gratification. Filial deprivation for parents is a process paralleling parental deprivation for children. [80; 81; 82] As part of a larger study some 430 parents were asked, "How did you feel the day your child was placed?" [82] Reactions identified included sadness, anger, bitterness, relief, thankfulness, worry, nervousness, guilt, shame, emptiness: 88 percent reported a feeling of sadness followed, frequently, by nervousness and worry; 30–39 percent reported feelings of guilt (usually mothers) and shame (usually fathers). These feelings were directed against themselves. About half the parents reported feelings of anger and bitterness, or thankfulness and relief; in most instances, such feelings were directed toward the agency. Anger and bitterness were likely to be felt when separation resulted from neglect and/or abuse; thankfulness, when it resulted from the physical illness of the mother; relief and guilt, when it resulted from the child's behavioral maladjustment. Unless some of these feelings are resolved, the success of the placement might be jeopardized and the child's adjustment to foster care made more difficult.

Without an awareness of his feelings, the biological parent may find it very difficult to be honest with the child if this involves an open confession that his return home is not likely. The tendency is to tell the child the good news he wants to hear rather than the bad news he has to hear. The biological parents may demand obedience, even in absentia, to themselves rather than to the foster parent. They may force the child to behave in allegiance to themselves rather than to the foster parents and thus use the child in their resentment against the foster parents, the "better" parent. Developing awareness of such feelings is the caseworker's responsibility.

The Child in Placement

The movement of the child from his own home to the foster home involves the process of separation, transition, and incorporation. The anticipation of separation elicits strong emotional reactions in the child, so that considerable preparation is required. The child supposedly struggles with the following kinds of reactions, many of them unconscious. [21; 57; 61; 100]

1. Feelings of rejection ("My parents don't want me"), which engender feelings of worthlessness.
2. Guilt ("I am so bad that they had to get rid of me"), which leads the child to feel he has contributed to breaking up the home.
3. Hostility ("I hope they get hurt for having rejected me"), which reinforces the guilt, because hostile feelings, particularly against one's own parents, are a punishable offense.
4. Fear of abandonment ("Will my parents want me back? What will happen to them while I am away?").
5. Fear of the unknown ("Where am I going? Will they like me?").
6. Shame ("Why can't my parents, like other parents, take care of me?").

Almost all social work literature contends that separation from the parents for placement in substitute care engenders these feelings in the child, but there is very little, except sparse anecdotal clinical excerpts, to confirm this contention. Such anecdotal material is not in the form of raw data but rather tends to be the reporter's interpretation of the child's feelings. All this, however, may be practical wisdom based on accurate perception by workers of the child's feelings, which are below the level of the child's awareness and so not capable of being articulated, except indirectly.

Of interest here is the fact that Meier, after lengthy interviews with sixty-one young adults who had spent considerable time in foster care, notes: "Current perception of most of the subjects as to why they could not remain with their own families is based on realistic appraisal of their home situation rather than an unrealistic self-blame." [114, p. 149] Most of the children in placement come from grossly deprived environments, in most cases from broken homes, and may have recognized their parents' inability to care for them.

Weinstein, in interviews with sixty-one children in foster care, asked about reasons that brought them there. He found that the age of the child at time of placement and at the time of the research was an important factor in determining his realism in assessing the situation. Most reasons given were external to the child and centered on the inability of his parents to care for him. It is significant, however, that there was considerable distortion in the child's memory of his home situation, indicating the operation of repressive factors. [183, pp. 32–33] Some of the contingencies requiring placement seem to be easier for the child to accept. Death—clear, unequivocal, and a matter of fate—is perhaps the easiest to accept. Mental illness is more difficult because the parent is apparently physically well, yet is unable to care for the child.

Despite the descriptive clinical reports, there is little empirical evidence of the effects on children of the separation necessitated by moving into a foster home or of the process of adaptation to the experience.

Thomas hypothesized that placement involves separation from, and loss of, objects that afforded the child gratification. [168] Such loss initiates a process of grief and mourning through which the child removes cathexis from libidinal objects from which he is now separated so as to make psychic energy available for investment in new objects, namely the foster parents. The process of mourning is supposedly reflected in a series of clearly identifiable behaviors: pre-protest, protest, despair, detachment. In studying the reactions to placement of thirty-five white school-age children (through detailed interviews with their foster parents), Thomas found that the children did experience some process of mourning, although its stages were not as clearly demarcated as he had hypothesized. Separation and object loss seemed less difficult for those children who had some clear idea as to what would happen to them. Surprisingly there was little difference in the process between those children who were visited very rarely by their natural parents and those children who received frequent visits.

There is far less discussion of the loss the child faces in being separated from siblings, though Meier, in her study of former foster children, found that sibling deprivation was keenly felt and keenly remembered. [114]

Because separation is difficult, because the agency is active in implementing separation, often the agency becomes the target of the child's hostility. An older foster child, in discussing her memory of separation with her caseworker, said, "You can't help being afraid and you have to hate someone. When I first met you I hated you because you were associated with the break-up of my home." [88, p. 101]

Bowlby suggests joint interviews with the parents and children "in which the whole situation is exhaustively reviewed and a common plan reached." [13, p. 120] This would make it more difficult for the child to support the fantasy that the agency is responsible for his placement and would help him to form a realistic understanding. Current interest in family interviewing reinforces Bowlby's suggested approach.

The social worker encourages the child to share his feelings, to be open with himself regarding his reactions to his natural parents and his foster parents, to talk about his disappointments and hostilities as well as his satisfaction in the placement. The worker helps the child to express his feelings, because unless these feelings are expressed and clarified in open discussion, they will create difficulties in adjustment.

These discussions are also designed to help the child correct any distortions he may have about the reasons for his being placed in foster family care—to let him know as clearly as possible what is going to happen next, to help him anticipate the experience, to permit him to meet the experience "in small doses" so that he can assimilate it emotionally. In all of this, the worker presents the situation as honestly and objectively as possible on a level that the child can understand, on a level that is meaningful to him. She includes the child as actively as possible as a participant in the entire process.

After a home has been selected, the child makes brief visits to his prospective home, accompanied by the worker, who acts as a supporting figure during the time the child is separating from one home but not yet incorporated in another. Sooner or later, however, the child has to make the transition. Supposedly, the best time to move a child into a foster home is early on Friday afternoon: he has time to get acquainted with the home before night, and the weekend permits contact with the whole foster family before the child (if he is old enough) is off to school on Monday. Nevertheless, the change is a radical one for the child.

> Everything the child has known in the past disappears. Everything he experiences is strange—the bed he sleeps in, the location of the bathroom and the closet for his clothes, the food, the family routine, the toys, the yard, the school, the people in close proximity to him. Nothing which happens from day to night is the same and there is no person to look to for a familiar response. [74, p. 3]

In his anxiety at the strangeness and the change, the child might regress: the toilet-trained child may become enuretic, the child who had begun to speak may stop speaking or speak haltingly, the child who was establishing some independence may begin to cling. These are the behavioral manifestations of inner tension.

Even after the move, there is a transitional period during which the child lives physically in the foster home but psychologically, to some extent, in the home he left behind. It is said that the child lives in one home and loves in another. During this transitional period the child is adjusting to his changed relationship to his biological parents and his new relationship to his foster parents. He is making some shift in his loyalties and affection. He is shedding old ways of doing things and learning new ones.

If the foster child is to fit into the foster family, he has to be socialized to its mores and daily customs, which may conflict with those of his natural family. Patterns of eating, recreation, toileting, dressing, speaking, thinking may be different. To learn one set of patterns is to unlearn another; to adhere to one is to be disloyal to the other. There is a period of transitional confusion, during which the child is trying to establish himself in this rather strange and demanding role of foster child.

The foster child has a dual family status—he belongs, in part, to both his foster family and his biological family. His "belonging" in the biological family may be purely formal and legalistic but by name and by kinship affiliation he is still part of that family system. As one foster child said to the foster mother, "I am my mother's daughter but your child."

The confusion is evident in the following excerpts from case records:

> I am not happy with my Aunty [foster mother]. She picks on me and there always upsets; she always wants to make me her little girl. I know my mother has to stay in the hospital and I was often naughty at home, but I still love my mother. I still have my own family even if I cannot live with them, and I can't join in with another family, just like that. I am very fond of Aunty but not in the same way as I am of my mother. And I don't want to be either. I don't want to take Aunty's surname, and I am not happy and don't want to stay. I think it would be better for everyone if I were to go. [88, p. 127]

> Pauline is continuing to make her adjustment, at a quicker rate than expected. At first she was unable to call the foster parents anything—neither *Aunt* and *Uncle* nor *Mother* and *Father*, admitting to her worker a feeling of great strangeness, since they were really not her relatives, and it seemed confusing to her to have two mothers. She thought it might be easier to call them just simply by their first names, something the worker could quite understand. Subsequently, however, there was a change in this and Pauline took the initiative in asking the foster mother whether she could call them *Mother* and *Father*. When assured that anything she would like to call them would be all right, she immediately started calling her foster parents *Mother* and *Father*. [86, p. 5]

The worker alleviates the child's anxiety by displaying an understanding acceptance of the child's ambivalent love-hate feelings toward his biological parents and by sanctioning his divided loyalties.

During the early period in the foster home, the child may be on his best behavior—the so-called "honeymoon" period of foster placement. This may give way to a period of testing, in which the child probes the limits of behavior the foster parents will accept. If separation symbolizes rejection for these children, then rejection is something they have actually experienced and are fearful of encountering again. Testing is the child's plea for reassurance that he is wanted in this home.

If the child remains in the home for some time and if the foster parents accept him and his behavior, he ultimately becomes incorporated in the new status. He has some clear idea of who he is, what is expected of him, and what he can expect of others. He makes some adjustment to the foster home and to himself as a foster child.

Throughout this process of separation, transition, and incorporation, the worker makes periodic visits to interview the child in the home. The purpose of these contacts is to help the child with any problems he may be having in adjusting to the foster parents, the siblings in the home, the new community, or the new school. They are also designed to help the child come to grips with the consequences of his status as foster child, which is different from the status of his peers. Because the child brings his past into his present home, the worker tries to help him deal with the residuals of the emotional and social difficulties most of these children have experienced in their own homes.

Because foster family care status is, as we noted, an unusual one involving simultaneous membership in two family systems, the worker helps the child to understand the meaning of foster care. As is true for any role, clear understanding of the placement situation is an important precondition of the child's adjustment to it. Ideally, the worker represents continuity for the child—the one stable relationship in the world of changing relationships. The worker was with the child before he met the foster parents and will be with him after he leaves them.

The child may experience conflict about sharing his problems with the worker. He may feel disloyal to the foster parents if he discloses their shortcomings and he may fear repercussions. He may feel that his relationship to the worker, too, is at stake. Because the worker chose the foster home, the child feels that any complaints will be viewed as a reflection on the wisdom of that choice. The child may use the worker as a shield against the foster parents and as a weapon against them. He may try to induce the worker to intercede in his behalf to obtain concessions from the foster parents.

The worker's conception of the purpose of these contacts may not be adequately communicated to the foster child, however. Weinstein undertook to interview sixty-one children in foster care. [183]   The children selected for interviewing were over five years of age and had been in a secure placement for some time. The interviews were designed to elicit the child's definition of the situation and his locus of identification. They included such questions as "What does *foster* mean?"; "What do you call your own parents? Your foster parents?"; "If you had some trouble or were worried, whom would you like to talk to about it?" In Weinstein's study, the children never perceived the social worker as having a responsibility to facilitate his return to his own parents. [183, p. 44]   Only in two cases did the answer to such questions as "If you had some trouble or were worried, whom would you like to talk to about it?" or "If you could pick anyone in the world to live with, whom would you pick?" indicate a predominant identification with the social worker. [183, p. 48]   Similarly, Gottesfeld, in a study concerned in part with foster children's reaction to foster care, finds that "While social workers should be ideal agents for helping the foster child to deal with the conflicts and problems of foster home care, the foster child does not perceive the social worker in this way. Less than half the foster children [in the study group] expressed a need to call their social workers about a problem." [62, p. 28]

Foster children complain that they see social workers infrequently and that the workers change so often that it is difficult for the children to get to feel comfortable with any one of them. Workers generally approach foster children with a problem-oriented attitude so that the child comes to feel that contact is unnecessary unless there is something actually or potentially troublesome. [62, p. 26]

The Foster Family in the Placement Process

The foster family is prepared for the child's placement in the home by the caseworker, who shares with the family the background information he has gathered—the reasons for the child's placement, his developmental history, his peculiarities and preferences, his special fears and special pleasures, his weaknesses and strengths. Yet foster parents sometimes complain that the agency does not provide them with sufficient background information—perhaps because, in their desire to find a place for the child the social worker might tend to describe him as less disturbed than he actually is.

The worker should, whenever possible, actively involve the foster parents in the planning process. They are the principal ingredients of a successful placement, and their thoughts and feelings need to be given serious and continuous consideration. Since the pattern of the relationship is set in the early contacts, it is during these contacts that the worker needs to actively solicit the participation of the foster parents, make certain that they are acquainted with what is going on and what the agency expects, and that any promises and requests are scrupulously made and acted upon.

The child's visits to the foster home help to prepare him to move in, help to prepare the foster parents for his coming. A room has to be made ready. Preparation for placement also involves the caseworker's sharing information about the natural parents, their visitation rights and privileges, and discussing with the foster parents a convenient schedule for visiting.

With the inclusion of the foster parents, the nature of the triangular relationships in foster care become clear. The foster parents have a relationship with both the child and the biological parents; the biological parents, with both the child and the foster parents; the child, with both sets of parents. The triangle, in uneasy equilibrium, is bound together by the agency, which serves the child, the biological parents, and the foster parents, and provides continuity in the process. With placement there is a redistribution of parental roles that is now shared among biological parent, foster parent, and agency worker. The process is affected by the distinctive attributes of the community in which it takes place. The configuration is illustrated in Fig. 9–1.

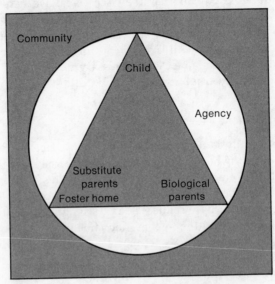

FIGURE 9–1. Configuration of relationships in foster care.

Foster Parent Role: Distinctive Aspects

The foster parent role presents a number of problems, some of which derive from the crucial differences between foster parenthood and biological parenthood. The foster parents enact the parental role in their day-to-day contact with the child, yet they do not have the full rights of the true parents. Because they are acting for the child's biological parents, not replacing them, and because they receive the child through the agency, they are only partial parents; they share control of the child with both the biological parents and the agency.

The foster parents want a child to board. Yet, in getting a child, they find they get an agency as well. The agency sets limits and advances directives as to how the foster parents are to behave toward the child—a situation not normally encountered by biological parents. The shared control and responsibility for the child is clearly set forth in the instruction pamphlets issued to foster parents. As one such pamphlet points out: "Disciplining a child must be done with kindness and understanding. Corporal punishment, which includes striking, whipping, slapping, or any other form of discipline that inflicts the child with physical pain, is prohibited. Don't forget that *prohibited* means *not allowed.* Disobey-

ing the regulation is cause for cancellation of the foster home license."
[28, p. 6] Another pamphlet says, "You are expected to give each child
six years old and over a monthly allowance. We insist on this as a
means of teaching the child the value of money." [67] No change in
the sleeping arrangements of the child may be made without the approval of the agency, nor may the child be taken out of the state on a
vacation trip without the prior approval of the agency. [32] The foster
parent is obligated to discuss the child's behavioral difficulties with the
agency.

Limited control implies limited responsibility as well. The fact that
the agency is responsible for the basic cost of maintenance of the child
indicates an essential difference between foster parenthood and biological parenthood. Furthermore, the foster parents are responsible for the
child for only a limited segment of his life span. And because the duration of their contact with the foster child is indefinite, the foster parents
cannot plan for the child's future, nor can they legitimately expect to
share in the child's future achievements. [111]

Although all parents are accountable in a general way to society,
there are no formal channels that periodically take a measure of their
performance. The foster parents, however, are accountable to an agency,
and the yearly relicensing is the procedure by which an accounting is
explicitly made. The decision as to whether the child remains or goes
rests with the agency. The state license usually includes a clause stipu-
lating that the foster parents must agree to the removal of the child upon
the request of the agency. Removal of a child from the biological parents'
home can be effected only after due process of law. Removal of the foster
child from the foster family home can be undertaken merely on the basis
of the agency's decision. The foster parents' relationship with the child
has no legal protection. If the foster parents value this relationship, this
situation must of necessity make them anxious and desirous of pleasing
—and sometimes even of placating—the agency.

The undesirable effects that derive from confusing the foster parent role with the biological parent role is illustrated in the following
case.

Mrs. D. applied for a baby to board when her own three children
were older—one married and out of the home, the other two,
teenagers. An infant was placed with her directly from the hospital
on a preadoptive boarding basis. From the beginning, the caseworker
warned her that the baby eventually would be placed for adoption,
which would mean his permanent separation from her. The caseworker visited the foster home consistently at weekly intervals to
share responsibility for medical planning with Mrs. D. and try to
make the role of the agency and her own role as a foster mother
real to her. As time went on, however, it became evident in the

way Mrs. D. handled the baby and talked about him that she had made him her own.

When the adoptive placement was finally made, Mrs. D. found separation from the baby extremely hard to take and told the caseworker that she felt that he had died. She sobbed, grieved, and mourned as if she had, indeed, been faced with death. The caseworker spent considerable time with her, supported her, and as Mrs. D.'s grief subsided, talked about the meaning of foster parenthood—the pleasures of giving to a child as well as the pain of giving one up. [112, p. 223]

The foster parents do not "own" the child; they are merely borrowing him for a time. Because the child belongs ultimately to the biological parents, the foster parents cannot encourage him to make a full emotional investment in themselves, nor can they permit themselves unrestrained expression of affection for the child because they must give him up at some point. In fact, the more the foster parents make the child "truly their own," the more guilt they might feel at "stealing" the child from his own family. The foster parents have to be able to let the child into the family easily, and out again just as easily.

All this suggests another difference between foster parenthood and biological parenthood. The biological parents expect to be rewarded for their care and affection by full, reciprocal affection from the child. Because full expression of emotional responsiveness must be inhibited in foster care, other sources of satisfaction need to be enhanced. One source of satisfaction is from a job well done—a successful job of parenting. Another source of satisfaction lies in the approbation and appreciation of the agency, from joint participation with the agency in a socially significant undertaking. Another legitimate source of satisfaction is the more adequate financial return. These kinds of satisfactions, however, tend to distinguish the foster parent from the biological parent.

Although explicit differences between foster parenthood and biological parenthood exist, foster parenthood remains an ambiguously defined role, and its enactment is likely to occasion difficulty. The foster parent is not always certain what is expected of him, and his definition of the situation may conflict with that of the public, the agency, the biological parents, or the child.

Wolins attempted to define the role of the foster parent empirically by interviews with nineteen child welfare workers, ninety-three foster parents and seventy-eight close neighbors of foster parents. [187] The interviewer posed for the respondent a variety of typical situations and attempted to elicit the respondent's conception of the appropriate role behavior. Among the questions asked were the following: "Fred is a very bright foster child. Who should make plans for his education after high school?" "John is a foster child who lives with the Joneses. He works after school and makes about $15 a week. Who has the right to the money?" The study of responses showed that the foster parents and neighbors tended to define the foster parents' role as an approximation of the biological parents' role. Few of the respondents defined the role in any unique or distinctive way. "More than three-fourths of our foster parents perceived themselves as most like a natural parent. For them, confusion is resolved when they understand others' expectations of them to be no different from those of a natural parent." [182, p. 30]

Ambinder *et al.* attempted to elicit foster parents' conception of their role. [2] Although the fifty parents included in the study were caring for disturbed children, their responses may be applicable to the more standard foster family care situation. Respondents were interviewed from one to one and one-half hours with reference to their foster care experiences and the interviews were supplemented by a detailed questionnaire. With regard to foster parents' perception of their own role, the "most clear-cut category" elicited was that of "natural parent surrogate." This is typified in the response "caring for these children would be like bringing up my own." Foster parents saw the caseworker as

. . . an ongoing contact person, supervising and helping with problems of the child. The emphasis is on the supervisory component of the caseworker's function and there is less perception and acceptance of the helping function. The foster parents' perception of their role and their perception of the caseworker's role are logically consistent. [2]

The data suggest that many of the foster parents wish to exclude the caseworker from significant involvement in the life of the foster home— a further manifestation of their desire to act as real parent surrogates, jealously guarding the prerogatives of this role from outside interference. As Weinstein points out:

There is little in the way of clean-cut formulations of the limits of responsibility and power to initiate or veto decisions associated with each of the positions in the [placement] system. In consequence, relationships develop in which there are disagreements about the rights and responsibilities of each of the parties. The child may be confronted with three sets of adults, all of whom have some stake in caring for him and planning for his future. In the absence of clearly structured role expectations, both power and responsibility may sometimes be shared, sometimes competed for, and sometimes denied by one or more of the three. [183, p. 15]

Role conflict is engendered when the foster parent acts as a biological parent to his own child and as a foster parent to the foster child. Similarly, it is difficult for a foster child to learn that appropriate behavior for the role of foster child is different from appropriate behavior for the role of biological child. Children who have had previous experience in foster homes, where they have had the opportunity to learn to be a foster child, tend to make more successful subsequent adjustments to the role.

Working with the Foster Parent

Because foster parenthood is a difficult, easily misunderstood situation, the agency seeks to help the foster parent in caring for the child. The worker visits regularly, discussing with the foster parents the child's adjustment and the family's reaction to the child. He acts, in these contacts, as an advisor-teacher, a counselor, and a source of psychological support, trying to allay anxiety, reduce guilt, and provide reassurance.

It is often difficult for the foster parents to understand the child's behavior. Although they have learned something of the child's past, which helps to explain his behavior, they need to experience it in order to appreciate the psychodynamic logic of what appears to be inappropriate behavior. The general interpretation given by the worker, in preparation for placement, as to what to expect has limited meaning. It comes to life as the foster parents actually encounter the child behaving in the ways which were anticipated. At these times, discussions with the caseworker are more likely to develop the kind of understanding the child needs from the foster parents.

It is hard for foster parents to understand how a child might still feel some affection for the natural parents, given the nature of the negative treatment he has received from them. The fact that the child continues to miss the natural parents and continues to talk about them might be seen by the foster parents as a rejection of them or a comment on the adequacy of their care. The worker reassures the foster parent that this is not the case.

The arrival of a foster child means a reworking of the old family configuration. The family interactional pattern grows more complex with the inclusion of another person, and although this may be a source of satisfaction and pleasure, it also may create problems in interpersonal relationships with which the caseworker attempts to offer help.

The foster parents may find it difficult to behave in an appropriately different way to their own children and to the foster child. Their status is different, yet to treat the foster child differently may occasion resentment and rebellion on the part of the foster child; to treat him as the others may cause difficulties with their own children.

As a consequence of his power to give and remove a child, the foster parents tend to see the caseworker as a parent figure. Technically, then, the situation presumably evokes transference reactions in which the foster parents act toward the worker as though he were their parent. This would then give the caseworker considerable influence with the foster parents. [91]

The foster mother knows the foster child better than the caseworker can ever know the child, but the caseworker knows foster children and general reactions to foster care situations, and can bring to the foster mother a perspective on foster care which is helpful.

> . . . [The caseworker] knows that fostering is largely a matter of trial and error, and that if a fostering fails it may be because he has not selected the right child or the right foster home, or that the child was not yet ready for a fostering experience, or that the interference of the real parents has made the success of the fostering impossible. But the foster parent does not have this experience of fostering as a guide. The foster parent . . . tends to feel that the success or failure of the fostering rests entirely on what the foster home has to offer to the child. To learn that this is not so will relieve the burden on the foster parents. [88, p. 116]

One of the most important contributions which the caseworker makes to the psychic comfort of the foster parents is his assurance that their occasional negative feelings toward the foster child are understandable, acceptable, and entirely normal; that an occasional failure in dealing with the foster child is inevitable; and that negative behavior on the part of the child is not a reflection of any inadequacy on their part as parents. Such reassurance, coming from a representative of the agency that has had experience with many foster placements, is often an effective antidote to the compulsive self-doubt which affects many foster parents as they encounter problems they had not anticipated in being surrogate parents to troubled children from troubled homes.

Furthermore, the caseworker's recognition, in the name of the agency which represents the community, that they are doing an important job satisfactorily, helps to compensate foster parents for the frequent disappointments felt in the slight emotional return they get from the child in response to the emotional energies they invest.

Foster parents more frequently ask for support and sanction than for instruction or advice. They recognize what the social worker recognizes but rarely makes explicit—that living day by day, all day, with the child, they know far more about his behavior than the social worker who visits briefly and infrequently. Consequently they are aware that social workers may not be able to provide them with magical answers that will change a difficult child into an angelic child. What they do want, and keenly appreciate, is a caseworker who does listen with empathy, sympathy, and interest, and who gives them the sanction of the agency for their efforts.

The caseworker brings a more professional knowledge of foster care and—equally important—the support of the agency resources. The agency, in addition to providing board payments, makes available all the resources of the community. It takes care of medical and dental treatment; it provides glasses, orthopedic appliances, and prescription medicine; it makes available psychological testing and psychotherapy for the child.

The caseworker's visits, then, are designed to help the foster family in discharging joint agency-foster family responsibility for care of the child. The foster family may see it differently, however.

> The worker may define the situation as one of consultation where he assists in the development of the child through advice based upon his professional knowledge. The foster mother may define the situation quite differently. What to the worker may be guidance, can be construed by the foster mother as an implicit attack on her adequacy as a parent. There may be an attempt on the part of the foster mother to curtail her relationship with the worker; in effect, to shut the agency out. [183, p. 11]

The mother may share with the agency only information which suggests that everything is fine or may dissimulate the true nature of the situation.

The assessment-selection process cannot assure the agency that the foster parents will actually act in a healthy manner toward the child. The assessment process is concerned with predicting behavior—always a dubious procedure. The actual behavior may be different. The agency can be of greatest value to the child in attempting to assess, and change if possible, the actual behavior of the foster parents. Foster parents, however carefully selected, may not always behave as anticipated. Ambinder and Sargent interviewed fifty foster parents representing thirty-one families caring for adolescent boys placed through a large public agency. [3] They were interested in finding out how foster parents handled unacceptable behavior on the part of the foster child. The "control techniques" were then sorted by two social workers and two psychologists in terms of three categories—techniques that seemed unlikely to enhance ego control and mature development, techniques that were neither helpful nor harmful in this respect, and techniques that seemed likely to enhance ego control and mature development. By far the greatest percentage of techniques employed (73 percent) fell in the first, supposedly harmful, category. These included threats to remove the child from the home, physical punishment, and ridicule. There was little realization on the part of these foster parents that the same techniques that had, perhaps, been used effectively with their own children had a different effect on the foster child because his situation was different. Instead, there was the persistent belief that the child's behavior was always under conscious control, wilfully deliberate and, hence, subject to change if the child wanted to change.

The study confirms the fact that the kind of parent the foster child needs and the kind of parental behavior the agency expects may be different from that prevalent in foster homes. It suggests the importance for the child of the agency's continuing participation in the foster experience.

Visits by the caseworker to the home are also designed to discharge the supervisory responsibility of the agency. As Kline says, "The foster parents' primary role is that of surrogate parents to the child within their own family setting under the supervision of an agency that is responsible and accountable for the child's care." [92, p. 220]   The caseworker visits to see how the child is getting along, what more needs to be done, and whether or not the child is adequately cared for. The supervisory components may be threatening to the foster mother and are apt to make her defensive. Some mitigation of the threat comes from the fact that the caseworker attempts to see the foster parents as persons in their own right, rather than as an "environment" for the child. He approaches the foster parents with some consideration for their needs and anxieties, assuming that they are not solely interested in justfying themselves and concealing their failings and difficulties but, rather, that they are eager to do a creditable job, to understand the child and whatever difficulties he has. The worker also appreciates that the foster parents have a direct and personal stake in the child's behavior and that they face direct and personal consequences of his behavior.

More recently agencies have been supplementing periodic visits with experimental family sessions—meetings with foster parents, their own children, and the foster child, all at the same time. [99]   Such an approach has the advantage of including the father and siblings, permits the worker to observe family interaction directly, and permits all the family members to know what the foster child is sharing with the social worker. In contrast to such an approach one foster parent said, "He [the foster child] called the worker [and said] that I was overprotecting him. They came to see him and talked to him in the car." [2]

The foster parent may perceive the worker as child-oriented rather than neutral, and consequently may feel some resentment. The following statement by a foster parent reflects his perception of the situation:

It has seemed to me that the uh . . . welfare workers have more or less taken the attitude that the children are always right. . . . It impressed me that the children kind of have that idea that, well,

the children are right and no matter what the foster parents do
to try and correct it, well they're being biased. . . . They're not
giving the child a fair chance . . . and I think that's wrong in
a way. . . . Well I know it was in our case . . . 'cause . . . [the
worker] thought that we should not punish him . . . by spanking
him . . . and uh . . . well last time I wanted to ask her if she
wanted to take him to live with her for a couple of weeks and see
what she would do. . . . Now maybe that's just . . . one worker.
. . . She said that she had kind of felt that way too . . . that she
tries to see things from the child's point of view rather than the
parents. . . .

Foster fathers tend not to be the passive partners they are generally
perceived to be by caseworkers. Their apparent passivity derives from
the fact that they see the child-rearing role as primarily the responsibility of the foster mother. Their peripheral relationship to the social
worker is reinforced by a "value system which precludes discussions of
child-rearing problems with women who are not related to them." [33,
p. 164] They have, by choice, little contact with the social workers,
who have, apparently also by choice, little contact with them and,
hence, little knowledge about them. The foster fathers, Fanshel notes,
are "quite strong and firm in the areas they perceive to be within their
proper area of functioning." [42, p. 151] A special study of forty-one
foster fathers tended to confirm Fanshel's findings. [33] With the
more accurate perception of foster fathers as heads of the family, it
has been suggested that foster care payments be made to them rather
than, as is often the case currently, to the mothers.

The phone might be more frequently, expeditiously, and economically employed to keep in contact with foster families. Phone interviews
can be as helpful as visits.

Visits

The periodic visits by the social worker call attention to an additional
penalty of foster parenthood: some loss of privacy. The agency has the
right and the obligation to intrude upon the foster parent-foster child
relationship. Furthermore, acceptance of the foster child involves acceptance of visitation rights by the natural parents. In getting a child
the foster parent not only gets an agency, he gets the child's family
as well.

Ideally, the relationship between foster parent and biological parent
should be one of mutual cooperation toward achieving what is best for
the child. Each recognizes and accepts the different responsibilities and
the different contributions the other can make toward seeing that place-

ment is least damaging to the child. Yet there is apt to be considerable deviation from the ideal relationship. As Weinstein notes:

> The foster mother may define the status of the natural mother as inferior in the relationship. She may be unwilling to entertain suggestions made by the natural mother on the grounds that she is inadequate by virtue of the child's being in placement. Any attempts on the part of the natural mother to participate may be resisted as unwelcome interference. The natural mother may see herself as superior in the relationship, according the foster mother a position similar to that of a "hired servant." She may see her position as the child's natural parent as entitling her to the right of unlimited critical review of the foster mother's actions. Such conflicting definitions of the situation may lead to open hostility. [183, p. 13]

Throughout the process the worker encourages contacts between the foster child and the biological parent through visits, letters, and phone calls. Such contacts help the child to make a positive adjustment to the foster home. Weinstein found that the average well-being of children (as judged by the caseworker) whose biological parents visited them regularly was significantly higher than that of children who did not have contact with their biological parents. This was the case even among children who had been in foster homes most of their lives and identified predominantly with their foster parents. "The correlations in this area are among the strongest to be found in the study." [183, p. 17]

Earlier, Cowan and Stout studied thirty children who had experienced complete and partial breaks in "environmental continuity." The results indicated that "a partial break in environmental continuity in the life of a child is less likely to be followed by behavior indicating insecurity (loneliness, enuresis, fears, sense of inadequacy, persistent disobedience) than is a complete environmental break." [30, p. 335] The authors suggest that the child's tendency to remember and discuss the past should be encouraged by letters and visits.

The earlier prescriptions of a "fresh-start" approach in foster care seem currently untenable. This approach was based on the assumption that removing the child from his home would result in a psychological as well as a physical separation, that the effects of his contact with his biological parents would be rapidly vitiated in the foster home. Actually, the difference that visiting makes on the adjustment of the child in the foster home suggests that the biological parents, although absent, continue to affect the life of the child. The biological parent cannot so easily abdicate his influence, and the ties that bind the child to the biological parent are not easily dissolved. However, the effects of prior contact with the biological parent, although they may be greater than had once been assumed, may be less than we currently suppose. Weinstein found that almost none of the unvisited children in placement showed a predominant pattern of identification with biological parents —the identification with them did not persist through the years of broken contact. "Thus, at least at the level being tapped in this study, carryover of identification would seem to require periodic reinforcement through contact." [183, p. 5]

Despite the difficulties inherent in the situation, the visits of the biological parents are important to the child because:

1. He identifies with his parents and perceives rejection of his parents, manifested by limited visiting privileges, as a rejection of himself.
2. He needs to see his parents occasionally, lest he develop ideal fantasies about them.
3. He misses them and mourns their absence.
4. He is helped by their visits to adjust to the realities of separation and to remember the objective reasons which required his separation from his parents. [101, pp. 18–19]
5. If the intent of foster care is temporary, substitute care visits between child and biological parent are required to maintain the continuity of the relationship.

However, studies confirm that visits are a source of considerable dissatisfaction and difficulty to the foster parents. [63; 101; 166; 187] Foster parents may resent the biological parents because

1. They visit at inconvenient times and are sometimes upset and demanding, sometimes drunk and argumentative.
2. The child might be upset by the parents' visits, and more difficult for the foster parents to handle.
3. They are threatened by the competition of the biological parents for the love and affection of the child or because they feel guilty about not having done enough (if one can ever do enough) for the foster child.
4. The parents' visit may present the child with an opportunity to pit foster parent and biological parent against each other.
5. Out of strong feelings of sympathy for the foster child, they may dislike the biological parent, for the harm their physical and/or emotional neglect has caused the child.

Sometimes the relationship is characterized by troublesome dependency. The biological mother in her visits seeks to act like a child toward the foster parent, discussing her troubles and seeking support and reassurance, thus perverting the foster care situation.

In the following material, some of the reasons for conflict between the foster parents and the biological parents are illustrated, as is the caseworker's approach to the problem:

Mrs. G. expressed her very strong disapproval of Mrs. S. as a mother and as a person. She was able to come out and say in no uncertain terms that she disliked Mrs. S. and thought she was a "hateful person." When I tried to discover some of the reasons for the foster mother's feelings, she told me that Mrs. S. had "no respect." I asked her what she meant by this and she said, "She didn't respect me or my home." She told me how she would come into her house smelling of alcohol and how she used to come in and bring men with her and about how she would smoke while she was there, even though Mrs. G. had told her that Theresa was allergic to smoke and that she did not like to have anyone smoke in the same room with Theresa. She said that Mrs. S. would complain about the care she was giving Theresa and told Theresa she was not being well cared for.

The foster mother said she knew Mrs. S. did not like her either and after this last incident, Mrs. S. had never been there again to visit Theresa. Mrs. G. felt that she had tried to be fair about it and had done as much as she could be expected to in allowing Mrs. S. to come into her home; that she felt she had to put up with just too much to let the mother come in and act the way she did. I asked Mrs. G. if she could think of any reason why the mother might act this way, and she said that she could not. She could not understand why people should find fault with someone who had taken care of their children whom they were not able to care for themselves, especially when the care she was giving to Theresa was good and she was feeding and clothing her well. I said these complaints were not surprising to me because we had found that many times parents could come into a foster home and complain about the way the foster mother cared for their children. We have found that the reason the parents did this was mostly because they felt guilty about not being able to care for their children and resented the fact that someone else was able to give them good care. Foster mother said she thought this was true and could see why they would feel that way. The foster mother went on to say she thought that if the mother had really wanted to take care of her children, she would find a way to do it, using the old expression "where there's a will, there is a way." I laughingly replied that if all parents could take care of their own children we would be out of business. [184, p. 9] *

* From Emily Wires, "Some Factors in the Worker-Foster Parent Relationship," *Child Welfare* (October 1954). By permission of Child Welfare League of America, Inc.

The visits look different from the point of view of the biological parent. According to Mrs. McAdams, a mother of six children who were placed when she became mentally ill,

> The fact that you are visiting your child in a foster home is a reminder that you are, at least for the time being, a failure as a parent. You are very sensitive, especially during the first visits. Sometimes a foster parent, in a well-meaning effort to let you know that your child is doing well in a foster home, will make comments on how well the child is eating, how neat he keeps himself and his room, how happy he is, etc. To me, this type of remark was just an implied criticism of the care I had given my child, and was a verbal slap in the face. . . .
>
> The foster parent who gives you orders and instructions in the presence of your child is another problem. You are told that you should have the child back in the foster home at 5 o'clock, and admonished not to be late, or you are told to be sure little Tommy doesn't go outside without his sweater, as he has just recovered from a cold. These instructions may be necessary, but your kid, no matter how young, is already aware of the fact that you have little authority at this time, and this only increases the child's concern as to how responsible you are. If it is necessary to give the natural parent instructions about taking the child away from the foster home on an outing, it would be better to do so out of the child's presence. . . .
>
> I think it is possible for foster parents and natural parents to have mutual respect for each other, but the very nature of their relationship makes it impossible to avoid elements of jealousy and competition. In the case of my children, finding themselves in the position of having foster parents whom they loved and admired and yet having to cope with me trying to strengthen their love for me and regain their trust was almost too much. This problem took a lot of effort at all levels, before they accepted the fact that love for one set of parents did not imply disloyalty to the other. . . .
>
> I know quite often children return from visits with the natural parents with all sorts of plans and promises given them during the visit. It is very difficult to deny a child any hope when the immediate situation seems to be pretty bleak. My kids were able to extract tentative promises of when we would all be reunited, because my pride was killing me and I didn't have the heart to say that I had no home, no money, and no definite time when I would have sufficient emotional and financial resources for getting these things. [110]

In this instance the children were returned home after several years after having been provided, the mother notes, with "a stable home environment and parental supervision at a time of crisis and emotional turmoil."

Recognizing their importance, the agency encourages visits and requires that the foster parents permit them. However, the agency also attempts to control the timing and frequency of visits. If visiting in the home is too upsetting to the foster family and the child, the agency arranges for such visits to take place in the office.

The worker has to prevent any hostility between biological parents and foster parents from affecting the child. Any derogation of the biological parent to the child as a consequence of such hostility is likely to be perceived by the child as a derogation of himself since he is identified with his parents. The agency seeks to mediate between the two sets of parents, maintaining some equilibrium between conflicting needs so that the situation does not harm the child's adjustment to the placement.

Replacement

The most desirable placement is one that permits the child to remain in the same home during the entire period of foster care. Removal from one foster home and replacement in another imposes on the child the emotional burden of repeated separation and change. Every replacement reactivates, and hence reinforces, previous separation and rejection experiences and tends to confirm for the child any predisposition he may have to regard himself as unacceptable to others. It increases the child's difficulty in determining who he is and where he belongs and in establishing a stable sense of identification. It is likely to increase his lack of trust in parental figures. The child is afraid to invest himself in relationship with others because of the experience of hurt, and such relationships are maintained at a shallow level. Frequent replacement makes it more likely that the child will manifest emotional problems and that subsequent placement will fail. [39]

A child may be moved from a foster home if the situation there is not conducive to his best interests, or if his behavior (or that of his parents) makes it very difficult for the foster parents to keep him, or if a change has taken place in the foster family situation—a foster parent becomes ill or dies, the foster family moves, and so on. Sometimes the move is a result of a deliberate plan on the part of the agency—perhaps from a receiving home to an appropriate foster home. It is difficult to know the frequency with which each of the discrete contingencies "causes" the removal of the child.

Trasler studied a group of fifty-seven children, all of whom had been removed at least once over a three-year period from a "long-term foster home" and subsequently replaced in another home. [175] In general, Trasler attributes failure to the child's inability to make an appropriate emotional response to the affection and care offered him by the foster parents—in short, to his inability to establish satisfactory interpersonal relationships. One group of children failed to respond because of prolonged institutional experience and lack of continuity in early mothering. Other children were afraid to invest themselves in an affectional relationship with the foster parents because they lacked confidence in the durability of such relationships. "Poor capacity for emotional response" and "effects of rejection experience" are among the principal causes of foster family care failure in 86 percent of the cases.

Frequently, causative factors are compounded. An emotionally disturbed child behaves in a way too difficult for the foster parent to tolerate and cope with, so that they take advantage of a situational change to request the child's removal. Disturbed behavior, then, is as often the cause of replacement as it is a result of it.

Given the problems for the child in discontinuous living experiences, in the perception of adults as hurtful figures and himself as unacceptable, the caseworker has a difficult decision to make. Are the dangers in the home so great, and the advantages of the next available foster home so unquestionable, as to warrant replacement? Often, of course, the decision is made for the social worker by foster parents who insist upon the child's removal. However, in those cases the worker should have been aware of the deteriorating situation and should have been discussing the foster parents' reactions to the difficulties. A precipitous removal made in the heat of a crisis is to be avoided.

When replacement must be made, it should be planned and as a result of mutual participation between the social worker, the child, and the foster parents. If possible, it should have the acceptance of the foster parents, so that they can help the child to move. This is difficult if the move is a result of the failure of the foster parents to cope adequately with the child's behavior, because the move itself is a symbol of their failure. Throughout the replacement procedure, the caseworker must be sensitive to the feelings of the foster parents and attempt to help them feel less anxious, less guilty, less threatened by the experience. As Herstein says, the caseworker should "present the reasons for replacement in terms which would be both realistic and within the boundaries of what the foster parents can emotionally and objectively accept." [72, p. 24]

The caseworker should also encourage the child's expression of feeling regarding the replacement, and help to interpret it in such a way that the child does not perceive the experience as another personal failure.

It would be helpful to both the child and the foster parents if they saw one another occasionally after the child has been replaced, so that the child's memory of the foster parents will not be distorted by anxiety-provoking fantasies and the foster parents will be reassured that the child is adequately cared for and does not hate them.

Termination

Ideally, once the child is in foster care, a plan should be formulated along three basic alternatives.

1. Planning for the child's return home by working with the biological parents and the child toward modification of those conditions which necessitated placement.
2. Planning for termination of parental rights and permanent parental substitution, when there is little likelihood that the home situation can be sufficiently modified. This involves working with the biological parents so that they consent to the child's release and placement for adoption.
3. Planning for long-term foster care when it is not likely that the child will ever be able to return to his own home and there is little likelihood that he can be placed for adoption.

Actually many of the key factors in the agency's choice of alternatives are shrouded in ambiguity and subject to change. The modifiability of the child's own home situation may not be clear at first, and the child's adoptability changes with the passage of time.

The first alternative terminates, of course, with the child's return home; the second, with adoption of the child; the third, with the child's achievement of his independence.

If termination involves the child's return to his own home, the social worker discusses with the child the implications of the impending change and, with the biological parents, some of the differences they might expect to find in the child as a result of his having lived away from them for a time. The foster parents are helped with their feelings about giving up a child for whom they have developed some feeling and the importance of their contribution is clearly acknowledged.

Foster family care is best terminated when the biological parents want the child home and can make a home for him. The parent may seek to terminate placement prematurely out of guilt or in response to the child's insistence that he be permitted to come home, or out of a fear that the child will forget him or reject him. These are reasons which make the success of the child's return home problematic.

Group Methods in Foster Family Care

Group methods have been used in working with foster parents. [7; 10; 14; 19; 25; 47; 51; 138; 146; 170] Membership in these groups is voluntary and the groups are small. In one instance, however, attendance was required as part of the responsibility parents assumed in caring for foster children. [170, p. 220] Sometimes the meetings are directed to foster mothers only, but more frequently they are designed for both foster parents. Although the groups often start with a didactic instructional format, they move to a more informal pattern in which the content for discussion is decided on by group members. Group activities include an annual foster parents' "recognition" party sponsored by the agency and highlighted by awards to foster parents.

On occasion, a more formal program of education may be sponsored jointly by the agency and an educational institution. A study of the changes in foster parents that resulted from one thirty-two week "group educational program" showed statistically significant differences between the changes achieved by the experimental and control groups in the relationship to the agency and the ability to understand and respond appropriately to needs and behavior of children. [163]

More frequently, however, evaluation of group meetings is in terms of general statements from foster parents. For instance, in one such evaluation report, "an experienced foster mother said that just knowing that other people had the same problems with foster children was very reassuring in relieving the anxiety of her husband and herself as foster parents." [47, p. 72]

Foster parents groups have discussed such topics as:

1. The feelings and problems that the child brings into placement.
2. The meaning of separation.
3. Child development.
4. The common problems of children in foster care, particularly enuresis, disobedience.
5. The differences in disciplining foster children and one's own children.
6. The attitudes of the community toward foster parents and foster children.
7. How to help children leave foster care.
8. The roles of the agency and the social worker in foster care.
9. The foster child with special needs.
10. Attitudes toward biologial parents.

The content and interaction of such discussion groups are illustrated in the following:

In discussing visiting parents, Mrs. J. said: "I think all visits with child and parents should take place in the agency office. Why isn't it done this way?" Mr. and Mrs. M. both spoke up, saying they had had problems with visiting parents—one mother had stayed until 1 a.m. and then had to be driven home because the buses were no longer running. Mrs. C. chimed in about the child she's boarding—the mother is supposed to come at 11 a.m. but doesn't show up until 3 p.m., and, since this mother is "mentally upset," Mrs. C. is afraid to say anything to upset her more. Mrs. J. asserted that she is incapable of taking care of problem parents—"that is the agency's job."

The leader said she wondered what experiences other foster parents had had. Mrs. A. said she and her husband never had any problems with visiting parents; they are just very definite with them. She added, "Don't let anybody take you for a fool." Mr. A. supported his wife, saying, "You have to be firm and definite." Mrs. M. asked how to do this since when you're nice to the mother she takes advantage of you. Mrs. K. stated she had been very firm with parents and told them to leave when the visiting time was up. Mrs. J. and Mrs. R. said that perhaps Mrs. A. and Mrs. K. could do this, but they could not tell parents they had to leave the house.

Mrs. C. and Mr. and Mrs. M. expressed relief that other people had this problem. They said they had wondered if they were doing wrong or not handling the problem correctly, and were encouraged to know that it must not be entirely their fault.

The leader raised the question of whether or not the foster parents had contacted the agency when problems had come up about visiting. They said they had hesitated to get in touch with the agency because they thought they should be able to handle the problems themselves. Mrs. A. pointed out that agency and foster parents work together and that the agency could be of help. The leader pointed out that the agency expects problems, and that while neither the agency nor the foster parents can handle every situation perfectly, both could do a better job through working together with confidence in each other.

At the end of the discussion, Mrs. C. and Mr. and Mrs. R. said that they have had bad experiences with visiting parents, but that they think they will be able to do a better job in this area in the future. [170, pp. 221–22] *

Group meetings with foster parents conducted by agency personnel have the following purposes and advantages.

1. To heighten the foster parents' identification with the agency and its program, and to develop loyalty to the program.
2. To widen the foster parents' concern and interest from their own foster child to all the children offered service by the agency.

* From Carolyn Thomas, "The Use of Group Methods with Foster Parents," *Children* (November–December 1961). By permission of the author and *Children*, U.S. Department of Health, Education, and Welfare, Social Security Administration, Children's Bureau.

3. To increase their knowledge and skills of foster parenthood and to improve their relationship with the foster child through increasing tolerance and understanding of the child's behavior.

4. To offer the foster parents an opportunity to discuss with other foster parents problems of mutual concern.

5. To enhance the status and, hence, the satisfactions of foster parents. They see themselves as a group specially chosen by the agency for a significant function.

6. To enable the agency to have a better understanding of the experiences encountered by foster parents in their day-to-day dealings with the child and their reactions to these experiences.

7. To enable foster parents to gain an appreciation of what is involved for the biological parent and child in the experience of separation. There is an opportunity for foster parents to develop a greater tolerance toward the natural parent as they learn something about the difficult life situations such parents face.

8. To enable the foster parents to gain a better appreciation of the agency's difficulties and problems. One father in one of the groups said, "I used to think the agency shouldn't make it so easy for parents to place a child. I thought it was like taking off an overcoat and saying 'here, take care of it' but I see it isn't so easy."

9. To develop a consensus about the role of the foster parent and the relative rights and obligations of agency and foster parents toward the foster child and toward the biological parents.

10. To help the foster parents realize that in some instances they may fail despite their best efforts, that failure in foster care may result from the child's deficiencies rather than any shortcomings on their part. They appreciate the truth of this as they listen to other foster parents discuss some of the problems they have encountered. It relieves the foster parents of a private evaluation of failure and guilt and feelings of frustration and discouragement.

11. To permit, in the safety of numbers, foster parents expression of dissatisfaction with agency policy, although some caseworkers fear the development of a foster parents' trade union which would bargain with the agency for better rates for foster parents. [138]

12. To permit a more expeditious discussion, with a large number of parents, of agency policy as it affects foster parents, and to obtain their help in formulating or reviewing policy.

13. To spark and plan recruitment programs for the agency, and help increase the supply of foster homes by reducing turnover. [106]

14. To give prospective applicants a clearer idea of what is involved in foster parenthood, and to help them to come to a decision. This permits judicious self-screening by some who find that the correction of their misconceptions has left them with no desire to continue. For those who decide to continue such group meetings help prepare

them for the home study so that they are in a better position to participate effectively.

The potential positive consequences of group meetings are that as a result, there would be a lower rate of foster parent turnover, fewer replacements of children, and a more capable foster parent available to the child during the time he is in placement.

Good intentions, however, go far beyond actual practice. A 1968 nationwide study of foster care agency practice reveals that "group work and community organization methods were reported by few respondents." [165, p. 27]

Evaluation

The nineteenth-century controversy over "placing out" of large numbers of children from metropolitan areas in the East to rural areas in the West and South produced a rash of evaluation studies, many of which were somewhat haphazard and biased. Some of the more respectable of these early studies have little relevance now because of the changed nature of the foster family care program. We will attempt, therefore, to review only the more recent studies.

In the early 1920's, the State Charities Aid Association in New York City evaluated all those children who had been under foster family care through the agency for at least one year and were, at the time of the study, at least eighteen years old. [16] This study was, as the agency contends, "the first serious effort to collect, at first hand, on a considerable scale, the facts as to the careers of an unselected group of foster children." Information was obtained on the basis of interviews by social workers with the foster child himself, or with the foster parents or relatives. The foster children were categorized by "experienced supervisors" as "capable"—subjects who are law-abiding, who manage their affairs with good sense, and who are living in accordance with good moral standards of their communities—or "incapable"—subjects who are unable or unwilling to support themselves adequately, who are shiftless, or who have defied the accepted standards of morality or order of their communities. Of 562 foster children in the group who were not subsequently adopted and on whom sufficient data for judging were available, 73 percent were judged "capable" and 27 percent "incapable" at the time of follow-up. Age at placement was significantly related to outcome: children who were five or younger when placed were more likely to be judged "capable." Outcome was not related to socioeconomic level of the home, but was related to the quality of foster parent-foster child relationships.

Baylor and Monachesi did a follow-up study of 478 children after discharge from foster care. For most of the children, the research was conducted four to six years after discharge. The Social Service Exchange was used to obtain follow-up information and "visits were made, sometimes several, in the homes of people concerned; employers were visited or sought by correspondence." [8, p. 414] The material assembled by field workers was evaluated independently by each of the authors. Of the 478 children for whom a "behavior evaluation" was attempted, 67.4 percent were found to be "behaving favorably" at the time of the follow-up. Children who had been placed for health reasons, because of a "broken home," or because of dependency and neglect, showed a much lower percentage of "unfavorable behavior" than children placed because of behavioral difficulties and/or delinquency. [8, p. 417]

The Dutch Child Caring Agency, Tot Steun, did a follow-up interview study in 1952–54 of 160 former foster children born between 1903 and 1920 who had been in care of the agency at one time for a "considerable length of time." [179] Interviews conducted by social workers ran for two to three hours. It was found that "more than half of all the respondents expressed strong negative feelings toward their foster parents" and most of these had severed "every contact with the foster parents after coming of age," as they had with their own parents. [179, p. 30] Those who had contact with their own families during foster family care and felt accepted by their own mothers were more accepting of the foster parents. "The feeling of being loved by their own mothers evidently helped their relationship with the foster parents," for these respondents "tended to speak kindly of their foster parents." This reinforces the findings of Weinstein and Cowan and Stout that positive contacts with the natural parents assist in the child's adjustment in the foster home. In summation, the report notes that "the situation of many of these former foster children at the time of the inquiry left much to be desired. Socially, many were rather well established. Only a few were unemployed or antisocial or had lost the parental rights to their own children. However, many felt unsuccessful, dissatisfied, and distressed." [179, p. 33]

Gil conducted follow-up interviews with twenty-five former foster children, or their relatives, five to six years after termination of agency service. [55] Judgments were made regarding the extent to which these foster children had realized their "developmental potential," previously evaluated on the basis of critical analysis of the significant data in the foster child's agency record. Twelve of the twenty-five subjects showed "considerable realization of preadmission developmental potential"; thirteen showed limited realization of such potential. [55, p. 235] The degree of realization was not related to the number of replacement experiences but was "markedly associated" with the quality of the foster home in which the subject had been placed. Tinker, too, found that when the foster family home meets the emotional needs of children, they tend to develop normally and healthfully. [172; 173; 174]   Murphy, reviewing the records of a Canadian agency, selected the records of mentally normal children who had been in continuous foster family care for more than five years, whose cases were closed at the time of the study, and who were at least eleven years of age at the time the case was closed. [120]   Two senior social workers, who had been with the agency throughout and who had "unusually complete memories," made available their knowledge of the outcome of each of the 316 cases selected for study. This was supplemented by agency records, which included post-closure contacts with foster child, foster parents, and "courts, hospitals, family agencies, and some employers in the city." The two senior officers divided the 316 former foster children into three categories:

1. Outcome satisfactory ("A") in terms of child's social milieu.
2. Outcome less satisfactory ("B"), but without signs of pathology or open disturbance.
3. Outcome unsatisfactory ("C"), usually with signs of pathology or disturbance. C ratings were given if there was a record of admission to a mental hospital, or involvement with the courts on other than a trivial charge.

Of the 316 cases, sixty-one, or 19.3 percent, were given a C rating; 151, or about 50 percent, received an A rating. [120, p. 392]   Murphy also found that the sex of the foster child is a significant factor related to outcome: if placement was the result of illegitimate births, the likelihood of failure in later life was significantly greater for the female child than for the male.

Ferguson did a follow-up study of some 140 young adults who had been cared for in foster family homes during childhood in Scotland. [48] At age twenty, 96 percent of the group were employed or in training and independently responsible for their own support. Rate of delinquency was high, however, 17 percent having been convicted of some crime before age twenty. It must be noted, however, that more than 50 percent of this group had tested IQ scores below 90.

Meier did a follow-up interview study of sixty-one adults between the ages of twenty-eight and thirty-two who had been in foster care in Minnesota for a period of at least five years. [114]   The criteria for outcome were based on the interviewers' ratings of the respondents' level of social effectiveness (employment and economic circumstances, care of the home and of the children, social relationships outside the home) and their feeling of well-being (feeling of adequacy, capacity to experience pleasure). Fifteen men and twenty-four women—some 64 percent of the total sample—had positive ratings in all areas of social functioning; the rest had a negative rating in at least one area, and three respondents had negative ratings in three areas. In summary, Meier notes:

> Current circumstances of these young adults as a group contrast
> sharply with family circumstances at the time of their placement;
> with few exceptions they are self-supporting individuals, living
> in conformity with the social standards of their communities.
> The children of most of them are well cared for. . . . In most areas
> of adaptation, current functioning compares favorably with that of
> the general population. . . . [114, p. 2]

Age at first placement and the number of placements were not found
to be significantly related to over-all social effectiveness and sense of
well-being, but they were related to specific aspects of functioning. Like
Murphy, Meier found that the sex of the foster child was a very important variable in determining response to foster care. The data suggested
that being reared away from his own family in itself damaged the male's
self-concept, whereas for the female, the content and quality of the
experience is of greater importance..

Children who were in foster care for long periods have in 70 to 80
percent of the cases grown up satisfactorily. Some of the associations
usually thought to be related to outcome, such as age at placement,
number of replacements, are not unequivocally supported in the studies.
Outcome seems to be differentially related to sex of the child and directly
related to interpersonal quality of the foster home.

Problems

1. One of the most serious problems faced by the foster home program is that for some children it fails to fulfill its purpose. The distinguishing aspect of foster care is that it is designed to be a temporary
arrangement. Currently, however, some children moving into foster care
never return to their own homes. [83, p. 87; 104, p. 379]

These are the children who are likely to grow up in foster care,
"orphans of the living," unvisited and unwanted by their parents, yet
not fully "belonging" to the foster family, living "in a placement that
goes on and on without termination but also without assurance of permanence." [97, p. 40]

As Sauber says in an extensive study of foster family care in one
community, "the typical [foster] child is not a three-year-old girl whose
mother will be in the hospital for six months and then reclaim the child.
The typical child is a boy of ten and one-half who has probably been in
foster care since he was six and has had more than one replacement."
[144, p. 25]

Agency response to a nationwide Child Welfare League study indicated that in 1968 the most common age of children coming into foster

family care was "under five years." The most common average length of stay in care was "twelve months or less," but about 25 percent of all placed children remained in care for more than thirty-six months. [165, p. 37]

The likelihood of the child's returning home is related to the factors which brought about his placement. Children who come to foster care because of physical illness of the mother are likely to return home after only a limited period of time. Children placed because they manifest problems of emotional disturbance are likely to remain in care for a longer period of time. When placement is initiated by the parents, the child is likely to remain in foster care longer than if it is initiated against their opposition.

Studies show that the longer a child has been in placement, the greater the likelihood that he will continue in placement. [44; 79; 103; 104; 149] Although parents have strong reactions to placement, their motivation to see the child returned home diminishes with time. Their sense of responsibility for the child, not being actively exercised, atrophies. Many gradually reorient their lives to the reality that they are no longer actually parents caring for their children, accepting employment and moving into smaller apartments. Having reorganized their lives in ways which do not include the child, his return would be disruptive and tends to be increasingly resisted. The separation becomes total—except in legal terms. Consequently, to optimize the chances of a child's returning home, maximum effort should be exerted early in the history of the placement.

2. A major component of foster care should be the effort to help the biological parents to effect changes that will permit the child's early return home. Yet here we encounter a second problem of foster care. Every study confirms the fact that little direct rehabilitative service is offered such parents. [54; 165] Maas, in his nationwide study, concludes, "Agency relationships with most fathers and mothers of the children in care are such that, if parental conditions are to be modified, the process will have to be one of self-healing without any assistance of casework service." [102, p. 5] A factor analysis of the study data indicated that long periods in care were associated with the fact that "casework of only the most superficial kind has been offered the natural parents of such children." [45, p. 128] A more recent national study of foster care practice concluded that, "once the child is in care, contact between parents and agency . . . generally [is] infrequent." [165, p. 28]

Some considerable component in this problematic situation rests with the kinds of families the agency is called upon to help. One study of the families of one hundred children, selected at random from the agency foster care case load, indicated that many "had such a serious degree of social and emotional incompetence as to render them in all probability beyond the hope of salvage for the particular child." [164, p. 27] The parents who need to place a child frequently have such limited strengths that even the best service will not result in rehabilitation. If, as the relevant studies indicate, lack of motivation to change is one of the factors in the behavior of the biological parents which determine the worker's decision to place the child, we can expect that this same lack of motivation would continue, after placement, to make more difficult rehabilitation of the home. It might be prudent, as Lawder suggests, not to confuse child welfare ideals with achievable goals. [95, p. 6]   Yet many of these children, although they no longer have much relationship or contact with their own parents, nevertheless legally "belong" to them and are not free for adoption. Of necessity, then, they live in an in-between world—between a family that does not want them and a family that cannot fully have them. These children, in reality, should be provided with an adoptive home.

In response to the child's need for a set of parents whom he could identify as his "own" with some assurance of permanence, many states have moved to simplify the process of termination of parental rights in cases where parents show no sustained interest in the child and where there is no foreseeable likelihood that the parents can, or will, plan for the return home of the child. One of the earliest of such plans of legislative action was taken in New York in 1959, to free the "permanently neglected" child for adoption. When the parents had forfeited their rights to the child by failure to discharge the obligations of parenthood, termination of parental rights without their consent was made permissible. [129; 130]   Previously, such children were available for adoption only if their biological parents gave their consent, or if the court found them abandoned. To declare a child abandoned, the court had to be satisfied that the parents had displayed "a settled purpose to forego forever all parental rights"—a severe test.

> The [new] law involves creating a new legal category, the "permanently neglected child" and giving jurisdiction to the children's courts to terminate parental rights over such a child in a proceeding initiated by the social agency having the child in its care and desiring to place him for adoption. [130, p. 1]

A "permanently neglected child" is defined as a child in foster care whose parents,

> . . . notwithstanding the diligent efforts of the agency to encourage and strengthen the parental relationship, failed substantially and continuously or repeatedly for a period of more than one year to maintain contact with, and plan for the future of the child although physically and financially able to do so. . . . [130, p. 2]

One of the real difficulties lies in the phrase *physically able*. Some children remain in foster family care over long periods because their mothers are hospitalized for mental illness. There is strong resistance to terminating parental rights in such instances, because mental illness is not the fault of the parent. The Children's Bureau suggests that, where mental illness is likely to continue "for a prolonged indeterminate period," the agency be given the sanction to press for termination of parental rights so as to free the child for adoption.

Of course, freeing foster children for adoption does not guarantee that they will be adopted. Children over two (see Chap. 10) and non-white children are difficult to place for adoption. However, the new laws may permit the agencies to move more expeditiously and plan adoption for some children before they grow too old or too disturbed to be easily placed for adoption.

A May 1970 survey conducted by the New York City Department of Social Services revealed that 6487 children in foster care were identified as having had no contact with either parent in the last six months. Although some 1600 of these children were legally adoptable, adoption was being actively considered for only about 225 of the children. [9]

3. There is a continuous problem in finding a sufficient number of adequate foster homes. An even greater problem is the difficulty of finding specialized foster homes for emotionally disturbed children, mentally defective children, and nonwhite children. Most foster parents want preschool children, while many of the children who need foster care are older.

A 1968 nationwide study of foster care agencies showed that the most important factor "adversely affecting quality of care" was "lack of facilities—both foster homes and group care resources." [165, p. 14] The shortage of homes limits the deliberate care with which the social worker can select a home for a particular child. Despite the practice view that priority should be given to the child's needs, in actuality not need but resources available often determines the decisions.

The difficulty of finding adequate foster family homes is likely to become progressively more severe. Women's liberation, zero population growth, the increasing percentage of working mothers—all contribute to the devaluation of parenthood and the child-rearing functions. The competition of the employment market, for which many more women can now qualify, and its substantially higher economic returns, will further reduce the number of women likely to be interested in foster care. The large families that once served as the training ground for many foster mothers are a thing of the past, and limited house space makes difficult the addition of another family member. The more open, working-class family, from which the foster parents traditionally come, is being replaced by the middle-class family, a compact nuclear group which discourages the entry of newcomers. [54, p. 85]   The fact is that there are, and probably always have been, relatively few people who are willing to accept the burden and responsibility of rearing someone else's child.

Foster homes are not only difficult to recruit but, once recruited, are difficult to retain. The average length of service by foster parents is four to six years. The single most frequent reason for giving up a foster care license was that the parents "were no longer interested." [165, p. 33]

4. The problem of recruitment is related to the problem of finances. The most recent national study indicates that in June 1970 the median basic maintenance payment for children under five was about $70 a month; for older children, $85–95. [66, p. 11]   In addition, agencies pay all medical and dental fees and meet costs for clothing, school supplies, and incidentals. Special board rates are paid for care of emotionally disturbed children. The report notes that "over half the [144] agencies [included in the study] reported that their rates do not cover costs" the foster parents incur in caring for the child. [66, p. 23]

Increases in maintenance rates have generally lagged behind increases in costs of living. Consequently, in a time of rapid increases in cost of living, foster parents are asked to accept even less in real income than previously. Board rates are not regarded as taxable income, and are not generally regarded as income in determining public assistance grants. But there is no payment for the time and energy devoted to the care of the child.

The Child Welfare League is frank and direct in calling for higher board rates. *Child Welfare*, the official organ of the League, calls attention to the fact that "children are 'stacked up' in temporary shelters awaiting more appropriate placement," while boarding rates are far lower than the rates usually received by babysitters and, in "most cities in the country, a cleaning woman can earn in two days more than foster parents receive in a week." [58, p. 56]

Foster family home placements have always been recruited on the basis of a quid pro quo. The nature of return for the foster parent has changed, however, with changing circumstances. At one time, almost all foster homes were free homes. Payment was the labor contributed by the child to the family. Urbanization required a money payment and put a new stress on the psychic satisfactions derived from fostering children. The relationship between money as a motivation for foster parents and their acceptability as applicants has rarely been tested empirically. An interesting experiment, conducted in Israel, indicates that a decent level of payment increases recruitment possibilities and that people who are attracted by such payment are also good prospects:

In an empirical test of motivation for fostering, students at a school of social work placed two advertisements at an interval of one month apart in the Israeli newspaper, *Maariv*. The first ad appealed for foster parents and mentioned "modest financial remuneration"; this attracted five applicants (who were then interviewed and the information or home study forwarded to the Child Welfare Division of the Ministry of Social Welfare), most of whom were deeply religious people. In the second ad the wording was identical to the first *except* for the fact that "reasonable financial remuneration" was offered. A total of 185 persons responded to the second ad. One of the striking conclusions derived from the students' interviews with foster care applicants was that there was no significant connection between the fact that an applicant applies purely for monetary reasons and his suitability or unsuitability for the role of foster parent. [76, pp. 17–18]

Analysis of what adequate board rates may cost the agency at the minimum wage rate indicates that the costs of foster care would be very substantially higher than they are now. [71] Society would have to agree to invest very considerably more in the foster family care program if payment were to be made for services rendered in addition to child maintenance payments.

Efforts have been made to study the effects on foster care of payment of a fee or a salary to foster parents for the time and effort devoted to child care. [77] In one experiment a salary of $200 a month was paid (in addition to the usual basic maintenance allowance), and the foster parents were viewed as agency employees. In a second experiment, a $100 service fee was paid. In general, the effects of such payments were positive.

1. The agencies were less defensive and apologetic in their relationship with the foster parents. The agency felt freer about making task assignments. One agency required that "the foster parents submit a brief monthly report of the child's adjustment." The requirement was met with regularity by most of the foster homes.
2. Agencies were less defensive in presenting the realities of the foster children's difficulties. The workers were less anxious about sharing the details of a child's behavioral difficulties for fear that the foster parents would reject the request for placement.
3. Payment for child care did not adversely affect the quality of care given. "Caseworkers gauged the over-all quality of foster parent functioning to be excellent or good in almost seven of ten cases." [77, p. 82]
4. The payments highlighted and made explicit the value to the agency and the community of the service performed by the foster parents.
5. The foster parents felt a greater sense of identification with the agency and perceived agency staff members as peers and colleagues.

It had been feared that such an arrangement might render foster parents vulnerable to the charge that they were mercenary in accepting salary for the care of a child, and that the children might react negatively to the fact that they were a source of income. Neither effect was confirmed by the studies.

In another experiment, which focused on a group foster home arrangement, foster parents were retained as salaried employees of the agency." There was no evidence of incompatibility between the employee status and the parenting role." [131, p. 27]   Nor was there any evidence that care of the children was adversely affected by the greater financial returns offered.

It is not certain that such procedures would lead to easier recruitment and longer retention of more foster homes. The limited empirical material available, however, suggests that a modest increment of homes might result. More adequate financial payments do enhance and support foster family care functioning. And for some the financial supports make possible the realization of a desire to become foster parents. Compassion and altruism, reinforced by an affective bond between foster parents and foster child, by some psychic recompense to the foster parent in meeting his own emotional needs, enable the foster parent to accept with more equanimity the burdens of foster parenthood. However, compassion and altruism, reinforced by psychic return and *adequate* financial reward, may provide a larger pool of foster homes than is currently available.

The problem is compounded by the fact that foster care is already very expensive. According to a recent study of cost factors in foster care, it is estimated that it cost $122,500 to provide foster care for an infant child who came into the system in 1971 and will stay in care for the full eighteen years of childhood. [46]

5. The problem of board rate payments is related to the problem of the agency's definition of its relationship to the foster parents. In one sense foster parents are "clients" of the agency because the agency has a resource—foster children—that can help to meet some of the foster parents' needs. In another sense, they are nonprofessional volunteer members of an agency staff, offering their homes and their services to meet the needs of children. In one sense they stand in a supervisee relationship to the supervisor worker assigned to the home. [57, p. 201]   In another sense they are colleagues cooperatively engaged with the worker in helping the child, each providing different kinds of help, offering skills at different levels of professionalization.

Differences in definition have implications for what is regarded as the appropriate agency-foster parent relationship. Those who define the foster parent as a client suggest that it is appropriate for the caseworker to offer casework treatment to the foster parent. In asking for a child the foster parents "are unconsciously seeking help with their own needs."

"Asking for a child may serve as a ticket of admission to the agency to enable the family to get its own needs met." [57, p. 199]   In this view the child is a therapeutic resource offered to the family by the agency.

If the foster parents are volunteer helpers, then any board rate payment is inappropriate. If they are paid employees and colleagues, then the level of board rate payment is inadequate.

There are recurrent suggestions that adequate levels of board rate payments would ensure a larger supply of applicants and resolve the confusion in the agency-foster parent relationship. It is suggested that foster parenthood be clearly established as a job title, that the agency pay adequate compensation, and that the foster parent be clearly recognized as an employee of the agency. This would further help to differentiate more clearly the foster parent role from the biological parent role. The foster parent would be defined as a person offering full-time physical, social, and emotional care to nonrelated children in a family setting as an employee of a child welfare agency.

If the foster parent is considered a trusted employee, then much of what is detailed in the literature regarding the contact between the caseworker and the foster family parallels the material on good employer-employee relationships—the need for recognition and appreciation of work well done, the need for support, reassurance, and understanding when the worker is facing some difficulty on the job, the need for maintaining a high level of morale.

As is true for any job, there are necessary elements of administrative supervision to assure the agency that the job is being competently performed. Caseworker visits to determine how the child is being cared for are also in line with the employee-employer relationship. The agency has to take some responsibility for developing skills, for educating the employee to meet the demands of the job. The educational-advising component in the caseworker's visits coincides with this aspect of the employer-employee relationship.

The agency employee concept makes more understandable, and more acceptable, an extensive evaluation study in selecting foster parents. As would be true for any job situation, it is understandable that the employing agency should have the right to make such study as it needs to assure itself that the applicant has the necessary qualifications for the position.

Opponents of this conception of the foster parent's role maintain that it would complicate and demean the foster child-foster parent relationship. If the foster parent is an employee, then the child can view his stay in the foster home as a business transaction, himself as a source of income, and any acceptance of himself as a person predicated on the desire for such income. He can use this as a lever to threaten foster parents with loss of their job. In response, however, it is pointed out that teachers, psychiatrists, and caseworkers ask for adequate compensation for services performed and yet present themselves as accepting children for their own sake and are deeply concerned with helping them. The interrelated problems of adequate recruitment, board payments, and the definition of foster parents' relationship to the agency remain currently unresolved.

Foster parents themselves are very ambivalent about employee status. As expressed in discussions of this at meetings of foster parents' organizations, the conflict between the humanitarian motive and the monetization of the child care becomes clear. But although foster parents reject salaries, they accept the need for better reimbursement. [139]

6. The field of social work also faces a problem in that it does not have clear title to the function of foster family placement. Children may be placed in an independent foster family home directly by their own parents. It is not known how many children are placed independently in foster homes, but one article noted that, in the state of Michigan, one-third of all children in foster care are in independent foster homes. [98] Parents do have the privilege of planning for their own children; the decision to place, when and where, rests primarily with the parents. Parents with money make this decision without controversy—by sending their children to boarding schools, camps, and so on. It is felt that people without money should have the same privilege. Yet the possibilities of abuse do exist, and because society does have a stake in what happens to the child, it has the right to regulate placements.

7. The rate of turnover of foster homes is lower than the rate of turnover among social workers assigned to such homes. [165, p. 34] A recent English study of foster care showed that the "rate at which child care officers replace one another is higher than the replacement rate of foster families." [54, p. 223] A study of twenty older children in long-term foster family care showed that, on the average, the children had lived in the same foster home for eight years from the date of placement, but had a different caseworker every year. [117, p. 193] Although the child's relationship with the caseworker is theoretically the only relationship on which the child can rely, the fact is that frequent personnel turnover makes for frequent changes in this relationship as well. It has been suggested, therefore, that stress be put on the child's relationship to the agency, which is always present and available, rather than on his relationship with the more transient caseworker. [50, p. 6] Actually, while considerable attention has been given to the problem of helping the child with his adjustment to a change of foster homes, much less consideration has been given to the problem of adjustment to a change of worker. [5]

Personnel turnover affects service to the foster parents as well. One study, involving lengthy interviews with 115 foster families, indicated that, as a result of such turnover, "about one-third of the mothers said that there have been times when they didn't know who their caseworker was." [185, p. 10]

Trends

1. The number of children coming into substitute care is increasing. This upward trend will be accompanied by a continuation of a trend toward increased responsibility of public welfare agencies for foster family care and a leveling off of the shift from institutional care to foster family care for children needing substitute care. While there was, throughout the 1960 decade, a consistent switch from institutions to foster family care, the rate of such change slowed down toward the end of the decade.

2. There is a trend toward a changing composition of children coming into foster family care. The development of services to children in their own homes implies that many situations that once led to foster care do not do so today. This suggests that the families of children needing foster family care are those that demonstrate the greatest disorganization, the greatest pathology. Children who have lived under such conditions for some time have suffered more deprivation and have more emotional difficulties than was true of children who come into foster care earlier in our history. A study by MacDonald at a Chicago agency, comparing children served by the agency at two different periods, tends to support this contention. [105]   Selig, basing her statements on a detailed knowledge of Jewish child care agencies, states that "disturbed children represent an increasing number of children in placement." [148, p. 74]

Because of the changing composition of the group of children placed in foster family care, more of the child-placing agencies offer an interdisciplinary service. The psychiatrist, the psychologist, and the educational consultant often help in making a diagnostic assessment of the child and the natural home.

3. The changing nature of the foster child places a heavier burden on the foster family home. This suggests a trend toward an explicit recognition of foster family care as a treatment resource. The more benign, more therapeutic environment of a good foster family, in itself, has treatment potential. It permits the actualization of the recuperative capacities of the child and permits the psyche an opportunity to mend itself. Just as many illnesses yield to rest, good food, and the reduction of outer stress, so a healthy emotional environment may encourage and support the health-striving tendencies within a child. There is a trend, then, toward actively enlisting the foster parents, wherever possible, in the treatment plan. The caseworker may instruct the foster parents to behave in such a manner, to respond in a particular way to the child, so as to reinforce and support casework efforts.

4. There is also a trend toward the exploration of groups in the population previously untapped for foster parenthood. For instance, in New York City the "continuance of the deplorable situation in which over 200 babies, mostly under two years of age, remain in the wards of public and voluntary hospitals while waiting for foster home placement" prompted recruitment of foster homes among the public assistance caseload. [53]   An arrangement was made so that board payment was not computed as a deductible income from the public assistance budget. AFDC families, despite the absence of a father in many of the homes, were a fruitful source of new foster homes. Although economically deprived, these families had achieved a level of emotional and social stability that offered considerable strengths. The report of the project notes:

> The potential project foster mother is an AFDC mother whose status has been stabilized for two or three years and who has school-aged children who are making an adequate adjustment in school. The family is integrated into the immediate community. The mother is active in a church or parents' group and maintains close ties with her family or a small group of neighbors [and is a good manager]. . . . We have found that the fatherless family home should not be categorically ruled out, particularly in a program such as ours in offering temporary care to babies. [53, p. 4]

Families were recommended by social workers assigned to the project and it was the pride and prestige in such selection, rather than the money, that seemed to be the more important factor in eliciting interest. As part of this trend attention has been called to the recruitment potential for foster homes among segments of the population not currently actively contacted, such as suburban homes [161] and low-income neighborhoods. [161]   Recruitment drives have been successfully conducted in ghetto areas for foster homes for nonwhite children (*The New York Times*, July 13, 1970). Thus the child continues to live in a familiar neighborhood and in a home that more nearly resembles his own.

5. There is also a trend toward greater diversification of foster homes. Besides receiving homes or group homes, there has been an attempt to develop specialized foster homes to offer care to the mentally defective child, the emotionally disturbed child, the physically handicapped child, the delinquent child, and the unmarried mother. [1; 24; 31; 49; 59; 73; 75; 84; 109; 135; 136; 142; 186]   The foster parents are selected because of their special interest in, and capacity for, working with children who present these problems. Most such families care for one or two children at a time, and are generally paid a premium beyond the usual board rate.

A report of a special project offering family care to emotionally disturbed children, some of whom were diagnosed as psychotic or brain-damaged, indicates the possibility as well as the difficulty of such service. [84]   The project, which involved intensive casework, psychiatric treatment, and adjunctive services (such as special camps and special schooling), served twenty-seven children over a twelve-year period. Of nine children on whom a follow-up report is given, five appear to be doing well, self-sustaining or in college, three are in mental institutions, the whereabouts of one is unknown. The impression given is that the five children who are doing well would not have been salvaged except for the project.

6. Since for many children foster family care is not a temporary expedient, more explicit attention is being devoted to planned long-term placement in a quasi-adoptive situation in which the foster parent is granted more autonomy than in the usual foster care arrangement. Until recently, long-term placements evolved without deliberate design as plans for the child's return home repeatedly failed. [18; 108; 182]

Long-term foster care has been accepted as desirable for children for whom adoption or return to the natural home is not advisable. Long-term care involves a contractual agreement between the agency and the foster family: the agency agrees not to remove the child, and the family agrees to accept responsibility for his continued care.

Several studies have confirmed that children can develop normally under long-term foster care. [87; 108]   One study, which compared the children in long-term foster care with a group of children in adoptive homes, found that "there were no statistically significant differences in the functioning of the two groups of parents nor in that of the two groups of children." [96, p. 74]

Permanent foster care, which is, in effect, a social adoption, is part of a trend toward the attenuation of the previously clear distinction between foster family care and adoption. As part of this trend, many agencies now permit foster parents to apply for the adoption of the child they are fostering if and when such children become available for adoption. [165, p. 31]

7. Foster parents have begun to organize nationally, and the First National Conference of Foster Parents met in Chicago in 1971. [23; 177] By 1972 some 200 foster parent associations had been formed across the country. [139]   In their local association meetings and at the National Convention, foster parents expressed gratification at the support and help they received from social workers. Yet dissatisfactions are also expressed by foster parents about social workers' activities. Foster parents want more specific help in dealing with children's problems, and often feel that workers are not equipped to offer such help. They tend to feel exploited by workers who visit irregularly and who are not readily available. They think that workers do not always frankly share with them the extent of the children's difficulties or of the biological parents' pathology. They are chagrined that workers often do not sufficiently credit the knowledge they have about the child, and they resent the

agency's power to place and remove the child. Foster parents generally want more autonomy and the right to participate in plans and decisions regarding the child. [89]

Foster parents recommend that some kind of review procedure be established to handle disagreements between the foster home and the agency; that foster parenting be given a career line so that experienced foster parents are utilized in the training and supervision of foster parent recruits; that, in addition to more adequate compensation, fringe benefits (Social Security, liability insurance, and so on) be provided. [43; 134]

8. Another aspect of the general trend toward the "professionalization" of the foster parent role is the increasing availability of formal training courses for foster parents. Education in foster parents role enactment provided by agency-sponsored group discussions [60; 116] is supplemented by specialized courses offered by schools of social work in cooperation with child-placing agencies. Such a course might meet for ten to fifteen weekly sessions and cover material on the basic developmental needs of children, the meaning of separation, the problem of adjustment to the foster home, and the place of the biological parents and the agency in foster care. [4; 69; 133]   Tuition for such courses is paid by the agency with help, in the case of public welfare agencies, from Federal funds.

9. There has been a trend toward amplifying the impact and effectiveness of professionals by team work with an auxiliary staff of less extensive education. One procedure in implementing this approach is the team model. This involves having a group of three or four college graduates function under the direction of a graduate social worker; responsibility for decision-making and treatment plans rests with the team leader but the plans and decisions are implemented by the team members. Reports are available of the rationale of the team model and suggestions for its implementation in the foster care program. [16]

10. In response to the fact that it is difficult for large public agencies to keep accurate track of children in foster care, efforts are being made to use computers to assure responsible and continuous assignment of every child in care.

11. There is a trend toward increasing interest in, and development of, group foster homes, but there is neighborhood opposition to such facilities. The New York Times (July 16, 1972) reported that "a plan to use a private house as a group home for nine children from New York City has thrown this middle-class mostly white neighborhood [in a city suburb] into an uproar." Neighborhood opposition is based not only on antipathy to lower-class, possibly disturbed children, but also on the fact that many of the children to be placed in group homes might be black.

Summary

Foster family care is substitute care in which the role of the biological parent is implemented by another set of parents. Unlike other forms of substitute care—institutional child care and adoption—foster family care is designed to be temporary and to offer the child care in a family setting. In general, children for whom foster family care is appropriate are those who cannot be cared for in their own home even if supportive and supplementary services are provided, and who can make use of, and contribute to, family life.

The children usually come from chronically deprived lower-class families facing crisis situations. While most of the children are white, there is a disproportionate number of nonwhite children.

The situation which most frequently precipitates the need for short-term foster care is the illness of the mother. Problems in parental role implementation due to death, divorce, desertion, and inadequate income, manifested frequently in neglect and/or abuse, bring a sizable group of children into long-term care. The child's disturbed behavior or physical and mental handicaps may also give rise to the need for long-term care.

Although there are several different kinds of foster family homes, the foster family boarding home accounts for some 95 percent of all foster family placements.

Foster families must be recruited, evaluated, and ultimately selected for a particular child. Agencies operate a constant recruitment service, assisted by special recruiting drives. Relatively few of those who indicate interest in foster family care ultimately become foster parents. Withdrawal of application accounts for the greatest percentage of such attrition. Rigorous selective standards are of considerably less importance in eliminating applicants.

Foster families tend to come from upper-lower- and lower-middle-class segments of the community. The mothers in such families regard child rearing as an important role, one from which they derive considerable satisfaction.

Casework with the biological parents is directed toward helping them with the feelings that are likely to accompany placement—guilt, shame, anxiety, sadness, and loneliness. It is also designed to help them to keep intact a relationship with the child through the structure of service, and to resolve their problems in order to permit the child to return home.

Casework with the child is directed toward helping him make the physical and emotional separation from his own home and the transition to the foster home. It is also designed to help him deal with his fears of abandonment, his feeling of rejection, his hostility toward his own parents, and his anxiety over acceptance by his foster parents. It also helps him to resolve the conflict of feeling toward his own parents and his foster parents, and to define his role as a foster child.

Casework with the foster parents is directed toward preparing them for placement, helping them to accept the child, and helping them with problems regarding the child's adjustment in the home. It is also designed to help them in their relationship with the child's biological parents, and to deal with the differences between the role of foster parent and that of biological parent. Group methods have also been used to supplement and support the casework approach in working with foster parents.

Evaluation studies of foster family care indicates that many children who have experienced such care grow up satisfactorily.

The following problems were identified as being of current concern:

1. Foster family care tends to become permanent for a sizable number of children.
2. A shortage of trained personnel and the pathology in the families from which the foster children come make unlikely the rehabilitation of the natural families.
3. Although many children remain in substitute care, their legal ties to their biological parents make them unavailable for adoption.
4. There is great difficulty in recruiting a sufficiently large number of desirable foster homes.
5. Board payments for foster care are inadequate.
6. There is no clear-cut definition of the foster parents' relationship to the agency, so that the parents are sometimes regarded as clients, sometimes as colleagues, sometimes as paid employees.
7. Personnel shortages and personnel turnover affect the recruitment of foster parents and the continuity of caseworker-child relationships.

Among the trends identified were the following:

1. An increase in the rate of children coming into foster care and increased public welfare responsibility for such placements.
2. Greater pathology in the families placing children and in the children placed.
3. More explicit recognition of the potential of the foster family as a treatment resource, in addition to its potential as a resource for child care.
4. A greater tendency to explore the possibilities for foster family care among families not previously considered, such as the AFDC homes.
5. A greater diversification of foster family homes and of the groups of children for whom such a resource might be used.
6. A more widely sanctioned use of permanent foster care for children who clearly need this resource and an attenuation of the differences between foster care and adoption.

7. The formal organization and education of foster parents and recommendations for changes in the relationship between foster parents and placement agencies.

Bibliography

1. ADAMS, MARGARET E. "Foster Care for Mentally Retarded Children: How Does Child Welfare Meet This Challenge?" *Child Welfare*, 49, 5 (May 1970), 260–69.
2. AMBINDER, WALTER, et al. "Role Phenomena and Foster Care for Disturbed Children." *American Journal of Orthopsychiatry*, 32 (January 1962).
3. ———, and DOUGLAS SARGENT. "Foster Parents' Techniques of Management of Preadolescent Boys, Deviant Behavior." *Child Welfare*, 44 (February 1965).
4. APPLEBERG, ESTHER. *A Foster Family Workshop Report*. New York: Wurzweiler School of Social Work, Yeshiva University, 1968.
5. ———. "The Dependent Child and the Changing Worker." *Child Welfare*, 48, 7 (July 1969), 407–12.
6. BABCOCK, CHARLOTTE. "Some Psychodynamic Factors in Foster Parenthood—Parts I and II." *Child Welfare*, 44, 9, 10 (November–December 1965).
7. BALL, GRACE M., and JONATHON G. BAILEY. "A Group of Experienced Foster Parents." *Case Conference*, 15, 12 (April 1969).
8. BAYLOR, EDITH, and ELIO MONACHESI. *The Rehabilitation of Children*. New York: Harper and Row, Publishers, 1939.
9. BELLISFIELD, G., et al. *Services to Children in Care Who May Need Adoptive Planning*. New York: New York City Department of Social Services, July 1971.
10. BISKIND, S. E. "The Group Method with Clients, Foster Families, and Adoptive Families: The Group Method in Services to Adoptive Parents." *Child Welfare*, 45, 10 (December 1966), 561–64.
11. BOEHM, BERNICE. *Deterrents to the Adoption of Children in Foster Care*. New York: Child Welfare League of America, December 1958.
12. ———. "Protective Services for Neglected Children." *Social Work Practice*. New York: Columbia University Press, 1968.
13. BOWLBY, JOHN. *Maternal Care and Mental Health*. Geneva: World Health Organization, 1951.
14. BRADLEY, DOROTHY. "Group Work with Foster Parents," in *Group Methods in the Public Welfare Program*. Ed. by Norman Fenton and Kermit Wiltse. Palo Alto, Calif.: Pacific Books, Publishers, 1963.
15. BREMNER, ROBERT H. *Children and Youth in America, A Documentary History*. Vol. 1:1600–1865. Cambridge, Mass.: Harvard University Press, 1970.
16. BRIELAND, DONALD. *Differential Use of Manpower: A Team Model for Foster Care*. New York: Child Welfare League of America, 1968.

17. Brubaker, Mary. "A Development in Public Agency Service for Parents." *Child Welfare,* **34** (October 1955).

18. Bryce, Martin, and Roger Ehlert. "144 Foster Children." *Child Welfare,* **50,** 9 (November 1971), 499–503.

19. Carter, Woodrow W. "Group Counseling for Adolescent Foster Children." *Children,* **15,** 1 (January–February 1968).

20. Cautley, Patricia W., et al. *Successful Foster Homes—An Exploratory Study of Their Characteristics.* Madison, Wis.: Wisconsin Department of Public Welfare, June 1966.

21. Charnley, Jean. *The Art of Child Placement.* Minneapolis: University of Minnesota Press, 1955.

22. Child Welfare League of America. *Standards for Foster Family Care.* New York, 1959.

23. Close, Kathryn. "An Encounter with Foster Parents." *Children,* **18,** 4 (July–August 1971), 138–42.

24. Cochintu, Anne, and Winifred Mason. "Foster Homes for Children with Medical Problems." *Child Welfare,* **40** (December 1961).

25. Collingwood, Ava. *A Study of Group Education for Foster Parents.* New York: Child Welfare League of America, 1939.

26. Colvin, R. "Toward the Development of a Foster Parent Attitude Test," in *Quantitative Approaches to Parent Selection.* New York: Child Welfare League of America, January 1962.

27. Community Council of Greater New York, Inc. *Foster Home Application Studies and Board Rates.* New York, July 1959.

28. Cook County Department of Public Aid. *Question and Answer Book for Foster Parents.* Chicago: Cook County Department of Public Aid, Children's Division, 1963.

29. Council of Social Agencies of Rochester and Monroe County, New York, Inc. *Finding More Foster Homes, A Special Readjustment Campaign.* New York, 1958.

30. Cowan, Edwina, and Eva Stout. "A Comparative Study of the Adjustment Made by Foster Children After Complete and Partial Breaks in Continuity of Home Environment." *American Journal of Orthopsychiatry,* **9** (1939).

31. Cox, Ruth W., and Mary H. James. "Rescue from Limbo—Foster Home Placement for Hospitalized Physically Disabled Children." *Child Welfare,* **49,** 1 (January 1970), 21–28.

32. Dane County Department of Public Assistance and Child Welfare. *You, Your Foster Child and the Agency.* Madison, Wis., 1961.

33. Davids, Leo. *The Foster Father Role.* Unpublished Ph.D. Thesis. New York University, New York, 1968.

34. De Cocq, Gustave. *The Withdrawal of Foster Parent Applicants.* San Francisco: United Community Fund of San Francisco, June 1962.

35. De Fries, Zira, et al. "Foster Family Care for Disturbed Children—A Nonsentimental View." *Child Welfare,* **44** (February 1965).

36. Dick, Kenneth. "What People Think About Foster Care." *Children* (March–April 1961).

37. Dingman, Harvey F., et al. "Prediction of Child-Rearing Attitude." *Child Welfare,* **41** (1962).

38. DINNAGE, ROSEMARY, et al. *Foster Home Care—Facts and Fallacies.* London: Longman Group Ltd., 1967.

39. EISENBERG, LEON. "Deprivation and Foster Care." *Journal of American Academy of Child Psychiatry,* 4 (1965), 243–48.

40. FANSHEL, DAVID. "Specialization Within the Foster Parent Role—Part I: Difference Between Foster Parents' of Infants and Foster Parents of Older Children." *Child Welfare,* 40 (March 1961).

41. ————. "Studying the Role Performance of Foster Parents." *Social Work,* 6 (January 1961).

42. ————. *Foster Parenthood—A Role Analysis.* Minneapolis: University of Minnesota Press, 1966.

43. ————. "Role of Foster Parents in the Future," in *Foster Care in Question.* Ed. by Helen D. Stone. New York: Child Welfare League of America, 1970.

44. ————. "The Exit of Children from Foster Care: An Interim Research Report." *Child Welfare,* 50, 2 (February 1971), 65–81.

45. ————, and H. MAAS. "Factorial Dimensions of the Characteristics of Children in Placements and Their Families." *Child Development,* 33 (1962).

46. ————, and EUGENE B. SHINN. *Dollars and Sense in the Foster Care of Children: A Look at Cost Factors.* New York: Child Welfare League of America, 1972.

47. FELLNER, I. W. "Group Meetings with a Special Group of Foster Parents," in *Group Methods in the Public Welfare Program.* Ed. by Norman Fenton and Kermit Wiltse. Palo Alto, Calif.: Pacific Books, Publishers, 1963.

48. FERGUSON, THOMAS. *Children in Care and After.* New York: Oxford University Press, 1966.

49. FINE, REBECCA. "Moving Emotionally Disturbed Children from Institutions to Foster Homes." *Children,* 13, 6 (November–December 1966), 221–26.

50. FLYNN, JAMES B. "Changing Patterns of Foster Family Care." *Child Welfare,* 42 (January 1963).

51. FLYNN, WILLIAM. "A Comprehensive Program of Group Meetings with Foster Parents," in *Group Methods in the Public Welfare Program.* Ed. by Norman Fenton and Kermit Wiltse. Palo Alto, Calif.: Pacific Books, Publishers, 1963.

52. FOLKS, HOMER. *The Care of the Destitute, Neglected, and Delinquent Children.* New York: The Macmillan Company, 1902.

53. GARLAND, PAT. "Public Assistance Families—A Resource for Foster Care." *Child Welfare,* 40 (September 1961).

54. GEORGE, VICTOR. *Foster Care: Theory and Practice.* London: Kegan Paul, Trench, Trubner & Co., 1970.

55. GIL, DAVID. "Developing Routine Follow-up Procedures for Child Welfare Services." *Child Welfare,* 43 (May 1964).

56. GLASSBERG, EUDICE. "Are Foster Homes Hard to Find?" *Child Welfare,* 44 (October 1965).

57. GLICKMAN, ESTHER. *Child Placement Through Clinically Oriented Casework.* New York: Columbia University Press, 1957.

58. GLOVER, E. ELIZABETH. "Is Child-Caring Important?" *Child Welfare*, **42** (February 1964).

59. GOLDBLATT, DOROTHY. "Foster Family Care for the Mentally Retarded Child." *Child Welfare*, **48**, 7 (July 1969), 423–26.

60. GOLDSTEIN, HARRIET, and ADOLINE DALL. "Group Learning for Foster Parents: I—In a Voluntary Agency; II—In a Public Agency." *Children*, **14**, 5 (September–October 1967).

61. GORDON, HENRIETTA. *Casework Services for Children*. Boston: Houghton Mifflin Company, 1956.

62. GOTTESFELD, HARRY. *In Loco Parentis—A Study of Perceived Role Values in Foster Home Care*. New York: Jewish Child Care Association of New York, 1970.

63. GRAY, P. G., and E. A. PARR. *Children in Care and the Recruitment of Foster Parents*. London: Social Survey, 1957.

64. GREENBERG, ARTHUR. "Agency Owned and Operated Group Foster Home for Adolescents." *Child Welfare*, **42** (April 1963).

65. GROW, LUCILLE, and ANN SHYNE. *Requests for Child Welfare Service—A Five-Day Census*. New York: Child Welfare League of America, December 1969.

66. ———, and MICHAEL J. SMITH. *Board Rates and Foster Family Care*. New York: Child Welfare League of America, 1971.

67. GUILFORD COUNTY, NORTH CAROLINA, DEPARTMENT OF PUBLIC WELFARE. *Your Foster Child*. Child Welfare Division. October 1961.

68. GULA, MARTIN. *Agency-Operated Group Homes*. Washington, D.C.: Government Printing Office, 1964.

69. HANWELL, ALBERT F., et al. *A Guide for Foster Parent Group Education*. Boston: Boston College Graduate School of Social Work, 1969.

70. HART, HASTING H. "Annual Report," in *Proceedings of the National Conference of Charities and Correction*. Boston: George H. Ellis, 1884.

71. HAYES, RUTH, and MURIEL STEEVES. "Allowances in Foster Care." *Children*, **2** (May–June 1955).

72. HERSTEIN, NORMAN. "The Replacement of Children from Foster Homes." *Child Welfare*, **36** (July 1957).

73. HIKEL, VIRGINIA. "Fostering the Troubled Child." *Child Welfare*, **48**, 7 (July 1969), 427–32.

74. HILL, ESTHER. "Is Foster Care the Answer?" *Public Welfare*, **15** (April 1957).

75. HUNT, ELIZABETH. "Foster Care for Delinquent Girls." *Children*, **19** (September–October 1962).

76. JAFFE, ELIEZER D. "Foster Placement in Israel." *International Child Welfare Review*, **13**, 2 (May 1969).

77. JAFFEE, BENSON, and DRAZA KLINE. *New Payment Pattern and the Foster Parent Role*. New York: Child Welfare League of America, 1970.

78. JENKINS, RACHEL. "The Needs of Foster Parents." *Case Conference*, **11** (January 1965).

79. JENKINS, SHIRLEY. "Duration of Foster Care—Some Relevant Antecedent Variables." *Child Welfare*, **46**, 8 (October 1967), 450–56.

80. ———. "Filial Deprivation in Parents of Children in Foster Care." *Children*, **14**, 1 (January–February 1967), 8–12.

81. ———. "Separation Experiences of Parents Whose Children Are in Foster Care." *Child Welfare*, **48**, 6 (June 1969), 334–41.

82. ———, and ELAINE NORMAN. *Filial Deprivation and Foster Care.* New York: Columbia University Press, 1972.

83. JETER, HELEN R. *Children, Problems and Services in Child Welfare Programs.* Washington, D.C.: Government Printing Office, 1963.

84. JEWISH CHILD CARE ASSOCIATION OF NEW YORK. *Follow-up Report on Treatment of Emotionally Traumatized Young Children in a Foster Home Setting.* New York, March 1965. Mimeo.

85. JOSSELYN, IRENE. "Evaluating Motives of Foster Parents." *Child Welfare*, **31** (February 1952).

86. JULIUSBERGER, ERIKA. *Phases of Adjustment in a Typical Foster Home Placement.* New York: Jewish Child Care Association of New York, 1961.

87. KADUSHIN, ALFRED. "The Legally Adoptable Unadopted Child." *Child Welfare*, **37** (November 1958).

88. KASTELL, JEAN. *Casework in Child Care.* London: Kegan Paul, Trench, Trubner & Co., 1962.

89. KENNEDY, RUBY. "A Foster Parent Looks at Foster Care," in *Foster Care in Question.* Ed. by Helen D. Stone. New York: Child Welfare League of America, 1970.

90. KINTER, RICHARD H., and HERBERT OTTO. "The Family Strength Concept and Foster Care Selection." *Child Welfare*, **43** (July 1964).

91. KLINE, DRAZA, and HELEN OVERSTREET. *Casework with Foster Parents.* New York: Child Welfare League of America, 1956.

92. ———, HELEN OVERSTREET, and MARY FORBUSH. *Foster Care of Children—Nurture and Treatment.* New York: Columbia University Press, 1972.

93. KRAUSE, JONATHON. "Predicting Success of Foster Placements for School-Age Children." *Social Work*, **16**, 1 (January 1971), 63–72.

94. LANGSAM, MIRIAM. *Children West*, Logmark ed. Madison, Wis.: The State Historical Society of Wisconsin, 1964.

95. LAWDER, ELIZABETH. "Can Long-Term Foster Care Be Unfrozen?" *Child Welfare*, **40** (1961).

96. ———, et al. *A Study of Black Adoption Families—A Comparison of a Traditional and Quasi-Adoption Program.* New York: Child Welfare League of America, 1971.

97. LEWIS, MARY. "Long-Time and Temporary Placement of Children," in *Selected Papers in Casework.* Raleigh, N.C.: Health Publications Institute, 1951.

98. LICHTY, LOIS R., and LEON H. RICHMAN. "Independent Foster Home Placement—A Child Welfare Concern." *Child Welfare*, **40** (June 1961).

99. LINDBERG, DWAINE, and ANNE WOSREK. "The Use of Family Sessions in Foster Home Care." *Social Casework*, **44** (March 1963).

100. LITTNER, NER. *Some Traumatic Effects of Separation and Placement.* New York: Child Welfare League of America, October 1950.

101. ———. "The Importance of the Natural Parents to the Child in Placement," in *Preliminary Conference Report First National Conference of Foster Parents.* Publication No. 72-5. Washington, D.C.: Department of Health, Education, and Welfare, 1971.

102. MAAS, HENRY. "Highlights of the Foster Care Project: Introduction." *Child Welfare*, **38** (July 1959).

103. ———. "Children in Long-Term Foster Care." *Child Welfare*, **48**, 6 (June 1969), 321–33.

104. ———, and RICHARD ENGLER. *Children in Need of Parents*. New York: Columbia University Press, 1959.

105. MacDONALD, MARY. "Children Placed by the Jewish Children's Bureau of Chicago in 1939 and in 1950–52." *Social Service Review*, **28** (1954).

106. ———, and MARJORIE FERGUSON. "Selecting Foster Parents: An Essay Review." *Social Service Review* (September 1964).

107. MacMAHON, MERLE E. "The Flexible Use of Foster Homes for Emergency Care." *Child Welfare*, **37** (June 1958).

108. MADISON, BERNICE, and MICHAEL SCHAPIRO. "Long-Term Foster Family Care: What Is Its Potential for Minority-Group Children?" *Public Welfare*, **27** (April 1969), 167–94.

109. MALUCCIO, ANTHONY N. "Selecting Foster Parents for Disturbed Children." *Children*, **13**, 2 (March–April 1966), 69–74.

110. McADAMS, MRS. "The Parent in the Shadows." *Child Welfare*, **51**, 1 (January 1972), 51–55.

111. McCOY, JACQUELINE. "The Application of Role Concept to Foster Parenthood." *Social Casework*, **43** (May 1962).

112. ———. "Motives and Conflict in Foster Parenthood." *Children*, **9** (November–December 1962), 222–26.

113. MECH, EDMUND V. "Decision Analysis in Foster Care Practice," in *Foster Care in Question*. Ed. by Helen D. Stone. New York: Child Welfare League of America, 1970.

114. MEIER, ELIZABETH G. *Former Foster Children as Adult Citizens*. Unpublished Ph.D. Thesis, Columbia University, New York, April 1962.

115. MILLER, CLARA. "The Agency Owned Foster Home." *Child Welfare*, **33** (November 1954).

116. MILLS, ROBERT B., *et al.* "Introducing Foster Mother Training Groups in a Voluntary Child Welfare Agency." *Child Welfare*, **46**, 10 (December 1967).

117. MOYNIHAN, WILLIAM. "Reader's Forum—Developing Foster Child's Identification with Agency." *Child Welfare*, **42** (April 1963).

118. MULREY, J. M. "The Care of Destitute and Neglected Children—Report of One Committee." *National Conference of Charities and Correction, 1899*. Boston: George Ellis, 1900.

119. MURPHY, H. B. M. *Foster Home Variables and Adult Outcome*. Mimeo.

120. ———. "Natural Family Pointers to Foster Care Outcome." *Mental Hygiene*, **48** (July 1964).

121. ———. "Predicting Duration of Foster Care." *Child Welfare*, **47**, 2 (February 1968), 76–84.

122. NAPIER, HARRY. "Success and Failure in Foster Care." *British Journal of Social Work*, **2**, 2 (Summer 1972), 187–203.

123. NAUGHTON, FRANCIS X. "Foster Home Placement as an Adjunct to Treatment." *Social Casework*, **38** (1957).

124. NOWAK, MARY J., and MARY REISTROFFER. *Foster Family Parent Education*.

Milwaukee, Wis.: University of Wisconsin, Department of Social Work, 1970.

125. OUGHELTREE, CORNELIA. *Finding Foster Homes.* New York: Child Welfare League of America, 1957.

126. PARKER, ROY. *Decision in Child Care.* London: George Allen & Unwin, Ltd., 1966.

127. PHILLIPS, MICHAEL H., et al. *Factors Associated with Placement Decision in Child Welfare.* New York: Child Welfare League of America, 1971.

128. ——, et al. *A Model for Intake Decisions in Child Welfare.* New York: Child Welfare League of America, 1972.

129. POLIER, JUSTINE WISE. *Parental Rights.* New York: Child Welfare League of America, June 1958.

130. POLIER, SHAD. "Amendments to New York's Adoption Law—the Permanently Neglected Child." *Child Welfare,* 38 (July 1959).

131. PRATT, CATHERINE. *The Development of Group Foster Homes for Children in Long-Term Care.* Washington, D.C.: Family and Child Services, June 1968.

132. RADINSKY, ELIZABETH, et al. "Recruiting and Serving Foster Parents." *Child Welfare,* 42 (January 1963).

133. REISTROFFER, MARY. "A University Extension Course for Foster Parents." *Children,* 15, 1 (January–February 1968).

134. ——. "Participation of Foster Parents in Decision-Making—The Concept of Collegiality." *Child Welfare,* 41, 1 (January 1972).

135. RICE, DALE, and SARA SEMMELROTH. "Foster Care for the Emotionally Disturbed Child." *American Journal of Orthopsychiatry,* 38, 3 (April 1968), 539–42.

136. RICH, MABEL. "Foster Homes for Retarded Children." *Child Welfare,* 44 (July 1965).

137. RICHMAN, LEON. "Trends in Child Care." *Jewish Social Service Quarterly,* 29 (1952–53).

138. ROBERTS, V. K. "An Experiment in Group Work with Foster Parents." *Case Conference,* 9 (November 1962).

139. ROSENDORF, SIDNEY. "Joining Together to Help Foster Children—Foster Parents Form a Natural Association." *Children Today,* 1, 4 (July–August 1972), 2–7.

140. RYAN, WILLIAM, and LAURA NORRIS. *Child Welfare Problems and Potentials—A Study of Intake of Child Welfare Agencies in Metropolitan Boston.* Monograph No. 3. Boston: Committee on Children and Youth, 1967.

141. SACKS, GERDA, and RUTH CASE. "Foster Home Recruitment—Problems and Solutions in the Large and Small Communities." *Journal of Jewish Communal Services,* 44 (Summer 1968), 350–59.

142. SARGENT, DOUGLAS A. "An Experiment in Foster Care for Seriously Disturbed Boys," in *Mental Health of the Child.* Ed. by Julius Segal. Washington, D.C.: National Institute of Mental Health, June 1971.

143. SAUBER, MIGNON. "Preplacement Situations of Families: Data for Planning Services." *Child Welfare,* 46, 8 (October 1967), 443–49.

144. ——, and SHIRLEY JENKINS. *Paths to Child Placement.* New York: Community Council of Greater New York, 1966.

145. Schaffer, H. R., and Evelyn B. Schaffer. *Child Care and the Family.* Occasional Papers on Social Administration No. 25. London: George Bell & Sons, Ltd., 1968.

146. Schick, B. G. "Group Activities with Foster Parents." *Child Welfare,* **34** (1955).

147. Schwartz, Miriam, and Isadore Kaplan. "Small Homes—Placement Choice for Adolescents." *Child Welfare,* **40** (November 1961).

148. Selig, Martha K. "Changes in Child Care and Their Implications." *Journal of Jewish Communal Services,* **33** (Fall 1956).

149. Shapiro, Deborah. "Agency Investment in Foster Care: A Study." *Social Work,* **17**, 3 (July 1972), 20–28.

150. Shinn, Eugene B. *Is Placement Necessary? An Experimental Study of Agreement Among Caseworkers in Making Foster Care Decisions.* Unpublished Doctor of Social Work Thesis. Columbia University, New York, 1968.

160. Shyne, Ann. *The Need for Foster Care.* New York: Child Welfare League of America, 1969.

161. Simsarian, Frances P. "Foster Care Possibilities in a Suburban Community." *Children,* **11** (May–June 1964).

162. Slingerland, W. H. *Child-Placing in Families.* New York: Russell Sage Foundation, 1919.

163. Soffen, Joseph. "The Impact of a Group Education Program for Foster Parents," *Child Welfare,* **41** (May 1962).

164. State Charities and Association. *Adaptability—A Study of 100 Children in Foster Care.* New York: Child Adoption Service, January 1960.

165. Stone, Helen D. *Reflections on Foster Care—A Report of a National Survey of Attitudes and Practices.* New York: Child Welfare League of America, 1969.

166. Swindell, Bertha E. "The Function and Role of the Natural Parent in the Foster Family Constellation." *Child Welfare,* **45** (February 1961).

167. Thies, S. Van S. *How Foster Children Turn Out.* New York: State Charities Aid Association, 1924.

168. Thomas, Carolyn B. "The Resolution of Object Loss Following Foster Home Placement." *Smith College Studies in Social Work,* **36**, 3 (June 1967).

169. ———. "Helping Foster Parents Understand Disturbed Children." *Child Welfare,* **50**, 3 (March 1971), 168–75.

170. ———. "The Use of Group Methods with Foster Parents." *Children,* **8** (November–December 1961).

171. Thurstone, Henry W. *The Dependent Child.* New York: Columbia University Press, 1930.

172. Tinker, Katherine. "Do Children in Foster Care Outgrow Behavior Problems?" *Minnesota Welfare,* **8**, 4 (October 1952).

173. ———. "Children in Foster Care Who Have Outgrown Problems." *Minnesota Welfare,* **8**, 5 (November 1952).

174. ———. "Children in Foster Care Who Remained Disturbed." *Minnesota Welfare,* **8**, 6 (December 1952).

175. Trasler, Gordon. *In Place of Parents.* New York: Humanities Press, 1960.

176. U.S. DEPARTMENT OF HEALTH, EDUCATION, AND WELFARE. *Child Welfare Services. How They Help Children and Their Parents.* Washington, D.C.: Government Printing Office, 1957.

177. ———. *Preliminary Conference Report First National Conference of Foster Parents.* Publication No. (OCD) 72-5. Washington, D.C.: Government Printing Office, 1971.

178. ———. *Children Served by Public Welfare Agencies and Voluntary Child Welfare Agencies and Institutions. March 1971.* Washington, D.C.: National Center for Social Statistics, March 1973.

179. VAN DER WAALS, PAULER. "Former Foster Children Reflect on Their Childhood." *Children,* 7 (January–February 1960).

180. VICK, J. E. "Recruiting and Retaining Foster Homes." *Public Welfare,* 25, 3 (July 1967), 229–34.

181. WAKEFORD, JOHN. "Fostering—A Sociological Perspective." *British Journal of Sociology,* 14 (December 1963).

182. WATSON, KENNETH. "Long-Term Foster Care: Default or Design?—The Voluntary Agency Responsibility." *Child Welfare,* 47, 6 (June 1968), 331–38.

183. WEINSTEIN, EUGENE. *The Self-Image of the Foster Child.* New York: Russell Sage Foundation, 1960.

184. WIRES, EMILY M. "Some Factors in the Worker-Foster Parent Relationship." *Child Welfare,* 33 (October 1954).

185. WISCONSIN DEPARTMENT OF PUBLIC WELFARE. *Focus on Foster Families.* Madison, Wis.: Wisconsin Department of Public Welfare, 1966.

186. WITHERSPOON, ARTHUR W. "Foster Home Placements for Juvenile Delinquents." *Federal Probation* (December 1966), 48–52.

187. WOLINS, MARTIN. *Selecting Foster Parents.* New York: Columbia University Press, 1963.

10

The Unmarried Mother
and the
Out-of-Wedlock Child

Introduction

Children born out of wedlock account for some 90 percent of adoptions by nonrelatives. Consequently, many of the agencies that offer adoptive services also offer services to the unmarried mother. The discussion of adoption services in Chapter 11 is, then, logically preceded by a discussion of out-of-wedlock pregnancy and services to the unwed mother.

Historical Background

The attitude toward illegitimacy is related to family structure. Negative attitudes toward illegitimacy are designed to protect the monogamous family and associated marital ties. Polygamous societies make little of technical illegitimacy. The Christian attitude toward monogamy and extramarital sexuality resulted in the development of a more punitive attitude toward illegitimacy. Religious sanctions were reinforced by secular motives during the Middle Ages to solidify such an attitude. As Krause notes:

It was natural that men, as legislators, would have limited their accidental offsprings' claims against them both economically and in terms of a family relationship, especially since the social status of the illegitimate mother often did not equal their own. Moreover,

478

their legitimate wives had an interest in denying the illegitimate's claim on their husbands, since any such claim could be allowed only at the expense of the legitimate family. Against these forces have stood only the illegitimate mother and the helpless child, and thus it is not surprising that our laws are inconsiderate of the child's interest. [51]

Under English common law, the illegitimate child was "son of no one" (*filius nullius*) or "son of the people" (*filius populi*)—without name, without right to support or inheritance. Yet the illegitimate child was not socially stigmatized in pre-Puritan England:

. . . until the sixteenth century bastardry had not been thought any great shame. Men took care of their bastards, were indeed often proud of them, and in many cases brought them home to their wives or mothers to be brought up. Children born out of wedlock were thus to be found growing up in their father's house with their half-brothers and sisters without a hint of disgrace either to themselves or to their natural parents. [79, p. 201]

The gradual hardening of attitudes arose not only from concern for the sanctity of the family but perhaps, more significantly, from concern for the burden on the community posed by illegitimate children. Nobody was seriously concerned about the fourteen illegitimate children fathered by Charles II, but there was widespread concern about the indigent illegitimate child.

The Poor Law Act of 1576,

made the first legislative provision for illegitimate children so many of whom were abandoned by their parents and left to be maintained from charitable or public sources. The preamble of the Act indicates the spirit in which this problem was approached. "Firste, concerning Bastards begotten and borne out of lawful Matrimony (an Offence againste Gods lawe and Mans Lawe) the said Bastards being now lefte to bee kepte at the chardge of the Parishe where They bee borne, to the greate Burden of the same Parishe and in defrauding of the Reliefe of the impotente and aged true Poore of the same Parishe, and to the evill Example and Encouradgement of lewde Lyef: It ys ordeyned and enacted. . . ." [79, pp. 206–20]

that the mother and putative father might be punished and both were responsible for support of the child.

The main concern of Parliament was the relief of public expenditure and the exposure of the moral failure of those who were responsible for bringing the child into the world. . . . Legal sanctions were to be employed against men and women whose bastards became a charge on the community; there were no legal penalties for those who could afford to support the fruits of their own indiscretions. [79, p. 207]

The principal ground of concern then, and one might add, now, "were the economics of maintenance rather than the circumstances of conception." [79, p. 220]

The English Poor Laws formed the basis for the even more punitive attitudes of Puritan colonists, who punished extramarital fornication and required the parents to support the child who was the result of fornication. Thus Anne Williams, in 1658, petitioned the court for maintenance from Richard Smith "for a child the defendant hath got by her." The court "ordered that the said Richard Smith maintain the child and that the woman for her fact committed, be whipped and have thirty lashes well laid on." [13, p. 52]

Throughout the nineteenth century resources available to the out-of-wedlock child for maintenance were the same as those available to any other child who needed help from the community. This included binding out in apprenticeship, and indoor and outdoor relief.

Over the last hundred years there has developed a more compassionate attitude toward the illegitimate child, a lessening of the distinctions between the legitimate and illegitimate child, and a reduction in the discriminations against the illegitimate child. Changing attitudes are reflected in changing terminology—from *bastard* to *illegitimate child* to *child born out of wedlock* or the less frequently employed *extramarital child* and *love child*. There are frequent citations of illustrious out-of-wedlock children—William the Conqueror, Erasmus, Leonardo da Vinci, Alexander Hamilton, Borodin, Willy Brandt.

The legal status of the child born out of wedlock differs from state to state but more frequently now such a child has a right to inherit from his mother and, where paternity is acknowledged, the right to inherit from his father. Many states have acknowledged the illegitimate child's rights to benefits under workman's compensation laws in case the father is injured or killed. Federal legislation has recognized the illegitimate child's rights to veteran's benefits and Old Age and Survivor's Insurance benefits from his father's account. But out-of-wedlock children still face substantial legal disadvantages in some states. [51; 52; 53]

The child's status is not indicated on the short-form birth certificate used for such purposes as school registration or job application, which merely lists name and time and place of birth.

Legitimation of the child can now be achieved by marriage of the parents after the child's birth, by petition to the court if the parents are not married, and by the father's acknowledgment of paternity. With legitimation, birth records are changed so as to delete any indication of the child's previous illegitimate status. If the father voluntarily acknowledges paternity, he is obligated to support the child. Bastardy proceedings or paternity proceedings can be instituted to establish the paternity of the child and to force the father to support the child. This is a civil procedure, which often, however, resembles a criminal action. If a man is judged to be the father but fails to make support payments, he can be prosecuted. But it is difficult to prove that a particular man is the father of the child. Blood tests merely exclude the possibility; they do not establish certainty. Paternity proceedings are usually instituted by the mother (often required in order to establish eligibility for AFDC assistance) but may be instituted by the state.

The mother is regarded as guardian of her child and as such has the right to custody, care, and control of the child and a right to the child's earnings. Currently there is increasing concern about the rights of the father. The father's right to custody is superseded by the mother's. Generally only the mother's consent is required to free the child for adoption. But if paternity has been acknowledged or legitimation established, the father's consent is also required. If the mother is a minor, some states require consent to adoption by her parents as well.

Scope

Although the number of illegitimate births has been increasing steadily since World War II, the illegitimacy rate (illegitimate live births per 1000 unmarried women fifteen to forty-four years of age) has leveled off during the last eight years. The increase in the number of illegitimate births is primarily a result of the larger number of fecund women aged 15–44 in the population. [105; 114]   The largest number of illegitimacies occur among women of twenty to twenty-four. The teenage illegitimacy rate has dropped slightly during the last half of the 1960's.

In 1969 there were a total of 360,800 out-of-wedlock births, representing some 10 percent of all live births. A more positive perspective is suggested by noting that the total of 360,800 unmarried mothers in 1969 represented only 8 percent of the total of some 43 million fecund women between the ages of fifteen and forty-four in the population at that time. A total of some 7–8 million people in the population are of illegitimate birth—about 4 percent of the total population.

Not all states collect, and make available, statistics on illegitimacy. Many populous urbanized states, such as California, Massachusetts, and New York are not included, because birth registration procedures in those states do not require that a distinction be made between in-wedlock and out-of-wedlock births.

White and Nonwhite Out-of-Wedlock Births

The nonwhite illegitimacy rate at the beginning of the 1970's was some six times larger than the white illegitimacy rate but the gap is narrowing. The contention that nonwhites are more "accepting" of illegitimacy is contradicted by interviews with some 340 black single pregnant adolescents, which revealed that "two-thirds of the girls were shocked and extremely upset when they first discovered they were pregnant" and 80 percent wished they were not pregnant. [32; 33]

A variety of factors help to explain the wide, although diminishing, differences between white and nonwhite illegitimacy rates.

1. The historical experience of the blacks under a slave system which had little regard for marriage and a high regard for black children, however fathered, is sometimes presented as a component of the cultural "causes" of illegitimacy in the present. Southern law did not recognize slave marriages, so that all slave children were, by law, illegitimate. Children fathered by a white but born of a slave mother inherited her status. It is suggested, then, that the historical experience in slavery is antithetical to the development of a concern that the child be born in wedlock.

2. An increase in illegitimacy rates has generally accompanied large-scale migrations. Families are temporarily disorganized and husbands and wives are separated for periods of time. Recently blacks have experienced a large-scale internal migration, from the South to the North and the West and from rural to urban locations.

3. Illegitimacy statistics imperfectly reflect the extent of extramarital coition. Between coition and illegitimate birth one can counterpose, in succession, contraception, abortion, or marriage before birth of the child. Each procedure reduces the number of children born out of wedlock, and each is less easily available to the nonwhite unmarried girl.

As Garland notes, "the middle or upper class white woman who becomes an out-of-wedlock mother biologically has greater opportunities of becoming an in-wedlock mother socially." [34, p. 85] The higher unemployment rate among black males and the more limited, lower-paying employment opportunities available to them understandably make many black single pregnant girls reluctant to "solve" a difficult situation by contracting a hazardous marriage. The objective situation perhaps favors the decision that "no marriage is bad; but no marriage is better than a bad marriage."

This may help explain the fact that in the Bowerman-Pope study of some 950 black and white unwed mothers, the black girls were less frequently interested in marrying the putative father. It was suggested that "Negro women perceive fewer advantages than white women in holding the marital rather than the single status. They receive fewer rewards for moving toward marriage." [82, p. 764] Between 1960 and 1964, fewer than one in five nonwhite women who became premaritally pregnant married within seven months, but three in five white women married. This implies that racial difference in premarital conception rates are smaller than racial differences in illegitimate birth rates.

4. Birth registration information has become progressively more complete over time as a higher percentage of women deliver their babies in hospitals. Nevertheless, whether a child is recorded as legitimate or illegitimate depends on information derived from the mother. Those mothers who feel greater shame about an out-of-wedlock birth, who have a greater sophistication about the implications of birth records, who are self-confident and assured in dealing with hospital personnel—in short, the older, better educated, white unmarried mother—is most likely to implement a decision to falsify the registration, which results in an underestimation of such illegitimacies. All white-black illegitimate births are reported as black when they could, with equal justification, be reported as white. This tends toward an overestimation of nonwhite illegitimacies.

The Governmental National Center for Health Statistics Study on Illegitimacy notes that "There is considerable evidence that socioeconomic composition is an important factor contributing to the white nonwhite differential in illegitimacy. It is likely that if it were possible to control for social class, much of the difference between those two groups would disappear." [105, p. 16]   Herzog similarly notes that if "illegitimacy estimates were related to income as well as color, the Negro-white difference would be drastically reduced." [43, p. 121]

The concern with illegitimacy stems from the higher risk such children present for community care. Consequently, the greater visibility of nonwhite illegitimacy results partially from the fact that the white girl may return to her nonmarried premotherhood status by giving up the child for adoption. The fewer opportunities for adoptive placement of the out-of-wedlock nonwhite child make continuing care and support of these children more of a community problem.

Determinants of Out-of-Wedlock Pregnancy

The social work approach to the single pregnant girl reflects the profession's thinking about the origin of the problem. This has undergone some changes over time. Before the Great Depression, the emphasis on personal and moral inadequacy led to the perception of the unmarried mother as morally promiscuous and/or mentally deficient. During the 1930's, the blame was placed on the socially deficient environment: the broken home, the poverty-stricken home were the factors which "explained" unwed motherhood. Studies of illegitimacy focused on class and color as factors determining attitudes toward extramarital intercourse and contraception.

After World War II, the emphasis shifted to psychological determinism. Out-of-wedlock pregnancy was seen as a symptom of some psychological need—conflict with a dominant mother, lack of response from a passive father, a desire for self-punishment, a search for a dependable love object, an attempt at self-assertion and independence.

Young noted that "Although a girl would obviously not plan consciously and deliberately to bear an out-of-wedlock child, she does act in such a way that this becomes the almost inevitable result." [113, p. 22] Out-of-wedlock pregnancy was seen as not only a symptom of individual disturbance but a symptom of family pathology.

The continuing search for causes has generated a series of studies of personality differences between the single pregnant woman and her single unpregnant sister. Results vary, some demonstrating personality disturbance in the unmarried mothers, some finding them essentially normal. [75, pp. 47–54]

Perhaps one of the most comprehensive and carefully controlled of these studies was that conducted by Vincent. One hundred young unwed mothers were matched in terms of crucial variables with an equal number of single girls who had never been pregnant. In psychological tests, the latter scored consistently at a more positive level of personality functioning, but differences between the two groups were smaller than anticipated and most of the scales showed no difference in the *direction* and *pattern* (italics in original) of the responses. [107, p. 119] The groups when compared in terms of developmental background showed an "absence of any statistically significant familial differences." [107, p. 117] Vincent concludes that "unwed motherhood is not the result of any one personality type, intrafamilial relationship, or social situation." [107, p. 179]

Furthermore, any personality differences that are revealed may be the response to the pregnancy rather than the cause of it. Pauker, who asked, "Are they pregnant because they are different or are they different because they are pregnant?" examined the personality profiles obtained *before* conception for a group of unmarried mothers and those of a matched group of nonpregnant peers and found them to be "very similar in shape and elevation." [75, p. 60] The unwed mothers' group showed no "striking personality difference from other girls," though it included a significantly larger number of girls who came from homes broken by separation or divorce. [75, p. 63]

A careful analysis by Cutright showed that such factors as level of religiosity, level of secularization of a society, divorce rates, decline of the authoritarian family, and levels of assistance granted the unmarried mother are unrelated to the changes in the illegitimacy rate. [24] In response to Young's contention that illegitimate pregnancy is, consciously or unconsciously, deliberately desired, Cutright, reviewing the relevant research, concludes that "there is substantial evidence that most unwed mothers would prefer to avoid the status." [24, p. 26]   As someone has said, "unmarried motherhood is a social status, not a psychiatric diagnosis."

Currently it is recognized that unmarried motherhood is too complex a phenomenon to yield a particular set of "explanations." There is a growing acceptance of the supposition that just as there is no juvenile delinquency but rather a series of different kinds of juvenile delinquencies, there is no unmarried motherhood but rather a series of different kinds of unmarried mothers who come to the experience through many different routes. Causation may differ with age, with social or racial background, and with personal experience. The determinants are cultural, personal, environmental, and—in some instances—accidental: contraceptives do fail and abortions are not always available.

Currently, social workers tend to emphasize factors such as psychosocial disturbances in the family (disturbed parent-child relationship, disturbed marital relationship, lack of parental affection and understanding, lack of communication among family members) and emotional disturbance in the individual (impulsivity, defective superego development, self-rejection, desire to punish parents, anxiety about sexuality, loneliness), but there is also serious consideration given to the general social situation (changing sex norms, changing attitudes in the relationship between the sexes and toward marriage, effects of socioeconomic conditions on establishing and maintaining a viable marriage). And as Perlman points out, the psychological explanation is more frequently applied to white unmarried mothers; the cultural explanation, to the nonwhite unmarried mothers. [77]   The white unmarried mother is seen as acting out a personal conflict; the nonwhite unmarried mother is seen as responding to a deprived socioeconomic environment.

Services for the Single Pregnant Woman

There are many different contexts for an out-of-wedlock pregnancy. The woman might be married, but to someone other than the father of the child she is carrying. The mother may be living with the father, but not be legally married to him. The woman may have been married and is now separated, widowed, or divorced, or the woman may be single and never married. The context for illegitimacy which the social agency most frequently encounters is the last—the single pregnant never-married woman.

The unmarried mother who receives service from a social agency is the exception rather than the rule. A 1960 nationwide study concluded that "about one out of six mothers who have illegitimate children in a year receive service either in public or voluntary agencies near the time of the pregnancy." [1, p. 43]   The younger the unmarried mother, the more likely it is that she will have had contact with a social agency. White unmarried mothers are more likely to make contact with voluntary agencies; nonwhite mothers, with a local Department of Public Assistance. A disproportionate amount of the total available social service time and energy has been directed toward white girls above the poverty level interested in placing their out-of-wedlock child for adoption. [85]

Because many unmarried mothers, while needing such service, either may not know of its availability or may be reluctant to use it, some states require hospitals to report all illegitimate births to the local Department of Public Welfare. A social worker then visits the mother, informs her of the services available, and helps her decide whether or not she wants to use them. In Wisconsin, which has such a law, a large percentage of unmarried mothers accept and use such service when it is offered.

The pregnancy is a crisis situation. The urgency of coming to a decision about the child, and the highly emotional responses which an out-of-wedlock pregnancy is likely to evoke, make the client temporarily more willing to accept help.

The unmarried mother needs two kinds of service from the agency: sociotherapy and psychotherapy. Sociotherapy includes income maintenance, housing (in many instances away from the family in a maternity home or a foster home), prenatal and obstetrical medical care, legal counseling, vocational counseling, and educational counseling. The psychotherapeutic services are intended to help with the problems of emotional disturbance, conflict, and tensions occasioned by the illegitimate pregnancy and related to the pregnancy. This includes counseling and emotional support for the woman's changing relationship with her own family, her relationship with the putative father, her changing relationship to peers, her reaction to the pregnancy and the anticipated birth experience, her plans for the child, changes in self-concept, and the total emotional configuration which might have motivated the girl to become pregnant.

In general, the single pregnant girl is likely to be more interested in sociotherapy than in psychotherapy. Most of the unmarried mothers to whom service is offered are likely to be more concerned with the specific, immediate problems posed by the pregnancy and the birth of the child.

Arranging for adequate medical care is an immediate consideration. The unmarried mother, in contrast to the married mother, tends to seek medical care later in the pregnancy and to get less adequate care when she does go. She is therefore more likely to have some complications during delivery, and runs a greater risk of dying. The younger the un-wed mother, the more she is apt to delay in obtaining medical services. [73]   The tendency to deny the pregnancy, a common reaction in most unwed mothers, is particularly pronounced among teenagers and causes a delay in going for help.

The illegitimate child, consequently, is more likely to experience a less hospitable physical and psychic intrauterine environment, to en-counter complications during delivery, to be born underweight or pre-maturely or with an abnormality, and runs a greater risk of infant mortality.

In all of this, the factor of the illegitimacy of the conception is com-plicated by factors of class, race, and age of mother. Many of the mothers are lower-class nonwhites, which makes adequate medical and nutritional care difficult to obtain in any circumstances. Teenage pregnancies, illegitimate or legitimate, are always high-risk pregnancies, and many of the unmarried mothers are teenagers. But despite the "normal" haz-ards of nonwhite lower-class teenage pregnancies, the fact of illegitimacy adds an additional and intensifying complication, making for some incre-ment in all of the risks encountered.

Medical care for unmarried mothers with limited resources can be financed through Medicaid. The older unwed mother may obtain finan-cial assistance under the AFDC program, if she is willing to file a com-plaint against the putative father. If paternity is established he will be required to contribute monthly toward support of the child. If the father is not known, not located, or not able to pay, financial assistance is available even before the birth of the child. The pregnant single woman is not eligible for unemployment insurance because she is not eligible for employment.

Housing is available in maternity homes and foster homes. The latter are often "wage" homes in which the girl receives room and board in exchange for babysitting and light housework.

The legal status of the teenage unmarried mother complicates the planning situation. Her parents' legal permission is often needed before she may receive medical care, enter a maternity home, or give up the child for adoption. The teenager may also find it difficult to obtain financial assistance unless her parents can satisfy the agency that they are not capable of supporting their daughter and are willing to apply for aid in her behalf.

The single pregnant woman faces not only the practical problems of medical care, finances, housing, etc., but emotional problems as well. For the married woman, pregnancy is a joyful occasion in which she is ap-plauded and supported by those who are close to her; for the single girl, it is occasion for regret, dejection, worry, and social disapproval. Al-

though society is currently more accepting, or at least less openly punitive, in its response to the unmarried mother, she is still considered
atypical and deviant.

Guilt and shame if manifested at all, are more likely to be evoked
by the pregnancy rather than by the sexual activity which caused it [98],
but the general situation in which the single pregnant girl finds herself
is apt to evoke strong feelings of anxiety and panic. Denial and distortion
of reality are understandable when the reality involves "having to
acknowledge that she has been abandoned by the baby's father, that she
is in social and economic jeopardy, and that she will either have to
relinquish a baby she may love or . . . keep a baby she is not sure she
is going to love." [7, p. 31] The social worker can help the unmarried
mother deal with her feelings about her situation.

Perhaps the first question which needs discussion is whether or not
to tell the parents about the pregnancy, and, if so, how to do this.
Parents frequently hate to be told, yet want to be told. Although learning
about the pregnancy excites guilt that they have failed as parents, they
are often capable of offering emotional support and concrete help. The
girl wants to conceal the pregnancy lest she hurt her parents, yet she is
relieved and comforted when they rally to her support. The relationship
between the unmarried mother and her parents may become particularly
difficult if the pregnancy is an interracial one or if parents and daughter
disagree on ultimate plans for the child.

While there is much in the situation which creates conflict between
daughter and parents, there is much that moves them toward reconciliation. The parents' guilt and compassion, the daughter's desire to
make amends for the pain she may be causing them may move them
toward reconciliation. The worker reinforces those tendencies which
move parents and child toward mutual forgiveness and attempts to resolve, or mitigate, the divisive elements in the situation.

For some girls the pregnancy may precipitate maturity. As a pregnant woman, the girl is perceived as an adult engaging in an adult
experience. As a consequence, she may decide to move away from home
and establish greater independence, or she may find that she is now
emotionally ready for marriage.

Most pressing is the need to discuss and resolve her feelings about
the child and to make plans for the child. Innocent though it may be,
the child has occasioned considerable difficulty for the mother, which
may make the mother feel resentment, and guilt and shame about her
resentment.

The social worker can help the mother to distinguish her feeling
about plans for the child from those of her family and/or of the child's
father. If a woman has a strong emotional need for the child but is
persuaded or coerced to give it up, she may incur another illegitimate
pregnancy in search of the lost child. The worker can also help the

mother to distinguish between what is desirable for the child and what is desirable for herself. As Crockett says, "Not only is it important that the unmarried mother reach the right decision but also that she reach it in a way that leaves her convinced that she has chosen wisely." [22, p. 77]

The decision to marry the putative father involves a decision to keep the baby. This suggests that the marriage starts with considerable economic, social, and emotional burdens, because the marital choice is being made under some duress. Marriages contracted while the girl is pregnant are much more likely to end in divorce than marriages in which no pregnancy is involved.

The unmarried woman who wants to keep her child must be helped to assess her capacity to care for the child as a single parent. If she seriously overestimates her capacity, she may later regret the decision. She may need clarification of the problems she is likely to face and information about the resources in the community which might be available to help her with those problems.

The woman who gives up her child must be helped to give up motherhood as well, and to resolve her feelings of loss. In most instances, despite a difficult period of transition, the girl resumes her place in society and in her own mind as a single childless woman.

A woman who has decided to give up her baby may feel threatened by, and guard herself against, feeling tender toward the child, since this may make implementing her decision more difficult. The girl who gives up her child may be haunted at intervals by thoughts of the child, wondering—without being able to find out—what is happening to him. She also has the problem of deciding whether or not to tell some man she may meet and plan to marry about this incident in her life.

The worker helps the mother to anticipate these feelings so that she is less likely to be overwhelmed by them and is better prepared to accept and resolve them.

Some of the conflicts experienced by unwed mothers are exemplified in the following case reports:

Miss E. was thankful that the baby had been born, since this meant she would have no problem in returning to college in March. I wondered if she still found it hard to talk about the baby. Her eyes filled with tears. Although she had not seen her, the doctor assured her that the baby was quite healthy. With much feeling, she hoped I did not think her "hard hearted." She just could not feel any love for the baby, although she did have some interest in her. During the few months at college she had a taste of something different for herself and didn't feel ready or able to give this up. I agreed with Miss E. that she was right to act on her own feelings. [22, pp. 82–83]

These were signs that Miss H. had been thinking more about the baby. In fact she told me that she had thought more about her in the last two days than ever before. Maybe this was because she had had a dream, a very vivid one, about her taking the baby home to her mother. Since then she had been wondering if the baby looked like the one she saw in her dream. A little timidly she asked what color hair he had, and when I told her it was light brown, she said, "That is just like the baby's father." Had she thought any more about seeing the baby? Miss H. thought it was best not to see him— that would only make it much harder. I accepted this but suggested that she might decide later to see the baby, as she might find that she was more worried in trying to imagine just what he looked like. Miss H. thought she might decide differently but right now it would be best not to see him. She spoke of the father of the baby, his desertion of her as soon as he knew that the baby was on the way, and her feeling that she never wanted to see him again. "It hurt me more the way he did that than it did about the baby." I guessed these two things were so close together that perhaps the baby could not mean anything good to her. Miss H. said the baby meant only trouble to her. [22, p. 83]

Until very recently, counseling of single pregnant girls excluded the possibility of abortion and contraception. Now abortion is one of the possible alternatives openly discussed. Discussion of contraceptives can help the single pregnant girl to choose from among the variety of contraceptive devices and procedures available.

Maternity Home

The maternity home is a specialized institutional facility developed to meet the needs of single pregnant women. The most recent survey showed that there were 201 such institutions (60 percent of them under denominational auspices) in the United States in 1966 offering service to about 25,000 women. [74]

Eligibility requirements are such that until recently they tended to restrict use of maternity homes to young, never married, not previously pregnant girls interested in placing their children for adoption. Until very recently, fewer than 10 percent of all residents in such homes were nonwhite although a large percentage of all single pregnant women are nonwhite. Rules and regulations, which frequently include a curfew, tend to discourage the older pregnant woman. Use of casework service and attendance at weekly group therapy sessions is mandatory in many maternity homes.

Such homes were established in the United States as early as 1836 but most were founded in the late nineteenth and early twentieth centuries. [74]   The largest network of such homes (forty-seven maternity homes in thirty states) is operated by the Florence Crittenton Association of America, founded in 1890 by a wealthy businessman, Charles Crittenton, in memory of his daughter. The earlier philosophy of the homes is expressed in the names they took—"House of Refuge," "Door of Hope," "Rescue Home," "House of Mercy," "Sheltering Arms."

Another large group of maternity homes is operated by the Salvation Army, whose mission was to rescue "fallen women" and "betrayed young girls."

Maternity homes provide care and rehabilitation as well as sanctuary. [84]   Many still rigorously protect their clients' identities.

Some homes have their own maternity units, while others arrange for delivery to take place at a local hospital. Some have nursery facilities so that the mother can care for the child for a short time after delivery.

Many women are interested in using the facilities of the maternity home, as they are in using social agencies generally, because they perceive such facilities as the best avenue to placing their babies for adoption. [65, p. 41]   The recently published diary of a single pregnant woman written during a stay in a Salvation Army maternity home gives a perceptive picture of the day-to-day living situation. [100]

The maternity home staff is concerned with helping the mother to prepare for the birth of the baby and for the decision she must make for her future. Individual and group counseling, educational and recreational activity, are included as part of the program of service. One of the desirable therapeutic aspects of the homes derives from the fact that a group of unmarried mothers are living together. This affords each woman a great measure of comfort and support as she compares notes and discusses common problems with others in the residence. It also makes possible the using of the therapeutic potential of a group sharing living experiences in group therapy sessions as a supplement to the casework interview. [50; 59; 94; 96]

Because the stay in a maternity home is relatively short, and because different residents are at different points in their pregnancies, people join and leave the group constantly. However, since all members share a common, highly affective experience, they rapidly get caught up in group discussions. One report of such a group program clearly indicates the objectives and illustrates some of the interaction:

> The primary purpose of the group is to help clarify and work through both current and future plans that the girls may have. Helping them understand their own behavior; their past and present relationships with their parents, boyfriends, and other significant people; and attempting to understand some of the reasons for their pregnancy are included.

Ann was an attractive twenty-four-year-old divorced woman

with a three-year-old son by her previous marriage. Her husband had deserted her shortly after the birth of this child, and Ann had considerable negative feelings about this man. The man by whom she became pregnant was the first person she had really dared to get close to since her divorce, and this, apparently, left her quite hostile toward all men. In the group, she talked about men taking advantage of her; she did not feel that she could ever trust another man. She planned to keep her baby and return home to live with her parents. In the group, there was little hesitation in discussing her hostile feelings and also her plan to keep the baby. The group was rather quick to question the strong hostility toward men and was able to point out to Ann that this was somewhat exaggerated. They also questioned the wisdom of keeping the baby, and one girl indicated considerable insight when she asked Ann how she would be able to love this child when she hated its father so much. Following that session, Ann discussed her plans for her baby with the Home caseworker; and just prior to the birth of the baby, she decided to place it for adoption. She told the group that she had changed her mind and decided that placement was a better plan for the baby. [28, pp. 225–26]

Intermediary group treatment has been successfully used to help prepare unmarried mothers to communicate in casework interviews. [68] After participation in a series of group meetings, they were more communicative in casework. [60]

Comfortable housing and health care of the unmarried mother is an easily achieved objective of the maternity home, which also provides a "safe shelter from a hostile environment." The social work objectives of helping the mother come to a decision about the baby are, however, more difficult to achieve and to assess. A British study notes, "Casework with unmarried mothers in a Mother and Baby Home could have two objectives: to support and assist a resident in making plans for her baby, and to help her resolve the most basic problems of adjustment of which the illegitimate pregnancy may be a symptom. Neither of these objectives seemed to be achieved." [65, p. 134]

Maternity homes are now facing a crisis: for the first time in their history they are facing a decline in applications, possibly because single pregnant women no longer want, or need, the concealment which the maternity home offers. As a consequence, many homes are making a more decided effort to attract black unmarried mothers, and the percentage of black residents has increased. [61, p. 16] They have also attempted to offer service on an outpatient basis to unmarried mothers.

Multiservice Centers for Single Pregnant School-age Girls and Group Programs

In the 1960's, there was a rapid development of multiservice, comprehensive, interdisciplinary programs for single pregnant women—from thirty-five such centers in 1968 to over 175 (serving some 40,000 clients) by February 1971. [25; 45]   The multiservice centers seek to provide, or coordinate, a comprehensive program of health, educational, and social services for pregnant school-age girls living at home. In meeting these needs, the local Board of Education works together with the local Department of Health and the local Department of Public Welfare.

One pioneer program of this nature—The Webster School in the District of Columbia—was organized in 1963. [46]   It enrolls only teenage pregnant girls and offers a program of educational, health, and welfare services provided by an interdisciplinary team of teachers, psychologists, social workers, doctors, public health nurses, and nutritionists. Another such program, the Oakland California Interagency Cyesis Program, involves the participation of the Departments of Welfare, Health, Education, and Recreation, the YWCA, community action groups, and voluntary agencies. Through such projects the girls continue their high school studies with teachers provided by the local board of education. In addition there are special classes in child care, health care during pregnancy, and home economics. Individual and group counseling is provided by social workers, who also help the girls make use of local social agency programs. Maternity care is provided by health personnel. Some of the projects offer pediatric care, family planning information, adoption placement, vocational training, and psychological diagnostic evaluation. Service is offered to the putative father and the girl's own family. But few of these programs provide continuing contact with the mother and child. Most girls, after they give birth, return to their regular school setting. [11; 37; 44; 56; 69; 110; 115]   Funds to implement such programs were made available through the Office of Economic Opportunity and through Title I of the Education Act.

Such services were developed in response to a growing sensitivity to the educational consequences of teen-age pregnancy. Many school systems require that the pregnant teenager leave school. Separated from her peers if expelled during the pregnancy and having lost a year of school, the girl is understandably reluctant to return to school after the birth of the child. As a result most of the girls never complete their education and are trapped in a cycle of low-paying jobs and limited income. School systems did attempt to provide continuing education for the pregnant teenager through instruction in the family home or through educational programs in the maternity home, but such resources were available only to a limited number of girls.

School policy affected health care. The danger of expulsion increased the girl's desire to conceal the pregnancy as long as possible, to the detriment of her own health needs and those of the child.

There have been few serious attempts to evaluate the multiservice programs. One such evaluation of The Webster School indicated that it was very successful in its principal aim of continuing the girls' education throughout their pregnancy so that they were able to return after childbirth to the regular school at the same level as their nonpregnant peers. It was successful in bringing the girls under prenatal care early in the pregnancy and insured their receiving such care consistently. As a consequence "the proportion of low-birth-weight infants, the infant mortality rates, and other indices were better for Webster girls than for various Negro populations in the District." [46, p. 49] However, "repetition of pregnancy among the girls was not reduced as a result of participation in the Webster program. Many girls had second babies within a relatively short period of time." [46, p. 57]

Group work programs in the community have been attempted. The groups were formed around the common problems faced by the single pregnant girl. [3] Group work has been offered the unmarried mothers in the community both before and after confinement. [12; 26; 48] Group programs conducted jointly by public health nurses and social workers and focused on the medical and social aspects of pregnancy and preparation for confinement seem to have greatest interest.

Evaluation

A study of the effectiveness of different approaches to treatment of unwed mothers in a traditional child welfare agency concluded that the methods "felt to be most effective are environmental manipulation, both direct and indirect, and sustaining, *i.e.,* offering encouragement and reassurance and fewer instances in which reflective discussion or consideration is involved." [81, p. 8]

The research included random assignment of ninety-one single pregnant women to one of three different treatment conditions—tangible environmental supportive service, intensive individual casework services, or intensive group counseling. Differences in functioning at the end of treatment were assessed by a casework research interviewer one month, six months, one year, and two years following delivery, and compared with an assessment of functioning at intake based on interviews and psychological tests. While environmental manipulation and sustaining were most successful, in general service did not effect any change in most clients. "Relatively few girls have grown through the experience. . . . The large majority resume their previous pattern of functioning as well as previous modes of adaptation." [81, p. 8]

Another study conducted in a similar kind of agency obtained its principal data from the unmarried mothers, whose responses to a checklist indicated that they perceived the agency as offering important services.

> They confirmed that their caseworkers had helped them get through the experience as soon as possible, had helped them keep their pregnancies secret, had helped them know how to answer questions about their absence from the community during their pregnancies, had helped them obtain vocational guidance, had helped those clients who wanted to keep their babies to make a suitable plan to do so, had helped those who wanted to place their child for adoption to sign the permanent surrender, had helped school-age girls get back into school and had helped some of the young girls to get back into their own homes. [67, p. 473]

Some 32 percent of the respondents indicated they had been helped by casework services to develop a greater understanding of themselves and their behavior.

A comprehensive program of services (casework, group work, medical and educational services) to a group of 240 teenage unmarried mothers and their families was evaluated by Bedger. Five key areas of functioning—the client's relationship with her family, her relationship with the putative father, the adequacy of her plans for the baby, her plans for her own future, and environmental stress—were rated at intake by the interviewer caseworker and at closing by the caseworker assigned to the case. The rating at closing showed greatest improvement in the client's relationships with her own parents and in the general family interaction. Over-all, "55 percent of the cases studied were rated [at closing] more positive in functioning on the five areas utilized. In 34.6 percent of the cases change was negative and in 9.6 percent of the cases there was no evidence of change." [5, p. 43] But since there was no control group, it is not clear that the positive results are ascribable to the comprehensive program offered.

A postpartum intensive group therapy project involving forty-seven weekly sessions for a limited number of unwed mothers showed participants manifesting a "significant increase in self-esteem," improved impulse control, and increased feminine identification as a result of the experience. Assessment was made on the basis of social work and psychiatric interviews and psychological tests before and after treatment. By contrast a control group of nonparticipant unwed mothers showed fewer positive changes during this period. [16]

The current situation with regard to effectiveness of service in response to the problem of illegitimacy is aptly summarized by researchers
who studied 134 black and white unwed mothers receiving agency service and concluded that

> . . . field observation and the response of the clients in the study
> raised little question about the capacity of the voluntary social
> agency to meet the *immediate* [italics in original] needs of the
> illegitimately pregnant girls who come or are brought for help.
> Plans are made, medical care is given and babies are placed for
> adoption when this is desired. . . . There seemed to be ample
> recognition of the value of agency services. . . . Difficulties in
> giving help arise in large measure from the fact that social agencies
> and the professionals they employ impose complex goals on them-
> selves which usually go far beyond the goal of meeting a crisis
> situation. Most agencies aim to give the client an experience of
> lasting value and to bring about long-run changes that are presumed
> to be constructive. [92, p. 64]

The Putative Father

For each out-of-wedlock child being carried by a single pregnant girl
there is, of course, a putative father. The putative father was once ignored or considered only as a source of financial support for the unwed
mother and her child. This was followed by a period during which
contact was attempted with the putative father because of what he could
contribute toward the emotional as well as financial support of the
unwed mother and because knowledge of the putative father was helpful
in adoptive planning for the child. Currently, contact with the putative
father is predicated on the recognition that he might want help in his
own right with the problems he faces relating to the out-of-wedlock
pregnancy.

The movement has been from seeing the putative father solely as a
resource for help to the unmarried mother to perceiving him as a person
in his own right who might be troubled about a difficult situation in
which he is a principal participant.

The current focus is on father-mother-child rather than exclusively
on the girl. [4; 7; 15; 29; 70; 71; 72; 80]

Characteristics

Studies of the background of the unmarried father indicate that he
is generally of the same age, social class, and educational level as the

single pregnant girl, and that he has known the girl for some time prior to the onset of the pregnancy. [40; 72; 83; 89]   He is usually not promiscuous. "Relationships between unwed mothers and unwed fathers are much more meaningful than popularly supposed and . . . unwed fathers have more concern for their offspring than is generally realized." [72, p. 85]   The relationship of the unmarried father to the mother cannot validly be characterized as either deviant or exploitative.

Only a small minority of pregnancies resulted from short-time contact with casually encountered strangers. In most instances the unwed father is far from the phantom figure one might expect if the mother was motivated to become pregnant in response to her own private needs and needed a man only for his biological contribution.

Social workers have tended to favor a psychological "explanation" for unwed fatherhood. The supposition is that, like unwed motherhood, unwed fatherhood is a symptom of some psychological need. The unwed father, it is believed, acts out of hostility toward women, or out of a desire to confirm his virility, or in rejection of authority and the core culture, or in reaction to fears of latent homosexuality.

But the responses of a group of unmarried fathers to the California Psychological Inventory substantially mirrors the standard profile. Modest deviations indicated less social maturity and responsibility and more self-centeredness. [72; pp. 103–106]   This lack of clear-cut differentiation between putative fathers and males in general is confirmed by other comparisons of the two groups. [76]

As Caughlan notes, the "act which initiates pregnancy" may range from "nothing more than a witless discharge of physiological tension" to the "fullest expression of the most mature relationship. . . . A great variety of psychosocial predisposing and precipitating factors can lead to the onset of this condition." [17, p. 29]

Services to the Unwed Father

The agencies which have made a special effort to offer service to the unmarried father have found that he is available, troubled, concerned, and frequently anxious to be of help. [15; 72; 80]

Perhaps the agency which has most actively and consistently attempted such a service is the Vista Del Mar Child Care Service in Los Angeles, which serves a predominantly urban middle-class white clientele. [70; 71; 72]   The agency notes that about 80 percent of the fathers whom they contacted were seen and that the majority of those had four or more interviews with the male caseworker. [72, p. 59, Table 17]

A public agency which attempted a program of service to unmarried fathers found that in at least 70 percent of the cases he was "available for interviews and frequently anxious to help in planning for his baby." [80, p. 537]

At least one agency requires that the unmarried mother accepted for service be willing to have the agency contact the unmarried father "for cooperation in giving history and consent to adoption." [15, p. 72]   The agency found that 83 percent of the fathers whom they attempted to reach "made themselves available for an interview." [15, p. 72]

A nationwide study of services offered by voluntary agencies to 20,000 unwed mothers in 1966, however, indicated that only about 7 percent of the putative fathers were interviewed by the social agencies. [40, p. 46]   If the putative father was a teenager, there was greater likelihood that he would be seen by the agency.

The unmarried father's fear that admission of paternity may make him legally responsible for continuing support of mother and child might lead him to refuse the invitation of the agency or to support a decision for adoption since adoption settles any question of the need for continuing financial support. Unwed fathers who are married and have legitimate children are reluctant to contact the agency out of the desire to protect their own families.

At the Vista Del Mar Agency, permission to contact the father is first obtained from the mother and, if possible, the mother arranges to bring the father for his first contact with the agency. A separate male worker is assigned to the father. Where the agency finds it necessary to make a direct contact with the father, it attempts to motivate his participation by stressing his importance in planning for mother and child and by stressing the help the agency can offer the putative father himself. If this fails to evoke his interest, "legal implication, such as statutory rape, etc. *may* [italics in original] have to be explained, at the worker's discretion, to impress upon the unmarried father the importance of his becoming involved with the agency." [72, p. 55]   Many fathers, however, do come when offered the opportunity.

The norms and values of the core culture require that a man protect and support the female he has impregnated and their child. There are, of course, many different ways in which the unmarried father mitigates any feeling of responsibility, guilt, or remorse. These range from "It may have been somebody else, not me," to "She didn't have to do it if she didn't want to and she should have taken proper precautions." Yet many men do feel remorse and shame if they fail to come to the support and assistance of the mother and child. Unlike the unmarried mother, the unmarried father does not have the physical and social discomfort of nine months of pregnancy and the pain of delivery through which some "atonement" is achieved.

The agency offering service to the putative father hopes to help him directly in the following ways:

1. By clarifying his attitude toward, and relationship with, the child, the agency may help him achieve a feeling of psychological father-

hood. This requires a reorientation of his self-concept and is more complex, of course, than the unthinking achievement of physical fatherhood. Without such help, the child remains for the father a shadowy fantasy rather than a living reality.

2. By clarifying his feelings of guilt and responsibility toward the mother and child, the agency may help him come to some decision about what he plans to do in discharging any responsibility he may feel. Contact with the agency can help the unmarried father clarify his financial responsibility to the mother and child and has resulted in substantial contributions toward both. [72, p. 95]

3. Contact with the agency can help the unmarried father clarify his relationship with the mother so that he can either dissolve it without excessive guilt or resolve his indecision about marriage.

4. Contact with the agency can help the father resolve any psychological emotional problem which may have contributed to his becoming a putative father and to reduce the possibility of recurrence.

5. The agency can offer information about any possible legal action against him as well as information regarding his entitlement to the child.

6. The agency helps the unmarried father clarify his indecision about whether or not to share with his own parents the problem he faces so as to obtain their support and help.

The agency is also interested in the indirect service to mother and child which might result from contact with the putative father. Discussion with the unmarried mother of the question of permitting contact with the unmarried father helps her clarify her relationship with him, what she hopes from him, and what she can realistically expect. Joint sessions among the unwed mother, father, and social worker can be helpful in dispelling any romantic, unrealistic fantasies the pair may have about each other and the nature of their relationship. The very fact that the father is taking some responsibility for the decision regarding the child is reassuring and supportive to the mother. As a consequence of sharing this responsibility the mother may feel more confident and less anxious.

For effective adoptive planning it is desirable to have detailed information regarding the child's paternal and maternal background. Contact with the putative father can provide more complete information of this nature. [2] Such knowledge might subsequently be communicated to the adopted child to give him a more complete sense of identity. The father's involvement is important to the child in other ways as well. Consent to the registration of paternity permits the child to claim, and obtain benefits, from the Social Security account of the father.

Currently the legal position of the unwed father is an unenviable one. He is responsible for support but the disposition of the child is decided by the mother. Recently agencies have supported changes so as to make paternity hearings more like civil proceedings and to grant the unwed father some legal entitlement in plans made for the child.

The trend in recent legal decisions has been to give the putative father a greater entitlement in the decision regarding plans for his out-of-wedlock child. While this may be a desirable recognition of the rights of the father, it may complicate and delay adoption for the child since consent of both the father and mother may be required before the child is legally free to be placed. [97]

The Decision to Keep or Place

While a very high percentage of nonrelative adopted children are illegitimate, only a small percentage of illegitimately born children are adopted. Most such children are kept and raised by the unmarried mother and/or her family. In 1969, for instance, some 361,000 children were born out of wedlock. In the same year only about 100,000 illegitimately born children were placed for adoption.

Whatever the reasons, it might be noted that the recent trend has been toward a greater proportion of unmarried mothers who keep their babies rather than surrender them for adoption.

This raises two questions which are of considerable interest to child welfare social work and which have been the subject of recurrent research: What distinguishes the unmarried mother who gives up her child for adoption from the unmarried mother who chooses to retain the child? [27; 35; 49; 57; 111; 112]   What has been the developmental experience of such children not placed for adoption? [20; 21; 23; 38; 55; 66; 73; 86; 88; 90; 109]

The factor of race is clearly associated with the decision to keep or surrender the child. Most (65–70 percent) white unmarried mothers give up their children for adoption, but relatively few (5–6 percent) black unmarried mothers do so. There is some controversy as to whether the decision of the black unmarried mother is freely made or a consequence of more limited adoption opportunities available to black children.

Until recently, many maternity homes (which serve as channels for adoptive placement) were not open to nonwhite women, and most of the adoptive agencies served white adoptive parents. But even now, when more adequate services are available to nonwhites, relatively few nonwhite children achieve adoption, because there is disproportionately a greater supply of such children. Recognition of this reality may have shaped the preference of the nonwhite unmarried mother.

Preference may have been shaped, too, by the historical antecedents of slave culture and subsequent rural living, both of which provide a tradition of extended family care of the black out-of-wedlock child in preference to giving him up. Whatever the determining factors, research reveals that black unmarried mothers express a stronger preference about keeping their children than do white unmarried mothers. Griswold found that black mothers "appear to be no more tolerant than their white counterparts toward sexual behavior that may lead to conception out-of-wedlock. . . . On the other hand, Negroes are far more opposed than whites to giving up illegitimate children for adoption." [39, p. 13] Shapiro found that one of the strongest and clearest differences in racial attitudes related to the adoption of the out-of-wedlock child: black unmarried women "heavily favored keeping children born out-of-wedlock." [91, p. 59]

Considerable research effort has been expended in trying to determine other social and psychological characteristics which distinguish the mother who keeps the baby from the one who gives it up for adoption.

Social factors associated with an increased likelihood of the child being retained by the white mothers include religion, education attainment, and age. The more highly educated, younger, non-Catholic clients who were still in school were more likely to surrender the child for adoption. Younger, dependent women were likely to be more responsive to the imposition of parental control dictating surrender of the child; the more highly educated women were likely to see retention of the baby as a handicap to further education and desirable career choices. Women who kept their babies were more likely to be older, Catholic, less educated, and more likely to have come from broken homes. Having grown up in a "one-parent home which they survived, they were more willing to chance a one-parent arrangement themselves." [27, p. 259]

Bowerman found that socioeconomic status and age were important variables: younger, less educated women of lower socioeconomic level were likely to keep their babies; older, more educated women of higher economic position were more likely to give them up. [10] He also found that a close relationship to the putative father, which suggested some hope of marriage, was related to the decision to keep the child. The factor of shame, not tested in most other studies, was directly related to the decision: those who felt a greater sense of shame in the pregnancy were more likely to divest themselves of its visible evidence.

Psychological tests of women who keep their children tend to indicate that they are likely to have more negative personality scores than women who surrender their children. Jones interprets this as suggesting that "surrender of the baby is associated with maturity and competence and this, in turn, related to conformance with the general norm of surrendering the baby so that legitimate nonmother status is restored." [49, p. 228] Vincent, who obtained his results through the California Personality Inventory, interprets them as indicative of the fact that "unwed mothers who keep their children have minimal positive identification as individuals with social groups who might communicate the traditional sex mores and the stigma concomitant with giving birth out of wedlock." Furthermore, "unwed mothers, in keeping their children, show their desperate need for at least one primary relationship in which they were needed and loved by someone whose dependence on them makes it safe for them to receive and return that love in their own ways." [107, p. 193]

Two caveats need to be clearly noted: both studies included only white women; and while the group scores between those who surrendered and those who kept their children were different, in individual instances, some women who kept their babies achieved more positive scores than some women who surrendered their babies. As Vincent notes, "It would be unfortunate if such group data were interpreted or misused to claim that any individual unmarried mother desiring to keep her child is, *ipso facto*, an inadequate mother and a disturbed person." [107, p. 199]

Timing

The timing and firmness of the mother's decision are important variables. The sooner the mother decides, the sooner the agency can began to make definite plans for disposition. If she decides upon adoption, the child can be placed in an adoptive home directly from the hospital in which he has been delivered. This reduces the possibility of discontinuity of mothering for the child, the problem of adjusting to a number of different mothers, and the trauma of separation after becoming adjusted to some mothering person.

It may be argued that an early decision is in the best interests of the mother as well. If giving up the child is an act of major psychic surgery, it might be less difficult before the mother builds a stronger affectional relationship to the child. However, it is also argued that the mother needs some time in contact with the child to resolve whatever decision she has made. A hurried decision entails the risk of subsequent regret and of attempts to reverse the decision with disruptive consequences for the adoptive parent and child. Hence the firmness of the decision is as important as its promptness.

Perhaps a two-stage process is desirable: a tentative conclusion before the baby is born and a final ratification afterward.

The agency's principal tenet is to encourage flexibility in decision making which permits each mother to come to her own decision in her own time. In general, research indicates that most mothers come to a firm, consistent decision either before or shortly after birth of the child. A study of 221 unmarried mothers in Scotland showed that "four out of every five single mothers reached their decision within a week after confinement." [101, p. 35]   Pannor found that most single pregnant women come to the agency having already decided disposition of the child. [72, pp. 86–88]   Bowerman, in interviews with about 500 white mothers, found that most had made their decision before the birth of the baby. [10, p. 265]   Those who intended to release the baby for adoption made the decision earlier than those who decided on other arrangements. About 82 percent of the white mothers said that, given, the opportunity, they would make the same decision again, indicating satisfaction with the decision they had made. [10, p. 232, Table 53]

The factors discussed above which appear to be related to the decision to place or keep the baby and the findings regarding timing and consistency of the decision feed into each other. The decision to place or keep is most strongly associated with situational circumstances—age, educational level, socioeconomic position—which are assessable even before birth of the child and act as principal constraints on the mother, limiting options and alternatives. The emotional relationship with the child and attachment to the child is not generally as important a factor in the decision. Realistically recognizing and evaluating her situation even before delivery, the mother generally comes to a decision as to what she can do and has to do. Contact with the child only infrequently results in a change of decision. Thus Yelloly found that, of 160 unmarried mothers, 68 percent made a decision very early in the pregnancy —a decision to which they held with consistency and upon which they finally acted. In most instances the decision was based on strong objective considerations such as the presence of other children of the mother, the married status of the putative father, and the attitude of the mother's parents. [111; 112]

In follow-up interviews with unmarried mothers who kept their children, Reed found that "72 percent of all mothers decided before the birth of the baby to keep the baby." Most were lower-class nonwhites. However, more than "half of the middle-class girls did not decide to keep the baby until after the birth of the baby." [86, p. 90]   Mothers who had few alternatives made a decision early; mothers with more options made the decision later.

The research further notes that mothers with prolonged ambivalence and strong conflicts about the decision are apt to be less emotionally stable and ultimately more likely to keep the child. [86]   This would suggest that these mothers are less responsive to the constraints of external reality and act more in response to internal emotional needs.

Of interest to social workers is the mother's perception of who helped her make the decision. In the overwhelming percentage of instances, the mothers studied by Bowerman said they turned to their parents for help—most frequently to their own mothers. Female relatives (sisters, aunts, grandmothers) were also frequently consulted. "The alleged father is brought into these considerations relatively rarely . . .

[and] it is very clear that the counsel of physicians, social workers, and other professionals (attorneys, clergymen, teachers) is sought by (or 'urged upon') but a small fraction of the respondents, almost all of whom are white." [10, pp. 197–99] Only about 1 percent indicated that a social worker had been most important in influencing the decision. It thus appears that in most instances the caseworker is faced with helping the mother confirm a decision and helping the mother implement a decision rather than helping the mother to make it.

Keeping the Child

The unmarried mother who places her child for adoption has been the primary concern of child welfare agencies. Yet it is recognized that a larger percentage of unmarried mothers keep their children and that frequently child welfare problems derive from this fact. However, there are few specific services directed primarily to this segment of the single-parent population.

There is little specific follow-up service to unmarried mothers who keep their children, but there have been studies which are concerned with what happens to the mother and out-of-wedlock child who stay together. The results generally are, once again, a tribute to the heterogeneity of the unmarried mother group and a confirmation of the fact that no stereotype is validly applicable to this group.

As Sauber says, "although these women shared the common experience of bearing a child out-of-wedlock and rearing that child, their lives as mothers followed many different paths. [90, p. 145] Many get married and merge into the two-parent family group; many remain single. Many have additional out-of-wedlock children; some do not. Some are employed full-time and self-supporting; some are employed part-time and receive supplementary help from relatives; some are wholly supported by relatives (including continuing contributions from the putative father); some are supported by public assistance. Some are living with relatives; some, with friends; many, alone. For most mothers, recreational and social life and involvement in community activity were limited and meager, but most resume their place among an accepting group of friends and relatives. A few have continued their education or received further vocational training; most, however, have not. A substantial minority faced financial difficulty and lived in substandard housing. A very high percentage indicated that, given the opportunity, they would decide once again to keep the child. [7; 8]

In almost all instances they appear to be reasonably adequate, concerned mothers who are doing a creditable job in rearing their children. Very few of the children had been placed in foster homes or with relatives; even fewer had been neglected and/or abused.

Since the decision to place the child for adoption is strongly associated with middle-class, better educated, white girls, it is not surprising that a substantial percentage of the mothers who kept their children are lower-class and nonwhite, with limited education and limited earning capacity, and living in more deprived neighborhoods in contact with relatives who themselves have limited resources to share.

One of the earliest follow-up studies of unmarried mothers, which involved interviews with fifty-four women some eight years after their confinement, concluded that "adoption was not necessarily the only desirable solution, as evidenced by the fact that some mothers who kept their children seemed to have done well by both the children and themselves." [55, p. 33]

A study by Reed published in 1962 reviewed the situation for 118 mothers, both black and white. [86]   Physical and psychological examinations of the children showed the largest majority of them to be "developing normally physically, mentally, and emotionally." [86, p. 107] Similarly, Wright's interview study of eighty unmarried mothers who kept their babies concludes that, "contrary to the original hypothesis, a majority of the children were judged to be fairing well." [109, p. 52]

The child-rearing practices of unmarried mothers who kept their children are not essentially different from those of comparative samples of low-income black and white mothers, although unmarried mothers were more concerned about restricting aggressive behavior and more likely to stress the importance of doing well in school. [20]

Oppel compared the care and development of black illegitimate children with a matched group of legitimate children. [66]   The findings did not support the "contentions that mothers of illegitimate children are more likely to give poor care to their children than are mothers of legitimate children." Nor is there any significant difference in development of the two groups of children. The researcher concludes that based on the findings there is no reason to single out illegitimate children "for long-term agency follow-up service nor should they be removed from their mothers on the assumption that illegitimacy is probably indicative of neglect."

The most elaborate and careful follow-up study of unmarried mothers who kept their babies was conducted by Sauber for the Community Council of New York. The study has reported on the adjustment of mother and child one and a half years after birth [88] and then again six years after birth. [90]   Some 90 percent of the 205 women still in the study when the child was six were black or Puerto Rican. A comparison between these children and legitimate children in the community studied by the Manhattan Survey of Psychiatric Impairment of Urban Children showed that they were essentially similar in emotional functioning. [90, p. 138]

The report echoes the implications of the studies already cited—that "more recognition should be given to the *strengths* [italics in original] of one-parent families rather than too hasty an attribution of pathology to them." [90, p. 45]   Sauber concludes:

> The study findings clearly challenge many myths about women
> who have had a child out of wedlock. For the great majority,
> this experience has not been the beginning of a life of promiscuity,
> instability, and dependency. Although some have suffered, the
> majority have coped very well, pursuing their lives in different ways,
> with the result that, six years after their first child was born, they
> have, in most respects, blended into the general population of
> mothers and children and exhibit the wide range of life styles and
> life situations found among families in the population generally.
> Perhaps the greatest service that could be rendered to this group
> is that they no longer be labeled "unwed mothers" but that they be
> viewed as parents, often single parents, of young children,
> and that they be provided with the respect and the social and
> economic supports necessary for them to carry out these roles.
> [90, p. 157]

Contrary to these general positive findings, however, are the results of a careful follow-up study in England which compared the development of out-of-wedlock children placed in adoptive homes with the progress made by out-of-wedlock children who remained in a single-parent home with their mother. On the basis of most of the criteria employed in the study, the adoptive child's adjustment and development were in advance of his nonadopted out-of-wedlock peer. [21]

The mother who keeps her child takes her place in the community along with all other single mothers who are rearing their children without benefit of a husband-father because of death or desertion or divorce or separation. The problems encountered by the single parent who comes to single parenthood through an out-of-wedlock birth are not significantly different from those encountered by other single parents. The services required by the unwed mother who keeps her child are, in essence, those required by all single parents—income maintenance, help with housing, day care, vocational education, job referral, help in finding adult companionship, help in making contacts with eligible males, help in finding satisfying leisure activity. Ultimately, these mothers do face a special difficult problem: explaining to their child the whereabouts of the father.

Only occasionally, as in AFDC application or housing project application, is any distinction made between out-of-wedlock single parenthood and other kinds of single parenthood, to the disadvantage of the former. In making application for AFDC, the mother has to name and initiate action against the putative father for support of the child. Housing projects frequently discriminate against unmarried mothers. But, in general, public policies and socioeconomic conditions helpful to the single-parent family headed by a woman are also helpful to the unmarried mother who keeps her child.

Here, as in adoption, the significant factor which differentiates this family from other single-parent families headed by a women lies in the nature of the genesis of the particular family. Once past genesis, however, the essential points of similarity between all single-parent families headed by a woman are overwhelmingly greater than any differences.

Problems

1. Providing adequate services to the unmarried mother and her child involves a very understandable ambivalence. Agencies can be, and are, criticized for doing "too much" by those whose concern is with conservatively maintaining social institutions and who see any help to the unmarried mother as an encouragement of illegitimacy; "too little" by those who are concerned with the needs of the unmarried mother and her child. The threat to the mores conflicts with compassion for the child. This is the classic dilemma which has consistently made difficult the offering of help needed by the unwed mother and her child.

A permissive attitude toward illegitimacy would suggest that the society attaches no great significance to marriage as the context for child rearing.

The question is whether or not such a conflict is as true as it is seemingly obvious. Certainly more punitive attitudes toward the unmarried mother and her child have not discouraged increases in illegitimacy rates, nor have more liberal public policies invariably resulted in sharp increases in illegitimacy rates. [108, pp. 323–24]

The 1957 edition of the Encyclopaedia Britannica in an article comparing world-wide illegitimacy rates comments that "the policies regarding illegitimate children have been especially liberal in the Scandinavian countries, and studies conducted in these countries have produced no evidence that such a liberal policy promoted illegitimacy." [47, Vol. 12, p. 85]

The persistent myth of a relationship between the adequacy of welfare programs available to the unmarried mother and increases in illegitimacy is very carefully examined both nationally (as it affects the AFDC program) and internationally, by Cutright, who found it to have no basis in fact. [24]   Apparently illegitimacy rates are not very responsive to positive changes in the level of such services and assistance.

Nor are they responsive to punitive measures, such as voluntary or compulsory sterilization, denial of public assistance, and criminal prosecution. In general, where such measures (particularly restriction of financial assistance) have been implemented, they have not resulted in any reduction in illegitimacy rates. They have, however, resulted in more deprived living conditions for the children affected by such policies.

2. There is a problem in developing procedures and approaches for reducing the illegitimacy rate. The slowly increasing illegitimacy rate is reflective of many pervasive aspects of the culture. Prominent public figures, such as actresses Vanessa Redgrave and Mia Farrow, and a member of the British Parliament, Bernadette Devlin, have proudly, openly, and without apology, borne children out of wedlock. Such examples both reflect and encourage a more matter-of-fact attitude toward unwed parenthood.

Furthermore, since black illegitimacy rates reflect some of the economic problems of the black male, they indirectly involve such questions as race relations and discrimination.

There is not yet unequivocal public support for programs of sex education or for government programs making contraceptive information and devices available to single teenagers and older women.

Pregnancy as a result of intercourse is the exception rather than the rule. "It has been estimated that there must be nearly one thousand such acts among the unmarried population as a whole for every pregnancy." [93, p. 13]   There is some substance, then, for the response so frequently encountered in studies when the unmarried mother, aware of contraceptives, is asked why she did not use them: "I didn't think I would become pregnant." She sees it as an unfortunate accident, something which just happened. She is victimized by an unlucky stroke of fate which her friends, engaged in the same behavior with the same lack of precaution, have escaped.

Contraceptives requiring a prescription are not always easy to purchase and even if the single younger girl obtains a prescription for the pill, she faces the problem of paying for a supply regularly. Diaphragms need to be fitted by a doctor and an intrauterine device needs to be placed by a doctor. The most readily available female contraceptives are nonprescription suppositories or jellies—which are apt to be less effective.

Even if the woman has contraceptives available, their use implies deliberate, planful anticipation of having intercourse. This presents the woman with a conflict, "for she cannot maintain her self-image as a 'nice girl' through rationally planning possibly 'not to be one.' . . . She would normally feel . . . 'immoral' if she recognized the possibility of sex relations being acceptable to her, while single, and prepared for the occasion." [10, p. 391]

Consequently, there tends to be a heavy reliance in such situations on the male contraceptive, the condom. Bowerman's study of white and black unwed mothers noted that "when contraceptives were used, the man was exclusively relied upon to provide the contraceptive protection in nine-tenths of the cases." [10, p. 419]   But since the man is not so heavily penalized for failure and because some men find that use of the condom diminishes pleasure, reliance on the man is apt to lead to more "accidents." For these reasons contraceptive programs, however widespread, are not likely to solve the problem of illegitimate pregnancies.

However, there is a need for more family planning education. A study of birth control information possessed by a group of black mothers indicated that 91 percent of them agreed with the statement "I don't know enough about how to use birth control." [33, p. 41]   The researchers conclude that "it seems that the failure to practice birth control stems more from limited knowledge and access than from any pattern of sexual promiscuity or cultural value supporting pregnancy outside of marriage." [33, p. 42]   Furthermore, preliminary reports of concerted efforts to offer contraceptive information to single women show a modest reduction in repeated illegitimate pregnancies [32, p. 55] as well as a reduction in rate of first illegitimate pregnancies. [114, p. 374]   Thus, whatever limited level in reduction in illegitimacy may be achieved by more extensive family planning education and provision of contraception to single women, such a policy change might be desirable. [30]   A widespread public program to make contraceptive devices easily accessible to married and unmarried members of all socioeconomic groups may have some effect.

But even if all single women exposed to risk of pregnancy used contraceptives, the level of failure is such that "one would still expect considerable numbers of illicit pregnancies." [24, p. 42]   Such a program, therefore, would need to be reinforced by the possibility of abortion on demand.

Hartley attributes the decline in illegitimacy rates in Japan to the widespread availability of abortion since the end of World War II. [41, p. 87]   Cutright notes that "for the Eastern European countries, the legalization of abortion on request appears to have had a significant effect in causing a decline in illegitimacy rates. In Czechoslovakia, Hungary, Yugoslavia, Poland, and Bulgaria, abortion on request for 'social' reasons was legalized between 1956 and 1958. In all these countries except Bulgaria, illegitimacy declined sharply following liberalization of the law—from 30 to 50 percent." [24, p. 33]   The illegitimacy rate in England, which had risen steadily since 1958, began to fall after the passage of a liberalized abortion act in 1968. During the first year of the implementation of the New York State liberal abortion law, out-of-wedlock births declined for the first time since statistics began to be collected in 1954, and all of the maternity shelters caring for single pregnant girls reported a sharp decline in the number of applications for admission. [73]

There is a problem of a more equitable distribution of services between black and white unmarried mothers and between those mothers who keep their children and those mothers who give up their children. Currently, service distribution tends to favor the white unwed mother who plans to give up her child.

Trends

1. The anticipated trend is a continued slow increase in illegitimacy rates. Even if the illegitimacy rate remained stable, the number of illegitimacies will increase within the next decade owing to the increase in the number of fecund women (fifteen to forty-four years of age) in the population during the 1970 decade. The anticipated increase may be offset and the number of illegitimacies may be reduced if abortion on demand becomes the general practice throughout the United States.

2. There is increasing public recognition of, and concern with, the problem. There is public concern over the fact that the percentage of children supported by AFDC who are illegitimate has increased—from 20.3 percent in 1958 to 28 percent in 1969 (see Table 10–1). [104; 106] And while incapacitation of the father was, in 1958, the single most frequent reason for a family's need for AFDC assistance, by 1969 illegitimacy was unequivocally in first place as the reason for need. Illegitimacy is thus imposing an increasing financial burden on the community.

But there is another element in the recent concern: the white middle-class community has gradually become aware that illegitimacy involves a growing percentage of its own sons and daughters. No longer is it a condition confined to blacks, or to the "promiscuous," the "feeble-minded," or the "products of broken homes." "The middle and upper social strata [now] feel threatened because of their growing sense that their own children are engaging in precisely the kinds of activities which they once thought were the exclusive properties of the lower class." [36, p. 272]

3. There also seems to be a trend among white unmarried mothers to keep their babies rather than give them up for adoption. This seems to reflect a growing acceptance of atypical family arrangements, and a growing appreciation of the strengths and possibilities of the single-parent family.

4. Social agencies are beginning to face the effective competition of many other organizations in offering services of prime interest to many unmarried mothers—agencies established by clergy, women's liberation organizations, grass-roots organizations representing the youth counter-culture. Every college newspaper, every underground press publication, carries ads or notices about the availability of contraceptive information and abortion counseling. Such groups, which have no official connection with social work, provide access to, and sometimes financial aid, for abortion and contraception to all women no matter what their age or marital status.

A testimonial to the growing number of recently developed services is the special listing *Problem Pregnancies* in the Yellow Pages of some phone books.

5. Agencies are beginning to note that they are receiving more requests from unmarried mothers who kept their children but who are finding, after a year or two of struggle, that they need help. There is a shift then to a greater concern with postnatal services. This includes the development of services for the unmarried mother and her child for some time after the birth of the child. For instance, the Louise Wise Agency in New York City, an adoption agency, runs a postnatal residence for unmarried mothers, where some twenty women might stay as long as six months after the birth of their babies.

We have previously discussed such trends as the development of multiservice centers for teen-age single mothers and the development of service to the putative father.

Summary

Out-of-wedlock births are the principal source of children for adoption. Consequently adoption agencies are very much involved with the problem of the single pregnant woman.

While the number of illegitimacies has increased over the 1960's, the rate of increase has diminished. The rate among nonwhites is considerably higher than that among whites, largely for historical and socioeconomic reasons.

The single pregnant woman needs medical, housing, and financial help as well as help in preparing for the birth of the child and in deciding whether to keep the child or give it up for adoption. The agency provides a variety of services to meet these needs, and also attempts to help the putative father.

Studies show that the woman who keeps her child is more apt to be Catholic, lower-class, and limited in education. There is limited support for the contention that she is likely to be somewhat less mature than the woman who gives up the child.

Follow-up studies of the mothers who keep their children show that care is adequate and child development generally normal. However, such children are at a developmental disadvantage when compared with children who have been placed for adoption. The mother who keeps her child faces essentially the same problems as do mothers who have lost their husbands.

Among the problems noted were:

1. The continuing stigma of illegitimacy and the ambivalence about helping single pregnant women.
2. The lack of consensus around procedures and policies designed to reduce the illegitimacy rate.
3. The relative lack of services for nonwhite single pregnant women.

Among the trends noted were:

1. Continuing legal efforts to give the out-of-wedlock child equal status and to safeguard the rights of the putative father.
2. The increasing number of out-of-wedlock children and increasing public concern with the problem.
3. The increasing number of mothers who keep their babies rather than surrender them for adoption and the decrease in maternity home applications.
4. The proliferation of agencies outside of social work concerned with this problem.
5. The development of multiservice centers to meet the needs of the teenage unmarried mother and services to the unmarried mother who keeps her child.

Bibliography

1. ADAMS, HANNAH. *Social Services for Unmarried Mothers and Their Children Provided Through Public and Voluntary Child Welfare Agencies,* Child Welfare Report No. 12. Washington, D.C.: Government Printing Office, 1962.
2. ANGLIM, ELIZABETH. "The Adopted Child's Heritage—Two Natural Parents." *Child Welfare,* 44, 6 (June 1965).
3. BARCLAY, LILLIAN E. "A Group Approach to Young Unwed Mothers." *Social Casework,* 50, 7 (July 1969), 379–84.
4. BECK, JOAN. *Our Unwed Teen Fathers.* Chicago: Florence Crittenton Association.
5. BEDGER, JEAN E. *The Crittenton Study—An Assessment of Client Functioning Before and After Services.* Chicago: Crittenton Comprehensive Care Center, April 1969.
6. BERNSTEIN, BLANCHE, and MIGNON SAUBER. *Deterrents to Early Prenatal Care and Social Services Among Women Out-of-Wedlock.* Albany, N.Y.: State Department of Social Welfare, 1960.
7. BERNSTEIN, ROSE. *Helping Unmarried Mothers.* New York: Association Press, 1971.
8. ———. "Unmarried Parents and Their Families." *Child Welfare,* 45, 4 (April 1966), 185–93.

9. Billingsley, Andrew, and Amy Tate Billingsley. "Illegitimacy and Patterns of Negro Family Life," in *The Unwed Mother.* Ed. by Robert W. Roberts. New York: Harper and Row, Publishers, 1966.

10. Bowerman, Charles E., et al. *Unwed Motherhood: Personal and Social Consequences.* Chapel Hill, N.C.: Institute for Research in Social Science, University of North Carolina, 1966.

11. Boykin, Nancy M. "A School-Centered Multidiscipline Approach to the Problems of Teen-Age Pregnancy." *Child Welfare,* **47**, 8 (October 1968), 478–87.

12. Bracken, March. "Lessons Learned from a Baby Care Club for Unmarried Mothers." *Children,* **18**, 4 (July–August 1971), 133–37.

13. Bremner, Robert H. *Children and Youth in America—A Documentary History. Vol. I: 1600–1865.* Cambridge, Mass.: Harvard University Press, 1970.

14. Brinton, Crane. *French Revolutionary Legislation on Illegitimacy, 1789–1804.* Cambridge, Mass.: Harvard University Press, 1936.

15. Burgess, Linda. "The Unmarried Father in Adoption Planning." *Children,* **15**, 2 (March–April 1968), 71–74.

16. Busfield, Bernard L., et al. *Out-of-Wedlock Pregnancy—What Happens Next. An In-depth Survey of Postnatal Unwed Mothers Treated by Long-Term Group Therapy.* Boston: Crittenton Hastings House, 1969.

17. Caughlin, Jeanne. "Psychic Hazards of Unwed Paternity." *Social Work,* **5**, 3 (July 1960), 29–35.

18. Chaskel, Ruth. "Changing Patterns of Services for Unmarried Parents." *Social Casework,* **49**, 1 (January 1968).

19. Connor, Lenora. "An Extended Service—A Halfway House for Unwed Mothers." *Child Welfare,* **45**, 4 (April 1966), 221–24.

20. Corrigan, Eileen M. "The Child at Home: Child-Rearing Practices of Unwed Mothers Compared to Other Mothers," in *Illegitimacy: Changing Services for Changing Times.* New York: National Council on Illegitimacy, 1970.

21. Crellin, Eileen, M. L. Kellmer Pringle, and Patrick West. *Born Illegitimate—Social and Educational Implications.* London: National Children's Bureau, 1971.

22. Crockett, Mary L. "Examination of Services to the Unmarried Mother in Relation to Age of Adoptive Placement of the Baby," in *Casework Papers.* New York: Family Service Association of America, 1960.

23. Crumidy, Pearl M., and Harold Jacobziner. "A Study of Young Unmarried Mothers Who Kept Their Babies." *American Journal of Public Health,* **56**, 8 (August 1966), 1242–51.

24. Cutright, Phillips. "Illegitimacy: Myths, Causes, and Cures." *Family Planning Perspectives,* **3**, 1 (January 1971), 26–48.

25. Cyesis Program Consortium. *Sharing.* Washington, D.C.: George Washington University, February 1971.

26. Danforth, Joyce, et al. "Group Services for Unmarried Mothers—An Interdisciplinary Approach." *Children,* **18**, 2 (March–April 1971), 59–64.

27. Festinger, Trudy Bradley. "Unwed Mothers and Their Decision to Keep or Surrender Children." *Child Welfare,* **50**, 5 (May 1971), 253–63.

28. FINCK, GEORGE H., *et al.* "Group Counseling with Unmarried Mothers." *Journal of Marriage and the Family*, **27**, 2 (May 1965), 224–29.

29. FLORENCE CRITTENTON ASSOCIATION. *The Unmarried Father.* Chicago, 1967.

30. FURIE, SIDNEY. "Birth Control and the Lower Class Unmarried Mother." *Social Work*, **47**, 1 (January 1966), 42–49.

31. FURSTENBERG, FRANK F. "Birth Control Experience Among Pregnant Adolescents: The Process of Unplanned Parenthood." *Social Problems*, **19**, 2 (Fall 1971), 192–203.

32. ———. "Premarital Pregnancy Among Black Teenagers." *Transaction*, **7**, 7 (May 1970), 52–55.

33. ———, *et al.* "Birth Control Knowledge and Attitudes Among Unmarried Pregnant Adolescents: A Preliminary Report." *Journal of Marriage and the Family*, **31**, 1 (February 1969), 34–42.

34. GARLAND, PATRICIA. "Illegitimacy—A Special Minority-Group Problem in Urban Areas—New Social Welfare Perspectives." *Child Welfare*, **45**, 2 (February 1966), 81–88.

35. GIL, D. G. "Illegitimacy and Adoption—Its Socioeconomic Correlates: A Preliminary Report." *Child Adoption*, No. 1 (1969), 25–37.

36. GOODE, WILLIAM J. "A Policy Paper for Illegitimacy," in *Organizing for Community Welfare.* Ed. by Mayer N. Zald. Chicago: Quadrangle Books, Inc., 1967.

37. GOODMAN, ELIZABETH M. "Trends and Goals in Schooling for Pregnant Girls and Teenage Mothers," in *Effective Services for Unmarried Parents and Their Children—Innovative Community Approaches.* New York: National Council on Illegitimacy, 1968.

38. GREENLEIGH ASSOCIATES. *Facts, Fallacies and Future—A Study of the Aid to Dependent Children Program of Cook County, Illinois.* New York, 1960.

39. GRISWOLD, BARBARA B., *et al.* "Illegitimacy Recidivism Among AFDC Clients," in *Unmarried Parenthood—Clues to Agency and Community Action.* New York: National Council on Illegitimacy, 1967.

40. GROW, LUCILLE. *Unwed Mothers Served by the Voluntary Agencies.* New York: Data Collection Project for Agencies Serving Unmarried Mothers, 1967.

41. HARTLEY, SHIRLEY. "The Decline of Illegitimacy in Japan." *Social Problems*, **18**, 1 (Summer 1970), 78–91.

42. HERZOG, ELIZABETH. "Some Notes About Unmarried Fathers." *Child Welfare*, **45**, 4 (April 1966), 194–95.

43. ———. "Unwed Motherhood: Personal and Social Consequences." *Welfare in Review*, **2**, 8 (August 1964).

44. HOWARD, MARION. "Comprehensive Service Programs for School Age Pregnant Girls." *Children*, **15**, 5 (September–October 1968), 193–96.

45. ———. *Multiservice Programs for Pregnant School Girls.* Washington, D.C.: U.S. Department of Health, Education, and Welfare, Social Rehabilitation Service, Children's Bureau, 1968.

46. ———. *The Webster School—A District of Columbia Program for Pregnant Girls.* Children's Bureau Research Report No. 2. Washington, D.C.: Government Printing Office, 1968.

47. "Illegitimacy," in *Encyclopaedia Britannica*, XII. Chicago, 1957, pp. 84–85.

48. JOHNSON, BETTY. "The Unwed AFDC Mother and Child Welfare Services," in *The Double Jeopardy: The Triple Crises—Illegitimacy Today*. New York: National Council on Illegitimacy, 1969.

49. JONES, WYATT C., et al. "Social and Psychological Factors in Status Decisions of Unmarried Mothers." *Journal of Marriage and the Family*, **25**, 3 (August 1962), 224–30.

50. KALTREIDER, NANCY, and L. DOUGLAS LENKOSKI. "Effective Use of Group Techniques in a Maternity Home." *Child Welfare*, **50**, 3 (March 1970), 146–52.

51. KRAUSE, HARRY D. *Illegitimacy: Law and Social Policy*. Indianapolis: The Bobbs-Merrill Co., Inc., 1971.

52. ———. "Equal Protection for the Illegitimate." *Michigan Law Review*, **65**, 3 (January 1967), 477–505.

53. ———. "Bringing the Bastard into the Great Society—A Proposed Uniform Act on Legitimacy." *Texas Law Review*, **44**, 5 (April 1966), 829–59.

54. LaBARRE, MAURINE. "The Triple Crises: Adolescence, Early Marriage, and Parenthood—Part I: Motherhood," in *The Double Jeopardy: The Triple Crises—Illegitimacy Today*. New York: National Council on Illegitimacy, 1969.

55. LEVY, DOROTHY. "A Follow-up Study of Unmarried Mothers." *Social Casework*, **36**, 1 (January 1955), 27–33.

56. McMURRAY, GEORGIA L. "Community Action on Behalf of Pregnant School-Age Girls: Educational Policies and Beyond." *Child Welfare*, **49**, 6 (June 1970), 342–436.

57. MEYER, HENRY J., et al. "The Decision of Unmarried Mothers to Keep or Surrender Their Babies." *Social Casework*, **39**, 4 (April 1956), 103–109.

58. ———, et al. "Unwed Mothers' Decisions About Their Babies—An Interim Replication Study." *Child Welfare*, **38**, 2 (February 1959), 1–6.

59. MIDDLEMAN, RUTH. "Social Group Work in a Maternity Home." *Child Welfare*, **38**, 2 (February 1959), 13–18.

60. MILES, HAVEN. "Implications of Intermediary Group Treatment for Readying Unmarried Mothers for Continued Casework." *Smith College Studies in Social Work*, **39**, 1 (November 1968), 80–81.

61. MILLER, SAMUEL. *Policy and Planning Paper on Maternity Homes*. Presented at Child Caring Institutions—A Working Conference on Policy and Planning, University of Chicago, April 1971. Mimeo.

62. MONOHAN, THOMAS. "Premarital Pregnancy in the United States." *Eugenics Quarterly*, **7**, 3 (September 1960), 133–46.

63. MORLOCK, MAUD, and HILARY CAMPBELL. *Maternity Homes for Unmarried Mothers—A Community Service*. U.S. Department of Labor, Children's Bureau Publication 309. Washington, D.C.: Government Printing Office, 1946.

64. NAIMAN, JAMES. "A Comparative Study of Unmarried and Married Mothers." *Canadian Psychiatric Association Journal*, **11**, 6 (December 1966), 465–69.

65. NICHOLSON, JILL. *Mother and Baby Homes*. London: George Allen & Unwin, Ltd., 1968.

66. OPPEL, WALLACE C. *Illegitimacy—A Comparative Follow-up Study.* Unpublished Ph.D. Thesis. National Catholic School of Social Services, Catholic University. Washington, D.C., 1969.

67. O'ROURKE, HELEN A. "The Agency as Seen Through the Eyes of Its Clients." *Child Welfare,* **47**, 8 (October 1968), 470–77.

68. ———, and FAYE CHANEY. "The Use of Group with Unmarried Mothers to Facilitate Casework." *Child·Welfare,* **47**, 1 (January 1968), 17–25.

69. OSOFSKY, HOWARD J. *The Pregnant Teenager—A Medical Education and Social Analysis.* Springfield, Ill.: Charles C Thomas, Publishers, 1968.

70. PANNOR, REUBEN. "Casework Services for Unmarried Fathers." *Children,* **10**, 2 (March–April 1963), 65–70.

71. ———, and BYRON EVANS. "The Unmarried Father: Demonstration and Evaluation of an Assertive Casework Approach," in *Illegitimacy: Data and Findings for Prevention, Treatment, and Policy Formulation.* New York: National Council on Illegitimacy, 1965.

72. ———, et al. *The Unmarried Father—New Approach to Helping Unmarried Young Parents.* New York: Springer-Verlag New York, Inc., 1971.

73. PAKTER, JEAN, and FRIEDA NELSON. "The Unmarried Mother and Her Child—The Problems and the Challenges," in *Illegitimacy: Data and Findings for Prevention, Treatment, and Policy Formulation.* New York: National Council on Illegitimacy, 1965.

74. PAPPENFORT, DONNELL M., and DEE M. KILPATRICK. *A Census of Children's Residential Institutions in the U.S., Puerto Rico and the Virgin Islands: 1966. Vol. 6: Maternity Homes.* Social Service Monographs, Second Series. Chicago: University of Chicago, School of Social Service Administration, 1970.

75. PAUKER, JEROME. "Girls Pregnant Out of Wedlock," in *The Double Jeopardy: The Triple Crises—Illegitimacy Today.* New York: National Council on Illegitimacy, 1969.

76. ———. "Research on Unmarried Fathers: Are They Different in Personality?" *National Council on Illegitimacy Newsletter* (Fall 1968).

77. PERLMAN, HELEN HARRIS. "Unmarried Mothers," in *Social Work and Social Problems.* Ed. by Nathan E. Cohen. New York: National Association of Social Workers, 1954.

78. Pierce, Ruth I. *Single and Pregnant.* Boston: Beacon Press, Inc., 1970.

79. PINCHBECK, IVEY, and MARGARET HEWITT. *Children in English Society. Vol. I: From Tudor Times to the Eighteenth Century.* London: Kegan Paul, Trench, Trubner & Co., 1969.

80. PLATTS, HAL. "A Public Adoption Agency's Approach to Natural Fathers." *Child Welfare,* **47**, 9 (November 1968), 530–37.

81. POWER, EDWARD, and MATHEW DE CHIRICO. *The Treatment of Unwed Parents—How Determined? How Effective?* Paper presented at Regional Annual Conference, Child Welfare League of America, March 1969, Pittsburgh. Mimeo.

82. POPE, HALLOWELL. "Negro-White Differences in Decisions Regarding Illegitimate Children." *Journal of Marriage and the Family,* **31**, 4 (November 1969), 756–64.

83. ————. "Unwed Mothers and Their Sex Partners." *Journal of Marriage and the Family*, **29**, 3 (August 1967), 555–67.
84. RAINS, PRUDENCE M. "Moral Reinstatement—The Characteristics of Maternity Homes." *American Behavioral Scientist*, **14**, 2 (November–December 1970), 222–35.
85. RASHBAUM, M., et al. "Use of Social Services by Unmarried Mothers." *Children*, **10**, 1 (January–February 1963), 11–16.
86. REED, ELLERY F., and RUTH LATIMER. *A Study of Unmarried Mothers Who Kept Their Babies.* Cincinnati, Ohio: Social Welfare Research, Inc., 1962.
87. REINER, BEATRICE SIMCOX. "The Real World of the Teenage Negro Mother." *Child Welfare*, **47**, 7 (July 1968), 391–95.
88. SAUBER, MIGNON. *Experiences of the Unwed Mother as Parent.* New York: Community Council of Greater New York, 1965.
89. ————. "The Role of the Unmarried Father." *Welfare in Review*, **4**, 9 (November 1966), 15–18.
90. ————, and EILEEN M. CORRIGAN. *The Six-Year Experience of Unwed Mothers as Parents.* New York: Community Council of Greater New York, 1970.
91. SHAPIRO, DEBORAH. "Attitudes, Values, and Unmarried Motherhood," in *Unmarried Parenthood—Clues to Agency and Community Action.* New York: National Council on Illegitimacy, 1967.
92. ————. *Social Distance and Illegitimacy—Report of a Pilot Study.* New York: Research Center, Columbia University, School of Social Work.
93. SHENKIN, A. M. "The Psychiatric Aspects of an Illegitimate Pregnancy," in *Unmarried Mothers—Their Medical and Social Needs.* Petershan, England: Standing Conference of Societies Registered for Adoption, 1967.
94. SHOENBERG, CARL. "The Expanding Nature and Purpose of the Maternity Home." *Child Welfare*, **43**, 1 (January 1964), 14–20.
95. SLAVSON, S. R. "Unmarried Mother," in *The Field of Group Psychotherapy.* New York: John Wiley & Sons, Inc., 1966.
96. STEINMETZ, MARTHA A. "Role-Playing in a Maternity Home." *Children*, **11**, 2 (March–April 1964), 61–64.
97. STEVENSON, NICHOLAS, and RITA DUKETTE. "The Legal Rights of Unmarried Fathers." *Social Service Review*, **47**, 1 (March 1973), 1–15.
98. TAYLOR, LILLIAN E. "Social Attitudes Toward Sexual Behavior and Illegitimacy," in *Illegitimacy: Data and Findings for Prevention, Treatment, and Policy Formulation.* New York: National Council on Illegitimacy, October 1965.
99. TEELE, J. E., et al. "Factors Related to Social Work Services for Babies of Mothers Born Out of Wedlock." *American Journal of Public Health*, **57**, 8 (August 1967), 1300–1307.
100. THOMPSON, JEAN. *The House of Tomorrow.* New York: Harper and Row, Publishers, 1967.
101. TRISELIOTIS, JOHN. "The Timing of the Single Mother's Decision in Relation to Adoption Agency Practice." *Child Adoption*, No. 3 (1969), 29–35.
102. UNITED NATIONS. *Demographic Year Book: 21st Issue, 1969.* New York: United Nations Statistical Office, Department of Economic and Social Affairs, 1970.

103. U.S. DEPARTMENT OF HEALTH, EDUCATION, and WELFARE. "Unmarried Mother." *Children,* **18**, 4 (July–August 1971), 159.
104. ———, Bureau of Public Assistance. *Illegitimacy and Its Impact on the Aid to Dependent Children Program.* Washington, D.C.: Government Printing Office, 1960.
105. ———, Public Health Service. *Trends in Illegitimacy—United States: 1940–1965.* National Center for Health Statistics, Series 21, No. 5. Washington, D.C.: Government Printing Office, 1968.
106. ———, National Center for Social Statistics. *AFDC—Selected Statistical Data on Families Aided and Program Operations.* NCSS Report H-4(71). Washington, D.C.: Government Printing Office, June 1971.
107. VINCENT, CLARK. *Unmarried Mother.* New York: The Free Press, 1961.
108. WIMPERIS, VIRGINIA. *The Unmarried Mother and Her Child.* London: George Allen & Unwin, Ltd., 1960.
109. WRIGHT, HELEN R. *Eighty Unmarried Mothers Who Kept Their Babies.* Department of Social Welfare, State of California, May 1965.
110. WRIGHT, MATTIE K. "Comprehensive Service for Adolescent Unwed Mothers." *Children,* **13**, 5 (September–October 1966), 171–76.
111. YELLOLY, MARGARET. "Adoption and the Natural Mother." *Case Conference,* **13** (December 1966), 270–77.
112. ———. "Factors Relating to an Adoption Decision by the Mothers of Illegitimate Infants." *Sociological Review,* **13**, 1, New Series (March 1965).
113. YOUNG, LEONTINE. *Out of Wedlock.* New York: McGraw-Hill Book Company, 1954.
114. YURDIN, MAZY O. "Recent Trends in Illegitimacy—Implications for Practice." *Child Welfare,* **49**, 7 (July 1970), 373–75.
115. ZOBER, EDITH. "The Pregnant School Girl." *Child Welfare,* **48**, 6 (June 1969), 362–66.

Some Additional Recent Books of Interest:

BOURNE, JOAN. *Pregnant and Alone—The Unmarried Mother and Her Child.* Roystone, Hertfordshire: Priory Press, 1971.
DEWAR, DIANA. *Orphans of the Living—A Study of Bastardy.* London: Hutchinson & Co. Ltd., 1968.
POCHIN, JEAN. *Without a Wedding Ring—Casework with Unmarried Parents.* London: Constable & Company, Ltd., 1969.
RAINS, PRUDENCE M. *Becoming an Unwed Mother—A Sociological Account.* Chicago: Aldine-Atherton, Inc., 1971.
ROBERTS, ROBERT W. (ed.) *The Unwed Mother.* New York: Harper and Row, Publishers, 1966.

11

Substitute Care: Adoption

Introduction

Adoption involves becoming a parent through a legal and social process rather than through a biological process. For the child, adoption involves a *permanent* change in family affiliation. It is an ancient process of providing children for childless parents and parents for parentless children. Adoption provides permanent substitute care for the child when his natural parents are unable, or unwilling, to care for him, and have been legally freed of any ties to the child. The effect of adoption is to create a new parent-child unit. According to the old Roman legal code, "Adoption imitates nature." According to the Greeks, "Adoption is a method of demanding from religion and law that which nature had denied." [99, p. 107]   A more formal definition of *adoption* suggests that "It entails the extinction of all present or future rights and obligations of the natural parents of the child and the transfer, by administrative or legal authority, of all these rights and obligations to a married couple who have no blood relationship with the child." [239, p. 63]

Biological parenthood cannot be shared. Psychosocial parenthood, however, is a complex of rights and obligations which can be "shared, acceded to, delegated, surrendered, or otherwise circulated among [different people] according to specific rules." [35, p. 8]

Historical Background

All of the ancient peoples—the Egyptians, the Babylonians, the Greeks, the Romans—sanctioned adoption. The Bible speaks of it. Pharaoh's daughter adopted Moses and Mordecai adopted Esther. The Code of Hammurabi mentions adoption and the protection that should be given the adoptive parent. Sargon, King of Babylonia circa 2800 B.C., was adopted. The inscription that tells his story reads:

> Sargon, the mighty king, King of Akkad, am I. My mother was a
> vestal, my father I knew not. . . . In my city, Azupirani, which
> is situated on the bank of the Euphrates, my mother, the vestal, bore
> me. In a hidden place she brought me forth. She laid me in a
> vessel made of reeds, closed my door with pitch, and dropped
> me down into the river, which did not drown me. The river carried
> me to Akki, the water carrier. Akki the water carrier lifted me up in
> the kindness of his heart. Akki the water carrier raised me as
> his own son. Akki the water carrier made of me his gardener. In
> my work as gardener I was beloved by Istar, I became the king,
> and for forty-five years I held kingly sway. [Quoted in 46, p. 598]

In earlier periods adoption was not so frequently resorted to in solution of the problem of childlessness, because a simpler solution was socially acceptable. If a wife was infertile, the husband took another woman to bear him children. Thus Sarah, who was childless, urged Abraham to take Hagar, her maid, as a concubine, with whom he then had a child. In ancient Greece and Rome, adoptions were arranged so as to acquire an heir to perpetuate the family or to manage extensive family property. Thus Solon, in Greece, sanctioned adoption as a means of providing continuity for a family line.

In early Rome one function of adoption was to permit a candidate for office to qualify under the provision "that a candidate who had children, or who had more children, was to be preferred to one who had none or fewer." [99, p. 113]

In India, adoptions were arranged so as to provide a male heir in order to meet the demands of religious ceremonials. Among the Hindus the adopting father declared to the adoptive son, "I accept thee for the fulfillment of religion; I take thee for the continuation of lineage." [99, p. 110] Among the Hindus, as among the Chinese, the need in adoption was specifically for a male child, because "Heaven awaits not one who has no male issue." The childless couple might adopt children so as to be sure of having care in their old age. This is the attitude expressed in a Hawaiian saying, "Feed human beings, for they can be sent on errands." [35, p. 27]

In some cultures, adoptions might be informally arranged between people who knew each other well and who were tied by bonds of mutual obligation. Parents who had too many children gave some to relatives or friends who had none or too few. In such arrangements there might be continuing and frequent contact between the two families, creating an additional parental relationship rather than a substitute parental relationship. [35]

In earlier periods of man's history, then, adoption served to meet the needs of adults; today it is supported primarily because it meets the needs of parentless children. There is no body of common law regarding adoption. Consequently, there was little precedent for adoption procedure in Colonial America. Abbott notes that "provision for care of dependent children by means of adoption was probably delayed by the development of the relation between master and apprentice" so that orphans and children of indigent parents could be bound out to obtain care in this way. [1, p. 461]

Prior to the passage of general adoption laws, state legislatures followed the practice of "passing special acts providing for the adoption of particular children by particular adults." [259, p. 29]

There is some question about whether Massachusetts or Texas was the first state to pass an adoption law. Nevertheless, it is clear that the Massachusetts statute enacted in 1851 became the model for many of the other state adoption laws passed during, or shortly after, the Civil War. It provided for

1. The written consent of the child's biological parent.
2. Joint petition by both the adoptive mother and father.
3. A decree by the judge if he was satisfied that the adoption was "fit and proper."
4. Legal and complete severance of the relationship between child and biological parents.

By 1929 every state had passed some kind of adoption legislation. The adoption laws indicate that "From the outset, most laws [at least as interpreted judicially] have had the welfare of the children as their main purpose." [259, p. 43]   Although the laws of the different states varied in effectiveness, the history of adoption has been a movement toward a greater emphasis on the protection of the principals affected by adoption —the biological parents, the adoptive parents, the community, and the child.

The early statutes were intended primarily to "provide evidence of the legal transfer of a child by the biological parents to the adopting parents and provision for a public record of the transfer." [2, p. 165] The judge's decision that the adoption was "fit and proper" was based only on his contact with the parties to the adoption. Recognizing that this was not sufficient to prevent adoption by unsuitable or unscrupulous parents, some states provided for more extensive inquiry regarding adoptive parents. Thus, in 1891 Michigan began to require that the judge make an investigation before finalizing an adoption. This law was later amended to provide for a social investigation by an agency that was, generally, in a better position to conduct such a study. In 1917, Minnesota passed the first law requiring detailed investigation by a local agency or the state Department of Public Welfare, and a written recommendation to the court regarding the advisability of permitting the adoption.

Before the introduction of community controls, advertisements such as the following, which appeared in the *Chicago Tribune*, were not uncommon:

PERSONAL—Wanted—Healthy Twins or Baby girl under 6 months, by couple able to give children wonderful home and future. Address KH 385, Tribune. (December 21, 1919)

PERSONAL—Wanted for adoption by wealthy Chicago couple, infant girl or boy. Address KH 386, Tribune. (December 21, 1919)

PERSONAL—Wanted to Adopt Baby month old, by responsible couple; good home. Address B 599, Tribune. (December 21, 1919) [Quoted in 24, p. 139]

Some of the unfortunate situations that might result were reported to a 1925 Commission appointed to study and revise Pennsylvania statutes relating to children:

CASE VII.
Frances, aged thirteen, recently made a personal application to a social agency stating that her foster father had been having sexual relations with her for the last two years. Upon investigation living conditions were found to be very bad. The foster mother corroborated the child's statements. Frances had been legally adopted in May 1918. She was sold to her foster parents by her mother for a quart of whisky. [Quoted in 24, p. 142]

Attempts to provide additional protection for the child included the introduction of a trial period between the time the child was placed in the adoptive home and the time the adoption was legally consummated. Also, an increasing number of states required that records of the adoption proceedings, once completed, be closed and sealed and that a new birth certificate for the child be issued at that time. All these changes indicated a shift from emphasis on the purely legal aspects of transfer of the child to a growing appreciation of the human aspects of adoption.

Scope

Adoptions are generally broken down into two principal groups—related and nonrelated. In related adoptions, the child is adopted by a stepfather, a stepmother, a grandparent, an uncle, and so on. Social agencies are not so directly concerned with such adoptions. In non-related adoptions, the child is adopted by persons who have no family ties to him. Social agencies are directly concerned in finding the home, evaluating it, and supervising it for a period of time after the child has been placed. Our interest, therefore, is primarily with nonrelated adoptions.

In 1971 about 169,000 children in the United States were legally adopted. Of these, 86,000—or about 51 percent—were adopted by relatives; 83,000—or about 49 percent—were adopted by nonrelatives. Although the absolute number of children adopted has increased from 80,000 in 1950 to 169,000 in 1971, the annual adoption rate has remained 20 to 21 per 10,000 children under twenty-one years of age for the period 1968 through 1971. [244] Currently there are about 1.5 million adopted children in the country—about 2 percent of all children.

The trend has been toward an increase in the percentage of non-relative adoptions made under the auspices of social agencies. While voluntary agencies still account for the greatest proportion of such placements, there has been a gradual increase of public agency activity.

The median age of the children placed for adoption in 1971 was about two months, and about two-thirds of all children adopted were less than three months old. Only 12 percent of the children placed for nonrelative adoption in 1971 were nonwhite. In 1971, for the first time, the number of children adopted decreased.

Sources of Children for Adoption

The sources of children for nonrelated adoptions are listed in descending order of importance:

1. Illegitimate children.
2. Abandoned, neglected children.
3. Orphans.
4. Legitimate children voluntarily surrendered for adoption by their parents.
5. Foreign-born children.

The principal source, by far, of nonrelated children available to adoptive parents are the illegitimate children. According to the Chil-

Thousands

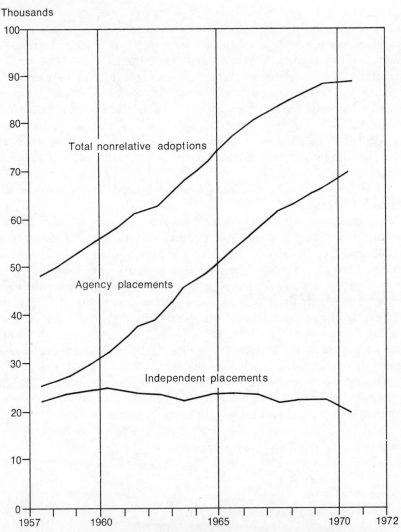

FIGURE 11–1. Children adopted by nonrelatives, by type of placement, 1957 to 1971. (*Adoptions in 1971,* U.S. Department of Health, Education, and Welfare, Social and Rehabilitation Service, National Center for Social Statistics, May 23, 1973.)

dren's Bureau, in 1971 about 87 percent of all the children adopted by nonrelatives were born out of wedlock. [244]

As the number of illegitimacies increase, the number of children available for adoption may increase if the rate at which mothers surrender children for adoption remains constant. However, an increasingly large percentage of unmarried mothers are deciding to keep their children.

Not all illegitimate children surrendered for adoption are actually placeable. In 1971, about 85 percent of all adopted children were white. Although about 55 percent of all illegitimate children are nonwhite, only 15 percent of the homes ready to take a nonrelated child for adoption were nonwhite. This indicates a serious imbalance, and suggests that the relationship between the increase in illegitimacies and the demands of unrelated adoptive applicants is a complicated one.

The social "orphans"—children whose parents have rejected, neglected, or deserted them—form a sizable group of the children available for nonrelated adoption. In such cases, society has to intervene to terminate the rights of the biological parents and to free the child for adoption (see Chap. 9). But it takes some time before society can establish, clearly enough to warrant court action, that parental rights need to be terminated. By that time many of the children are hard to place because they are older.

The full orphans—the children whose parents have died—form a smaller number of children available for adoption. Although in 1920 1.9 percent of all children were full orphans, in 1971 only 0.1 percent of all children were so deprived—a very limited segment of the child population.

Little is known about married couples who voluntarily give up their children for adoption. [60; 103; 157] It is the impression of social workers in contact with such parents that conditions such as "economic pressures, unsatisfactory housing, unwillingness to accept family responsibilities . . . [and] emotional problems involving rejection of the child" account for such voluntary relinquishment. [44, p. 8] Agency studies confirm that only a small number of mothers relinquish for adoption a child fathered by their own husband with whom they are still living. [186]

A final source for adoption are foreign children. Some are adopted abroad by U.S. citizens, others are brought into the country for purposes of adoption. These are children who have been orphaned or abandoned in their home country and who, for one reason or another, could not have been adopted there. In 1970, about 2400 foreign children were adopted—56 percent from Asia, 24 percent from Europe. An increasingly large percentage of such adoptions are being arranged via social agencies. [3]

The list of sources of children available for adoption suggests that adoption is appropriate under the following conditions:

1. When the biological parents are unable to care for the child because the family was never completely organized—as in the case of the illegitimate child, who never had a father.
2. When the biological parents are unable to care for the child and are

not likely to be able to do so in the future—as in the case of the child whose parents have died or have deserted him.

3. When the biological parents have proved unable and/or unwilling to care adequately for the child.
4. When the parents voluntarily relinquish their rights to the child.

Adoption is not appropriate under the following conditions:

1. When the child with close family ties has parents and/or relatives who might be helped to care for the child adequately in his own family home.
2. When the child is so physically, mentally, or emotionally handicapped that he cannot live in a normal family setting, develop normal relationships with parental figures, and function adequately in a family.

Child-Applicant Ratio

The principal source of adoptive parents is the infertile couple. Less frequently the applicants have a child, or children, of their own, cannot have additional children, and are interested in increasing the size of the family through adoption. More recently, some fertile couples concerned about population growth deliberately choose to adopt a child already born rather than give birth to one of their own.

Not all infertile couples are interested in adoption. As a matter of fact, one study of couples who had come to a hospital infertility clinic showed that only about half of those who were infertile resorted to adoption. [108]

One of the most significant statistics determining agency practice and procedure is the ratio of adoptive applicants to children available for adoption. When this ratio is high, the agency can be highly selective; when it is low, the agency tends to modify, relax, or eliminate various eligibility requirements.

The ratio of adoptive applicants to available children has varied widely over the past twenty years. During the 1950's, there were decidedly more applicants than infants; during the 1960's a rise in the number of illegitimate births increased the supply of children, while the demand decreased (the group of young adults most interested in adoption was relatively small, owing to the lower birth rates of the period 1933–43). As a consequence, agency procedures were relaxed and many of the eligibility requirements regarding age, infertility, children in the family, and mother's employment were applied flexibly, if at all. More recently, the trend has reversed, the number of potential applicants increasing and the number of infants available for adoption sharply reduced.

The facts regarding the changes in ratio have been documented by periodic studies conducted by the Child Welfare League of America with the cooperation of their member agencies. [95; 96; 196; 220; 221] These reports note that "the most consistent trend during . . . [1969, 1970, and 1971] had been the rapidly declining number of white children accepted for adoption in both voluntary and public agencies." [221, p. 373]

Changes in supply and demand are summarized in the ratio statistics: In 1958 there were 158 applicants for every 100 children available; in 1962, 129 applicants for every 100 children available; in 1967, 104 applicants; in 1970, 150 applicants; in 1971, 200 applicants for every 100 children available.

In response to the increase in demand for, and a decrease in the supply of, adoptable white children, some agencies began to close their intake of applications for white nonhandicapped children in the early 1970's. Otherwise the imbalance would have been even more decided than the statistics indicate.

The principal factor in the decrease of white, nonhandicapped children available for adoption is the greater availability of contraception and abortion, as a consequence of which the rise in illegitimate births has been slowed and, in some places, reversed. More significant, fewer unmarried mothers give up their babies for adoption, because more adequate social services enable more of them to keep and raise their children, while the stigma attached to unmarried motherhood is fading. Interestingly enough, the same factors are also reducing the number of children available for adoption abroad. [241]

At the same time, the potential demand for adoption has increased as the large numbers of children born in the late 1940's and early 1950's began reaching the age of adoptive application and concern with population increase led to growing acceptance of adoption by fertile couples who deliberately choose not to bear their own children. A poll conducted in 1971 by a Presidential Commission on Population Growth found that 56 percent of respondents indicated "They would consider adopting a child if they already had two children and wanted a larger family." [50, p. 147]

On the other hand, counteracting technological and ideological factors may decrease the level of adoptive demand. Remedies for infertility and sterility have steadily eroded the number of couples who have to resort to adoption. Greater control over the childhood diseases that once caused sterility and the venereal diseases that once resulted in miscarriages and stillbirths has increased the ability of some women to conceive children and carry them to term. Perfection of artificial insemination techniques and growing acceptance of this procedure may further reduce the number of couples who seek to meet the problem of childlessness through adoption. [73; 151; 207] One authority states that over 20,000 pregnancies originate annually from artificial insemination, and that the number of such inseminations "has soared since 1941." [13, pp. 58–59]

The Women's Liberation movement emphasis on satisfying, alternative roles and life styles for women other than motherhood has tended to make parenthood a less desirable status than was previously the case. Also, population growth is beginning to be seen as a threat to society, and pressure is developing to revise public policy measures so as to limit and discourage childbearing. This changing point of view affects attitudes toward parenthood generally. Parenthood is not so firmly equated with the ultimate symbol of adulthood as was once the case, and full adult status can be achieved without it. Instead of being regarded as a deprivation, childlessness is currently being more frequently seen as a desirable option.

The decided imbalance in the ratio of applicants to available white nonhandicapped infants has resulted in the reappearance of the black and gray adoption market (*New York Daily News*, September 19, 1971; *The New York Times*, July 18, 1971).

Actually, however, there are two different adoption supply-and-demand situations—one applies to the white nonhandicapped child, another to the "child with special needs" or the "hard-to-place child"— the nonwhite child, the older child, the handicapped child. The largest group of hard-to-place children is composed of nonwhite children. According to the Child Welfare League, in 1971 there were 133 approved adoptive homes available for every 100 white adoptive children, but only 71 approved homes for 100 nonwhite children.

Diminished availability of white, nonhandicapped children increased the demand for, and placeability of, all "children with special needs" and in 1970 "about three-fourths of the agencies report[ed] that they have put greater emphasis on adoption planning for nonwhite children." [96, p. 405]

Requirements of Adoptive Parenthood

In order to adopt a child through a social agency, the applicant must meet certain requirements set by the agency. In 1954 the Child Welfare League of America made a nationwide study of the practices of adoption agencies, devoting a major section of the study to explicating eligibility standards. The study was updated by a less extensive review by Brieland in 1958. [27] The eligibility requirements for adoption through social agencies, as reviewed in such studies, are reflected in the recommended standards established by the Child Welfare League of America, and form the basis for this discussion. [43] Actual adherence to these requirements differs with the agency, the circumstance, and the particular applicant. The requirements themselves change with time and with changes in the adoption picture.

In the context of a ratio which is favorable to the adoptive applicant, agencies can move, as they have, toward a shift in emphasis in their relationship to the applicant from assessment and evaluation to facilitation and enabling. [164; 166] Where the ratio of applicants to children is such that almost all applicants can be provided with a child, the social worker can be concerned with helping the applicants accept and prepare for adoptive parenthood rather than centering on determining which applicant is the most acceptable. [166] The tendency then is to broaden the definition of the "adoptable" parent, and to "screen people in" rather than "screen people out." When the number of infants is limited, however, "requirements" are employed not only, as is usually the case, for the primary purpose of the interests of the child, but also for the administrative purpose of managing application work load. High ratio of applicants to children available not only makes selectivity possible, it requires greater selectivity. Rules of eligibility tend to be applied more stringently if the staff is not to be overwhelmed by the need to interview applicants sympathetically and skillfully and complete studies of applicants without too great a delay. Currently the emphasis is on applying standards in a relaxed, flexible manner, as guidelines to be modified by the worker in terms of his professional assessment of the individual situation.

Some of the criteria considered important and given emphasis are definite and objective, e.g., age, physical health, marital status etc.; some are ambiguous and subjective, e.g., emotional health, capacity for parenthood, motive for adoption, etc.

Age

Desirable age of adoptive parents for adoption of an infant lies between thirty-five and forty-five. There are several reasons for this requirement. First, it increases the probability that the parent will be alive throughout the sixteen to eighteen years of the adoptive child's dependency. Having lost one set of parents, the adoptive child would be doubly deprived if the adoptive parents died before he was ready to assume independence. The age requirement follows the folk saying "late child, early orphaned." Furthermore, too great an age spread between the adoptive parents and the child increases the possibility of intergenerational difficulties in understanding. The older adoptive parent would be too far removed in time to empathize with the child. Too great difference in age also limits the energy available for the physically burdensome demands of child care, and decreases the possibility of parental participation in the activities of the adopted youngster. Finally, too great an age spread between parents and child is discrepant with the normal family situation. The atypicality calls attention to the fact that this family is different from others.

In the case of the older child being proposed for adoption, however, the desirable age of the applicant can be raised while still maintaining a constant difference in age between parent and child.

Physical Health

The agencies also require some assurance of good physical health—again, to insure the child against loss of another set of parents. It also assures the agency that the applicants have the requisite physical capacity to care for the child adequately. It prevents the possibility of infection of the child where the applicant suffers from an infectious condition. In the case of the father, poor health or a disability raises some question about employment security and the ability to provide for the child's economic needs.

Marital Status

The applicants for adoption should be married. Most agencies require that the marriage have been in existence for some minimum period—generally from three to five years. Thus the marriage has had a chance to prove itself and to achieve some stability, and there has also been an opportunity for the couple to achieve parenthood by natural means. The divorce rate is highest during the first five years of marriage. Requiring that this minimum time lapse gives the child greater assurance that the family into which he is moving will remain intact.

Infertility

The couple must have medical proof that achievement of parenthood through natural means is doubtful. If the couple is fertile but has deliberately chosen to complete the family through a legal procedure, one might legitimately question the degree of their acceptance of parenthood. There is, furthermore, some concern about the differences in treatment of the adopted child and a natural child which might be born to fertile parents after completing adoption. Permitting a fertile couple to adopt an infant when other, less fortunate, couples are competing for such a child might be regarded as an inequitable disposition of available resources.

In many instances infertility can be established on the basis of medical examination. In some cases, however, a history of unsuccessful experience in trying to conceive, or a series of miscarriages, establishes the fact of infertility. Furthermore, childlessness for reasons other than sterility is justification for completing a family through adoption. When pregnancy clearly represents a hazard to the health of the mother, or when there is a strong likelihood that a hereditary difficulty will be transmitted, the applicants are likely to be considered.

Religion

In many states the law specifies that, wherever practical, a child be placed in a home of the same religious persuasion as that of his biological parents. In line with this requirement, applicants must have some religious affiliation, even if merely of a *pro forma* nature.

Financial Stability

Financial stability, rather than any minimum income, is a requirement set by most adoptive agencies. The agency would like some assurance that the family can count on a steady, even if limited, income to meet its needs; that it will be able to carry the extra burden of child care without imposing a strain on the stability of family relationships.

Emotional Health

Although the agencies are looking for "emotionally healthy" parents, the term itself is open to considerable differences in definition. Even if clearly defined, it would be difficult to measure. Emotional health, as stated in the adoption literature, implies, among other things, a clear understanding of oneself, a relaxed acceptance of all one's weaknesses and strengths, a minimum of unresolved developmental conflicts, adequate enactment of principal social roles, an ability to postpone gratification and to deny self-gratification out of consideration for the needs of others, a flexible conscience that can accept some failure, some occasional sinfulness without crippling guilt, a capacity to form satisfying and permanent interpersonal relationships, the ability to be independent and yet be capable of dependency if it is objectively justified. It is said that in order to be a happy parent one must first be a happy person.

Capacity for Parenthood

This factor is tied to the factor of emotional health, because the emotionally healthy person supposedly possesses the essential prerequisites for competent parenthood. Yet capacity for parenthood goes beyond emotional health—it includes the capacity to love, accept, and offer emotional security to children; the capacity to permit them to grow in terms of their own individuality; a readiness to accept, understand, and meet the inevitable behavioral problems of children. The good parent is flexible in his expectations and is realistic in accepting the child's limitations; he accepts the child as an end in himself rather than as a means toward some parent-defined end; he likes children and enjoys them.

Some idea is given about the applicant's attitude toward children in his statement regarding the kind of child he would like to have. The question of expressed preference itself is not as significant as the tenacity and rigidity with which the statement of preference is held. This suggests that the applicant has a strongly preconceived idea as to what the child should be like and that, unless the child comes up to such expectations, he faces the danger of rejection.

In assessing the capacity for parenthood, the agency explores with the applicants their own experiences as children. Such background information is important because this experience materially affects their enactment of the parental role. If they have had a satisfactory experience, they are likely to have developed positive patterns of identification with a good parent. A negative experience implies not only the absence of such patterns of identification but also residual problems in the parent-child relationship area that are likely to be reactivated when they themselves become parents.

Adjustment to Sterility

Because the problem that brings the applicant to the adoptive agency is one of inability—for whatever reason—to have children naturally, the nature of the applicant's adjustment to this deprivation is an important consideration. The adoptive child is a constant living reminder of the adoptive parents' deficiency. If the problem has not been adequately resolved, it is likely to make for difficulties in the parent-child relationship. The applicants' reaction to the agency's request for medical certification of their fertility status might be regarded as indicative of their attitude toward their infertility. If they resist strongly the need for the medical examination, or if they are made excessively anxious by the requirement, this might lead to some question as to how successfully they have accepted the condition.

Quality of the Marital Relationship

Although the length of time married says something about the quality of the marriage, more than this needs to be assessed. Because the child is likely to be affected by the dynamics of marital interaction, the agency would like to assess the degree of mutual emotional satisfaction the applicants derive from their marriage. Factors such as mutual participation in decision making (particularly with reference to the decision to adopt), the extent to which each of the partners comfortably accepts his sexual identification, the degree of mutual sexual satisfaction, the acceptance of allocated roles within the family—all are regarded as important considerations. A happy family starts with a happy marriage.

Motives for Adoption

The agency is also interested in the motives that have prompted the applicant to apply for adoption. Some motives are regarded by the agency as less desirable and more indicative of possible future difficulty. In general, motives that focus on the needs of the adoptive parents are regarded as less acceptable, more suspect, than those that center on the needs of the child. However, the same expressed motive can have a positive meaning in the life configuration of one couple and a negative meaning as viewed in terms of another couple's situation. A desire to help a child grow may have positive connotations as expressed by an accepting, understanding couple; but in the case of a rigid, self-centered couple, it may indicate a desire to push the child to fulfill the prospective parents' needs and ambitions.

Couples who wish to adopt a child for the purpose of stabilizing a shaky marriage or as a "replacement" for a recently deceased child are classically suspect, although some may be acceptable.

One important dimension is the extent to which the applicant has conscious recognition of his motivations. "Undesirable" motivation of which the applicant has some awareness is subject to modification and change; consequently, even undesirable motives of which the applicant is aware are likely to be acceptable to the agency.

Natural parenthood can be achieved without giving any explicit thought to why one wants children. The adoptive couple's decision to become parents is a voluntary, deliberate step, which requires that motives for parenthood be made explicit because they must be shared with the agency.

The records of successful adoptive parents give some idea of the varied motivations for parenthood.

Mrs. M., who could not conceive a child because of congenital absence of the uterus, said that both she and her husband had come from large families. "There always had been many nieces and nephews running in and out of the home. She felt that a home was rather lonesome or just too quiet without children. She compares the way the house is when her nieces and nephews are visiting and after they leave. It's so enjoyable having the children around and it's pretty lonesome when the children leave, so that it makes them want to have their own all the worse. It's very lonesome with just the two of them in the house."

Mrs. W. and her husband, a machinist, could not have children because of an insufficiency of sperm. She said she had always wanted a child. "Playing with a child, dressing it up, teaching it right from wrong, was about the best life that one could imagine. She felt that there are so many little things she loves to do, such as sewing, making lampshades, decorating, collecting things out of doors, that she would like to do with a child. Things don't seem to be quite complete without a child to share it with. Children fill up a home."

A manufacturer of electrical equipment, whose wife had three miscarriages, said that "raising children would give them a purpose in life. There would be more to life than just having fun and having one's own selfish gratification. If they were able to provide satisfying home experiences to children and could help them to grow into healthy normal adulthood, to be good citizens, they would feel that there was some purpose to their lives. Living as a married couple without children was just too selfish a way of life. He felt, too, that what he and his wife had earned and accumulated for themselves should be passed on."

Mr. A., a lawyer, and somewhat older than most adoptive applicants, said that "having a child would keep them from getting in a rut. Both he and his wife had observed this tendency in other couples who are childless. They become selfish, self-centered, and self-satisfied when they get to be fifty. They become smug and sufficient unto themselves. They have a great deal of love that is going to waste and which will be wasted if they wait much longer to try to adopt a child."

These are some of the typical responses of would-be parents who were asked to tell why they decided they wanted children. Companionship, a significant goal, interest and purpose in life, pleasure in helping a child to grow and develop, pleasure in seeing the world fresh again through sharing a child's experience, a bridge into the future, satisfaction in a duty to be performed, the opportunity to share one of life's more significant experiences with friends, the desire to share affection with a child and receive affection from a child, were among the reasons explaining a desire for children.

Paradoxically, even the penalties are sought as pleasures—the noise, the work, the activity, the anxiety that comes with rearing children. These seem to be an antidote to boredom, an insurance against selfish overconcern with one's own narrow desires.

Attitudes Toward Illegitimacy

Since most of the children available for adoption are born out of wedlock, the applicants' attitude toward illegitimacy is significant. A negative, punitive attitude might condition the parents' response to the adopted child.

Attitude of Significant Others

It is also important for the agency to get some idea of reactions to the idea of adoption on the part of people who are close to the applicants. If the applicants' parents, for instance, are strongly opposed to the idea of adoption, this might increase problems in adjustment to the adoption on the part of the applicant.

Table 11-1 lists some of the less categorical factors that are involved in the agency's decision regarding an applicant's eligibility.

TABLE 11-1. Rating Sheet for Prospective Parents

Some Criteria in Evaluating Couples Who Wish to Adopt a Child

---

Total personality	*Feelings about children*
Family relationships	Basic love for children
Work adjustment	Ability to deal with developmental prob-
Relationship with friends	lems
Activity in community	Sensitivity to, and understanding and
	tolerance of, children's difficulties
Emotional maturity	Ability to individualize child
Capacity to give and receive love	
Acceptance of sex roles	*Feelings about childlessness*
Ability to assume responsibility for care,	*and readiness to adopt*
guidance, and protection of another	
person	Absence of guilt regarding infertility
Reasonable emotional stability	Mutual decision to adopt
Flexibility	Ability to tell child he is adopted
Self-respect	Attitudes toward biological parents and
Ability to cope with problems, disap-	illegitimacy
pointments, and frustrations	
	Motivation
Quality of marital relationship	Desire to have more nearly complete
	life
Successful continuance of marriage not	Desire to accept parental responsibility
dependent on children	Desire to contribute to development of
Respect for each other	another human being
Capacity to accept a child born to other	Desire to love and be loved
parents	

It might be noted that stability is a recurrent criterion—physical stability, emotional stability, financial stability, marital stability. The agency is responsible for acting for the community in behalf of the child too young to choose wisely for himself. The agency needs to guarantee the child a permanent home. Stability presupposes continuity and the likelihood of permanence.

But what confirmation is there that the agency can make a reliable decision regarding such criteria? Brieland designed a study to determine the reliability with which social workers make decisions regarding adoptive applicants. [26] He taped the intake interviews that one caseworker conducted with five different adoptive applicant couples. Brieland then played the tape of these interviews to 182 caseworkers in twenty-eight different agencies in thirteen states. Each worker was given a transcript of the interviews to follow while listening to the tapes. Having heard the tape, each worker was asked to decide whether or not the agency should continue contact with the couple. The percentage of agreement among the 184 workers varied from couple to couple, ranging from 89.1 percent agreement in the case of one couple to 61.4 percent agreement in the case of another couple. Over-all agreement for the total of the five cases was 73.6 percent, so that, for the total sample, percentage of agreement was at a statistically significant level. Although these results suggest some general tendency toward agreement between worker and worker as to how they evaluated each couple, they also indicate some considerable percentage of disagreement. (Brieland himself has offered a critical analysis of the research problem of such a study and the limitations of the results. [28])

In 1970 Brown replicated Brieland's study, using video tapes of interviews for presentation to eighty-four workers in adoptive agencies. [29] There was 72 percent agreement regarding decisions on the five couples—but again substantial deviation from the consensus.

The social worker is called upon to assess ambiguously defined entities such as the applicants' maturity, their marital relationship, their reaction to infertility, their attitude toward children, and their capacity for rearing a child. The behavioral criteria by which these factors are measured are nowhere adequately delineated. Furthermore, he is asked to predict their behavior in the future, in complex interaction with some unknown child. Ripple, in a follow-up study of adoption, found "little evidence that potential for good parenting can be assessed with confidence." [197, p. 494]

Even the applicant who wants to be honest and open with the worker may not be able to accurately evaluate how he will react to adoptive parenthood. The following is the case record of an adoptive home from which a school-age boy was removed:

Mrs. R. shared with the worker how terribly upset and guilty she was feeling. . . . She commented that she had always thought of herself as having more patience than most people and it was a great surprise to her to learn that she was not patient. . . . She was very critical of herself, feeling that she should have been able to accept John and work with him longer than she did. She continues to be surprised to learn that she does not have the patience she thought she did and that she can get so nervous and upset.

Mrs. R. had presented herself in the application interview as patient and accepting, which she honestly perceived herself to be.

Many applicants, knowing what the agency worker is looking for, try to project the image of acceptable adoptive parents. Isaac suggests how to produce a favorable impression:

> Use the pronoun *we* not *I*; share the fact that you have problems but that you have "handled" them maturely; while on good terms with own parents indicate that you are not on such good terms so as to seem dependent; if the wife works she should indicate that she is happy on the job—but not too happy so that she is ready to give it up for motherhood; indicate that the marriage is a satisfying one, that there are, however, disagreements and conflicts, but these are satisfactorily resolved, etc. [112]

Such efforts on the part of applicants to act the role of acceptable applicants further confounds the worker's difficulty in making an accurate assessment.

However, despite these difficulties, which need to be explicitly acknowledged, the fact is that workers in both the Brieland and Brown studies cited above agreed with each other on selection of applications at a level which was statistically significant. This reflects some consensus on selection criteria employed and some consensus on assessment of applicants. This confirms the findings of an earlier study. [153]

Process in Adoption

From Application to Placement

The agency seeks to obtain from a variety of sources the information it needs in making a decision. The principal source, of course, is the adoptive applicants themselves. The agency caseworker will schedule office interviews with the couple and with each member of the marital pair separately. The interviews generally include discussion of the following:

1. How interest in adoption developed.
2. Motivation for adoption.
3. Attitude toward childlessness and infertility.

4. Understanding of children and experiences with children.
5. History of the marriage and current patterns of marital interaction.
6. Developmental history.
7. Educational and employment history.
8. Patterns of social participation.
9. Attitude of extended family toward adoption.
10. Attitude toward illegitimacy and the out-of-wedlock child.
11. Problems anticipated in adoption and how they must be handled.
12. Attitudes toward working with the agency.

If all goes well, the interviews will be followed by a series of home visits, during which the caseworker will have an opportunity of seeing the couple react in an informal, familiar setting. He will also be able to obtain some information about the physical resources of the home and the neighborhood. References, submitted by the applicant, are contacted for whatever additional information they can provide. They not only help the caseworker to see the applicant through the eyes of other people but also indicate the extent to which the applicants are integrated into the community and the attitude of the community toward adoption. Psychological tests such as the Rorschach have occasionally been used to supplement the interview and reference material. [138]

Throughout all of these contacts, the agency, acting for the child, is assuring itself that these applicants will provide an adequate, stable home for the child. It is also helping the adoptive applicants to decide that this is what they really want to do and helping them to adjust to the idea of impending parenthood. The nine months of pregnancy provide the opportunity to biological parents for adjusting to the idea of the significant changes in their lives that will follow the birth of their child. The study period provides an opportunity for thoughtful self-examination, anxious anticipation, and hopeful delay which entails the kind of emotional reorganization that is involved in actual pregnancy. It helps prepare the applicant, emotionally, for parenthood. It is highly desirable that the adoptive parents be active participants in this process of mutual exploration since, as Campbell says, "For successful adoption, children need to be 'taken' by the adoptive parents, not merely given by the agency." [33, p. 184]

A letter from one adoptive parent regarding the study experience notes:

By the end of our interviews we felt that, even if we were not accepted by the agency, we had gained a valuable experience that would enable us to approach adoption from other sources with a much greater understanding of its problems and difficulties than we had before.

An adoptive mother, in a retrospective analysis of her experience, said:

> In our thoughts about adoption, my husband and I had raised
> many questions and hypothetical situations to each other concerning
> an adopted child. Two of these neither of us could answer satis-
> factorily. One dealt with the discipline of an adopted child who
> might remind you that since you are not their real parent they do
> not have to obey you, and how to cope with an adopted child's
> curiosity about his natural parents. By answering these questions,
> the social worker made us feel that at this point the interview really
> began. We began to see the social worker's role as a dual one. The
> interviews are not only to serve the purpose of finding out about
> you, but are there to help you and answer any doubts that you
> may have in regard to an adopted child.

Agencies also see the contact as providing a possibility of helping applicants to deal with those problems that might militate against a successful adoption.

> We discussed with Mr. M. his feeling toward children born out of
> wedlock since his child, if he was offered one for adoption, would
> in all likelihood be illegitimate. During the early part of the contact
> he was anxious about "a child of a promiscuous woman" but toward
> the later interviews, as a result of our interpretation, he felt more
> comfortable with the fact that "sinfulness" is not inherited.

How does the application study process actually work out in practice? Bradley studied the processing of some 400 applicants in eight agen-cies. [21] The process was completed within four or five interviews, indicating that it is not a prolonged, elaborate procedure. The median amount of time between application for, and placement of, a child was seven to nine months, closely approximating the usual pregnancy time lapse.

Of the applicants 26 percent were rejected by the agencies; another 6 percent might have been encouraged to withdraw but withdrew volun-tarily. Interestingly, the most highly professionalized agencies had the lowest percentage of rejection; the least professionalized, the highest. [21, p. 110]

Bradley checked the social workers' assessments against the deci-sions actually made in order to determine factors associated with selec-tion. Those factors having the highest association with acceptance were "positive qualities of couple interaction in their marriage, flexible and outgoing characteristics of both husband's and wife's personalities, the couples' openness, their nonneurotic motivation for adoption, their adequate marital role performance, and their acceptance of infertility." [21, p. 22]   However, applicants were also accepted who "tended to be marginal couples who were considered more suitable for marginal children"—hard-to-place children. [21, p. 188]   In other words, there were two alternative but nonsimultaneous routes that led to a positive impression of couples as adoptive prospects with the "better" couple seen as suitable for the "better" child and the marginal couple seen as more suitable for the marginal child. [21, p. 189]

This confirms an earlier study, which indicated that applicants who presented qualifications which differed from those generally accepted by the agency sought to improve their chances by indicating a willingness to accept a hard-to-place child. [119]   A more recent study of the application process in English agencies found that, "in the case of hard-to-place children, agencies compromised considerably in their expectations of adoptive applicants." [240, p. 88]

Once the applicants have been approved for adoption, the agency is faced with the problem of selecting a child for them. Some effort is made to match child and parents in terms of ethnic background, physical appearance, temperament, and intelligence potential. Having been selected as adoptive parents, at this point they are selected as adoptive parents for a particular child.

When the agency has determined on a mutually advantageous selection of child and parents, the adoptive parents are called in and given background information on the child. Any questions or doubts they may have are discussed and, if possible, resolved. If all goes well on the verbal presentation, the parents meet the child and a decision is made. [12]   One study of this point in the process notes:

> One factor which increases the anxiety and discomfort of adoptive parents during the placement process is that, unlike natural parents, they can "back out" if they choose. When parents are having their own children, however worried they may feel, they have no choice but to accept it; therefore they have no decision to make. [155, p. 145]

In the case of older children, aware of what is going on, an effort may be made to have the prospective parents meet the child by arranged "accident" in the park, supermarket, and so on. This gives the adoptive parents an opportunity to see the child without his feeling rejected if they decide against taking him.

The caseworker is also involved in working with the child. If the child is an infant, little preparation for the impending change is possible. However, the agency arranges for a thorough physical check of the child and informs the adoptive parents of the results. With older children, an effort is made to prepare them for the change by discussing with them the meaning of adoption and some of the problems they will experience in moving into a new home with a new set of permanent parents. For the older child, a gradual process of placement can be arranged. This might involve an overnight visit to the adoptive parents or a series of such visits before the final move is made. [6]

From Placement to Adoption

After the child is placed in the home, there is a trial period, usually six months to a year, during which the child is still under the legal guardianship of the agency. At the end of a year, if it is agreeable to both the agency and the adoptive parents, the final adoption takes place through appropriate court action.

The trial period or postplacement service, as it is sometimes more neutrally designated, is based on the recognition that not even the most acute, perceptive study can confidently predict how the adoptive parents will actually feel when confronted with rearing the adopted child. At best, the study "can differentiate between the potentially good prospects and more or less poor risks." [70, p. 16] This period, then, can be viewed as an extension of the home study. At this point the parent is actually performing as a parent rather than talking, imagining, or anticipating parenthood. The period thus serves a protective function, ensuring that the child has, in fact, been placed in a desirable home. This time is, consequently, a threat to the adoptive parents, for the agency might decide to remove the child if problems become serious. Actually, only rarely is a child likely to be removed after placement and before final adoption. Studies (see p. 572) indicate that removal occurs only in about 2 percent of the cases.

The trial period protects the adoptive parent as well. If the child is not developing normally, if a physical or mental handicap has become manifest, the parent has a right to reconsider before the adoption is made final.

The agency, however, would like to emphasize that this period is one of helping the parents and the adopted child develop a sense of kinship and of helping them with the inevitable problems that arise as a result of such a radical change in their life situation. The agencies see this supportive function as taking precedence over the protective function.

Here the perception of adoptive parents seems to be at variance with the intent of the agency. An interview study of fifty-seven adoptive couples in Minnesota indicated "that they rated the 'probation' function as their opinion of the primary purpose of the continued contact by the agency," whereas caseworkers unanimously regarded help in successful integration of the adoptive family as the primary purpose. Forty percent of the families felt that postplacement interviews had not been particularly helpful; 19 percent felt that the visits had been of "substantial" help. [89, p. 9]   The clients' view of postplacement service as primarily protective is confirmed by another, more limited, study of client reaction. [263]

Few of the parents felt that a clear, unambiguous statement of the purpose of the trial period had been communicated by the agency. When it had been, parents were more likely to feel the contacts were helpful—especially in two general areas: "reassurance (such as reassurance that they were doing a good job, that their child was developing properly or that the agency would not take the child away) and problem solving (such as provision of child care and developmental information and legal procedural information or help with specific adoption problems such as how to tell their child about adoption)." [88, p. 322]   "The single area of service that the greatest number of adoptive parents considered the most helpful was reassurance that they were doing a good job as parents." [89, p. 10]

Studies indicate that the actual contacts between the agency and the family during this period are generally infrequent. Gochros [89] found that visits were made about once every three months, and Triseliotis found that an average number of 1.6 visits were "paid to each case during the average six months probationary period." [240, p. 106]

Some adoptive parents might resent the implication that they cannot be adequate parents without agency help. Continuing contact serves to remind them that they are not biological parents and that the child is not yet their own.

While most adoptive parents feel that adoption services are helpful in preparing them for their adoptive role, few have voluntary contact with the agency after adoption, preferring to turn to family, friends, and their pediatrician for help with parent-child problems. [226, pp. 499–500]

Problems of Adoptive Families

The Adoptive Parent

Once the child is adopted, the family is like all other families—yet different. Consequently they have the same problems all other families face but, in addition, some unique problems which derive from the fact of adoption. Biological parents require no intermediary in achieving parenthood; adoptive parents require the agency. Biological parents pass no test of adequacy; adoptive parents must satisfy the agency of their adequacy. Biological parents can count on the child's appearance within a given period of time; adoptive parents do not know when—or if—the child will come. Adoptive parenthood, unlike biological parenthood, cannot be achieved in private in a moment of impulse; it requires a deliberate process in which motivation must be made explicit and shared with others. Adoptive parents can control the sex of the child, can ensure that the child is without serious defect, and can avoid the discomforts of pregnancy and childbirth; at the same time they miss the experience of unity with the child in developing life and giving birth.

Once past the point of genesis, the differences between adoptive and biological families grow smaller and the similarities grow larger. Even the most perceptive observer would be hard put to distinguish an adoptive family from a biological family in a restaurant, at the beach, in a department store. [125]

Parenthood is primarily a social role and title to the status *parent* should be reserved for those who actually perform its functions. The Talmud says, "He who raises up the child is called 'father'; not he who begot the child." The playwright Schiller noted, "It is not flesh and blood, but the heart, which makes us fathers and sons." Krugman observes, "The differentiation to be made is not between two sets of parents ('natural' and 'adoptive') but between *parents* and those who *give birth* to the child" [italics in original]. [137]

As *parents*, then, adoptive parents face all of the problems of adjustment and change in accepting the child into the home that all other parents face with the birth of a child. These have been described by LeMasters in his study of the crises of parenthood. [146] And they continue to face those problems encountered by all parents in conscientiously trying to raise a biologically, socially, and emotionally healthy child.

But society is ambivalent about granting full endorsement to the adoptive parent. The very words *natural mother* or *real mother* suggest that the adoptive parent is "unnatural" and/or "unreal," reflecting society's attitude that biological relationships are more important than social relationships, that "giving birth" is more important than "caring for," and that we are obliged to honor biological relationships for their own sake. Our vocabulary, reflecting our thinking, our mores, and our legal procedures, suggests that adoption is a second-best route to parenthood. More recently adoptive parents organizations have been suggesting the use of the term *biomother* or *bioparents* to distinguish the birth parents from the adoptive parents.

At any rate, adoptive parents do have some particular problems which derive from their unique status. They are members of a minority group who have achieved parenthood in a special way. [132] Given a choice, adoptive parents would have preferred to conceive as well as rear their children. They usually come to adoption out of necessity, not by choice.

There are no readily available role models of adoptive parenthood which would help socialize adoptive parents to their status. While the biological parent role almost uniformly elicits from others comments indicating support and approbation, the adoptive parent role frequently elicits comments which contain components of hostility, derision, and rejection.

With adoption the parent faces the problem of accepting his status publicly. Application for adoption may be kept secret, but with the arrival of the child, the extended family and the immediate neighbors become aware of the adoption. The loss of anonymity raises such questions as what to tell friends and relatives about the child's background. But of somewhat greater difficulty is the fact that the adoptive parents now risk public recognition of their infertility. Questions will be raised about why they needed to resort to adoption.

Adoptive parents may bring to parenthood some special feelings about the child. Because adoptive parenthood is achieved with the consent of the community through selection by a community agency, adoptive parents may feel a greater sense of accountability for their performance as parents. They may, on occasion, feel guilty that they are not living up to the expectations of the community, that better parents might have been chosen for the children. As one adoptive parent said "The yardstick by which the adoptive parent, as a parent, is measured is a longer one." They may feel that, because the child has been once deprived, they have an obligation to be more indulgent with him. They may feel that, because some part of the child belongs irrevocably to the natural parent, they cannot be as firm in disciplining him—that he might reject them. The adoptive parent is aware that he shares the child, at least in fantasy, with the biological parents. He may be concerned that the child will, ultimately, seek out and make contact with the biological parents.

The adoptive parent may be concerned about his entitlement to the child, possibly feeling somewhat equivocal about the completeness of his relationship to the child. There is a feeling that a social-emotional relationship is less binding, more fragile, than the relationship between biological parent and child in which the social-emotional component is reinforced by the mutual bond of blood. The problem for the adoptive parents is that of really feeling the child "belongs" to them.

Raleigh, in a study of adoptive families at a child guidance clinic, noted that adoptive mothers "tended to be more overanxious about their children's problems and were more overprotective in their attitudes," which suggests "that the adoptive mothers tended to feel more insecure in their parental role" and had a greater need to appear concerned. [189, p. 70]   Adoptive mothers were also more inconsistent in their disciplining than natural mothers and felt less secure in coping with their children's unacceptable behavior. [189, p. 69]

However much the adoptive parent may have moved toward the conviction that environment is the more important component in the child's development, there are still some residual feelings about the unknown hereditary elements behind the child's behavior. Because most of the children are illegitimate, uneasy feelings about "bad blood" and the child's destructive impulses may make the parents anxious.

Problems of Adoptive Children

The adopted child faces all the general problems of development encountered by his nonadoptive peers. In this sense he is a child among other children. But, in addition, like the adoptive parents, he faces some special problems which are related to the fact that he is an adopted child.

The fact that the "birth parents" of the adoptive child are different from the "bread parents," those who actually perform the role of parents, presents the child with special problems. The child faces the problem of "genealogical bewilderment," of accepting the fact that he is the biological product of parents whom he does not know and never will know. Who are the people who gave him birth? What were they like? The process of self-identification is a more difficult one for the adopted child.

Freud points out that every child, when faced with the reality of some rejection by his parents, imagines that he is really a stepchild or an adopted child and that his real parents are all-loving and all-permissive. [81]   Sooner or later, however, the child accepts the fact that his parents are both loving and rejecting. However, because the adopted child does, in fact, have two sets of parents, he can separate the components of this ambivalence by letting one set of parents embody the negative, rejecting component and the other set of parents represent all that is loving and accepting. The task of fusing the two aspects of the parental image is consequently more difficult for the adopted child and the tendency to idealize the unknown biological parent is greater. Yet the very fact that the first set of parents gave him up for adoption raises doubts in the child's mind about his acceptability, posing a difficulty for the development of a positive self-image. [122]

As the child grows older, he may want to know why his own parents could not care for him. The significant question, for the child, is whether or not he was so bad, so unacceptable, that his parents needed to reject him. Some assurance must be given to the child that his placement for adoption did not result from anything bad or wrong on his part. "Just as parents need to feel that they are worthy of parenthood, so too the most important question in any child's mind is not 'How did I get here' but 'Are you glad I am here?' " [147, p. 274]

With adolescence, another problem arises. Many adopted children are aware that they are illegitimate. Identified, to whatever limited degree, with natural parents who engaged in illicit sex, of which they are the living evidence, the child faces the problem of resolving any predisposition to think that "like father, like son; like mother, like daughter." He also may have greater difficulty in establishing independence because his feelings of gratitude and obligation toward his adoptive parents conflict with the need to break away from them.

While these are the special problems that might be faced by adoptive parents and children, there is little empirical evidence to show how frequently such problems actually do arise. Kadushin found that adoptive parents perceived the differences between themselves and biological parents but rarely considered them problems. [125]   Research on the emotional problems of adopted children reveals that the psychosocial development of such children is, in most instances, indistinguishable from that of their peers.

Telling

The most difficult, most troublesome, unique aspect of adoption is the problem of "telling." "Telling" involves the process of gradually sharing with the child the information that he is adopted and helping him to understand and emotionally accept the fact. This proves to be a problem for adoptive parents as well as for their children. Many of the problems already discussed are activated or exacerbated by the necessity for "telling."

The question "How shall I tell my child he is adopted?" contains within it a second question: "How do I accept myself as an adoptive parent?" "Telling" makes explicit the fact of infertility; "telling" makes explicit the fact that the child had other biological parents; "telling" introduces the natural parents' image into the family system and threatens the exclusiveness of the relationship between adoptive parents and child. Deutsch notes that, in explaining to the child that "she is not his real mother . . . [the adoptive mother] must revive the ghosts that she tries painfully to chase away from her own psychic life, unleash again the pain and estrangement that she mastered or still must master. The adoptive mother fears the burden she must impose upon the child, his disappointment, his subsequent questions and explorations." [57, p. 425]   Comfortable "telling" thus requires not only that the adoptive parents resolve their feelings about their infertility but also that they are sufficiently confident of the strength of the child's emotional kinship with them so that it is not threatened by the fact of a biological kinship with others. As Kirk puts it, "telling" conflicts with the requirement for "integrating" the child into the family because it "differentiates" the child from the family. [131, p. 319]   "Telling" also is anxiety provoking because it raises the whole question of sexuality—how babies are conceived, how babies are born. Parents may be diffident about "telling" because they feel uncomfortable with such questions.

"Telling" forces both adoptive parent and child into an explicit recognition of their adoptive status. Parents may be reluctant to impose the burden of this atypicality on the child, the knowledge of this difference from his peers. They may be anxious to spare the child the knowledge that he was born out of wedlock, or that his parents were neglectful.

"Telling" also raises questions relating to an additional "public" not in the picture when the placement was made. What if the child's friends ask about his being adopted? Should the school be informed when he is first enrolled? Should neighbors be told when the family moves to a new neighborhood?

There is some clinical support for the supposition that adoptive children contend with these feelings and questions. Schechter, drawing on his experience with adopted children in private psychiatric practice, notes that the child made aware of his adoption has to "cope with the knowledge of the rejection by the original parents, representing a severe narcissistic injury." [203, p. 31] This gives rise to recurrent anxiety in the children for, "having been given up once for undetermined reasons, they may be given up again at some future time, also for undetermined fantasied reasons." [203, p. 31] Eiduson reports similar clinical findings. [61] But Schwartz, comparing the Thematic Apperception Test responses of twenty-five adopted children with those of twenty-five non-adopted peers, concludes that "there were more similarities than differences between the two groups" and that "for the child adopted in infancy, his first allegiance is to the adoptive parents and, within a relatively stable family situation, the family romance is of no greater significance for him than it is for any child." [209, p. 390]

Despite the difficulties involved, it is generally agreed that it is desirable for the adoptive parent to tell the child that he is adopted. Aside from the fact that not telling falsifies the relationship and requires that the adoptive parents live a lie, it is possible that the child might discover, through other sources, that he is adopted. The parents' silence, then, might be taken to mean that there is something bad about the fact of adoption. An interview study of twenty-eight adoptive families concerned with attitudes toward telling indicated that all felt the child should know of the adoption and "none wanted to risk the child's discovery of this through outside sources." [63, p. 121]

> The adopted mother said that she and her husband were resting
> secure in the feeling that their son had no idea that he was an
> adopted child, when suddenly in his last year of high school he
> began to act very strange and distant, going out a great deal and
> letting his school work lag, where previously he had been close,
> confiding, and a good student. Finally, a relative visited and
> told the parents that the son knew he had been adopted, as he heard

the relative's daughters talking about it. The adopted mother said she and her husband put in a night of horror wondering what to do and finally decided to tell him the next night.

The following night after dinner, the father called the adopted son in the living room, "both of us crying. I took it on myself to tell him, told him I couldn't have a baby, how we picked him out and loved him as our own."

But the adopted mother and father were crestfallen when he turned away and walked out of the room, because they thought they had lost him. In a few minutes he came back and said, "What difference does it make? I'm your baby." The adopted mother said, "You'll always be my baby." The son then went over to the dad and said, "It doesn't make any difference, you'll always be my dad, everything will go on as usual." The adopted mother said that after the tension they all laughed hilariously and "felt very close. Everything has gone on as usual." [258, pp. 78–79]

Adoptive children who accidently learned of their adoption or who learned of it precipitously in some crisis situation described their reaction as that of "panic," "profound hurt," "rejection," "having been deceived." [97; 181]

"Telling" is not only desirable because it requires adoptive parents and children to clarify between themselves the nature of their relationship, not only is it pragmatically expedient because of the great risk of exposure, it is also ethical: the child is entitled to know his true origins. Furthermore, rather than threatening the relationship, "telling" may intensify positive feeling between parents and child as they acknowledge their "shared fate." Some research findings suggest that those adoptive families which openly accepted the idea of adoption, implied in "telling," were apt to be better adjusted to adoption. [63, p. 126; 132, pp. 95–99]

There is some controversy, however, over when "telling" should take place. The agencies recommend that "telling" begin early in the child's life and be reintroduced for discussion at progressively higher levels of complexity. Parents are advised to introduce the word early, to apply the word and concept in appropriate situations, and to tell the child about adoption simply and directly as one of the facts of life that the child needs to know.

More recently some psychoanalysts have advised that "telling" should be delayed until the child is beyond the Oedipal stage in development. "Telling" the younger child supposedly feeds his fantasies and makes more difficult the resolution of the Oedipal conflict. It is suggested that when the child is between six and twelve, he has a better grasp of reality and can develop a more realistic image of the adoptive situation. [7; 182] The material in support of this view is very limited, restricted to isolated clinical examples, and contradicted by Witmer's study, which found that a delay in "telling" was associated with heightened negative reactions on the part of the child. [259, p. 392]

The level of interest in adoptive status is not uniform throughout the child's life. There is a peak period around eight or nine when his peers become explicitly aware of, and raise questions about, adoptive status. When the adolescent is struggling with self-definition, questions about his origins become more insistent. And at each level there is progressively deeper understanding of the meaning of adoption as it is explained in a different context. To the young person approaching marriage, it might be explained that marriage is, in effect, a procedure through which husband and wife "adopt" each other and develop a relationship more intense than any blood relationship. Perhaps, however, full understanding is not achieved until the adopted child becomes a parent himself. One adoptee said, "I never saw anybody of my own flesh and blood until I held my baby in my arms."

There are also suggestions on "how" to "tell." The general advice is that the parents should share the information confidently, realistically, positively, without anxiety or apology. All of this suggests that the parents would have to feel very comfortable with the idea of adoption.

Overemphasis is as much an indication of discomfort with the idea as is vigorous avoidance. The adoptive parents of the child who said, "I knew. They knew I knew. I even told them I knew. But they still refused to talk about it" are clearly uncomfortable with the fact of adoption. But discomfort is also present in the case of the family of the adopted child who said, "It was good to know that I was adopted, but I wished that they would stop talking about it."

As McWhinnie notes, in summarizing the reaction of adopted adults whom she interviewed,

> None of these adopted children wanted their adoptive status shrouded in complete secrecy. . . . Equally they did not want constant reference to it. They wanted something in between, where their adopted status was acknowledged without embarrassment and then overtly forgotten so that they were treated exactly as if they were the biological sons and daughters of their adopted parents. . . . Thus they were emphatic that they did not want to be introduced as an "adopted son" or an "adopted daughter." They wanted to feel they belonged in the family and were completely accepted there as a son or daughter. [159, p. 249]

Emphasis in telling might be more productively placed on what the child has gained, a home with accepting parents, rather than on loss of the biological parents.

Adoptive parents must feel, and communicate to the child, that adoptive parenthood and adoptive childhood are as desirable as biological parent-child relationships; that the adopted child belongs just as certainly and securely in the adoptive family as the biological child does in his family.

"Telling" at its best can be an expression of love and acceptance of the child. The account of how he came to be adopted can reinforce feelings of belonging and identity. However, "telling" can also be used as a weapon. Depending on the spirit of the communication, it may be designed to make the child feel obligated for all the adoptive parents did for him or as a threat that the child might be "returned" if he did not give satisfaction.

Adoptive parents have to accept responsibility for "telling." Earlier studies indicated that adopted children were indifferent toward adoption. [168, p. 13; 63, p. 122; 204, p. 42] Apparently children rarely took the initiative of asking questions. More recent studies suggest, however, that children are eager to know but, despite their curiosity, felt that they could not initiate discussion about origins, that the information had to come from the adoptive parents on the initiative of the adoptive parent. As adopted children, they felt hesitant about taking responsibility for raising these questions, out of fear of hurting, or upsetting, or appearing disloyal to the parents.

Agencies generally recommend that parents introduce the child early and gradually to the idea of adoption, through the judicious use of such books as *The Chosen Baby* [251] or *The Family That Grew*. [198] Announcement cards, used to inform others of adoption, tend to emphasize the "chosen baby" motif. One of the more popular ones runs

> We have a brand new baby,
> And there isn't any doubt
> We got just what we wanted—
> Because we picked our baby out!

However, the "chosen child" concept places a great burden on the child of living up to some great expectations. It is clearly inappropriate in those situations where there is a biochild in the family. Furthermore, the "chosen child" explanation is essentially false. As one adopted child said, "I was not chosen as an individual; my parents just wanted a child." The idea of being "wanted" rather than "chosen" is closer to the realities of the adoptive situation.

A more difficult question, of more pressing concern to the adopted child is, "Why did his biological parents give him up?" Frequently the answer is, "Because they could not care for you and loved you so much that they wanted the best for you." But the idea that "they loved you so much" is rejected by adopted adults. One woman said:

First of all I don't think it is possible to feel true potential love
for a newborn or growing child. This comes from living together.
Also if my real parents loved me so much, why did they give me up?
I used to think, "Are my adoptive parents going to give me up,
too, because I know they love me?" It is more honest to say
that there are circumstances which make it necessary to place
the child for adoption. It is a question of the ability to be a parent,
not a question of love. [97, p. 27]

Another difficult question concerns the kinds of information about
the biological parents that should be shared with the child in "telling."
The agency, too, must determine how much of its knowledge about the
bioparents should be shared with the adoptive parents.

Generally the agency provides only information that would help
the adoptive parents in their child-rearing responsibilities or has bearing on the child's development. Information given adoptive parents
might therefore include medical information about the child's birth,
immunization history, special health problems, sleeping patterns, and
food preferences; information about the biological parents' ages, educa-
tions, and general appearance, and the nature of the relationship between
the child's father and mother. Many agencies prefer not to burden the
adoptive parents with too many details of the child's background so that
they can truthfully tell the child that they do not know much about the
biological parents. However, what can be truthfully pointed out is that,
whatever reason occasioned the inability of the natural parent to care
for the child, he showed enough concern for the needs and welfare of
the child to give him up for adoption.

It is difficult to discuss adoption without implying that the child has
been rescued from inadequate parents, yet to imply this may make it
difficult for the child, who is, to some extent, identified with his biological parents. The adoptive parents must therefore communicate background information in an accepting, understanding tone. This in itself
may be difficult for many adoptive parents: having been highly motivated to have a child, they find it difficult to empathize with, or understand, a mother who has given up her baby. A recent follow-up study
found that there "appeared to be a link between the adoptive parents'
attitudes to the natural parents and the difficulty they found in telling
the child he was adopted. Though none considered telling to be easy,
those who actually disapproved of the natural parents found it to be
more difficult." [212, p. 149]   For all, there is the problem of conveying
understanding and acceptance of the unmarried mother without implying the moral and practical desirability of out-of-wedlock pregnancy.

Recent research involves interviews with adult adoptees who shared,
retrospectively, their experience in the "telling" process. [159]   Another
study was based on small group meetings by adult adoptees who met

over a period of six months to discuss their experiences in adoption. [97] The adoptees, to a considerable extent, agreed that it was crucial for the parent to share with the child the fact that he was adopted, that integration of the meaning of adoption takes place gradually and that real understanding is not achieved until adolescence or even early adult-hood, and that while it is necessary to reiterate the fact of adoption, it should be referred to only on those occasions where the situation calls attention to adoptive status.

Adoptive parents may exaggerate the adopted child's desire to seek out his biological parents. Even when information about the biological parents is legally available to the adopted child, relatively few take advantage of the option. In Scotland it is possible for an adopted child, on reaching the age of seventeen, to apply for information about his bio-logical parents from the original birth certificate. While some 1500–2000 adoptions are completed each year in Scotland, between 1958 and 1968 an average of only thirty-four adoptees annually called at Register House, where such information is made available. [161, p. 38]   Few of these go on to seek out their parents. The knowledge of the name of the parents "often appears sufficient to satisfy the adopted person's curi-osity." [225, p. 31]

Both South Dakota and Virginia permit the adopted child, on reach-ing legal age, to learn the identity of and other available information about his biological parents, without a court order. The adoption con-sultant for the State Department of Public Welfare in South Dakota noted, however, that less than a half dozen children a year attempt to obtain this information (Rapid City Journal, October 9, 1969).

In most states an adopted child can petition the court for the release of information. "A check of several Minnesota courts revealed that this type of petition is rare." [148, p. 47]

Or the adopted child can, if he knows the agency which handled the adoption, return to the agency for information. An experienced English adoptive agency worker, reviewing her agency's experience, says that "of all the children who are placed for adoption by an agency each year, comparatively few ever come back asking for more information. . . ." [261, p. 23]

On the other hand, there have been organizations formed, such as The Adoptees Liberty Movement Association (The New York Times, July 25, 1972) and Orphan Voyage, which presume to speak for adoptees who are actively interested in establishing legal procedures which would give them the right to identify their bioparents. [181; 225]

It is difficult to meet the justifiable, but conflicting, needs of all the parties involved. While the child is entitled to knowledge about his origins, the biomother who gave up her illegitimate child for adoption has the right to be protected from exposure. Because of this conflict of interests and rights, both courts and agencies handle requests for information on the part of the adopted child with considerable care.

With very few exceptions, a group of adult adoptees who discussed the question in a series of group meetings indicated they "did not want to locate their biological parents." As one woman stated, "What would you say to complete strangers? You would just be people who had no meaning for each other." [97, p. 28]   They felt that their real identity stemmed from their adoptive parents rather than their biological parents. One remarked, "It is rather ironic for your biological mother to be called your 'real' mother for in fact she is very unreal."

They were curious about their bioparents' age, height, coloring, education, occupation. But although they were curious about them as people they did not have a feeling about them as parents. They thought of them more as a "concept" than as "flesh and blood" people. The motive for knowledge about their background was not tied to a desire to contact the biological parents, but rather to the desire to understand themselves better and develop some feeling of continuity with their past. Thus the sharing of such information with the adopted child does not necessarily threaten his loyalty to, and relationship with, his adoptive parents.

Adoption may not itself be the cause of difficulty in the parent-child relationship, but it may become a weapon if difficulties exist. Children who are denied a satisfactory parental relationship in adoption may seek an alternative relationship with their bioparent. [113; 159]

The principles of "telling" might be summarized as follows:

1. The child's receptivity to the fact of his adoptive status is best assured if the parents themselves accept it and are convinced of the importance of "telling."
2. The child need be told at any one time only as much as he can understand, so that "telling" is a gradual process.
3. There will be many different opportunities to tell the child, and repetition in different contexts is useful. Everyday use of the word, when appropriate, helps make it comfortably acceptable.
4. Overemphasis, like avoidance, has some dangers. Telling the child he was "chosen" may burden him with the need to live up to excessive expectations.
5. The parent must take the initiative in offering information about adoption.
6. Sharing of such information is not likely to threaten the relationship between adoptive parents and children if the relationship is an essentially positive one.

Group Approaches in Adoption

Group methods have been used effectively in adoptions. Some agencies arrange for a group meeting of applicants to review some general ideas about adoption and agency procedure in processing an application. The content of these meetings tends to be primarily "factual, and the method of presentation instructional," although the aim is partly to reduce an applicant's anxiety. [231, p. 88]

As a result of these orientation meetings, couples who are interested in continuing contact with the agency are better informed about what to expect and what is expected of them. [223]   Some decide not to submit an application—couples who are very ambivalent about adoption or who clearly cannot meet the eligibility requirements. [249, p. 102]

Attempts have been made to use group meetings for getting to know the applicants. [58; 127; 256; 257]   It was hypothesized that use of group meetings for the home study "would make it possible to neutralize the study so that fear of the power of the worker would be diminished, defensiveness lessened . . . and preparation for parenthood enhanced." [127, p. 128]   As Biskind notes, "Parents in the group situation are freer to acknowledge their perplexities and fears." [15, p. 145]

Group meetings have also been used during the period between placement and adoption and after final adoption. Conklin found that one of the advantages of the use of groups between placement and final adoption lay in countering the defensiveness of workers in contact with the family during this period. The caseworkers who had made the placement and, for purposes of continuity, were assigned responsibility for contact with the family during this period, tended to defend the correctness of their decision to place the child by failing to recognize incipient problems. The opportunity to observe the adoptive couples in group meetings permitted the agency to get a more objective picture of their reaction to adoption. [51]

Group support may help to overcome the diffidence and anxiety new adoptive parents feel in the period immediately after placement—precisely when they feel least free to share doubts and misgivings and difficulties with the workers. [38; 184; 211]

One agency arranges a group meeting shortly before final legal adoption as a sort of graduation exercise. [237]   Other agencies have experimented with group meetings after final adoption. [33; 47; 160; 199]   Most legal adoptions take place before the children are two years of age. Some of the most difficult problems of adoptive parenthood are only theoretical at this point. When adoptive parents actually encounter the full impact of the child's questions about adoption—when he is five or six—they might want then to discuss them with the agency and with other adoptive parents. The following are excerpts from notes taken at the first meeting of one such group:

There was considerable discussion on the pros and cons of sharing illegitimacy with children. Mr. Doyle felt that, if adoptive parents do not see illegitimacy as a stigma, and the child has the security and love of his parents, he need not feel this as a stigma either. Mrs. Grau decided that, when her child asks why his own parents gave him up, she would explain very simply that children can be born to married parents and to unmarried persons, and that when a mother does not have a husband to help care for the child she cannot do this alone, and feels that the child should have the advantage of being cared for by two parents.

On the whole, the group objected to "killing off" the natural parents. Mrs. Nash and Mrs. Wexler said they don't like to lie, and Mrs. Grau said that if the child subsequently learns that this was not true it will result in his losing confidence in the parents. She added that the child may ask where his parents are buried. Others also felt that, if told that the biological parents died, the child may fear the death of the adoptive parents.

However, Mrs. Hall felt that death was the best "story." She expressed fear that, if the child knows his parents are alive, he might look for them. She also objected to burdening the child with the knowledge of illegitimacy. To her it was quite simple to tell the child his parents were married, and the fact that it is not true does not bother her. She said, "Why not make our own truth?" The others in the group took exception with Mrs. Hall's point of view. [30, p. 20]

The number of adoptive couples engaged in such postadoptive meetings is, as yet, small. One agency, a pioneer in such activity, has, over a six-year period, met with a total of 150 families. [199, p. 250] This is partly because postplacement contact is a process which differentiates adoptive parents from other parents and is consequently resisted by adoptive parents. In an adoptive follow-up study of 160 families, the question was asked whether or not it was desirable for the agency to hold group meetings for adoptive parents; 70 percent of the white parents and 56 percent of the black parents said no. [197]

The Rejected Applicant

Not all applicants are successful in becoming adoptive parents. As Michaels notes: "If it is occasionally necessary to choose between a possible injustice to a family and possible injustice to a child, the agency must, by virtue of its essential responsibility, protect the child." [163, p. 370]

The agency, however, has a responsibility to deny the applicants in a way that results in minimum damage to their psychic health. The appli-

cants are generally vulnerable: they have applied because of a condition
—inability to have a child by natural means—which, in itself, is a deep
narcissistic wound. However the agency handles the situation, "there is
no softness that can remove entirely the sting of being denied parenthood for the second time—first by life, and then by society." [163, p.
372]

The agency strives to help the applicants come, on their own, to the
same conclusion reached by the agency—that they are not ready for
adoption and, in pressing their application, they are doing themselves a
disservice. If the agency is successful, the applicants withdraw their
application as a matter of choice and the agency has performed a helpful
service both to the adoptive applicants and to its pool of adoptable
children. The following is an example of such a situation:

> Mr. and Mrs. W. came about the adoption of an infant. It had
> not been absolutely determined that they could not have their own
> child, although the chances were slim and Mrs. W. felt that she
> did not want to wait any longer for a child. Mr. W. brought
> out many questions about the effects of heredity on a child and how
> adopted children turn out. The worker, recognizing his fear,
> helped them see that they had some difference in their readiness for
> adoption, and Mr. W. could say that he would still prefer to have
> his own child. Both felt that Mr. W. was the sort of person who
> needed to examine the risks and possibilities of an important new
> venture thoroughly before entering into it. The worker agreed
> that certainly adoption was important, and that people should be
> sure they wanted to take the risks involved before attempting it.
>
> The worker commented that evidently Mr. W. was not sure he
> could feel comfortable about being a parent to a child strangers
> had borne. He enlarged on his own question and fear. The worker
> told them about the shortage of children, and the need of the
> agency to limit applications drastically, saying that one of the things
> the agency needed to know in deciding which families to add to
> the long waiting lists was which were most likely to feel like
> parents to children placed with them, and that it would be hard
> for us to know this when the W.'s did not yet know it themselves.
> The worker suggested that perhaps this was something they needed
> to settle for themselves first.
>
> Mr. W. seemed very relieved, and Mrs. W. agreed that they
> should withdraw their request for the present, and explore the
> possibilities of having their own baby. They could then decide
> whether, if they absolutely could not have their own, they preferred
> to accept the risks Mr. W. feared in adoption or the possibility of
> a childless marriage. [163, p. 373]

Frequently the applicants will dispute, rather than consider, their lack of readiness for adoption or their failure to meet the agency's requirements. This problem is met more easily when the agency can honestly point to the large number of applicants and hide behind assertions that it is "being forced to turn down even very fine families because of the shortage of children." [163, p. 375] The objective situation, rather than any applicant deficiency, is stressed. As Michaels notes, "As far as possible the onus of failure to obtain a child should be placed on the external adoption situation beyond the . . . [applicants'] control and the agency's." [163, p. 375] A second line of defense is to explain the rejection, wherever possible, in terms of the applicants' failure to meet certain specific requirements—age, housing, religion, and so on. Applicants who do not meet specific minimum requirements are weeded out early in the process. Some applicants are rejected because they are judged by the agency to have "limited capacity for parenthood," because of "immaturity" or psychosocial deficiencies. These are, of course, as real and as important as specific requirements of age, health, and income. Having decided, however, that the applicants do not meet agency standards in these regards, the agency must interpret this decision to the client. The problem has not been entirely resolved. Aronson notes that the key to the approach "lies in awareness of the fact that telling the whole truth may, instead of being a virtue, actually be an act of the crassest cruelty and may throw into disequilibrium a situation which has some stability. . . . [Under] these circumstances we must not only permit but encourage rationalization" [9, pp. 23, 33] by which the applicants can explain acceptably, to themselves, the agency's rejection. The principle dictates that the agency leave helpful psychic defenses intact. Accordingly, Brown suggests that the agency interpret rejection so as to direct the applicants' hostility toward the agency rather than against each other. [31, p. 160] It is helpful to stress the acceptability of the applicants as individuals despite the fact that the agency questions their acceptability for a particular social role—that of parenthood. At the same time, the agency can point to their competence in many other social roles—as husband or wife, as employee, as friend. The negatives which have prompted the agency's decision are related to one particular sector of their lives and there is no imputation of their adequacy in terms of other roles.

Rejection of an application may be easier if the agency shares some of its doubts and misgivings with the couple as they arise. [128] The final decision is then something for which they have been partially prepared.

International Adoptions

In response to a humanitarian concern for the many children abroad who were displaced, abandoned, or orphaned as a result of postwar upheaval and because there were, for a time, more adoptive applicants than adoptive infants available in this country, an increased interest has developed in the adoption of foreign children. Such interest was stimulated also by the mobility of American families, many of whom lived abroad for extended periods with the Armed Forces or in the employ of foreign branches of American concerns.

There are several social agencies with international affiliates that handle such adoptions. The principal officially recognized agency is International Social Service (ISS), a voluntary nonsectarian social welfare agency with headquarters in Geneva, Switzerland. It has branches in many countries, the American branch of ISS having been established about forty years ago. Each of the branches is staffed and supported by the country in which it is located.

Before a child is moved for adoption from his country of origin, ISS establishes the fact that the child is "an orphan or deprived of normal family life and that there is no prospect for him to be adopted unless he comes to the United States." [104, p. 4] The preadoption requirements of the state of the child's proposed residence must be met and assurance received from an "appropriate social welfare agency that the social investigations have been satisfactorily completed in both countries, that the prospective adoptive home is recommended, and that the child has been found suitable for adoption" before the U.S. Immigration and Naturalization Service will process the child's immigration. [104, p. 4]

This would suggest that the international adoption program has reasonable built-in safeguards, that it is not likely to be exploited as a procedure to "dump" foreign children, and that it offers the American child seeking adoption only limited competition.

Currently intercountry adoptions are an additional resource for meeting the demands of adoptive parents. As Adams notes in reviewing intercountry adoption statistics, "With the developing shortage of 'adoptable' white infants in the United States, American parents are beginning to look overseas for children." [3, p. 218] In 1970 about 2400 such children were admitted for adoption.

The new language that must be learned, the new foods to which the child must become accustomed, the new customs and new ways that must be learned—all complicate the process of adjustment for the adopted foreign child. In addition, most of these children are older, so that they face the general problems that older children encounter in becoming truly integrated into a new family. Despite this combination of problems, and despite greatly deprived early developmental experiences faced by these children, many of whom were abandoned, follow-up studies reveal good adjustment to American homes and adoption success. [42; 59; 94; 248; 254]

Despite the existence of international agencies, such adoptions are hampered by the fact that there are differences in the adoption laws of various countries. As a consequence, the first World Congress on Adoption and Foster Placement held in Italy in 1971 petitioned the United Nations to convene an international conference for the purpose of establishing a World Convention on Adoption Law and formulating a uniform code.

Legal Aspects of Adoption

Adoption is regulated by state law. [144]   As a consequence, there is considerable variation from state to state in the legal procedure and philosophy associated with adoption. Although a national adoption law has been proposed, there is little active support for it.

Legal procedure for adoption is initiated by filing a court petition. The courts responsible for handling adoption proceedings might be the probate court in one state, the juvenile court in another, and the superior court in still another. The petition, generally filed in the county in which the adoptive parents live, includes the pertinent information regarding the child, the adoptive parents, and the biological parents. Consent to adoption must be obtained from the biological parents. In many instances the agency has obtained guardianship of the child, and it is the agency that gives consent to adoption. In other instances, it has obtained a signed "surrender" of the child by the biological parents, which authorizes the agency to place the child for adoption. But parental surrender or relinquishment of the child is more ambiguous than clear termination of parental rights through judicial action. "Only with such judicial termination is there a complete divestment of all legal rights, privileges, duties, and obligations of the parent and the child with respect to each other." [245, p. 10]   When the child is fourteen years of age—in some states, as young as ten years of age—his consent to adoption is also required.

The petition having been filed, a notice of proceeding is given to alert those people affected by the adoption. An official investigation of the circumstances regarding the adoption is then ordered by the court and is usually carried out by the public welfare agencies. When the child has been placed by an agency, the agency adoption study is the relevant material offered the court. The investigating agency makes a recommendation to the court based on the information it has obtained.

A hearing is then held, usually in a closed court, at which time the court meets with the adoptive parents, the child, and any witnesses it deems should be heard. The court then makes a decision based on material made available during the hearing and on the report from the agency authorized to study the adoption. The decision is made in terms of the best interests of the child. The adoption petition may be approved or denied, or decision may be deferred to some later date.

This order is usually temporary or interlocutory. The final order will not be granted until after the passage of some time, six months to a year. During this time, the child will be living in the home of the adoptive parents but will not yet legally belong to them. At the end of the trial period, the final order for adoption is approved. Before issuing the final order, the court generally asks for a recommendation from the supervising agency. Once the final decree has been issued, there is the possibility of annulment, but this is rare: the child is the legal child of the adoptive parents.

In many states there is no provision for an interlocutory order; but it is necessary for the child to have lived in the home of the petitioner for some time, usually six months to a year, before a petition for adoption can be initiated. Because, in such instances, the investigations are made after the child has been living with the adoptive couple for some time, the court is likely to decide adversely only in unequivocally disadvantageous situations. Registration with a public welfare agency *before* taking a child into the home, as is currently required by some states, permits the agency to make an investigation of the desirability of the home before such a relationship is established.

The effect of a final decree is to establish a parent-child relationship between the petitioner and the adopted child and to terminate all relationships between the child and the biological parents. When the final adoption order is granted, the child legally assumes the surname of his adoptive parents. A new birth certificate may be issued in this new name and the record of the adoptive proceedings is sealed.

For the most part, with the final decree the legal rights, duties, privileges, and obligations of the biological parents and child exist between the adoptive parents and child. But, although the child may inherit from his adoptive parents, he does not, if he is an alien, gain their citizenship. This has created a special problem in international adoptions, requiring special legislation by Congress to provide for the issuance of nonquota visas to permit "eligible" foreign children to come to the United States for adoption even though the immigration quota of their native country is oversubscribed.

When the child and the adoptive parents are not residents of the same state, the petition for adoption may be initiated in the state where the child lives, but it is more desirable if the action is initiated in the state in which the adoptive parents reside. This expedites the social study of the adoptive applicants, upon which rests the decision of the court to grant or deny the petition. However, bringing the child into the state in which the adoptive parents reside also presents a problem. Most states require the permission of the state department of public welfare before a child is permitted to enter the state for the purpose of adoption. This is to protect the state from the necessity of supporting a dependent child if the adoption is not consummated.

Although some thirty states have laws making independent placement by an intermediary a punishable offense, in most of these states the mother herself is permitted to place the child. Only Connecticut and Delaware require that "no petition for [nonrelative] adoption may be presented unless the child has been placed for adoption by an authorized agency." [171, p. 64]

All states have provisions for licensing agencies which are granted authority to place children for adoption. Generally, the state department of public welfare sets the minimum standards required for obtaining such a license and is given the responsibility of seeing to it that licensed agencies operate in accordance with these standards.

The Children's Bureau suggests that the parental rights of the biological parents be terminated through consent or judicial decree with proper due process, that the child be placed through a social agency, and that some time elapse between placement and final petition for adoption. Judicial decision should take into consideration the recommendations of the social agency based on its study of the home, and should provide confidentiality through issuance of a new certificate following adoption and sealing of the adoptive records. The recommendation for exclusive control of adoption by a social agency is perhaps the most controversial. The public is not yet convinced that agency placement is clearly more advantageous to the child than independent and/or third-party placements.

Independent Adoptions

The adoption process outlined above describes only a limited number of the nonrelated adoptive placements consummated each year. Sizable proportions of nonrelated adoptive placements are achieved each year outside this route. These are the independent adoptions. In 1971, for instance, of the total of about 83,000 children adopted by unrelated persons, 65,000 (79 percent) were placed by social agencies; 17,000 (21 percent) were placed independently. [244]   There has been a steady change in the last twenty-five years in the proportion of children placed through agencies and those placed independently with unrelated persons. In 1944, of the 26,000 adoptive children placed, 12,700 (49 percent) were placed through agencies, while 13,300 (51 percent) were placed

independently. Despite the steady change in favor of the agency placement, the fact that in 1971 some 21 percent of the children placed for
adoption with unrelated persons were placed independently indicates
that this is still an important problem for the adoption field.

The term *independent adoption* applies to a number of different
procedures. The natural parents may make their own contact with a
person whom they know, through one source or another, is desirous of
adopting a child. Or a doctor or lawyer may know of parents unable, or
unwilling, to care for a child, and a childless couple seeking a child, and
may act as the intermediary. This is sometimes termed the *gray market*
in adoptions. [247]   A third kind of independent placement involves
an actual business transaction. In this case, a "black marketeer" under-
takes to sell a baby to a couple eager to adopt. No statistics are available
that indicate how many of the independent placements are of one type or
another.

Independent placement involves dangers and disadvantages to the
child, the adoptive parents, the biological parents, and ultimately to the
community.

As was noted above in the section concerned with a discussion of
child-applicant ratios, the gray and black markets, after a period of
quiescence, began to emerge, once again, as a problem in the early
1970's. This makes relevant a brief review of the possible dangers of
such procedures.

The rights of the child to a good home are not as securely guaranteed
in independent placement. The gray market and the black market are
oriented to the needs and desires of the adoptive couple rather than to
the needs of the child. The agency makes the best effort, however falli-
ble, to find a good set of parents for the child. The couple with whom
the child is independently placed has been subject to no assessment
process. The only eligibility requirement, in many instances, is ability
to pay, which bears little direct relationship to capacity for parenthood
and is no guarantee of an emotionally healthy environment for the child.

It might seem, from the adoptive parents' point of view, that there
are obvious advantages in independent adoption—no "red tape," no
elaborate interviews, no need to meet what are perceived as restrictive
agency eligibility requirements, no need to satisfy a social worker of
their capacity for parenthood. Yet the seeming advantages may, in fact,
be disadvantages. Becoming a parent is not an unmitigated pleasure nor
is the desire for parenthood unequivocal. The agency's interviews with
prospective adoptive parents are designed as much to help the applicants
clarify for themselves their decision about parenthood as it is to satisfy
the agency that their home will be a good one for a child. Frequently,
on the basis of the exploration in which the agency procedure involves
the adoptive couple, they decide they do not really want to adopt a baby.

The independent adoption procedure gives the couple no explicit opportunity to discuss, with someone experienced in such matters, the problems involved in adoption, the burdens they are undertaking, and the changes this will occasion in their lives—problems, burdens, and changes they may choose not to accept once they are made evident.

The supposed advantages of getting a child without agency entanglements is also a disadvantage during the period between placement and final adoption. The adoptive parents are, in some respects, different from biological parents, and there are many unique aspects in the adopted child–adopted parent relationship. The independent adopter's freedom from agency entanglements also means "freedom" from the opportunity of agency help in dealing with the social and emotional consequences of adoption—the problems attendant upon the assumption of this unique role.

Assurance of confidentiality of the adoption may be less firm in independent adoptions than in agency adoptions. Contact between natural parents and adoptive parents, which is deliberately broken in agency adoption, is a greater possibility in the independent adoption. When the natural parents themselves have arranged for placement, they know the identity and, in all likelihood, the whereabouts of the adopters. In adoptions through the gray or black market, the identity of the adoptive parents may be kept secret but the degree to which such secrets are maintained depends on the intermediary's moral and ethical standards. If babies are sold for a price, might not the identity of the adopting parents be sold for a price?

Social agency adoption procedures generally involve the agency's obtaining clear title to the child so it is in a position to assure the prospective adoptive parents that there will be no difficulty in their legal title to the child. Some independent placements occasion great anxiety for the adoptive couple because they may not be sure that the natural parents will consent to adoption.

Finally, because in some independent placements the sole concern is providing the adoptive parents with a child at a price, any information that is likely to increase the adoptive parents' hesitancy to accept the child may be falsified.

Independent placements involve disadvantages for the unmarried mother as well. Instead of being helped to arrive at her own decision regarding disposition of the child, she is pressured to make one decision —to surrender the child for adoption. She is also deprived of help with the personal and/or social difficulties which might be related to the out-of-wedlock pregnancy. Nor is there, of course, any effort made either to contact or to help the father.

An extensive investigation of black market adoptions, undertaken in 1955 by the Kefauver Subcommittee to Investigate Juvenile Delinquency, revealed some of the dangers involved for the child, the biological parents, the adoptive parents, and the community. [246] The

testimony given by one couple who had obtained a baby through a
Canadian black market operator (previously convicted of forgery) is
reflected in the Committee's report:

> Mr. and Mrs. W. were instructed by a friend, who had already
> gone through the procedure of adopting a child from Mr. B., to call
> Mr. B. During this call, Mr. B. told them he had a child available
> for them and should fly to Montreal as soon as possible. The
> price for this child would be $2100. Within the next day they flew
> to Montreal and upon their arrival, Mr. B. accompanied them
> to a house on the outskirts of Montreal. . . .
>
> Mr. and Mrs. W. were able to select a child that appealed to
> them from a group of five or six which were at that time in his house.
> The selection was done just on the appeal, the emotional appeal
> that the child made upon them. They selected a little girl who
> was just then about five days old. After their selection, the choice
> of this little girl, they returned to Mr. B.'s office, where they paid
> him in United States currency the sum of $2100.
>
> Mr. B. then took Mr. and Mrs. W. to the office of the
> registrar of births where, while Mrs. W. was in an outer room,
> Mr. W. was instructed by Mr. B. to give specific information to
> the registrar as though actually his wife had given birth to that
> baby girl.
>
> B. assured them that this copy of the registration of birth was, in
> effect, the final paper that they would have received if they had
> gone through the Canadian Social Welfare Court. . . .
>
> During the summer of the same year Mrs. W. called Mr. B.
> and said she was living in fear because she knew that the paper
> she had in her possession was a falsified document.
>
> She later returned to Montreal and tried to thresh the matter out
> with Mr. B.: this time he very crassly and cruelly told her that if
> she wasn't satisfied with the arrangements she should return
> the child, and he would return the money—much like you would
> ask for a refund.
>
> Of course, this was impossible for the W.'s to do after having
> had the child in their home for a period of three or four months.
> [246, pp. 59–60].

The danger for the adoptive parent lies in the illegality of the birth
record and the tremendous anxiety and uncertainty this occasions; the
danger for the child lies in the process of selection of adoptive parents,
the criterion for which, in this instance, was $2100.

Social workers point out that providing families for parentless children is too important to the community to be left unregulated. Social
agencies are keenly aware of the dangers cited. Their procedures are

designed to protect the child so that he gets the best possible home and the best possible care while waiting for a home. They are also designed to protect the adoptive parents by freely disclosing any of the child's shortcomings, by assuring confidentiality, by making certain of the legal availability of a child, by helping them to make a reasoned decision regarding adoption, and to resolve those problems that might endanger the adoption. They are also designed to protect the unmarried mother by giving her support, care, and protection during her pregnancy, helping her come to a firm decision regarding disposition of the baby, and helping her with those problems that may have led to her pregnancy. In addition, agency adoptions offer the following advantages:

1. A professional qualified staff with a special knowledge of adoption problems.
2. A pool of adoptive homes from which to select the one that meets the needs of a particular child.
3. Consultants—psychiatrists, psychologists, geneticists, pediatricians—who aid the agency staff in dealing with special problems.
4. Uniform records of all transactions in line with the agency's accountability to the community.
5. Alternative resources—foster homes, institutions, and so on—are available to care for the child while he is awaiting adoption or if he proves to be unplaceable.

And only the social agency discharges another important community function: it actively seeks to find homes for children who are hard to place.

Evaluation

Many studies have attempted to answer questions regarding the "success" of adoptive placements. Available studies have been summarized in Table 11–2.* Only those studies are included in which definite information was presented regarding sources of data and criteria of outcome and in which some attempt was made at statistical analysis of data. The studies cited vary in the level of methodological precision with which they were conducted, in the nature and detail of data obtained, in the criteria of outcome employed, in the procedure used in making judgments of outcome, and in the statistical rigor with which data were analyzed. The study population of the research cited in Table 11–2 is

---

* Bibliographical citations provide information about the source of the material included in Table 11–2 for the convenience of those readers interested in reviewing the studies directly.

TABLE 11-2. Adoptive Outcome Studies

Study and Date	Size of Study Group and Lapse of Time Between Placement and Study	Outcome		Data Used for Follow-up Assessment	Auspices
		Outcome Criteria for Categorization	Number and Percentages		
Van Theis (1924)	235 (adults) 12–18 years after placement	"Capable" "Incapable"	207 (88.1%) 28 (11.9%)	Interviews with adoptive children, adoptive parents, and "other persons" by project interviewer	Agency
Morrison (1950)	24 (children) 10–17 years after placement	"Getting along satisfactorily" "Unsatisfactory adjustment"	18 (75%) 6 (25%)	Interview with adoptive parents by agency workers	Agency
Brenner (1951)	50 (families) median of 4.4 years after placement	"Successful" "Fairly successful" "Unsuccessful"	26 (52%) 18 (36%) 6 (12%)	Observation of children in home, interviews with adoptive mothers by agency workers, psychological tests of children	Agency
Neiden (1951)	138 (adults) 15–20 years after placement	"Very good" "Good" "Indifferent" "Bad"	35 (25%) 62 (45%) 29 (21%) 12 (9%)	Records and interviews with adoptive parents by agency social workers	Agency
Armatruda (1951)	100 (children) at time of placement	"Good" "Questionable" "Poor"	76 (76%) 16 (16%) 8 (8%)	Agency study of adoptive home, study of child by Yale development clinic	Agency

Study and Date	Size of Study Group and Lapse of Time Between Placement and Study	Outcome		Data Used for Follow-up Assessment	Auspices
		Number and Percentages	Outcome Criteria for Categorization		
Armatruda (1951)	100 (children) at time of placement	46 (46%) 26 (26%) 28 (28%)	"Good" "Questionable" "Poor"	Agency study of adoptive home, study of child by Yale development clinic	Independent
Fairwether (1952)	18 (children) 3–4 years after placement	18 (100%)	"Good"	Interviews with adoptive mothers by agency workers, psychological tests of children	Agency
Edwards (1954)	79 (children) 5 years after placement	69 (87%) 9 (12%) 1 (1%)	"Very happy" "Some problems" "Serious problems"	Information not available	Agency
National Association for Mental Health, England (Estimated 1954)	163 (children) minimum of 2 years after placement	142 (87.1%) 21 (12.9%)	"Satisfactory" "Unsatisfactory"	Agency records	Agency
Davis and Douck (1955)	396 (children) 1 year after placement	371 (93.7%) 25 (6.3%)	Not removed Removed	Agency records	Agency
Fradkin and Krugman (1956)	37 (children) during first year after placement	27 (73%) 6 (16%) 4 (11%)	"Good" "Intermediate" "Poor"	Ongoing contact with parents during first year of supervision, tests of infant	Agency

TABLE 11-2. Adoptive Outcome Studies—(Cont.)

Study and Date	Size of Study Group and Lapse of Time Between Placement and Study	Outcome		Data Used for Follow-up Assessment	Auspices
		Number and Percentages	Outcome Criteria for Categorization		
Witmer et al. (1956–57)	484 (children) most 9 years after placement	324 (67%) 39 (8%) 121 (25%)	"Excellent to fair" "Not definitely unsatisfactory" "Definitely unsatisfactory"	Interviews with parents and teachers by project interviewers, psychological tests of children	Independent
McWhinnie (1967)	52 (adults) 16–66 years after placement	21 (40.5%) 21 (40.5%) 10 (9%)	"Good" and "Fairly good" "Adjustment in all areas" "Reasonable adjustment in some fundamental areas" "Adjustment poor in many areas"	Interviews with adoptive children as adults	Independent
Ripple (1968)	160 (children) 9–10 years after placement	75 (47%) 47 (29%) 38 (24%)	"Within the normal range" "Some problems in adjustment" "Serious emotional or behavioral problems"	Agency records, interviews with father, mother, child	Agency
Kornitzer (1968)	233 children and adults (time lapse varied)	96 (41.2%) 85 (36.5%) 45 (19.3%) 7 (3.0%)	"Success" "Average" "Problems" "Bad"	Interviews with mother by researcher, some fathers interviewed	Agency and independent

Study and Date	Size of Study Group and Lapse of Time Between Placement and Study	Outcome		Data Used for Follow-up Assessment	Auspices
		Number and Percentages	Outcome Criteria for Categorization		
Lawder et al. (1969)	200 (families) 8–15 years after placement	29 (14%) 98 (49%) 53 (27%) 20 (10%)	"Superior" "Good" "Fair" "Poor"	Interviews with fathers and mothers together and alone	Agency
Jaffee and Fanshel (1970)	100 (adults) 20–30 years after placement	33 (33%) 34 (34%) 33 (33%)	"Low problems" "Middle range" "High problems"	Interviews with father and mother separately, questionnaire completed independently by parents	Agency
Bohman (1970)	122 (children) 10–11 years after placement	34 (28%) 28 (23%) 33 (27%) 25 (20%) 2 (2%)	"No symptoms" "Slight symptoms" "Moderate symptoms" "Problem child" "Requiring institutional care"	Interviewed father and mother together and alone	Agency
Seglow et al. (1972)	145 (children) 9 years after placement	19 (82%) 23 (16%) 3 (2%)	"Very well" "Not well adjusted" "Disturbed"	Interviews with adoptive mothers, some adoptive fathers	Agency

almost exclusively that of white, nonhandicapped, infant adoptive placements.

The recapitulation (Table 11–3) indicates that 65 percent of the adoptions were judged unequivocally successful; an additional 18 percent were judged to be of fair, moderate, or average success; 17 percent were judged to be failures. It would seem, therefore, that adoptions are most frequently successful.

TABLE 11–3. Recapitulation of Adoptive Outcome Studies

Outcome	Number	Percent
UNEQUIVOCALLY SUCCESSFUL "Satisfactory" "Very good" "Good" "Success" "Superior" "Low problems" "No symptoms or slight symptoms" "Excellent to fair" "Within normal range" "Very well adjusted"	1583	65
INTERMEDIATE SUCCESS "Not definitely unsatisfactory" "Fairly successful" "Indifferent" "Questionable" "Some problems" "Intermediate" "Average" "Moderate symptoms" "Not well adjusted"	439	18
UNSUCCESSFUL "Unsatisfactory" "Poor," "low" "Problematic" "Unsuccessful" "Incapable" "High problems" "Problem child" "Disturbed"	418	17
Total	2440	100.0

But how do agency placements compare with independent placements? And how does the success of adoptive families compare with the success of biofamilies? In the absence of normative data regarding the "success" rate of biofamilies, the latter question is impossible to answer at this time. The material in Table 11–2, however, permits some tentative answers to the first question.

Only Witmer's study is exclusively concerned with nonagency placements, though the studies by Armatruda and by Kornitzer offer some additional material. Armatruda's study, although frequently cited to show the superiority of agency placements, is not a true follow-up study because assessment of the home was made at the time of placement. Kornitzer's study shows that only 14.4 percent of agency placements, but 25.6 percent of "third-party and direct placements," were categorized as problems or failures. [135, p. 159] Witmer's study shows a failure rate of 25 percent for nonagency adoptions.

If the data from Witmer's study, and those from the Kornitzer and Armatruda studies concerning children independently placed, are deleted from Table 11–2, the failure rate for agency placements become 14.8 percent—considerably lower than the 25 percent failure rate in Witmer's study and the 25.6 percent failure rate of independent placements in Kornitzer's study. Any conclusions must remain tentative because of the differing levels of validity of the data used in the different studies. Justifying the cautionary note is the fact that the information in Table 11–6 indicates that adoptive children who are referred for psychiatric treatment are just as likely to have been placed through a social agency as to have been independently placed.

Another set of outcome studies might be cited as relevant to the question of evaluation of adoptive outcome. These studies of adoption outcome employ a standard, objective criterion for identifying failure: removal of the child from the home at any time between placement and legal adoption (in most states, a year). Table 11–4 recapitulates the results of these studies. Most of the follow-up adoption studies cited earlier are concerned with family functioning five or ten years after placement, by which time the validity of the agency's decision to place a child in the home cannot be clearly distinguished from the many intervening variables that may have affected the outcome. Checking the placement within the one-year period is a better test of the agency's decision.

Except for Thomas' study (which focused on children with special needs) most of the studies included only white, nonhandicapped children who were infants at time of placement. All the children were placed through social agencies. Of approximately 35,000 placements, only 673, or 1.9 percent, were failures (*i.e.*, the child was removed from the home during the period between placement and final legal adoption). It might be noted that many of the children listed in these studies who were removed were subsequently successfully placed in other adoptive homes.

Another series of outcome studies (summarized in Table 11–5) focus on children who "were hard to place" or, more euphemistically, "chil-

TABLE 11-4. Summary of Studies Relating to Failed Adoptive Placements

Study	Agency Auspices	Period Covered by Study	Children Placed	Children Returned to Agency	Failure Rate
Davis and Douck [53]	Public	3 years (1951–53)	396	25	6.3%
Calif. Citizens' Adoptions Comm. [32]	Public-voluntary	1 year (1962)	4470	85	1.9%
Kornitzer and Rowe [136]	Voluntary	1 year (1966)	9614	109	1.1%
Edmonton, Canada [56]	Public	2 years (1967–68)	3086	43	1.4%
Kornitzer [135]	Public-voluntary	Unclear	664	15	2.2%
L.A. County Dept. Adoption [149]	Public	2 years (1965–66)	4910	129	2.6%
Lefkowitz [145]	Voluntary	5 years (1965–69)	8040	82	1.0%
Kadushin and Seidl [126]	Public	8 years (1960–68)	2945	85	2.8%
Goldring and Tutleman [91]	Public	1 year (1968–69)	2384	75	3.1%
Thomas [236]	Voluntary	4 years (1967–70)	735	25	3.4%
TOTAL			35,244	673	1.9%

dren with special needs"—older children, handicapped children, non-white children, and foreign-born children. All placements were made by social agencies.

Table 11–5 indicates that even problem placements are likely to be successful. The general conclusion, then, which can be derived from the studies summarized in Tables 11–2, 11–3, 11–4, and 11–5 is that most adoptions turn out well, and adoptions under agency auspices are somewhat more likely than independent adoptions to succeed.

Emotional Disturbance in Adopted Children

Another series of studies focuses on the frequency of referral of adopted children to guidance clinics or psychiatric services. A higher

TABLE 11-5. Adoptive Outcome Studies of Hard-to-Place Children

Study and Date	Nature of Placement Difficulty	Size of Study Group and Lapse of Time Between Placement and Study	Outcome		Data Used for Follow-up Assessment
			Number and Percentages	Outcome Criteria for Categorization	
Graham (1957)	Foreign-born children (transracial adoption)	50 children (2–10 years after placement)	32 (64%) 13 (26%) 5 (10%)	"Satisfactory positive adjustment" "Only fair" "Poor or very poor adjustment"	Interviews with parents and teachers
Rathbun et al. (1964)	Foreign-born children (transracial adoption)	33 children (6 years after placement)	5 (15%) 16 (49%) 10 (30%) 2 (6%)	"Superior" "Adequate" "Problematic" "Disturbed"	Joint interviews with parents
Franklin-Massarik (1969)	Moderate or severe handicap	71 children (4–12 years after placement)	26 (37%) 29 (41%) 16 (22%)	"Excellent" "Good" "Doubtful"	Joint interviews with parents, unstructured observation of child

TABLE 11–5. Adoptive Outcome Studies of Hard-to-Place Children—(Cont.)

Study and Date	Nature of Placement Difficulty	Size of Study Group and Lapse of Time Between Placement and Study	Outcome		Data Used for Follow-up Assessment
			Number and Percentages	Outcome Criteria for Categorization	
Kadushin (1970)	Older—age 5–12 at placement	91 children (4–10 years after placement)	67 (73%) 8 (9%) 18 (16%)	"High ratio of parental satisfactions to dissatisfactions" "Balance between satisfactions-dissatisfactions" "Low ratio of satisfactions to dissatisfactions"	Joint interviews with parents, questionnaire responses
Raynor (1970)	Nonwhite children	51 children (1–4 years after placement)	43 (83%) 5 (10%) 3 (6%)	"Very good" "Adequate" "Problematic"	Structured joint interview with parents
Zastrow (1971)	Nonwhite children (transracial adoption)	44 children (1–6 years after placement)	36 (88%) 5 (11%) 1 (1%)	"Extremely satisfying" "More satisfying than dissatisfying" "Half and half"	Interview with parents
Fanshel (1972)	Nonwhite children (transracial adoption)	97 children (starting with 1st year after placement, repeated annual interviews for 5 years)	51 (53%) 24 (25%) 10 (10%) 11 (11%)	"Problem-free" "Adequate" "Adequate but guarded" "Poor"	Joint interviews with parents, interviews with father-mother alone (repeated over 5-year period)

574

rate of referral for emotionally disturbed behavior among adopted children would suggest that child rearing is less successful in the adoptive family than in the biofamily. Table 11–6 lists the relevant studies and summarizes the findings.

The research data show that 4.4 percent of the patients at the facilities studied were nonrelative adoptees. Since it is estimated that only about 1 percent of all children are nonrelative adoptees, it would appear that such children are clearly overrepresented in the clinic population. The rate is higher than the rate for children from biofamilies. It may, however, be lower than that which we have a right to expect given the insults to psychic health which the adoptive family has encountered. As Fanshel says, "The controversy revolves around the question whether adoptive children and natural-born children have the same odds working for them with respect to the opportunity to develop stable personalities and successful life adjustments."

It is argued, in explanation, that the adoptive family population is more apt to seek professional help for solving problems. Having resorted to an agency for adoption, they are more likely than other families to resort to agencies again. But Schechter, in his second study, sought to test this theory by examining the tendency of adoptive couples to use pediatric clinics; he concluded that adoptive parents were no more "agency-prone" than bioparents. [204]

Some specific characteristics of the adoptive family may create special stresses for the adoptive child. Most adoptive parents receive their first child in their early thirties, whereas most biological parents have their first child in their early twenties. Patterns of marital interaction and family ritual may have become less flexible with time and may be difficult to change in response to the incorporation of a child in the family system. The adoptive child is more apt to be a first child of older parents and more likely to be an only child. Furthermore, adoption is still an atypical procedure for achieving parenthood and the family may react to the stress of minority-group status.

The child must deal with the "rejection" by his biological parents, some "genealogical bewilderment" over origin, and the problem of fusing "good" and "bad" parental images. Adoptive parents must resolve their feelings about infertility and fear of competition from the child's biological parents. Further, however short the period between birth and adoption, every adoptive child faces some experience of early separation and some discontinuity in mothering. All these factors impose possible stresses on the adoptive family.

Research suggests that congenital factors may contribute to the problem. Most adopted children are born out of wedlock to young women for whom this is the first pregnancy. Such a pregnancy is apt to be highly stressful and some of the mother's tension and anxiety might adversely affect the fetus. Furthermore, such mothers are apt to get less

TABLE 11-6. Studies of Adopted Children Referred for Psychiatric Treatment

Study	Total Number in Study Group	Number of Adoptees in Study Group	Percent of Adoptive Children Referred for Service	Percent of Referred Adoptees Placed by Agency	Adoption Status—Relative or Nonrelative
Stonesifer (1942)	2000	48	2.4%	—	Both
Holman (1953)	100	7	7.0%	—	Nonrelative
Pringle (1961)	2593	210	8.3%	—	Both
National Association of Mental Health, England (1954)	1152	17	1.5%	—	Both
Schechter (1962)	120	16	13.3%	50% [e]	Nonrelative
Toussieng (1962)	357	39	10.9%	51%	Nonrelative
Humphrey and Ounsted (1963)	2700	80	2.9%	50%	Nonrelative
Sweeny (1963)	292	21	7.2%	—	Nonrelative
Goodman (1963)	593	14	2.4%	50%	Nonrelative
Ketchum (1964)	196	20	10.7%	"Most often"	Both

Study	Total Number in Study Group	Number of Adoptees in Study Group	Percent of Adoptive Children Referred for Service	Percent of Referred Adoptees Placed by Agency	Adoption Status—Relative or Nonrelative
Schechter (1964)	—	159 [c] (41 adults, 118 children)	6.6% [d] (average from three psychiatric facilities)	46%	Nonrelative
Borgatta-Fanshel (1964)	2281	123	5.5%	—	Nonrelative
Menlove (1965)	1314	59	4.6%	—	Nonrelative
Simon-Senturia (1966)	1371	35 [b] (29 children, 6 adults)	2.6%	—	Nonrelative
Kirk, et al. (1966) [a]	2117	132	6.2%	—	Both
Jameson (1967)	390	42	10.8%	55%	Nonrelative
Reece-Levin (1968)	1017	30	2.95%	56%	Nonrelative
Work-Anderson (1971)	1282 (outpatients) 363 (inpatients)	56 34	4.3% 9.3%	— —	— —

[a] The table includes only those tabulations from Kirk's study that were presented by the author as having high or medium reliability. [See Kirk, Jonassohn, and Fish, 133, Table 5, p. 297]

[b] This figure includes 29 children and 6 adults.

[c] This figure includes 118 children and 41 adults.

[d] This percentage represents an average from three psychiatric facilities.

[e] These data were given in the 1964 study.

TABLE 11-6.   Recapitulation

Study	Total Number in Study Group	Number of Adoptees in Study Group	Percent of Adoptive Children Referred for Service	Percent of Referred Adoptees Placed by Agency
Total relative and nonrelative adoptions (excluding Schechter, 1964)	20,238	983	4.8%	—
Total non-relative adoptions	10,535	466	4.4%	51%

adequate nutritional and medical care during pregnancy and less emotional support. The higher mortality rate, higher congenital anomaly rate, and lower birth weight associated with such pregnancies cited in Chapter 10 is confirmation of the stressful context of such a pregnancy for the child. [158]   One study of the patients at a pediatric hospital unit showed that a disproportionate percentage of adopted children had "minimal brain damage." A review of the developmental records led to the conclusion that "indifferent prenatal medical care may have been crucial in determining brain injury." [129, p. 29]   Electroencephalographs of adopted and nonadopted children suggest that "adopted children as a group, due to various biosocial deprivation and insults, sustain a high percentage of neurological damage." [150, p. 4]   This may be related to the finding, confirmed by a number of different studies, that when adopted children are disturbed, they are more apt to demonstrate aggressive, hostile, hyperactive behavior than other kinds of disturbed behavior.

The emphasis that we have placed on the emotional difficulties of adoptive children requires some correction in perspective. Despite the overrepresentation of adopted children in psychiatric facilities, for whatever explainable reasons, the fact of the matter is that relatively few adopted children receive treatment for emotional disturbance. After reviewing the relevant material, Kadushin notes that about 98 percent of the adopted children in the community apparently have never been referred for psychiatric treatment. [120; 121]   As Humphrey notes, "Since only a small proportion of adoptive parents ever seek psychiatric advice, it seems that most adoptions work out happily for both parents and children. . . ." [109, p. 607]

Another series of studies can be cited which confirms this conclusion and further tends to confirm that emotional disturbance in adopted children is the exception rather than the rule. The studies listed in Table 11–6 are studies of selected samples of adopted children identified by their referral to a psychiatric facility. Comparisons of a random sampling of adopted children with a random sampling of a matched group of nonadopted peers reveal—with a few exceptions—that adopted children develop as healthfully, physically and emotionally, as their nonadopted peers.

One of the earliest studies, that by Nemovicher, is one of the few exceptions: in comparing thirty adopted children with thirty nonadopted classmates he found that adoptive children were apt to be significantly more "hostile," "fearful," and "tense." [174]

Witmer compared 448 adopted children with a matched group of nonadopted peers on the bases of such items as the California Test of Personality, sociometric measures, school achievement tests, and teacher observation of behavior. When those adopted children who had been older when placed were eliminated from the analysis, "all but one of the differences between adopted and [nonadopted] control children disappeared. The one difference that remained was in aggressive maladjustment, the adopted children having a slightly higher average score than their controls." [259, p. 246] Matching in this study, as in other studies to be cited, was in terms of age, sex, class grade, and intelligence level of the two sets of children. Hoopes et al. compared one hundred adopted children with a matched control group of one hundred nonadopted children using teachers' rating, the California Test of Mental Maturity, the California Test of Personality, and the Thematic Apperception Test. "There was no evidence of greater emotional disturbance or psychopathology in the sample of one hundred adopted children than in the control group of children living with their natural parents." [106, p. 50]

Mikawa compared twenty adopted children with twenty matched nonadopted children on the basis of a Sense of Attitude Test, Anxiety Scales, Thematic Apperception Tests, and observer rating of behavior. "No significant differences were found between the adopted and nonadopted group on any of the measures used." [165, p. 277]

Bohman compared 168 Swedish adopted children with a group of 222 nonadopted peers. Information was obtained from school performance and health records, teachers' reports, and parents. There was a statistically significant difference between the adopted boys and the nonadopted boys in terms of school adjustment and manifestation of nervous symptoms, but no significant level of difference between adopted and nonadopted girls. [18, pp. 140–41]

The Perinatal Mortality Survey in England provided an opportunity for a nationwide comparison of adopted children with other peers. Information was gathered on every baby born in England, Scotland, and Wales during the week of March 3–9, 1958. These 17,000 children were subsequently followed up for school testing, health testing, teacher reports, and parental interviews. By the time the children were seven years old, about 180 had been adopted by nonrelatives.

Analysis of available data in a study by Seglow, Pringle, and Wedge indicates that the adopted children were just as healthy as the non-adopted children living with their biological parents. [212] There was no difference between the two groups of children in terms of school achievement and attainment or in terms of behavior and adjustment in school. [212, p. 75] However, when the records of adopted children were sorted by sex, a larger percentage of adopted boys proved to be "maladjusted" than their nonadopted peers; the percentage of "maladjusted" adopted girls was lower than the percentage of nonadopted maladjusted girls.

Elonen, reporting on a longitudinal study of adopted children, concludes that "the total adopted group compares closely with a comparable nonadopted living with their natural families" and that "being adopted is not a causative factor *per se* in the emotional problems of adopted children." [62, pp. 76, 78]

Bratfos, comparing the difficulties manifested by 250 Norwegian adopted children with those of the general population as reflected in national statistics, concludes: "The incidence of mental deficiency, schizophrenia, and minor mental disorders in persons who have grown up in adoption houses does not appear to deviate to any great extent from what can be expected in a population, neither is crime more prevalent." [23, p. 383]

Thus, though adopted children are significantly overrepresented in the clientele of psychiatric facilities and more frequently manifest aggressive behavior, adopted children are, on the whole, very similar to their nonadopted peers in terms of development and adjustment. This is a tribute to the adoptive parent-child relationship, for adopted children start life with some initial handicaps and adoptive families must struggle with some unique problems.

Another kind of "success" criteria, of interest to the community taxpayers, might be cited. Every child placed for adoption in infancy saves the taxpayers some $122,000 which the community would have had to expend if the child continued in foster care through his dependency. "It might be economical to assign a caseload of only 5 children to an (adoptive) homefinder, since success in finding a suitable adoptive family for only one child would more than compensate for the workers annual salary." [70, p. 25]

Factors Associated with Adoption Outcome

Extensive research has provided information on the success of adoption and has helped to determine the relationship among the various factors that influence outcome. Such research was designed to test the validity of the criteria traditionally applied in selecting adoptive homes.

In general, background factors in both the child and the parents appear to have little relation to adoptive outcome. This runs contrary to the premise that developmental history is an important consideration that needs to be carefully reviewed in adoptive interviews. The number of placements experienced by the child, his history of institutional placement, his socioeconomic background, and his history of preadoptive deprivation do not appear to be related to adoptive outcome. Age at placement is generally negatively related to outcome, but a very high percentage of older children are successfully adopted.

The child's background variables seem to have less and less significance as prognostic factors from placement to follow-up. This is a tribute to the resilience of children in surmounting earlier developmental deficiencies, to the coping capacity of the adoptive parents, and to the rehabilitative potential of a good adoptive home.

Similarly, parental background is of questionable significance. Starr *et al.* attempted to test the relationship of developmental experience to adoptive outcome. On the basis of social history data obtained through self-report questionnaires and inventories, they selected two groups of adoptive parents: one was composed of applicants who had experienced a happy, loving childhood in a harmonious, affectionate home; the other consisted of applicants who had experienced some rejection or neglect in homes in which there was marital conflict and psychic stress. Forty-three adoptive couples in each group were interviewed at follow-up to evaluate their functioning as adoptive parents. "The findings indicated that early life experiences were only minimally associated with performance as adoptive parents." [226, p. 494]

The age of adoptive parents, the length of their marriage, their religious affiliation, and the number and status of other children in the home show little relation to outcome. Assessments of parents' motivation for adoption are of questionable significance as a predictor of adoptive success, as are their attitudes toward infertility and childlessness. Socioeconomic status, education, and income are only feebly related to positive outcome.

None of the research shows matching between adoptive parents and children to be a factor in adoptive outcome. The general factors most clearly related to adopted success are the attitude of the parents toward the child and the nature of their relationship with the child. Acceptance of, and satisfaction in, adoptive parenthood—coupled with warmth toward, and acceptance of, the child—were invariably associated with adoptive success. Conversely, the factor most clearly related to difficulty is parental rejection, although it is not clear whether the rejection causes the difficulty or the difficulty causes the rejection.

The child's sex is clearly related to outcome. Adoptive boys seem to be more likely to be maladjusted than either adoptive girls or nonadoptive peers.

While we have attempted to list and assess the effect of the discrete factors on adoptive outcome in any particular situation, the various factors interact with each other so as to modify the effects of the contribution of any one factor to the overall result. Ultimately it is the configuration of factors that determines outcome.

The Hard-to-Place Child

The Nonwhite Child

One of the most serious problems in the field of adoption concerns the children who are legally free for adoption, who benefit from, and contribute to, normal family living but who are hard to place because they belong to minority groups (black, chicano, Indian, and so on); because they are older; because they are physically, mentally, or emotionally handicapped; or because they are a part of a group of three or four siblings who should be placed together.

The largest group of unplaceable children belong to minority groups. The Federal Office of Child Development, planning for the establishment of a special Black Adoptive Project to stimulate adoption of black children estimated in March 1971 that "about 80,000 minority children are now in foster care, of whom some 20,000 are known to be in long-term care. It is also estimated that about 40,000 to 50,000 children of unwed mothers are, or would be, available for adoption if the services were offered." [242]

The very considerable gap in placement possibilities for black children is indicated by the fact that the CWIA 1971 nationwide survey reported 133 approved homes for every 100 white children available but only 71 approved homes for every 100 nonwhite children available. [220, Table 1]

Herzog concluded that two-parent black families above the poverty line were adopting at about the same rate as comparable white families. [100]   A statistical review in March 1971 confirms her findings. [100] The report notes that the "difference in (adoption) rates for Negro and white families is probably slight." [243]   Improving the economic position of the nonwhite community would increase the proportion of black families available for the adoption pool by increasing the number of two-parent families with above poverty-level income.

Recent studies have attempted to identify deterrents to adoption on the part of nonwhites. [101; 102]   Parent-centered reasons related to lack of knowledge about the magnitude of the problem; anxieties about undesirable traits in the child or damage as a result of early developmental experience; anxiety about economic insecurity; agency-centered reasons related to a perception of the agency as being evaluative, threatening, and demanding in its approach to applicants. The agency was perceived as having a middle-class bias, a white-racist orientation, and a readiness to reject. Agency "red tape," requirements, procedures, and length of time between application and placement were mentioned as agency-centered deterrents, the applicant being "overevaluated" and "overinterviewed."

The most frequently reported deterrent was economic insecurity. "Again and again it is pointed out that black families have lower incomes, less job security, fewer economic reserves than most white families, and that the incomes, though generally lower, more often represent two wage-earners." [101, p. 8] This conclusion is supported by those of other studies. [54; 68; 75; 76] Detailed interviews with 129 middle-class black families in Hartford, Connecticut, revealed that "overwhelmingly our informants attributed the problem [shortage of black adoptive homes] to the prevalence of low income, poor employment, and inadequate housing among blacks." [75, p. 48]

The reality is that adoption is a low-priority problem in the black community as compared with other problems, that the deterrent of economic insecurity and anxiety is still a powerful reality, and that the black community of two-parent families above the poverty line is, and has been, adopting at about the same rate as white parents. This suggests that there is little "give" for a substantial, disproportionate, increase in black adoptive homes that are likely to be available.

Some agencies have succeeded in placing an increasing number of black children in black homes. A review of the procedures which are related to their greater effectiveness in meeting the problem indicates the following. [200] These agencies made a definite effort to involve members of the black community in the development of programs, policies, and procedures, as board members, workers, volunteers, and interpreters of agency need and service. They actively cooperated with local departments of public welfare, and conducted continuous mass media campaigns to "present" children needing adoption. District offices were opened in the black community. Changes in agency procedure permitted the scheduling of evening interviews in the home immediately after application. Agency requirements relating to age, length of marriage, number of children in the family, income, infertility, and mother's employment were relaxed in an effort to "screen in" rather than "screen out" applicants. The time between application and placement was reduced, so that some of the agencies completed home studies and placed children within two to four months after application.

Available statistics, however, show that the increase in the number of black children placed in black homes as a consequence of such special, concerted efforts is very modest. [13; 74; 116]

A study of adoptions of black children by Wachtel shows a strong correlation between the frequency of agency placement of such children and the proportion of the agency's social workers who are black. [250, p. 6]

Earlier research had suggested that the drop-out rate, once application had been made to an agency, was higher for blacks than for white applicants. [21; 68; 76]   However, a more recent study showed that this was not the case. [72, p. 24]

In order to see what might be done to lower the withdrawal rate of blacks who applied for adoption, Festinger conducted telephone interviews with desirable applicants—eighty black women and eighty-six white women—who had withdrawn. [72]   Black appplicants more often than white applicants attributed their withdrawals to agency rules and procedures—the "number of forms, interviews, and questions." Yet this was a major reason in only 17.5 percent of the cases. Factors over which the agency had little or no control accounted for 51.6 percent of the major reasons explaining withdrawal of black applicants—pregnancy following application, financial difficulty, unanticipated circumstances (illness, job transfer, and the like), ambivalence about adoption. Interestingly enough, while some of the black applicants had been seen by white workers, this was never listed as a factor explaining withdrawal.

The researchers conclude that the black withdrawal rate might be reduced if the agency were clearer and more direct about its expectations and procedures. The results of the study parallel the findings of Shireman's similar but less extensive study in Chicago. [216]

Transracial Adoptions

The transracial adoption program is one of the programs recently developed to meet the adoptive needs of nonwhite children. [82]   The National Urban League Foster Care and Adoption Project was established in 1953; New York City set up an Adopt-a-Child program in 1955; San Francisco organized MARCH (Minority Adoption Recruitment of Children's Homes) in 1955; Minneapolis set up PAMY (Parents to Adopt Minority Youngsters) in 1961; the U.S. Bureau of Indian Affairs and the Child Welfare League of America sponsored a nationwide Indian Adoption Project in 1958. [4; 152; 154]   These projects have been reviewed by Billingsley. [13]

Statistics indicate that transracial adoptions increased sharply during the latter part of the 1960's, tripling between 1968 (700) and 1971 (2574). [177]   By 1971 there were an estimated 10,000 transracial adoptive families in the United States and Canada involving black, Indian, or Oriental children.

As Billingsley notes, interracial adoption follows a "continuum based on skin color," as well as a continuum reflecting community attitude toward a particular racial minority. [14]   It is easier to place the lighter-skinned child; it is easier to place black children in Canada, where they form a small proportion of the population, but harder to place Indian children in those sections of Canada where there are many Indians; Oriental children are easier to place than blacks. Transracial adoptions most frequently involve children of mixed racial background. Thus, in a report of the placement of 115 nonwhite children placed in white homes over a twelve-year period, 107, or 92 percent, were part white. [86]

Researchers have attempted to identify the special characteristics of parents who accept children of another race. [66; 67; 69; 183; 188; 192; 214; 224; 262]   Such parents are likely to have higher occupational levels and higher educational attainment than adoptive families generally; they are more distant socially and geographically from their relatives; they are more likely to be fertile and to have had children in the family prior to adoption; their motive is more likely to be that of providing a home for a child who might otherwise not be adopted; they tend to be somewhat more individualistic and inner-directed, and to have a higher self-concept. As Fanshel notes, "Repeatedly, the element that has been most noteworthy in the self-descriptions of the [parents] . . . has been a certain independence, often self-referred to as a 'stubborn streak.' . . . It is not that they would not care what their neighbors think; it is rather that they would not allow themselves to be guided in their actions by such considerations." [69, p. 322]

They are not necessarily without prejudice, since some who accepted Indian children made it clear that they would not accept a black child, and those who accepted a child of black-white parentage would not have accepted a full-blooded black child. Their voting habits and political ideologies reflect diverse convictions; only a minority viewed transracial adoptions as a gesture expressing their conviction about an integrated society.

Some were prompted to accept transracial adoptions in order to ensure that the agency would place a child with them as soon as possible. As is true for the placement of all of the hard-to-place children group, agencies have been ready to relax standards and make concessions in order to increase the number of applicants willing to adopt transracially.

Frequently it appears that the applicant who has accepted a hard-to-place child was initially interested in adopting a child; only later, after some discussion of the situation with the agency, did he consider a minority-group child, an older child, or a handicapped child.

Available research clearly indicates that applicants interested in such adoptions are not meeting some neurotic need or expressing a sense of rebelliousness. It further suggests that the worker's attitude toward the feasibility and desirability of transracial adoptions is an important determinant of the applicants' response. Applicants are sensitive to the worker's attitudes and respond positively when transracial adoptions are presented in a flexible, nondefensive manner. A 1972 study "strongly suggests that caseworkers responded more favorably to requests for transracial adoption than to requests about adopting a white child" [213, p. 120] which indicates the receptivity of workers to such adoptions.

The trend toward transracial adoptions has created a countertrend—an active opposition on the part of nonwhites to the placement of their children in white homes. [34; 40; 101; 116]   Blacks who oppose such placements say that, "Black families build in mechanisms to handle living in a racist society. White families could not provide these for a black child. . . . Identity is all-important and no white family can provide this for a black child. . . . I question the ability of white parents—no matter how deeply imbued with good will—to grasp the totality of the problem of being black in our society—I question their ability to create what I believe is crucial for these youngsters—a black identity." [116, pp. 40–41, 157]   In April 1972 the National Association of Black Social Workers went on record as being in "vehement opposition" to the placement of black children with white families and called transracial adoptions "a growing threat to the preservation of the black family" (*The New York Times*, April 12, 1972).

We, perhaps, need to be reminded that this position is not very different from the position of denominational agencies. Catholic adoption agencies were long committed to the principle that any Catholic child could be placed for adoption only in a Catholic home. [20]   The "child saving" activity of one group is perceived as a "child snatching" activity by another group. One of the most vehement controversies in the history of child welfare took place in late nineteenth-century America, when Catholic organizations charged that placement agencies such as the Children's Aid Society were "maintained for the purpose of bribing poor destitute Catholics to abandon their faith." Placing Catholic children in Protestant homes was not charity, it was claimed, but sectarian zeal designed to destroy a child's faith in the religion of his parents. [140, pp. 48–50]

Currently, in addition to the charge that transracial adoption results in a loss of the child's identification with the black community, there is the further accusation that transracial adoption is a procedure designed primarily to meet the needs of white adoptive applicants who lack white children to adopt rather than the needs of nonwhite children, and that a more concerted effort could be made to find nonwhite homes. Transracial adoptions would then be only one approach—and a limited one at that—of a more comprehensive campaign involving a number of different procedures to find homes for nonwhite children.

Despite the controversy about the ultimate desirability of transracial adoption, it is regarded as more desirable than foster home care or institutional care. Still, questions about the advisability of transracial adoption derive from the special problems which such adoptions present to the adoptive children and parents—acceptance of the child by siblings, playmates, peers, relatives, and neighbors, and, most difficult of all, the problems related to resolution of racial identification. Being Oriental, or Indian, or black, and living with Caucasian parents in a Caucasian environment, how can the child be helped to develop a stable, secure concept of racial identification? How will the white community react when the child reaches adolescence and begins dating? The child's affectional ties are with the white world of his parents, which constitutes his reference group for socialization. However, the world outside the family responds to him in terms of his visible racial affiliation. [40; 67]

Agencies and parents, dealing with these problems in anticipation, adhere to general principles of mental health. "All children have problems of identification in adolescence, this is just more of the same"; "if the child can be helped, through love and acceptance, to resolve his identity as a human being, he will then be able to resolve his racial identity"; "building a good self-concept through parental trust, love, and acceptance will provide the necessary secure foundation for healthy resolution of the problem."

In addition, parents have been advised to learn something about the art, literature, history, and life style of the child's race, and to attempt to convey these to the child so that he can develop some pride in his heritage. Further, it is recommended that the family develop social and professional contacts with people of the child's racial background or move to a racially mixed neighborhood so that the child may play with children of his own race. It has also been suggested that the parents attempt to identify and resolve any racist feelings they may have which might intrude upon their relationship with the child.

If "telling" involves a discussion of sex, "telling" in transracial adoptive parents involves a discussion of race as well. To say, "God made people differently. . . . All people are colored; some people are colored white, some black. . . . Just as people have different color hair and eyes, they have different skin colors. . . ." may be sufficient for the young child. However, the questions and answers grow more complex in interpreting the reality of racial difference and racial conflict as the child grows older in twentieth-century America.

Parents and agencies indicate that the seriousness of the problems which will be encountered by these children is a function, in a large measure, of the state of race relations when they reach adolescence. It may be, they say, that the level of racial tension and discrimination will be lower in the future.

One resource, developed by the parents themselves, may be helpful:

associations of transracial adoptive families, which meet to discuss common problems and share solutions. The meetings permit the sharing of a common experience and members provide social and emotional support for each other. The Open Door Society of Montreal was the earliest of such organizations. There are now Open Door Societies in Indiana, Missouri, Illinois, and Wisconsin. Other organizations include The East-West Society, the Council on Adoptable Children, Families for Interracial Adoption, and the Interracial Family Association. In 1969, such organizations began sponsoring an annual North American Conference on Adoptable Children, devoted in large measure to problems of transracial adoption.

Transracial adoptions are recent and the children are still quite young. Follow-up research available at this point indicates that sibling acceptance is not much of a problem; grandparents are more resistive at first but later appear to welcome the children; young playmates and peers accept such children readily; the negative reaction of neighbors is private, as yet not public; explicitly manifested prejudice is unfashionable and infrequent. Parents frequently encounter stares of curiosity, but rarely overt hostility. As a matter of fact, parents note that it is more embarrassing to have to cope with gushing comments of approbation. Transracially adopted children who are old enough to be in school have experienced heckling and teasing, but this has been neither frequent nor persistent. The adustment of the children seems to be positive in a great majority of the cases. Most of the adoptions are successful, but at the point of study most of the children were still young.

Zastrow, in a study comparing the responses of in-race and transracial adoptive parents, found the levels of satisfaction in the adoption, by both groups, to be equally high. [262] Falk found transracial adoptive parents to have lower levels of satisfaction and to be somewhat more less likely to say that they would repeat the experience. [66]

Fanshel's study of the transracial placement is the most comprehensive and rigorous of such research. [69] As a result of a cooperative effort of the U.S. Bureau of Indian Affairs and the Child Welfare League of America, 395 Indian children were placed with white families over a ten-year period. Annual interviews were conducted with the families of ninety-seven of these children for five years after placement. Fathers and mothers were interviewed jointly and separately, and the adjustment of the child was studied in detail. The over-all conclusion "was that the children are doing remarkably well as a group." Health and cognitive development were normal:

> . . . [In] personality and behavior patterns there are more incipient
> signs of difficulties than in other areas, [but] this is true of only
> 30 percent of the children, and most of these are seen to have mod-
> erate rather than serious problems. The children appear to be

well-imbedded within their adoptive families and the relationships appear to be as close and devoted as one would find in other kinds of adoptive families or in biological family units. [69, p. 323]

It seems clear that whatever problems might be encountered in the future the transracial adoptive experience is less problematic than had been anticipated during childhood and latency.

The Older Child

Another sizable group of adoptable, but hard-to-place children is composed of older children. Schapiro, Boehm, and Kadushin note age as a handicap for placement, and the general difficulties in the adoptive placement of the older child have been discussed. [11; 17; 39; 45; 64; 98; 118; 142; 143; 156; 202; 215; 227] For adoptive purposes, a child of two is "middle-aged" and a child of five is "old."

By the time a child is five years of age, he has already developed some relationship, of which he is explicitly aware, with parents, parent-substitutes, siblings, and other relatives. He has a vivid memory of a life lived with other people in other places. The adoptive parents have to establish themselves in the child's life either in addition to, or in opposition to, such memories. Thus parents who adopt an older child can less easily fantasize that the child is truly their own.

An older child is therefore apt to face a problem of competing or conflicting loyalties. Having developed emotional ties of some intensity to either his biological parents or his foster parents, he cannot permit himself to "belong" unconditionally to the adoptive parents without betraying his love for the adults to whom he previously felt some allegiance. Adopting an older child deprives the adoptive parents of the affectional contact with an infant and the satisfactions in shaping the child's life during the time when he is most malleable.

The older child comes to adoptive parents with an established name, an established way of dealing with the problems of daily living that may or may not fit into the adoptive family's way of doing things. The adoptive parents must, in some measure, accept the child as he is; they are deprived of the opportunity of socializing the child, from the start, in terms that are acceptable to them.

The older child is more likely to be a "damaged" child. Having lived for some years under conditions that are not generally conducive to stable emotional development, he is likely to have developed some emotional disturbances. The older the child, the older the problem and the less susceptible it is to therapy. This is less likely to have happened to infants available for adoption who have had, by virtue of their age, only limited exposure to pathogenic conditions.

Having overtly experienced rejection, older children are apt to anticipate rejection. They are likely, then, to be reticent about allowing themselves to feel love for the adoptive parents or to express affection. They are more likely to test the adoptive parents' patience and endurance in order to prove their acceptability. The adoptive parents, thus, are in for a harder time and, at least initially, fewer satisfactions.

Selection of an adoptive home for an older child requires his active participation, for he is consciously and explicitly aware of the experience. Unlike the infant, the older child measures the acceptability of the prospective adoptive couple and any doubts or hesitancies he may have must be given consideration.

However, there are advantages. The older child can participate in family activities, communicate with parents, and be talked to. There is less of the drudgery in training and caring for a totally dependent child and there is less anxiety about "telling" since the child has experienced the placement and knows he is adopted. Parents who have adopted older children stress these advantages:

Father: You can build rapport more easily, I think. You have a youngster who can talk and you got a youngster who can do things. . . . I mean . . . you get a tiny infant in the home and they lay in the basket or you take them out and give them a bath and dress them and feed them and that's just about the extent of it. Where you take the six- to eleven-year-old, these youngsters have already interests and you can cultivate those interests, you can even build new interests. And this, I think to me, was the . . . was one of the nicest factors in adopting an older child.

Mother: Babies are so routine and you don't get much enjoyment out of them . . . you know just sterilizing bottles and washing diapers whereas I think someone older is much more interesting. Older people if they would take an older child would find it more enjoyable.

Father: You have a child that wants to be adopted . . . like he did and that's one thing in your favor . . . and he knows it. . . . I mean he's aware of it . . . that his folks can't keep him. He's already trying to adjust, because he wants to and he's old enough to understand . . . to realize.

Father: We adopted an older child so that we didn't have to go through this diaper wash, two o'clock feeding, walk the floor bit.

Father: I think that's one advantage . . . of adopting an older child. . . . The child knows it's being adopted . . . with an infant you . . . you'd always have to wonder—well, gee—when should I tell her or should I ever tell her . . . and with the older child . . . it's just a fact when she comes. . . .

Kadushin interviewed ninety-one families with children who had been placed for adoption at five years of age or older. [124] The greatest majority of such placements were successful and the children appeared to be adjusting well. Yet all these children had spent their infancy and early childhood under very deprived circumstances. In almost all instances the biological parents' rights to the child had been terminated by the courts as a consequence of neglect and/or abuse.

The study shows the older children, despite memories of earlier attachments, do develop strong relationships with their adoptive parents and learn and accept the ways of the new family. In the recuperative environment of a healthy, permanent family, old emotional wounds are healed. [124]

But there is still great resistance to accepting the older child. [37] Of course, when a shortage of adoptable children continues for a long time, the tendency is, of necessity, for adoptive parents to move gradually down the hierarchy of preferences. By 1972 there were indications that the older child was more frequently proposed for adoption because sizable numbers of such children were still available.

Any initial deterrent to placeability ultimately results in additional deterrents. Because the Negro or handicapped child is initially hard to place, the delay results in his becoming an older child who is now doubly difficult to place. In addition, he is likely to have developed emotional problems that further reduce his placeability. Boehm notes that opportunities for adoption diminish as the child grows older, not only because he is no longer the infant that most families prefer, but because "for the child in foster care emotional difficulties tend to increase with the passage of time." Because adoptability is greatest during the early stages of contact, "the most effective service to the hard-to-place child is to prevent his becoming hard to place." [17, p. 28]

The Handicapped Child

That the existence of a physical, emotional, or mental handicap should make a child difficult to place for adoption is almost self-evident. Schapiro lists children with physical or mental handicaps as among those with special needs and, consequently, hard to place. [202] Beaven presents a cogent defense of the right to adoption of the mildly, or moderately, mentally retarded child. [10] Colville, Fowler, Fradkin, Hornecker, Lake, and Taft have presented case discussions of the adoptive placement of physically and mentally handicapped children. [49; 77; 78; 107; 139; 233]

Children who are physically handicapped, or mentally retarded, require more than the normal amount of parental time and energy; they require specialized knowledge and facilities, and they are apt to impose a greater burden of medical expense as well as medical care; they are less likely than the normal child to enable the adoptive parents to derive satisfactions from his achievements; they are likely to remain dependent for a longer period.

Children with such medical conditions as cleft palate, hernia, asthma, crossed eyes, deafness, blindness, congenital heart defects, or mild cerebral palsy can be, and have been, successfully placed for adoption. In most instances, however, the physical handicap has been mild or correctable. Less frequently, mildly retarded children have been placed for adoption, but neither the moderately or severely retarded child is regarded as a likely candidate for adoption. [84; 134]

Franklin and Massarik, who conducted intensive follow-up interviews with 169 families who adopted handicapped children, conclude that "children with medical conditions of all degrees of severity and correctability can be successfully placed and reared in adoptive homes." [80, p. 399] Most of the children were between five and twelve years of age at the time of the interview. While the families ultimately proved adaptive and resilient in meeting the handicapped child's special needs, a majority of the parents had expressed some concern at the time when the child was presented to them. Only a small minority of the couples had themselves initiated a request for a handicapped child; in most instances, the agency initiated discussion of the possibility of placement for such a child. The agency, in finding homes for such children, tended to be more flexible in applying eligibility criteria and to move more expeditiously in processing applications. [80, p. 463] Some of the adoptive parents had originally been foster parents to the handicapped child. An attachment to, and relationship with, the child had developed and adoption resulted. Initial placement for foster care may be a desirable procedure in the case of the hard-to-place child. It permits the parents to develop a commitment to the child without initially feeling an obligation to make the child a full member of the family.

In this study, as in other studies of adopted children with special needs, parents interviewed frequently urge the researchers to stress two points: first, many of the problems for which the agency had prepared them, and which they had anticipated, did not occur; second, there was decided pleasure in having these children, some special rewards in the feeling of performing a useful, significant function, and some special understandings to be derived. Anderson, who wrote about his own experiences in adopting three transracial children, sees these children "as children of special value who enrich and deepen human experience in uncommon ways." [5, p. 181] He is seconded in this way by the novelist Jan deHartog, who perceptively recounts his own experiences in adopting Asian children. [55]

Problems in Adoption

1. Although there is a trend toward greater public acceptance of adoption, there still are residuals of derogatory community attitudes regarding adoption. Kirk notes that in a study of comments encountered by adoptive parents, some 32 percent had been told, "How lucky you are that you didn't have to go through all the trouble of pregnancy and birth like I had"; 22 percent had encountered such comments as "How well you care for the child, just like a real mother"; 82 percent heard "Tell me, do you know anything about the child's background?" All these comments are subtle devaluations of adoptive parenthood. [132, p. 30] Even the seemingly complimentary comments ("Isn't it wonderful of you to have taken this child") encountered by 92 percent of the respondents tended to differentiate the adoptive parent from the biological parent.

Another aspect of this problem is that the public is still not fully aware of, and does not fully accept, the viewpoint of social agencies regarding adoption. Adoption workers are still often accused of being arbitrary, of "playing God," of unnecessarily withholding children from adoptive parents, and so on. It is partly because of this feeling that the public has not more vigorously supported efforts to legislate against independent placement, and there is still considerable controversy as to whether social workers should be given primary control of such adoptions. Clearly, adoption concerns social relationships. Adoption "creates" parent-child relationships and directly affects the marriage. Clearly, then, according to our definition of *child welfare*, it is within the professional responsibilities of the social work profession. Yet social workers have not succeeded in convincing the public that they should be primarily, if not exclusively, responsible for bringing parentless children and childless "parents" together.

Lawyers argue against this. TenBroek states that "the competition of independent adoptions (if the regulation of them can be made effective) has a salutory effect upon agencies. The agencies are stimulated to improve their efforts and services by the existence of the alternative machinery." [234, p. 347] An English Parliamentary Committee on adoption, in noting the number of independently arranged nonrelative adoptions, argues:

> In the present state of our knowledge, it would not be right to
> fetter all this good will. No careful research into the comparative
> results of adoptions carried out through the agency of adoption
> societies, local authorities, or third parties or arranged direct,
> has, so far as we know, been undertaken and, in the absence of
> reliable data, no conclusion as to the relative value of these methods
> can be drawn. [105, p. 12]

The burden of proof, the Parliamentary Committee suggests, lies with the social work profession. As Kirk says, "if a group seeks a monopoly of practice through public licensing, it must of necessity claim special competence," a special competence it must ultimately prove. [132, p. 22]

There is a recognition on the part of agency critics, however, that adoptions are of too great a concern to the community to permit haphazard operation. The argument then is not between the black market and the agency, but between social agency monopoly of adoption and some reasonable regulation of independent adoptions.

2. The religious qualification requirement in adoption is currently the subject of considerable controversy and hence another problem for the field of adoption. [173]   One aspect of the problem results in the decided imbalance between supply and demand for some religious groups. Because there are relatively few illegitimate Jewish children available, the ratio of Jewish adoptive applicants to Jewish adoptable children is higher than for other religious groups, forcing the Jewish applicant into the gray or black adoption market. Thus at a time when the median ratio was three adoptive couples to every white infant, the ratio in agencies serving Jewish couples was eight adoptive couples to every white infant. [27, p. 24]

An even more significant and more general difficulty is related to the inequity imposed on the nonreligious applicant. He is penalized for his agnosticism by his inability to qualify as an adoptive applicant. The American Ethical Union, a society of humanists, expresses the dilemma and point of view of this group of potential adopters. Because Ethical Culture is not a religion, there are "literally no babies for them to adopt." They comment:

> Americans, providing that they meet all other standards, deserve
> equal opportunity to adopt children openly, without having to
> profess a religion to which they do not honestly subscribe, through
> legitimate adoption channels. In this area, as in any other, there
> should be no discrimination on the basis of religious beliefs
> (*The New York Times*, October 11, 1959).

The Child Welfare League of America suggests that, although the religious faith of the natural parents should be respected and—wherever possible—followed in selecting an adoptive home for the child, "placement of children should not be restricted, in general, to homes with formal church affiliation." [43, p. 25]   This point of view is rejected by the National Conference of Catholic Charities, which has been the most active organization advocating the retention and extension of the religious requirements in adoption. The Conference feels that "Among the factors that play a part in successful adoption, the weightiest, although not the sole element, is the religious status" [of prospective adopters]. [43, p. 26]

A third aspect of the problem lies in the fact that, supposedly, the adoption of children is denied or delayed if there are no coreligionist applicants available at the time they are released for adoption. There is no study that substantiates such denial of adoption, except in some few instances. [36; 48]

But there is the question of the right of the relinquishing parent to determine this aspect of the child's future life. If the parent's power to determine where the child shall live, how he will be raised, educated, and cared for is terminated, why not the control of religious affiliation? [173] Religious matching of adoptive applicants and child "wherever practicable" (as most state laws require) involves, in effect, the determination of the child's religious affiliation by the bioparent. [190]

The more recent trend has been toward an easing of the religious qualification in adoption. In 1971 the New Jersey Supreme Court overturned a lower court ruling which denied an adoption petition in the case of parents who were professed atheists. In 1970 Massachusetts and Maryland revised their legislation so as to permit adoption without reference to the child's religious background. A New York State revision permits the biomother to express her lack of preference for a particular religion for her child's future home. A mother who professes no religious preference usually signs a waiver giving the agency power of decision regarding the religious factor in placement.

3. With the decrease in the number of children available for adoption, adoptive agencies are beginning to face a question of survival. In the early 1970's such agencies were beginning to diversify their functions, moving out from adoption to family counseling and family life education. Such diversification provides the agency with a useful service to occupy staff. A small percentage of agencies have chosen to discontinue their adoption service in response to the changing situation.

In response to the shortage of white, unhandicapped infants available for adoption in the early 1970's the agencies were beginning to feel the competition of black and gray market operations in adoption (*The New York Times*, February 20, 1973). The director of the Child Welfare League of America estimated in 1973 that the "black market in babies equals about four or five percent of the yearly adoption rate and that the average price is about $5,000 to $10,000 an infant" (*San Francisco Sunday Examiner and Chronicle*, February 4, 1973).

Trends

We have previously noted some trends in adoption which can now be summarized. There has been a steady increase in the number of children placed for nonrelative adoption, although the rate of increase has been leveling off. Children are being placed sooner after birth, more often under agency auspices and increasingly under public child welfare agency auspices. There are fewer white healthy infants available for adoption, so efforts have increased to place nonwhite, older, and handicapped children.

One result of these efforts is the increase in transracial adoptions. Other innovative procedures include greater variety in recruitment approaches, acceptance of single-parent adoptions, development of a national adoptive exchange program, and use of adoptive subsidies.

1. There is a trend toward greater flexibility in recruitment procedures in order to develop interest in the hard-to-place child. One approach involves a vigorous program of publicity. This has required some re-evaluation of confidentiality. This implied that children would not be identified publicly but had the unintended effect of concealing their need. The Louise Wise Adoption Service, in deciding on a program of publicity for adoptable physically handicapped children, said, "We believe it is more important for . . . [the children] to find loving, permanent homes of their own than to go unphotographed, unpublicized, and homeless." Brief descriptions of each of six physically handicapped children, as well as photographs, were made available to newspapers. The response to this particular campaign was immediate and overwhelming—over five hundred couples responded. The agency evaluated applicants immediately, and within three months four of the six children were placed. Weingarten, the public relations consultant who supervised the campaign, argues that confidentiality implies that the "agency will use information responsibly in the client's behalf, that this responsibility involves not only protection against improper disclosure but sharing appropriate information with appropriate persons at appropriate times in order to provide the client with the best possible service." [253]

The Los Angeles County Bureau of Adoption at one time published a quarterly bulletin, The Top Ten Tots, about hard-to-place children. In Canada over 130 Ontario newspapers carry a syndicated column called "Today's Child," which presents children needing adoption. The pioneer use of television by the Minnesota Division of Child Welfare as an aid in recruiting homes for hard-to-place children has now become standard procedure. [83] The Los Angeles County Department of Adoptions "shows" adoptable children each week as part of a regularly scheduled television program. In almost all cases these are hard-to-place children. By January 1970, of 286 children who had appeared on the program over a two-year period, 202 had been placed for adoption and an additional fifty were in the process of being placed. Children under two years of age are personally presented; pictures of older children are shown. There is no indication that children are hurt by this procedure, although some object to what they call the commercial sale of children.

Some agencies have used closed-circuit television and one-way mirrors to present adoptable children to parents without their being aware that they are being observed for possible placement. Video tape has also been used to "show" a child who lives in one section of the country to prospective parents living elsewhere. [180]

Some cities have arranged an Adoption Week to promote adoption. [201] An Adoptive Father of the Year is selected, and all the babies available for adoption are brought to a picnic arranged at a local park for all adoptive families in the area.

2. *Adoption resource exchange* has been defined by the Child Welfare League as "an organized means of exchanging information among agencies about children for whom they have difficulty in finding appropriate homes and about adoptive applicants for whom they have no suitable children." [71, p. 26] Ohio was the first to originate a state-wide exchange, and most tend to be an intrastate resource. However, such a resource can be extended to a regional level and, ultimately, to a national level.

The adoption exchange has the advantage of increasing the opportunities for placement because it makes available a larger pool of potential adopters for the child, and a larger pool of children for the applicant. [115] Agencies list children available for placement with a Central Adoption Resource Exchange. A summary of essential descriptive data accompanies each name. At the same time the agencies send summaries of data on adoptive parents who are waiting for children and who have expressed interest in, and capacity for, accepting hard-to-place children.

Adoption exchanges are of greatest immediate benefit to the hard-to-place child. Schapiro notes that "state experience with adoption clearance services shows that almost all of the children placed through them are children of minority groups and mixed racial parentage [and] those who are older [or] handicapped. . . ." [202, p. 46] Leatherman cites the Texas Adoption Exchange as an important factor in the adoptive placement of a sizable number of older children. [143]

In 1967 the Child Welfare League of America established a national adoption research exchange which includes Canadian agencies and is known as ARENA (Adoption Resource Exchange of North America). Most of the children listed present special problems for adoption:

Girl, two years old, of white-black parentage; born with congenital hemolytic anemia; her present functioning is above average. Agency is prepared to negotiate medical expenses.

Girl, year-and-a-half old, described as affectionate, loving, and active. Cynthia is retarded. She will be capable of education at a trainable level, although her potential is limited.

Boy, four-and-a-half, mixed racial heritage; friendly, alert, precocious.

Two girls, aged five and eight and their brother three. Average children with normal problems. Important that they remain together as a family unit. Needed is an adoptive family with space, finances, and desire for a ready-made family.

Listed with the exchange are families such as the following:

A college professor and his wife want to adopt an infant of Mexican-American heritage. There are no such children available in the community in which they live.
A family with four children, one of whom is blind, would like to adopt a blind child. Because of their experience with their blind son, they feel they have something special to offer such a child.

Between 1967 and 1973 ARENA registered about 2300 children needing adoption and 3000 families seeking to adopt. About 650 children were placed during this period.

The California Department of Social Welfare's Adoptions Resource Referral Center was the first adoptions exchange in the country to computerize its operations. The first child placed through the system was a racially mixed three-year-old from a public agency in southern California adopted by a white family registered with a private agency in northern California. Legislation has been introduced in the U.S. Senate which would authorize the establishment of a Federally financed computerized national adoption information exchange program.

Increasing agency success in placing the usual hard-to-place child has resulted in more frequent listing by adoption exchanges of the child with multiple handicaps—the older child with a physical handicap, the mentally retarded black child, and so on.

3. In subsidized adoption, the agency continues to make financial contributions to the adoptive family after the legal adoption of the child. [41] Agencies have for some time subsidized the adoption of physically handicapped children by continuing to pay for the medical care of the child. Agencies have also subsidized the joint placement of a group of siblings. In special instances, agencies have subsidized adoptive parents for a limited period so that psychiatric treatment might be provided for an adoptive child. An agency might agree to a time-limited subsidy to permit a family to adjust to the loss of a wife's earnings when she leaves her job upon placement of the child. These are special, time-limited transitional uses of subsidy to insure the success of the placement. [229; 255]

Subsidized adoption, approved in twenty-two states by 1973, is quite different. It provides that the community will make a monthly grant to the adoptive family to meet the routine expenses of rearing the adopted child. It thus makes adoption possible for low-income families that could not otherwise afford to adopt a child. The Presidential Commission on Population Growth and the American Future recommended in its 1972 report that subsidies be offered to qualified families unable to assume the

full financial cost of a child's care. [50, p. 148]   The legislation is designed to make more adoptive homes available to hard-to-place children.
For instance, the Illinois State Department of Children and Family
Services may provide subsidies to "persons who adopt physically or mentally handicapped, older, and other hard-to-place children." The California legislation is designed to encourage the adoption of children for
whom "permanent homes were not readily available because of age,
physical handicap, or ethnic background."

The first statistics available on the operation of the New York program reveal that the great majority of subsidized adoptions involved
black children. [87]   Of the 345 subsidized homes approved in Illinois
in the first two and a half years of program operation, 156 of the children
were black, 102 were handicapped, and 154 were over six years of age.
[210, p. 4]   The legislation often restricts subsidization to adoptive
parents who previously cared for the child on a foster care basis. This
permits the foster parent to adopt the child without loss of board care
support.

There is some support for the contention that subsidization increases
adoption. A Chicago study of the principal agencies concerned with substitute care found that caseworkers estimate that "over 30 percent of the
children currently in their foster homes are adoptable and would be
adopted if subsidies to current foster parents could be paid." [217, p. 7]
Most of the children adopted as a result of the availability of subsidization were, in fact, formerly foster children in the home. To encourage
this trend, New York State passed a law which required that, if a child
became available for adoption after having been in a foster home for two
years, the foster parents be given preference in applying for adoption
of the child. All of this tends to make foster and adoptive home less
distinctively different and more conceptually interchangeable. The trend
toward permanent or long-term foster care has blurred the previously
sharp distinction between foster care and adoption; subsidized adoptions
tend to obscure it further. If one difference between foster care and
adoption was the fact that one was temporary and the other permanent
substitute care, another clear difference was that foster parents received
payment for care of the child while adoptive parents did not. Permanent
foster care runs counter to the first distinction; subsidized foster care
nullifies the second distinction.

Adoptive subsidy involves a means test and an annual review to
determine if the subsidy needs to be continued. In New York State,
which passed the first adoption subsidy legislation in March 1969, a
family with less than $11,000 income could receive financial support of
up to $125 a month for an adopted child.

Since the subsidy program requires a yearly review of income for
subsidy adjustment, it continues the involvement of the adoptive family
with the agency. Agencies and some adoptive parents see this continu-

ing contact as reassuring and helpful. [90]   Some contend that such periodic checks are not necessary. Maryland's program, for instance, requires "no annual reporting on income." [187, p. 58]   As Watson says, "The task is to devise a system of fiscal accountability for subsidized adoptions that does not insist on the casework involvement of the family, that does not give the impression of checking up to see how the adoption is working out, and that does not imply that the agency has any continuing responsibility." [252, p. 228]   An annual affidavit from the family as to its financial situation may be the answer.

Unresolved questions relate to whether or not independent and stepparent adoptions are to be eligible and whether or not use of casework services by the family is to be a requirement.

4. Single-parent adoptions have also been selectively sanctioned for placement of children with special needs. Applications from nonmarried adults are accepted only when two-parent families are not available. Such placements have been made with single, divorced, or widowed women and, occasionally, with single men. [22; 52; 117; 123]   Single applicants, to be acceptable, must have close contact with an extended family (to provide help and male relatives as surrogate fathers), and a healthy sexual identification without hostility toward the opposite sex. She must also have good health, since illness would rob the child of his one parent, the financial capacity to care for the child without working, or a reasonably permanent, viable plan for child care. She must be a mature, stable person whose motive for adoption is primarily oriented toward the child's needs.

A five-month-old girl was placed with Mrs. N., a widow:
Mrs. N. works on an assembly line from 4:30 p.m. to 1 a.m.
These hours allow her to be with the child most of the day. Mrs. N.'s sister and her family live next door to her, and take care of the child while Mrs. N. is at work.

Mrs. N. is the sixth child of a large, closely knit family. All but one of her brothers and sisters live in Los Angeles County, as do both her parents. She also has eighteen nieces and nephews, fifteen of them children and three adults. Before the adoption, Mrs. N. was the only childless member of her sibling group.

Mrs. N. manages well. She owns a car, which is fully paid for— as is all her furniture. She carries adequate life insurance, and enough health insurance to cover medical expenses for herself and her child. She has completed a course as a grocery checker, which she expects will help her obtain employment with a better salary. Moreover, she may eventually have the support of a husband, for she is a handsome, warm, cheerful woman who gets along well with men. [22, p. 106]

Single parents face some special problems in "telling," and the agency will have to help the single parent develop some response to the feelings the child might have about having been denied a two-parent home.

Single-parent adoption also requires some change in the counseling of the unmarried mother. Currently, social workers help the unmarried mother deal with her guilt and hesitancy in giving up the baby by assuring her that she is making it possible for the child to have a "normal" family. Greater emphasis needs to be given to the fact that some single women are in a better position to provide adequate child care, that these are the women the agency would select.

One strong deterrent to the acceptance of single parents for children needing a home is the attitude on the part of social workers that the one-parent family is inherently, and necessarily, productive of pathology. Research does not support this. Most children raised in single-parent homes become emotionally healthy adults and socially productive members of the community. A one-parent home may be more desirable than a conflict-ridden two-parent home.

5. There is a trend toward insuring greater parity between adoptive parenthood and bioparenthood. Some firms which provide maternity allowance benefits to the biomother are granting similar allowances to adoptive mothers. A bill has been introduced in the U.S. Senate permitting income tax deductions of expenses incurred in adoption (legal fees, agency fees, medical fees). Civil service regulations permit the use of sick leave and vacation time so that an expectant mother can take paid leave before and after delivery. She may continue on unpaid leave for a time without jeopardizing her job. There is growing demand to permit an adoptive mother to remain at home with the child for a short period of time after placement without jeopardizing her position.

6. There has been a trend toward organizing adoptive parents on local and national levels. The National Council of Adoptive Parents Organizations, with local branches throughout the country, boasts a distinguished advisory board and publishes a news bulletin—*National Adoptalk*. Opposed to exclusive control of adoptions by social agencies, the organization distributes bumper stickers which proclaim, "Room for one more? Adopt."

Summary

Adoption, a second form of substitute care, involves legal and permanent transfer of parental rights and obligations from the biological parent to the adoptive parent.

Adoptive parents may be related to the child, or they may be people who were formerly total strangers to the child. The latter are termed *nonrelative adoptions* and constitute about 83,000 (49 percent) of the total of 169,000 adoptions consummated in 1971.

Children available for nonrelative adoption are most frequently (87 percent) illegitimate. Children of parents whose parental rights have been terminated by the courts because of neglect constitute another important source of adoptive children. Infertile married couples form the majority of nonrelative adoptive parents.

The agency, in selecting among adoptive applicants for the children available, takes the following factors into consideration:

1. The age of the parents in relation to the age of the child.
2. Adequate physical health.
3. Stability of marriage.
4. Fertility status.
5. Religious affiliation.
6. Emotional health and maturity.
7. Capacity for parenthood.
8. Adjustment to sterility.
9. Motivation for adoption.
10. Reaction of significant others in the applicant's family.

Interviews with the couple are followed by individual interviews with husband and wife, home visits, and contact with references. After the study, a child is selected; the applicants are informed, and arrangements are made for a meeting between the applicants and the child. If the reactions of both the agency and the applicants are positive, the child is placed. After a period of six months or a year, legal steps are initiated to make the adoptive couple the legal parents of the child. During this period, the agency helps the parents and the child to make the adjustment to this socially established parent-child relationship.

Some of the recurrent problems related to adoption are the following:

1. Desirable procedures for sharing with the child the knowledge that he is adopted.
2. The parents' acceptance of their status as adoptive parents.
3. The special difficulties adoptive parents may have in child rearing.
4. Desirable procedures for sharing with the child the fact that he is adopted.
5. Legal procedures in completing the adoption.

Group approaches have been effectively used at different points in the process of adoption—at intake, during the interim period between placement and legal completion of adoption, after legal adoption.

Nonrelative adoptions may also take place outside agency channels—in the gray market, in which doctors and lawyers act as intermediaries, often without fee, and in the black market, in which children are "sold" for a profit. These independent adoptions carry certain potential dangers to the child, the biological parents, the adoptive parents, and the community.

A recapitulation of evaluation studies of completed adoptions indicates that about 65 percent are unequivocally successful and an additional 18 percent achieve some intermediate level of success; 17 percent are deemed unsuccessful. The over-all success rate of agency adoptions was computed at about 85.2 percent, as contrasted with a success rate of 75 percent for independent adoptions.

A recapitulation of studies of adoptive children receiving service at guidance clinics and psychiatric facilities shows a rate of 4 percent of nonrelative adoptees at such agencies as compared with an estimated rate of 1 percent of such children in the general population. However, adoptive children do not tend to show any unique symptoms—except, perhaps, greater aggressiveness, and it would appear that such children are no more disturbed than nonadopted children.

The following problems regarding adoptive services were identified and discussed:

1. The problem of the hard-to-place child.
2. Problems regarding transracial adoptions.
3. The controversy over agency control of adoption and independent placements.
4. The problem of religious qualifications for applicants.

The following trends were identified and discussed:

1. The trend toward increased numbers of adoptions, particularly under agency auspices, although the adoption rate remains steady.
2. The trend toward a decrease in the availability of white, nonhandicapped infants and a changing applicant-to-child ratio.
3. The trend toward increasing concern with, and placement of, nonwhite, older, or handicapped children.
4. The trend toward innovative procedures in recruiting adoptive parents, the development of adoption exchanges, the subsidization of adoptive families, and acceptance of the single applicant.
5. A trend toward greater parity between adoptive parents and bioparents.

Bibliography

1. ABBOTT, GRACE. "Adoptions." *Encyclopedia of Social Science.* Ed. by Edwin R. Seligman. New York: The Macmillan Company, 1937.
2. ———. *The Child and the State,* Vol. I. Chicago: University of Chicago Press, 1938.
3. ADAMS, JOHN E., and HYUNG KIM. "A Fresh Look at Intercountry Adoptions." *Children,* **18,** 6 (November–December 1971), 214–21.
4. ADOPT-A-CHILD. *Adopt-a-Child—A Midpoint Report.* New York, January 1955–June 1956. Mimeo.
5. ANDERSON, DAVID C. *Children of Special Value—Interracial Adoption in America.* New York: St. Martin's Press, Inc., 1971.
6. ANDREWS, ROBERTA. "The Transitional Method in the Adoption Placement of Older Infants and Young Toddlers." *Child Welfare,* **40** (May 1961).
7. ANSFIELD, JOSEPH G. *The Adopted Child.* Springfield, Ill.: Charles C Thomas, Publishers, 1971.
8. ARMATRUDA, CATHERINE, and JOSEPH BALDWIN. "Current Adoption Practices." *Journal of Pediatrics,* **38** (February 1951).
9. ARONSON, HOWARD. "The Problem of Rejection of Adoptive Applicants." *Child Welfare,* **39** (October 1960).
10. BEAVEN, PAUL. "The Adoption of Retarded Children." *Child Welfare,* **35** (April 1956).
11. BELL, VELMA. "Special Considerations in the Adoption of the Older Child." *Social Casework* (June 1959).
12. BERNARD, VIOLA. "First Sight of Child by Prospective Parents—A Crucial Phase in Adoption." *American Journal of Orthopsychiatry,* **15** (1945).
13. BILLINGSLEY, ANDREW, and JEANNE GIOVANNINI. *Children of the Storm—Black Children and American Child Welfare.* New York: Harcourt Brace Jovanovich, Inc., 1972.
14. ———, and JEANNE GIOVANNINI. "Research Perspectives on Interracial Adoption," in *Race Research and Reason: Social Work Perspectives.* Ed. by Roger Willer. New York: National Association of Social Workers, 1969.
15. BISKIND, SYLVIA. "The Group Method in Services to Adoptive Families." *Child Welfare,* **45,** 10 (December 1966), 561–64.
16. ———. "Helping Adoptive Families Meet the Issues in Adoption." *Child Welfare,* **45,** 3 (March 1966), 145–50.
17. BOEHM, BERNICE. *Deterrents to the Adoption of Children—Foster Care.* New York: Child Welfare League of America, December 1958.
18. BOHMAN, MICHAEL. *Adopted Children and Their Families—A Follow-up Study of Adopted Children, Their Background Environment and Adjustment.* Stockholm: Proprius, 1970.
19. ———. "A Comparative Study of Adopted Children, Foster Children and Children in Their Biological Environment Born After Undesired Pregnancies." *Acta Paediatrica Scandinavica,* Supplement 221 (1971).
20. BOWERS, SWITHEN. "The Child's Heritage—From a Catholic Point of View," in *A Study of Adoption Practice,* Vol. II. Ed. by M. Schapiro. New York: Child Welfare League of America, 1956.

21. BRADLEY, TRUDY. *An Exploration of Case Workers' Perceptions of Adoptive Applicants.* New York: Child Welfare League of America, 1966.

22. BRANHAM, ETHEL. "One-Parent Adoptions." *Children,* **17,** 3 (May–June 1970), 103–106.

23. BRATFOS, OLE, et al. "Mental Illness and Crime in Adopted Children and Adoptive Parents." *Acta Psychiatrica Scandinavica,* **44,** 4 (1968), 376–84.

24. BREMNER, ROBERT H. (ed.). *Children and Youth in America: A Documentary History, Vol. II: 1866–1932,* Parts 1–6. Cambridge, Mass.: Harvard University Press, 1970.

25. BRENNER, RUTH. "A Follow-up Study of Adoptive Families." *Child Adoption Research Committee* (March 1951).

26. BRIELAND, DONALD. *An Experimental Study of the Selection of Adoptive Parents at Intake.* New York: Child Welfare League of America, 1959.

27. ———. "Practices in Selecting Adoptive ,Parents." *Child Welfare,* **38** (May 1959).

28. ———. "The Selection of Adoptive Parents at Intake." *Casework Papers, NCSW—1960.* New York: Columbia University Press, 1961.

29. BROWN, EDWIN G. *Selection of Adoptive Parents—A Videotape Study.* Unpublished Ph.D. Thesis, School of Social Service Administration, University of Chicago, Chicago, August 1970.

30. BROWN, FLORENCE. "Services to Adoptive Parents After Legal Adoption." *Child Welfare,* **38** (July 1959).

31. ———. "What Do We Seek in Adoptive Parents?" *Social Casework,* **32** (April 1951).

32. CALIFORNIA CITIZENS' ADOPTIONS COMMITTEE. *Serving Children in Need of Adoption.* Los Angeles, June 1965.

33. CAMPBELL, ANNE. "Principles of Social Work Applied to Adoption Practice, Policy and Procedure." *Social Work and the Preservation of Human Values.* Ed. by William Diton. London: J. M. Dent & Sons, Ltd., 1957.

34. CARROLL, JEROME. "Adoption by Whites of Children of Afro-American Heritage—Some Issues for Consideration." *Adoptalk,* **6,** 2, 3 (March–April, May–June 1970).

35. CARROLL, VERN (ed.). *Adoption in Eastern Oceania.* Honolulu: University of Hawaii Press, 1970.

36. CAWLEY, C. C. "The Outlaws." *The Christian Century* (April 3, 1957).

37. CHAMBERS, DONALD. "Willingness to Adopt Atypical Children." *Child Welfare,* **49,** 5 (May 1970), 275–79.

38. CHAPPELEAR, EDITH, and JOYCE FRIED. "Helping Adopting Couples Come to Grips with Their New Parental Roles." *Children,* **14,** 6 (November–December 1967), 223–26.

39. CHEMA, REGINA, et al. "Adoptive Placement of the Older Child." *Child Welfare,* **49,** 8 (October 1970), 450–58.

40. CHESTANG, LEON. "The Dilemma of Biracial Adoption." *Social Work,* **17,** 3 (May 1972), 100–105.

41. CHILD CARE ASSOCIATION OF ILLINOIS. *Subsidized Adoption—A Call to Action.* Moline, Ill., 1968.

42. CHILD WELFARE LEAGUE OF AMERICA. *Adoption of Oriental Children by American White Families—An Interdisciplinary Symposium.* New York, 1960.

43. ———. *Standards for Adoption Service*. New York, 1968.
44. CITIZENS' ADOPTION COMMITTEE OF LOS ANGELES COUNTY. *Natural Parents Who Relinquish Children for Adoption*. Los Angeles, June 1952.
45. ———. *Our Children in Foster Care—A Study of Children Needing Adoption*. Los Angeles, 1953.
46. CLOTHIER, FLORENCE. "Some Aspects of the Problem of Adoption." *American Journal of Orthopsychiatry*, 9 (1939).
47. COLLIER, CATHERINE. "A Postadoption Discussion Series." *Social Casework*, 41 (April 1960).
48. COLUMBIA LAW REVIEW. "Religion as a Factor in Adoption." *Columbia Law Review*, 54 (1954), 376–403.
49. COLVILLE, ANITA. "Adoption for the Handicapped Child." *Child Welfare*, 36 (October 1957).
50. COMMISSION ON POPULATION GROWTH AND THE AMERICAN FUTURE. *The Report of the Commission on Population Growth and the American Future*. New York: New American Library (Signet), 1972.
51. CONKLIN, LLOYD, et al. "Use of Groups During the Adoptive Post-Placement Period." *Social Work*, 7 (April 1962).
52. COSTIN, LELA B. "Adoption of Children by Single Parents." *Child Adoption* (November 1970), 31–33.
53. DAVIS, RUTH, and POLLY DOUCK. "Crucial Importance of Adoption Home Study." *Child Welfare*, 34 (March 1955).
54. DEASY, FEILA C., and OLIVE W. QUINN. "The Urban Negro and Adoption of Children." *Child Welfare*, 41 (November 1962).
55. DEHARTOG, JAN. *The Children—A Personal Record for the Use of Adoptive Parents*. New York: Atheneum Publishers, 1969.
56. DEPARTMENT OF PUBLIC WELFARE. *Report on Adoptions*. Edmonton, Alberta, Canada, 1969. Mimeo.
57. DEUTSCH, HELENE. *The Psychology of Women*, Vol. II. New York: Grune & Stratton, Inc., 1945.
58. DILLOW, LOUISE. "The Group Process in Adoptive Home Finding." *Children*, 15, 4 (July–August 1968), 153–57.
59. DIVIGLIO, LETITIA. "Adjustment of Foreign Children in Their Adoptive Homes." *Child Welfare*, 35 (November 1956).
60. DOTY, ROSEMARIE, and RICHARD MERWIN. "Parents Relinquishing Rights to First-Born Legitimate Children." *Child Welfare*, 48, 2 (February 1969), 100.
61. EIDUSON, BERNICE, and JEAN LIVERMORE. "Complications in Therapy with Adopted Children." *American Journal of Orthopsychiatry*, 23 (1953).
62. ELONEN, ANNE, and EDWARD SCHWARTZ. "A Longitudinal Study of Emotional, Social and Academic Functioning of Adopted Children." *Child Welfare*, 48, 2 (February 1969), 72–78.
63. EPPICH, ETHEL, and ALMA JENKINS. "Telling Adopted Children." *Studies of Children*. Ed. by Gladys Meyer. New York: King's Crown Press, 1948.
64. EPSTEIN, LAURA, and INRMGARD HEYMANN. "Some Decisive Process in Adoption Planning for the Older Child." *Child Welfare*, 46, 1 (January 1967), 5–9.
65. FAIRWEATHER, O. E. "Early Placement in Adoption." *Child Welfare*, 31 (1952).

66. FALK, LAWRENCE L. "A Comparative Study of Trans-racial and In-racial Adoptions." *Child Welfare,* **49**, 2 (February 1970), 82–88.

67. ———. "Identity and the Transracially Adopted Child." *Lutheran Social Welfare,* **9**, 2 (Summer 1969), 18–25.

68. FANSHEL, DAVID. *A Study in Negro Adoption.* New York: Child Welfare League of America, January 1957.

69. ———. *Far from the Reservation: The Transracial Adoption of American Indian Children.* Metuchen, N.J.: Scarecrow Press, Inc., 1972.

70. ———, and EUGENE B. SHINN. *Dollars and Sense in the Foster Care of Children—A Look at Cost Factors.* New York: Child Welfare League of America, 1972.

71. FELTON, ZELMA. "The Use of Adoption Resource Exchange." *Child Welfare,* **31** (June 1953).

72. FESTINGER, TRUDY BRADLEY. *Why Some Choose Not to Adopt Through Agencies.* New York: Metropolitan Applied Research Center, Inc., 1972.

73. FINEGOLD, WINIFRED. *Artificial Insemination.* Springfield, Ill.: Charles C Thomas, Publishers, 1964.

74. FISCHER, CLARENCE D. "Homes for Black Children." *Child Welfare,* **50**, 2 (February 1971), 108–11.

75. FOOTE, GWENDOLYN, and ROSALIND L. PUTNAM. *Negro Attitudes Toward Adoption in Hartford.* New Haven: The Connecticut Child Welfare Association, September 1965.

76. FOWLER, IRVING. "The Urban Middle-Class Negro and Adoption: Two Series of Studies and Their Implications for Action." *Child Welfare,* **45**, 9 (November 1966), 522–24.

77. FOWLER, LOWA. "Problem of Adoption Placement in British Columbia." *Social Welfare and the Preservation of Human Values.* Ed. by William Diton. London: J. M. Dent & Sons, Inc., 1957.

78. FRADKIN, HELEN. "Adoptive Parents for Children with Special Needs." Discussion by Ruth Taft. *Child Welfare,* **37** (January 1958).

79. FRANKL, ANNI W. "Work with Adoptive Parents." *Child Welfare,* **38** (April 1959).

80. FRANKLIN, DAVID S., and FRED MASSARIK. "The Adoption of Children with Medical Conditions: Part I: Process and Outcome; Part II: The Families Today, Part III: Discussion and Conclusions," *Child Welfare,* **48**, 8, 9, 10 (October–November–December 1969), 459–67, 533–39, 595–601.

81. FREUD, SIGMUND. "Family Romances," *Collected Papers,* Vol. V. London: Hogarth Press, Ltd., 1950.

82. FRICKE, HARRIET. "Interracial Adoption: The Little Revolution." *Social Work,* **10** (July 1965).

83. ———. "T.V. or Not T.V.—Minnesota Settles the Question." *Child Welfare,* **35** (November 1956).

84. GALLAGHER, URSULA M. "The Adoption of Mentally Retarded Children." *Children,* **15**, 1 (January–February 1968), 17–21.

85. ———. "Adoption Resources for Black Children." *Children,* **18**, 2 (March–April 1971), 49–51.

86. GALLAY, GRACE. "Interracial Adoptions." *Canadian Welfare,* **39**, 6 (November–December 1963), 248–50.

87. GENTILE, ANGELA. "Subsidized Adoption in New York: How the Law

Works and Some Problems." *Child Welfare*, **49**, 10 (December 1970), 576–83.

88. GOCHROS, HARVEY. "A Study of the Caseworker–Adoptive Parent Relationship in Postplacement Service." *Child Welfare*, **46**, 6 (June 1967), 317–25.

89. GOCHROS, HARVEY. *Not Parents Yet—A Study of the Postplacement Period in Adoption*. Minneapolis, Minn.: Division of Child Welfare, Department of Public Welfare, 1962.

90. GOLDBERG, HARRIET L., and LEWELLYN H. LINDE. "The Case for Subsidized Adoptions." *Child Welfare*, **48**, 2 (February 1969), 96–99.

91. GOLDRING, HOWARD, and JANIE TUTLEMAN. *Adoption Failures at the Los Angeles County Department of Adoptions*. Unpublished Master's Thesis, University of Southern California, School of Social Work, June 1970.

92. GOODACRE, IRIS. *Adoption Policy and Practice*. London: George Allen & Unwin, Ltd., 1966.

93. GOODMAN, JEROME. "Adopted Children Brought to Child Psychiatric Clinics." *Archives of General Psychiatry*, **9** (November 1963).

94. GRAHAM, LLOYD. "Children from Japan in American Adoptive Homes," in *Casework Papers*. New York: Family Service Association of America, 1957.

95. GROW, LUCILLE J. *A New Look at Supply and Demand in Adoption*. New York: Child Welfare League of America, May 1970. Mimeo.

96. ———, and MICHAEL SMITH. "Adoption Trends, 1969–1970; January–June 1971." *Child Welfare*, **50**, 7 (July 1971), 401–407; **50**, 9 (November 1971), 510–11.

97. HAGEN, CLAYTON, et al. *The Adopted Adult Discusses Adoption as a Life Experience*. Minneapolis: Lutheran Social Service of Minnesota, 1968.

98. HALLINAN, HELEN. "Adoption for Older Children." *Social Casework*, **33** (July 1952).

99. HASTINGS, JAMES (ed.). *Encyclopedia of Religion and Ethics*. New York: Charles Scribner's Sons, 1908.

100. HERZOG, ELIZABETH, and ROSE BERNSTEIN. "Why So Few Negro Adoptions?" *Children*, **12** (January–February 1965).

101. ———, et al. *Families for Black Children: The Search for Adoptive Parents. I: An Experience Survey*. Washington, D.C.: Government Printing Office, 1971.

102. ———, et al. "Some Opinion on Finding Families for Black Children." *Children*, **18**, 4 (July–August 1971), 143–48.

103. HILLER, ELSIE. "Applications by Married Parents for Adopted Placement of Their In-Wedlock Child." *Child Welfare*, **45**, 7 (July 1966), 404–409.

104. HOCHFIELD, EUGENIE. "Across National Boundaries." *Juvenile Court Judges Journal*, **14** (October 1963).

105. HOME OFFICE, SCOTTISH HOME DEPARTMENT. *Report of the Departmental Committee on the Adoption of Children*. London: Her Majesty's Stationery Office, 1958.

106. HOOPES, JANET, et al. *A Follow-up Study of Adoptions*. Vol. II: *Postplacement Functioning of Adopted Children*. New York: Child Welfare League of America, 1970.

107. HORNECKER, ALICE. "Adoption Opportunities for the Handicapped." *Children*, 9 (July–August 1962).

108. HUMPHREY, MICHAEL. *The Hostage Seekers*. Essex, England: Longmans Group Ltd., 1969.

109. ———, and CHRISTOPHER OUNSTED. "Adoptive Families Referred for Psychiatric Advice—I: The Children." *British Journal of Psychiatry*, 109 (1963).

110. HUNT, ROBERTA. *Obstacles to Interstate Adoption*. New York: Child Welfare League of America, 1972.

111. HYLTON, LYDIA. "Trends on Adoption." *Child Welfare*, 44 (July 1965).

112. ISAAC, RAEL J. *Adopting a Child Today*. New York: Harper and Row, Publishers, 1965.

113. JAFFEE, BENSON, and DAVID FANSHEL. *How They Fared in Adoption: A Follow-up Study*. New York: Columbia University Press, 1970.

114. JAMESON, GRACE. "Psychiatric Disorders in Adopted Children in Texas." *Texas Medicine*, 63, 4 (April 1967), 83–88.

115. JAQUITH, ESTHER. "An Adoptive Resource Exchange Under Private Auspices." *Child Welfare*, 41 (May 1962).

116. JONES, EDMOND D. "On Transracial Adoption of Black Children." *Child Welfare*, 51, 3 (March 1972), 156–64.

117. JORDON, VELMA L., and WILLIAM F. LITTLE. "Early Comments on Single-Parent Adoptive Homes." *Child Welfare*, 45, 9 (November 1966), 536–38.

118. KADUSHIN, ALFRED. "The Legally Adoptable, Unadopted Child." *Child Welfare*, 37 (December 1958).

119. ———. "A Study of Adoptive Parents of Hard-to-Place Children." *Social Casework*, 43 (May 1962).

120. ———. "Adoptive Parenthood: A Hazardous Adventure." *Social Work*, 11, 3 (July 1966).

121. ———. "Letter to the Editor." *Social Work*, 12, 1 (January 1967), 127–28.

122. ———. "Psychosocial Problems in Adoption." *Wisconsin Psychiatric Newsletter* (Fall 1967), 15–17.

123. ———. "Single-Parent Adopters: An Overview and Social Research." *Social Service Review*, 44, 3 (September 1970).

124. ———. *Adopting Older Children*. New York: Columbia University Press, 1970.

125. ———. "Adoptive Status—Birth Parents vs. Bread Parents." *Child Care Quarterly Review*, 25, 3 (July 1971), 10–14.

126. ———, and FREDERICK SEIDL. "Adoption Failure: A Social Work Postmortem." *Social Work*, 16, 3 (July 1971), 32–37.

127. KAPLAN, IRVING H. "A Group Approach to Adoptive Study." *Journal of Jewish Communal Services*, 47, 2 (Winter 1970), 127–35.

128. KASPORWICZ, ALFRED. "Interpreting Rejection to Adoptive Applicants." *Social Work*, 9 (January 1964).

129. KENNY, THOMAS, et al. "Incidence of Minimal Brain Injury in Adopted Children." *Child Welfare*, 46, 1 (January 1967), 24–29.

130. KETY, SEYMOUR S., et al. "Mental Illness in the Biological and Adoptive Families of Adopted Schizophrenics." *American Journal of Psychiatry*, 128, 3 (September 1971), 302–306.

131. KIRK, H. D. "A Dilemma of Adoptive Parenthood—Incongruous Role Obligation." *Marriage and Family Living*, **21** (November 1959).

132. ———. *Shared Fate*. New York: The Free Press, 1964.

133. ———, KURT JONASSOHN, and ANN FISH. "Are Adopted Children Especially Vulnerable to Stress?" *Archives of General Psychiatry*, **14** (March 1966).

134. KNIGHT, IRIS. "Placing the Handicapped Child for Adoption." *Child Adoption*, **62**, 4 (1970), 27–35.

135. KORNITZER, MARGARET. *Adoption and Family Life*. New York: Humanities Press, Inc., 1968.

136. ———, and JANE ROWE. *Some Casework Implications in the Study of Children Reclaimed or Returned Before Final Adoption*. Surrey, England: Standing Conference of Societies Registered for Adoption, May 1968. Mimeo.

137. KRUGMAN, DOROTHY. "Reality in Adoption." *Child Welfare*, **43**, 7 (July 1964).

138. KUHLMANN, FRIEDA, and HELEN ROBINSON. "Rorschach Tests as a Diagnostic Tool in Adoption Studies." *Journal of Social Casework*, **32** (January 1951).

139. LAKE, ALICE. "Babies for the Brave." *Saturday Evening Post* (July 31, 1954).

140. LANGSAM, MIRIAM Z. *Children West*. Madison, Wis.: State Historical Society of Wisconsin, 1964.

141. LAWDER, ELIZABETH, et al. *A Follow-up Study of Adoptions: Postplacement Functioning of Adoption Families*. New York: Child Welfare League of America, 1969.

142. ———. "A Limited Number of Older Children in Adoption—A Brief Survey." *Child Welfare*, **37** (November 1958).

143. LEATHERMAN, ANNE. "Placing the Older Child for Adoption." *Children* (May–June 1957).

144. LEAVY, MORTON. *Laws of Adoption*. Dobbs Ferry, N.Y.: Oceana Press, 1954.

145. LEFKOWITZ, MORRIS. Director of Services, Children's Home Society of California. Personal communication, December 12, 1969.

146. LEMASTERS, ERSEL. "Parenthood as a Crisis." *Marriage and Family Living*, **19** (1957).

147. LE SHAN, EDA. *You and Your Adopted Child*. New York: Public Affairs Committee, 1958.

148. LINDE, LLEWELLYN H. "The Search for Mom and Dad." *Minnesota Welfare*, **19**, 2 (Summer 1967), 7–12.

149. LOS ANGELES COUNTY DEPARTMENT OF ADOPTIONS. *Biennial Report 1965–67*. Los Angeles, October 1967.

150. LOSBOUGH, BILIE. "Relationship of E.E.G. Neurological and Psychological Findings in Adopted Children (75 cases)." *A Medical Journal of E.E.G. Technology*, **5**, 1 (January 1965), 1–4.

151. LOVSET, J. "Artificial Insemination: Attitudes of Patients in Norway." *Fertility and Sterility*, **2** (1951), 415–29.

152. LYSLO, ARNOLD. "The Indian Adoption Project." *Child Welfare*, **40** (May 1961).

153. MAAS, HENRY. "The Successful Adoptive Parent Applicants." *Social Work*, **5** (January 1960).

154. MARCH. *Adoptive Placement of Minority Group Children in the San Francisco Bay Area—A Study by MARCH.* San Francisco, 1959.

155. McCORMICK, REA. "The Adopting Parents See the Child," in *Studies of Children*. Ed. by Gladys Meger. New York: King's Crown Press, 1948.

156. McCOY, JACQUELINE. "Identity as a Factor in the Adoptive Placement of the Older Child." *Child Welfare*, **40** (September 1961).

157. McKAY, GORDON H. "Today's Controversial Clients: Married Parents Who Place Legitimate Children for Adoption." *Child Welfare*, **37** (January 1958).

158. McNEIL, THOMAS F., and RONALD WIEGERINK. "Behavioral Patterns and Pregnancy and Birth Complication Histories in Psychologically Disturbed Children." *Journal of Nervous and Mental Disease*, **152**, 5 (May 1971), 315–23.

159. McWHINNIE, ALEXINA M. *Adopted Children—How They Grow Up.* London: Kegan Paul, Trench, Trubner & Co., 1967.

160. ————. "Group Counselling with Seventy-Eight Adoptive Families." *Case Conference*, **14**, 11–12 (March–April 1968).

161. ————. "Who Am I?" *Child Adoption*, **62** (November 1970), 36–39.

162. MENLOVE, FRANCES L. "Aggressive Symptoms in Emotionally Disturbed Adopted Children." *Child Development*, **36** (June 1965).

163. MICHAELS, RUTH. "Casework Considerations in Rejecting the Adoption Application." *Social Casework*, **28** (December 1947).

164. MIDDLESTADT, EVELYN, *et al.* "Adoption Counseling—A New Opportunity for Growth." *Child Welfare*, **46**, 7 (July 1967), 365–70.

165. MIKAWA, JAMES, and JOHN BOSTON. "Psychological Characteristics of Adopted Children." *Psychiatric Quarterly Supplement*, **42**, 2 (July 1968), 274–81.

166. MONDLOH, RAYMOND. "Changing Practice in the Adoptive Home Study." *Child Welfare*, **48**, 3 (March 1969), 148–56.

167. MORGENSTERN, JOSEPH. "The New Face of Adoption." *Newsweek* (September 13, 1971), 66–72.

168. Morrison, Hazel. "Research Study in Adoption." *Child Welfare*, **29** (1950).

169. MULREY, J. M. "The Care of Destitute and Neglected Children." National Conference of Charities and Correction, 1899. Boston: George Ellis, 1900.

170. NATIONAL ASSOCIATION FOR MENTAL HEALTH, ENGLAND. *A Survey Based on Adoption Case Reviews.* London: National Association for Mental Health, 1954.

171. NATIONAL ASSOCIATION OF SOCIAL WORK. *Social Work Encyclopedia.* New York, 1965.

172. NATIONAL CONFERENCE OF CATHOLIC CHARITIES. *Adoption Practices in Catholic Agencies.* Washington, D.C., 1957.

173. NATIONAL COUNCIL OF CHURCHES OF CHRIST IN THE UNITED STATES. "Religious Factors in Child Adoptions—A Study Document." *Lutheran Social Welfare Quarterly*, **5** (March 1965).

174. NEMOVICHER, JOSEPH. *A Comparative Study of Adopted Boys and Non-*

adopted Boys in Respect to Specific Personality Characteristics. Unpublished Ph.D. Thesis, New York University, 1960.

175. NIEDEN, MARGARETE Z. "The Influence of Constitution and Environment Upon the Development of Adopted Children." *Journal of Psychology,* **31** (1951).

176. OFFORD, D. R., *et al.* "Presenting Symptomatology of Adopted Children." *Archives of General Psychiatry,* **20,** 1 (January 1969), 110–16.

177. OPPORTUNITY. *1971 Survey of Adoption of Black Children.* Portland, Ore.: Boys' and Girls' Aid Society of Oregon, 1971.

180. PAGET, NORMAN. "Use of Video Equipment in a Child Welfare Agency." *Child Welfare,* **48,** 5 (May 1969), 296–300.

181. PATON, JEAN M. *The Adopted Break Silence.* Philadelphia: Life History Study Center, 1954.

182. PELLER, L. "About 'Telling the Child' of His Adoption." *Bulletin of the Philadelphia Association of Psychoanalysis,* **11** (1961), 145–54.

183. PEPPER, GERALD W. *Interracial Adoptions: Family Profile, Motivation, and Coping Methods.* Unpublished Ph.D. Thesis, University of Southern California, 1966.

184. PETTIGREW, BRENDA. "Group Discussions with Adoptive Parents." *Child Adoption,* **1** (1969), 39–42.

185. PETTIS, SUSAN. "Effect of Adoption of Foreign Children on U.S. Adoption Standards and Practices." *Child Welfare,* **37** (July 1958).

186. PLATTS, HAL K. "Facts Against Impressions—Mothers Seeking to Relinquish Children for Adoption." *Children,* **17,** 1 (January–February 1970), 27–30.

187. POLK, MARY. "Maryland's Program of Subsidized Adoptions." *Child Welfare,* **49,** 10 (December 1970), 581–83.

188. PRIDDY, DREW, and DORIS KIRGAN. "Characteristics of White Couples Who Adopt Black-White Children." *Social Work,* **16,** 3 (July 1971), 105–107.

189. RALEIGH, BARBARA. "Adoption as a Factor in Child Guidance." *Smith College Studies in Social Work,* **25** (October 1954).

190. RAMSEY, PAUL. "The Legal Imputation of Religion to an Infant in Adoption Proceedings." *N.Y.U. Law Review,* **34** (April 1959), 649–90.

191. RATHBUN, CONSTANCE, *et al. Later Adjustments of Children Following Radical Separation from Family and Culture.* Paper presented at the Annual Meeting American Orthopsychiatric Association, Chicago, 1964.

192. RAYNOR, LOIS. *Adoptions of Nonwhite Children—The Experience of the British Adoption Project.* London: George Allen & Unwin, Ltd., 1970.

193. ———. "Agency Adoption of Nonwhite Children in the United Kingdom." *Race,* **10,** 2 (October 1968), 153–62.

194. REECE, SHIRLEY, and BARBARA LEVIN. "Psychiatric Disturbances in Adopted Children: A Descriptive Study." *Social Work,* **13,** 1 (January 1968), 101–11.

195. REEVES, A. C. "Children with Surrogate Parents—Cases Seen in Analytic Therapy and an Aetiological Hypothesis." *British Journal of Medical Psychology,* **44** (1971), 155–71.

196. RIDAY, EDWIN. "Supply and Demand in Adoption." *Child Welfare,* **48,** 8 (October 1969), 489–92.

197. RIPPLE, LILLIAN. "A Follow-up Study of Adopted Children." *Social Service Review,* **42**, 4 (December 1968), 479–97.

198. RONDELL, FLORENCE, and RUTH MICHAELS. *The Family That Grew.* New York: Crown Publishers, 1951.

199. SANDGRUND, GERTRUDE. "Group Counseling with Adoptive Families After Legal Adoption." *Child Welfare,* **41** (June 1962).

200. SANDUSKY, ANNIE LEE, et al. *Families for Black Children—The Search for Adoptive Parents. II: Program and Projects.* Washington, D.C.: Government Printing Office, 1972.

201. SARMIENTO, J. M. "Adoption Week: A Publicity Project in Adoptive Recruitment." *Child Welfare,* **48**, 3 (March 1969), 166–69.

202. SCHAPIRO, MICHAEL. *A Study of Adoption Practice,* Vol. III: *Adoption of Children with Special Needs.* New York: Child Welfare League of America, April 1957.

203. SCHECHTER, MARSHALL. "Observation on Adopted Children." *AMA Archives of General Psychiatry,* **3** (July 1960).

204. ———, et al. "Emotional Problems in the Adoptee." *General Archives of Psychiatry,* **10** (February 1964).

205. ———, et al. "Adoption Problems and the Physician." *Current Medical Digest* (June 1967), 821–37.

206. ———. "Psychoanalytic Theory As It Relates to Adoption." *Journal of American Psychoanalytic Association,* **15**, 3 (July 1967).

207. SCHELLEN, A. C. M. C. *Artificial Insemination in the Human.* New York: American Elsevier Publishing Co., Inc., 1957.

208. SCHRAGER, JULES. "After Adoption: An Agency-Sponsored Program." *Children,* **4** (July–August 1957).

209. SCHWARTZ, EDWARD. "The Family Romance Fantasy in Children Adopted in Infancy." *Child Welfare,* **49**, 7 (July 1970), 386–91.

210. SCHWARTZ, ELAINE J. *Subsidized Adoption—Sound Practice or Expedient Solution.* Child Welfare League of America, Midwest Conference, Winnepeg, Canada, 1972. Mimeo.

211. SCHWARTZ, WILLIAM. "Group Work in Public Welfare." *Public Welfare,* **26** (October 1968), 348–56.

212. SEGLOW, JEAN, et al. *Growing Up Adopted—A Long-Term National Study of Adopted Children and Their Families.* Windsor, England: National Foundation for Educational Research in England and Wales, 1972.

213. SEIDL, FREDERICK. "Transracial Adoptions: Agency Responses to Applicant Calls." *Social Work* (May 1972), 119–20.

214. SELLERS, MARTHA. "Transracial Adoption." *Child Welfare,* **48**, 6 (June 1969), 355–56.

215. SHARRAR, MARY L. "Some Helpful Techniques When Placing Older Children for Adoption." *Child Welfare,* **49**, 8 (October 1970), 459–63.

216. SHIREMAN, JOAN F. "Adoptive Applicants Who Withdrew." *Social Service Review,* **44**, 3 (September 1970), 285–92.

217. ———. *Subsidized Adoption: a Study of Use and Need in Four Agencies.* Chicago: Chicago Region Child Care Association of Illinois, 1969. Mimeo.

218. ———, and KENNETH W. WATSON. "Adoption of Real Children." *Social Work,* **17**, 1 (July 1972), 29–38.

219. SIMON, NATHAN, and AUDREY SENTURIA. "Adoption and Psychiatric Ill-ness." *American Journal of Psychiatry*, **122** (February 1966).

220. SMITH, MICHAEL J. "Adoption Trends: January–June 1971." *Child Welfare*, **50**, 9 (November 1971), 510–12.

221. ———. "Selected Adoption Data for 1969, 1970, and 1971." *Child Welfare*, **41**, 6 (June 1972), 373–74.

222. SOCIAL PLANNING COUNCIL OF METROPOLITAN TORONTO, CANADA. *The Adoption of Negro Children—A Community-wide Approach*. Toronto, July 1966.

223. SPRINGER, HELEN. "Sharing Responsibility with Applicants to Adopt." *Child Welfare*, **35** (March 1956).

224. ST. DENNIS, GERALD. *Interracial Adoptions in Minnesota: Self Concept and Child Rearing Attitudes of Caucasian Parents Who Have Adopted Negro Children*. Unpublished Ph.D. Thesis, University of Minnesota, 1969.

225. STANDING COMMITTEE OF AGENCIES REGISTERED FOR ADOPTION. "Adoptees' Right to Know." *Child Adoption*, **53** (1968), 30–31.

226. STARR, PHILIP, et al. "Early Life Experiences and Adoptive Parenting." *Social Casework*, **51** (October 1970), 491–500.

227. STARR, J. "Adoptive Placement of the Older Child." *Casework Papers*. New York: Columbia University Press, 1954.

228. STATE CHARITIES AID ASSOCIATION. *Facts to Build on—A Study of Adoption in New York State*. New York: State Charities Aid Association 1962.

229. STERNAU, AMELIA. "Short-Term Financial Aid for Adoptive Parents." *Child Welfare*, **38** (October 1959).

230. STONESIFER, ELSIE. "The Behavior Difficulties of Adopted and Own Children." *Smith College Studies in Social Work*, **13** (1942).

231. STUMPF, MARGARET. "Group Meetings for Prospective Adoptive Applicants," in *Group Methods in the Public Welfare Program*. Ed. by Norman Fenton and Kermit Wiltse. Palo Alto, Calif.: Pacific Books, Publishers, 1963.

232. SWEENY, DOLORES, et al. "A Descriptive Study of Adoptive Children Seen in a Child Guidance Clinic." *Child Welfare*, **42** (November 1963).

233. TAFT, RUTH. "Adoptive Families for 'Unadoptable' Children." *Child Welfare*, **32** (June 1953).

234. TENBROEK, JACOBUS. "California's Adoption Law and Programs." *Hastings Law Journal*, **6** (April 1955).

235. THEIS, SOPHIE VAN SENDEN. *How Foster Children Turn Out*. New York: State Charities Aid Association, 1924.

236. THOMAS, MORLAIS. "Foster/Adoptive Home Breakdowns." *Child Adoption*, **66** (1971), 29–33.

237. THUNEN, MARGARET. "Ending Contact with Adoptive Parents—The Group Meeting." *Child Welfare*, **37** (November 1958).

238. TOUSSIENG, POVL. "Thoughts Regarding the Etiology of Psychological Differences in Adopted Children." *Child Welfare*, **41** (February 1962).

239. ———. *European Seminar on Inter-Country Adoptions. Lysin, Switzerland, May 1960*. Geneva: United Nations Technical Assistance Office.

240. TRISELIOTIS, J. P. *Evaluation of Adoption Policy and Practice*. Edinburg University, Department of Social Administration, 1970

241. ———, and Valerie Lobban. "Recent Developments Affecting Adoption Numbers and Adoption Practice." *British Journal of Social Work*, 1, 3 (Autumn 1971), 333–44.

242. U.S. Department of Health, Education, and Welfare, Office of Child Development. *Progress Report: A Three Year Plan for a Black Adoption Project*. September 17, 1971.

243. ———. *Negro Adoption Rates*. March 31, 1971. Mimeo.

244. ———. Social and Rehabilitation Service. *Adoption in 1971*. Washington, D.C.: National Center for Social Statistics, 1973.

245. ———. *Legislative Guide for Termination of Parental Rights and Adoption*. Washington, D.C.: Government Printing Office, 1961.

246. U.S. Senate. *Hearing Before the Subcommittee to Investigate Juvenile Delinquency of the Committee on the Judiciary*. Washington, D.C.: Government Printing Office, 1956.

247. University of Chicago. *The Gray Market in Child Adoption*. University of Chicago Round Table No. 879. Chicago: University of Chicago Press, February 18, 1955.

248. Valk, Margaret. *Korean-American Children in American Adoptive Homes*. New York: Child Welfare League of America. September 1957.

249. Vieregge, Elizabeth. "Experience with Applicants in a Single Preadoption Group Meeting," in *Group Methods in the Public Welfare Program*. Ed. by Norman Fenton and Kermit Wiltse. Palo Alto, Calif.: Pacific Books, Publishers, 1963.

250. Wachtel, Dawn D. *Adoption Agencies and the Adoption of Black Children*. Washington, D.C.: Adoptions Research Project, 1972.

251. Wasson, Volintina. *The Chosen Baby*. New York: Cormick and Evans, 1939.

252. Watson, Kenneth. "Subsidized Adoption: A Crucial Investment." *Child Welfare*, 51, 4 (April 1972), 220–30.

253. Weingarten, Victor. "Breaking the Barrier of Confidentiality." *Child Welfare*, 37 (April 1958).

254. Welter, Marianne. *Comparison of Adopted Older Foreign Born and American Children*. New York: International Social Service, 1965.

255. Wheeler, Katherine B. "The Use of Adoptive Subsidies." *Child Welfare*, 48, 9 (November 1969), 557–59.

256. Wiehe, Vernon. "The Group Adoptive Study." *Child Welfare*, 51, 10 (December 1972), 645–49.

257. Wingfield, F. "Prospective Adopters Groups: An Experiment." *Social Work*, 26, 4 (October 1969), 14–16.

258. Winsor, Geraldine. *The Adopted Parent Speaks*. Unpublished Master's Thesis, School of Social Work, University of Wisconsin, Madison, Wis., 1962.

259. Witmer, Helen, *et al. Independent Adoptions*. New York: Russell Sage Foundation, 1963.

260. Work, Henry H., and Hans Anderson. "Studies in Adoption: Requests for Psychiatric Treatment." *American Journal of Psychiatry*, 127, 7 (January 1971), 948–50.

261. Young, Joyce. "The Adoption Agency and the Adopted Person." *Child Adoption*, No. 66 (1971), 21–28.

262. ZASTROW, CHARLES. *Outcome of Negro Children—Caucasian Parents' Transracial Adoptions.* Unpublished Ph.D. Thesis, University of Wisconsin, Madison, Wis. 1971.

263. ZOBER, EDITH. "Postplacement Service for Adoptive Families." *Child Welfare,* **40** (April 1961).

12

The Child-Caring Institution

Introduction

The child-caring institution is a third facility that offers total substitute care for the child whose parents cannot and/or will not implement their parental role. The boarding home is a temporary facility; the adoptive home, a permanent one. Both provide the child with family care. The institution, like the boarding home, provides temporary substitute care; like the adoptive home, it offers permanent care; but, unlike either, it offers group care rather than family care.

A *children's institution* is defined as a twenty-four-hour residential facility in which a group of unrelated children live together in the care of a group of unrelated adults.

There are many different kinds of institutions serving different kinds of children. Among them are the following:

1. Institutions for normal but dependent and neglected children. This is the closest modern analogy to the old orphan asylum.
2. Institutions for physically handicapped children. There are separate institutions for children who are blind, deaf, crippled, asthmatic, and so on.
3. Institutions for mentally retarded or mentally defective children.
4. Institutions for the confinement and rehabilitation of juvenile delinquents. These are often called *training schools.*

5. Institutions for emotionally disturbed children; these are known as *residential treatment centers.*

There are other institutions that do not necessarily serve a special population of children but that are distinguished by their special purpose. These include:

1. Emergency facilities that accept children on a short-term basis while a study is made of the situation to determine the best plan for their care. Such a facility might also be used for children who need short-term care.
2. Diagnostic or observation centers to which a child is referred for the explicit purpose of undergoing a detailed physical, psychological, and social study.

Although institutions deal with the child who faces some problem in the parent-child relationship network, many institutions are not under social work child welfare auspices. This may result from the fact that the central problem is perceived as a medical problem in the case of the physically handicapped child; as a problem of law enforcement in the case of the juvenile delinquent; as a medical or educational or vocational problem in the case of the emotionally disturbed or mentally deficient child. Hence institutions operate under the auspices of many groups.

The heterogeneous responsibility for the child-caring institutions stems also from the fact that well into the 1920's, the social work profession saw the child-caring institution as a somewhat disreputable last resort. Only after World War II did professional social work "accept" the institution as a specialized service to be selectively and appropriately used for some groups of children.

The different institutions serving different groups of children are, of course, apt to differ in many essential details. All have in common the fact that they are group-care facilities that provide total substitution of the biological parents' care of the child. This implies, then, that many significant elements are common to all institutions. Our concern in this chapter is with those general factors that are characteristic of all institutions. However, whenever we do encounter a need to be concerned with the more particular practice of institutions, we will focus on institutions for the dependent and neglected and on residential treatment centers for emotionally disturbed children. These institutions employ the bulk of social workers working in institutional child care. Furthermore, Federal statistics on institutional child care are listed in terms of these two kinds of institutions. [109]

Historical Background

The institution has a long history. The *xenodocheion* established by the Council of Nicaea in 325 to give shelter to the sick and the poor became asylums for abandoned children—a fact that led some of them to be called *Brephotrophia*. In 787, Datheus, Archbishop of Milan, established an institution to care for children. Concerned about the abandonment of children, he noted: "These horrors would not take place if there existed an asylum where the adulterer could hide her shame but now they throw the infants in the sewers or the rivers and many are the murders committed on the new-born children. . . ." [46, p. 294] Similarly, the pitiful condition of the many abandoned children in fifteenth-century France attracted the sympathy of St. Vincent de Paul, who established homes for the *enfants trouvés* in 1633.

But, although there existed a limited number of institutions exclusively concerned with caring for children, the more typical pattern was to have the children share an institution with other deprived groups in the population. Admission records of the New York City Almshouse note that some 15 percent of the admissions between 1736 and 1746 involved "young and parentless children—the orphaned and the deserted —who would remain until the beginning of their apprenticeship." [92, p. 39] Only a few institutions for dependent children had been established by the end of the eighteenth century. One had been established in New Orleans, as a result of the need to care for a large number of children orphaned by an Indian massacre at Natchez. Another was established as a result of a yellow fewer epidemic in Philadelphia. More frequently, however, children requiring institutional care were consigned to mixed almshouses "to live with the aged, the insane, the feeble-minded, and the diseased. They were usually cared for by the ignorant employees; their physical needs were neglected. . . . Those who survived knew only the life and routine of a pauper institution." [1, p. 4] Some almshouses did make an effort to see that children's needs were met, however. The Rules and Orders for the Management of the Work House in Boston, dated 1739, noted

> . . . That when any children shall be received into the House,
> there shall be some suitable women appointed to attend them;
> Who are to take care that they be wash'd, com'b and dress'd every
> morning, and be taught to Read and be instructed in the Holy
> Scriptures . . . and that the rest of their time be employ'd in such
> work as shall be assigned them. . . . [Quoted in 113, p. 397]

Although additional institutions for children were built early in the nineteenth century, the number of children in mixed almshouses continued to grow. As investigation after investigation confirmed the undesirable conditions under which the children lived, a growing dissatisfaction led to increasingly insistent demands that this method of caring for children be prohibited. Thus, the Board of Public Charities for the State of Ohio, in its report for 1869, declared:

> Nearly one thousand children in the poor-houses of Ohio! What is to be done with them? Think of their surroundings. The raving of the maniac, the frightful contortions of the epileptic, the driveling and senseless sputtering of the idiot, the garrulous temper of the decrepit, neglected old age, the peevishness of the infirm, the accumulated filth of all these; then add the moral degeneracy of such as, for idleness or dissipation, seek a refuge from honest toil in the tithed industry of the county, and you have a faint outline of the surroundings of these little boys and girls, all more or less intelligent, many of them bright and beautiful, in such homes as these. How deeply must every human sympathy be touched with the reflection, that to these little children the poor-house is "all the world." [1, p. 52]

There were some attempts at compromise by making separate institutional facilities available to children on almshouse grounds, but these attempts were few and unsatisfactory.

During the latter part of the nineteenth century, many states prohibited almshouse care for children. Thus New York State, in 1875, declared that children should "be removed from almshouses and provided for in families, asylums or other appropriate institutions." This meant that alternative forms of care had to be provided for the literally tens of thousands of children who had to be removed from almshouse care in one state after another. By this time, both foster care and institutions exclusively concerned with children, such as orphanages, had been developed. And, as Thurston notes, "as children were withdrawn or refused admission to almshouses, the tendency to build orphan asylums —already strong—was stimulated." [103, p. 90] The rapid use of the orphan asylum is exemplified by New York State, which had only two such institutions in 1825 but more than 60 in 1866.

The asylum was seen as shelter, sanctuary, and training school for the child. Moralism dictated the routine and the orientation put a premium on order, obedience, and character development through work. Institutions were developed under the auspices of benevolent organizations, charitable individuals, and religious groups. An early history of social work notes:

> Institutions are in favor with the benevolent because the work done is so manifest. . . . Buildings are obvious and the money that goes into them takes a concrete form gratifying to contributors.

> The churches prefer such life for the children dependent on them
> because the children can be so easily isolated from teachings
> other than their own and there is opportunity for catechetical
> instruction. [111, p. 134]

Public institutions were also developed under municipal, county, and state auspices. The first state institution was established by Massachusetts in 1866, and many states followed Michigan's pattern of housing dependent children in one central institution and placing them in families as soon as possible. The nineteenth century also witnessed the development of special institutions for the care of the physically handicapped, the deaf, the blind, the mentally retarded, and the delinquent. Thus, by 1923, the U.S. Census on Children Under Institutional Care listed 1558 "orphan asylums." [103, p. 39]

But even while the special institution for children was superseding the almshouse, serious questions were being raised about the advisability of any kind of institutional care for children. The late nineteenth and early twentieth centuries witnessed a continuous, prolonged, and often acrimonious debate in child welfare circles between the proponents of institutional care for children and the advocates of family foster care. [118] A growing recognition of the importance of the family to the child's healthy psychosocial development resulted in a growing preference for family foster care. The prevailing negative attitude toward the institution was supported, and strongly reinforced, by a United Nations report, *Maternal Care and Mental Health*, by John Bowlby (1951), which provided a detailed review of a considerable body of research showing the deleterious effects of institutional care on child development. [15]

Child welfare workers developed a hierarchy of preferences: the child's own home, even if inadequate, was felt to be better than the best boarding home; a boarding home, even if inadequate, was felt to be better than the best institution. More recently, however, the controversy regarding the relative merits of the boarding home and the institution has been redefined in different terms. The institution is no longer viewed in terms of a hierarchy of preferences but, rather, in terms of its appropriateness for certain groups of children who cannot be served by any other kind of facility. Institutions and boarding homes have come to be seen as complementary, rather than competitive, resources. Each is necessary and appropriate for different groups of children, and each has a particular place in the total pattern of child care services.

The resolution of the controversy resulted not only from the redefinition of the problem, but also from a more critical attitude toward Bowlby's major thesis—that institutional care was likely to be harmful to the child. More recent research has softened the negative attitude toward the institution and contributed toward the growing readiness to use it when it meets the needs of the child. [25; 27; 73; 115; 116; 117; 119]

The "Uniqueness" of the Institution

The fact that institutional care is group care in a separate, twenty-four-hour, residential, physically defined community gives it some unique advantages that can be exploited to meet the special needs of some particular groups of children.

1. The institutions offer opportunities for a diluted emotional relationship with parental figures. Because the child in the institution has to share the houseparents with many other children, his relationship with them is apt to be attenuated. This permits the child to maintain a certain "safe" psychological distance from the parental figure and to modulate his contact in accordance with his emotional needs. Just as the child may want less from institutional parent figures, they, in turn, make fewer demands on the child. Specific portions of the houseparents' "time and energy have been purchased in relation to therapeutic purposes." [97, p. 2]   As employees, they are less apt than foster parents to demand psychic repayment from the child.

2. The institution provides the child with a greater variety and choice of parental figures. If the child feels uncomfortable with the houseparent, he may develop a relationship with the resident teacher, or the resident social worker, or the resident maintenance man. There is a greater chance in the institution that the child will find the kind of person with whom he wants to identify.

3. The institution offers greater tolerance for all sorts of behavior that could not, and would not, be accepted in the community. "The greater symptom tolerance in an institution applies not only to acting-out behavior, but to withdrawn or bizarre behavior—for example, a child who sits by himself and will not talk or one who refuses to bathe for weeks." [59, p. 107]   A child can also be permitted a greater range of destructive behavior in an institution than in a normal home. None of the staff "owns" the institution, so that destructive behavior, although deplored, does not arouse the same intense reaction it might evoke from foster parents whose furniture was being ruined. The institution is in a better position than a private home to "absorb" such losses. By the same token, "the diffusion of the child's hostility among many adults makes it easier for any one staff member to take." [29, p. 7]

4. The fact that institutional living requires rules, regulations, and a certain routine may be an advantage to many children who need the tight structure of precise routine to reinforce their own efforts at self-control. The regularity, consistency, and stability of the institutional structure, and the routines of orderly living, provide the kind of support some of the children need. Many have experienced the anxiety that comes from living in an uncertain situation. Many of these children have never had a pattern of regularity in their daily routine. The explicit structure of regulation relieves the child of responsibility for making decisions regarding his behavior, decisions which may occasion anxiety. Routine simplifies the child's life and permits him to know, with some assurance, what to expect.

5. Also, the institution is allied with those components of the child's ambivalence that strive to maintain control and to manifest acceptable behavior. Internal controls, which are weak in the child's own character structure, are built into the institution to help the child control himself. The child recognizes that the staff will support him in his efforts to refrain from impulsive, unacceptable behavior. Those kinds of behavior which the child might manifest in the open community—running away, truancy, sexual promiscuity, and so on—are not permitted in the more controlled, closed environment of the institution. Furthermore, unlike parental controls, institutional controls have the force of law and, because they are impersonal, uniform, and imposed on every member of the group, they are more difficult for the child to fight. [44] The institution carries the stamp of authority and, unlike parental controls, institutional controls are less likely to be seen as a personal attack.

6. The fact that the child lives his daily life as a member of a peer group means that the group has power to control his behavior. Group pressure can be applied to motivate the child to change his behavior so as to be less deviant, more conforming. Intimate, daily living with a peer group provides the possibility of exploitation of group interaction as a catalyst for change. Through identification with the peer group, the child is able to accept and want what the peer group accepts and wants. For instance, one boy at first resented contact with the institutional social worker. The worker, consequently, delayed scheduling an appointment.

> All of H.'s group went to their regular appointments with their workers and H. became increasingly annoyed by this "neglect" when he received no appointments. After two months, he finally asked, "What the hell is the matter with that jerk of a social worker? Can't that guy write? Why doesn't he send me a pass for an appointment?" The worker, at this point, finally sent H. his appointment. The boy immediately was involved in an intensive treatment relationship. [95, p. 322]

7. Of great importance is the fact that residential group care permits the institution to plan the child's daily living experience so that it will be optimally therapeutic. It can provide the child with an environment that is planned and controlled so as to help the child. A child who is having

difficulty with peers in one cottage can be moved to another cottage, and another peer group, within the same institution. An institutional staff can deliberately select children for a cottage group in accordance with some explicit considerations as to what kinds of friends each of the children needs. The institution can regulate the demands it enforces on the child in line with the child's inadequacies. It can particularize the details of his living situation, and, within limits, it structures his reality to meet his clinical needs.

> . . . [It can provide] a flexible low-pressure environment for the deeply disturbed sensitive child, a clearly defined, more rigidly organized environment for the acting-out aggressive child who needs help in controlling his impulses. The environment for the young impulse-driven schizophrenic child with little personality structure must give greater weight to such considerations as the use of space, the allotment and scheduling of time. It might provide for greater emphasis on order and regularity and movement in personal routine. [5, p. 131]

Also, because many institutions control the child's educational program, they can provide a more individualized curriculum, permitting a slower pace with more intensive personal tutoring.

8. Because the institution has specially trained personnel and special facilities, it can meet the unusual needs of the blind, the mentally defective, the emotionally disturbed, and so on. The institution, with its professional staff, can provide special physical rehabilitation programs, special medical treatments, and special remedial educational programs. The institution makes the child available and accessible to treatment— contact with personnel offering therapy is facilitated by virtue of the fact that the child is living on the grounds. The child is available for diagnostic study as well. The staff can observe his behavior at first hand rather than have to depend on reports from parents, teachers, and so on.

Situations for Which Institutional Care Is the Appropriate Resource

Institutional care is appropriate in many of the situations in which the child must be removed from his own home and placed under substitute care for some indefinite period (see Chaps. 9 and 10). Those children referred for institutional care are more likely to have been removed from their homes as a result of their inadequacy in implementing their roles, primarily because of emotional, physical, or mental handicaps. Children who are removed from the home because of parental inadequacy are more likely to be placed in a foster family or made available for adoption. Despite this difference, the primary decision is whether to remove the child from his own home. Referral to foster family or institutional care is a secondary decision.

The choice of institutional care may be predicated on what the child brings, or fails to bring, to the situation. The child, for one reason or another, may be unable to make use of the substitute family situation found in boarding or adoptive care. He may be emotionally incapable of developing a satisfactory relationship with parental figures, neither accepting nor responding with affection to them. Trasler notes the reactions of such children to the foster care that had been inappropriately selected for them:

> The foster parents complained that M., the illegitimate child of a feeble-minded woman, "showed no signs of affection for them and appeared to be indifferent to their demonstrations of affection for her. They felt that she would never be able to adjust herself to their family group." [104, p. 21]

> S.'s mother had been committed to a mental hospital and she had been shuttled from one home to another. Her foster parents asked that she be removed from the home because of her "apparent lack of real affection for them." They told the social worker "how often they had been hurt and grieved by S.'s complete lack of loyalty or any positive feeling for them. She does not harmonize with them at all and they feel quite unable to regard her as a member of the family." [104, p. 37]

Such children need, for a time, the kind of parent-child relationship provided by the institution—attenuated relationships, emotional distance, and limited involvement.

This same advantage of the institution may make it the most appropriate placement for a child who is very closely tied to his natural parents. Placement in a foster family home for such a child would excite a conflict of loyalties between allegiance to his own parents and affection for the foster parents. Placed in an institution, without obligation to respond to a close relationship with parental figures, the child is spared the problem of competitive allegiances.

This aspect of institutional life also makes it an appropriate placement for the adolescent. The adolescent is faced with the problem of emancipating himself from close family ties, reducing his emotional investment in the family, and increasing his emotional investment in the peer group. For the adolescent the institution offers a less intense relationship with parental figures and easy access to a peer group.

The institution is also appropriate for the child whose behavior makes him difficult to live with in a normal family setting. If the child is very aggressive and/or destructive, he cannot live satisfactorily in the close give-and-take of the normal family. Furthermore, the community might find it difficult to tolerate his behavior; his aggressiveness may present a danger to other children and to community property. The child who set fires or engages in repeated acts of vandalism and who is beyond the control of parents needs an institution. The child who masturbates constantly and openly, who soils himself, who demonstrates extreme withdrawal behavior and unrelieved apathy is not likely to be acceptable in a boarding home. Such children, in fact, have often been rejected by a succession of foster parents and need the temporary permanence of an institution. The acting-out child needs the controls, limits, structure, and orderliness of the institution. The child manifesting bizarre, neurotic behavior needs the greater tolerance for deviation that the institution can provide.

The following are descriptive statements of children who were referred to a residential treatment center:

> "Screaming fits and unmanageable at home"; "timid, fearful and withdrawn, screaming and fear of adults"; "found to be carrying out 'an under-cover reign of terror' in the school"; "picks fingers raw, frightful temper"; "mother at wits' end—boy has violent temper, antagonistic to everyone"; "soiling, enuresis, destructive behaviors"; "unaccountable bursts of sobbing; preoccupied with fire; a considerable danger in the home"; "sleeps badly, screams at night, night terrors"; "never spoke in the house; 'used to cry if you looked at him,' no life, no spontaneity, no interests"; "destructive, unruly, disobedient, spiteful, and uncontrollable"; "restless, completely uninhibited, acting on strong instinctive impulses, very difficult, and has terrible rages in which he kicks and bites and nothing is safe from him"; "truancy and unwillingness to go to school, suffers from sudden and extreme panics and anxieties." [6, pp. 137–67]

Such children—the child who acts out and the child who is unable to form any kind of satisfactory relationship with parental figures—are unable, because of their emotional handicaps, to implement adequately their roles as children in the normal family setting.

Other groups of children are unable to implement their roles adequately because of physical or mental handicaps. The blind, the deaf, the crippled, and the mentally deficient may, for a time, be unable to live in a family group because of the excessive demands they impose on the parent-child relationship. Such children require special care and special handling. The institution, with its special facilities and professional staff, is better geared to meet the needs of such children.

The decision to offer institutional care may be based not on what the child brings, or fails to bring, to the situation but on the parents' responses. The natural parent who is greatly threatened by the loss of his child's affection to foster parents may be better able to accept his child's placement in an institution. The fact that the child has to share the institutional parent figures with a group of children reduces the natural parent's anxiety. Furthermore, the institution is perceived as being sufficiently different from family living that the parent may feel less guilty if the institution succeeds where he has failed with the child. The parent can attribute such success to the special facilities and professional staff of the institution.

Choice of an institution may also be predicated on the need for short-term care. As Lerner says, "The institution, because it demands less in terms of emotional involvement, protects the child from making ties that must soon be broken." [59, p. 108]

Also, a large group of siblings who want to, and should, be kept together have found this to be possible only through institutional placement:

Eight of nine children in one family orphaned by an auto accident will shortly pile into two automobiles for the seventy-mile ride to Kannapolis where they will enter an orphanage in answer to their plea to remain together.

The children, who range in age from four to fourteen, now are in five foster homes. A ten-month-old infant is still in another home. The orphanage won't accept him until he is two.

"I talked to them as a group," said the social worker. "I explained to them this may be the only way they could remain together." *

Institutional placement is supposedly contraindicated for infants and very young children. Such children are too young to profit from group living and require the more intensive relationship and mothering that are more likely to be available in a family setting.

Ideally, then, institutional placement is offered the child and the family after some considered assessment of the situation. Ideally, the child should not end up in an institution simply because more desirable alternatives are not available. Institutional care should be "treatment by choice rather than treatment by default." [95, p. 319] It appears, however, that here, as elsewhere, there is a gap between the ideal and reality.

The Maas-Engler study of children in care reveals wide variations from community to community in the relative proportions of children placed in foster care and in institutions. Thus, in one community, 90

---

* From Associated Press dispatch from Lenoir, N.C., printed in *The Capital Times*, Madison, Wis., June 1963. By permission of The Associated Press, New York.

percent of the children in substitute care were in institutions and 10 percent were in foster homes. In another community of similar size, the pattern was almost exactly the reverse: 85 percent of the children were in foster homes and 15 percent were in institutions. [62, p. 15]   Wolins and Piliavin, analyzing state statistics, demonstrate variations from state to state in the extent to which use is made of foster family care or the institution. [118]   Because it is not likely that there are wide variations in the children's situations, the differences in the frequency with which the institution is used are attributed to expediency and to the lack of availability of alternative resources. [118, p. 43]

A national survey of 2000 children's institutions indicated that 36,000 children had been accepted or retained because this was the only expedient and feasible plan, though not the best. [79, p. 457]   At the same time the institutions did not have room for some 54,000 children that they felt needed, and should have gained, admittance. In summary, over a "one-year period, directors of children's institutions reported that they made 126,829 decisions about children in need that they personally considered contrary to the best interests of the child in question, simply because of administrative problems or because the appropriate resource was not available." [79, p. 458]

Maluccio and Marlow, after reviewing the relevant literature, concluded:

> The decision to place a child in residential treatment is presently a highly individualized matter based on a complex set of idiosyncratic factors defying categorization. The literature does not indicate agreement on consistent criteria or universal guidelines and it is not certain whether institutions diverse in origin, philosophy, policy, and clientele can agree on a basic set of premises. [65, p. 239]

Like some decisions in foster care, the decision to refer a child to a residential treatment center may be often "more a decision of desperation than of deliberation."

One of the advantages of the institution is its greater availability. In the absence of sufficient foster homes or adoptive homes, the institution stands ready to accept the child. As Lewis says, "Whenever there is a strain on the placement facilities, it has always been easy to look to the institution as a general refuge to get a roof over the heads of children in need. It seems simple to add one more bed and one more place to such an on-going residence." [60, p. 141]   This very advantage, then, acts as a disadvantage in encouraging use of the institution on the basis of expediency.

Briar attempted an experimental study of how social workers go about making the decision to offer the child an institution or foster care. [17; 18]   Although the research has been criticized for its methodological deficiencies, it indicates that social workers do take into consideration the extent of the child's emotional disturbance and the preferences of the biological parents. [36]   Greater emotional disturbance in the child and opposition by the biological parents to foster care were associated with choice of the institution rather than a foster home. This is clearly in line with a decision based on diagnostic assessment. However, the study also showed that social workers in an agency that stressed foster care tended to recommend such care, whereas workers in agencies committed to institutional care tended to recommend this kind of care. This, then, is another factor influencing the decision process, which violates the principle that the decision regarding the use of the institution be based on diagnostic considerations.

Scope

Table 12–1 lists the number of children under 18 years of age living in institutions in 1968–70. In September 1965 there were some 3763 residential institutions for children in the United States. Institutions for dependent and neglected children comprised the largest single category—40 percent; residential facilities for mentally retarded children, 19 percent; correctional facilities for delinquents, 17 percent; institutions for the physically handicapped, 10 percent; institutions for

TABLE 12–1.   Children in Institutional Care Under 18 Years of Age, 1970

Type of Institution	Number	Percent
Welfare		
Homes for dependent and neglected children	43,867	18
Homes for unwed mothers	2,351	1
Homes for the aged and dependent	2,368	1
Correctional		
Training schools for juvenile delinquents	51,932	22
Prisons, reformatories, and local jails	10,180	4
Detention homes	9,709	4
Diagnostic and reception centers	n.a.	n.a.
Mental Disabilities		
Home and schools for the mentally handicapped	69,752	29
Mental hospitals and residential treatment centers	26,792	11
Physical Disabilities		
Homes and schools for the deaf	7,873	3
Homes and schools for the blind	4,742	2
Other homes and schools for the physically handicapped	3,874	2
Hospitals for tuberculosis and chronic diseases	4,650	2
TOTAL	238,090	99

Source: *Persons in Institutions and Other Group Quarters*, U.S. Bureau of the Census, July 1973.

emotionally disturbed children, 8 percent; maternity homes for un-married mothers, 6 percent. Fifty-two percent of all institutions were under private voluntary auspices, the majority sponsored by religious denominations; a third were public facilities; some 15 percent were privately operated. [98, p. 5]   Although most of the institutions are under private auspices, a substantial portion of their funds comes from public sources. Public social services agencies, arranging for the place-ment of a child in institutional care, pay the costs for care of the child.

Institutions for the mentally retarded account for the largest number of children in institutional care [78],   followed by training schools for juvenile delinquents. The residential treatment center, defined by the Children's Bureau as an "institution for the treatment of emotionally disturbed children in which planning is based on clinical study and in which treatment is carried out according to recommendations emerg-ing from such a clinical study," serves only a small percentage of children in institutional care. [77]

In 1969 there were some 260 residential treatment centers in the United States, housing about 21,000 children, a modest percent of the children in institutional care. The majority were small privately owned institutions, two-thirds providing service to fewer than fifty children and none accepting children under six years of age. [108]   Most of these institutions were established after World War II and many had been institutions for the dependent and neglected which had "adjusted their program to meet changing definitions of need." [77, p. xxxiv]

Institutions for the dependent and neglected, comprising a large per-centage of all the institutions for children and caring for a large percent-age of children in institutions, are defined by the U.S. Bureau of the Census as follows:

> This class of homes covers orphanages and other institutions which provide long-term care for children; it also covers institutions generally known as receiving homes or shelters which provide temporary care primarily to children whose homes have been broken by illness, desertion, death, and social crises.

Most of these institutions are under private—usually denominational—auspices. In fact, twenty-three states listed no public institution for the dependent and neglected in 1966. [76, Table 1, p. 2]   The mean age of children living in these institutions in 1966 was twelve years and four months. Only 1.8 percent of the population of the institution was under two years of age. [76]   The population of residential treatment centers was slightly older. In institutions for the dependent and neglected, the population was 57.2 percent male and 42.8 percent female, but in resi-dential treatment centers it was 70 percent male and only 30 percent female.

Statistics show that such institutional placement is not long-term substitute care. The average stay in residential treatment centers is two to two-and-a-half years [77, Table 222, p. 237]; in homes for the dependent and neglected, it is likely to be somewhat longer—two-and-a-half to three years. [76, Table 23, p. 29]

Social Work and Institutional Care

Preparation for Placement

Before the agency can seriously consider the institution as a resource in any particular instance, it has to study the child and the family. The parent is helped to explore the nature of the situation requiring substitute care for the child, and to discuss possible alternatives.

One study notes that intake discussions with parents considering institutionalization of a mentally deficient child often resulted in decisions to keep such children in the home. [31] Hagen reports, without further amplification, that, "at a certain small multiple-service children's agency that has a strong casework service, 80 percent of the parents applying for institutional service decided they would keep their children with them and work out their problems within the home." [43, p. 4]

This was confirmed by an experiment in Israel in which "two local public welfare offices were operated for a period of eighteen months by a university-guided team of social workers to test the effects of innovative work on rate of institutional placements for dependent children." [47, p. 7] The two experimental offices emphasized explorations of solutions other than institutional care. Two control offices, which accepted the clients' initial requests for institutional care, showed a significantly larger proportion of institutional placements than the two experimental offices.

In many instances, the decision to institutionalize the child has come after frustration and disappointment in attempts to use supportive and supplementary services to maintain the child at home. Many emotionally disturbed children have received treatment at child guidance clinics or by psychiatrists in private practice before being committed. A study of children at the Junior Village, Washington, D.C., indicated that supportive and supplementary services had been utilized by many of the families—28 percent had used local psychiatric facilities, 72 percent had applied for AFDC, and "about a third" were known to the local Family and Children Service. [107, pp. 125–27] A detailed study of the work of twenty-one residential treatment centers indicated that 53 percent of the children at the centers had previously received some kind of therapy for their emotional problems. [46, p. 126] And a study by

Bloch and Behrens shows that 75 percent of the children referred for residential treatment had been separated from their homes before request for institutional care was made; 40 percent had lived in four or more foster homes or institutions before the referral. [14] It is likely, too, that some attempt has been made to maintain the physically handicapped at home while receiving treatment on an outpatient basis prior to application for institutional care.

If institutionalization is the only feasible alternative, the parents need help in coping with their possible sense of failure and guilt at their inability to care for their child and in accepting surrender of their child. They have to be prepared to accept the fact that the substitute parents in the institution may succeed in helping the child make the kinds of changes that he was not able to make at home. At the same time helping the parents to resolve doubts about the plan for placement is helpful to the child. The child can better accept the placement if his parents do so.

It is hoped that many children will return home after temporary institutionalization. Consequently, an effort must be made to maintain the ties between the natural parents and the child. Discussion of the structure of service-visiting procedures, support of child while institutionalized, and so on, helps to accomplish this by stressing the continuing responsibility of the parents for the child. As Gula says, "The institution should be an interim, not a terminal, resource." [40, p. 20]

Because the necessity for removing the child from his own home results from some failure in the parent-child relationship, acceptance of the child for institutional care presumes involvement of the parents with the agency so that the parents may be helped to change or to effect changes in their social situation. It is important that the parents' responsibility as clients be made clear to them, and that they be helped to accept this aspect of the contract between agency and family.

At this point, parents are asked to sign a board agreement statement indicating what regular payments they will be making for support of the child. The payments are set according to their capacity to pay. At the same time, unless the child is being sent to an institution by order of the court, a written consent is obtained from the parents for institutionalization of the child.

The parents are also involved in the social study of the child conducted by the agency in preparation for placement. The institution, if it is to do its job effectively, must know something about the child's developmental history, his particular difficulties, his particular pattern of response to parents and peers, and so on. The parents are the principal source of such information. When the child to be placed is older, he, too, is involved in the social study. A report summarizing the background information on the child is sent to the institution for the guidance of institutional personnel.

Preparation for placement involves a visit to the institution before admission, by both the child and his parents. During this visit, the child might meet with the housemother and some members of the group with whom he will be living. Frequently, these institutions make available literature specially prepared for the child, which answers some of the most frequent questions children are likely to ask about living in an institution.

Preparation *with* the child, rather than merely *for* the child, involves more than providing reading material or arranging for a visit. It requires active discussion between caseworker and child of the fears and doubts that are aroused by separation from the parents and placement in the institution. It requires discussion of why institutionalization is necessary, what is going to happen, and when and under what circumstances the child will be returning home.

The institutional staff should be prepared for the child's arrival, and they, in turn, should have prepared the group with which the child is to live. The social worker and the institutional staff should discuss how the child is likely to affect the group to which he is assigned and how the members of the group are likely to affect him. This implies that the group has been selected with some thought as to how its composition will further the treatment plans for this child. Also, "some institutions have a 'Welcome Committee' of two or three children in each cottage or section to introduce the new child and help him to feel at home." [106, p. 38]

The importance of preparing the child is based on the recognition that institutional placement is a very radical change in the child's life. As Beedell says, "The variety of new contacts with adults and other children which face a child joining a residential unit are almost comparable to those an adult would face who moved to a new town, changed her job, broke an engagement to marry, and contemplated another all on the same day." [8, p. 34]   More difficult yet is the fact that the child is asked to live with peers whom he has no say in choosing. "Each child had to adjust in some way to children he has never seen before, who may or may not like him, and whom he may or may not like and with whom he will be constantly thrown." [56, p. 34]

The Child in Care

Caseworkers have a continuing responsibility to work with the child once he is moved to the institution. They must help him adjust to the setting and make optimum use of what the institution has to offer. At the same time, they act as a bridge between the child's past—his own home and parents—and his present life in the institution. The social worker seeks to help the child deal with the problems of separation from his old life and integration into the life of the institution, of adjustment to institutional regulations and demands, of interaction with the peer group and the institutional staff.

The treatment rationale of the institution in helping the child to change is predicated on two complementary approaches. In delineating these approaches we are using the residential treatment center as a model because, although it currently serves only a limited number of the children in institutional placement, it serves as the prototype for the more progressive institutions of all kinds. The two complementary approaches involve individual psychotherapy, and the structuring of a total therapeutic environment through which the child can be helped to change.

On the basis of a significant relationship with the caseworker, the child is helped to explore the dynamic basis for his behavior, to understand why he behaves as he does, and to change his behavior. Psychotherapy in the institution is more likely to center on the dynamics of present behavior rather than on material out of the child's past. This, as a matter of fact, is an advantage to the caseworker because he can reach the child at a time of emotional stress to discuss conflicts through which the child is living. Treatment moves out of the office into the child's world and his immediate reality for on-the-spot therapy.

> When S., a thirteen-year-old youngster, was adamant in refusing
> to return to her group and marched up and down the institution's
> "campus," it was her [case] worker who joined her in the march.
> The material handled during this time was not at all dissimilar
> to the content of their interviews: the child's feeling that she was too
> sick to be helped, that her rejection by the family was devastating
> and motivated these overwhelming feelings of hopelessness.
> When she marched past the gate, she said she could not control
> herself and not even the worker could control her. On the ensuing
> three-mile hike through neighboring towns and the final return
> to the grounds of the institution, the child received not only the
> demonstration of the worker's ability to control her, which
> diminished her feelings of anxiety, but also some insight into her
> current concern about her mother's illness and its relationship
> to the incident. [95, p. 322]

But individual psychotherapy is only one way in which the institution hopes to effect change in the child—and for those children whose ability to develop an emotionally involved relationship with any therapist is limited, it is not the most effective way. The second approach lies in a procedure unique to institutional living. Because the administration has the possibility of controlling the nature of the child's world, an explicit effort is made to structure his daily experiences so that all aspects of his environment have a therapeutic intent and impact. "Residential treatment differs significantly from outpatient and other treatment methods by taking responsibility for total management of the child's current experience-in-living. It attempts to monitor and modify, for therapeutic gain, all facets of the child's life." [26, p. 37] Thus, treatment infiltrates all areas of a child's life. Food, recreation, education, allowances, chores, peer-grouping, discipline, personal hygiene, visiting —all the daily activities have, in addition to their manifest meaning, some psychological meaning for the child.

For example, food is a physiological necessity and a source of pleasure. Beyond this, however, feeding is a symbol of the parents' acceptance of the child, their willingness to care for him, and of the child's dependence on them. It is a bridge to a relationship between the child being fed and the adult doing the feeding. Food is food, but it also signifies love. It can be used, therefore, to help a child toward emotional health as well as physical health. Thus snacks, extra portions, sweets, the regularity of mealtimes, and special permission to dawdle over food might be employed as a part of an explicit design to give the child the kind of experience he needs. Anna Freud tells of her experiences with a group of children in a residential treatment center who needed, and were permitted, to sprinkle sugar over all food—meats, green vegetables, potatoes, pickles, and so on.

By the same token, play is a physiological necessity and a source of pleasure. It releases tension and hostility, permits the acting out of unresolved experiences, relieves anxiety, and helps develop a feeling of self-confidence and a more acceptable concept of self. It results in a more positive relationship with peers and with the adults who supervise play. Play can be explicitly employed to provide the child with a corrective living experience. The director of an agency responsible for one of the most advanced residential treatment centers discussed play as a factor in building the therapeutic environment:

> Recreation is, at one and the same time, recreation and therapy. It offers pleasurable leisure-time experience for the children and utilizes the child's experience in the group to implement the treatment plan for him. This is accomplished by providing specially selected ego-building activities and utilizing these to condition the interrelationship between the children in the group to each other and to the leader. [5, p. 120]

The same director speaks of the therapeutic implications of work assignments in the institution:

> Work is a medium for building a sense of achievement as well as a bridge to meaningful interpersonal ties between child and adult.

A sense of increased mastery of the world around them that
comes through success in ordinary or even simple tasks is obviously
of great importance to our children who have experienced failure
in many aspects of living. . . . Over and over again we see the
effectiveness of work as a medium for significant relationships
between child and adult. Doing things together remains the most
solid foundation for positive identification. The most meaningful
relationship some of the children form are with the handy
man and the chauffeur. [5, pp. 117–18]

These daily activities, then, are structured to induce, encourage, and
support positive changes in behavior. The living situation is the therapeutic tool and, in an environment conditioned to meet his needs, the
child lives therapy. Clinical reports confirm the contention that the
therapeutic milieu itself, even without accompanying psychotherapy, is
capable of effecting considerable change in the behavior of disturbed
children. [57]   Psychotherapy and the therapeutic milieu are complementary aspects of the total treatment program.

Today we conceive of the residential treatment settings as a
psychodynamically determined environment in which the total
living experiences of the child are contrived and integrated with
individual treatment comprising a unified therapeutic plan. The
total life of the child, including his group living experiences,
relationships with adults and children, school classes, work
assignments, and recreational activities, becomes part of the
therapeutic experiences of the child. . . . The experimental aspects
of the child's life are consistent, parallel, and intermesh with the
process of individual treatment. [95, p. 319]

Psychotherapy, in the institution, is largely a responsibility of the
casework staff. Hylton, in a study of twenty-one treatment centers,
reports that, "considering the total number of children in individual
therapy during the year, 70 percent of the residential group were in
therapy with social workers and 35 percent were in therapy with psychiatrists." [46, p. 129]

A more recent study of over 600 residential treatment centers notes
that they employed about 1600 full-time social workers, the greatest
majority of whom had a master's degree. "Social workers along with
school teachers were employed more universally in residential treatment
centers than other types of professional personnel. . . . and were utilized to a greater extent than [members of] any other professional discipline." [108, pp. 11–12]   A 1966 nationwide study of children's
institutions in general revealed that psychiatrists were seeing 10,000

children for treatment or counseling, while social workers were offering service to 65,000 children. [79, p. 453]

If social workers and psychiatrists share total responsibility for individual psychotherapy, the entire staff shares responsibility for creating and maintaining the therapeutic environment. Although all share in this task, it is the particular responsibility of the child care worker. These workers go under different names in different institutions—*cottage parent, houseparent, group parent, counselor, group counselor, residential worker, group living staff.* Whatever the differences in title, the principal task is the same: the day-to-day care of the child. He is the nearest thing to a full-time parent assigned to the child. He lives with a small group of children in a cottage, or in a circumscribed section of a building. He sees to the children's feeding and eats with them; he gets them to bed on time and wakes them up; he is concerned with their personal hygiene and their clothing needs; he settles fights and disputes among them and disciplines those needing discipline; he cares for and comforts them when they are sick; he gets them off to school and is there to greet them when they come home; he makes sure they do their homework and often helps them with it. He is responsible for the daily living arrangements for the individual child, for the needs of the group as a group, and for the maintenance of the living quarters. The Child Welfare League indicates that "the child care staff is the heart of the program in an institution for children." [29, p. 61]   A rich literature is being developed directed toward the education of houseparents and concerned with the day-to-day problems encountered by houseparents. [9; 10; 19; 23; 29; 56; 58; 63; 67; 68; 69; 70; 94; 105; 110]

The professional clinical staff—the social worker, the psychiatrist, the psychologist—have ultimate responsibility for diagnosing the child's problem and planning his treatment. But the child care worker—in direct, intimate, continuous contact with the child—has the primary responsibility for implementing the treatment plan. It is he who, in disciplining the child and arranging for his daily needs and activities, organizes the child's life in accordance with the treatment plan and provides the content of the therapeutic living experience.

The social worker consults with the child care worker, explaining what the child needs, getting feedback information about how the child is behaving from day to day in reaction to the treatment plan and in soliciting the help of the child care worker in reformulating the treatment plan.

The social worker has a similar relationship with other institutional personnel who may be playing a significant part in the child's life. This requires a cooperative relationship of respect among all members of the institutional staff. The need for such a relationship between child-care worker and social worker is particularly important. It is somewhat disappointing, then, to note that the one empirical study available on the relationship between social workers and cottage parents at two different institutions indicates a relationship often characterized by resentment, differences of opinion, and lack of mutual respect. The caseworkers in one of the residential treatment centers studied resented the cottage parents' emphasis on control, their intrusions into the caseworker's counseling responsibilities, and their failure to carry out treatment plans developed by clinic workers and agreed upon in case conferences. The cottage parents, on the other hand, felt that the caseworkers were either unrealistic in their treatment of youths or in their appraisal of the possibilities of program implementation within cottages. In addition, they voiced resentment about the deprecating appraisal of them by clinic personnel. While cottage parents did not deny that they at times departed from established treatment plans or counseled members of their cottages, their rationale for these actions was at variance with that of clinicians. First, all the cottage parents stated that maintaining order within their cottages was one of their primary responsibilities and that, when implementation of treatment plans interfered with control, this implementation had to be postponed. Furthermore, some of them felt that counseling or advising the boys was an appropriate cottage parent function. Cottage parents believed resident staff may be more important than clinic workers for purposes of treatment. The caseworkers held the diametrically opposite view. [82, p. 21]

At the second institution, the relationship between the two groups was characterized primarily by indifference. The researcher, in summation, states: "Given, then, the importance of informal communication in institutional settings, the findings of this research are striking, for they reveal that such communication was rare between cottage parents and caseworkers at both of the institutions studied." [82, p. 22] Some of the same difficulties are noted by Mayer in descriptive accounts of child care staff activity. [69]

Child-care workers and social workers, having different responsibilities, have, necessarily, different perspectives on what they regard as important. In studying the residential treatment center, Polsky found that child-care workers emphasized activities concerned with meeting institutional demands: cottage housekeeping, maintaining the institutional standards regarding language or dress, and the child's relationship to subsystems in the institution, such as school, work, and appointments with therapists. [86; 87] Social workers concerned with therapy emphasized individualization and flexible interpretation of institution regulations in terms of the need of the particular child. The child-care worker, more concerned with smooth cottage management and functioning, sees such an orientation as destructive of the orderly housekeeping job he is requested to do. The child-care worker is apt to be oriented to the cottage group as the unit of treatment and concern; the social worker, to the individual child. Both are concerned with seeing that the children adhere to institutional norms, and both discourage behavior which is disruptive of the social system of the institution, but social workers are more likely to give precedence, where there is a conflict, to those activities which presumably facilitate the child's therapy, change, and psychological development. [35]

Differing expectations lead to conflict. The child-care worker may expect that the social worker will provide clear and explicit "solutions" for coping with behaviors which disrupt cottage life. The social worker finds it difficult to communicate the fact that there are often no ready-made "solutions."

On the other hand, the social worker expects the child-care worker to implement a treatment program in the cottage, and the child care worker may find it difficult to communicate the view of the disruptive consequences of the social worker's recommendations. Confidence and respect between the two groups are eroded and conflict develops. As one houseparent said, "I can't get through to the social worker what the kid is like in the cottage."

The child-care staff needs to be autonomous in its operation of the cottage. If the houseparent too frequently has to defer a decision because he needs to discuss the situation with the social worker, this tends to derogate his position in the eyes of the child. It is more difficult for the child to identify with the houseparent as symbolizing the independent adult.

Some institutions have developed a team approach in dealing with such staff problems. Social workers visit each cottage and take part in the deliberations of each cottage team. The team—the teacher, the social worker, the cottage parents, the recreation leader—meet to plan and coordinate their efforts and direct them toward an agreed objective. For example, the child in question is shy, withdrawn, isolated: the social worker helps him express his feelings and explains the motives for his behavior; the teacher helps him establish contact with the children in the classroom; the recreation leader plans activities which might involve the child; the cottage parents utilize living situations to build a bridge between the child and other children.

Even so, there are potential sources of disagreement between the two groups. Studying the interaction in one institution which provided this kind of arrangement, Sternbach and Pincus found that the child-care workers were more concerned with the extent to which the children conformed to institutional norms, maintained the cottage, and adhered to institutional routines, while the social workers were more concerned with the extent to which peer group interaction was harmonious and satisfying, and the extent to which the group was capable of operating autonomously and democratically. [99]

Yet houseparents and social workers do frequently cooperate to help the child: the child-care worker receives support and encouragement from the social worker, his concerns are respected, and his attachment to the children is credited.

The size of the cottage group varies, but it is rarely under eight and rarely more than fifteen. This is the primary group, the family of peers with whom the child lives. In the area or cottage assigned to the group, the child is allotted a private place, his own bed, his own furniture for his clothes. He eats with his group in the dining area in the cottage. He may attend the regular community schools, or he may be assigned to the school on the institutional grounds organized in accordance with a curriculum approved by the local board of education and staffed by licensed teachers. The institution provides recreational facilities—television in the cottage, playing fields, scheduled movies—and, in addition, the child might be involved in the recreational programs of community agencies—YMCA, Boy Scouts, Little League. The children are also given an allowance and are expected to perform the kinds of chores normally demanded of a child in the family—making their beds, helping with the dishes, and so on. Older children may be paid for performance of institutional maintenance tasks—working in the yard, cutting wood, assisting in the library and in the canteen, and so on.

While the child is in the institution, the caseworker continues to work with the parents to prepare for the child's return home. Parents are advised of the child's progress and are encouraged to visit him regularly. Visits can assist the child in making progress, for they indicate the parents' concern for and attachment to him and assure him that he has not been abandoned. At the same time, they present difficulties because, for many children, their relationship with the parents is a source of conflict, and the visits reactivate such conflicts. The caseworker tries to structure the visits so that they have an optimum beneficial effect. The caseworker might, for the good of the child, control the timing, frequency, and length of such visits. [2] The visits may be restricted to institutional grounds, or the parents may be encouraged to visit with the child away from the institution. Workers may help the parents to plan the visits and suggest things to do with the child for those parents who seem at a loss after the first few minutes of contact.

Parental visits can be dealt with more therapeutically in the institution than in the foster family. Because the staff with which the parent comes into contact on such visits is either professionally trained or under professional supervision, the response to parents' behavior—even that which is disruptive to the child's placement—is more likely to be accepting and understanding. The child-care worker is less apt to feel that he is a rival of the natural parents for the child's affection and, hence, less apt to feel threatened by their visits. As Mayer says, parents on visits "frequently try to show the child-care worker that he is not so perfect either. They may find the living room disorderly, the tablecloth torn, the floor dirty, and may become unduly upset about it, even though they may be poor housekeepers themselves." [70, p. 146] Social workers help the child-care worker to accept with understanding some of the critical reactions parents exhibit as an expression of their guilt at having others care for their child. Furthermore, institutional rules and regulations can be applied to control parents' visits without their feeling that such limitations are a personal attack.

Some institutions previously sought to reduce contact between the child and his parents, because the parents had "done enough harm already." The child was fenced in and the parent was fenced out. The institution now sees itself as the ally of the parents in helping the child; consequently, it encourages their active involvement in the life of the child and the services of the institution. As Mayer says, "Child care workers must always remember the adage that one can take children away from parents but one cannot take parents away from children." [70, p. 145]

Currently many institutions have moved from rejection to toleration, to passive acceptance, to active encouragement of parent participation in treatment plans with the child. Currently, parents might help to care for the child in the institution for limited periods, participate in institutionally sponsored children's outings, be included in periodic evaluation of child progress. [54] There is a growing recognition that the greater the involvement of the family in preplacement and placement planning and the greater the involvement with the child during the period of residence, the more likely the child will be to accept the placement and the more likely it will be that he will return home. [33; 72]

The adjustment of children returned from a residential treatment center is related, as might be expected, to parental pathology and difficulties in parent-child relationship. Prognosis is likely to be unfavorable for a child returning to a family in which little change had occurred in the parent-child relationship. Recognizing that placement has profound effects on the family as well as the child, social workers employed by the institution are taking greater direct responsibility for working with the child's family rather than working through the social worker in the local agency. They have organized discussion groups and counseling groups for parents and have offered sociobehavioral training programs in child management techniques. [45]

Contact with parents varies with institutional setting. Since many children in institutions for the dependent and neglected come from broken, multiproblem homes, fewer of these parents are seen by the agencies as being amenable to treatment, and 47 percent of the institutions for the dependent and neglected did not provide casework or therapy with the families. [76, Table 250, p. 267] However, of the residential treatment centers 83.7 percent provided casework or therapy with parents. [77, Table 250, p. 267]

Group workers have been assigned special functions in the child-caring institutions. [55; 93]   Most frequently they are concerned with the supervision and coordination of special recreational services. In the more advanced institutions, they might be asked to develop programs of group psychotherapy or to organize meetings of cottage groups offering guided group interaction. Groups have been used not only as a therapeutic corrective device to aid in the child's normal development, but also as an aid in management of the institution. [64; 66]   The cottage unit meets to decide on cottage living rules. "Campus councils," representing the child population of the institution, meet as a group to help legislate for the institution as a whole. [7]   There are also reports of group psychotherapy with parents of children in a residential treatment center. [114]

Termination

Once a child has been in an institution for some time, a periodic review of the situation is advisable. This will reduce the child's chances of being "overlooked" and remaining in the institution longer than is necessary. Termination should come when the child has received maximum benefits from institutional care. To hold him beyond that point is to deny him some measure of a more normal life. Just as the social worker helps the child to make the transition into the institution, so he should help the child to make the transition into the community.

Intake, life in the institution, and discharge from institutional care are all different steps in a single process. Preparation for, and help with, the return to the community is an important unit in the process. As Kahn says:

> Rehabilitation must ultimately take place in the community. Institutionalization is, at best, a successful period of removal from the community in order to help the individual increase, equip, and prepare himself for his return. The after-care worker aspires to create optimum conditions for the return to the community and also to provide emotional support, concrete help, and protection of community interests during the process. [53, p. 14]

Efforts to help the child make the transition from the institution to the community involve follow-up services to the child in his own home or on an outpatient basis, foster care, group homes, or halfway houses. A 1966 nationwide survey indicated that about half of the institutions were providing some kind of after-care service to former residents. [79, p. 455]   Institutions for emotionally disturbed children were among those most likely to have established some specific provisions for such service.

Termination may involve an intermediate stage between the institution and the return home. In some cases, foster family care is indicated for the child as further preparation for living in the normal family setting. Some children cannot go home because they have no home to go to or because their parents are still not ready to accept them. They, too, might need foster care. However, foster care is not always available for these children or, if available, may not be desirable because the child is in late adolescence.

For such children transitional residence clubs have been established. These are extensions of the institution, located in the city. The child lives in the residence club, as he might live in a large hotel. He has greater freedom, more autonomy, and more responsibility for organizing his life than he had in the institution. In addition, the residence club staff stands ready to assist the child with personal, vocational, and educational guidance. Staff members are assigned to every floor of the residence and are readily available for interviews. Bellefaire, a residential treatment center in Cleveland, operates a number of group homes accommodating four or five children. [39] The homes are "one-family dwellings in a middle-class suburban area and are indistinguishable from other homes on the street."

It has been suggested that institutions coordinate the need of institutional children for contact with some interested adult with the need for after care. Thus foster parents could be selected a year in advance of the child's planned discharge. They might visit the child at the institution and have the child visit with them on weekends and holidays. They would be paid on a standby basis even before the child is placed in their home.

Residential treatment centers are developing a postdischarge foster care program of their own. For instance, the Astor Home for Children in New York had fourteen licensed foster homes in operation in 1969.

The institution, or the parent agency administering the institution, takes responsibility for after-care follow-up of those children who can return to their own homes. The contact enables the family and the child to have the continued support and help of the agency as the child is reincorporated into his own home. If all goes well, fewer and fewer interviews are scheduled, and ultimately contact is terminated.

Evaluation

Evaluation of the work of the child-caring institution is complicated by the fact that the term covers many different kinds of facilities serving distinctively different groups. The criteria for assessment of outcome for the residential treatment institution for emotionally disturbed children is different from the criteria for assessing outcome of a training school for delinquents—and these, again, are different from the criteria applicable to an institution serving the blind.

Social workers have a greater professional investment and interest in some child-caring institutions than in others. It is clear that the residential treatment center is one such kind of institution. We will, therefore, focus on evaluation studies of the residential treatment center.

Johnson and Reid studied the outcome of treatment of 339 children accepted for treatment at the Ryther Child Center in Seattle, Washington, during the period 1936–45. [50] Treatment was categorized as "successful" if the child was subsequently able to adjust to his own home or a foster home, if he was getting along well in school or at work, and if he was living in accordance with community legal standards. Seventy-five percent of the group was rated "satisfactory" by these criteria. There was limited information available for assessment in some cases, but in general children who were younger at the time of admission to care were more likely to have been successfully treated.

Rausch conducted a detailed observational study of a small group of six emotionally disturbed children in residential treatment. [89] The behavior of each of these children "was characterized by such overwhelming aggressiveness that they could not be tolerated by community, schools, foster parents, or parents." [89, p. 10] Trained observers taped details of a particular child's behavior in six different kinds of interactional situations. The observational protocols were coded by at least two coders working together to categorize the nature of the behavior that had been observed. Observations were repeated after the child had been in residential treatment for eighteen months.

> Over a year and a half, the interpersonal behavior of the children shifted considerably. The major changes were in the relations of the children with adults. Here there was primarily a decrease in hostile, dominant behavior and an increase in passive, friendly behavior. The appropriateness of the behavior increased both in relations with children and adults. The patterns of change were consistent with treatment aims, and they seemed, at least in part, a function of the treatment program. [89, p. 25]

Black and Glick used the Glueck Prediction Scale to evaluate the success of the treatment program at Hawthorne Center. [13] Applying the scale to one hundred delinquent boys, they determined "that the relative chances of the Hawthorne boys for making a good community adjustment," if they had not received treatment, "were slight." In only eight of the one hundred cases "was there an even chance of not recidivating." Follow-up study of the group five years after discharge revealed that actually 74 percent of the boys had not committed any offense for which they might have been arrested. [13, p. 39] The difference between the high prediction and the actual rate is attributed to treatment received at Hawthorne. The validity of the results depends, of course, on the validity of the Glueck Prediction Scale.

Silver reports on a study of fifty-four children placed by the Jewish Family and Children's Service of Detroit in two different residential treatment centers. [96] He notes that 60 percent evidenced some positive change in behavior as a result of their stay at the residential treatment center, 20 percent showed no change, and an additional 20 percent showed a negative change. There is no indication in the report as to how the judgment was made. Success in treatment was related to the diagnosis: Silver states that, "in the neurotic group, there was a preponderance of positive outcome; on the other hand, in the combined category of character disorder and psychotic," there were fewer children who had positive outcome. Success in treatment was related to time in treatment, but not to whether the children and/or the parents had an awareness of their need for treatment.

Allerhand conducted a follow-up study of fifty boys discharged from Bellefaire, a residential treatment institution in Cleveland. [4] Data for the study included a two-hour taped interview with each boy, interviews with his parents, and psychometric examinations of the boys. Included among the eleven different areas of social functioning assessed by the researchers were participation in family life, dating patterns, stability of school or work situation, presence or absence of disciplinary actions in the community with regard to the boy. On the basis of the assessment, 64 percent of the fifty children were manifesting successful social performance at the time of the follow-up study.

One of the more significant findings is confirmation of the fact that adaptation at point of discharge is not in itself indicative of adaptation at follow-up. The incongruence between expectation at discharge and actual performance at follow-up was related to the level of stress or support provided by the living situation to which the boy returned: "It is the supportive or stressful nature of the post-institutional milieu that appears to be the critical factor in success, without regard to the within-institution career pattern." [4, p. 142] Only at the extreme end of the continuum were the boys' adaptations at discharge impervious to the effects of the postdischarge environment. For some, capacity for adaptation had been so strengthened by the institutional experience that they could successfully cope with postdischarge stress; for others, who had been unable to respond even to the benign environment of the institution, no amount of postdischarge support seemed sufficient to enable them to adapt with adequacy. Postdischarge levels of adaptation were also a function of the extent to which recommendation of Bellefaire staff for after-care living had been implemented. The researchers point out that institutional living prepares the child for institutional living, but since the child ultimately needs to take his place in the community, the institution needs to provide the opportunity for more direct exposure to community demands.

The results of this study receive support from a follow-up of children who had been treated at Children's Village, a residential treatment center in Connecticut. The researchers found that "continuity and support following residential treatment was essential to postdischarge adaptation" and that "the greater the degree of support in the postdischarge environment the greater the degree of the child's adaptation to the environment." [100, pp. 50–51] Work with the child's family is clearly indicated. More descriptive studies that present clinical accounts of success in residential treatment are those by Redl and Wineman, and by Bettelheim. [11; 12; 90; 91]

In recapitulation, then, the few studies available do support one another in suggesting that residential treatment in an institution does have positive effects on the child's behavior.

Problems

1. A significant aspect of evaluation is concerned with the deficiencies inherent in institutional care. The earlier concern that institutionalization traumatizes the child because it imposes maternal deprivation and stimulus deprivation seems to have given way to a more critical analysis of the problem. [25; 27; 73; 115; 116; 117; 119] It is conceded that a reasonably well-organized institution with a decent child-staff ratio can provide the child with the affectionate care and stimulation he needs for adequate growth. [115, p. 81] The research on infant deprivation, which was the basis of so much of the concern, is not applicable to institutional populations which are composed largely of children between ten and twelve years of age—well beyond the critical period for maternal deprivation.

It is difficult, however, even for those institutions with a low child-staff ratio and adequate resources, to provide continuity of care, which requires a relationship with a nurturing adult who has primary responsibility for care of the child over a significantly long period in the child's development. Discontinuity in care in the institution results from the fact that a twenty-four-hour caretaking day is likely to require three sets of different parents, that caretakers need days off and vacations, and that all institutions have a very high staff turnover. A constant problem for institutional management is the shortage of trained staff and the associated problem of high staff turnover. Many, particularly younger, workers view the position as a temporary one. As Mayer says, they are hired for a job rather than for a career and for a particular agency rather than for an occupational field. Given their low status in the institution, the low pay, the lack of a career line and promotional possibilities, the lack of an occupational reference group with which they can identify, and the emotionally stressful nature of the job, it is easy to understand why 30–40 percent of child care workers quit within a year. When directors of child care institutions were asked in a nationwide study to list their recommendations for change, the one most frequently listed was for "raising the quality of the child care staff through recruitment at higher salaries and/or increasing in-service training." [79, p. 458]

2. The distinctive features of the institution present problems as well as advantages. One of the most distinctive features of institutional care is that it is a group situation. In constant, intimate interaction with one another, the children themselves informally assign social roles to members of their group, so that it has a definite social structure—leaders and followers, exploiters and exploited. The group also develops its own code of behavior, to which it expects members to conform if they want to be accepted by, and included in, the group.

It is to be remembered that most of the children served by the institution are teenagers. Distrust of, and hostility toward, adults are at their height at this time, even among teenagers who have not experienced difficulty—and these children have known little except hurt and pain from the adults they have encountered. Furthermore, the need for acceptance by the peer group and dependence on the peer group is very great during adolescence. The peer group can, therefore, exercise considerable control over those who refuse to conform to its code by threatening to reject them.

Given these considerations, it is not unusual to find that the social structure and the code of the group are developed without consultation with adults on the staff and that children in the institution feel a strong pressure to accept them. As long as the social structure and the code of the group reinforce the aims of the official structure of the institution, the group is an additional powerful resource that helps the child to change in the desired direction.

The problem is, however, that this informally developed social subsystem might operate to encourage and support behavior that is in opposition to that officially sanctioned by the institution. In such a case, group living—the distinctive feature of the institution—provides the basis for a serious problem of competition between the formal, official system and the often incompatible, informal subsystem. The contention that such a problem does, in fact, exist is supported by the analysis of the "inmate subculture" of training institutions by Ohlin and Lawrence. [75] It is supported even more directly by the detailed empirical study by Polsky of one cottage in a residential treatment center. [85]

The reports indicate that the group code generally discourages the kind of intimate, psychologically open relationship with institutional staff that is necessary to the achievement of the therapeutic aims of the institution. According to Ohlin, "Under existing circumstances, the inmate as a client must run the risk of social rejection by his peers to gain full advantage of the treatment experience." [75, p. 9] Furthermore, the social structure of the group is built along autocratic lines, leaders and followers having markedly unequal status, interpersonal relationships being characterized by the exploitation of the weak by the strong. This, too, is in contravention to what the institution is trying to teach about democratic group living characterized by understanding and acceptance.

Various suggestions have been made to reduce the differences between the formal official system of the institutional staff and the informal, unofficial system of the client group. The most frequently cited one is that the group which communicates and enforces the informal system—the cottage group—be the principal unit for treatment.

> The first step necessary for change is to acknowledge the existence of the delinquent subculture with all its ramifying importance for individual and group rehabilitation. The next step is to fashion an institutional arrangement whereby we can place at the center of the cottage a professional person who works directly with the boys on a cottage level. [84, p. 10]
> It would seem profitable to restructure the institutional situation so treatment interaction is focused directly on the group. . . . It would be desirable if the worker would be relocated at the central part of the most vital interaction with inmates' experience. In most instances this would mean close and intimate working relationships and shared experience with cottage personnel. [75, p. 12]

The client to be worked with would be the cottage group, and the social worker, then, would spend more of his time with the cottage group, sharing more intimately their day-to-day experiences, and attempting directly to influence the cottage social system. A more radical solution would require that the social worker become the houseparent or that the houseparent become the social worker. As a congregate care facility dealing with a sizable group of children, the institution needs regulations and rules. There arises, thus, a conflict between the need for some regimentation and the therapeutic need to individualize the situation for each child. Individualizing regulations in response to the therapeutic needs of a particular child makes for conflict in the institution. Children are confused and upset when they see one child treated one way for an infraction of the rules and another child treated another way for an infraction of the same rules. The problem is to reconcile regulations and individualization in a situation where the procedure is open to the scrutiny of the client group.

Group living also creates conflict between the individual needs of one child and the individual needs of another and involves some loss of privacy. The problem is one of reconciling the conflicting needs of individual children in a group and to establish a structure that guarantees some sense of privacy.

Furthermore, the institution is apt to be child-centered and, for this reason, unreal. In the normal family situation the childs' life is not so "egocentrically structured." Frequently there is adult talk directed to adult concerns, and frequently adult concerns must be given precedence over the child's needs.

One advantage of the institution—the fact that the social worker is directly aware of the child's problems and, in fact, injects himself into the child's reality—also serves to create a problem. The workers are called upon to make recommendations that directly affect the lives of the children—recommendations regarding a child's visit home or a parent's visit to the institution, recommendations regarding a child's discharge from the institution, recommendations regarding the disciplining of the child when he breaks the rules. The worker is, then, no longer a neutral figure to whom the children can freely confide all. The child becomes aware of some of the real-life consequences of his sharing. The problem is one of reconciling the power of the worker over the child's life and the therapeutic neutrality needed for the best worker-child contact.

Another advantage—the variety of adults available from among whom the child can select an object for identification—may give rise to conflict. The adults might be working at crosspurposes with one another, each teaching and advocating different things. The problem is one of integrating the activities of the different adults in contact with the child so that their different contributions to the child reinforce, rather than conflict with, one another.

3. Another problem faced by the institution is that the people who have the greatest responsibility for therapy and who have the greatest functional power for therapy have the least education and status. [97] Mayer points out that, "while the child-care workers have far less professional education and experience than other people on the staff, they spend more time with the child than anyone else. They are exposed more acutely to his pathology and have to deal with it more directly than any other member of the staff." [68, p. 83] Despite the fact that they have responsibility for dealing with the day-to-day and hour-to-hour reactions of the children, despite the fact that they have responsibility for structuring the details of the therapeutic situation, the child-care workers are under the direction of others and must, because of their more limited education, defer to the professional clinical staff of social workers, psychiatrists, and psychologists.

4. Another of the current problems of the institution is one we tend to associate with a past period in our history. As recently as 1950, Albert

Deutsch published a detailed, and shocking, nationwide report of child-caring institutions that were guilty of neglect and exploitation of the children living in them. [34]   He described training schools in which the housing was dilapidated and overcrowded; the food scanty, monotonous, and inedible; the educational and recreational resources primitive or nonexistent; and the care of the children, at best, indifferent, and at worst, clearly irresponsible. In May 1964 *The Daily Oklahoman* ran a series on a children's institution, Miracle Hill, in which seventy-two youngsters, forty-eight of them under ten years of age, were cared for by a staff of five, all without any training in child care. [32]

> Twenty-nine windows were broken out, stained broken ceiling boards sagged above a makeshift shower in the boys' bathroom. In an unkempt food storeroom, canned goods spilled out of a pasteboard carton across the floor. A gaping hole, large enough for a normal person to walk through, was torn in a wall of the boys' dormitory. . . . As newsmen entered, a mouse sneaked from under a cardboard box and darted across the floor into a pile of debris in one corner. . . . Inside . . . [the children] moved cafeteria-style along a wooden table as four older girls dished up the evening's meal—cornbread, navy beans, and ice water.

The existence of such an institution was made possible by the fact that the state of Oklahoma had no power to enforce minimum acceptable standards of child care in the institutions. [101]   Most states enforce maintenance of such standards through the use of licensing procedures. Authority for investigating the conditions, facilities, and program of the institution, and for granting the license to operate, is generally lodged with the state department of public welfare. Currently, most states have such licensing requirements, but the rigor with which such statutes are written, the kinds of exceptions and exemptions permitted, vary. Oklahoma, in 1964, had some licensing procedures, but they were ambiguous enough to permit Miracle Hill to operate. It might be presumed that similar ambiguities in licensing procedures permit other such institutions to operate in other states. A report, published in 1970, of conditions in children's institutions around the country mirrored the 1950 findings. [49]

This is an example of a general problem facing child-caring institutions—the problem of the gap between the reality and the ideal. Often it is, as Gula says, "The best choice representing the best compromise between what is desirable and what is available." [40, p. 11]

5. Another problem is the uneven distribution of residential treatment institutions so that many sections of the country are without such a facility. Other communities do not have temporary shelters or detention

homes. The result is that some children, who clearly do not belong there, are committed to adult wards of psychiatric hospitals or held in prisons. Also, many institutions are understaffed, lacking social workers and other professionally trained people. As a result, such institutions see custody as the only service they can offer. The problem of personnel is compounded by high turnover rates. For instance, a study of the staff in residential treatment centers showed that 41 percent of the staff on duty at the beginning of the year terminated employment during the year. [46, p. 155]

6. Institutions also face a problem of public acceptance. An article in the August 17, 1961, edition of *The London Times* indicates the nature of the problem:

> . . . A national children's organization, making an application to buy a large home in a residential area, had been refused permission by the local town council.
>
> The report notes that Mr. B. Grant, speaking for the children's organization, said that they considered the house ideal. "Eighteen children would live there with a staff of six. They would occupy three separate flats as individual family groups."
>
> "The old idea of an institution-type home with communal meals, and uniforms is dead," he said. "Instead, the children will go to ordinary schools, use public parks and facilities, be invited into homes of their friends, and be able to invite friends back. In short, they will lead a perfectly normal existence."
>
> The reasons given for refusing the application to purchase were that "the heavy traffic constituted a danger, that the house and grounds were too small, and that a children's home in a residential area could be detrimental to neighboring properties." It was specifically stated that the town council was not "influenced by the notion that institutional children are not as good as children residing in the area."

The problem is revealed again in a dispatch to *The New York Times*, October 24, 1965:

> An ordinance that would have banned construction of a school for emotionally maladjusted children in this sedate community of 2500 was defeated in a referendum here today, 585 to 545.
>
> The argument over construction of the school began when Mrs. Adrian Van Sinderen decided to turn over 120 acres of the seventy-five-year-old family estate here to the Devereux Foundation of Pennsylvania, a nonprofit organization, to build a school for emotionally maladjusted children.

The foundation is considered one of the largest in the country studying and treating functional and nervous disorders in adolescents.

Mrs. Van Sinderen's action aroused some resentment among residents, who felt that if the community gets to be known as a "mental institution town" it will be dead economically.

Trends

We have previously noted some of the trends in institutional child care—the stabilization of the relative distribution of children between foster family care and the institution for children needing substitute care; the increased efforts to include the participation of parents in the treatment program; the increased concern with after-care programs.

1. A principal trend in institutional care is the change in the nature of the population served. The development of supportive and supplementary services has reduced the number of children requiring substitute care. Now the children who require it are more frequently those who are so disturbed or who come from a situation so disorganized that even supportive and supplementary care would not permit them to be kept in their own or in foster homes. And even if the situation is so precarious as to require substitute care, the foster home is usually the first choice. Thus the institution receives those children who not only require substitute care but who are unable to use family-type substitute care. The institution, then, tends to serve the most difficult of the most difficult cases.

Gula cites this trend when he states:

. . . the more severely disturbed, aggressive[ly] delinquent, and severely retarded children are squeezed to the top and referred to institutions. Since these children have more complex treatment needs, institutions are being asked to provide more specialized care and treatment. [40, p. 4]

2. With the diversification of child welfare services, and the changes in the nature of the children institutionalized, there has been a change in the nature and the purpose of the institution. From a general placement setting for children needing substitute care the institution has become a specialized kind of agency serving a special population. The trend is to modify the essential purpose of the institution from custody to treatment. The modern institution is said to be a "filling station, not a parking lot." Yesterday's "inmate" is today's "patient."

There is hardly a children's institution today that will not say that providing treatment is its primary responsibility. This has become such a fashionable cliché that it is not uncommon for some children's institutions called a home, a school, a village, or a farm to be described as "analytically oriented," as "a clinical setting," or as "a residential treatment center." [20, p. 77] But this trend is more a result of a change in the nature of the children served than a result for increased status on the part of the institution. The nice children that we used to get . . . pale, with sorrowful faces and shy, quiet manners . . . [have been replaced by] unhappy children who express their longing for understanding and tenderness in a language which is natural to them; swearing and pestering and using foul language, kicking and punching and stealing, playing truant, bad table manners, sex talk, smoking, and boasting. [52, p. 42]

3. This change in the program of the institution has resulted in increased professionalization of staff. Custody and care do not require professional services; treatment does. Hence, there is a trend toward an increase in the number of social workers, psychiatrists, psychologists, and remedial teachers working in the institution. This corresponds with a trend toward upgrading the nonprofessional staff in the institution, particularly the crucially important houseparent staff. Many schools of social work have developed special, noncredit courses for houseparents, generally covering such topics as normal child development, the meaning of separation, the impact of institutional living on children, the use of living routines in meeting children's needs, discipline in the institution, the child and his relatives, dynamics of group living. The Child Welfare League of America acts as a clearing house of information about such programs. [10; 30] By 1970 institutions of higher learning in twenty-one states were offering courses in preparation for child care work, many at the junior college level. [67]

4. The change in the nature of the institution also requires greater individualization of approaches to the child and, hence, diversification of institutions available. Thus there are now institutions specializing in service to the asthmatic child, the autistic child, and so on.

5. There is a long-term trend to deinstitutionalize the institution and permit the child an experience that more closely approximates noninstitutional living. In the old institution, children slept in dormitories, ate in large mess halls, wore uniforms, and marched in line. In the new institution, children live in small cottage units, have their own rooms, eat with a small group in the cottage dining room, and dress according to their individual taste. Pyle notes: "Institutions at one time provided mass care. They now provide group care." [88, p. 13]

Another element in deinstitutionalization is the trend toward a closer link between the institution and the neighborhood community. Children now move from the institution into the community, attend community schools, use local recreational facilities, join in local activities, shop in community stores, use the local library, and so on. Community volunteers act as special tutors for the children, serve as scout leaders, take children to swimming lessons in the community, and the like. As the institution becomes smaller, as it moves into the community, the larger foster group residence meets and merges with it and the two become indistinguishable.

6. New experiments are being attempted in order to meet the problems of staff shortage. One imaginative effort, the foster grandparent program, initiated and supported by funds from the Office of Economic Opportunity, involves hiring older people on an hourly basis to come into the institutions and care for the chidren. This permits an increased ratio of staff to children and more personalized care for each child. The greatest help has been provided to institutions for mentally deficient and physically handicapped children, which house many younger children who need to be fed, and played with, and have their clothes and bedding changed. [51; 74; 102]

7. There has been a move toward racial integration of children's institutions. The fact that segregated institutions could be denied public funds acted as an effective stimulus for desegregation. [42]   Desegregation not only meant acceptance of minority-group children, but a change in staffing pattern so as to open employment in institutions, at all levels, to minority-group applicants.

Desegregation was complicated by the fact that some institutional charters were written to exclude racial minority group children; some communities with which institutions interpenetrated were segregated. Black children residing at the institution might be going to all-white schools, pools, theaters, and so on. Parents of white children in the institution might object to their children living in such close, intimate association with minority-group children. Despite these difficulties, many institutions have successfully integrated both staff and children population.

8. There is a trend toward diversification of approaches in treating children in institutional care. The dominant approach is still psychoanalytic or modified psychoanalytic, deriving from the work of Aichorn, Redl and Wineman, and Bettelheim. But now there is also the social systems model approach, which emphasizes therapeutic manipulation of the "fabricated" society of the institution, planned changes in the social interactional system, and changes in the structure and management of the institution as procedures for changing behavior, and the behavior modification model, which emphasizes directed learning as a procedure for change. [21; 83]

9. There is currently a negative attitude toward institutional care of whatever kind, and a trend toward retaining people in the community. To implement such a program, specialized community resources have been developed. For example, a planned Los Angeles Community Mental Health Center will include twenty-five beds for acute treatment, a community rehabilitation center, a remedial school, and five duplex family homes, each of which will house six disturbed children. Therapeutic preschool facilities, special classes for emotionally disturbed children, community-based mental health centers, walk-in twenty-four-hour emergency clinics, specialized family foster homes, and group homes for emotionally disturbed children might reduce the number of children referred for institutional care.

Summary

The child-caring institution is a third form of substitute care, which provides congregate group care rather than substitute family care. The group care it offers permits some unique advantages.

1. The child is not pressured, or obligated, to develop a close relationship with parental figures.
2. The peer group itself can be used as a catalyst for helping the child to change.
3. The routine required in group living, and the regulations which the institution is required to enforce, offer security to the child and support him in controlling his impulses.
4. The institution can tolerate a wider range of behavior than is acceptable in the community.
5. Special facilities for care, treatment, rehabilitation, and vocational training can be made available to a group of youngsters burdened by the same disability.

The distinctive attributes of institutional living suggest the kind of child to whom institutional care might be selectively offered when substitute care is needed.

1. The child who, because of previous negative emotional experiences with parents, is unable to relate positively to them and hence cannot make effective use of family care.
2. The adolescent, who faces the developmental task of dissolving ties to parents and for whom, therefore, a situation permitting attenuated parent-child relationships is desirable.
3. Youngsters requiring special facilities or programs—emotionally

handicapped, impulsive, delinquent youngsters requiring the structure of controls rather than open community living, the physically handicapped, and the mentally deficient.
4. Youngsters whose behavior is a danger to themselves and the community, or whose behavior cannot be tolerated by the community.
5. Youngsters whose parents are threatened by the thought of another family succeeding where they failed, but who can accept the institution as a form of substitute care.

The institution, in helping the child, also takes advantage of the unique properties of group living. In addition to individual psychotherapy, the institution attempts to structure the child's daily living experience so that it encourages and supports healthy change. This can be done in the institution because the staff controls the nature of the child's environment—who he lives with, where and how he eats, sleeps, plays, goes to school, and so on.

Problems faced by the institutions include the following:

1. The difficulty in providing continuity of care because of great staff turnover.
2. The potentially negative effects of group living. Children living in groups set up their own social system and code of behavior, which may oppose, rather than support, the aims of the institution.
3. The contradiction between the need for regulations and the need to individualize; the conflict between the needs of the individual child and the needs of the group.
4. The disparity between the education and status of the child-caring staff and their therapeutic significance to the child.
5. The public's ambivalent attitude toward the institution and the children it serves.

Among the major trends noted were the following:

1. The increased use of the institution as a special resource for special children.
2. The stabilization of the rate of children referred to institutions but the increased severity of the problems presented by children referred.
3. The movement from custody to treatment as the major service offered and the diversification of treatment approaches.
4. The increased professionalization and upgrading of staff, including houseparents, and the increased diversification of institutions.
5. The attempt to deinstitutionalize and desegregate the institution, and the increasing tendency to involve the parents in the treatment program.

6. Increasing concern wih after-care programs.
7. Continued attempts to find alternatives for institutionalization.

Bibliography

1. ABBOTT, GRACE. *The Child and the State*, Vol. II. Chicago: University of Chicago Press, 1938.
2. ADDESSA, SYLVESTER. "The Elements and Structure of Therapeutic Milieu," in *From Chaos to Order—A Collective View of the Residential Treatment of Children*. New York: Child Welfare League of America, 1972.
3. ————, and AUDREY LAATSCH. "The Therapeutic Use of Visiting in Residential Treatment." *Child Welfare*, 44 (May 1965).
4. ALLERHAND, MELVIN E., et al. *Adaptation and Adaptability: The Bellefaire Follow-up Study*. New York: Child Welfare League of America, 1966.
5. ALT, HERSCHEL. *Residential Treatment of the Disturbed Child*. New York: International Universities Press, Inc., 1960.
6. BALBERNIE, RICHARD. *Residential Work with Children*. Elmsford, N.Y.: Pergamon Press, Inc., 1966.
7. BAXTER, MARY JANE. "House Council—An Integral Part of Residential Treatment for Disturbed Children." *Catholic Charities Review* (May 1963), 46–47.
8. BEEDELL, CHRISTOPHER. *Residential Life with Children*. New York: Humanities Press, Inc., 1970.
9. BEKER, JEROME, et al. *Critical Incidents in Child Care*. New York: Behavioral Publications, Inc., 1972.
10. BERMAN, SAMUEL P. "A Report on a Child Welfare League of America Pilot Project to Train Child Care Workers." *Child Welfare*, 49, 3 (March 1970), 156–60.
11. BETTELHEIM, BRUNO. *Love Is Not Enough*. New York: The Free Press, 1951.
12. ————. *Truants from Life*. New York: The Free Press, 1955.
13. BLACK, BERTRAM, and SELMA GLICK. *Recidivism at the Hawthorne-Cedar Knolls Schools*. New York: Jewish Board of Guardians, 1952.
14. BLOCH, DONALD, and MARJORIE BEHRENS. *A Study of Children Referred for Residential Treatment in New York State*. New York: New York State Interdepartmental Health Resources Board, 1955. Mimeo.
15. BOWLBY, JOHN. *Maternal Care and Mental Health*. Geneva: World Health Organization, 1951.
16. BREMNER, ROBERT H. (ed.). *Children and Youth in America—A Documentary History. Vol. I, 1600–1865*. Cambridge, Mass.: Harvard University Press, 1970.
17. BRIAR, SCOTT. "Clinical Judgment in Foster Care Placement." *Child Welfare*, 42 (April 1963).
18. ————. "A Reply to Dr. Fanshel's Critique." *Child Welfare*, 42 (May 1963).

19. BROTEN, ALTON M. *House Parents in Children's Institutions—A Discussion Guide*. Chapel Hill, N.C.: University of North Carolina Press, 1962.

20. BROWNE, CLIFTON T. "Some Problem of Children's Institutions in Achieving Maturity." *Child Welfare*, **42**, 2 (February 1963).

21. BROWNING, ROBERT M., and DONALD O. STOVER. *Behavior Modification in Child Treatment*. New York: Aldine Publishing Company, 1971.

22. BURMEISTER, EVA. *Forty-five in the Family*. New York: Columbia University Press, 1949.

23. ———. *The Professional House Parents*. New York: Columbia University Press, 1960.

24. ———. *Roofs for the Family*. New York: Columbia University Press, 1954.

25. CASLER, LAWRENCE. "Maternal Deprivation—A Critical Review of the Literature." *Monograph of the Society for Research in Child Development*, **26** (1961).

26. CHILD WELFARE LEAGUE OF AMERICA. *From Chaos to Order: A Collective View of the Residential Treatment of Children*. New York, 1972.

27. ———. *Maternal Deprivation*. New York, January 1962.

28. ———. *A National Directory of Child Care Training Courses*. New York, 1969.

29. ———. *Standards for Services of Child Welfare Institutions*. New York, 1964.

30. ———. *Training for Child Care Staff*. New York, June 1963.

31. CLANCI, VINCENT. "Home Supervision of the Mentally Deficient." *American Journal of Mental Deficiency*, **51** (January 1947).

32. "A Crisis at Miracle Hill." *Daily Oklahoman*, Oklahoma City, Okla. (May 17–26, 1964).

33. CRISS, FLORENCE L., and RAY C. GOODWIN. "Short-Term Group Counseling for Parents of Children in Residential Treatment." *Child Welfare*, **49**, 1 (January 1970), 45–48.

34. DEUTSCH, ALBERT. *Our Rejected Children*. Boston: Little, Brown and Company, 1950.

35. DICK, HARRY. "Nature and Significance of Changes in the Houseparents' Role in Institutions for Children." *Journal of Health and Human Behavior*, **12**, 4 (December 1971).

36. FANSHEL, DAVID. "Commentary on Clinical Judgment in Foster Care Placement." *Child Welfare*, **42** (April 1963).

37. FANT, RAYMOND. "Use of Groups in Residential Treatment," in *Healing Through Living*. Ed. by Morris F. Mayer and Arthur Blum. Springfield, Ill.: Charles C Thomas, Publishers, 1971.

38. FOSTER, GENEVIEVE W., et al. *Child Care with Emotionally Disturbed Children*. Pittsburgh: University of Pittsburgh Press, 1972.

39. GREENBERG, ARTHUR, and MORRIS F. MAYER. "Group Home Care as an Adjunct to Residential Treatment." *Child Welfare*, **51**, 7 (July 1972), 423–35.

40. GULA, MARTIN. *Child-Caring Institutions*. Washington, D.C.: Government Printing Office, 1958.

41. ———. "Children Who Need Treatment," in *From Chaos to Order: A*

Collective View of the Residential Treatment of Children. New York: Child Welfare League of America, 1972.

42. ———. *Quest for Equality.* Children's Bureau Publication 441. Washington, D.C.: Government Printing Office, 1966.

43. HAGEN, HELEN. *The Institution as a Casework Agency.* New York: Child Welfare League of America, February 1958.

44. HECHLER, JACOB. "Social Controls in Institutional Treatment." *Social Work*, 1 (April 1956).

45. HEITING, KENNETH H. "Involving Parents in Residential Treatment of Children." *Children*, 18, 5 (September–October 1971), 163–67.

46. HYLTON, LYDIA. *Residential Treatment Center, Children Program Costs.* New York: Child Welfare League of America, 1964.

47. JAFFE, E. D. "The Impact of Experimental Services on Dependent Children Referred for Institutional Care." *Social Work Today*, 1, 2 (May 1970), 5–8.

48. ———. "Professional Background and the Utilization of Institutional Care of Children as a Solution to Family Crisis." *Human Relations*, 23, 1 (1970), 15–21.

49. JAMES, HOWARD. *Children in Trouble—A National Scandal.* New York: David McKay Co., Inc., 1970.

50. JOHNSON, LILLIAN, and JOSEPH REID. *An Evaluation of Ten Years Work with Emotionally Disturbed Children.* Seattle: Ryther Child Center, 1947.

51. JOHNSTON, RUTH. "Some Casework Aspects of Using Foster Grandparents for Emotionally Disturbed Children." *Children*, 14, 2 (March–April 1967), 46–52.

52. JONSSON, GUSTAV. "Introduction to New Staff," in *Children Away from Home—A Sourcebook of Residential Treatment.* Ed. by James K. Whittaker and Albert E. Trieschman. New York: Aldine Publishing Company, 1972.

53. KAHN, ALFRED. *When Children Must Be Committed.* New York: Citizens' Committee for Children of New York, June 1960.

54. KEMP, CLAIRE J. "Family Treatment Within the Milieu of a Residential Treatment Center." *Child Welfare*, 50, 4 (April 1971), 239–42.

55. KONOPKA, GISELA. *Group Work in the Institution*, revised. New York: Association Press, 1970.

56. ———. "What Houseparents Should Know," in *Children in Care.* Ed. by J. N. Tod. Essex, England: Longman Group Ltd., 1968.

57. LANDER, JOSEPH, and RENA SCHULMAN. "The Impact of the Therapeutic Milieu on the Disturbed Personality." *Social Casework*, 41 (May 1960).

58. LEIBROCK, JOHN B. *Manual of Skilled Houseparentry.* Philadelphia: Whitmore Publishing Co., 1967.

59. LERNER, SAMUEL. "The Diagnostic Basis of Institutional Care for Children." *Social Casework*, 33 (March 1952).

60. LEWIS, CLAUDINE. "Selective Intake and Placement in a Children's Institution," in *Creative Group Living in a Children's Institution.* Ed. by Susanne Schulze. New York: Association Press, 1951.

61. LOW, SETH. *America's Children and Youth in Institutions, 1950, 1960, 1964: A Demographic Analysis.* Washington, D.C.: Government Printing Office, 1966.

62. MAAS, HENRY, and RICHARD ENGLER. *Children in Need of Care.* New York: Columbia University Press, 1959.

63. MAIER, HENRY W. "The Child Care Worker," in *Children Away from Home—A Sourcebook of Residential Treatment.* Ed. by James K. Whittaker and Albert E. Trieschman. Chicago: Aldine Publishing Company, 1972.

64. ——— (ed.). *Group Work as Part of Residential Treatment.* New York: National Association of Social Workers, 1965.

65. MALUCCIO, ANTHONY N., and WILMA D. MARLOW. "Residential Treatment of Emotionally Disturbed Children: A Review of the Literature." *Social Service Review,* **46**, 2 (June 1972), 230–50.

66. MAYER, MORRIS F. "The Group in Residential Treatment of Adolescents." *Child Welfare,* **51**, 8 (October 1972), 482–93.

67. ———, and JOHN MARSUSHIMA. "Training for Child Care Work: A Report on a National Conference." *Child Welfare,* **48**, 9 (November 1969), 525–32.

68. ———. *Supervision of Houseparents.* New York: Child Welfare League of America, 1965.

69. ———. "Differentials in Training Child Care Workers," in *Training for Child Care Staff.* New York: Child Welfare League of America, June 1963.

70. ———. *A Guide for Child Care Workers.* New York: Child Welfare League of America, 1958.

71. MEYER, MARGARET. "Family Ties and the Institutional Child." *Children,* **16**, 6 (November–December 1969), 226–31.

72. MORA, GEORGE, *et al.* "A Residential Treatment Center Moves Toward the Community Mental Health Model." *Child Welfare,* **48**, 10 (December 1969), 585–90.

73. MOYLES, WILLIAM E., and MARTIN WOLIN. "Group Care and Intellectual Development." *Developmental Psychology,* **4**, 3 (1971), 370–80.

74. NASH, BERNARD. "Foster Grandparents in Child Care Setting." *Public Welfare,* **26** (October 1968), 272–80.

75. OHLIN, LLOYD, and WILLIAM LAWRENCE. "Social Interaction Among Clients as a Treatment Problem." *Social Work,* **4** (April 1959).

76. PAPPENFONT, DONNELL, *et al. A Census of Children's Residential Institutions in the U.S., Puerto Rico and the Virgin Islands: 1966. Vol. II: Institutions for Dependent and Neglected Children.* Chicago: University of Chicago School of Social Service Administration, 1970.

77. ———, *et al. A Census of Children's Residential Institutions in the U.S., Puerto Rico and the Virgin Islands: 1966. Vol. IV: Institutions for the Emotionally Disturbed Children.* Chicago: University of Chicago School of Social Service Administration, 1970.

78. ———, *et al. A Census of Children's Residential Institutions in the U.S., Puerto Rico and the Virgin Islands: 1966. Vol. I: Seven Types of Institutions.* Chicago: University of Chicago School of Social Service Administration, 1970.

79. ———, and DEE MORGAN KILPATRICK. "Child Caring Institutions 1966: Selected Findings from the First National Survey of Children's Residential Institutions." *Social Service Review,* **43**, 4 (December 1969), 448–59.

80. ———, et al. "Children in Institutions 1966—A Research Note." *Social Service Review*, **42**, 2 (June 1968), 252–60.

81. PAYNE, GEORGE H. *The Child in Human Progress*. New York: G. P. Putnam's Sons, 1916.

82. PILIAVIN, IRVING. "Conflict Between Cottage Parents and Caseworkers." *Social Service Review*, **37** (March 1963).

83. PIZZAT, FRANK. *Behavior Modification in Residential Treatment of Children*. New York: Behavioral Publications, February 1972.

84. POLSKY, HOWARD. "Changing Delinquents' Subculture: A Social Psychological Approach." *Social Work*, **4** (October 1959).

85. ———. *Cottage Six—The Social System of Delinquent Boys in Residential Treatment*. New York: Russell Sage Foundation, 1962.

86. ———. *Social Systems Perspectives in Residential Institutions*. East Lansing, Mich.: Michigan State University Press, 1968.

87. ———, and DANIEL S. CLOSTER. *The Dynamics of Residential Treatment —A Social Systems Analysis*. Chapel Hill, N.C.: University of North Carolina Press, 1968.

88. PYLE, MARY L. *Institutions for Child Care and Treatment*. New York: Child Welfare League of America, February 1947.

89. RAUSCH, HAROLD. "The Interpersonal Behavior of Children in Residential Treatment." *Journal of Abnormal and Social Psychology*, **59** (January 1959).

90. REDL, FRITZ, and DAVID WINEMAN. *Children Who Hate*. New York: The Free Press, 1951.

91. ———. *Controls from Within*. New York: The Free Press, 1953.

92. ROTHMAN, DAVID J. *The Discovery of the Asylum*. Boston: Little, Brown and Company, 1971.

93. SCHULZE, SUSANNE. *Creative Group Living in Children's Institutions*. New York: Association Press, 1951.

94. ———, and FRITZ MAYER. *Training House Parents*. Children's Bureau, Social Security Administration. Mimeo. n.d.

95. SHULMAN, RENA. "Treatment of the Disturbed Child in Placement." *Jewish Social Service Quarterly*, **30** (Spring 1954).

96. SILVER, HAROLD. "Residential Treatment of Emotionally Disturbed Children: An Evaluation of Fifteen Years' Experience." *Journal of Jewish Communal Service*, **38** (1961).

97. SIMON, ABRAHAM. "Residential Treatment of Children." *Social Service Review*, **30** (September 1956).

98. STAR, SHIRLEY A., and ALMA KUBY. *Number and Kinds of Children's Residential Institutions in the U.S.* Washington, D.C.: Government Printing Office, 1967.

99. STERNBACH, JACK, and ALLEN PINCUS. "Differences in Perception of the Group by Cottage Parents and Social Workers." *Child Welfare*, **49**, 6 (June 1970), 327–35.

100. TAYLOR, DELORES A., and STUART W. ALPERT. *Continuity and Support Following Residential Treatment*. New York: Child Welfare League of America, 1973.

101. THOMAS, CLARKE. *No Miracles at Miracle Hill*. New York: Child Welfare League of America, 1965.

102. Thompson, Benevive M., "Foster Grandparents." *Child Welfare*, **48**, 9 (November 1969), 564–68.
103. Thurston, Henry. *The Dependent Child*. New York: Columbia University Press, 1930.
104. Trasler, Gordon. *In Place of Parents*. London: Kegan Paul, Trench, Trubner & Co., 1960.
105. Trieschman, Albert E., *et al. The Other Twenty-three Hours*. Chicago: Aldine Publishing Company, 1969.
106. United Nations. *The Institutional Care of Children*. New York, 1956.
107. U.S. Congress. *Hearing Before the Public Health, Education, Welfare, and Safety Subcommittee of the Committee on the District of Columbia, U.S. Senate, 89th Congress, May 10, 1965*. Washington, D.C.: Government Printing Office, 1965.
108. U.S. Department of Health, Education, and Welfare, National Institute of Mental Health. *Residential Treatment Centers for Emotionally Disturbed Children 1969–1970*. National Health Statistics Series A, No. 6. Washington, D.C.: Government Printing Office, 1971.
109. ———, Social Rehabilitation Service. *Children Served by Public Welfare Agencies and Voluntary Child Welfare Agencies and Institutions—March 1971*. Washington, D.C.: Government Printing Office, 1973.
110. Vincent, Ben. *Begone Dull Care—An Informal Guide to the Residential Care of Children*. London: Her Majesty's Stationery Office, 1968.
111. Warner, Amos G., *et al. American Charities and Social Work*, 4th ed. New York: Thomas Y. Crowell Company, 1942.
112. Whittaker, James K., and Albert E. Trieschman (eds.). *Children Away from Home—A Sourcebook of Residential Treatment*. Chicago: Aldine Publishing Company, 1972.
113. ———. "Colonial Child Care Institutions: Our Heritage of Care." *Child Welfare*, **50**, 7 (July 1971), 396–400.
114. Winder, Alvin, *et al.* "Group Therapy with Parents of Children in a Residential Treatment Center." *Child Welfare*, **44** (May 1965).
115. Witner, Helen, and Charles P. Gerhenson. *On Rearing Infants and Young Children in Institutions*. Children's Bureau Research Reports No. 1. Washington, D.C.: Government Printing Office, 1968.
116. Wolins, Martin. "Group Care: Friend or Foe." *Social Work*, **14**, 1 (January 1969), 35–53.
117. ———. "Young Children in Institutions—Some Additional Evidence." *Developmental Psychology*, **2**, 1 (1969), 99–109.
118. ———, and Irving Piliavin. *Institution or Foster Family—A Century of Debate*. New York: Child Welfare League of America, September 1964.
119. World Health Organization. *Deprivation of Maternal Care—A Reassessment of Its Effects*. Geneva. World Health Organization, 1962.

13

Child Welfare Services in Other Countries

Introduction

All countries have child welfare problems which are similar to those encountered in this country. This is not unanticipated. All of the world's children are dependent for a long time and are cared for, primarily, in families. And all over the world parents fall ill, die, desert, have children out of wedlock, struggle with limited resources, and so on. Children who suffer from neglect, abuse, and physical, mental, and emotional handicaps are encountered everywhere in the world.

Madison, after a comprehensive recent review of family and child welfare services in the Soviet Union concludes that "the Soviet definition of child welfare services would not differ essentially from the definition currently used in the United States." [49, p. 175] While child welfare services in all countries are not identical, there are similarities which suggest common problems and analogous solutions.

The following three case studies from three widely separated countries—Poland, Zambia, Japan—are a testimonial to the universality of child welfare problems.

Poland

A social inspectress learned, during her supervision of the guardianship of little Mania, that the latter loved her "guardian" so much that she wanted to become her real daughter. Mrs. N. shared the same desire. She had taken in the child when a baby from the hands of her mother, a girl in great despair, who had subsequently disappeared. The guardian had taken preliminary steps with a view to adopting the little girl, but the formalities had seemed too complicated. Mania bore, in fact, the name of her mother, and it was first of all necessary to initiate a long procedure in order to clear up the situation. With the help of the guardianship court and the police, our inspectress had a search carried out in several provinces, and ended up by finding the mother. The latter was married, had three children, and her husband knew nothing of the fourth. The mother at once consented to the adoption of her first illegitimate child, and everyone was happy. [118, pp. 24–25]

Zambia

Joan Mulonga, aged twelve, came to the office and complained she had no school uniform and was not getting enough to eat—all because her father is sick with asthma and out of work; her mother works as a nursemaid but does not earn enough to keep them. Asked her to ask one of her parents or both to come and see me as soon as possible.

Mr. Mulonga came as requested. He knew his daughter had been to see me; he had in fact sent her himself. He had had an attack of asthma and had not been able to come himself. Said he has had asthma for twelve years or so. He is a chef by profession and is married to a Coloured woman from South Africa. Because of his asthma he cannot keep a job—he is always getting attacks and employers say they cannot afford to keep sick men. He has been to many doctors who have failed to cure him. Is now undergoing treatment at . . . Clinic. His wife is working as a nursemaid but does not earn enough for the family. He has considered taking a light job as an office orderly so that his asthma will not bother him but he has not been able to find one yet. Has also thought of returning to his village in the Fort Janeson area but with his Coloured wife who is not accustomed to village life he cannot do this. They are presently short of food and his daughter requires school uniforms. He thought we might help. I said we were prepared to help but would have to look into the situation more fully. Issued him with a voucher for rations pending inquiry. [12, pp. 19–20]

Japan

Mrs. F., age thirty, a graduate of junior high school, has a husband, a university graduate, age thirty-three, a son, five, and a daughter, two. Because Mr. F. is an only son, the couple live with Mr. F.'s mother and are partially dependent on her. Mrs. F. came to our agency saying she could not tolerate the home situation longer because of the over-close relationship between Mr. F. and his mother and the fact that his mother was trying to dominate her. The couple had married for love immediately following Mr. F.'s graduation from university and after he had secured his first job. From the beginning his earnings were insufficient and mother helped financially. Mrs. F. complained that they had no privacy even in the bedroom and that the grandmother not only gave "blind love" to the two grandchildren but also that she insisted on controlling everything in the family, doling out money to Mrs. F., and making her account for what she spent. Mrs. F. felt that her mother-in-law treated her like a maid and when she complained about this Mrs. F., Sr., scolded her for acting superior. We worked with Mr. F. and tried to help him play a more dominant role in the family. But the two women could not get along so the young couple decided to live separately from Mrs. F., Sr., and we closed our case. [18, p. 121]

There are differences, however, in the frequency with which different kinds of problems are encountered, and in the nature and pattern of services that have been developed to deal with them. Among the factors that determine differences in the programs are the following:

1. Attitudes toward "preventative" solutions—contraception, abortion, abandonment, and so on.
2. Child dependency ratios.
3. Level of economic wealth of the community.
4. Political and administrative development.
5. Prevalent attitude toward women and children.
6. Position of the nuclear family vis-à-vis other social institutions in the community.
7. Historical antecedents in coping with child welfare problems.

"Preventive" Solutions

Some of the "preventive" solutions to child welfare problems are acceptable in other countries. Contraception is, of course, widespread and has gained great acceptance. Abortion is available in Japan, England, Poland, Hungary, the Soviet Union, and other countries—with more or less official government sanction. [10; 16; 68; 90]   "In Russia, abortions are freely performed in government clinics if required for medical reasons. They cost five rubles ($5.50) in all other cases" (*The New York Times*, June 9, 1963). Abortion, having been made illegal in the Soviet Union in 1936, was made legal in 1955 [63]   "in order to respect the constitutional rights of women and allow them freedom to arrange their own lives." [47, p. 21]   Nevertheless, the government maintains a campaign to discourage abortion and will not legally permit termination of pregnancy after twelve weeks. By 1970, Hungary, Bulgaria, and Rumania, concerned about declining birth rates, adopted more restrictive abortion policies than they had had, and Czechoslovakia was considering a similar change in legislation. [45, p. 1]

In other countries an attempt is made to help the family with the decision regarding abortion. The Mother's Hygiene Bureau in Oslo employs an "abortion counselor," whose task it is "to offer advice and guidance to women who consider applying for legal abortion." [39, p. 74] In Denmark, the Mothers' Aid Centers, through their publicly supported local committees, process applications for abortion. This processing includes a discussion with the applicant to clarify the decision.

In most instances, abortions in these countries are requested by married women who want to delay having a family for economic or educational reasons, or who want to limit the size of the family they already have because of lack of income and/or space to care for additional children.

Many countries have begun to develop explicit population policy programs in order to control population growth. For instance, mainland China provides contraceptive devices to all women at no charge and a small army of "barefoot doctors," paramedical personnel with special training, "are assigned to a commune or urban block organization where they dispense contraceptives and supervise their use" (*The New York Times*, February 20, 1972). "Abortion has been legal in China since 1957 and women have the right to fifteen days of paid vacation following an abortion" (*The New York Times*, April 30, 1972). Vasectomies are available to men. [14, p. 286] Early marriage is actively discouraged and the relatively late average age at marriage (twenty-eight years for men, twenty-five years for women) also acts to reduce birth rates.

Abandonment of children as a solution for the parents, if not for the community, is practiced in some underdeveloped countries. A special report from Brazil to *The Milwaukee Journal* on July 15, 1962, notes: "As police make their rounds, they pick up starving children, abandoned and helpless. Sometimes they find them lying on the street, sometimes even thrown into garbage cans." A dispatch from Bogotá, Colombia, to *The New York Times* on September 9, 1962, details the living situation for a colony of 1200 vagrant children between seven and twelve years of age who live together on the streets, in parking lots, on construction sites, without families and without homes. A dispatch to *The New York Times*, regarding the effects of food shortages in Afghanistan in 1972, details the abandonment of children as one consequence of the country's poverty.

The boy's spindly body sank slowly to the dusty gravel road. He lowered his head to the pebbles, resting his sunken cheek on his hand. His dry, cracked lips did not close. He tried to cover his feet, but the torn, dirt-encrusted rags he wore were not long enough. He placed an empty tin can, his only possession, near his stomach. And then he started to cry.

No one knows how many children, abandoned by parents who had no food for them, have died or are dying in Afghanistan (*The New York Times,* June 16, 1972).

Child labor as a solution to child welfare problems is still widespread. In the Latin American countries, for instance, "an appreciable proportion of the labor force is still under fifteen." [113, p. 48]

Dependency Ratios and Levels of Industrialization

Dependency ratios—the ratios of productive adults to dependent children in the country—vary widely. The United Nations reports that in 1965, in the more developed regions of the world, 63 percent of the population were in their productive years (ages fifteen to sixty-four). These adults were responsible for caring for 28 percent of the population that were dependent because of childhood (ages ten to fourteen). In the less developed regions, however, only 55.1 percent of the population were in their productive years and faced with the necessity of caring for the 41.6 percent of the population composed of children. [111, p. 26]   It is predicted that by 1985 there will be, in the developed countries, sixty-three adults caring for twenty-six dependent children; in the developing countries fifty-six adults will be faced with the care of forty dependent children. [111, p. 26]

The dependency ratio is significant because it reflects the burden imposed by the unproductive group on the productive group. Where the relative number of producers is small, production is limited and has to be thinly distributed. The special programs required by the dependent must be funded from these already scarce resources.

The differences for children in the two sectors of the world, resulting from the contrasting dependency ratio situation, is further exacerbated by a growing maldistribution of wealth between the two sectors. During the 1960's, the world total gross national product increased by some $1100 billion. About 80 percent of this increase went to the developed sectors, which contain only one-quarter of the world's population; "only 6 percent of the increase went to countries where per capita incomes average $2000 or less, but which contain 60 percent of the world's population." [91, p. 3]

The United Nations notes, "No country can afford to move into programs of social entitlement until its economic resources have reached a point where a substantial amount can be made available for social expenditure." [100, p. 109]

Not only are developing countries characterized by high dependency ratios and limited resources, but they also face a heavy requirement for investment capital for economic development. Investment of capital in industry may, in the long run, result in more adequate child welfare resources and services. In the short run, however, the needs for such resources and services compete with the needs for child welfare services.

The problem is not only one of allocating limited financial resources but also one of allocating limited human resources. When there are few people in the country who have an opportunity for professional training of one kind or another, social work cannot easily compete with such professions as medicine, teaching, or engineering. As a United Nations report indicates, the limitations of the social service programs in the underdeveloped countries are dictated by their absolute poverty of resources in money, personnel, and institutional structure. [100, p. 106]

In the last analysis, the wealth of the community is the essential basis for any system of social welfare. And the degree of industrialization is decisive in determining the level of wealth. However, even if sufficient wealth were available, it might be deployed for child welfare services only if there is a favorable attitude toward the needs of the child. Thus, in some developing countries, the emphasis on investment in industry is sometimes balanced by the recognition not only that children are the beneficiaries of economic development programs, but that they are themselves an investment. Adequate provisions for children then become part of the national economic strategy. It is as necessary to improve the quality of human resources as it is to increase the supply of capital resources.

Dependency ratios and the level of industrialization of the economy not only dictate the amount that might be made available for social welfare, they also determine the kinds of social problems to which social welfare has to accord priority. It is not likely that the highly developed program of child welfare services will be given priority in countries where most people live in villages, "where there is little transportation, no telephone, no school, no doctor, only the most primitive housing and few, if any, literate people." [102, p. 41] Priority in these countries must be given to the most basic needs—keeping the child alive, keeping him fed, providing him with the beginnings of an education.

In many parts of the world, children suffer from chronic semistarvation. [80] Undernourishment resulting from lack of food is compounded by malnourishment arising from lack of the all-important proteins required by the growing child. Milk is still a luxury food in many underdeveloped countries. *Kwashiorkor,* a widespread diet deficiency disease of children in such countries, comes from an African word that, literally translated, means *first-second.* It connotes "the disease the first child gets when the second is expected," and is associated with weaning and denial of the mother's milk.

Many childhood diseases are widespread in underdeveloped countries, sapping the energy and vitality of children and reducing their capacity and motivation for learning. Malaria, trachoma, bilharziasis, diarrhea, parasitic infestations, yaws, and chronic hunger make these children dull and apathetic. Despite improvement in health conditions and the resulting reduction in infant mortality rates in the developing countries in recent years, these rates are still, in some instances, four and five times higher than they are in more economically advanced countries. [108]   And those countries that are still confronted with the most elementary problems of food needs, health needs, and educational needs for all children can hardly be expected to develop great concern for services needed by groups of specially deprived children. Where all are deprived those who are specially deprived lose any claim to special treatment. (See Fig. 13–1.)

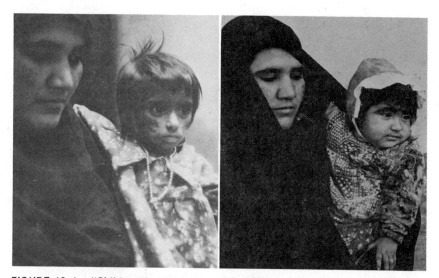

FIGURE 13–1. "Child welfare" in an underdeveloped country (Iraq)—a case of malnutrition, before and after treatment. (UNICEF photo.)

Three-quarters of the world's children, nearly a billion of them, live in developing countries. Of the hundred children born every half minute in these areas, twenty will die in their first year; two-thirds of the remainder are likely never to see adolescence and only one in four reaches "old age"—which, in terms of the average length of life in some of these countries, is about thirty-eight years. Of 100 children born in India and 100 American children more American children will live to age sixty-five than Indian children will live to age five. [28, p. 2]

Only a little more than half of those who survive to age five in the developing countries will ever set foot in a classroom. Fewer than 40 percent of that half will complete the elementary grades. [111]

Large numbers of children live on the pavements in Bombay and Calcutta or grow up under the most deprived environmental circumstances in the *favelas* or *ranchos* of Latin America or the *bustees* or *shuggies* of India. Makeshift housing in one shantytown or another is "home" for a sizable percentage of the world's population of children—a "home" without water, heat, electricity, sewerage, or garbage disposal system. [112]

In the mid-1960's the United Nations reported:

> . . . while in North America and western Europe, men and women ate on an average about 3000 calories and eighty to ninety grams of protein a day; in Latin America, with the exception of Argentina, the average fell to 2400 calories and some seventy grams of protein; in Asia, 2100 calories and fifty grams; and in Africa, the protein consumption was lower still. [114, p. 56]

Excluding mainland China, 72 percent of the world's children live in countries with a per capita income of less than $500; 47 percent of these children live in countries with a per capita income of less than $100. [114, p. 12]

Illegitimacy rates are ten times greater in some countries than in the United States. "In some areas in Latin America the illegitimacy rate is as high as 60 to 70 percent of all births; in these circumstances what is needed is a policy to organize the family rather than one to strengthen it." [113, p. 12–13]

Table 13–1 shows some of the differences between the developed countries and the underdeveloped countries in regard to some essential factors affecting the welfare of the child.

TABLE 13–1. International Comparison of Selective Factors

Economically Advanced Nations		Developing Nations	
Female Life Expectancy at Birth in Years [a]			
Netherlands (1968)	76.4	India (1960)	40.5
United States (1968)	74.0	Burundi (1965)	38.5
Czechoslovakia (1966)	73.6	Nigeria (1966)	36.7
Infant Mortality Rates (Deaths Under One Year per 1000 Live Births) [b]			
USSR (1970)	24.4	Liberia (1970)	131
United States (1970)	19.8	Madagascar (1970)	102
Netherlands	12.7	Chile (1968)	91.6

TABLE 13–1. International Comparison of Selective Factors—(Cont.)

Economically Advanced Nations		Developing Nations	
Percentage Illegitimacies per 1000 Live Births [c]			
Sweden	15.1	Guatemala	67.4
United States	9.7	Mozambique	34.3
Japan	0.9	Paraguay	43
Per Capita National Income Expressed in U.S. Dollars, 1968 [d]			
United States	3578	Chile	449
Sweden	2294	Camaroon	140
Israel	1158	India	71
Net Food Supplies—Calories per Day, 1967–1968 [e]			
New Zealand	3290	Bolivia (1966)	1980
United States	3200	Iran (1966)	1890
Denmark	3150	Algeria (1966)	1870
Inhabitants per Physician [f]			
United States (1969)	669	Chad (1970)	64,000
Austria (1970)	540	Nigeria (1969)	56,670
Czechoslovakia (1969)	500	Indonesia (1968)	27,560
Children of Primary School Age Attending School [g]			
North America	98%	Latin America	55%
Europe and USSR	97%	Asia	45%
Oceania	95%	Africa	40%

Dependency Ratio—Percentage of Population 0–14 Years of Age and 15–64 Years of Age, Major World Areas, 1965 [h]

Region	0–14	15–64	Region	0–14	15–64
Europe	25.4	64.1	Africa	43.5	53.7
North America	31.0	59.8	South Asia	43.0	54.0
USSR	30.5	62.1	Latin America	42.5	53.9

[a] [109] United Nations. *Statistical Yearbook—23rd Issue, 1971.* New York: United Nations, 1972.
[b] [108] United Nations. *Demographic Yearbook—21st Issue, 1969.* New York: United Nations, 1970.
[c] [108] United Nations. *Demographic Yearbook—21st Issue, 1969.* New York: United Nations, 1970.
[d] [110] United Nations. *Yearbook of National Accounts Statistics.* New York: United Nations, 1970.
[e] [109] United Nations. *Statistical Yearbook—23rd Issue, 1971.* New York: United Nations, 1972.
[f] [109] United Nations. *Statistical Yearbook—23rd Issue, 1971.* New York: United Nations, 1972.
[g] [106] United Nations. *1970 Report on the World Social Situation.* New York: United Nations, 1970.
[h] [111] United Nations. *Trends in Social Situation of Children—Report of The Secretary General.* New York: United Nations, January 8, 1970.

The limited development of general community services for health, education, and welfare in the underdeveloped countries means that a great deal of child welfare is concerned with the problem of inadequate role enactment resulting from deficiencies in community resources. These difficulties lie outside the parent-child relationship network but affect it adversely.

Thus, although child welfare services in the more advanced countries may have to be provided on an individual basis for those children who lack the normal arrangement for care—the child of the broken family, the emotionally disturbed child who cannot make good use of the family that is available—child welfare in the underdeveloped countries is more concerned with providing for all children, on a mass basis, those essential primary conditions necessary for normal, healthy development. Whereas child welfare is concerned in the United States with the handicapped child who cannot use the available schools, the problem for child welfare in the underdeveloped countries is to make a school available.

Political and Administrative Development

The development of child welfare services and associated social security programs is dependent on the ability of the country to develop a sophisticated administrative and fiscal apparatus. It requires birth registration procedures to determine how many children there are and where they are located, and it permits the certification of age for social security. Yet a United Nations report on child welfare services in Africa noted that "only about a third of the nations in the region had birth registration programs in 1964." [103, p. 23]   The provision of services requires the opening of local offices, the establishment of forms and procedures for record keeping, accounting, and a communications system so that people can be reached, checks sent, appointments made. A workman's compensation program requires associated medical services; an unemployment insurance program requires associated job-finding and vocational retraining services. A network of social services requires the recruitment, training, and deployment of many workers who possess the necessary skills. An efficient social insurance program requires the acceptance of a strong central authority so that a uniform program can be administered in a standardized manner throughout a country.

The Relationship of the Nuclear Family to the Community

The nature of child welfare services is also affected by the existence of other institutional arrangements available to meet the needs of children. In the relatively simple, localized, self-sufficient society, which until recently characterized Africa, "The family and tribal pattern of relationship and responsibility function to meet the recognized social needs of its members. Not only the parents but the larger family group assumed responsibility for the rearing of children." [100, p. 105] Family and tribal organizations furnished protection against some of the same risks and difficulties for which social services are organized in the more highly industrialized countries. A United Nations report on child welfare services in Africa notes:

> The concept of adoption is new in Africa as is also the concept of illegitimacy. By virtue of the extended nature of the family system, adoption has not been necessary in the past and has been looked down upon. Children have been valued in and of themselves and relatives have considered it their obligation to look after orphans and neglected children. For example the response from Sierra Leone comments, "There are no adoption laws, but the family system is such that as a rule there are hardly unwanted children. Children are cared for even by nonrelatives." [103, p. 26]

Such solutions to child welfare problems, however, become progressively less feasible as a society becomes more industrialized. With movement to urban areas the extended family disperses and traditional solutions no longer apply. Hasen, discussing social security in India, points out that "the joint family is disintegrating with increasing urbanization" and that the "family is losing both the capacity and the willingingness to act as the sole agent responsible for providing social security." [26, pp. 193–94]   A process of "detribalization" takes place. The movement to the city brings a dependence on wage employment, on a money economy. The authority of the father is diminished, for he no longer is head of a family productive unit. With this decline in paternal authority comes a painful reallocation of role responsibilities and privileges between the different generations within the family group and between husband and wife. The United Nations notes that in the new industrialized, urbanized society the family "may have no tie to any group which feels a direct responsibility for its welfare. At the same time, the instability of the urban family results in increasing numbers of deserted mothers and abandoned children." [30, p. 124]   Urbanization, then, increases the likelihood of child welfare problems while it simultaneously denies the availability of a structure through which such problems were previously resolved. [94]   The network of tribal mutual aid and support weakens and there arises a need for institutionalization of child welfare services. "In developing societies, social welfare services emerge to meet human needs that can no longer be satisfied exclusively through the traditional institutions of a more static period." [102, p. 10]

Attitude Toward Women and Children

Industrialization and urbanization change the position of women in the family. A changing attitude toward the child is tied to a changing attitude toward the mother. More adequate care for the child requires more adequate education of the mother and a greater concern for her needs. The mother suffering from "maternal depletion syndrome"— resulting from early marriage, frequent pregnancies, inadequate diet, and overwork—can hardly be expected to meet the needs of the child. An important aspect of child welfare in the developing countries, then, is concerned with the child indirectly through concern with the mother. A changing, more positive attitude toward the needs of women is expressed in the establishment of women's clubs and social centers, set up side by side with children's clinics, devoted to the teaching of mother-craft and homemaking and to helping women with the problems they face.

Poverty of resources alone does not always explain difficulties encountered in providing for adequate care of the child. Sometimes cheap, healthy foods, such as peanuts, are available, but it may not be traditional to offer these to children. Up to a point, improvement of children's health may be more directly affected by educating the parents than by increasing the supply of doctors or medicine. But this often requires programs directed toward the reduction of illiteracy, particularly that of women.

The Influence of Historical Precedent

The pattern of child welfare services is determined by the nature of earlier institutionalized approaches to similar problems. [101]   Countries previously under British control, in accordance with the British pattern, rely heavily on voluntary agencies; former French colonies associate social service with health and nursing activity and stress family allowances; Latin American countries stress social service offered under the auspices of the Catholic Church.

Countries that, like the United States, value independence, autonomy, individualism, self-reliance, and self-fulfillment are likely to be more resistant to welfare legislation than are countries that value the idea of community responsibility for the welfare of all of their citizens. Different countries also give different priorities to groups in the population in allocating welfare resources. France is strongly child-oriented; Denmark is more strongly oriented to its old people.

Some Selective Comparisons:
Child Welfare Service, Here and Abroad

Having discussed some of the factors that affect the development of child welfare programs generally, we shall now review the different categories of services—supportive, supplemental, and substitutive—and point to variations and modifications found in other countries. Because of the possible appropriateness of these variations and modifications to our own child welfare problems, most of the countries cited are similar to the United States in levels of industrialization and standards of living.

It would be an impossibly lengthy task to review in detail the child welfare programs of even a representative group of countries, so we must be quite selective. Our purpose is to call attention to those aspects of these programs that we might consider in strengthening our own child welfare programs. Consequently, the result is not likely to be a fair comparison. To do justice to our own program, we would have to cite

FIGURE 13-2. Meeting essential physical needs is the child welfare priority in some countries. Photo shows homeless children in Bombay. (UNICEF photos by Jack Ling.)

the weaknesses of the foreign programs to which we call attention. If we were to present a balanced picture, for instance, of the Soviet welfare system as it affects children, we would have to note that the social insurance system does not cover some agricultural workers as adequately as it does industrial workers, that there is no unemployment insurance system in the Soviet Union, that political "undesirables" can lose their rights to social security, that there are no statistics available on adoption, and no published evaluations of Soviet services, that mothers of young children may be denied financial assistance if they refuse to accept work or work training, that income maintenance programs for divorced or deserted mothers are inadequate, and so on. [83] However, given the aim of stimulating thinking toward a broader, less ethnocentrically based perspective on child welfare services, a selective presentation of alternative approaches appears justified.

Supportive Services

Great Britain is one of the relatively few countries to have developed a highly professionalized program. It has a network of family service agencies, many of which are affiliated with the national council of family casework agencies. Operating under the auspices of some family service agencies are the Family Discussion Bureaus, which offer marital counseling through psychoanalytically oriented casework. The government provides grants-in-aid to such organizations.

The work of the Family Service Units in Great Britain started during World War II, when conscientious objectors founded the Pacifist Service Units to care for disorganized, bombed-out families in large English cities. As a result of their contact with the families, and the realization that many of the difficulties presented by the families were not the result of the war, the units began to work toward helping the families resolve some of their basic problems. Although casework is the principal method of aid, the units operate in a distinctive way. The staff lives together in a house in the district they serve and its members are available to families in the district on a twenty-four-hour basis. The staff attempts to demonstrate, in this home, that standards can be maintained even though the housing is poor. In establishing a relationship with families he could not reach through "talk" alone, the caseworker may go into the home and assist the family directly by scrubbing floors, washing clothes, caring for the children, cooking a meal, and so on. [54; 66]

Holland has attempted to help the multiproblem family in an even more comprehensive way. It has set up special villages, known as *reeducation centers*, to which the family is moved. Employment for the father is obtained in the neighborhood, and the children go to the village school. Through demonstrations, teaching, and counseling by social workers who visit daily, the families learn how to manage the home, how to budget, and how to live together with less friction.

For many parents seeking help, the complexity of social services is baffling. They not only need help in determining where to go, they also need help in understanding the eligibility requirements and the procedures. The British have established a network of Citizens' Advice Bureaus to help people find their way around the complex world of social services. Simple explanations are offered, information as to what is available is given, and referrals are made to the proper agency. [34; 43; 135]

Another supportive service of interest is the subsidized vacation. The Norwegian government provides subsidies to families in order to enable housewives to have an annual two-week vacation, preference being given to housewives with small children. France and Germany maintain family holiday homes—nonprofit establishments designed to permit the family to vacation together. The Swedish government supports, through grants-in-aid, holiday homes for housewives. During their absence, vacationing mothers may arrange for homemakers from the local social welfare bureau to prepare meals for their husbands and children and do housecleaning. Such homemaker service is at community expense if the family of the vacationing mother cannot afford to pay. [92, p. 17]

If protective services are included as supportive services, we might note that most countries provide sanctions in the case of neglect by parents of their duties toward their children. In England, women convicted of child neglect may be sent to training homes for mothers. The institutions offer courses in elementary "housewifery and mothercraft." The mothers take with them, to the training homes, their children under five years of age. [3, p. 6]

The United States celebrates Father's Day and Mother's Day, but East Europeans celebrate International Children's Day: in Bulgaria, it is regarded "as a big public event in which it is the duty of all to participate" [120, p. 13];   in Poland, the motto for the day is "the upbringing and the education of children is the responsibility of all." [118, p. 51]

Supplementary Services: Social Insurance, Homemaker Service, Day Care

The 1971 compilation by the U.S. Department of Health, Education, and Welfare of social security programs throughout the world lists material from 125 countries. [116]   All have some type of social security program. A workman's compensation program is the oldest and most widespread social security measure (122 countries); the least frequently listed program is unemployment insurance (thirty-four countries). Over one hundred countries have some kind of program providing for old age, disability, and survivors' insurance; sixty-eight have some kind of sickness and maternity insurance programs; and sixty-three countries had a family or children's allowance program. However, the mere fact that a country has a particular program may be deceptive. Agricultural workers, who often constitute a majority of the economically active population, are frequently not included in the programs. [22; 25]

The most widespread kind of social insurance of direct interest to children is the family allowance. Originally adopted in France to encourage a higher birth rate, its spread to more than sixty countries was based on the idea that the existence of dependent children should not give rise to undue inequalities in family levels of living. The program provides for the payment of a regular allowance to every family for the support of each child and corrects the imbalance between family income and family need. The allowance is designed for adopted and foster children as well as natural children. [24; 27; 42; 116]   In some countries, allowances are paid to all families with dependent children regardless of employment status or family income. In other countries, they are paid only to families with limited income; only to people in certain occupations; or only upon the birth of the second or a third child.

Family allowances are usually financed by a tax on employers or out of general governmental revenue. Generally there is a cutoff point for eligible children, which ranges between fourteen and eighteen years; however, this cutoff point may be extended for children who are in school, or who are sick or handicapped.

Before 1972, "Japan and the United States were the only industrial nations which did not include a national system of cost allowances for children among the social security programs." [38, p. 39]   In January 1972, after ten years of debate, Japan adopted a family allowance program whose goal is "to lead to the healthy upbringing of children and the stability of life at home." Currently the United States is the only highly industrialized nation without such a program.

France, which instituted the family allowance in 1858, has one of the most substantial programs. "Average gross earnings for an unskilled worker in the Paris area are approximately $120 a month (1966). The family allowance, assuming three children under ten years of age, would amount to approximately $36." [77, p. 18]

In 1969 the allowance for a family with three children constituted 23 percent of its estimated average monthly earnings in France; 17 percent in Sweden; 10 percent in England; and 6 percent in West Germany. [24, Table 2, p. 23]   In other countries the allowance is more modest. In 1969 Canada, for example, paid $6 a month for each child up to the age of nine and $8 for older children. Yet Madison concludes that "the welfare of Canadian children, including children who do not live in their own homes, has been contributed to considerably by the allowance." [46, p. 140]

One might point to our own income tax reductions for each dependent child as an indirect family allowance program; however, most of the countries which provide family allowances do so in addition to allowing income tax reductions.

Unlike the United States, most European countries have government-operated health insurance programs. [116]   The particular significance of this for child welfare, aside from the increments to family income that result from the fact that the insurance pays the family's medical bills, is that it provides prenatal, delivery, and postnatal medical care for every mother, and guarantees the possibility of adequate medical attention for every child. This may help account for the fact that in 1970 the United States ranked fourteenth in the world in infant mortality rates. [19; 108] In 1970 infant mortality in the Netherlands was 12.7 percent per 1000 live births against 19.8 in the United States. (See Fig. 2–3, p. 61.) Most of the countries with lower infant mortality rates—Sweden, the Netherlands, Australia, Great Britain, Denmark—have national health insurance programs. Free health services in the Soviet Union are not only guaranteed by the State but organized to "provide preventively oriented, readily available, and geographically accessible care." [115, p. 3]

In addition to health insurance, which provides free medical care, many countries protect the working mother and child by offering maternity benefits. [32]   Maternity benefits compensate the family for the loss of the mother's wages during pregnancy, enable her to stop work earlier in the pregnancy, and permit her to remain home with the baby for at least a minimum period after birth. Thus, the working Soviet mother receives maternity benefits at the rate of 100 percent of pay for a sixteen-week period—eight weeks before and eight weeks after confinement. Italy's social insurance system provides 80 percent of earnings up to thirteen weeks before and eight weeks after confinement. In Yugoslavia, "working women are entitled to 133 days of paid maternity leave and subsequently their working day is reduced by four hours until the child reaches three years of age." [76, p. 23]   Israel grants working women a three-month leave at 75 percent of salary at the time of confinement. The women may return to work and "be permitted an hour less work per day until the end of the year at the expense of the employer." [61, p. 298]   France, and some thirty other countries, provides a lump sum maternity allowance to the family at the birth of a child, the amount varying with each birth; the payment is designed to help the family meet the extra costs of welcoming a new child into the family.

As a protection to both mother and child, maternity benefits are frequently made on condition that the mother use the free medical care during the pregnancy. For instance, France pays a prenatal allowance with the onset of pregnancy, "the nine monthly payments due for the period of pregnancy are divided into three, each being paid after the medical examination and provided that the examination has taken place at the proper time." [43, p. 53] With this kind of inducement, 95 percent of all Finnish expectant mothers, for instance, are under medical care. [8, p. 22] After maternity leave, a woman worker who is breast-feeding her child has the right to some time off. In the Soviet Union, for example, working mothers are allowed a breastfeeding break of at least half an hour every three-and-a-half hours.

Health insurance plans provide medical care, sickness insurance, and substitute income when the wage-earner is ill. Although most of the industrialized nations make sickness insurance available as part of the social insurance system, the United States does not. Those countries having social insurance sickness benefits increase the insurance or provide supplementation when the wage-earner has dependent children. [98, pp. 17–18] Sickness allowance is also paid when a working mother is needed at home to care for a sick child. [37, p. 56] For instance, in Bulgaria should a child under the age of three fall ill the working mother can obtain paid leave to care for the child. [120, p. 6] In East Germany single parents who need to care for a sick child receive sick pay during their absence from work. [52, p. 91]

Indirect procedures have also been adopted to help maintain family income at a level that would permit adequate care of the child. Hot school lunches at little or no cost and free distribution of food to low-income families supplement the family budget. Rent allowances go further than subsidies of low-cost housing. Denmark, for example, has a system of differential rents for families with three or more children living in flats built especially for such families. Rent reductions of up to 70 percent are given according to the number of children, and "about half of all families with two or more children under sixteen years receive rent subsidies." [20, p. 145] In France housing allowances can range up to 85 percent of the rent for families with four or more children.

In Denmark, low-income families may also receive textile discount coupons of specified value to be used toward the purchase of children's clothing. In Belgium, Greece, France, and Scandinavia, large families are given special reductions of 50–75 percent on train and bus fares. Sweden provides free holiday travel, once a year, to a place of rest and recreation for members of low-income families.

Most industrial nations have complementary programs of public assistance which, like those in the United States, are designed to cover groups in the population not protected—or not adequately protected— by the social insurance programs. While such assistance programs attempt, as in England, to advertise and offer the program so that recipients are not stigmatized, such an objective is difficult to achieve. Assistance programs involve a means test and, most frequently, inadequate grants. The concept of guaranteed minimum income for all citizens is rarely implemented. The People's Republic of China has, apparently, a program which assures every family a minimum standard of living: a subsidy is granted a worker with a certain number of children whose income is below the government level established for a family of that size (*The New York Times,* June 3, 1971, p. 16).

The continued persistence of pockets of poverty in countries with a comprehensive social insurance system has led to a re-examination of the efficiency of such services. [1; 13]   Family allowance programs, now available to all without a means test, may be revised so that more money can be channeled to those in greater need of such aid.

In general, then, many of the other highly industrialized nations have a more comprehensive social welfare program than the United States. According to the International Labor Office, the United States, in 1963, ranked twenty-eighth of fifty-six countries studied in percentage of gross national product devoted to social security benefits. [31, pp. 296–301]   Part of the difference results not from variations in comprehensiveness of coverage, but from the fact that the social security program in the United States is of more recent origin than the programs in other industrialized countries. More people are likely to be drawing benefits under programs which have been established for longer periods of time.

The larger percentage of gross national product devoted to transfer payments through the welfare programs in other countries may help to explain in part differences in income distribution between the United States and some other countries. Chandler concludes a study of such differences by noting:

> The lowest-income fifth in the United States received a 5.0
> percent share of total household income after taxes, compared
> with 6.4 percent in Germany, and 8.3 percent in the United Kingdom.
> Thus, in terms of either comparative dispersion or aggregate
> income, there was apparently a greater inequality in income
> distribution in the United States than in other countries. [9, p. 56]

These comparisons, however, are subject to rapid change. [86]   Between 1965 and 1970, social welfare expenditures in the United States increased about 12–14 percent each year and increased 17.5 percent in 1971. As a consequence, social welfare expenditures from public funds constituted, in 1971, more than half of all government expenditures. Such expenditures amounted to 16.5 percent of the gross national product in 1971 as compared with 11.8 percent in 1965. The standing of the United States was, in all likelihood, considerably higher in 1971 than in 1963 (the latest date for which comparative information is available), although still lower than that of some other comparably industrialized countries such as France, West Germany, and Australia. [35, p. 11]

In the Soviet Union, social services are more closely tied to social insurance than they are in the United States, which permits a much wider access to family problems than is true for social insurance agencies in the United States. Similarly, Australia has organized a special casework service within its general social security administration and "French social security agencies employ social workers to perform *polyvalent* social duties, which include family casework and the handling of problems with which families may be faced." [99, p. 30]   France, too, combines social services and the social insurances:

> One of the characteristic features of the French social security
> system is that it links a program of health and social services to the
> agencies that administer benefit payments. That means that these
> organizations are not merely administrative and financial agencies,
> but that they use part of their resources to activate a true
> program of services for the benefit of their members." [41, p. 182]

The French family allowance system, for instance, makes available such services as homemaker service, day care, family holidays to family allowance recipients. [71, p. 317]

Homemaker service is more highly developed in some countries than it is in the United States. In Great Britain, homemaker service is one of the programs offered as part of the National Health Service Act— Britain's socialized medicine plan. In 1967 England and Wales had 62,000 homemakers—one for every 760 people. [29, p. 3]   At the same time there were some 8000 homemakers employed in the United States —only one for every 25,000 people. [60, Table 12, p. 218]   In Finland, legislation requires that there be homemakers available in every public health district to work closely with midwives and public health nurses. As a result the number of homemakers per capita is much higher than in the United States. In the Scandinavian countries, the homemaker programs are supported by public funds. In Norway, for example, in the case of certain illnesses, the cost of homemaker service is borne by health insurance payments.

Although there is no formally established program of training for homemakers in the United States, several European countries have such a program. Holland has an eighteen-month curriculum; France, which classifies homemaker service as a social profession, offers a seven-month program; Finland has schools offering a two-year course in homemaker training; Sweden offers a fifteen-month homemaker training course in fourteen schools scattered throughout the country. [62]   In every instance, the courses offer a combination of theoretical material and practical field work in a hospital, child-care institutions, or supervised placement in families. [96]   In addition, Germany has a special organization that offers homemaker service to large families, on the theory that giving the mother of a large family an opportunity for a break from unremitting child care is sensible preventative therapy.

The expansion in employment of married women gives rise everywhere to the problem of the need for day care. Many European countries apparently do not share our reluctance to have a day-care facility associated with the mother's place of work nor our reluctance to offer group care to children under three years of age. [3; 7; 15; 65]   Consequently, especially in the East European countries, the factory *crèche*, or infant nursery, is quite common. [96, pp. 18–44]   Part of the greater need for and, hence, acceptability of group care is predicated on the fact that a significantly larger percentage of women in East Europe work outside the home than is true in the United States. In addition, the housing shortage there makes home care less feasible.

However, perhaps a more significant factor is the ideological one. In the United States the natural parents are clearly and unequivocally the primary parents and only in unusual circumstances does the state exercise its parental right to the child. In the Soviet Union, however, the state assumes a more active responsibility, even in ordinary circumstances, and the natural parents' rights over the child are more clearly delegated rights than primary rights. [5; 49]   There is a closer, more explicit partnership between state and natural parents in child rearing. It is felt that if the "New Soviet Citizen" is to emerge from the process of socialization, the state cannot entirely trust the parents, or the family system, to do the job correctly. To live in a collective society and adapt to the collective means socialization to collective living from the start. [5; 51]   In the words of Makarenko, the Soviet educator who was to Soviet child rearing what Spock was to American child rearing, the child is to be brought up "in the collective, by the collective, for the collective." Responsibility for child socialization in the Soviet Union rests largely with community agencies and the children's collective—the group of age mates whose motto is "mine is ours; ours is mine." Hence group care is not only expedient, but also desirable. Ideology also helps explain the group child-rearing practice of some of the Israeli collectives —the kibbutzim. [4; 69; 87; 126]

Other countries provide group day care for more children, for younger children, for longer periods of time than is true in the United States. In the Soviet Union care provided for children on a group basis in *crèches*, in extended kindergarten programs, and in "children's homes" administered by the Ministry of Education, is very extensive. [5; 11; 55; 63; 70; 127; 128; 129]   All-day nurseries, organized on a district basis or as adjuncts to factories, accept children from the age of seven months to three years.

Currently all new Soviet apartment buildings are required to reserve a minimum of 5 percent of space for a *crèche*, and "all enterprises employing more than 500 workers must provide nursery and *crèche* facilities." [70, p. 31]   By the end of 1970, the network of preschool facilities had expanded to serve 12.5 million Russian children between the ages of two to three months and seven years. Thus about 50 percent of all Russian children under the age of seven (when elementary school begins) were cared for in some preschool day-care facility. Bronfenbrenner estimated in 1970 that 10 percent of all Soviet children *under* two years of age were enrolled in public nurseries. [5, p. 15]

Every effort is made to provide adequate care. A "patronage nurse," implementing the role of a social worker, visits the homes of children whose families are applying for day care to help integrate the child's experience in the day-care center and the home. [63]   The nurseries which enroll children at three months of age have one "upbringer" for every four children at the younger age levels.

Czechoslovakia has developed a national system of day-care service "completely financed by the national government without charge to the parents (except a small fee for meals). Every Czechoslovakian who works outside the home has a monthly deduction from his paycheck—based on income and family size—and he and his family then become eligible for all day-care programs without cost." [112, p. 29]

China, too, provides widespread day-care facilities for children and infants. Such services are necessary since almost 90 percent of all Chinese women are in the work force. Children are admitted to commune "receiving room" care when they are fifty-six days old, move to a nursery school when they are a year-and-a-half old. [82, p. 33]   Nursery rooms are available in most factories and other work places. [14, pp. 287–91] There are some full-time nurseries open day and night, and some parents take their children home only on weekends (*The New York Times*, April 21, 1971). Approximately 50 percent of the children between one-and-a-half to three years of age are cared for in communal nurseries; grandparents care for an additional large group of children. [81]

In Japan the Sony Company operates a day-care center for its many women employees. Twice a year the children are given complete medical checkups. The children study English from the age of two-and-a-half years old through Sony tape recorders. [3]

Research reports from Poland and France (see Chap. 8) stress the healthy development of children under three years of age in day-care centers. [131, pp. 112–37, 147–89]   Some recent reports from Czechoslovakia and other East European countries, however, express some doubts about the outcomes. [40; 55; 56]

Besides day-care centers and the infant's nursery or *crèche*, Norway has a large number of "park aunts," who look after children of preschool age in parks and playgrounds. The mother who needs to shop or visit a clinic, or who merely wants to catch her psychic breath, may leave the young child with the park aunt for part of the day. In Sweden " 'after-noon homes' and 'walking tours' are provided in many neighborhoods. Under this arrangement one of the women in the neighborhood takes care of the children of employed mothers and, when the weather will permit, takes them on tours." [74, p. 82]

Substitute Care: Foster Care, Adoptions, Institutions

The United States appears to be ahead of other countries in the pro-vision of substitute care. This is particularly true of foster care and adoptions. Early in the century, adoption was of little importance as a child welfare service in Europe. However, as a result of the large number of children orphaned by two world wars, European countries became more interested in adoption. Legislation legalizing adoption was passed in countries where no such legislation had previously existed, and existing adoption laws were revised to give greater protection to the child and the adoptive parent. Current legislation in most European countries is, for the most part, similar to that in the United States. [23; 57; 93; 95]

Unlike procedure in the United States, however, a foreign child adopted by a British citizen is automatically granted British citizenship. This ensures for the child a greater feeling of identification with the adoptive family and suggests that he has the same status as a natural child.

In an effort to control black or gray market adoptions, some countries have national regulations that parallel the legislation passed by some of our states. Great Britain forbids the payment, or acceptance, of any payment or reward for arranging an adoption, and prohibits the publica-tion of advertisements either offering or seeking children for adoption. Denmark stipulates that, before an adoption order is granted, informa-tion shall be elicited as to whether a fee has been paid or is to be paid any of the interested parties.

The attitude toward religious preference in adoption tends to be permissive. In Denmark there is no legal provision in the adoption law concerning the child's religion, and no legal bar to placing a child of one religious affiliation with adoptive parents of another. In England the mother may express a religious preference, which then determines the religious affiliation of the adoptive couple with whom the child is placed, but when unmarried mothers do not indicate a preference the agency is permitted to place the child with a family of any religious affiliation. An Agnostics Adoption Society is available to offer service to those adoptive couples who are reluctant to declare a religious affiliation or who have none.

The shortage of children available for adoption is even greater in some European countries than in the United States. As a matter of fact, some American children who could not be placed for adoption here have been placed in Sweden. This was true of a black child with a heart defect placed through the help of an American agency (*The New York Times*, August 20, 1972).

Israel's experience with adoption is significant for our own, because Israel has struggled with a problem of "two nations." One group of Jews, the Ashkenazim come from Europe and are indistinguishable in appearance from most Western white Europeans. The second group of Jews, the Sephardim, come from North Africa or the Near East and are often dark-skinned. The Ashkenazim hold the positions of leadership in the country, most of the better jobs, and most of the enrollment in institutions of higher learning. The Sepharadim hold the lower-paying jobs and constitute the principal group receiving public assistance. They also contribute the largest percentage of illegitimate children available for adoption.

> The dominant pattern in Israeli adoptions is one of Sepharadi
> children being adopted by Ashkenazi parents. This is an interesting
> finding since the coloring of the Sepharadi children, as well as
> other features, often differ from that of Ashkenazi children, yet
> the Israeli adoptive parents seem not to find this as great a barrier
> to accepting the child as is the case with interethnic adoptive
> applicants in other countries. [33, p. 11]

The lesson might be that where two people regard themselves as one nation, barriers to adoption may not be so great.

Israeli adoptive laws, like those of Scotland, legally permit the adopted child access to background material upon reaching adulthood. In Israel, however, each case is reviewed to determine whether the material should first be presented orally to the adoptee by the Ministry of Welfare Chief Adoption Officer to prepare for any surprises which the record may hold concerning the child's past.

Some attempts have been made in Europe to develop distinctive types of institutions for dependent and neglected children. The most notable example is the "children's village," established originally in Austria by Hermann Gmeiner. The village consists of a series of about ten to sixteen cottages, each with a "mother" and, ideally, nine children, boys and girls of various ages from babyhood to adolescence. Only those children who are healthy enough emotionally and physically to live in a family without receiving special attention are accepted. The "mother" is given a budget for each child and cares for them as though they were her own. The children attend the local school and are a part of the local community. The mother buys food at the village store and the "family" may supplement the budget by planting and tending a kitchen garden. The "mothers" are carefully selected, undergo a four-month training period, and are either unmarried or childless widows. [17; 121; 122; 130] The *Dorfleiter*, or village manager, provides the only "fathering" that is officially available. Familiar with each child in the village, he has responsibility for advising the "mothers" and serving as a combination judge, mediator, and father confessor. Every village has a corps of "family helpers," often cottage mothers in training, who assist the "mothers" or substitute for them during time off or vacation, or when they are ill. There is some evidence that a sense of family develops among the children in a particular cottage and that the movement is successful in achieving its aim of healthy child rearing for many of the children it accepts. [130]

The SOS Children's Federation, which sponsors the children's villages, has built about one hundred such villages throughout the world and by 1972 had facilities in forty countries on five continents. [17]

Institutions for children in Europe include, as a key staff member, a professional known as an *educateur*, who has no counterpart in American institutions. The *educateur* has the responsibility of resocializing the child assigned to the institution, organizing the child's activity in such a way as to insure changes in the child's behavior. [30; 44; 67] The distinctive difference in the approach of the *educateur*, sometimes called an *orthopedagogue*, lies in the techniques he uses for resocializing the child.

> [This may include use of] ceramics, painting, weaving, woodwork, metal craft, puppets and marionettes, home economics, interior design, music, dance, body movement and expression, hobbies, and physical and vocational re-education. In addition the *educateurs* are trained to use radio, television, and films, cultural events, holidays, birthdays, and sporting events as techniques for activating and re-educating the maladjusted child. [44, p. 322]

The idea is to reach the child through meaningful activity which involves interaction between child and *educateur*.

Unlike the houseparent in this country, the *educateur* is not responsible for the maintenance of the child's living facilities. In France some of the *educateurs* work with gangs in the slum areas and are employed in youth centers.

The European *educateur* function, with its emphasis on resocialization, has influenced the development of programs in this country. The Re-Ed (re-educational) experimental programs for disturbed children here are patterned on the *educateur* model.

The Unmarried Mother—The Illegitimate Child

Some of the legislation regarding the unmarried mother–illegitimate child pair is more humane in the Scandinavian countries than in the United States. In Norway, for instance, the state, rather than the mother herself, takes responsibility for establishing paternity. In Denmark, once the question of paternity is established and the father's contribution to the care of the child determined, the mother is entitled to advance payments of the father's contribution from public funds; the authorities then undertake to recover the amount from the father. Such advance payments are also made to the divorced mother when the father defaults in making support payments. In these countries, once paternity has been established, the child's right to inherit from his father is also granted. [59; 133]

Private agencies in France have been experimenting with housing for the unmarried mother and the illegitimate child. These are known as *Hôtel Maternelle*. While the mothers are working, infant nurses, and later kindergarten teachers, care for the child. The mothers pay for their upkeep, and, in general, finance the maintenance of the home.

Britain has developed a somewhat similar arrangement—working mothers' hotels. The mother and child live at the hotel for a period of a year or two after the birth of the baby. The hotel staff cares for the child while the mother goes out to work. The hotels are open to widowed mothers and deserted wives as well as unmarried mothers. Similar housing is available in Denmark. [133, p. 145]

New Zealand has a statutory provision that a child welfare worker must be notified, in confidence, in every case of illegitimate birth. This gives the social worker the opportunity of making an offer of help to every unmarried mother. [2, p. 4]

Whereas some 70 percent of white unwed mothers place their child for adoption in the United States, in England and the Scandinavian countries, only some 20–25 percent of the mothers make this decision. [21, pp. 9, 23]   Not only is the percentage of out-of-wedlock children placed for adoption smaller than in this country, but the trend is toward a decline in the percentage of children placed. The decline is attributed "to the improved condition of the solitary mothers, who have better opportunities for keeping their children and because of a certain change of attitude on the part of the general population to the illegitimate child and his mother, the unmarried mother being more generally accepted than before." [34, p. 116]

Recognizing that from the start in life the out-of-wedlock child is handicapped by virtue of a lack of a father's protection, European countries provide for the appointment of a public guardian to the child. [125, pp. 333–40]   In Germany the Local Youth Board provides a guardian at the birth of the child to assist the mother and protect the child through development of a personal relationship with the family. In Sweden the child welfare guardian "sees that the child receives the financial benefits to which he is entitled and can start executive proceedings against a father who neglects to pay maintenance." [124, p. 5]   In Finland a "communal godfather" is appointed to each illegitimate child. Sometimes the appointed guardian is a professional social worker; sometimes he is a lay volunteer selected by the child welfare board. The trend has been toward reducing the guardian's control over the family and making his appointment voluntary rather than automatic.

Sex education is an accepted part of the school curriculum in Scandinavian countries. Contraceptive information is available in Denmark, through the network of Mothers' Aid Centers, to everyone over the age of fifteen, single or married, with or without their parents' consent. The aim of Mothers' Aid Centers is to give all pregnant women personal, social, and legal assistance before and after the birth of the child. It also offers information and advice concerning sex education, family planning, and abortion. Through the Mothers' Aid Centers, Denmark has established a nationwide adoption exchange program which permits the matching of available children with parents in any part of Denmark. [84, p. 26]

Organization of Child Welfare Services

One of the most persistent problems faced by American child welfare is the coordination of the work of the many different agencies dealing with various aspects of the child's situation. The social agencies in Paris have been experimenting with a plan to meet this problem. The city is divided into districts. All the public and private agencies in the district offering family service coordinate their efforts under a combined staff. The combined staff, in effect, forms a new agency that represents all of the agencies. The workers in the coordinating group remain staff members of the agencies which employ them, but they form a unified social work department offering the family services in the district. The workers of the united agency elect a director—usually an outstanding, experienced worker—to coordinate the work of the members of the combined family service unit. [78]

A recent comprehensive review of social welfare programs in Britain by the Seebohm Committee made radical suggestions for total reorganization of the pattern of service. [79]   The proposal adopted by Parliament in 1970, was to unite all government-supported social workers in a community in one department under their own administrative control and supervision. Service would be offered by a team of ten to twelve social workers through area offices serving populations of 50,000–

100,000 people. Separate child welfare services would merge with other personal services to individuals and families, to form a comprehensive, community-based, family-oriented agency offering a wide variety of services.

The Soviet Union and other European countries organize their child welfare services in a pattern different from ours. In these countries "all social service functions are considered ancillary to some other primary concern. Thus family counseling and service for young children are provided by health agencies; those for older children and young people, by educational agencies." [100, p. 112; see also 72]

Although no particular, explicitly designated professional social work group exists in the Soviet Union, the functions that the social worker performs for the child are just as necessary there as elsewhere. In the absence of a profession of social work these functions are performed principally by the schoolteacher, the nurse, and the trade union. [47; 48; 49; 50; 104; 119] The teachers have the responsibility for being aware not only of the educational progress of the child but of his psychosocial development as well. In discharging this responsibility, the Soviet teacher is aided by the fact that she moves with the child through the first four years of schooling. The teacher visits with the parents regularly in the home and in the school to discuss problems and give advice regarding the upbringing of the child. The schools may recommend to the local district Soviet government the removal of children from the care of their parents (in case of neglect) and may be asked by the local government to consider adoptive homes for children who are available for adoption. The work of the teacher is supplemented by the children's inspector, who is also an employee of the educational system. He is responsible for dealing with truancy and behavior problems, investigates complaints of child neglect, and supervises placement of children on the very few occasions when foster care is employed.

Child welfare functions are performed by the "patronage" or "social" nurses, operating out of district clinics, each clinic composed of a team of one pediatrician and two patronage nurses responsible for service to 1000 children. "Since the team serves the same children throughout their childhood and adolescence both in their home and in the clinics, it becomes thoroughly acquainted with them, their families, and their total life situation." [50, p. 322] The nurses are primarily concerned with the health problems of the children, but they also have the responsibility of helping the family with the social and emotional problems encountered by the child as well as with problems of housing, financial assistance, guardianship, and so on. "It is compulsory for a nurse and a doctor attached to the local infant welfare clinic to visit the child in his home on the day he leaves the hospital or on the following day. They examine the state of health and living conditions of the newborn baby and give advice to the mother." [115, p. 103] The district clinic is the central organization to which the family relates in meeting the physical and health needs of the child throughout childhood. This provides not only integrated care but also continuity of care.

The work of the teacher and the patronage nurse is supplemented by the trade unions, which have been given the responsibility for discharging some of the "helping" functions in connection with social problems faced by families of union members. The trade unions have developed child welfare programs and attempt to involve their members as "patrons" for children who need help.

> The "good" trade union committee concern themselves not only
> with providing summer camps for the children of the employees
> but also with giving emotional supportive help to the widow
> who is losing control over her adolescent son or to the unmarried
> mother who is rearing her youngster single-handedly. [48, p. 200]

More emphasis is placed on use of volunteers in direct work with parents around parent-child problems. A teacher concerned about a child might request that members of the union committee in the plant where the father works talk to the father. The local Soviet may ask a "good" mother to make a visit to give advice to the family.

Comradeship courts in factories, housing blocks, or collective farms, with "judges" elected by their peers, use "measures of social pressure" to "help" neglectful or ineffective parents become more competent. The comradeship courts stand behind parents committees made up of neighbors who take the initial responsibility for seeing that parents adequately care for their children. Parents committees "are composed of parents who have been successful in raising their own children." [119, p. 133] They help the parent to relate to the child and offer practical assistance such as seeing that the children attend school and helping an overburdened mother with child care.

All the child-care manuals emphasize the fact that all citizens have a concern for all children. What might be regarded as meddling in someone else's affairs in the United States is an act of good citizenship in the Soviet Union. It is, in effect, an implementation of the principle of child advocacy.

Many European countries demonstrate a greater willingness to involve lay local leadership and volunteers in responsibility for child care. For instance, in Sweden the child welfare boards take responsibility for major services in the local community. Members of local child welfare boards are judges, teachers, physicians, nurses, who serve as citizens rather than in their professional capacity. The board has the right to employ professional social workers to implement its decisions, but it has the ultimate responsibility for seeing that child welfare services are provided to any child in the community who needs them.

In Holland many dependent and/or delinquent children are placed under the supervision of a family guardian, a private person of good conduct who volunteers to devote his time to helping the child and the family without pay. Organizations of family guardians serve as a link between the volunteer and the juvenile judge, and also recruit, train, and supervise family guardians. The family guardian generally is assigned one or two children and their families. While there is some difficulty in recruiting family guardians, most of the child welfare experts note with surprise that many people still volunteer for such work and are very consistent in discharging their responsibility. As a matter of fact, there is less turnover among family guardians than among professional social workers; families assigned a family guardian have greater continuity of care. A report from the Dutch Ministry of Justice points out that the activity of the volunteer family guardian is "not typical casework. It is rather a matter of pedagogic influencing through a confidential relationship. The family guardian represents a bit of healthy society within the family." The help offered may vary "from practical advice connected with the choice of school or a profession to serious, penetrating talks." [73, p. 22]

In Denmark volunteers are used as supervising guardians to assist the family with advice and guidance in matters relating to children. And in Poland "social guardians" are appointed to offer assistance to families in trouble in an effort to "improve the financial, social, and educative condition, cooperate in the fight against alcoholism, hooliganism, prostitution, ill treatment of children, and against all social scourges." [118]   The People's Councils in Rumania, composed of lay volunteers, perform similar functions, offering "legal and social assistance services taking the form of surveillance, primarily of a preventative nature, which intervene effectively only if and when the physical development, education, upbringing, vocational training of the child are endangered by the improper behavior of the parents or their negligence manifested in its upbringing." [105, pp. 51–52]

Supranational Child Welfare

There are organizations which offer child welfare service across national boundaries. International Social Service [ISS] conducts an intercountry adoption program; the International Union for Child Welfare, publishers of the *International Child Welfare Review*, conducts international child welfare seminars and conferences and stimulates child welfare research; the United Nations International Children's Emergency Fund, better known as UNICEF, is active in combating disease and hunger, has equipped maternal and child health centers throughout the world, inoculated millions of children against a variety of infectious diseases, distributed billions of pounds of food to hungry children, and trained thousands of midwives. The United Nations Bureau of Social Affairs collects and disseminates information regarding child welfare problems throughout the world; various agencies of the United Nations offer technical assistance to nations in developing their child welfare services in a demonstration of international mutual aid.

In 1959 the United Nations adopted a Declaration of the Rights of the Child, which explicitly recognizes the right of the child to grow up with affection and acceptance with his own parents in a home that provides adequately for his physical, social, emotional, and spiritual needs. It stipulates, furthermore, that the child should be given special protection by the community against all forms of neglect, abuse, and exploitation. The Declaration of the Rights of the Child stands as an explicit statement of what the people of the world hope they can achieve for their children.

Summary

.The problems that require child welfare services are universal. The services available in each country to meet children's needs are a function of such factors as the economic resources available for caring for dependents, the ratio of dependents to productive adults, the general attitude toward the child, the availability of alternative patterns of mutual aid in the primary group.

Developing countries are currently facing some of the same problems in organizing social services that were faced by the more economically advanced nations two or three centuries ago. Child welfare services in such countries are primarily concerned with meeting the basic health, educational, and housing needs of the child population.

A review of the supportive, supplementary, and substitutive child welfare services in nations similar to our own suggests that the social insurance plans of such countries, as they affect the child, are more comprehensive than our own. They include family allowances, maternity benefits, medical care, and sickness insurance. Some additional details were noted regarding differences between child welfare services here and abroad.

The greater availability of some social services as day care and homemaker service abroad suggests a more institutional approach to child welfare. The institutional approach implies that these services cover all children rather than primarily those who are underprivileged or handicapped. The Russian, Chinese, and Israeli programs, which give the community greater responsibility for the child earlier in life, suggest a greater willingness to consider alternatives to the nuclear family.

Bibliography

1. Abel-Smith, Brian, and Peter Townsend. *The Poor and the Poorest.* London: George Bell & Sons, Ltd., 1965.

2. Anderson, Lewis G. "Child Welfare in New Zealand." *Indian Journal of Social Work,* **24,** 1 (April 1963).

3. Bayh, Marvella. "Russian and Japanese Ahead in Day Care." *Voice,* **3,** 2 (February 1970), 3–4.

4. Bettelheim, Bruno. *The Children of the Dream.* New York: The Macmillan Company, 1969.

5. Bronfenbrenner, Urie. *Two Worlds of Childhood—U.S. and U.S.S.R.* New York: Russell Sage Foundation, 1970.

6. British Central Office of Information. *Children in Britain.* London: Her Majesty's Stationery Office, 1959.

7. Brown, Ruth. "Day Care Centres and Child Welfare in Denmark." *Canada's Health and Welfare,* **16** (June 1961).

8. Central Union for Child Welfare in Finland. *Child Welfare in Finland.* Helsinki: Central Union for Child Welfare, 1968.

9. Chandler, John. "Perspectives on Poverty—An International Comparison." *Monthly Labor Review,* **92,** 2 (February 1969), 32–62.

10. Chapin, Emerson. "Japan's Birth Rate—The Trend Turns." *The New York Times Magazine* (October 25, 1964).

11. Chauncey, Harry. *Soviet Preschool Education. Vol. II: Teachers' Commentary.* New York: Holt, Rinehart & Winston, Inc., 1969.

12. Clifford, W. *A Primer of Social Casework in Africa.* New York: Oxford University Press, 1966.

13. Coates, Ken, and Richard Silburn. *Poverty: The Forgotten Englishmen.* Baltimore: Penguin Books, Inc., 1970.

14. Committee of Concerned Asian Scholars. *China: Inside the People's Republic.* New York: Bantam Books, Inc., 1972.

15. David, Henry P. (ed.). *Child Mental Health in International Perspective.* New York: Harper and Row, Publishers, 1972.

16. DeMoerloose, J. "Abortion Throughout the World." *Child Adoption,* No. 2 (1972).

17. Dodge, James. "SOS Children's Villages Throughout the World: Substitute or Superior Service." *Child Welfare,* **5,** 6 (June 1972), 344–53.

18. Dessau, Dorothy. *Glimpses of Social Work in Japan—Revisited.* Kyoto: Social Workers' International Club of Japan, 1968.

19. Falkner, Frank. "Infant Mortality—An Urgent National Problem." *Children,* **17,** 3 (May–June 1970), 83–90.

20. Friis, Henning. "Issues in Social Security Policies in Denmark," in *Social Security in Perspective.* Ed. by Shirley Jenkins. New York: Columbia University Press, 1969.

21. Garmezy, Edith. "Meeting the Problems of Illegitimacy—The Danish Way," in *Effective Services for Unmarried Parents and Their Innovative Community Approaches.* New York: National Council on Illegitimacy, 1968.

22. Gerig, Daniel S. "Social Security in the New African Countries." *Social Security Bulletin,* **29,** 1 (January 1966).

23. GREBLER, ANNE M. "Adoption in European Countries." *Child Welfare*, **42**, 10 (December 1963).

24. HAANES-OLSEN, LIEF. "Children's Allowances: Their Size and Structure in Five Countries." *Social Security Bulletin*, **35**, 5 (May 1972), 17–28.

25. ———. "Social Security Abroad." *Social Security Bulletin*, **32**, 10 (October 1969), 30–32.

26. HASAN, SAIYID Z. "Social Security in India: Limited Resources—Unlimited Need," in *Social Security in International Perspective*. Ed. by Shirley Jenkins. New York: Columbia University Press, 1969.

27. HEER, DAVID M., and JUDITH G. BRYDEN. "Family Allowances and Population Policy in the USSR." *Journal of Marriage and the Family*, **28**, 4 (November 1966), 514–19.

28. HEILBRONER, ROBERT L. *Mankind's Children—The Story of UNICEF.* New York: Public Affairs Pamphlet, 1959.

29. HUNT, AUDREY. *The Home Health Services in England and Wales.* London: Her Majesty's Stationery Office, 1970.

30. *International Child Welfare Review.* Special Issue—"The *Educateur*" (February 1971).

31. INTERNATIONAL LABOR OFFICE. *The Cost of Social Security—6th International Inquiry.* Geneva: International Labor Office, 1967.

32. ———. *Maternity Protection—A World Survey of National Law and Practice.* Geneva: International Labor Office, 1965.

33. JAFFE, ELIEZER. *Child Welfare in Israel—An Overview of Institution Care, Foster Home Care and Adoption*, 1969. Mimeo.

34. JENSEN, ORLA. *Social Welfare in Denmark.* Copenhagen: Det Danske Selskab, 1961. With supplementary data to 1966.

35. KADUSHIN, ALFRED. *Developing Social Policy in Conditions of Dynamic Change—U.S. Report to 16th International Conference on Social Welfare, 1972.* New York: U.S. Committee of the International Council on Social Welfare, 1972.

36. KAHN, ALFRED, et al. *Neighborhood Information Centers—A Study and Some Proposals.* New York: Columbia University School of Social Work, 1966.

37. KAKOL, KAIMIERZ. *Social Rights and Facilities in Poland.* Warsaw: Polonia Publishing House, 1959.

38. KIRKPATRICK, ELIZABETH K. "Children's Allowances in Japan." *Social Security Bulletin*, **35**, 6 (June 1972), 39.

39. LANGHOLM, MAGNE. *Family and Child Welfare in Norway.* Oslo: Norwegian Joint Committee on International Social Policy, 1961.

40. LAGMEIER, J., and Z. MATEJCEK. "Psychological Aspects of Collective Care in Czechoslovakia," in *Child Mental Health in International Perspective.* Ed. by Henry P. David. New York: Harper and Row, Publishers, 1972.

41. LAROQUE, PIERRE. "Social Security in France," in *Social Security in International Perspective.* Ed. by Shirley Jenkins. New York: Columbia University Press, 1969.

42. LEBEL, ROLAND, and ZARCO CVEJIC. *Family Allowances—Developments in Legislation Since 1953.* International Social Security Association, Report XVI. Geneva, 1965.

43. Leissner, Aryeh. *Family Advice Services.* Essex, England: Longman Group Ltd., 1967.

44. Linton, Thomas E. "The European *Educateur* Model—An Alternative—Effective Approach to the Mental Health of Children." *Journal of Special Education,* **3,** 4 (Winter 1969), 319–27.

45. Lewit, Sarah. *International Consultants Report—1970.* New York: Association for the Study of Abortion, 1970.

46. Madison, Bernice. "Canadian Family Allowances and Their Major Social Implications." *Journal of Marriage and Family Living,* **26,** 2 (May 1964).

47. ———. "Contributions and Problems of Soviet Welfare Institutions." *Social Problems,* **7,** 4 (Spring 1960).

48. ———. "Social Welfare: Soviet Model." *Social Service Review,* **38,** 2 (June 1964).

49. ———. *Social Welfare in the Soviet Union.* Stanford: Stanford University Press, 1968.

50. ———. "Welfare Services for Children in the Soviet Union, 1945–1963." *Child Welfare,* **42,** 7 (July 1963).

51. Makerenko, A. S. *The Collective Family: A Handbook for Russian Parents.* New York: Doubleday & Company, Inc., 1967.

52. Manpel, Siegfried, and Kane Hawk. *Social Policy in the Soviet-Occupied Zone of Germany.* Bonn: Federal Ministry of Labour and the Social Structure, 1966.

53. Marsden, Dennis. *Mothers Alone—Poverty and the Fatherless Family.* Baltimore: Penguin Books, Inc., 1969.

54. McKie, Eric. *Venture in Faith.* Liverpool: Liverpool and District Family Service Unit, 1963.

55. Meers, Dale R. "International Day Care: A Selective Review and Psychoanalytic Critique," in *Day Care: Resources for Decisions.* Ed. by Edith H. Grotberg. Washington, D.C.: Day Care and Child Development Council of America, Inc., 1971.

56. ———, and Allen E. Maraus. "Group Care of Infants in Other Countries," in *Early Child Care—The New Perspectives.* Ed. by Laura L. Dittman. New York: Atherton Press, Inc., 1968.

57. Moore, Joyce. "Adoption in Denmark." *Child Adoption,* No. 54 (1968).

58. ———. "Adoption in Kenya." *Child Adoption,* **64,** 2 (1971), 19–34.

59. Morisey, Patricia Garland. "From Scandinavia to the Urban Ghetto—Implication of Scandinavian Welfare Programs for Services to Unwed Mothers," in *Effective Services for Unmarried Parents and Their Children —Innovative Community Approaches.* New York: National Council on Illegitimacy, 1968.

60. National Council for Homemaker Services. *Readings in Homemaker Services.* New York: National Council for Homemaker Services, 1969.

61. Neipris, Joseph. "Social Service in Israel—A Review of Programmes and Policies." *Journal of Jewish Communal Services,* **47,** 4 (Summer 1971), 289–315.

62. Nordstrom, Margarita. "Social Home Help Services in Sweden," in *Readings in Homemaker Services.* New York: National Council for Homemaker Services, 1969.

63. Orlova, Nina V. "The Protection of Children's Rights and Interests in

the U.S.S.R." *International Child Welfare Review*, **23**, 4 (October 1969), 15–21.

64. OSBORN, ROBERT J. *Soviet Social Policies—Welfare Equality and Community*. Homewood, Ill.: Dorsey Press, Inc., 1970.

65. PALTIEL, FREDA L. "Day Care in Europe: The Scandinavian Experience." *Social Worker (Canada)*, **39**, 4 (November 1971), 145–50.

66. PHILIP, A. F. *Family Failure*. London: Faber & Faber, Ltd., 1963.

67. PERCH, PAUL. "The Specialized *Educateur*, the Institution and the Community." *International Child Welfare Review*, **25**, 1 (February 1971).

68. POTS, MALCOLM. "Legal Abortions in Eastern Europe." *Eugenics Review*, **59**, 4 (December 1967), 232–50.

69. RABIN, A. I. *Growing Up in the Kibbutz*. New York: Springer-Verlag New York, Inc., 1965.

70. RADIN, NORMA. "Preschool Programs of the U.S.S.R." *Child Welfare*, **49**, 1 (January 1970), 29–36.

71. RODGERS, BARBARA N., *et al. Comparative Social Administration*. New York: Atherton Press, Inc., 1968.

72. ROLLINS, NANCY. *Child Psychiatry in the Soviet Union—Preliminary Observations*. Cambridge, Mass.: Harvard University Press, 1972.

73. ROOD-DEBOER, M. *Child Care in the Netherlands*. The Hague: National Foundation for Child Welfare, 1966.

74. ROSENTHAL, ALBERT H. *The Social Programs of Sweden—A Search for Security in a Free Society*. Minneapolis: University of Minnesota Press, 1967.

75. SALVESEN, KAARC. *Social Legislation in Norway*. Oslo: The Norwegian Joint Committee on International Social Policy, 1967.

76. SCABERNE, BRONISLAV. "Child and Youth Welfare in Yugoslavia." *International Child Welfare Review*, **23**, 1 (October 1969), 22–35.

77. SCHNITZER, MARTIN. *Guaranteed Minimum Income Programs Used by Governments of Selected Countries*. Paper No. 11. Material Prepared for the Use of the Joint Economic Committee. Congress of the United States, 90th Congress, 2nd session. Washington, D.C.: Government Printing Office, 1968.

78. SCHORR, ALVIN. *Social Security and Social Services in France*. U.S. Department of Health, Education, and Welfare, Social Security Administration Research Report No. 7. Washington, D.C.: Government Printing Office, 1965.

79. SEEBOHM, FREDERIC, Chairman. *Report of the Committee on Local Authority and Allied Personal Social Service*. London: Her Majesty's Stationery Office, 1969.

80. SICAULT, GEORGE. *The Needs of Children*. New York: The Free Press, 1963.

81. SIDEL, RUTH. *Women and Child Care in China*. New York: Hill and Wang, 1972.

82. ———, and VICTOR SIDEL. "The Human Services in China." *Social Policy*, **2**, 6 (March–April 1972), 25–34.

83. SIMANIS, JOSEPH. "Recent Changes in Russian Social Security." *Social Security Bulletin*, **35**, 12 (October 1972).

84. SKALTS, VERA. *Mothers' Aid in Denmark—The Organization and Activity*

of the Danish Maternity Aid Centres. Copenhagen: Det Danske Selskab, 1965.

85. SKARDAL, DOROTHY B. Social Insurance in Norway. Oslo: The Norwegian Joint Committee on International Social Policy, 1960.

86. SKOLNIK, ALFRED, and SOPHIE DALES. "Social Welfare Expenditures, 1970–71." Social Security Bulletin, 34, 12 (December 1971), 3–16.

87. SPIRO, MELFORD. Children of the Kibbutz. New York: Schocken Books, Inc., 1968.

88. SWEDISH INSTITUTE. Social Benefits in Sweden. Stockholm: The Swedish Institute, 1966.

89. STEIN, HERMAN (ed.). Planning for the Needs of Children in the Developing Countries. New York: United Nations, 1965.

90. TIETZE, CHRISTOPHER. "Abortion in Europe." American Journal of Public Health, 57, 11 (November 1967), 1923–32.

91. TITMUSS, RICHARD. Developing Social Policy in Conditions of Rapid Change—The Role of Social Work. 16th International Conference on Social Welfare. The Hague, August 1972. Mimeo.

92. UHR, CARL G. Sweden's Social Security System, U.S. Department of Health, Education, and Welfare, Social Security Administration Research Report No. 14. Washington, D.C.: Government Printing Office, 1966.

93. UNITED NATIONS. Study on Adoption of Children. New York, 1953.

94. ———. Processes and Problems of Industrialization in Underprivileged Countries. New York, 1955.

95. ———. Comparative Analysis of Adoption Laws. New York, 1956.

96. ———. "Family and Child Welfare." International Social Service Review, 1 (January 1956).

97. ———. "Objectives in Social Policy for Improving Family Levels of Living." International Social Service Review, 5 (September 1959).

98. ———. "Social Insurance and the Family." International Social Service Review, 5 (September 1959).

99. ———. "Social Security and the Social Services." International Social Service Review, 5 (September 1959).

100. ———. 1963 Report on the World Social Situation. New York, 1963.

101. ———. Patterns of Social Welfare Organization and Administration in Africa. New York, 1964.

102. ———. Family, Child and Youth Welfare Services. New York, 1965.

103. ———. Family, Child and Youth Welfare Services in Africa. New York, 1966.

104. ———. Organization and Administration of Social Welfare Programmes —A Series of Country Studies: The Union of Soviet Socialist Republics. New York, 1967.

105. UNITED NATIONS DEPARTMENT OF ECONOMIC AND SOCIAL AFFAIRS. Organization and Administration of Social Welfare Programmes—A Series of Country Studies: Rumania. New York, 1967.

106. ———. 1970 Report on the World Social Situation. New York, 1971.

107. ———. Compendium of Social Statistics—Series K. No. 3. New York, 1967.

108. ———. Demographic Yearbook—21st Issue, 1969. New York, 1970.

109. ———. Statistical Yearbook—23rd Issue, 1971. New York, 1972.

110. ———. *Yearbook of National Accounts Statistics.* Statistical Office of the United Nations Department of Economic and Social Affairs. New York, 1970.
111. ———. Commission for Social Development. *Trends in the Social Situation of Children—Report of the Secretary-General.* New York, January 8, 1970.
112. ———. Economic and Social Council. *Children and Adolescents in Slums and Shanty-Towns in Developing Countries.* New York, March 1971.
113. UNITED NATIONS CHILDREN'S FUND. *Children and Youth in National Development in Latin America—Report of a Conference.* New York, 1966.
114. ———. *Strategy for Children.* New York, 1968.
115. U.S. DEPARTMENT OF HEALTH, EDUCATION, AND WELFARE, PUBLIC HEALTH SERVICE. *Special Report: The First U.S. Mission on Mental Health to the U.S.S.R.* Public Health Service Publication No. 1893. Washington, D.C.: Government Printing Office, 1969.
116. ———. *Social Security Programs Throughout the World—1971.* Office of Research and Statistics Research Report No. 31. Washington, D.C.: Government Printing Office, 1972.
117. ———. *Height and Weight of Children in United States, India, and the United Arab Republic.* Rockville, Md.: National Center for Health Statistics, September 1970.
118. VEILLARD-CYBULSKA, HENRYKA. "Aspects of Child Welfare in the People's Democracies. II: Poland." *International Child Welfare Review*, **20**, 1 (1966), 5–61.
119. ———. "Aspects of Child Welfare in the People's Democracies. I: U.S.S.R." *International Child Welfare Review*, **19**, 3 (1965), 101–32.
120. ———. "The Welfare and Protection of Children and Adolescents in Bulgaria." *International Child Welfare Review*, **23**, 4 (October 1969), 3–13.
121. WACHSTEIN, SONIA. "An Austrian Solution to the Problem of Child Placement." *Child Welfare*, **42**, 2 (February 1963).
122. WAGNER, MARSDEN G., and MARY M. WAGNER. "Day Care Programs in Denmark and Czechoslovakia," in *Day Care: Resources of Decisions.* Ed. by Edith H. Grotberg. Washington, D.C.: Day Care and Child Development Council of America, Inc., 1971.
123. WECHSBERG, JOSEPH. "A House Called Peace." *The New Yorker* (December 22, 1962).
124. WESTER, ASTRID. *The Swedish Child.* Stockholm: The Swedish Institute, 1970.
125. WIMPERES, VIRGINIA. *The Unmarried Mother and Her Child.* London: George Allen & Unwin, Ltd., 1960.
126. WEINGARTEN, MURRAY. *Life in a Kibbutz.* Jerusalem: Zionist Organization, Youth and Hachalutz Department, 1959.
127. WOLINS, MARTIN. "Another View of Group Care." *Child Welfare*, **44**, 1 (January 1965).
128. ———. "Political Orientation, Social Reality and Child Welfare." *Social Service Review*, **38**, 4 (December 1964).
129. ———. "Some Theory and Practice in Child Care: A Cross-Culture View." *Child Welfare*, **42**, 8 (October 1963).

130. ———. *The SOS Kinderdorf: Families in a Village.* 1969. Mimeo.
131. WORLD HEALTH ORGANIZATION. *Care of Children in Day Care Centers.* Geneva, 1964.
132. ———. *Maternal and Child Health in the U.S.S.R.* Geneva, 1962.
133. WYNN, MARGARET. *Fatherless Families.* London: Michael Joseph Ltd., 1964.
134. ZIEGLER, STAN. "Residential Treatment of Emotionally Disturbed Children in Norway." *Child Welfare*, 51, 5 (May 1972), 290–96.
135. ZUCKER, MILDRED. "Citizen's Advice Bureaus—The British Way." *Social Work*, 10, 4 (October 1965), 85–91.

14

The Sociology of the Child Welfare Worker

Introduction

The sociology of occupations is a well-developed specialization, its justification deriving from the fact that each distinctive occupation is a subculture. It has its own language, its own special patterns of thought, its own special values, its own special ways of relating to other occupational groups with which it cooperates, its own concerns and problems, its own knowledge and skills, and its own demography. Each occupation has its particular pressures and anxieties, and particular areas of conflict between the mores of the occupation and the mores of the surrounding culture. Each occupation is a miniature social world, with its own distinctive sociopsychological milieu. One of the principal responsibilities of professional education is socialization of recruits to the professional subculture, the "community of occupation." [21, p. 195]   Greenwood notes:

> The transformation of a neophyte into a professional is essentially
> an acculturation process wherein he internalizes the social values,
> the behavior norms, and the symbols of the occupational
> group. In its frustrations and rewards, it is fundamentally no
> different from the acculturation of an immigrant to a relatively
> strange culture. [25, p. 53]

Here *socialization* means

701

the process by which people selectively acquire the values and attitudes, the interest, skill, and knowledge—in short the culture— current in the groups of which they are, or seek to become a member. It refers to learning social roles. [46, p. 287]

In this chapter *socialization* refers to the role of the child welfare social worker.

As is true for a distinctive ethnic group, members of the occupational subculture have a sense of mutual identification, a recognition of their special differences from other people in the wider community. This is sometimes called the *professional self* or the *sense of the professional identity*—the explicit self-awareness on the part of a person that he is a social worker and that he behaves in accordance with the way people identified as members of this occupational group should behave. Differential association, the need to associate primarily with members of the occupation on the job and the choice of such associates during leisure time, tends to reinforce the effects of professional education in shaping the occupational identity.

This solidarity is further enhanced by some homogeneity in the kind of people selecting an occupation. The nature of the occupational tasks tends to act as a screening device attracting and selecting people with particular kinds of personality attributes, while repelling and rejecting other kinds of people. However, having selected a profession and having been selected by a profession, the individual finds that those personality characteristics that are useful to the profession are emphasized and reinforced while other personality attributes are attenuated by disuse or actively discouraged. In this sense, then, the occupation ultimately tends to shape personality. "If personality is the subjective aspect of culture, then a man's work, to the extent that it provides him a subculture and an identity, becomes an aspect of his personality." [28, p. 23]   Lubove, in reviewing the history of the profession of social work, says, "The profession was not only a career but a way of life which shaped personality by offering it a means of expression." [42, p. 118]

This suggests the basis for a sociological approach to child welfare social work. The approach sees child welfare social work as a circumscribed social institution within the larger community and child welfare social workers as an identifiable, organized subgroup in society.

Child welfare has a specialized language in terms such as *placement*, *T.P.R.*, *U-M*, and *home study*. Child welfare workers have special interests and shared values, a good deal of social interchange, and in-group gossip. Differential association, in-group language, in-group gossip and humor tend both to reflect and reinforce the sense of identity as a child welfare worker. Solidarity is further intensified by special publications such as *Child Welfare* and periodic meetings such as the annual regional meetings sponsored by the Child Welfare League of America. As a consequence, practitioners develop a distinctive way of thinking about the problems and people that are so much a part of their daily activities. This special point of view becomes part of the subcultural configuration which distinguishes the child welfare worker.

Profile of the Child Welfare Worker

No national study of social workers has been conducted since 1960. [51] A 1968 survey of the membership of the National Association of Social Workers, by far the largest organization of social workers, indicates that "child welfare services in various settings (institutional, non-institutional, court, and school) continue to command the largest single group of respondents. In 1961 23 percent of all respondents were so employed; in 1968 this figure is up to 27 percent." [76, p. 39; see also 70] This would indicate that the child welfare social workers are the largest single identifiable group of social workers, and growing.

Social work is regarded as a woman's profession. In 1970 approximately two-thirds of all social workers were women; one-third, men. It is estimated that 80 percent of all child welfare workers are women. Some areas within child welfare, however, have a particularly heavy concentration of male workers—for example, work with children in court settings or in correctional training institutions.

Simpson and Simpson review the unique aspect of the "semiprofessions" which contain a preponderance of women—nursing, teaching, librarianship, social work. [74] They note that for many women the occupational role competes with the wife-mother role, which takes precedence. This makes for a lower commitment to work as a primary source of satisfaction and a tendency to give up work whenever family roles demand. "While men are being promoted or gaining experience that will equip them for promotion, many women are at home tending babies, their skills growing rusty and their knowledge lagging behind new developments in the field." [74, p. 229] Women's goals and values make professional competition secondary to good personal relationships on the job and lessen the tendency for a strong ambitious drive. Less concerned with advancement, seeing the occupation as a series of jobs rather than as a career, sharing the general cultural deference to men, women are more ready to accept bureaucratic controls which limit professional autonomy. All of this may undergo rapid change, however, with the spreading effects of the women's liberation movement. [8; 71]

Farson points out that many of the characteristics which are associated with the desirable counselor or caseworker orientation are also the attributes associated with the female sex. Adjectives such as *tender*, *gentle, loving, understanding, warm, passive, receptive, accepting* typify both the good counselors and females in general. [17; see also 43]

The average male social worker is younger than his female colleague and a higher percentage of men are married (86 percent of the men, 52 percent of the women).

A comparison of the socioeconomic status of social workers with that of their parents' status indicates that in becoming social workers the group was upwardly mobile. This is much truer for male social workers, who tend to come from upper-lower-class or lower-middle-class backgrounds than for female social workers, who are more likely to come from upper-middle-class or lower-upper-class families. [50]

The profession is disproportionately white. Blacks constitute some 12.8 percent of the total population, but only 9.5 percent of social workers. This situation may be changed during the 1970's as a result of a concerted effort on the part of schools of social work to attract members of ethnic and racial minorities. The results of these efforts to recruit nonwhites to social work are revealed in a 1972 report, which indicates that about 16 percent of practitioners in child welfare agencies with a master's degree were black, as were some 24 percent of practitioners without a master's degree. [12, Table 3] Compared to the general population, Jews are overrepresented and Protestants and Catholics are underrepresented in the profession. [41]

Social workers are most likely to be employed in urban areas and tend to be concentrated in the Mid-Atlantic region. The Pacific Coast, however, has the largest number of child welfare workers in proportion to the population. States with lower income levels, higher incidence of poverty, and lower levels of urbanization lack social work manpower to a greater degree.

A small percentage of those people occupying a position with the title *social worker* have full professional training. Most are college graduates, but only "approximately 25 percent . . . had completed graduate social work education and held a master's degree." [16, p. 100]

Numbers and Need

The best estimate is that there were about 30,000–35,000 child welfare social workers employed in public and voluntary agencies in 1970, with a continuing trend toward an increase in the percentage of social workers employed by public agencies.

The most recent authoritative prognostication was made by the U.S. Department of Labor in March 1972. [88] Figure 14–1 charts the projected employment requirements for a variety of professions during the 1970's. Social work opportunities are expected to increase more sharply than those of most other professions.

However, earlier optimistic estimates of rapid increase in employ-

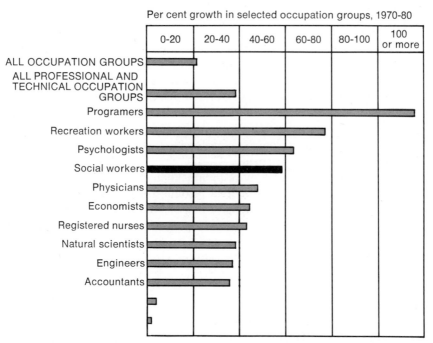

Per cent growth in selected occupation groups, 1970-80

	0-20	20-40	40-60	60-80	80-100	100 or more
ALL OCCUPATION GROUPS						
ALL PROFESSIONAL AND TECHNICAL OCCUPATION GROUPS						
Programers						
Recreation workers						
Psychologists						
Social workers						
Physicians						
Economists						
Registered nurses						
Natural scientists						
Engineers						
Accountants						

FIGURE 14–1. Employment requirements will rise much faster in some professions than in others. (*Manpower Report to the President—U.S. Department of Labor,* transmitted to the Congress, March 1972, Washington, D.C.: U.S. Government Printing Office, 1972, p. 112.)

ment opportunities were not fulfilled. [29; 39; 99] Although the number of social work positions increased markedly during the 1960's, by the end of the decade holders of bachelor's degrees were finding it difficult to obtain jobs as social workers, while holders of master's degrees had fewer jobs from which to choose and some difficulty in finding them.

Growing public disillusionment with social reform and with social work led to a leveling off in appropriations for social service programs by the end of the 1960's. Also, with adoption of the "Scheuer Amendment" to the Economic Opportunity Act in 1966, the Federal government required that efforts be made to employ members of economically deprived groups as "paraprofessionals," "subprofessionals," and "case aides." Subsequently the requirement was incorporated in Federal legislation supporting a wide variety of social service programs. As a consequence, an increasing number of entry-level jobs in public welfare agencies, some of which had previously been allocated to holders of bachelor's degrees, are now reserved for such "new careerists." These factors, plus a leveling off in the growth of the population of children, suggests a slower growth of job opportunities in the 1970's.

Salary

A 1973 nationwide study of salaries in primarily voluntary child welfare agencies indicated that the median salary for executive directors is about $26,650; for supervisors, about $13,800; for practitioners with professional degrees, about $11,100, for practitioners with no graduate training, about $8,750. [75]   Salaries in public child welfare agencies were at about the same levels. These compare favorably with salaries paid in other "women's" professions, such as elementary school teaching, nursing, librarianship. During the 1960's, salaries for child welfare social workers rose more rapidly than the cost of living, so that there was an actual increase in real income. By the end of the decade, however, the rate of salary increase had slowed down, so that between 1971 and 1972 salary increases were only slightly in advance of the increase in cost of living.

It is interesting to note that in a profession in which some 70 percent of the personnel are women, only 22 percent of the executive directors are women, and their median salary in 1973 was some $3700 less than the median salary for men executive directors. [75, p. 18]   Median salaries for all female social workers lag behind those of their male colleagues. [76, p. 41; see also 98]   Nevertheless, some 31 percent of all male social workers held a part-time job in addition to their full-time employment. [76, p. 38]

Social workers, like nurses and teachers, are responsive to "a dedicatory ethic" which elevates service motives and denigrates material reward as the proper motivation for work. The work is seen not as a "job" but as a "calling." However, there is a growing tendency to see dedication as a form of subsidy to the welfare system which social workers are no longer willing to grant.

The Public Image

The potential for attracting recruits is partly a function of the public's perception of the occupation. In general, studies suggest that the profession is viewed in favorable terms. When asked to select adjectives to describe the social worker, people are apt to choose words such as *sympathetic, understanding, humane, tolerant, patient, generous, likeable, warm,* and *friendly.* [2; 4; 79]   An interview study of attitudes toward welfare programs indicated that child welfare programs were more likely than other programs to elicit strong support. [63, p. 29]

Although the image of social work is now generally positive, the same studies suggest other difficulties. [4, p. 21]   People "are extremely vague about what social work is, what it does, who does it, and with what success. . . . Unlike such fields as medicine and law, and so on, which people can define clearly, social work is amorphous and extremely diverse; hence, very difficult to picture clearly." [4, p. 18]   Social work is most frequently perceived as being concerned only with the destitute, the needy, and the deprived. The layman sees no relationship between the activities of the profession and any problem he might have. He rejects, in general, any identification of himself as a possible social work client. [2, p. 66]

An important factor regarding the sociology of an occupational group is its prestige level—the rank in the hierarchy of value which any occupation holds relative to any other occupation. No studies are available to indicate the prestige level of the child welfare worker vis-à-vis other occupational groups, but studies of the prestige level of social work in general might be taken to reflect that of child welfare. In general, such studies show that social work ranks high in prestige when compared with all occupational groupings, but it ranks low when compared with other professions. Its prestige ranking compares favorably with other traditional women's professions—teaching, nursing, librarianship —but, like these, it is considered a minor, if not a marginal, profession. [35]   Social work is ranked high on education, high on contribution to society, but low on financial return. A person interested in coming into social work may be less concerned with the general prestige ranking of social work but specifically concerned with whether or not a particular aspect of the profession which is of concern to him has prestige. Social workers themselves feel that they rate high on their contribution to society and their ability to help people. [60]

The insecurity generated by the marginal status of the profession gives rise to a great concern about professionalism and professional behavior. What Devereaux says about a somewhat analogously positioned profession, nursing, is applicable here:

> The status problem of the nurse is comparable to the lower-middle
> classes who have to cling stubbornly to their "respectability"
> for fear of being "down-graded" socially. The nurse is, therefore,
> forced to display an excessively professional attitude. . . . By
> contrast, an established physician, secure in his position, can
> and usually does unbend and act human. . . . In brief, what
> "respectability" as a badge of membership in the middle classes
> means to the lower-middle classes, a professional attitude means to
> the nurse. [14, p. 633]

The marginal status of social work within the family of the professions may have had a similar effect on social workers. [25; 61]

Who Chooses Social Work? When? Why?

An occupation perpetuates itself by attracting and selecting new recruits from the potential candidates for the professions. Whom does child welfare social work tend to attract? When do they make the decision to select child welfare, and what are the reasons that prompt their decision?

The best data available come from studies made of all first-year students entering schools of social work in the United States and Canada. The studies, conducted in the fall of 1960 and replicated in 1966, will be referred to as the Pins studies. [56; 57]

More women than men enter social work because its functions accord with the role responsibilities of women in society. There are, however, additional reasons for the attractiveness of social work to women.

Because most women are either supplementary wage-earners or responsible only for their own support, the matter of relatively low salaries is not a great deterrent to their choice of social work as a profession. Furthermore, women are still actively discriminated against in the professions. The proportion of women students in schools of law, medicine, engineering, and dentistry was not very much larger in 1965 than it was in 1910. The fact that social work does not discriminate against women tends to act to attract them to the profession. The fact that it is a "woman's field," conversely, might tend to attract some men. The National Manpower Council suggests: "The best way for a man to insure his advancement is to prepare for a field of work in which most employees are women." [49, p. 240]   Men are promoted more rapidly and more frequently to administrative and supervisory positions, earn more for comparable jobs, and are more likely to publish in social work journals. [68]

Social workers, including those in child welfare, make their occupational choices relatively late. This is partly a function of the low visibility of social work as a profession. [34]   Although most children encounter teachers and doctors and nurses, relatively few ever see a social worker. The same limited visibility is characteristic of social work in mass communication media. There has been only one, relatively brief, television series in which the social worker was the central person. The profession lacks distinctive ceremonial garb, insignia, or gadgetry by which it might be clearly identified and remembered.

Another reason for the relatively late selection of social work as a career choice lies in the undifferentiated nature of preparation. Social work does not require a definite commitment either in high school or in college. Students majoring in a wide variety of fields can still obtain social work positions upon graduation from college and can apply for admission to graduate schools of social work. Early specialization and early commitment encourage early crystallization of choice.

The Pins study notes:

> As a group, social work students become aware of this field at a
> relatively late state in their education. Direct contact with social
> work and social workers (in pre-professional employment
> in social work) as well as college courses and instructors were
> the major sources of information for students about social
> work. . . . Social work was not seriously considered or decided on
> until last year in college or after graduation. [56, pp. 31–34;
> see also 10]

For many of the students, social work was a second occupational
choice. These students had initially been interested in other fields of
human service—the ministry, teaching, psychology, and so on.

The summer work programs established by social work agencies as
an aid to recruitment enable many young people to "discover" social
work. Similarly, many people "discovered" social work while in the
Peace Corps. Frequently, however, people discover social work when
they seek employment after graduation from college. As college students, they may have been interested in sociology or one of the other
social sciences, but one needs to tie this to an occupational outlet. Social
work is one of few possible occupational expressions of such interest.

According to the Pins studies, most of the students entering graduate
schools of social work majored in the social sciences in college and
received average grades, were active in school organizations, and had
professional work experience in social work. About one-third of all
students in the Pins study listed the "important contributions of social
work to individuals and society" as one of the major reasons for their
choice of social work as a career. An almost similar proportion listed
the fact that they enjoyed working with people as one of the major reasons for their choice. "Only 14 percent included status and monetary
remuneration as one of the two reasons they chose social work." [56,
p. 138]   Nor was job security an important factor in choice. Frequently,
the students saw social work as involving the kind of work they would
enjoy doing and as an occupation in which they could succeed. They
perceived the values and technical concerns of the profession as being
congenial to their personal interests and predispositions. About 10 percent of the students felt that social work could help them "to become a
better person, parent, marriage partner." [56, p. 115]   There is little
empirical support for the contention that social work attracts people
who become interested in the profession because they themselves are
emotionally disturbed.

In general, then, intrinsic satisfaction in the work—satisfaction in
service, satisfaction in working with people, satisfaction in indulging a
technical interest in human behavior—is more frequently stressed by

those who choose social work than extrinsic job satisfactions—salary, professional status, job security, and so on. The task rather than the reward is a principal source of attraction.

The general conclusions of the Pins studies are confirmed by other studies. For example, Rosenberg, in a study of the occupational values of some 2500 undergraduate college students, found that students interested in social work were more likely than others to emphasize that the "ideal job must permit me to work with people rather than with things" and "give me an opportunity to be helpful to others." [67]   The social work group scored very low on the external-reward-oriented value complex, which stresses high earnings, status, prestige. On a personality typology analysis, social work students showed greater concern than others with being liked, wanted, needed, approved of, and appreciated.

In comparing the responses of a sample of clinical psychologists, psychiatrists, and social workers to the Strong Vocational Interest form, Klein noted that clinical psychologists and psychiatrists were alike but that the social workers differed from both. The social worker had lower scores on scales suggesting "scientific values and interests" and higher scores on scales concerned with "altruistic" values. [37, p. 179]

McCornack and Kidneigh, in a study of approximately 1200 social workers, delineated the interests of male and female social workers as distinguished from those of men and women in general. They found that "a strong liking for verbal activities and a dislike of the physical sciences seem to be the distinctive interests of social workers." [44, p. 163]

A 1961 national study compared 990 social work seniors with some 19,000 other seniors who were identified with education and social sciences. Values constituting a service dimension ("opportunity to work with people rather than with things"; "opportunity to be helpful to others or useful to society") more strongly characterized individuals selecting social work as a career than those who chose education or social science. However, social work majors gave lower responses to such items as "opportunity to be original and creative" and "living and working in a world of ideas." Response to such items as "freedom from supervision in my work" and "a chance to exercise leadership" indicated social work majors as being less concerned with independence and autonomy than others. They placed "unusually high value on jobs or careers which gave them an opportunity to be of service; they . . . [were] relatively uninterested in jobs which contain an intellectual component; they . . . [were] relatively uninterested in monetary rewards and the opportunity to operate independently on the job." [50, p. 24; see also 19; 20]

Walther, in a study of over 500 social workers, concluded that social workers are "oriented more toward people than to things . . . more accommodating than self-assertive in their relations to people," do not place high value on intellectual achievement, are uncomfortable with highly structured routine situations, and value themselves "most through being sympathetic, understanding, unselfish, and helpful to others." [90, p. 11]

In general, then, the typical social worker might be characterized as a white, female, of urban origin, of middle- or lower-class background, with strong social service and social interaction interests, who makes the choice rather late in her academic career often after having seriously considered other alternatives.

The Career Line

After one has selected child welfare social work, how does he obtain a position and what is likely to be the subsequent course of his career? Currently there are two principal routes into the profession: through civil service examinations for public child welfare positions following graduation from college; through professional training in graduate school. Fully trained workers are more likely to work in voluntary child welfare agencies; workers not fully trained are likely to work in public agencies. However, in agencies in which fully trained workers work side by side with those not fully trained, there is little difference in the tasks assigned to them and little difference in the work they do. [33]

Attempts are currently being made to define, with greater precision, which responsibilities can be delegated to workers with a bachelor's degree—and, it is to be hoped, with a social work major. [3; 9; 64; 69; 94] Thus the Children's Bureau has developed a "Guide for Class Specification for Positions in State and Local Child Welfare Programs," which specifies different tasks for the social worker with a master's degree in social work and a child welfare assistant with a college degree. [85; 87]

The career line of the fully trained worker offers more possibilities. The line of promotion in the profession leads to administration—from direct services in a casework position, to supervision or consultation, to executive duties. The movement away from direct service is characteristic of professions practiced in an organizational setting (teaching, engineering, librarianship, and so on). It is less likely to be true in the entrepreneurial professions: the doctor or lawyer advances by developing a larger, more select, more remunerative practice, so that, while advancing, he stays with direct service. The pressure toward vertical mobility is even greater in social work than in most professions practiced in organizational settings. This derives from the large number of positions open and the few fully trained candidates for them. Each fully trained professional then has to magnify his potential impact on the client group. One trained child welfare caseworker can service just so many clients. The same trained worker, acting as supervisor to six or seven child welfare workers, can affect, albeit indirectly, a larger client group.

Vertical mobility is not open to the worker without graduate training. For this worker, advancement is along horizontal lines. While continuing in the same kind of job the worker with experience and seniority is rewarded with a smaller, more desirable caseload, a better office, more autonomy and freedom, more respect and prestige from peers, better secretarial service, and, of course, higher pay. But the limited job openings and promotional possibilities for the workers who are not fully trained prompt many of them eventually to complete their graduate education. This tendency is encouraged by a sizable stipend program, sponsored by the Federal and state governments, which generally involves payment of all educational expenses and additional financial support for the academic year.

There is clear recognition, however, that more needs to be done to make child welfare positions more attractive to those who have only a bachelor's degree, if they are to be induced to remain on the job. Such concern also implies an explicit recognition that the two career lines do exist and are likely to typify the personnel pattern of public child welfare agencies for the foreseeable future. The two careers have been designated in the Federal literature as the social worker career line and the graduate social worker career line. [87, p. 11] More recently a third level, that of case aide paraprofessional worker, has been introduced and is receiving explicit visibility.

The tendency of fully professionally trained workers, both men and women, is to remain in social work. However, there is a relatively high turnover rate of workers in voluntary child welfare agencies, and an even higher one in public agencies. [36; 58; 80; 86] Studies indicate separate rates of around 30 percent, which is considerably higher than the 8 percent rate among schoolteachers or the 12 percent rate among all civil service employees. [36, p. 138] However, many people who leave one social work position seek, and accept subsequent employment in, another. Women tend to resign for family-related reasons; men for job-related reasons—higher salaries, better opportunities for advancement.

In child welfare, as in other fields, the woman's career pattern is likely to be discontinuous. After graduation, the woman moves into the job market and stays until she marries or has her first child, when she resigns from the job. When her last child is no longer dependent, she may return to her career.

The career pattern of the single, professional female child welfare worker is analogous to that of men, but she is less likely to move frequently from one job to another.

Interviews with people who left social work positions indicate that while situational demands (pregnancy, residential relocation, child-care problems) account for some of the departures, dissatisfaction with the job situation was a more frequent reason. Such dissatisfaction included "overwhelming job demands; poor atmosphere and morale within the agency; inability to be of real help to the client; poor supervision; little respect, encouragement, and support from agency administration; and little opportunity to use one's own initiative and be creative." [36, p. 137]   Salary and fringe benefits were rarely the most important reasons for leaving, although these are significant contributing factors in the decision.

Weinberger found that salary (once this reaches an acceptable level) was not related to job satisfaction, but that autonomy in the work situation, opportunity for direct work with clients, and a more professional agency climate providing more opportunity for interaction with colleagues were. [95]   Principal satisfactions on the job come from contact with clients and contact with colleagues. On the other hand, beginning social workers were most frequently discontented "with the organizations in which they practice, the policies that governed their professional behavior, and the administration which made and enforced those policies." [48, p. 9]   In short, the content of the job was a source of satisfaction; the context was a source of dissatisfaction. Relatively little turnover results from discharge or induced resignations.

One interesting and disconcerting finding was that those beginning social workers in the New York City Department of Public Welfare who had achieved the highest scores on the civil service examination required for the appointment were most likely to leave the agency within nine months or less. [58, p. 12]

The Apparatus of the Profession

Every professional group seeks to develop some institutional apparatus for the dissemination of information, the protection of its interests, the establishment and maintenance of standards, and the control and discipline of its members. In response to these needs professional associations are established.

The professional association acts as a lobby for the profession; it protects the integrity and status of the profession and seeks to obtain a greater measure of control over the field of practice; it acts to guarantee performance on the part of individual members and agencies in accordance with professional standards; it educates the public concerning the functions of the profession and its contribution to society; it acts as liaison between the profession and allied professions, government, the universities, and so on. The professional association also seeks to define the content of the professional training program and to define the procedures for licensing, certification, or registration, and assists the service agencies in recruiting, training, and directing personnel.

The National Association of Social Workers, formed in 1955, is the principal social work association. Until 1970 membership was open only to those who had received a master's degree from an accredited school of social work; currently full membership is also open to social workers who have completed an undergraduate program approved by the Council on Social Work Education, and associate membership is open to holders of any bachelor's degree employed by social agencies. In 1972 of 170,000 social workers in the United States, some 56,000 were members. The organization publishes *Social Work*, which is concerned with professional problems in social work, as well as additional regular bulletins concerned with career opportunities. Although there is no special employee membership organization for child welfare workers, the Child Welfare League of America is a membership organization of child welfare agencies, and publishes *Child Welfare*, which is concerned with the special problems of the child welfare worker.

Because professional training is the legitimate avenue into child welfare work, there must be some institutionalized apparatus for controlling the selection and training of those seeking professional education. The Council on Social Work Education serves this purpose. It establishes the curriculum for professional education and ensures, through its accreditation power and procedure, that such a curriculum will be offered recruits to the profession.

To some extent, an institutional apparatus seeks to enhance the status of the group, to protect and extend the prerogatives of the profession. [28]   But it is also designed to protect the client, who is not in a position to assess the competence of the individual worker or the quality of his work, nor to ensure himself that the worker will act ethically in relationship to him. Professional organizations protect the client by guaranteeing some minimal competence through their control of selection and education of candidates and assuring ethical behavior by their authority to police and control their members.

The Child Welfare League of America does this for the child welfare client indirectly by developing and publishing standards of service. It has published a detailed statement of standards of service in foster care, adoptions, institutional child care, and so on. It accepts for membership only those agencies that conform to its standards.

The professional organizations exercise control over individual members of the profession through selective use of promotional opportunities, special career and research grants, membership on national committees, and invitations to lecture, lead institutes, and act as consultants. These opportunities can be offered to those who adhere to professional practices and denied those who offend or violate the mores of the profession. But only in a limited number of states have social workers been able to translate available sanctions into force of law through licensing of practitioners. In 1973 eleven states plus Puerto Rico had statutes calling for registration, certification, or licensing of social workers and generally reserving use of the title to those holding a master's degree, while allowing the title *associate social worker* to those with a bachelor's degree and some experience. [32; 41]

Social work can, and does, control membership in the National Association of Social Workers, which represents the profession and speaks for it. This becomes one way of differentiating those who have some training from those who do not.

But the control that the apparatus of the social work profession can exercise over the profession's activities is severely limited because anyone hired by an agency can legally practice social work.

Occupational Problems

Every profession has occupational problems, which grow out of the work it does, the way it does it, and the context in which it does it. This is equally true for child welfare. There tends to be some disparity between the ideology of the child welfare worker and that of the society in which he operates. Rapoport calls attention to this problem:

> Social work seeks to embrace and implement some principles and values which may be essentially unpopular and uncongenial to the dominant social order. Hence, in some respects, social work seems to be outside the main stream of society. . . . This particular role of the profession gives it the attributes of a minority group in society. [62, p. 63]

It contributes to a feeling of marginality, a feeling of being different, on the part of the worker. The child welfare worker has to resolve the impact of society's ambivalence toward the job it is asking him to do. Two contradictory orientations contend for acceptance in the mind of the public. [24; 78] One orientation is an expression, however modified, of social Darwinism and the Puritan ethos, which suggest that man is the architect of his own destiny, that he is in full rational control of his fate and situation, and that failure is indicative of weakness and inadequacy, of some "unfitness."

> The needy, the poor, the sick, the unemployed, the unemployable, the delinquent, the unadjusted—these are the social analogies of the biologically unfit: the extension of assistance to such groups involves a negation of the natural process and results in the enfeeblement of society. Social Darwinism is exemplified by the rugged individualist with his contempt for failure. [24, p. 8]

The other orientation is that of the Judeo-Christian ethic of social responsibility for those dependent and in need—the young, the physically handicapped, the mentally handicapped, the mother with young children, the aged. The humanitarian ethos suggests that there are no "strong men," only men who have been spared; that those who have not needed help are taking pride in a self-sufficiency that derives, to a very considerable extent, from a more fortuitous situation. Those who grow up in an unbroken family, blessed with a healthy, normal body and a healthy, normal mind, born with the right color, in the right country at the right time, are counted among the "fit." A change of circumstance—a crippling accident, the sudden death of a parent, the birth of a mentally defective child—and the thin line between self-sufficiency and dependency is wiped out. Because everyone is potentially dependent, the humanitarian ethos is pragmatic. It ensures the obligation of support for ourselves when we need the support of the community.

The profession of social work stands clearly and unequivocally with the humanitarian orientation. Practice has repeatedly confirmed the fact that a punitive attitude toward the client does not help the social worker to help the client. Assessment of blame and assignment of punishment is the responsibility of such institutions as the police and the courts, primarily concerned with social control. Social work is given responsibility for helping the client to deal more adequately with a social problem. The only effective technical approach that has been developed in discharging this responsibility is one centered on understanding and accepting the client.

Neither modified social Darwinism nor humanitarianism has won a clear victory in our society. We cannot permit the dependent child of the unmarried mother to die—this is a victory for the humanitarian orientation. However, we grant our support grudgingly, hesitantly, with considerable doubts about the wisdom and morality of what we are doing—this is the victory of the Puritan ethic and social Darwinism. Society asks the child welfare worker to perform certain tasks, and then denies him adequate resources to achieve that goal.

It may be that society is not really concerned about the effectiveness of child welfare services. The mere existence of such services, whatever their effectiveness, acts to assure society that something is being done about social problems which excite the conscience of the group. [52; 53; 55] For such "institutions to be viable it is not, in fact, necessary for them to be efficient." [53, p. 144]

Society supports social work agencies because they are part of the necessary apparatus for social control. They act to mitigate the effects of situations which might lead to social conflict, and to alleviate the most egregious effects of social dysfunction. The limited support given to child welfare agencies allows them to perform this secondary function. The support necessary to carry out their primary functions—to provide adequate measures for prevention and/or rehabilitation—society is not yet willing to grant.

The child welfare worker, therefore, has to implement a policy that reflects society's ambivalence, and has to resolve, within himself and in contact with the client, the behavioral implications of that ambivalence. He has to implement a policy that conflicts, to some degree, with the values of the profession. This conflict creates a stress for the worker in contacts with his peers. Acculturation to the professional ethos means that the social worker is likely to be more understanding of deviancy than is true of the laymen with whom he associates. [60]   He finds himself "explaining" the delinquent child, the broken family, the neglectful parent, the unmarried mother to friends and relatives who feel punitive toward such groups.

Yet the worker is a member of that same society from which he differentiates himself in implementing his role as a social worker. As a member of the general society, he holds some of the same attitudes, and he might still not have resolved many of the moral dilemmas encountered in his work—dilemmas posed by the unmarried mother, the self-centered parents who neglect their children, the deserted mother living with a succession of "boy friends," the AFDC mother who "cheats" on the agency, the unmarried teenager's request for abortion or contraception, the family's request for institutionalization of a mentally deficient child. The worker thus frequently faces the stress of making decisions and taking action in the face of moral, ethical, and value questions about which he is himself still undecided.

The nature of the problems with which child welfare workers are concerned, and the tasks required of them, also present occupational problems. [1; 40; 46; 73]   These are problems with which every human being has had to contend in growing up. "Living on a job that is so closely allied to life itself makes separation of work from other areas of life exceptionally difficult. Since, in social work, the work task and living are often simultaneously experienced, anxiety is greater than in many other fields of endeavor." [1, p. 417]   In this work, more than in many other kinds of work, there is an interpenetration of different areas of one's life.

The worker who has been disappointed in his own parents is predisposed to overidentify with the deprived child. In studying adoptive parents or foster parents for the child, he is likely to be highly critical and demanding. Rejecting the application of couples who apply to become adoptive or foster parents may be a highly satisfying opportunity for the worker to "punish," symbolically, his own parents. Conversely, the need to reject clearly unacceptable applicants may conflict with the worker's fear of symbolically rejecting his own parents. Working with the unmarried mother reactivates the woman social worker's own anxiety about the possible failure to control her impulses and desires. Encountering separation experiences, the worker is predisposed to react in terms of his own remembered separation experiences—the hospitalization or death of a parent, the threat of divorce, and so on. The worker might picture himself as a "rescuer" of children from rejecting parents, or as a "superior" parent protecting the victimized child, or as an "avenging angel" acting in the child's behalf.

That such feelings do, in fact, affect the worker's attitudes and activity with a child he is called upon to help is suggested by a study done by Rosen. [66]   Although subjects for the study were child-care workers in a residential treatment program, the conclusions have relevance for social workers. Depth interviews eight to ten hours long were conducted with child-care workers and were concerned with the workers' developmental history and their reactions to the children at the center. It was found that "strong positive feelings toward a child were associated with the worker's perception of that child as being similar to his childhood self. Strong negative feelings toward a child were associated with a worker's perceiving the child as dissimilar to his childhood self," or as having traits which the worker rejected in himself. [66, p. 260]

The fact that the worker is constantly called upon to help in situations that reflect his own experiences requires him to develop a high degree of self-awareness. This is fostered and encouraged by the profession. The child welfare supervisor's responsibility involves helping the worker to examine himself to see how, and under what circumstances, his own needs and feelings intrude in his handling of a case situation. Some workers delight in such introspective self-examination and the self-awareness to which it leads. Others are made uncomfortable by it and resent it.

Some occupational stress is occasioned by the responsibilities of the job. The decisions the worker is called upon to make generally have great implications for the future of children. This is an awesome responsibility, and conscious awareness of the possible consequences of one's activities is apt to create emotional tensions. Furthermore, the child welfare worker deals with people who are living under considerable stress and strain. He encounters them at a time of crisis, when their emotional reactions are overt and strong. The need to deal with a great deal of raw emotion—anxiety, anger, depression, grief—and the constant exposure to highly charged emotional situations, while under the necessity of controlling one's own emotional responses—is highly enervating. As Feldman notes:

> The worker, face to face with the client in the interview, is exposed continually to an onslaught of unrepressed primitive feelings. The avalanche of feeling with which the . . . social worker is confronted is an unusual stress situation peculiar to the task of extending

psychological help. It is, in a sense, an occupational hazard. [18, p. 153]

He encounters "clients" who have neither asked for nor want agency service and who are hostile and resistive to his efforts to help. Despite such hostility and the worker's own very human reaction of antipathy to some clients, professional practice principles require that he act acceptingly. [45]

There is an additional stress involved in working with children. The barriers between impulse and behavior, between emotion and acting out, are not as solid for the child as they are for the adult. Hence the worker who deals with children has to face the unnerving prospect of dealing with a greater measure of impulsive behavior, a greater measure of direct, open expression of feeling. [11] Because the child has limited capacity for verbalization the worker has to learn a new language in helping the child—the language of gestures, the language of play.

The occupational danger of emotional exhaustion results also from the constant need to give of oneself emotionally on the job. The flow of emotional supplies goes one way, from the worker to the client, and it may lead to the emotional depletion of the worker.

The most important instrument in the child welfare worker's work is the child welfare worker himself. Failure in a case may not only reflect the worker's competence as a technician, but it might be also regarded by him as a reflection on his competence as a person. More so than in most other jobs the child welfare worker *is* his work. Failure, then, is apt to be more keenly felt and it is likely to be personalized.

Some of the occupational stress to which the child welfare worker is subject stems from ambiguity about what he should be doing and how he should be doing it. Techniques and approaches for helping the client are not so clearly established as to provide clear-cut guidelines for the worker's behavior. For many situations there is no validated professional consensus as to the most effective approach. In addition to incomplete, or imperfect, mastery of available knowledge, the worker has to accept the limitations of professional knowledge itself.

In some situations there is no clear consensus as to desirable aims. For instance, should the AFDC mother be encouraged to work, or to stay home with her children? Should a child be removed from his home, or should an attempt be made to maintain him in a home with neglectful parents?

Child welfare social work shares this problem with other human relations professions. Hughes states: "In the factory there is at least fair consensus about what the object produced shall be. There is often no such consensus in institutions where things are done for, or to, people." [28, p. 76] The worker also has to live with the absence of clear and objective standards of performance. As Polansky says, "This is no field which can count units of production, volume of sales, or even Trendex ratings." [59, p. 314] The worker, therefore, has to have a high tolerance for ambiguity and an ability to live with the responsibility for acting decively while uncertain as to aims and outcome.

Many situations encountered by child welfare workers have all the essential elements of the classic Greek tragedies. They involve conflicting but legitimate interests and needs. There may be conflict between the justifiable needs of the parents as they conflict with the justifiable needs of children; it may be a conflict between the rights and privileges of a foster parent and the rights and privileges of a natural parent. The child welfare worker has to act so as to recognize and understand the conflicting needs of all parties in the situation. Even if the child's needs have priority, it is not always clear how those needs can best be met. Would it be best to keep the child in the home while working with the parents to effect change? When are parents ready to receive a child back from substitute care?

> About a month after Mrs. Y. returned from the state mental hospital she expressed a desire to have her children back. Hospital prognosis was ambiguous. A telephone call to the attending physician was not helpful. Mrs. Y. refused to see a psychiatrist in an outpatient clinic. She clamored for her children. She seemed to be in fairly good shape as far as the worker could tell. [92, p. 97]

And there is the problem of decision regarding competing needs of one child client and another child client. Devoting a considerable amount of time to one child's adjustment to his placement may mean that another is left in limbo for a longer period of time without any foster home available. As one worker put it:

> The conflict that I felt was not only between the regulations and the clients but between client and client. If you want to help clients get schooling or job training or discuss personal problems with people who may be very eager to talk to you about them, you do so with the knowledge that you are not using this time to help get basic material things to people who just as desperately need them. [47, p. 24]

Some difficulties arise from the nature of the problem situations which are the principal concern of child welfare and the specialized expertise which the profession has developed, or has failed to develop, in helping with such problems.

A profession claims a monopoly in providing a particular service on the basis of superior knowledge and skills. They are granted sanction for the monopoly when the profession is successful in "persuading society that nobody else can do the job and it is dangerous to let anybody else try." [22, p. 279]   The community justifies granting that monopoly on the grounds that only a special group, with special knowledge and special training, has the skills to perform the service effectively, efficiently, and without damage to the client. "It is felt that not just anybody can do the job, so the job territory is marked 'off limits' to the amateur, often by law." [22, p. 284]   Thus only the lawyer who has been admitted to the bar can practice law; only the licensed physician can practice medicine. Almost anyone, however, is free to use the title of social worker, and everyone claims some expertise in parent-child relationship problems.

Furthermore, there is no clear "manifest disaster criterion" applicable in child welfare, as there is in some other professions. Doctors warn that the patient will die; the engineer can predict that the bridge will collapse; the dentist can assert the tooth will be lost. Rarely can social workers assert that such immediate disasters will follow from failure to utilize the skills of the profession. Nonqualified performance, then, is accepted by the public with little anxiety about outcome. All of this makes it difficult for the profession to establish the exclusive prerogative of professionally trained social workers to perform what the profession defines as child welfare social work tasks. The lay public cannot recognize the need for special competence in an area where everyone is "expert." As Charles Dollard put it, "Social work has had to fight a constant rear guard action against the pervasive notion that any man with love in his heart can do the job." [quoted in 15, p. 147]   The profession holds that what is needed is "not uninhibited love of humanity, spontaneous sentiment, or undisciplined emotion and compassion, but rather a scientific, trained intelligence and a skillful application of technique." [42, p. 122]   However, society is reluctant to grant child welfare social workers the legitimacy of such special competence because they have, as yet, been unable to unequivocally demonstrate that they "command esoteric knowledge and skills which enable them to accomplish their task much more efficiently and with better results than 'any other enthusiastic amateur.' . . ." [15, p. 147]

There is no area of child welfare activity for which the worker has clear monopoly. He shares control of homemaker service with public health nurses, of day care with educators, of protective service with the police, and so on. And, in many states, adoption is, with public sanction, independently arranged by lawyers and doctors. Such a situation is, in effect, a derogation of the special skill and knowledge possessed by the child welfare worker and, consequently, the occasion for some occupational stress.

The agency context in which child welfare tasks are performed imposes an occupational stress. The worker faces some problems that derive from the conflict between the ideology of the profession and the needs of agency structure, between the professional culture and bureaucratic needs. [5; 34; 89]   An agency is a bureaucracy, with a formal hierarchic organization. Different workers are assigned to the performance of different tasks, and there is a formal chain of command, control, and supervision. In order for any sizable organization to operate efficiently, rules, regulations, and procedures must be formulated and followed. Bureaucratic red tape is inevitable, particularly in social agencies supported by public funds and accountable to the public. The worker desires to devote his energies to service, and finds himself enmeshed in red tape; he accepts the profession's broad commitment to help the client, and finds that his ability to help is limited by the more restrictive procedures of the agency.

The professional commitment is to individualize the client: bureaucratic efficiency requires that the client be categorized, and his eligibility judged according to uniform regulations. Regulations and procedures restrict the professional exercise of autonomous judgment and decision.

The professional orientation emphasizes ends rather than means—offering the best possible service to the client, helping the client to solve his problems, and so on. The bureaucratic orientation emphasizes means rather than ends—offering the service in compliance with rules and regulations, following agency procedures, and so on. Billingsley, who has studied this conflict in child welfare agencies, notes:

> In spite of the social worker's intellectual and emotional commitment to meeting the needs of his client, it is apparent that these needs must be met within the framework of structured approaches imposed by the agency and the profession even over the worker's own estimation of the needs of the client. This is consistent with findings in studies of other professions. [5, p. 403]

The conflict between the two orientations leads to a strain between the agency demand that a given number of units of work be performed and the desire of the professional to do the best possible job. Billingsley identifies this as the conflict between quantitative output and qualitative performance.

Control over the worker's decision in the agency is frequently determined by nonprofessionals—members of the agency board and legislators. The agency regulations they formulate limit the autonomy of the professional worker, and are designed to protect the taxpayer, the community, or the agency budget rather than the client.

In the agency, as in any bureaucratic organization, there is an informal structure that exists side by side with the formal structure. The formal organization is "owned" by the professional trained workers who occupy, or who will occupy, the positions of administrative and executive power in the formal structure. Workers without professional training, who remain in direct service, form a well-organized clique. The bureaucracy represents the more orthodox professionalized ideals and seeks to run the agency in accordance with these ideals. The informal clique tends to oppose, in significant ways, the aims of the supervisory staff and to modify such approaches.

The conflict between the formal and informal structure is illustrated in a study by Bogdanoff and Glass. [7] Anthropologists by training, they were employed as caseworkers by the Cook County Department of Public Welfare. While employed there, they undertook to study the behavior of welfare workers, and kept a detailed diary of "bull sessions," talk during coffee breaks, conversations overheard, and so on. The researchers report that, although it would appear that the agency hierarchy controls the administration of casework,

> we have noted that there exists within the welfare agency a sub-system, the clique group. It is this subsystem which exercises much greater control over the way in which public casework is administered. During our investigation, we noted that the opinion-molding aspect of the group was influential in areas of conceptions toward recipients, methods of casework, attitudes toward the official agency. [7, pp. 77–79]

The study indicated that the vertical hierarchy (supervisor, administrator) educates the worker in accepted agency practice while the horizontal hierarchy of peers carries on a program of informal "in-service training" as to what is acceptable practice. A great deal of solidarity develops among clique members—a solidarity permitting the enforcement of sanctions against members who violate acceptable patterns of clique behavior. This can be almost as powerful as the rewards (promotions, raises, and the like) used by the vertical hierarchy. [30; 100] For the many child welfare workers who are not fully trained, there may be occupational stress occasioned by the conflict between the demands made on him by the formal structure of the agency, as represented by his supervisor, and those imposed by the clique.

In addition, every worker in every profession faces the problem of adjusting to what has been termed *reality shock,* the discrepancy between the norms inculcated by professional training and the actual requirements of practice. [77]

Wasserman followed the careers of twelve graduates of a school of social work who obtained positions in 1966 as child welfare workers in a public agency. The actual work situation encountered was quite different from what they had expected. Instead of handling limited caseloads which would permit a leisurely review of a situation and a reasoned professional decision, the workers were constantly faced with emergency situations which required immediate action. Sheer physical and emotional fatigue resulted from "the cumulative impact, perhaps the cumulative terror, of a large number of cases—by the human suffering, deprivation, disorder, ignorance, hostility, and cruelty the worker must face as part of his everyday work situation." [92, p. 96]   In addition there was the frustration which resulted from trying to deal with difficult situations with limited resources available to help—limited financial help, foster homes, day-care centers, homemakers, and so on.

Blau describes some of the aspects of reality shock encountered by workers in a public assistance agency in Chicago. The new worker, he says,

> . . . encounters clients who are very different from what he had expected and with whom he must establish a working relationship.
>
> Most persons who took a job in the welfare agency were partly motivated by an interest in working with and helping poor people. They tended to look forward to establishing a warm, although not intimate, relationship with deserving and grateful clients, and considered the caseworker as the agent of society who extended a helping and trusting hand to its unfortunate members. Newcomers generally deplored the "means test" and cared little about protecting public funds by investigating whether clients meet eligibility requirements, feeling that a trusting attitude should accompany financial aid in the best interest of rehabilitation. The attitudes of most new caseworkers toward clients were strongly positive, if somewhat sentimental and idealistic. Contacts with clients put these views to a severe test, which often resulted in disillusion.
>
> Recipients of public assistance constitute the most deprived segment of the population, especially in a period of relative prosperity. In this Northern metropolis, disproportionate numbers of them were Negroes, in-migrants from the South, unmarried mothers, alcoholics, and generally people with handicaps in the labor market. The mores and folkways of most of these people were quite different from those prevailing in the American middle or working class. Strong moral condemnation of desertion, illegitimacy, or physical violence, for example, was not part of the values of their subculture. Such differences in values and customs made it difficult for middle-class workers to maintain their positive feelings for clients, but another factor was even more important in changing their orientation. Clients were in dire need, since the assistance allowance, originally set low, never caught up with the inflationary trend. They were, therefore, under strong pressure to conceal what slim resources they might have had and try to get a little more money from the agency, even if this required false statements. People under such deprived conditions tend to look

upon government organizations as alien forces that must be tricked into yielding enough money for survival, and consequently some clients, although by no means all, tried to cheat. In fact, the situation in which recipients found themselves made honesty a luxury. The new caseworker was typically full of sympathy for clients' problems, but as he encountered clients who blamed him personally for not helping them enough, even though agency procedure limited him, and clients met his trusting attitude by cheating and lying, the newcomer tended to experience a "reality shock" just as new teachers do whose first assignment is an overcrowded class in a slum. [16, p. 34] *

The same study shows, however, that workers who stay with the job and accept its realities do tend to find their major satisfaction in their contact with the clients and in helping the client.

The content of reality shock, the disenchantment, and the subsequent recovery of "faith" is graphically described by a New York City Youth Board worker assigned to a gang of delinquent girls.

It's not easy to love a delinquent girl. She's vulgar, she's coarse, she's loud. She denies her girlhood and flaunts her sex. She despises the world, her life, herself.

Offer her love, and she's suspicious. Treat her with respect, she's on guard. Be her friend, and she will use you. Come to her aid, she'll be astonished, but refuse her just once and she'll turn on you.

She will test you, deceive you, disappoint you, exhaust your patience, and shake your resolve. Her demands are endless, her gratitude nonexistent. You try to remember what you really believe, that the noise and bravado and selfishness hide a hungry child. Hungry for love, for attention, for respect, and decency—and, all too often, hungry for food. You will teach and preach, instruct and persuade.

A youth worker's voice can get very tired.

Then one day she'll decide you're for real. You don't have an angle and you're not a kook. She doesn't understand it, but she accepts it. You'll begin to see the signs. She manages to sit next to you in the candy store. She asks you to let her fix your hair different. You hear familiar words—yours—coming out of her mouth, and you realize she's caught the meaning of what you've been saying.

---

* From Peter M. Blau, "Orientation Toward Clients in a Public Welfare Agency," *Administrative Science Quarterly* (December 1960). By permission of the author and *Administrative Science Quarterly*.

You'll begin to see little signs of respect—for you and for herself.

It doesn't always happen that way, of course. Not eight times out of ten, or even five times out of ten. But it happens. And when it does, you'll know that even if it happens only one time out of a hundred, it's enough. [27, pp. 20–21]

And, as a psychiatrist once said on reflecting on the realities of his profession, "every once in a while we are, beyond a doubt little saviors: and help weather a crisis, dispel a dread, release a growth, . . . a lasting change for the better." [38, p. 36]

Summary

Child welfare, as a social institution established by society to perform specific functions in meeting human needs, has a defined structure, designated statuses and roles, an explicit value system, goals, and operational principles. It can, then, like any social system, be described in sociological terms.

The typical child welfare worker is a white woman of middle-class background working as a caseworker in a public child welfare agency located in an urban, industrialized area. She made a decision to go into social work during her last years in college, or shortly after graduation, after majoring in social science and attaining average grades. She is not likely to have a master's degree in social work. In one out of four cases she is likely to leave the agency because of marriage, childbirth, or to move with her husband to a new job. In 1973 she was earning about $11,100 a year. She was attracted to social work because she likes to work with people, because it offers an opportunity for service to others, and because she felt she had the attributes and interests that would make for success in the profession. She tends to be less interested in the extrinsic rewards such a position could offer. If she remains with the agency, promotional opportunities are likely to be limited because of her lack of full professional training.

A smaller group of child welfare workers do have a master's degree in social work, and their career line involves promotion upward in the agency hierarchy and away from direct service to the client. Salaries for fully trained workers were some $2375 a year higher than those for holders of bachelor degrees, and salaries for men were generally higher than those for women. Men also advanced more rapidly than women to positions of executive responsibility.

The prestige level of social work is high among all occupations, but relatively low within the family of the professions. The public image of social work is a positive one, even if there is considerable vagueness as to what social work is and what the social worker does.

The profession has established an organizational apparatus for the promotion of professional interests, the maintenance of standards, the protection of the client, and the induction and training of recruits. The relevant organizations for the child welfare worker are the National Association of Social Workers, the Child Welfare League of America, and the Council on Social Work Education.

Some of the more significant occupational problems faced by the child welfare worker include the following:

1. Conflict between the value orientation of the occupational subculture and the wider community.
2. The failure of the child welfare field to obtain control over the qualifications for the title *child welfare worker* and monopolization of child welfare services.
3. The interpenetration of life and work.
4. The responsibility for formative life experiences without clear consensus as to techniques and aims and without sufficiently definitive knowledge in many areas.
5. The constant exposure to emotionally evocative experiences.
6. The conflict between bureaucratic structure and professional ideology and between the professionalized formal structure and the informal, nonprofessional clique structure.

A Personal Comment

This is an objective, analytical account of the sociology of the child welfare worker. Yet something is missing—something that eludes the kind of summarization of factors characterizing an occupational subculture.

Throughout the text, the writer has consciously and deliberately refrained from intruding himself into the material. At this point, he is taking the liberty of editorializing. The impulse to make a personal comment stems from a firm commitment to child welfare social work, the values for which it speaks, and the task it is asked to do. It stems from a conviction that child welfare workers are engaged in one important sector of the most significant task of any community—the task of rearing the next generation. Nothing—not all our building, not all our production, not all our scientific advances—can equal in importance the work of helping, in whatever way, to ensure that our children, who constitute our eternity, grow to adulthood healthy in mind, body, and spirit. Socrates, at his wisest, noted this:

If I could get to the highest place in Athens, I would lift my voice
and say, "What mean ye, fellow citizens, that ye turn every stone
to scrape wealth together and take so little care of your children
to whom ye must one day relinquish all?"

The most meritorious of societies is that which welcomes the question, "Is it well with the child?" and answers, truthfully, "All is indeed well."

The Talmud, emphasizing the importance of each individual life, says, "If, during the course of your own life, you have saved one life, it is as if you have saved all mankind." Few occupations give us the opportunity of participating in the saving of a life. The everyday work of the child welfare worker is concerned with just that—reclaiming a child for life. It is to be expected that such a task would be very difficult. It is also to be expected that there are few, if any, tasks that offer the same degree of satisfaction and the same sense of accomplishment.

The task is large and difficult. The aims and hopes have to be commensurately modest. The medieval medical dictum is applicable and appropriate here—"to cure some time, to relieve often, to comfort always."

The red wine of life, the passion in the encounter with children denied a childhood, needs to be included here as an addition to the factual data regarding the child welfare worker. It is included in the child welfare worker's job.

Bibliography

1. BABCOCK, CHARLOTTE. "The Social Worker in a World of Stress." *Social Service Review*, **25**, 2 (March 1951).
2. BAILEY, MARGARET. "Community Orientations Toward Social Casework." *Social Work*, **4**, 3 (July 1959).
3. BARKER, ROBERT L., and THOMAS L. BRIGGS. *Differential Use of Social Work Manpower*. New York: National Association of Social Workers, 1968.
4. BARLOW, WALTER. *Public Understanding of Social Welfare*. Columbus, Ohio: National Conference on Social Welfare, 1963.
5. BILLINGSLEY, ANDREW. "Bureaucratic and Professional Orientation Patterns in Social Casework." *Social Service Review*, **38**, 4 (December 1964).
6. BLAU, PETER M. "Orientation Toward Clients in a Public Welfare Agency." *Administrative Science Quarterly*, **5**, 4 (December 1960).
7. BOGDANOFF, EARL, and ARNOLD GLASS. *The Sociology of the Public Assistance Caseworker in an Urban Area*. Unpublished M.S. Thesis, University of Chicago, Chicago, March 1964.
8. BRAGER, GEORGE, and JOHN A. MICHAEL. "The Sex Distribution in Social

Work—Causes and Consequences." *Social Casework,* **50**, 10 (December 1969), 595–601.

9. BRIELAND, DONALD, et al. *Differential Use of Manpower: A Team Model for Foster Care.* New York: Child Welfare League of America, 1968.

10. CHATTERJEE, PRENAB. "Recruitment in Law, Medicine and Social Work: Some Comparative Trends." *Social Work Education Reporter,* **21** (December–January 1973), 24–27.

11. CHETHIK, MORTON. "The Emotional 'Wear and Tear' of Child Therapy." *Smith College Studies in Social Work,* **39** (February 1967), 147–56.

12. CHILD WELFARE LEAGUE OF AMERICA. *Representation of Racial and Ethnic Minorities on CWLA Member Agency Staffs and Boards.* New York Child Welfare League of America Research Center, June 16, 1972.

13. DAVIS, ANNE J. "Self-Concept, Occupational Role Expectations, and Occupational Choice in Nursing and Social Work." *Nursing Research,* **18**, 1 (1969), 55–59.

14. DEVEREAUX, GEORGE, and FLORENCE WEINER. "The Occupational Status of Nurses." *American Sociological Review,* **15**, 5 (October 1950).

15. ETZIONI, AMITAI (ed.). *The Semiprofessions and Their Organization— Nurses, Teachers, Social Workers.* New York: The Free Press, 1969.

16. FANSHEL, DAVID. "Child Welfare," in *Encyclopedia of Social Work,* 16th Issue. Ed. by Robert Morris. New York: National Association of Social Workers, 1971.

17. FARSON, RICHARD E. "The Counselor Is a Woman." *Journal of Counseling Psychology,* **1**, 4 (1954), 221–23.

18. FELDMAN, YONATTA, et al. "One Aspect of Casework Training Through Supervision." *Social Casework,* **34**, 4 (April 1953).

19. GOCKEL, GALEN L. "Social Work as a Career Choice," in *Manpower in Social Welfare—Research Perspectives.* Ed. by Edward E. Schwartz. New York: National Association of Social Workers, 1966.

20. ———. "Social Work and Recent College Graduates: A Report on Two National Surveys." *Social Work Reporter,* **15**, 2 (June 1967).

21. GOODE, WILLIAM. "Community Within a Community—The Profession." *American Sociological Review,* **22**, 2 (April 1957).

22. ———. "The Theoretical Limits of Professionalization," in *The Semiprofessions and Their Organization—Teachers, Nurses, Social Workers.* Ed. by Amitai Etzioni. New York: The Free Press, 1969.

23. GREEN, A. D. "The Professional Social Workers in the Bureaucracy." *Social Service Review,* **40**, 2 (March 1964), 71–83.

24. GREENWOOD, ERNEST. *Toward a Sociology of Social Work.* Special Report Series No. 37. Research Department, Welfare Counsel of Metropolitan Los Angeles. Los Angeles, November 1953.

25. ———. "Attributes of a Profession." *Social Work,* **2**, 3 (July 1957).

26. GROW, LUCILLE J., and MICHAEL J. SMITH. *Salary Study 1971.* New York: Child Welfare League of America, March 1971.

27. HANSON, KITTY. *Rebels in the Streets.* Englewood Cliffs, N.J.: Prentice-Hall, Inc., 1958.

28. HUGHES, EVERETT. *Men and Their Work.* New York: The Free Press, 1958.

29. HYLTON, LYDIA. "Projected Social Welfare Staff Needs." *Child Welfare,* **45**, 2 (February 1966).

30. JACOBS, JERRY. "Symbolic Bureaucracy: A Case Study of a Social Welfare Agency." *Social Forces*, **47**, 4 (June 1969), 413–22.
31. JEHU, DEREK. "The Connotative Meaning of Social Work—A Semantic Differential Analysis." *Social Work* (English), **27**, 1 (January 1970).
32. JOHNSON, DONALD. "Legal Regulation of the Social Work Profession." *Social Casework*, **51**, 9 (November 1970), 551–55.
33. JONES, BETTY L. "Nonprofessional Workers in Professional Foster Family Agencies." *Child Welfare*, **45**, 6 (June 1966), 313–25.
34. KADUSHIN, ALFRED. "Determinants of Career Choice and Their Implications for Social Work." *Recruitment for Social Work Education and Social Work Practice*, **6** (April 1958).
35. ———. "Prestige of Social Work—Facts and Factors." *Social Work*, **3** (April 1958).
36. KERMISH, IRVING, and FRANK KUSHIN. "Why High Turnover? Social Work Staff Losses in a County Welfare Agency." *Public Welfare*, **27**, 2 (April 1969), 134–39.
37. KLEIN, FREDERICK, *et al.* "Strong Vocational Interest Blank Scores of Clinical Psychologists, Psychiatrists and Social Workers." *Journal of Counseling Psychology*, **9** (1962).
38. LEDERER, WOLFGANG. "Stalking the Demons." *The Progressive*, **31**, 9 (September 1967), 34–37.
39. LEVINE, MORTON. "Trends in Professional Employment," in *Manpower in Social Welfare—Research Perspectives*. Ed. by Edward E. Schwartz. New York: National Association of Social Workers, 1966.
40. LITNER, NER. *The Strains and Stresses on the Child Welfare Worker*. New York: Child Welfare League of America, 1957.
41. LOAVENBRUCK, GRANT. "NASW Manpower Survey." *National Association of Social Workers News* (March 1973), 10–11.
42. LUBOVE, ROY. *The Professional Altruist*. Cambridge, Mass.: Harvard University Press, 1965.
43. McCLAIN, EDWIN W. "Is the Counselor a Woman?" *Personnel and Guidance Journal*, **46**, 5 (January 1968), 444–48.
44. McCORNACK, RITA, and JOHN KIDNEIGH. "The Vocational Interest Patterns of Social Workers." *Social Work Journal*, **35**, 4 (October 1954).
45. MAYER, JOHN E., and AARON ROSENBLATT. *Sources of Stress Among Student Practitioners in Social Work: A Sociological View*. 1973. Mimeo.
46. MERTON, ROBERT K., *et al*. *The Student-Physician—Introductory Studies in the Sociology of Medical Education*. Cambridge, Mass.: Harvard University Press, 1957.
47. MILLER, RONALD, and LAWRENCE PODELL. *Role Conflict in Public Social Services*. New York: Office of Community Affairs, Division of Research and Innovation, 1971.
48. MILLER, SAMUEL. *Components of Job Satisfaction for Beginning Social Workers*. October 1970. Mimeo.
49. NATIONAL MAN POWER COUNCIL. *Women Power*. New York: Columbia University Press, 1957.
50. NATIONAL OPINION RESEARCH CENTER. *Silk Stockings and Blue Collars*. Chicago: University of Chicago Press, April 1966.

51. NATIONAL SOCIAL WELFARE ASSEMBLY. *Salaries and Working Conditions of Social Welfare Manpower in 1960.* New York, 1961.

52. NOKES, PETER. *The Professional Task in Welfare Practice.* New York: Humanities Press, 1967.

53. ————. "Purpose and Efficiency in Humane Social Institutions." *Human Relations,* **13**, 2 (May 1960), 141–55.

54. OHLIN, LLOYD, et al. "Major Dilemmas of the Social Worker in Probation and Parole." *National Probation and Parole Journal,* **2**, 2 (July 1956).

55. PEIRCE, F. P. "A Functional Perspective of Social Work." *Social Work Education Reporter,* **18**, 1 (March 1970), 48–61.

56. PINS, ARNULF M. *Who Chooses Social Work? When? and Why?* New York: Council on Social Work Education, 1963.

57. ————, et al. *Students in Schools of Social Work.* New York: Council on Social Work Education, 1972.

58. PODELL, LAWRENCE. "Attrition of First-Line Social Service Staff." *Welfare in Review,* **5**, 1 (January 1967), 9–14.

59. POLANSKY, NORMAN. "The Professional Identity in Social Work," in *Issues in American Social Work.* Ed. by Alfred Kahn. New York: Columbia University Press, 1959.

60. ————. "Social Workers in Society." *Social Work Journal,* **34**, 4 (April 1953).

61. POLLAK, OTTO. "The Culture of Psychiatric Social Work." *Journal of Psychiatric Social Work,* **21** (1952).

62. RAPOPORT, LYDIA. "In Defense of Social Work—An Examination of Stress in the Profession." *Social Service Review,* **34**, 3 (March 1960).

63. REGIONAL RESEARCH INSTITUTE OF SOCIAL WELFARE. *Public Opinion Poll of Social Services.* Los Angeles: School of Social Work, University of Southern California, March 1971.

64. RICHAN, WILLIAM C. "A Theoretical Scheme for Determining Roles of Professional and Nonprofessional Personnel." *Social Work,* **6**, 4 (October 1961).

65. ROE, ANNE, and MARVIN SIEGELMAN. *The Origin of Interests.* Washington, D.C.: American Personnel and Guidance Association, 1961.

66. ROSEN, JACQUELINE L. "Personality Factors in the Reaction of Child Care Workers to Emotionally Disturbed Children." *Psychiatry,* **26**, 3 (August 1963).

67. ROSENBERG, MILTON. *Occupational Values and Occupational Choice.* Unpublished Ph.D. Thesis, Columbia University, New York, 1964.

68. ROSENBLATT, AARON, et al. "Predominance of Male Authors in Social Work Publications." *Social Casework,* **51**, 7 (July 1970), 421–30.

69. RUSSEL, ELLERY. "Case Aides Free Casework Time." *Child Welfare,* **37**, 4 (April 1958).

70. SCHWARTZ, ARTHUR. "The Southern New Jersey Chapter of NASW: A Study in the Sociology of the Profession." *Social Service Review,* **41**, 4 (December 1967), 401–10.

71. SCOTCH, C. BERNARD. "Sex Status in Social Work's Quest for Women's Liberation." *Social Work,* **15**, 3 (July 1970), 5–11.

72. SCOTT, W. RICHARD. "Professional Employees in a Bureaucratic Structure:

Social Work," in *The Semiprofessions and Their Organization—Teachers, Nurses, Social Workers*. Ed. by Amitai Etzioni. New York: The Free Press, 1969.

73. SHURLEY, JAY T. *Emotional Stresses Encountered in Social Work Practice.* First Annual University of Texas Social Work Conference, May 1954. Mimeo.

74. SIMPSON, RICHARD L., and IDA H. SIMPSON. "Women and Bureaucracy in the Semiprofessions," in *The Semiprofessions and Their Organization— Teachers, Nurses, Social Workers*. Ed. by Amitai Etzioni. New York: The Free Press, 1969.

75. SMITH, MICHAEL, and BARBARA L. HARING. *Salary Study—1973.* New York: Child Welfare League of America, March 1973.

76. STAMM, ALFRED. "NASW Membership: Characteristics, Deployment and Salaries." *Personnel Information*, **12**, 3 (May 1969), 1, 34–45.

77. STYZA, LARRY. "Reality Shock in a Public Welfare Setting." *Public Welfare*, **30**, 3 (Fall 1972), 43–46.

78. SZUREK, S. A. "The Social Plight of the Social Worker." *American Journal of Orthopsychiatry*, **12**, 1 (1942).

79. TIMMS, NOEL. "Knowledge, Opinion, and the Social Services." *The Sociological Review*, **9**, 6 (November 1961).

80. TOLLEN, WILLIAM B. *Study of Staff Losses in Child Welfare and Family Service Agencies.* Washington, D.C.: Government Printing Office, 1960.

81. TOREN, NINA. *Social Work: The Case of a Semiprofession.* Beverly Hills, Calif.: Sage Publications, 1972.

82. TREUDLEY, MARY B. "American Cultural Themes and Social Work." *Social Forces*, **28**, 3 (March 1950).

83. U.S. DEPARTMENT OF HEALTH, EDUCATION, AND WELFARE. *Child Welfare Statistics—1970.* Washington, D.C.: Government Printing Office, 1971.

84. ———. *Differential Use of Staff in Family and Child Welfare Services— With Particular Reference to Subprofessional Staff: A Guide.* Washington, D.C.: Government Printing Office, 1971.

85. ———. *Guide for Class Specifications for Positions in State and Local Child Welfare Programs.* Washington, D.C.: Government Printing Office, 1963.

86. ———. *Research Report Overview Study of the Dynamics of Worker Job Mobility.* Washington, D.C.: Government Printing Office, 1971.

87. ———. *Utilization of Social Work Staff with Different Levels of Education for Family Services in Public Welfare.* Washington, D.C.: Government Printing Office, December 1965.

88. U.S. DEPARTMENT OF LABOR. *Manpower Report to the President.* Washington, D.C.: Government Printing Office, 1972.

89. VINTER, ROBERT. "The Social Structure of Service," in *Issues in American Social Work.* Ed. by Alfred Kahn. New York: Columbia University Press, 1959.

90. WALTHER, REGISTT, et al. "The Occupation Culture of Policemen and Social Workers." *Experimental Publications System*, Issue Ms. No. 314–256, American Psychological Association, December 1970.

91. WARKOV, SEYMOUR. "Social Work Students and Other Graduate Students: A Comparison," in *Manpower in Social Welfare—Research Perspectives.*

Ed. by Edward E. Schwartz. New York: National Association of Social Workers, 1906.

92. WASSERMAN, HARRY. "Early Careers of Professional Social Workers in a Public Child Welfare Agency." *Social Work*, **15**, 3 (July 1970), 93–101.

93. ———. "The Professional Social Worker in a Bureaucracy." *Social Work*, **16**, 1 (January 1971), 69–95.

94. WEED, VERNE, and WILLIAM DENHAM. "Toward More Effective Use of the Nonprofessional Worker: A Recent Experiment." *Social Work*, **6**, 4 (October 1961).

95. WEINBERGER, PAUL. *Job Satisfaction and Staff Retention in Social Work.* School of Social Work, San Diego State College, January 1970. Mimeo.

96. WILENSKY, HAROLD. "Work Careers and Social Integration." *International Social Science Journal*, **12**, 3 (Fall 1960).

97. ———, and CHARLES LEBEAUX. *Industrial Society and Social Welfare.* New York: Russell Sage Foundation, 1958.

98. WRIGHT, HELEN. "Employment of Graduates of the School of Social Service Administration." *Social Service Review*, **21**, 3 (September 1974).

99. ZIMBALIST, SIDNEY E., and CLAIRE M. ANDERSON. "The Social Welfare Manpower Crisis Revisited: A Study of Personnel Needs in the Chicago Area." *Social Service Review*, **44**, 4 (December 1970), 452–59.

100. ZIMMERMAN, DON. "Tasks and Troubles—The Practical Bases of Work Activities in a Public Assistance Organization," in *Explorations in Sociology and Counseling.* Ed. by Donald A. Hansen. Boston: Houghton Mifflin Company, 1969.

Author Index

Subject Index